SWEET TOOTH BOOK ONE

CRUNCHY

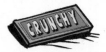

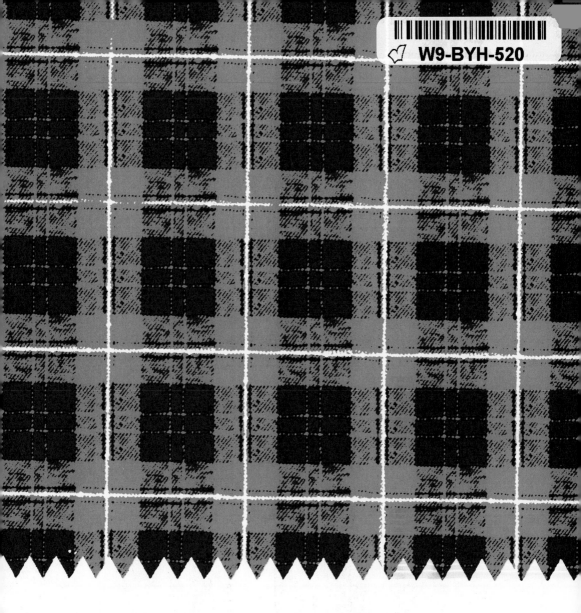

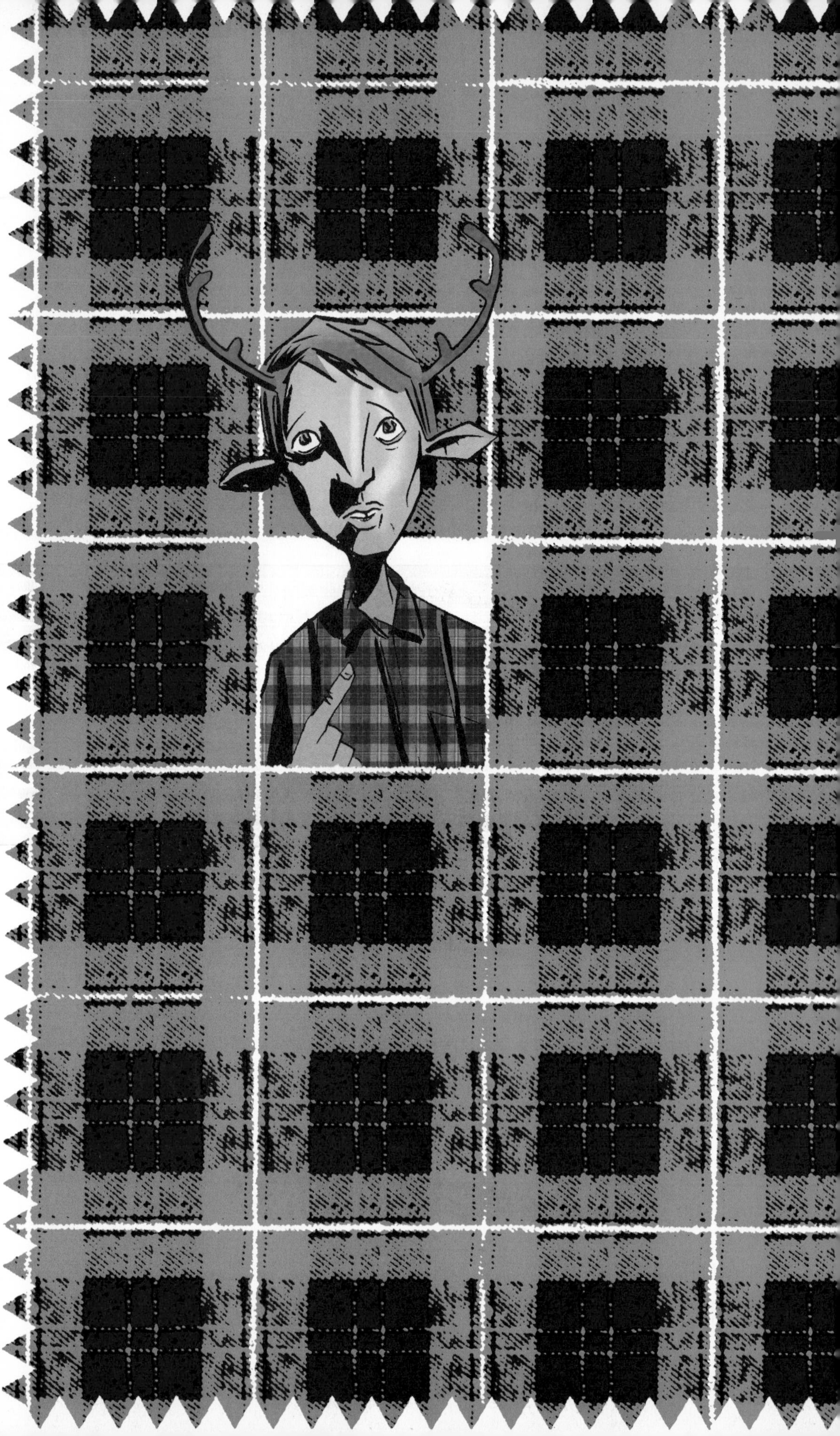

SWEET TOOTH

BOOK ONE

JEFF LEMIRE story & art
JOSÉ VILLARRUBIA colors
PAT BROSSEAU letters
JEFF LEMIRE collection cover art & color
SWEET TOOTH created by JEFF LEMIRE

Pornsak Pichetshote
Brandon Montclare
Bob Schreck Editors – Original Series
Robin Wildman Editor – Collected Edition
Steve Cook Design Director – Books
Louis Prandi Publication Design

Marie Javins Editor-in-Chief, DC Comics

Daniel Cherry III Senior VP – General Manager
Jim Lee Publisher & Chief Creative Officer
Joen Choe VP – Global Brand & Creative Services
Don Falletti VP – Manufacturing Operations & Workflow Management
Lawrence Ganem VP – Talent Services
Alison Gill Senior VP – Manufacturing & Operations
Nick J. Napolitano VP – Manufacturing Administration & Design
Nancy Spears VP – Revenue

SWEET TOOTH BOOK ONE

DC Comics, 2900 West Alameda Ave., Burbank, CA 91505
Printed by LSC Communications, Owensville, MO, USA. Third Printing.
ISBN: 978-1-4012-7680-5

Library of Congress Cataloging-in-Publication Data is available.

PEFC Certified
This product is from sustainably managed forests and controlled sources
PEFC
PEFC/29-31-337
www.pefc.org

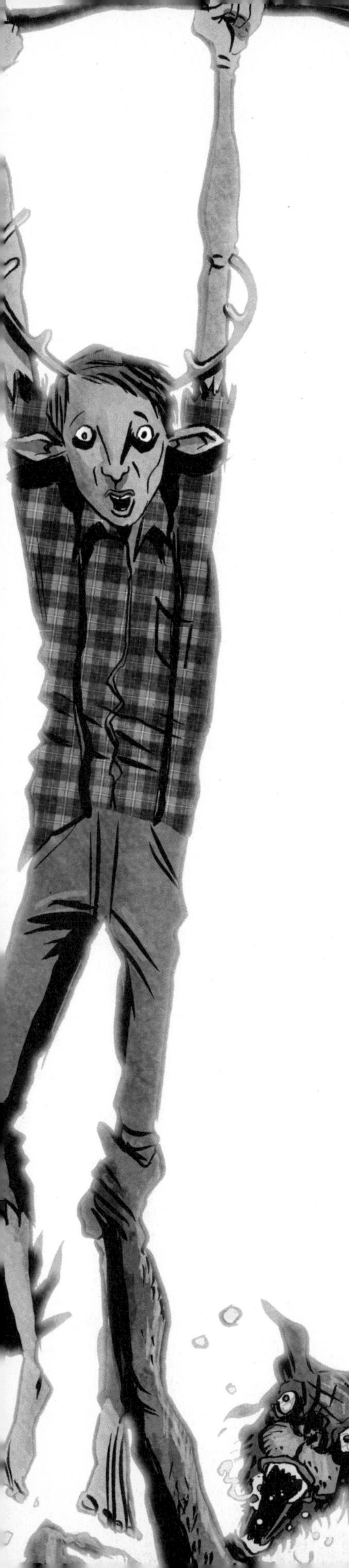

FOREWORD
by Michael Sheen

"Never, EVER leave the woods." The number one rule—leaving the woods is a sin, disobedience against God, and like with Adam, the first man, it must be paid for. But it was only through disobeying God that man could begin his long journey of awareness. With awareness came knowledge, and with knowledge came the potential for arrogance. Hubris, the Greeks called it. An overreaching pride, punishable by the gods.

Heading downriver toward the darkest of hearts in *Apocalypse Now*, Captain Willard warns, "Never get out of the boat. God-damn right. Unless you were going all the way." Well, hold on to your antlers, folks, because this one goes all the way...

The beginning of the end, we're told, "This is the story of a little boy with antlers who lived alone in the woods." And so it is. A little boy with antlers and a lot of names. Sweet Tooth. Gus. 171. The Boy-King. But he doesn't like the name Sweet Tooth. And where 171 is too clinical, the Boy-King seems too grandiose. So let's stick to the name his father gave him—Gus. His father, the janitor-prophet, a voice crying out in the Nebraska state wilderness, preparing the way of his ward. No ordinary birth for Gus. Like others of his ilk, who spring from thighs or issue forth of virgin births, his beginnings are both humble and portentous. Like the Hindu god Shiva, he is both creator and destroyer, savior and scourge, the end and the beginning. With an innocent taste for both plaid and chocolate.

Where there is Innocence there must also be Experience. The one working upon the other, altering it, shaping it, moving toward the corruption of one or the redemption of the other. So if there is Gus, there must also be Jepperd. Jepperd. The man of violence. The Big Man. The White Demon. The Shepherd. He enters the story with a denial of God, an ex-hockey player looking for a Frank Miller story to self-destruct in. "I could always fight. It's the rest of it I ain't ever been no good at." You could imagine Brando's Terry Malloy saying that in *On the Waterfront*.

Together they touch on something very deep within us. There's an archetype at work here. You can trace it through our cultural history, like strata within a rock. The man of violence and the special child, bound to each other and propelled across a bitter landscape. It's there when the Hound delivers Arya in *Game of Thrones*, when Frodo encounters Boromir and when the gunslinger Roland Deschain and the boy Jake Chambers follow their Ka across Mid-World in Stephen King's *Dark Tower* saga. It's there as we watch a taxi driver find redemption through violence for the sake of a young girl in Scorsese's New York urban nightmare, and also in Bogdanovitch's *Paper Moon* as Moses Pray and little Addie Loggins travel across a black-and-white Depression-era Kansas. In Japan, we see it in the many adventures of *Lone Wolf & Little Cub*, and as we move deeper through the psychic strata, it's there as Abraham takes his son Isaac on their dark journey to Mount Moriah. Perhaps most significantly, it's present when St. Christopher, "terrifying both in strength and countenance," unknowingly carries the Christ child across the raging river. And on down, deeper and deeper into the rock of the collective unconscious, beyond popular culture, beyond religion, beyond primitive beliefs and into a place of pure archetypes. Like a cavern of ancient doorways waiting beneath the scientific structures of man.

What was the first post-apocalyptic wasteland-wandering story? Was it in Genesis, when Adam and Eve were cast out of Eden to roam the bleak landscape beyond God's garden? Or was it their son Cain? Doomed to wander a cursed earth after his brother's murder makes him a fugitive. We find fratricide plays a part in SWEET TOOTH, too. These are epic, primal, ambitious themes that Jeff Lemire is exploring here. And they require a visual language of real depth and substance to render them on the page.

From the first time I came across Jeff's work, which was when I read his brilliant tale of budding heroes and sparring ice hockey brothers, *Essex County*, with its rough-hewn carvings of broken noses and homemade capes, I was enthralled by his artwork. In SWEET TOOTH, it reaches Goya-like dimensions at times. Look at paintings like *Witches' Sabbath*, *The Great He-Goat* or the so-called Black Paintings. Or look at Van Gogh's *The Potato Eaters*. The dark, oily strokes where crude, heavy lines belie a rich complexity. Conversely, as Gus sails out and journeys into Death, where you'd expect darkness, Jeff and José Villarrubia combine to conjure a delicate and sinuous watercolor world like something out of Blake.

In the language of film, Jeff's sense of where to be in the frame is impeccable. Without ever thinking about it, you're always seeing things from exactly where you want to be. Split screen, jump cuts, time lapse, tracking shots. He plays with the form, uses it and takes risks, breaks rules and manipulates structure so creatively. Every panel, every page, every sequence so explored and mined for fresh and innovative uses. But never drawing attention to its creator—always in service to the story. Form and content in perfect harmony. Multiple realities intertwine and intersect, obscuring then revealing. Moving around in time with an ease and a confidence that in other hands might be jarring, creating new and surprising rhythms, a poetry of chronology.

Look at the page that ends SWEET TOOTH #5. From high above, we look down on Abbot's compound. On one side of the fence, we see Gus being carried off to a seemingly hideous fate. On the other, Jepperd walks away, his deal done, only his shadow stretching out ahead of him to remind him of his betrayal at every step. The same high viewpoint of the same place repeats itself later in the story, as we see the moment in the past when that very same deal was struck. Or in later issues, when time folds in on itself as Jepperd and Louise simultaneously leave their home and return to it on the same page, but much later and in vastly different circumstances, time bridged by the Big Man's promise. These scenes and others like it are visual echoes, sounding backwards and forwards through time, disturbances rippling out through the story in multiple directions simultaneously, haunting and resonant.

This is the kind of work that rewards multiple viewings. A book of infinite revelations. I hope this doesn't make it all seem too dry or ponderous. As Jepperd reminds us, "It's what happens next that really matters." And above all, SWEET TOOTH keeps you wanting to know what happens next. For all its vast themes and epic complexity, it is a blood-pounding page-turner of a tale.

When I finished the last chapter for the first time, I immediately wrote to Jeff. I found the email recently. Here's the end of it: "I had tears running down my cheeks for the whole last section of the story. Endings are so strange with truly great stories, because the journey at their heart seems like it should never end. I suppose because it is our story, our journey, it resonates so much for us, because it is the journey we are still in the middle of struggling with. So, to be able to break through that natural resistance to the portrayal of its mortal conclusion is a real achievement. To do what you have done here though is a sublime act. So incredibly powerful. This is a landmark work, I think. So huge in scope, yet so personal and intimate at the same time. Coruscating and hopeful. An extraordinary achievement. And one that will stay and grow with me forever."

If you do choose to disobey and leave the woods, I hope your journey goes all the way. And that it, too, will stay and grow with you forever.

—Michael Sheen

Award-winning actor and director Michael Sheen has drawn acclaim for his many roles in film and television, including Frost/Nixon, The Queen, Midnight in Paris *and the Showtime series* Masters of Sex. *He is also an unabashed fanboy at heart.*

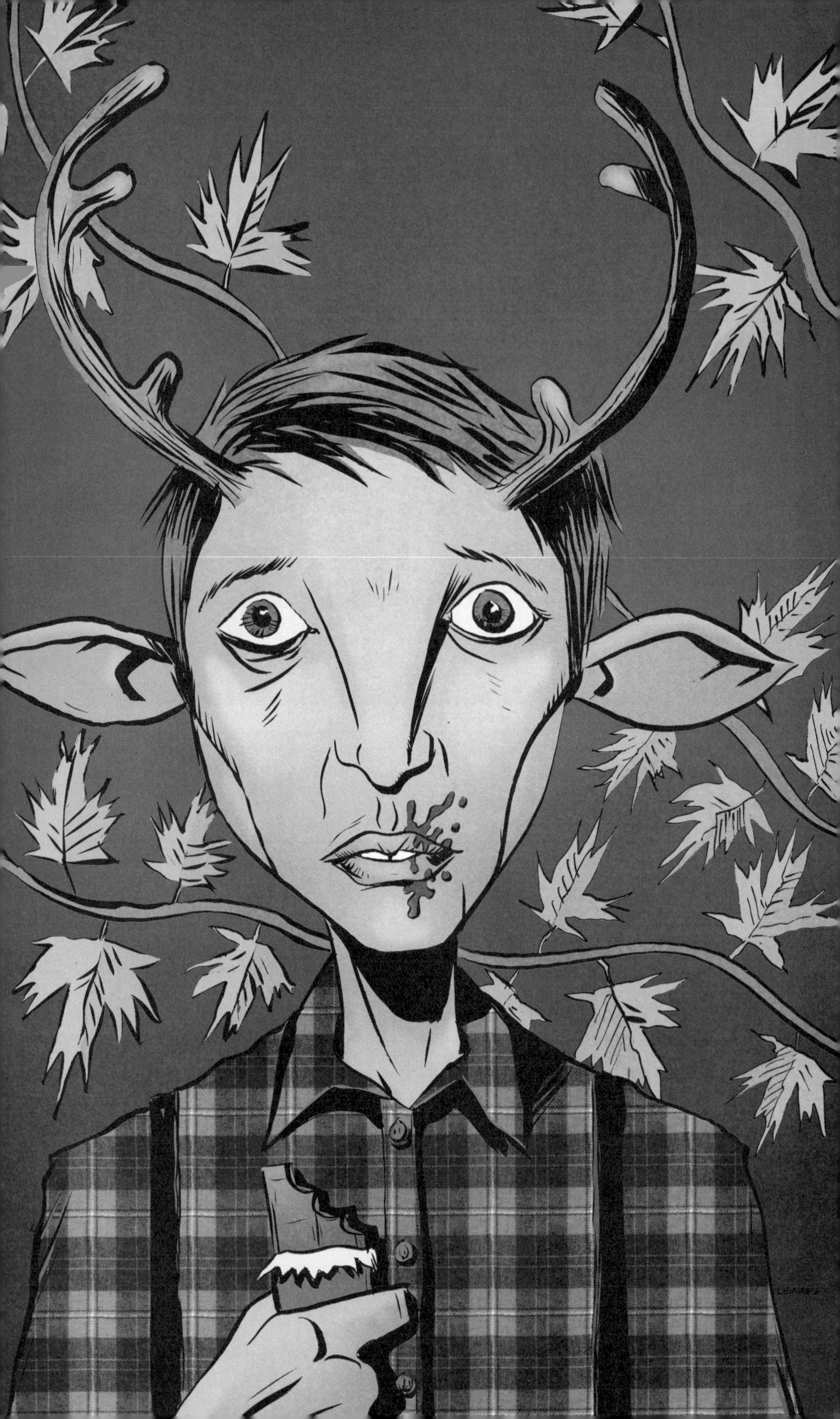

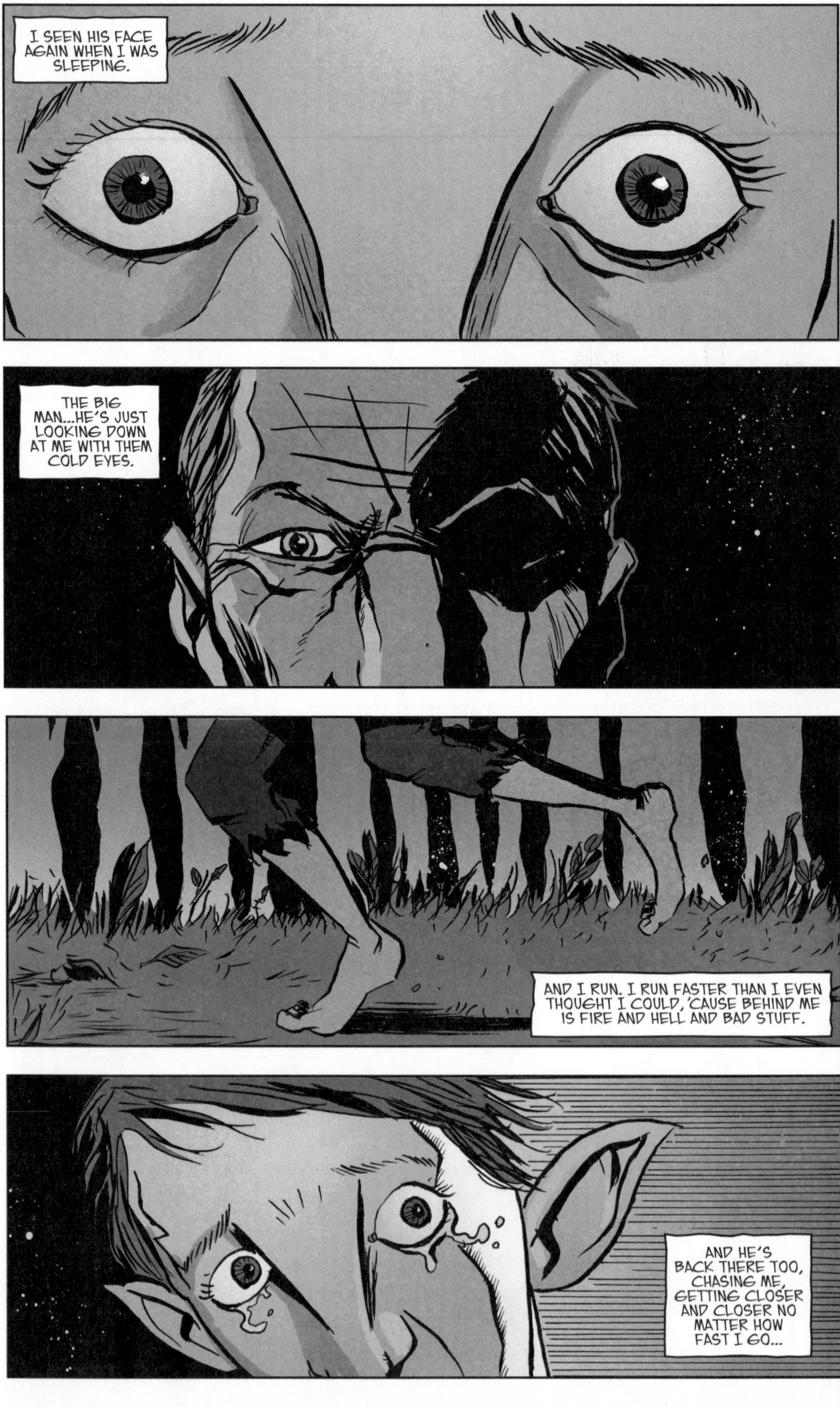
I SEEN HIS FACE AGAIN WHEN I WAS SLEEPING.
THE BIG MAN...HE'S JUST LOOKING DOWN AT ME WITH THEM COLD EYES.
AND I RUN. I RUN FASTER THAN I EVEN THOUGHT I COULD, 'CAUSE BEHIND ME IS FIRE AND HELL AND BAD STUFF.
AND HE'S BACK THERE TOO, CHASING ME, GETTING CLOSER AND CLOSER NO MATTER HOW FAST I GO...

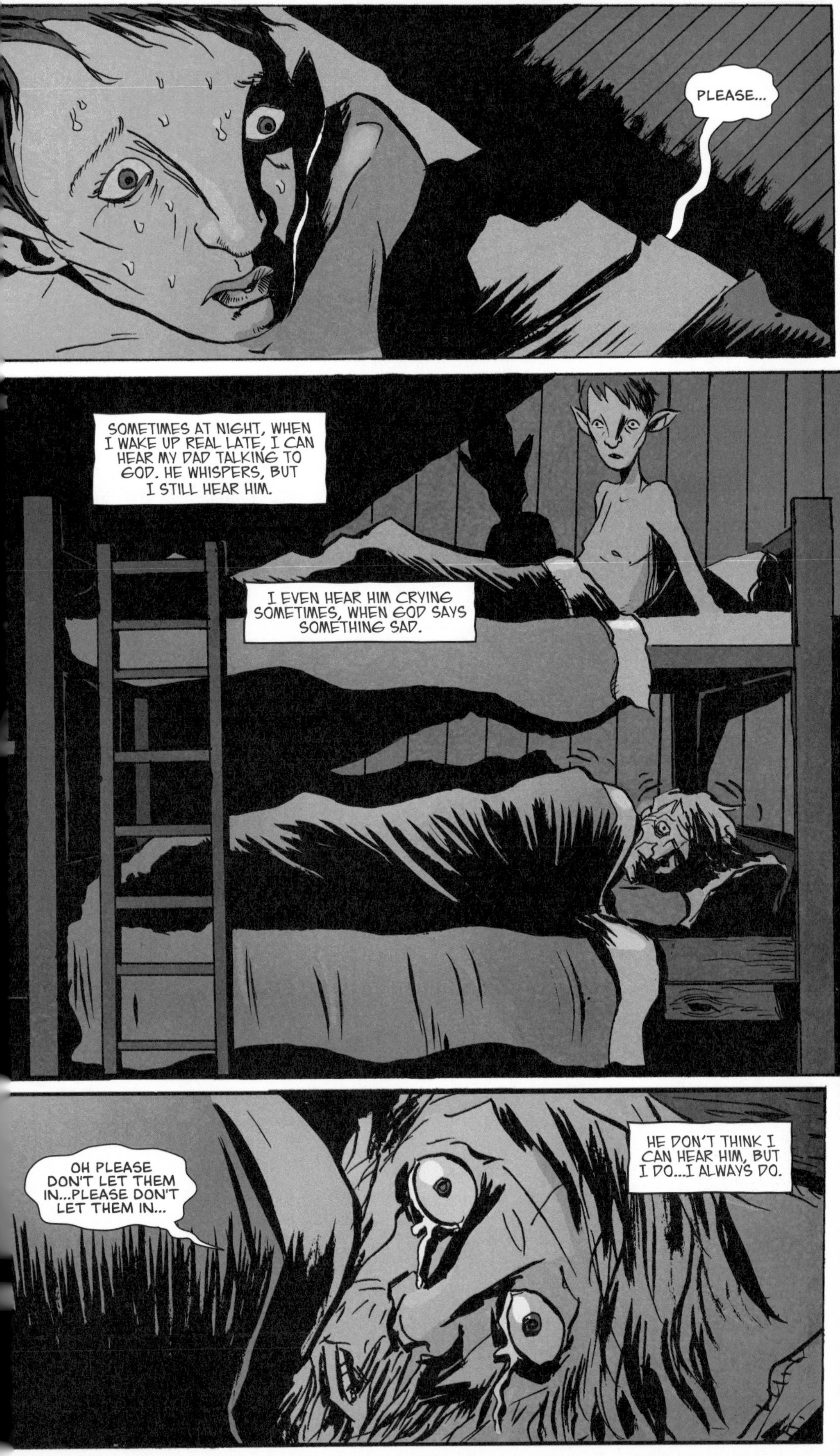
PLEASE...
SOMETIMES AT NIGHT, WHEN I WAKE UP REAL LATE, I CAN HEAR MY DAD TALKING TO GOD. HE WHISPERS, BUT I STILL HEAR HIM.
I EVEN HEAR HIM CRYING SOMETIMES, WHEN GOD SAYS SOMETHING SAD.
OH PLEASE DON'T LET THEM IN...PLEASE DON'T LET THEM IN...
HE DON'T THINK I CAN HEAR HIM, BUT I DO...I ALWAYS DO.

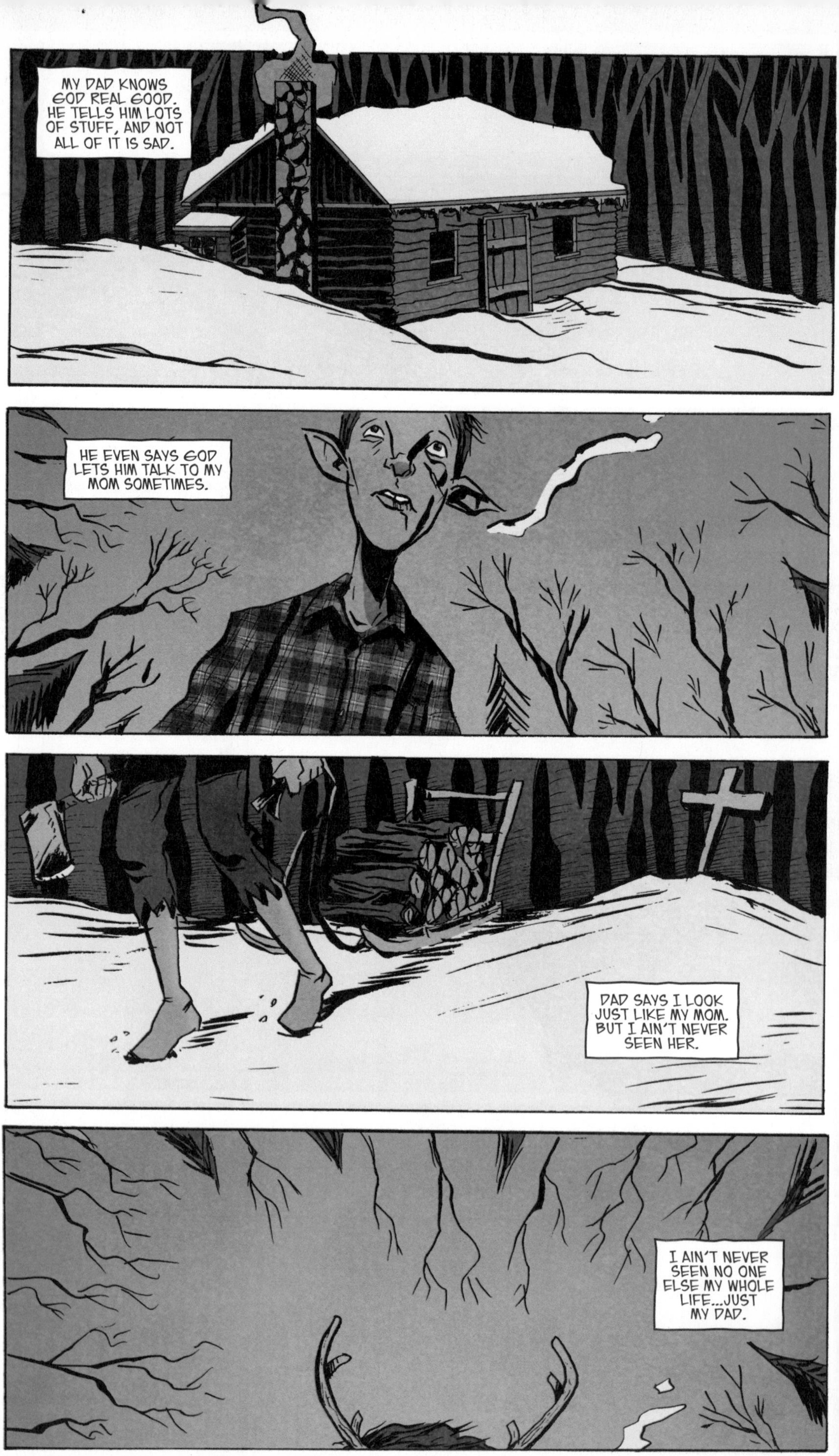
MY DAD KNOWS GOD REAL GOOD. HE TELLS HIM LOTS OF STUFF, AND NOT ALL OF IT IS SAD.
HE EVEN SAYS GOD LETS HIM TALK TO MY MOM SOMETIMES.
DAD SAYS I LOOK JUST LIKE MY MOM. BUT I AIN'T NEVER SEEN HER.
I AIN'T NEVER SEEN NO ONE ELSE MY WHOLE LIFE...JUST MY DAD.

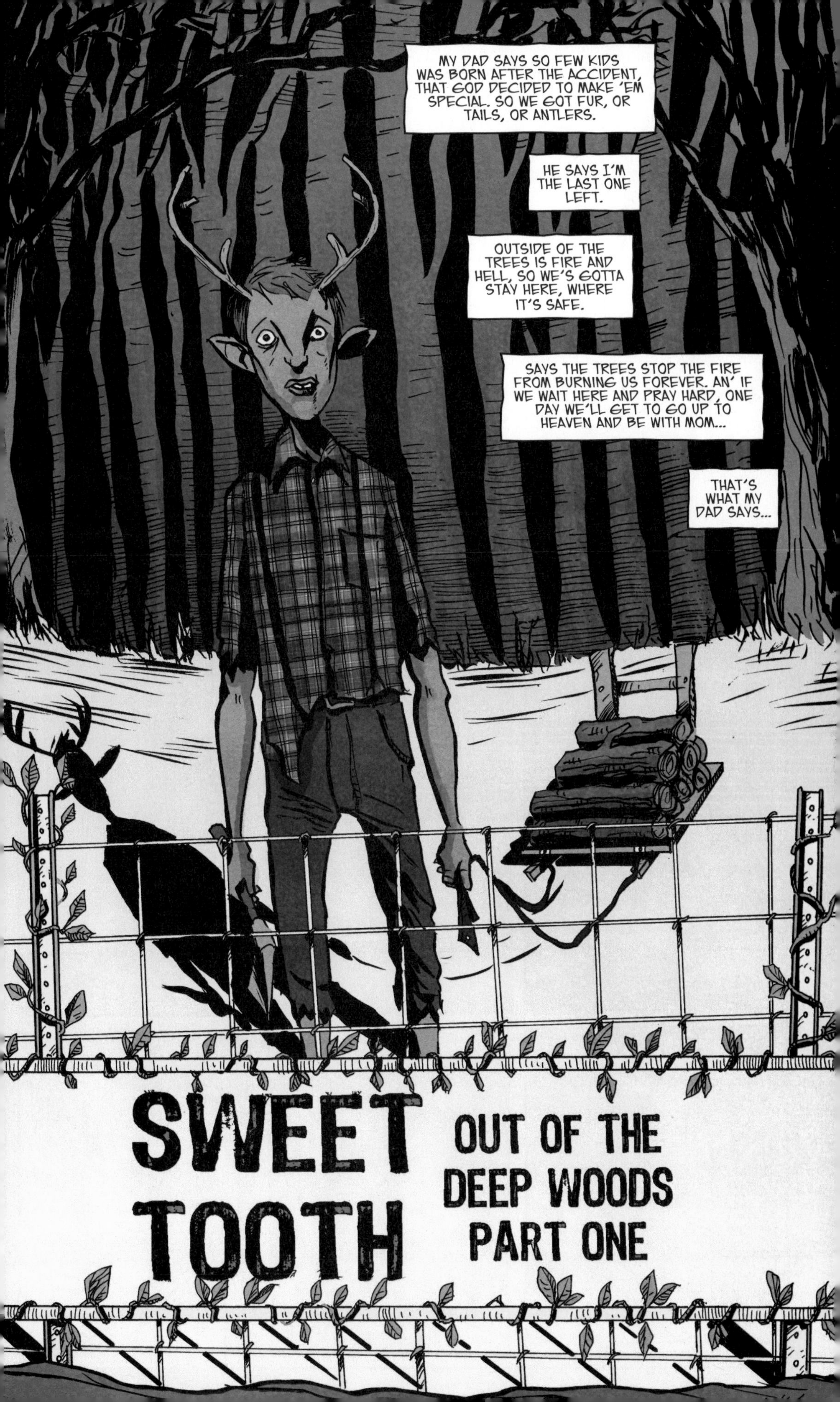
MY DAD SAYS SO FEW KIDS WAS BORN AFTER THE ACCIDENT, THAT GOD DECIDED TO MAKE 'EM SPECIAL. SO WE GOT FUR, OR TAILS, OR ANTLERS.
HE SAYS I'M THE LAST ONE LEFT.
OUTSIDE OF THE TREES IS FIRE AND HELL, SO WE'S GOTTA STAY HERE, WHERE IT'S SAFE.
SAYS THE TREES STOP THE FIRE FROM BURNING US FOREVER. AN' IF WE WAIT HERE AND PRAY HARD, ONE DAY WE'LL GET TO GO UP TO HEAVEN AND BE WITH MOM...
THAT'S WHAT MY DAD SAYS...
SWEET TOOTH
OUT OF THE DEEP WOODS PART ONE

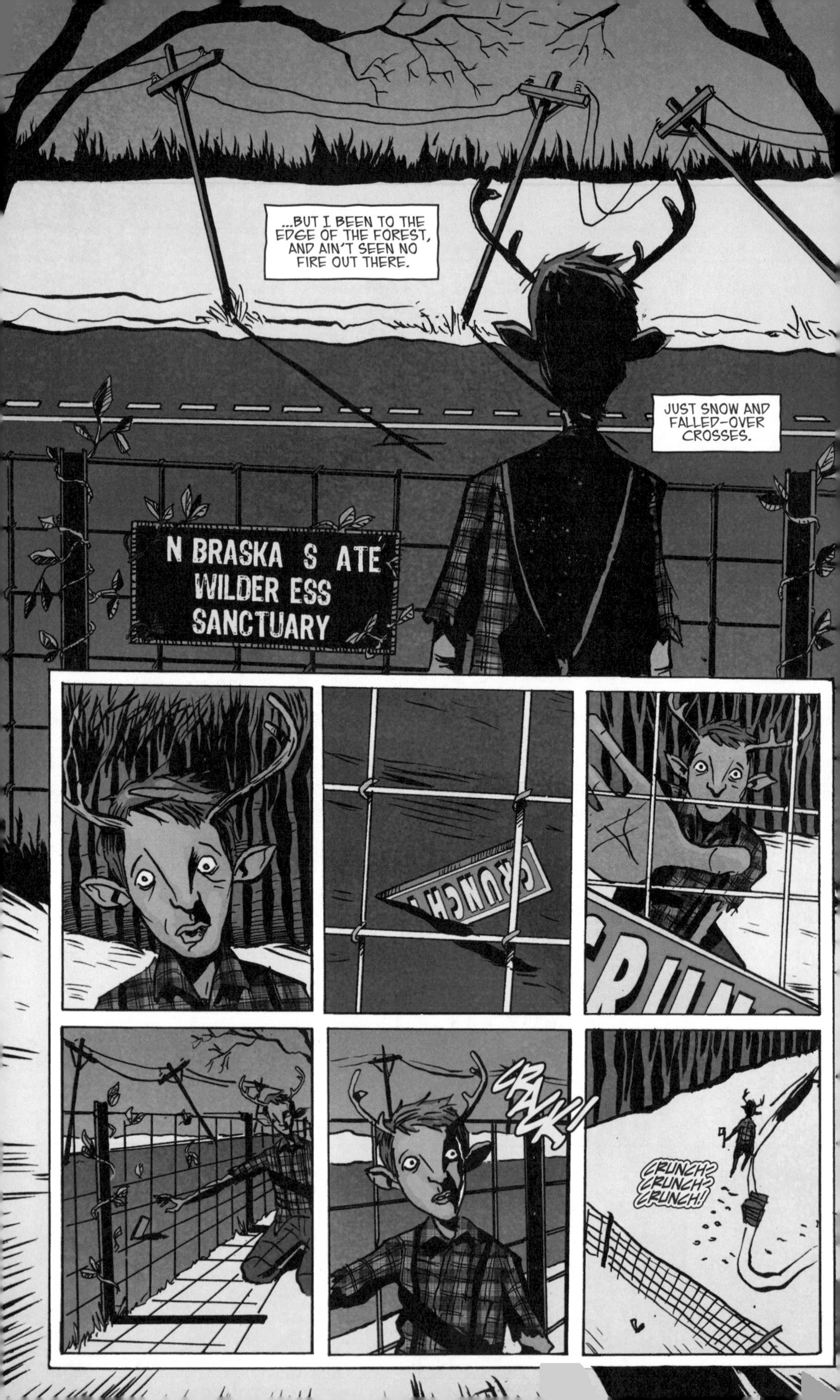
...BUT I BEEN TO THE EDGE OF THE FOREST, AND AIN'T SEEN NO FIRE OUT THERE.
JUST SNOW AND FALLED-OVER CROSSES.
N BRASKA S ATE WILDER ESS SANCTUARY
CRUNCH!
CRACK!
CRUNCH CRUNCH CRUNCH!

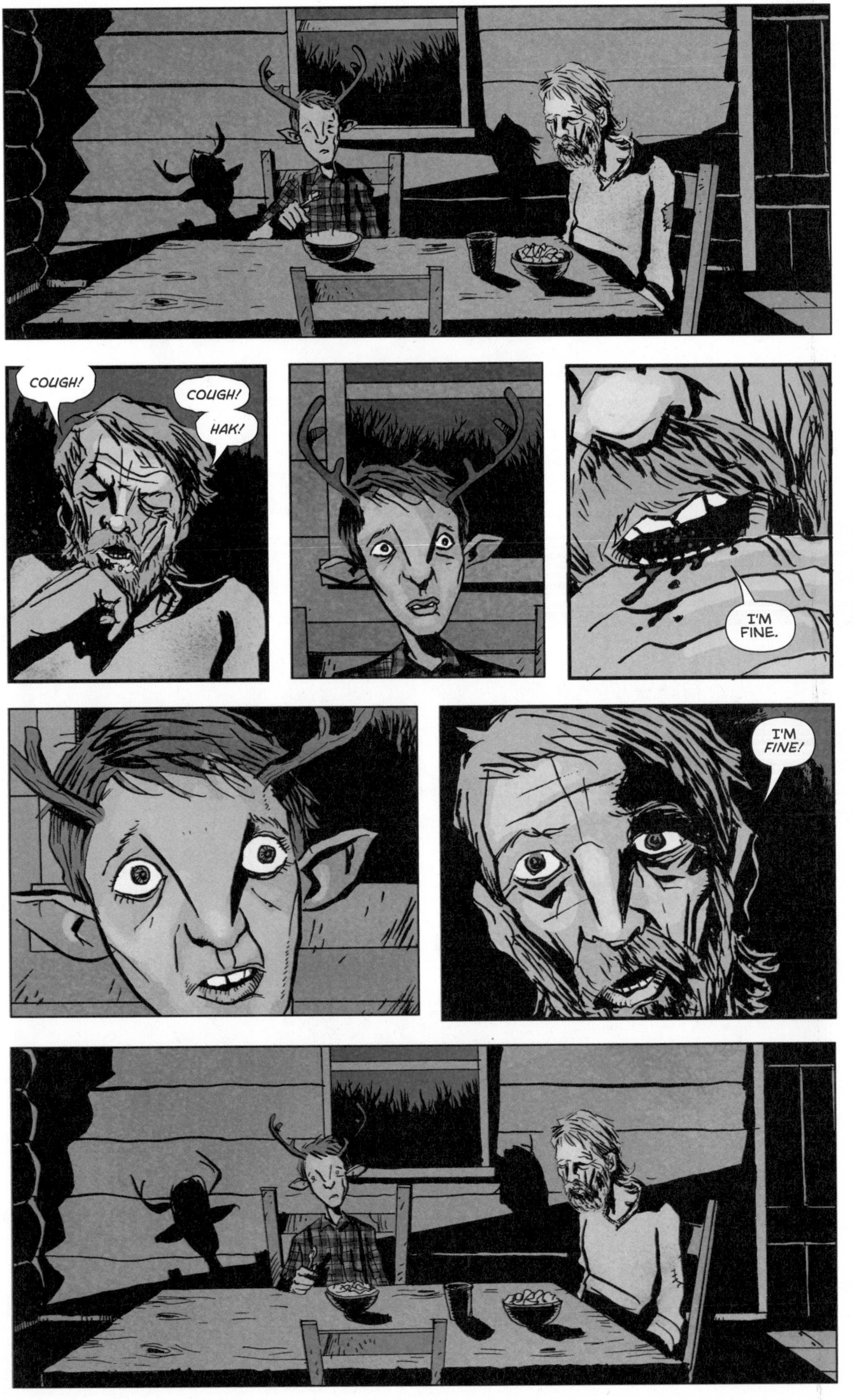
COUGH!
COUGH!
HAK!
I'M FINE.
I'M FINE!

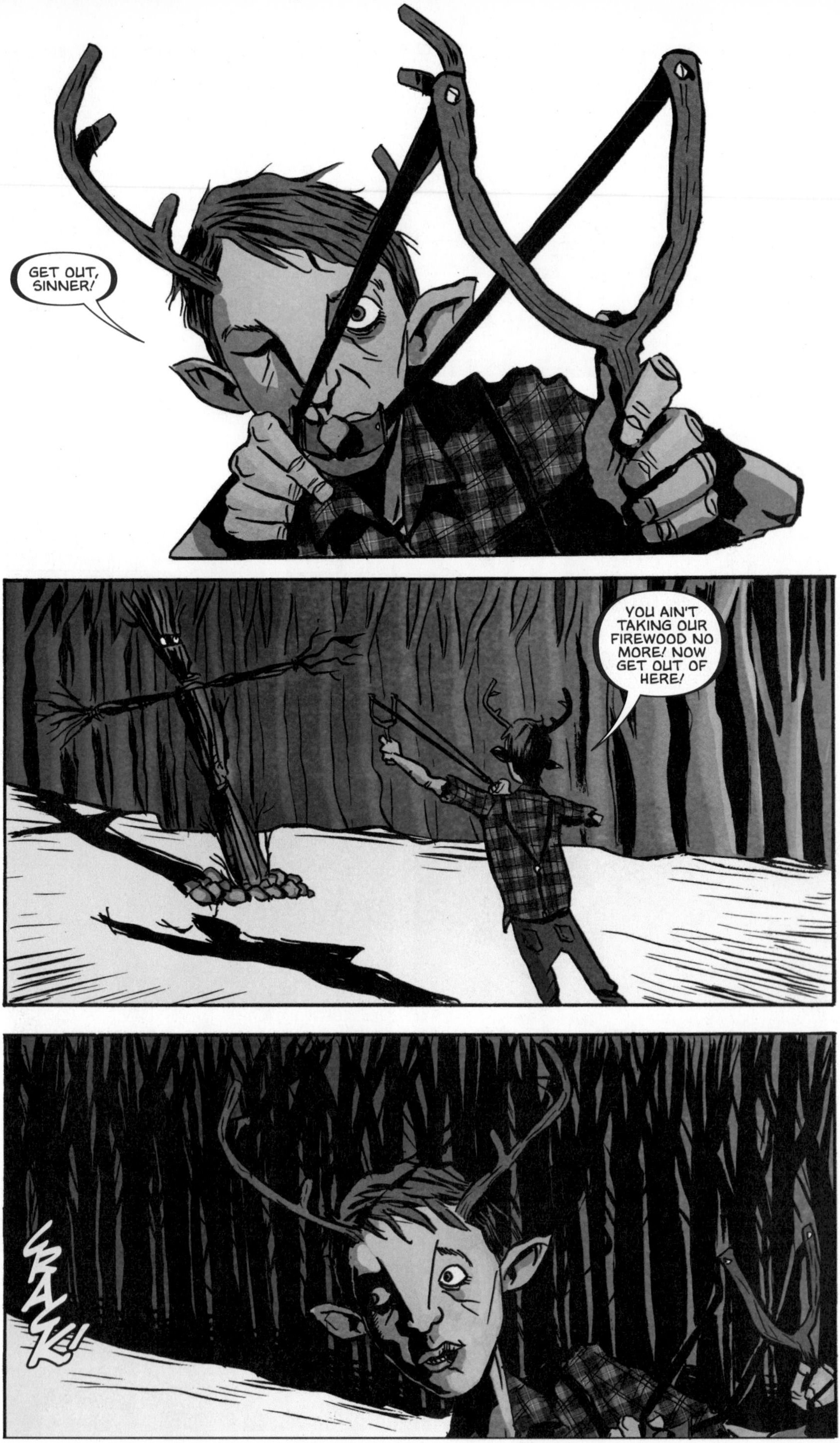
GET OUT, SINNER!
YOU AIN'T TAKING OUR FIREWOOD NO MORE! NOW GET OUT OF HERE!
KRAKK!

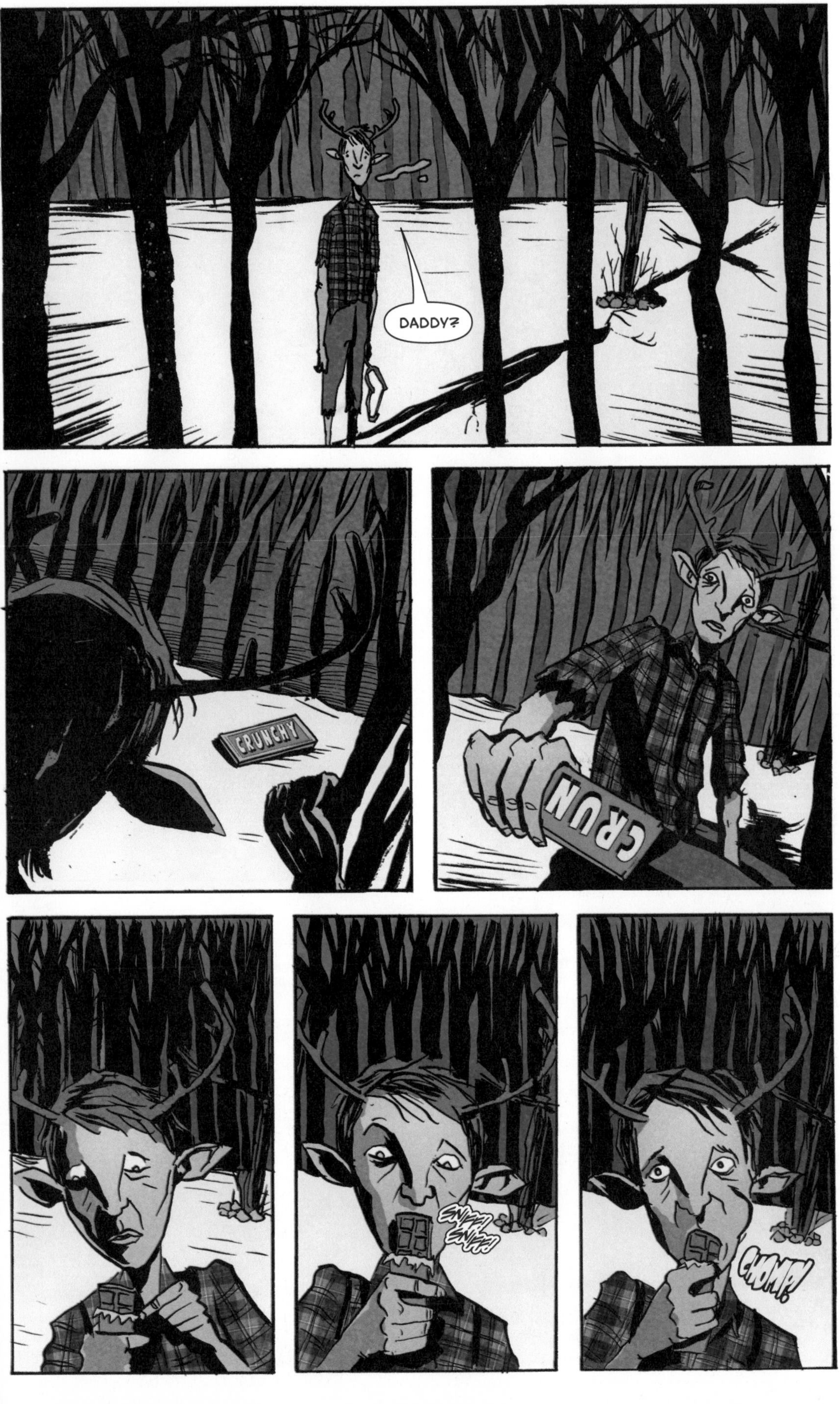
DADDY?
CRUNCHY
CRUN
SNIFF! SNIFF!
CHOMP!

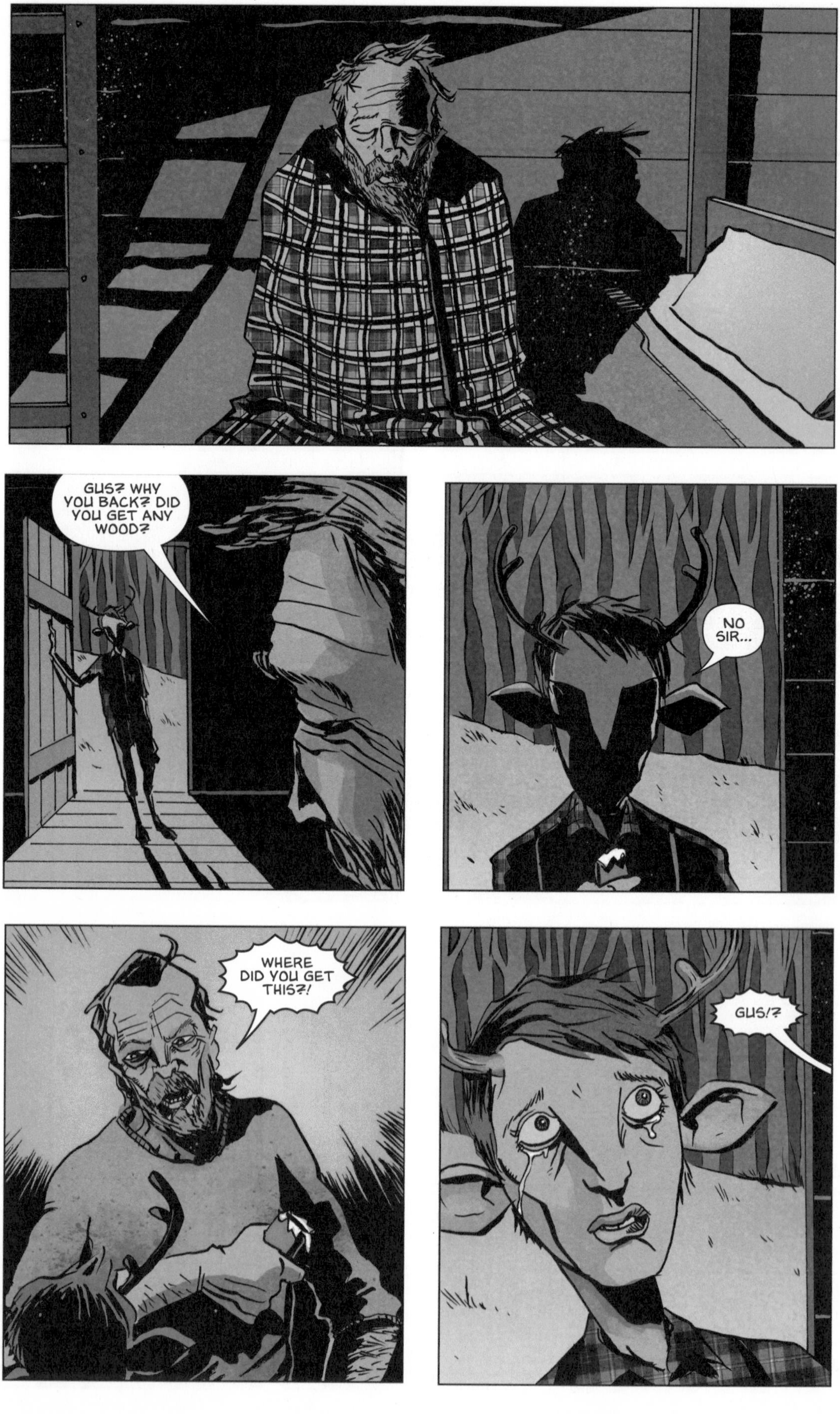
GUS? WHY YOU BACK? DID YOU GET ANY WOOD?
NO SIR...
WHERE DID YOU GET THIS?!
GUS!?

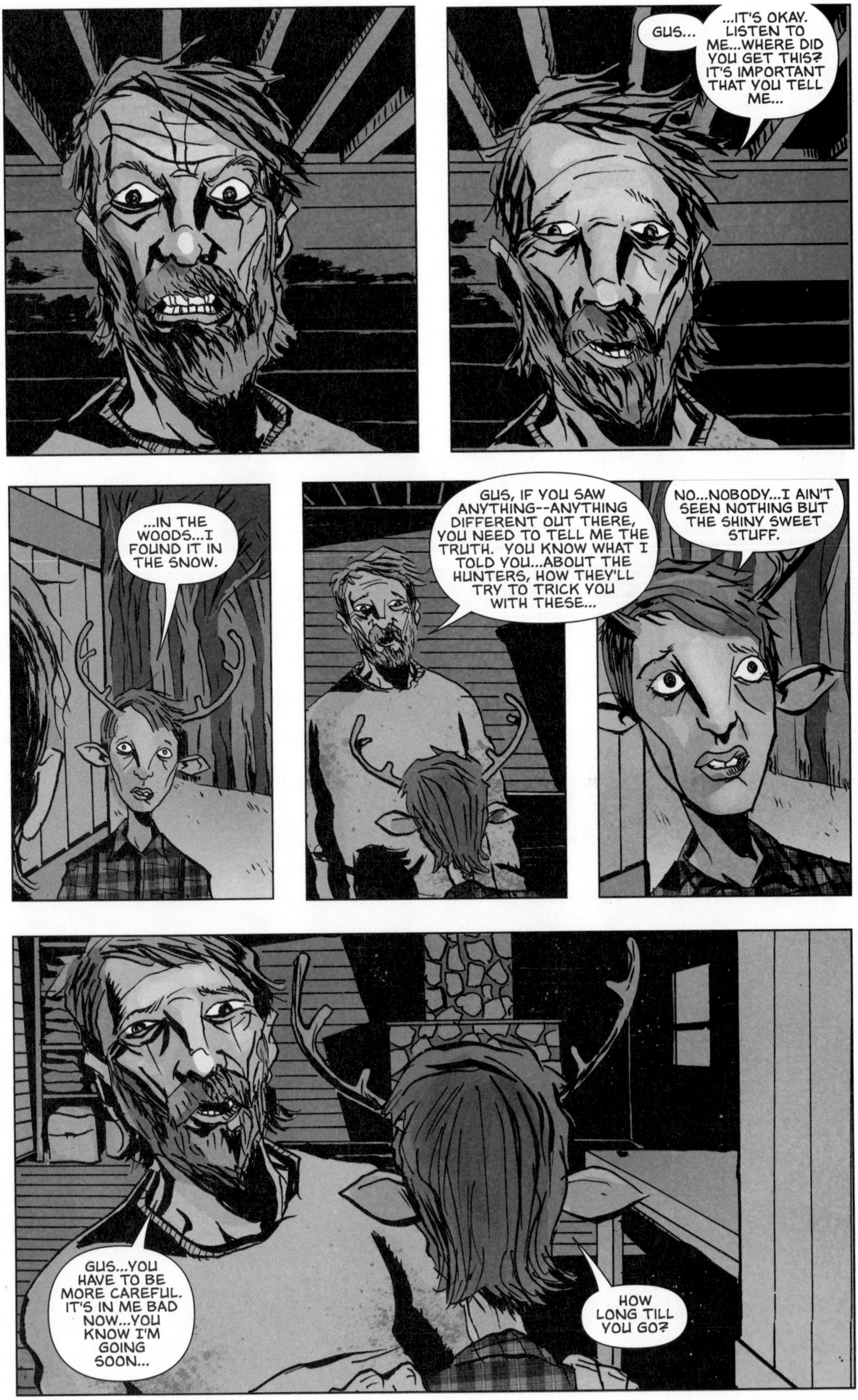
GUS...
...IT'S OKAY. LISTEN TO ME...WHERE DID YOU GET THIS? IT'S IMPORTANT THAT YOU TELL ME...
...IN THE WOODS...I FOUND IT IN THE SNOW.
GUS, IF YOU SAW ANYTHING--ANYTHING DIFFERENT OUT THERE, YOU NEED TO TELL ME THE TRUTH. YOU KNOW WHAT I TOLD YOU...ABOUT THE HUNTERS, HOW THEY'LL TRY TO TRICK YOU WITH THESE...
NO...NOBODY...I AIN'T SEEN NOTHING BUT THE SHINY SWEET STUFF.
GUS...YOU HAVE TO BE MORE CAREFUL. IT'S IN ME BAD NOW...YOU KNOW I'M GOING SOON...
HOW LONG TILL YOU GO?

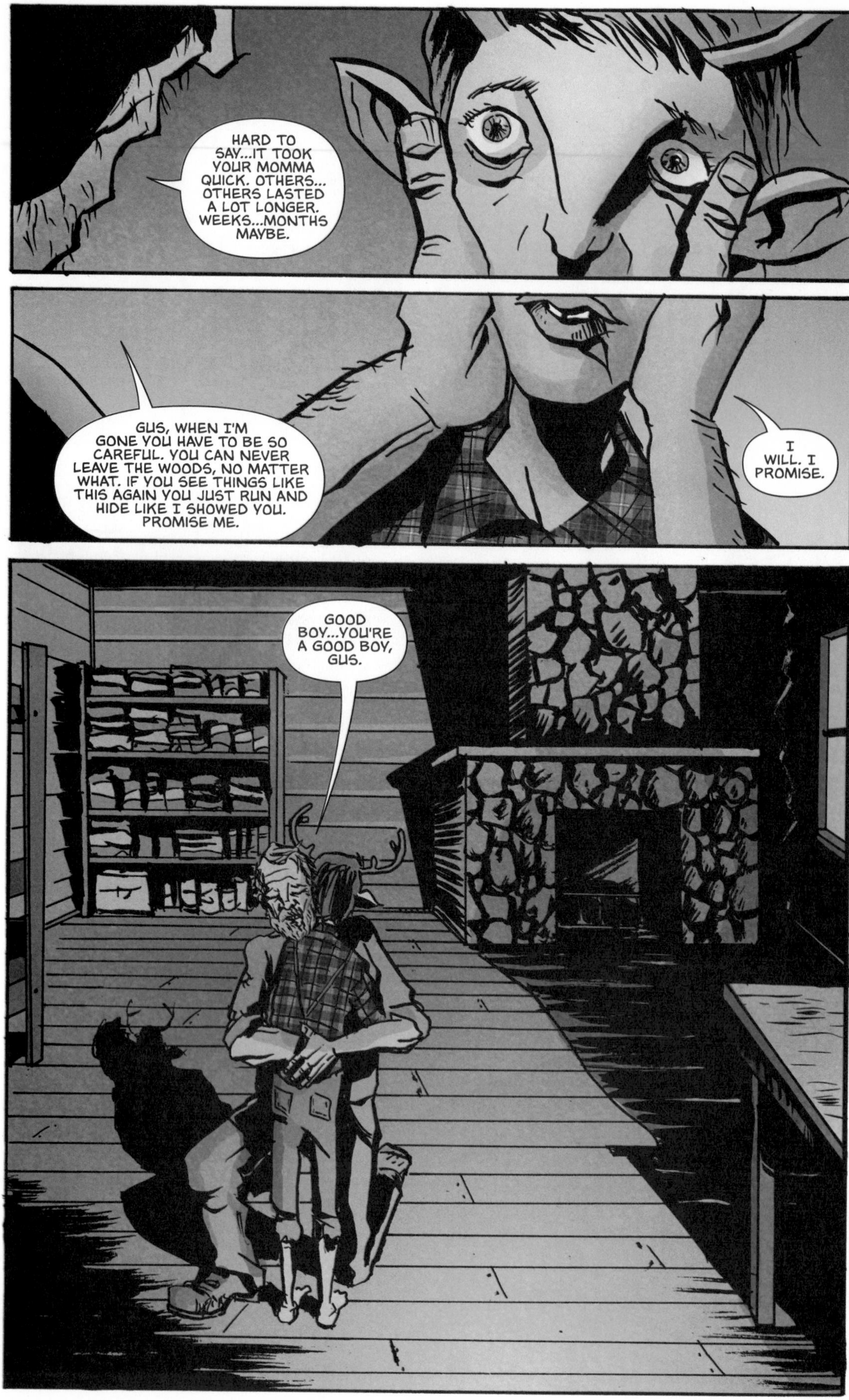
HARD TO SAY...IT TOOK YOUR MOMMA QUICK. OTHERS... OTHERS LASTED A LOT LONGER. WEEKS...MONTHS MAYBE.
GUS, WHEN I'M GONE YOU HAVE TO BE SO CAREFUL. YOU CAN NEVER LEAVE THE WOODS, NO MATTER WHAT. IF YOU SEE THINGS LIKE THIS AGAIN YOU JUST RUN AND HIDE LIKE I SHOWED YOU. PROMISE ME.
I WILL. I PROMISE.
GOOD BOY...YOU'RE A GOOD BOY, GUS.

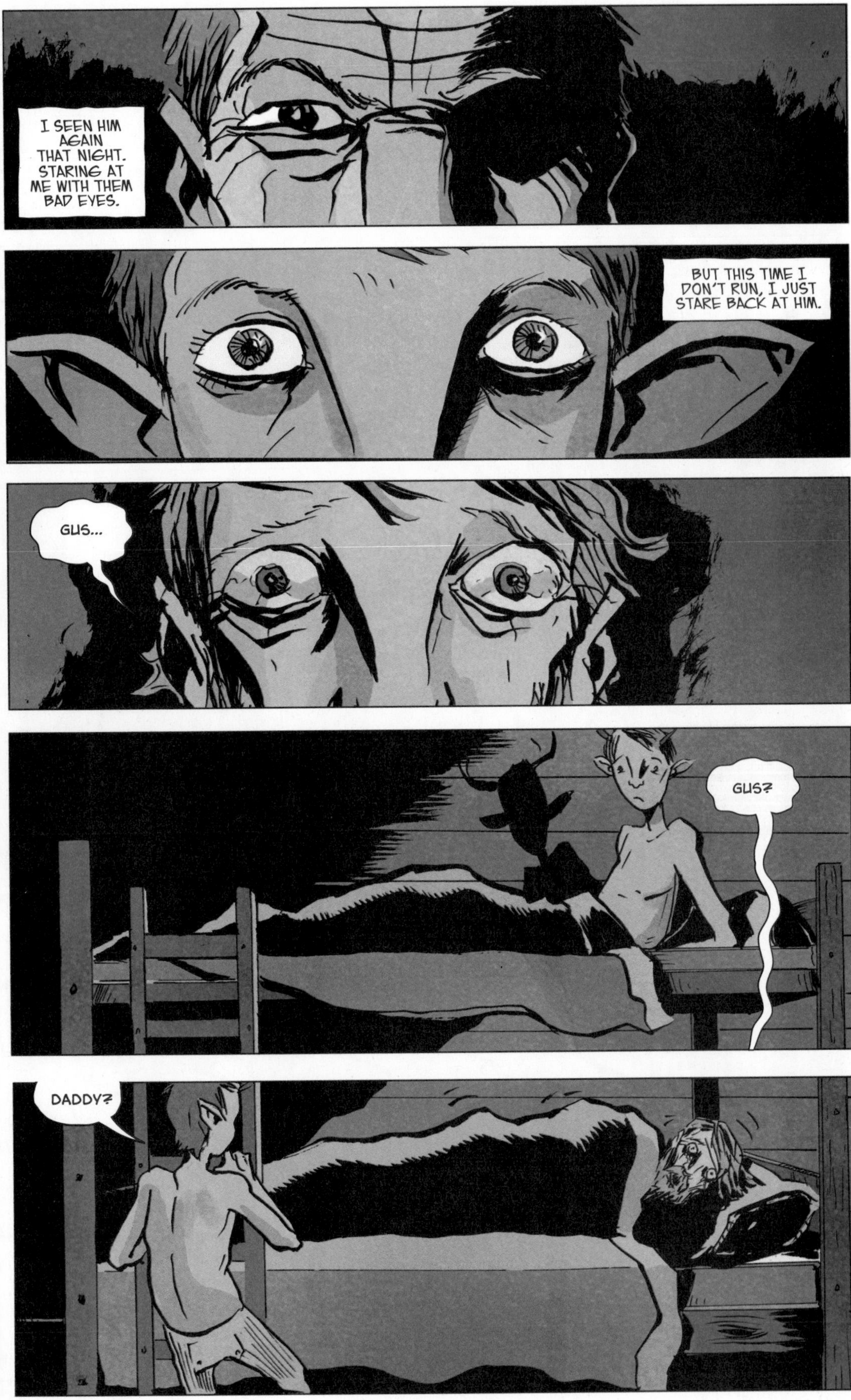
I SEEN HIM AGAIN THAT NIGHT. STARING AT ME WITH THEM BAD EYES.
BUT THIS TIME I DON'T RUN, I JUST STARE BACK AT HIM.
GUS...
GUS?
DADDY?

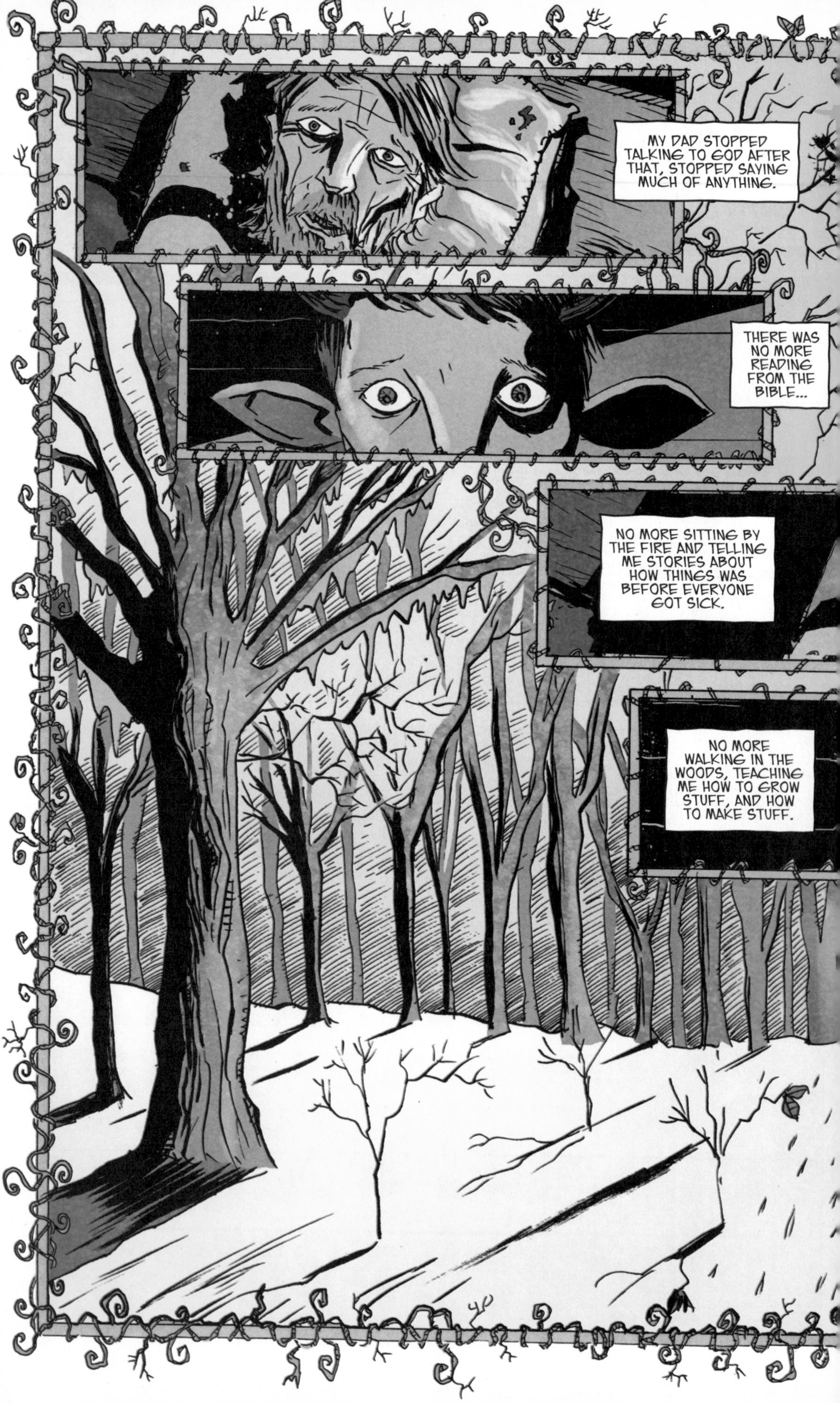
MY DAD STOPPED TALKING TO GOD AFTER THAT, STOPPED SAYING MUCH OF ANYTHING.
THERE WAS NO MORE READING FROM THE BIBLE...
NO MORE SITTING BY THE FIRE AND TELLING ME STORIES ABOUT HOW THINGS WAS BEFORE EVERYONE GOT SICK.
NO MORE WALKING IN THE WOODS, TEACHING ME HOW TO GROW STUFF, AND HOW TO MAKE STUFF.

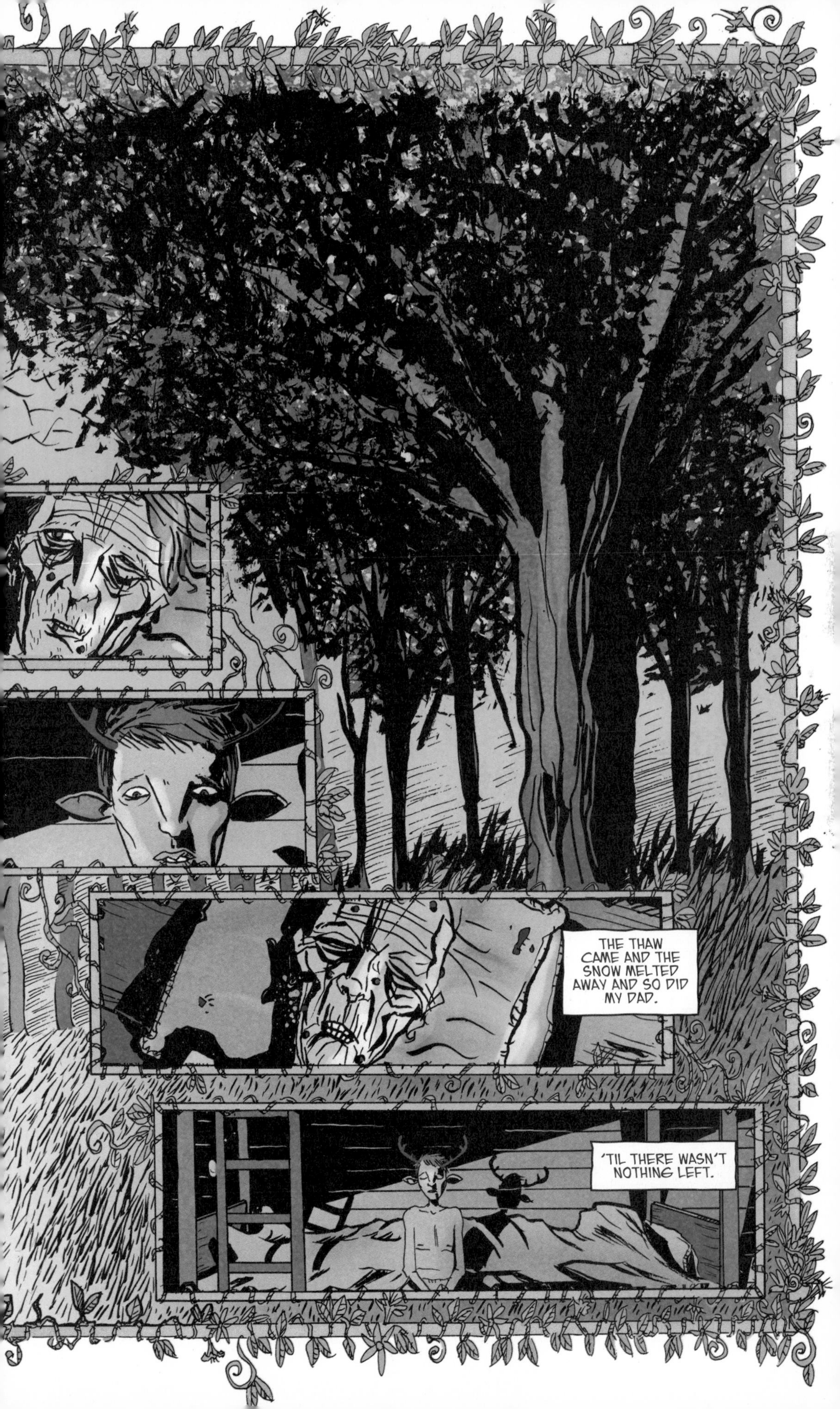
THE THAW CAME AND THE SNOW MELTED AWAY AND SO DID MY DAD.
'TIL THERE WASN'T NOTHING LEFT.

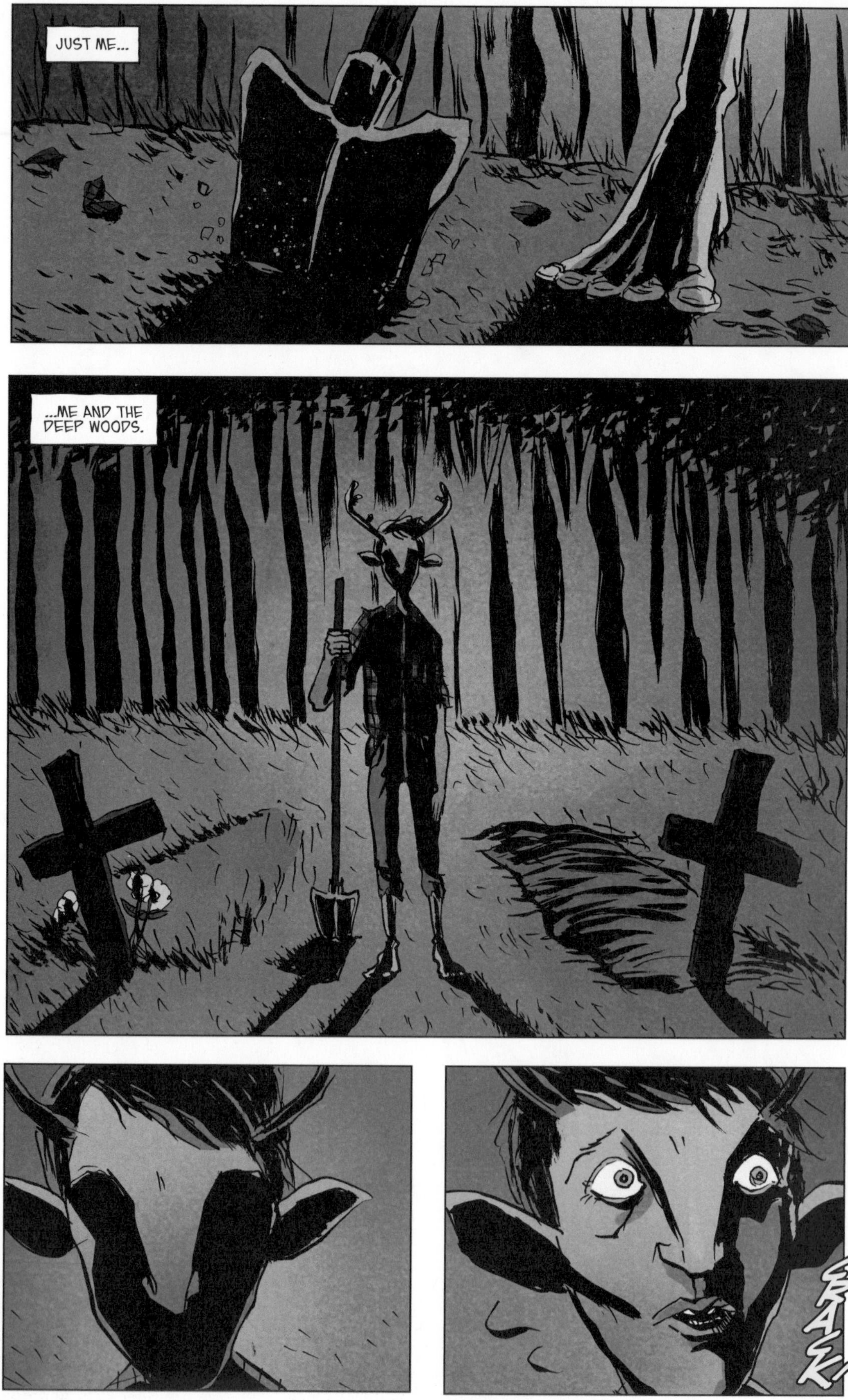
JUST ME...
...ME AND THE DEEP WOODS.
CRACK!

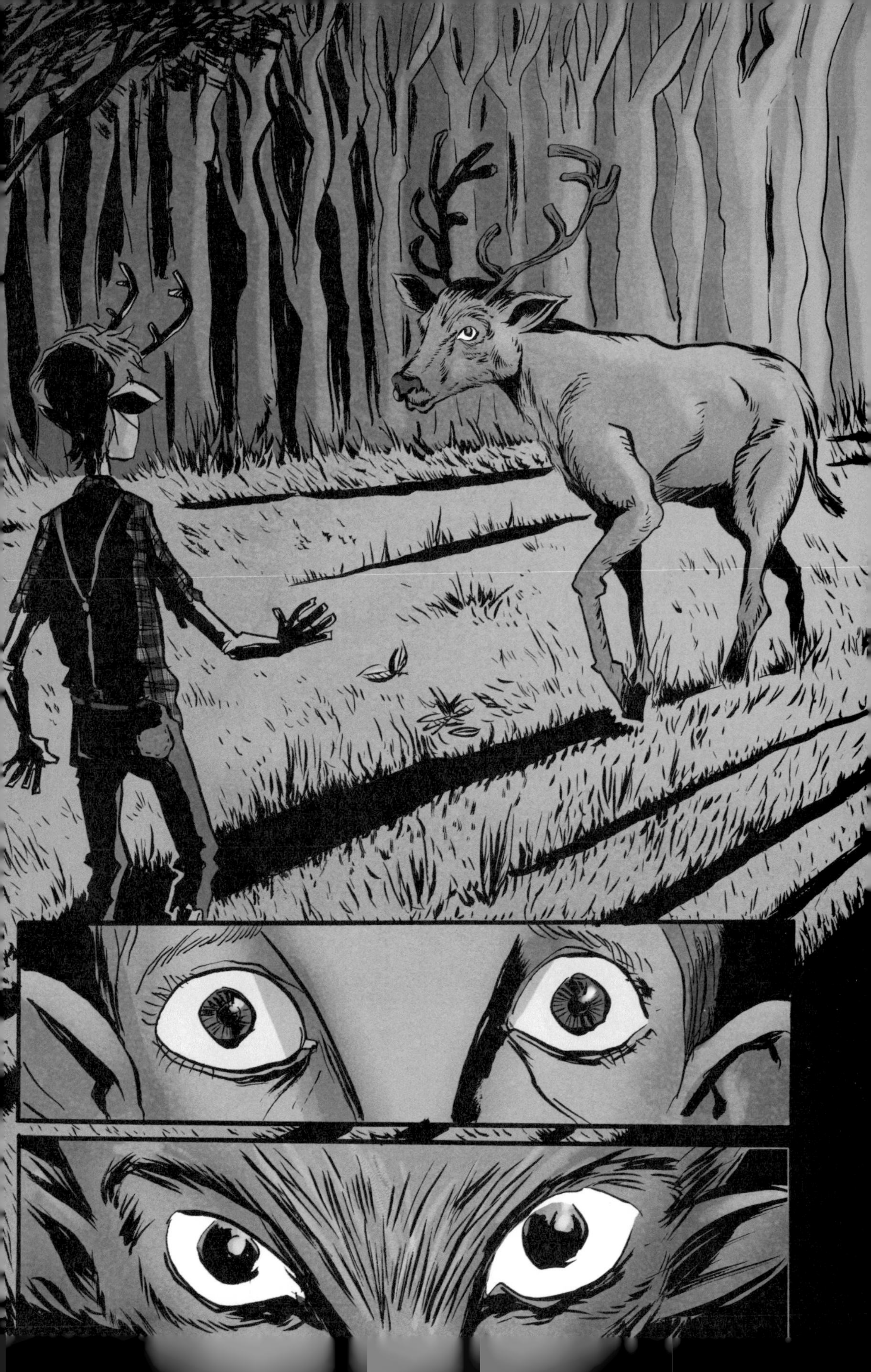

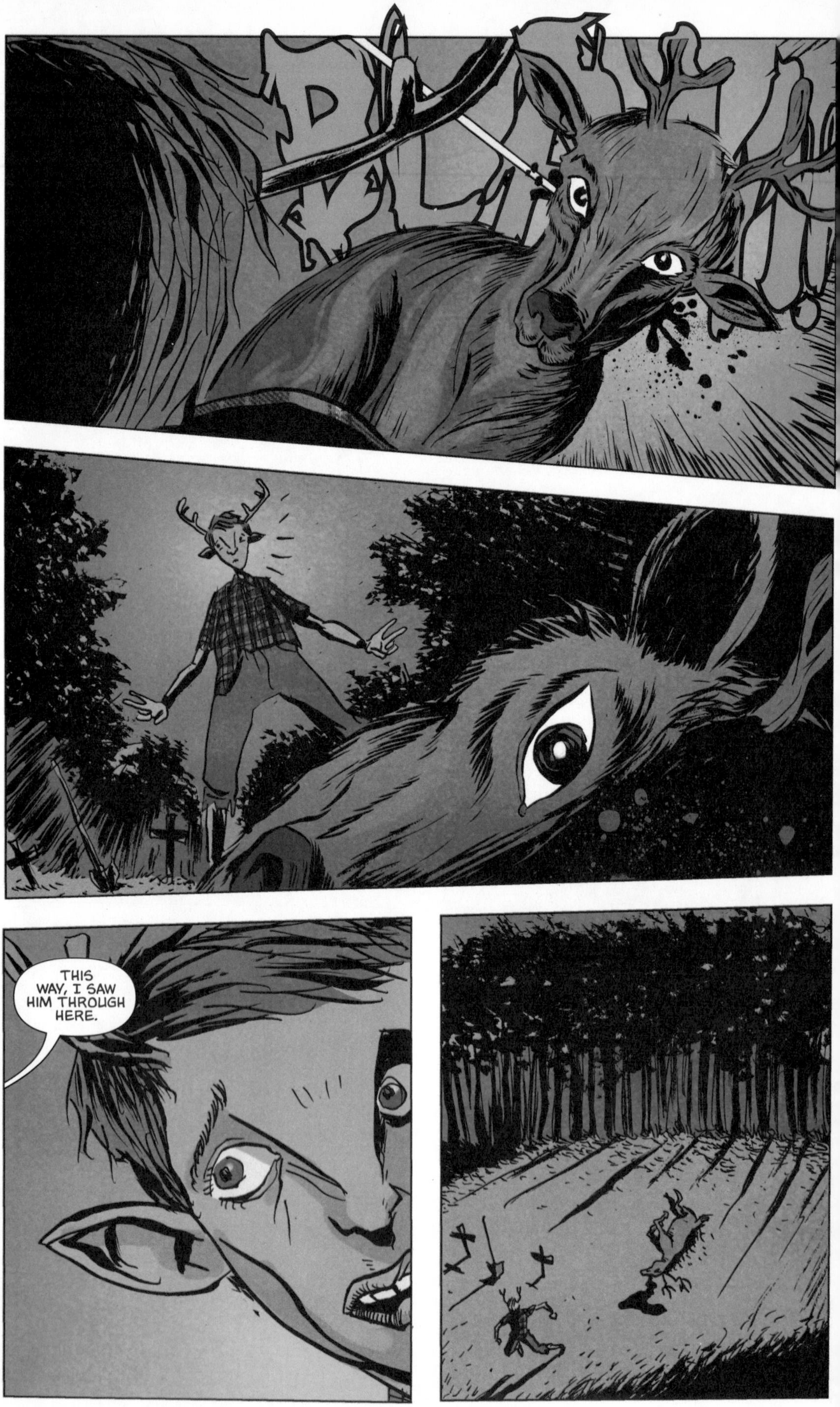
THIS WAY, I SAW HIM THROUGH HERE.

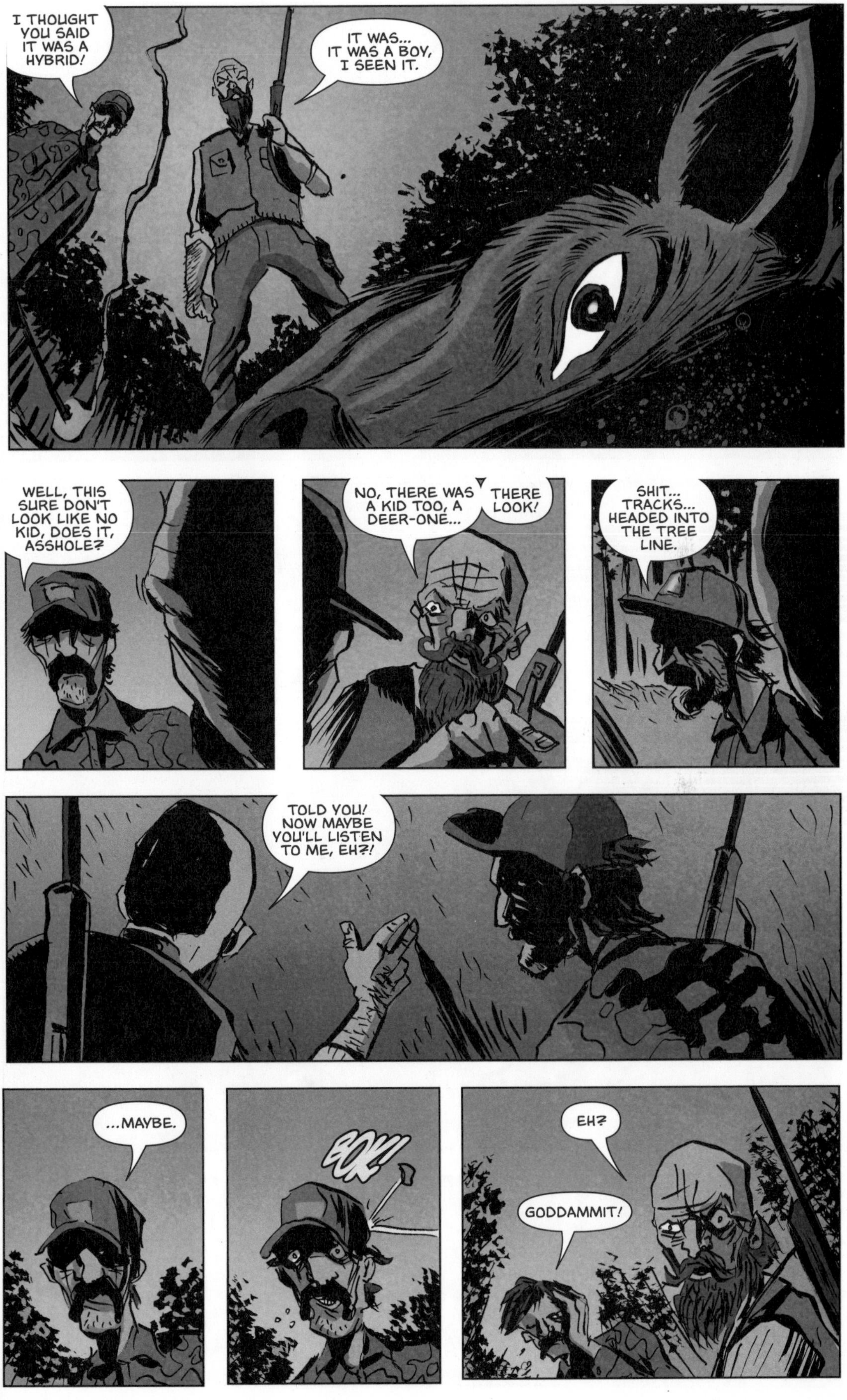
I THOUGHT YOU SAID IT WAS A HYBRID!
IT WAS... IT WAS A BOY, I SEEN IT.
WELL, THIS SURE DON'T LOOK LIKE NO KID, DOES IT, ASSHOLE?
NO, THERE WAS A KID TOO, A DEER-ONE...
THERE LOOK!
SHIT... TRACKS... HEADED INTO THE TREE LINE.
TOLD YOU! NOW MAYBE YOU'LL LISTEN TO ME, EH?!
...MAYBE.
BOK!
EH?
GODDAMMIT!

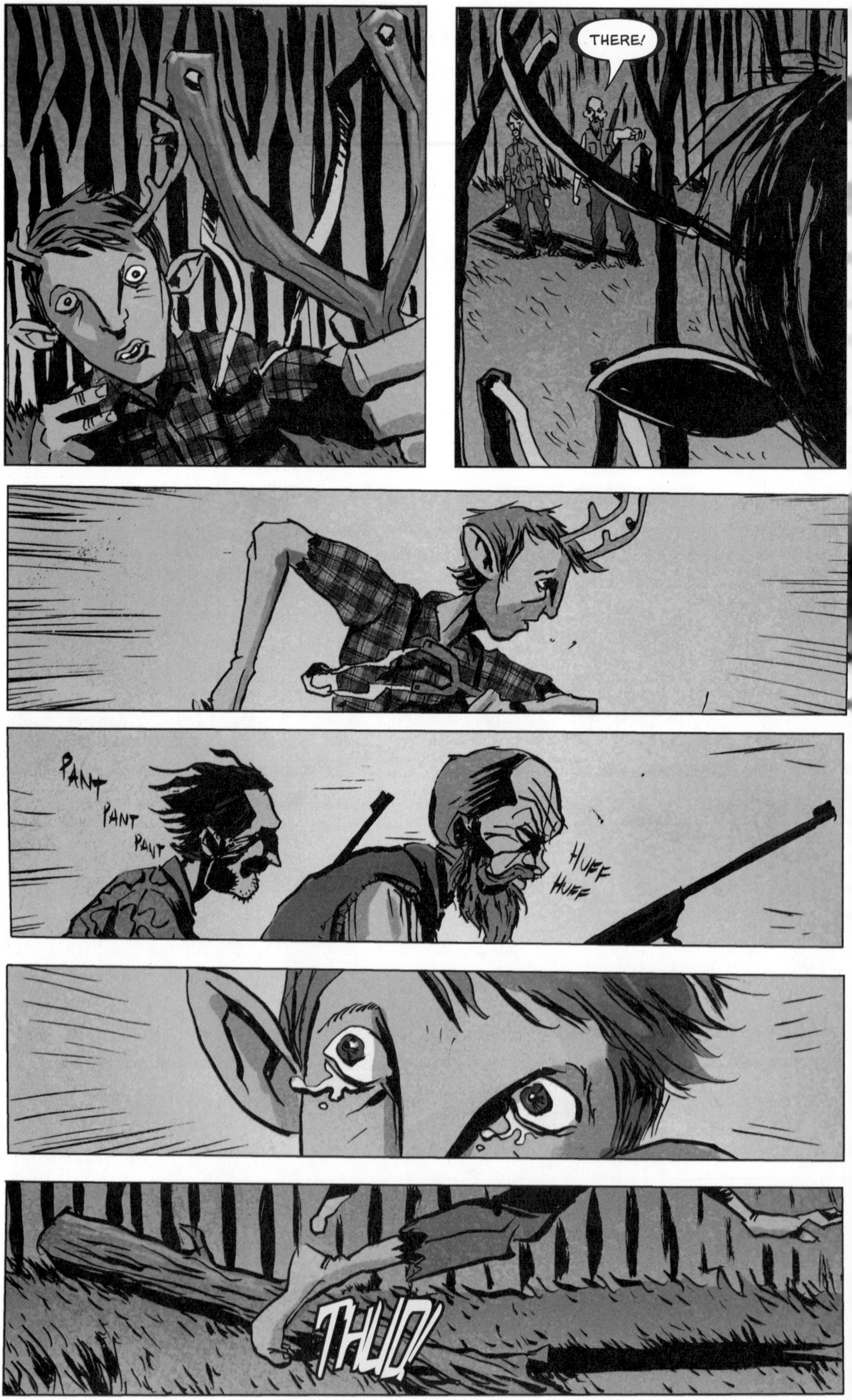
THERE!
PANT PANT PANT
HUFF HUFF
THUD!

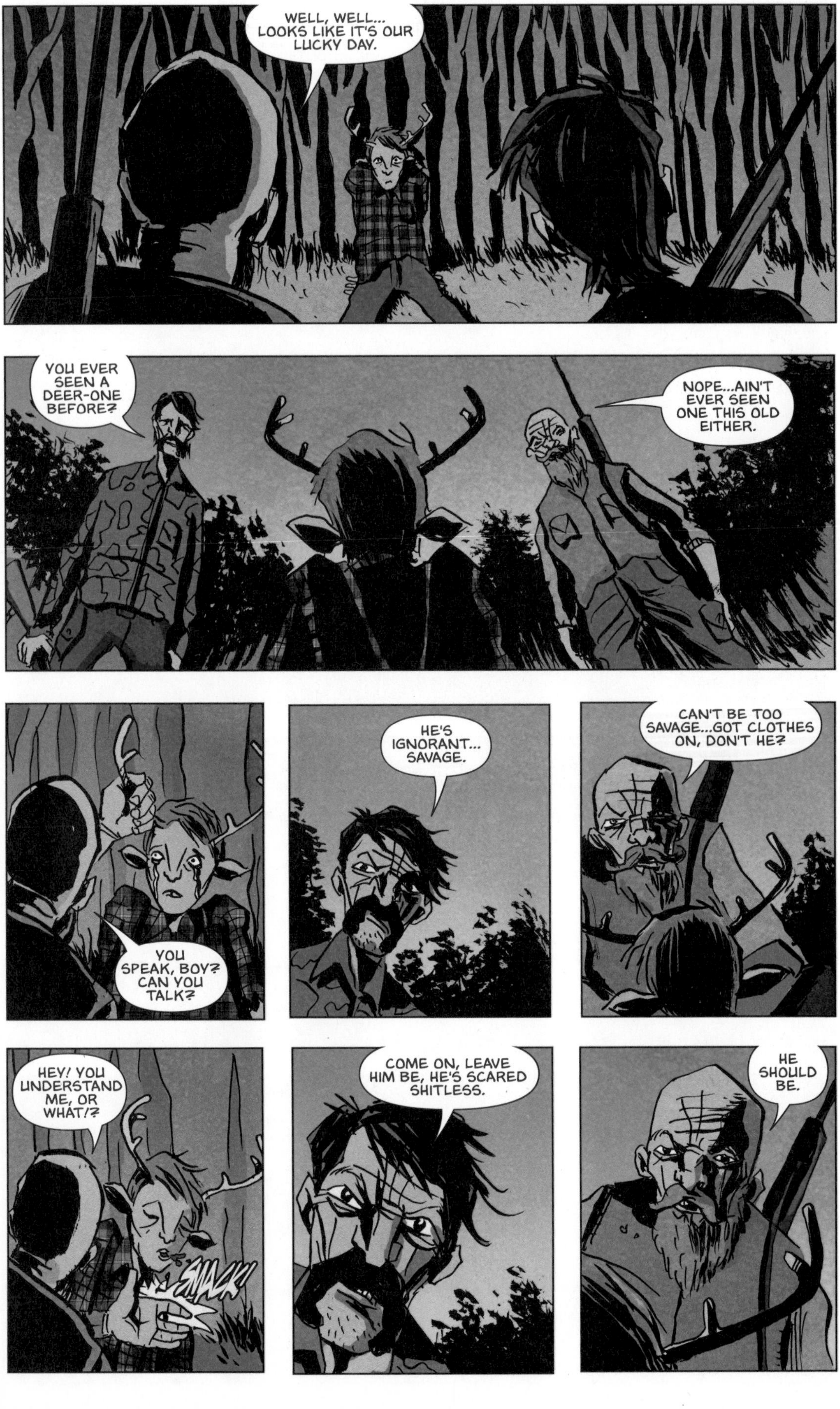
WELL, WELL... LOOKS LIKE IT'S OUR LUCKY DAY.
YOU EVER SEEN A DEER-ONE BEFORE?
NOPE...AIN'T EVER SEEN ONE THIS OLD EITHER.
YOU SPEAK, BOY? CAN YOU TALK?
HE'S IGNORANT... SAVAGE.
CAN'T BE TOO SAVAGE...GOT CLOTHES ON, DON'T HE?
HEY! YOU UNDERSTAND ME, OR WHAT!?
SMACK!
COME ON, LEAVE HIM BE, HE'S SCARED SHITLESS.
HE SHOULD BE.

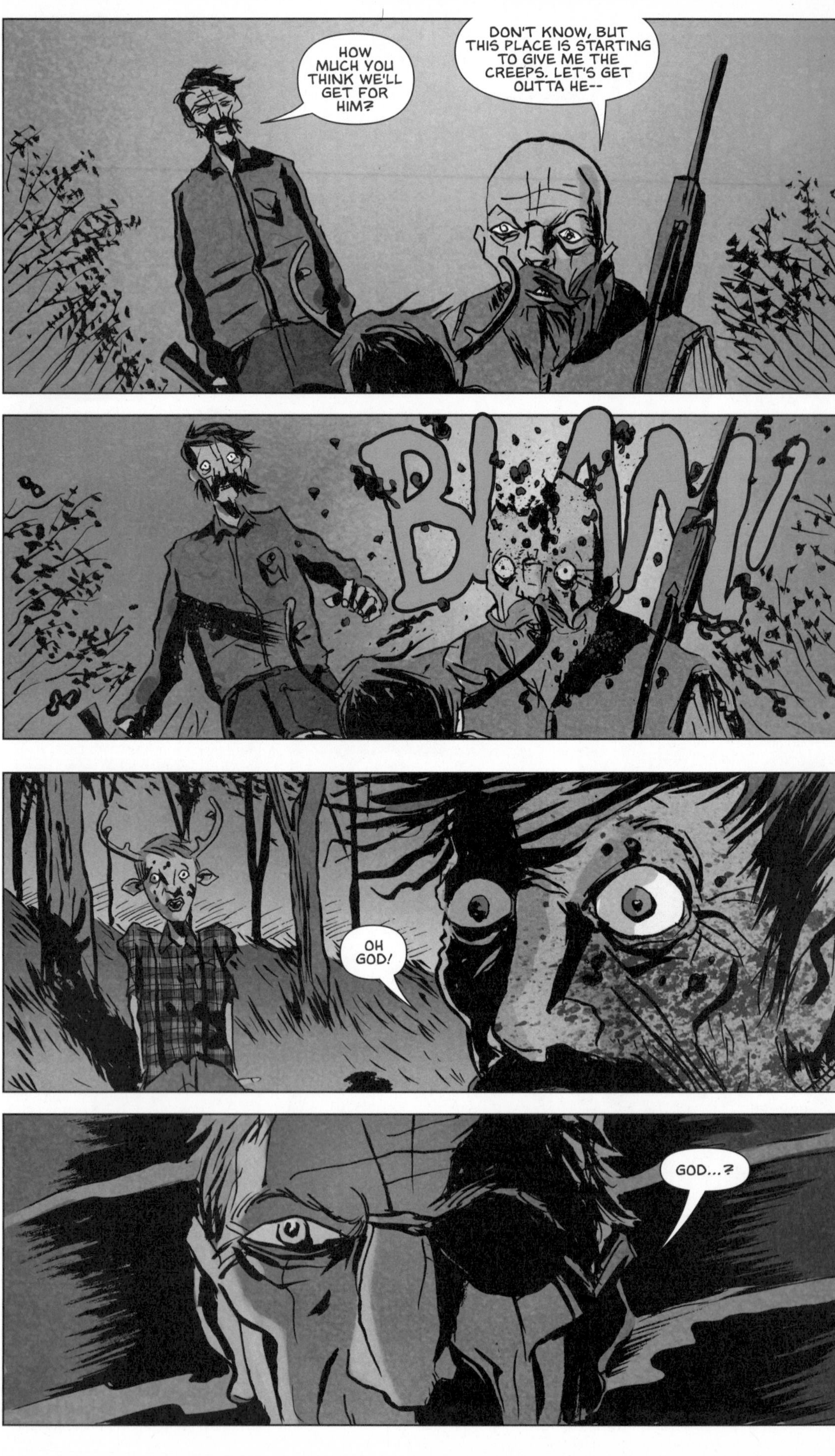
HOW MUCH YOU THINK WE'LL GET FOR HIM?
DON'T KNOW, BUT THIS PLACE IS STARTING TO GIVE ME THE CREEPS. LET'S GET OUTTA HE--
BLAM!
OH GOD!
GOD...?

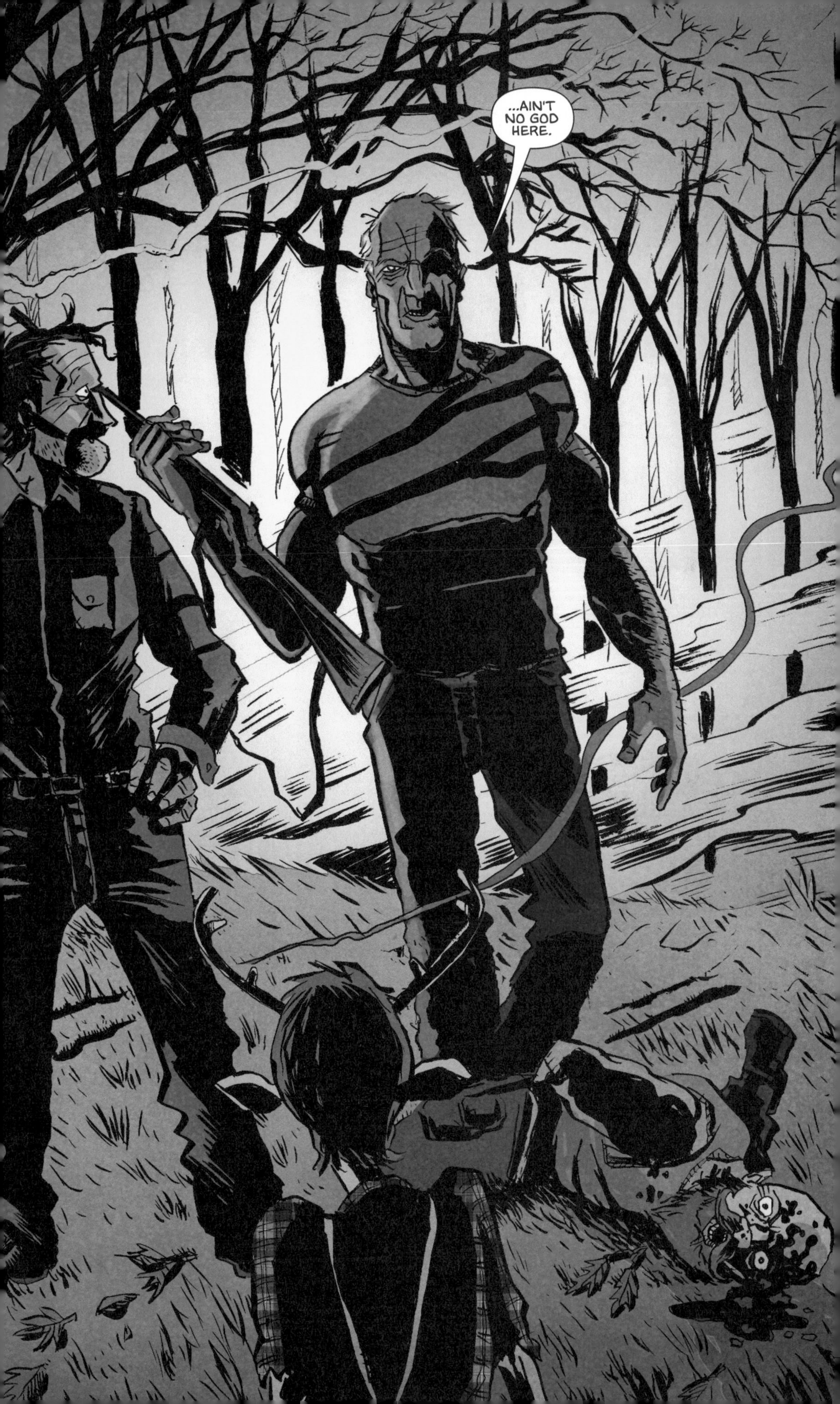
...AIN'T NO GOD HERE.

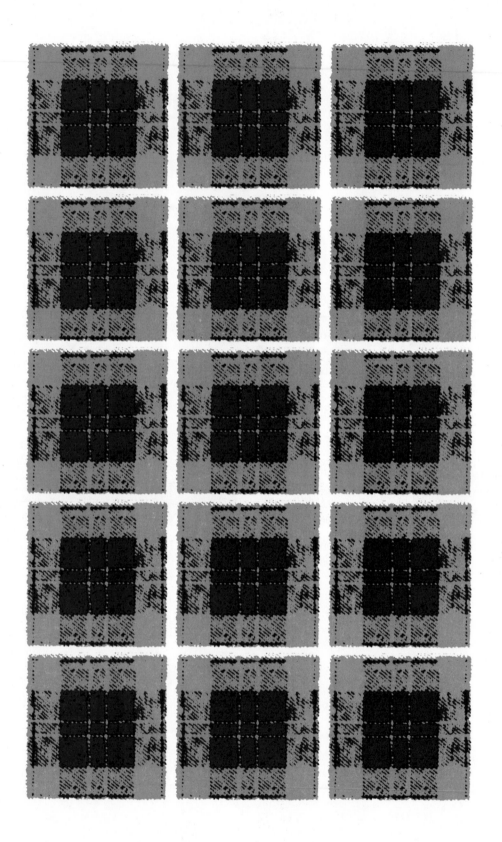

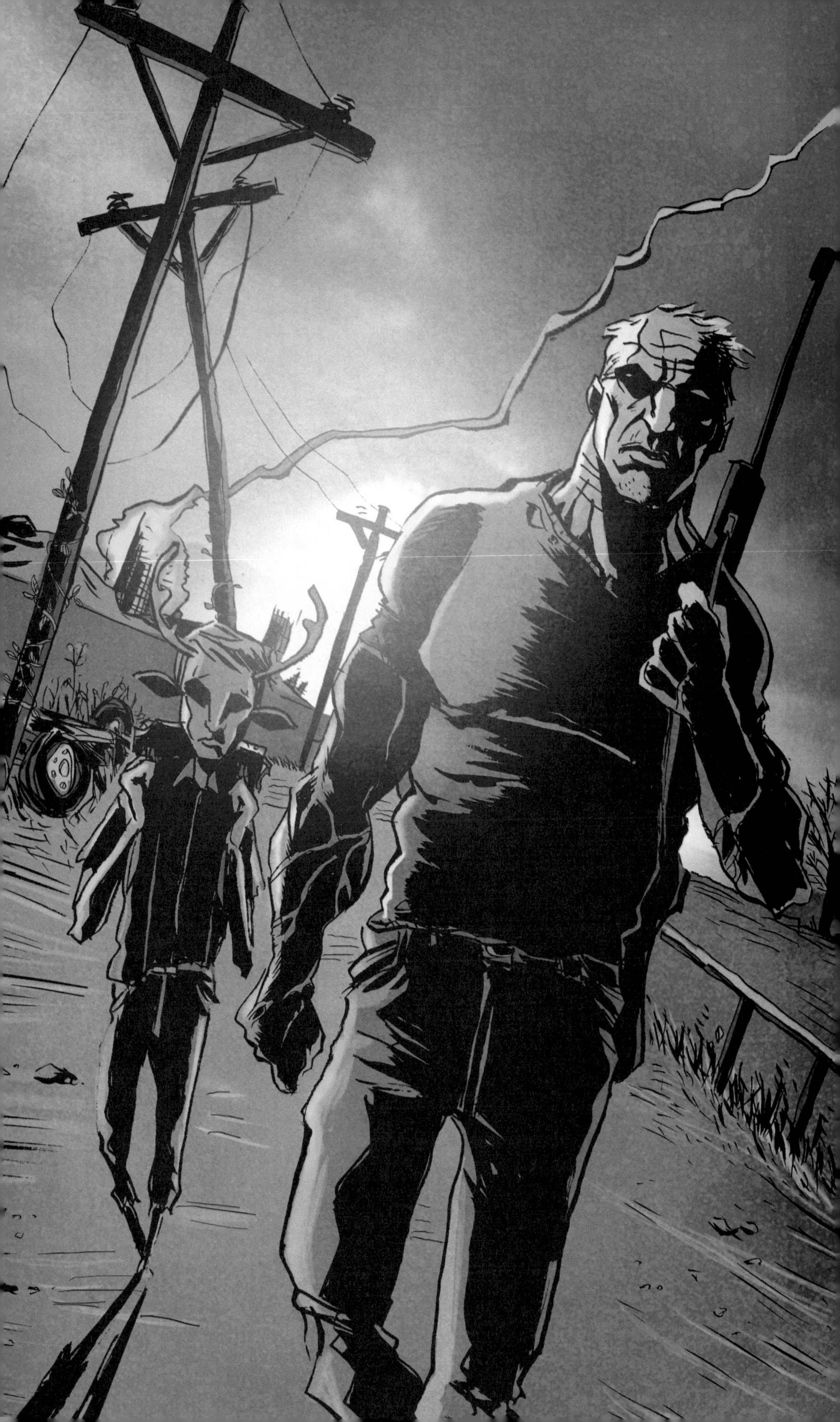

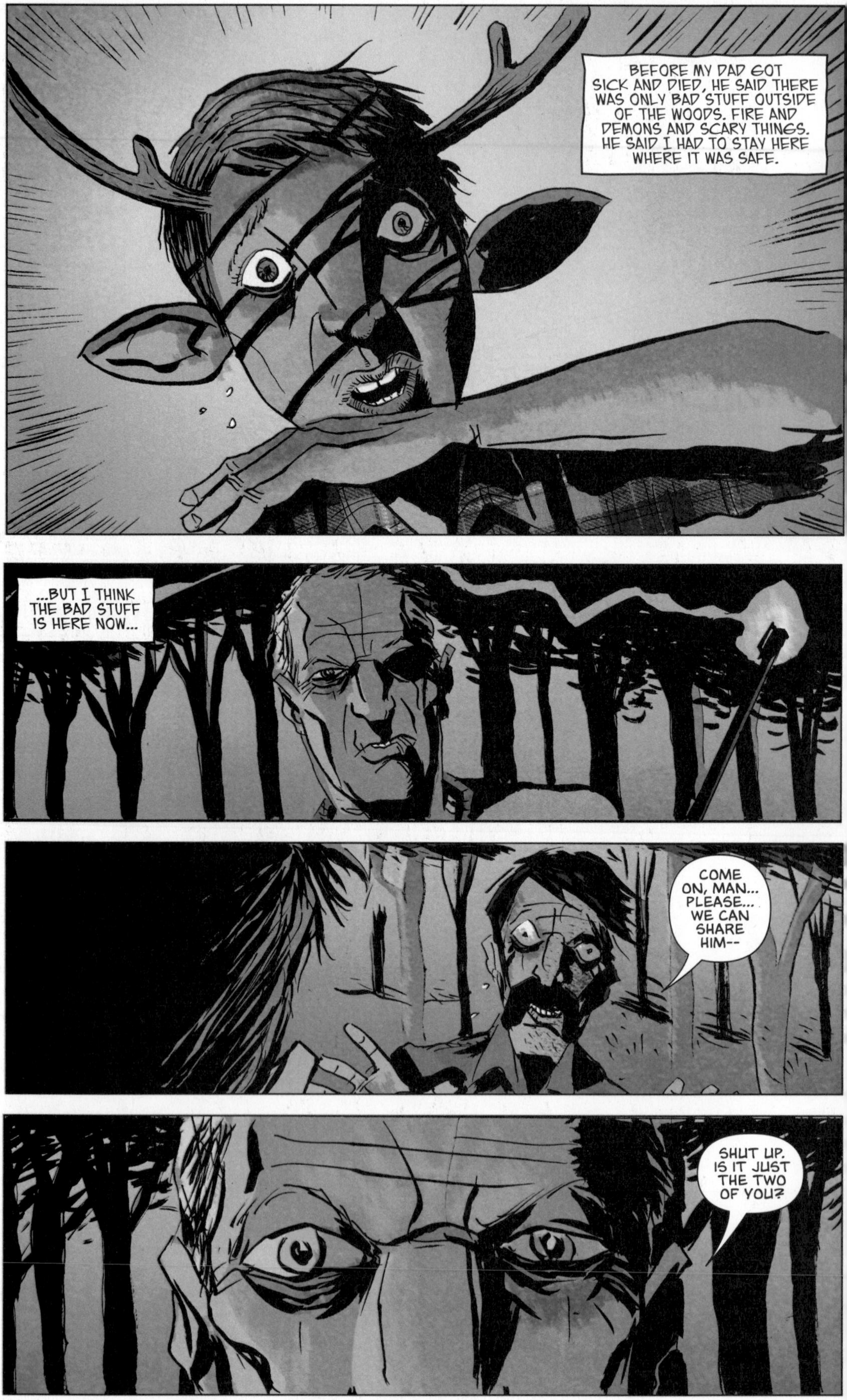
BEFORE MY DAD GOT SICK AND DIED, HE SAID THERE WAS ONLY BAD STUFF OUTSIDE OF THE WOODS. FIRE AND DEMONS AND SCARY THINGS. HE SAID I HAD TO STAY HERE WHERE IT WAS SAFE.
...BUT I THINK THE BAD STUFF IS HERE NOW...
COME ON, MAN... PLEASE... WE CAN SHARE HIM--
SHUT UP. IS IT JUST THE TWO OF YOU?

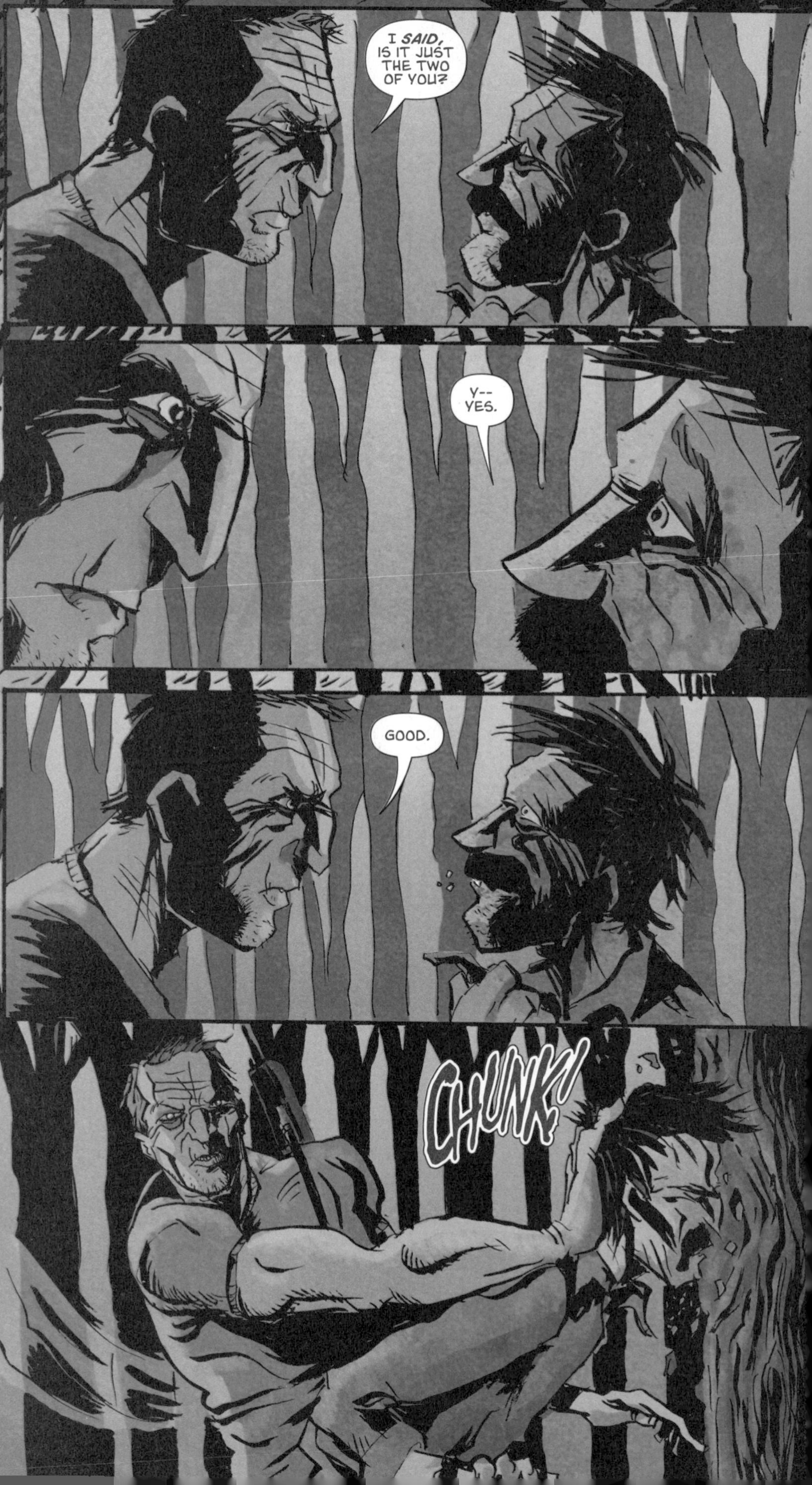
I *SAID*, IS IT JUST THE TWO OF YOU?
Y-- YES.
GOOD.
CHUNK!

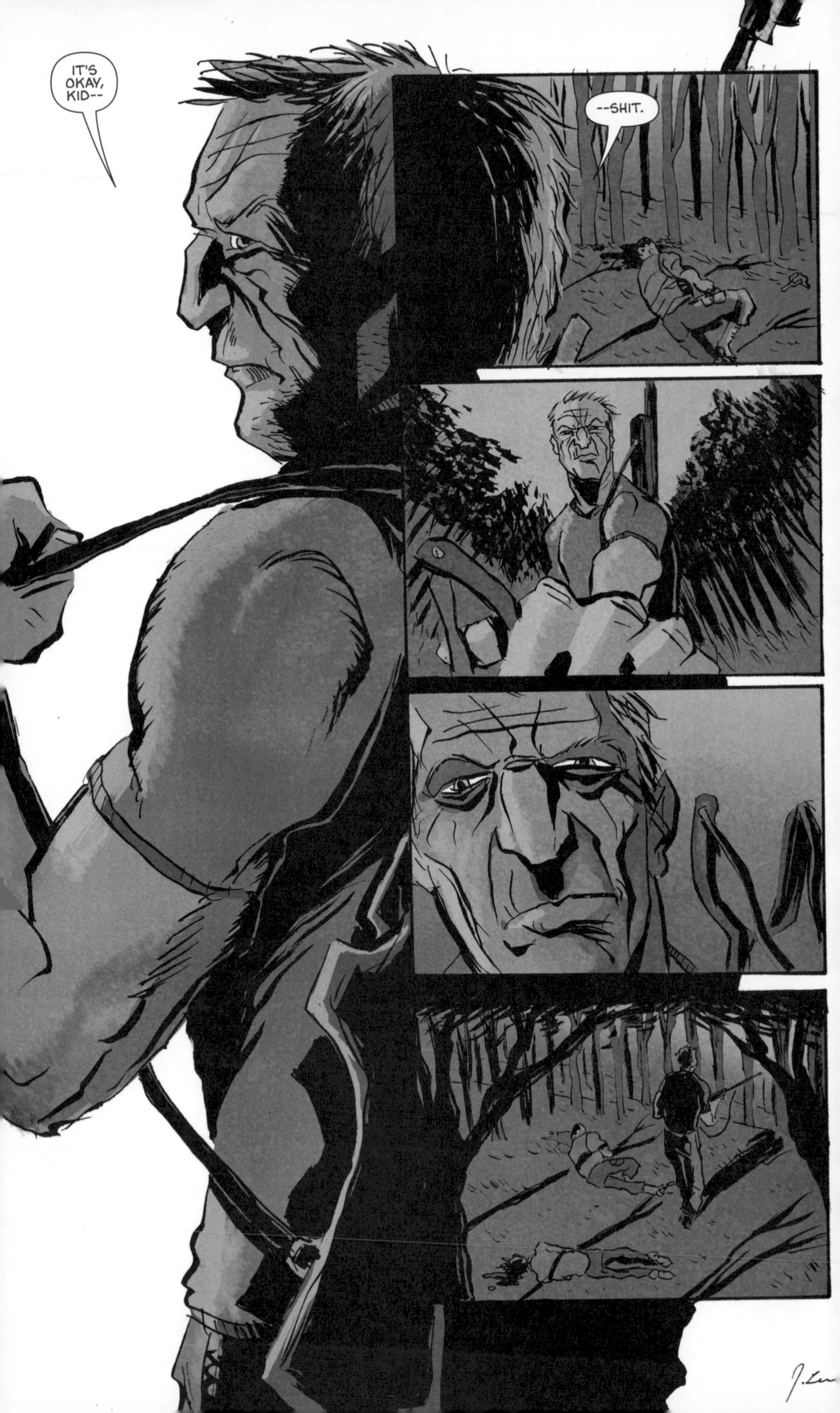
IT'S OKAY, KID--
--SHIT.

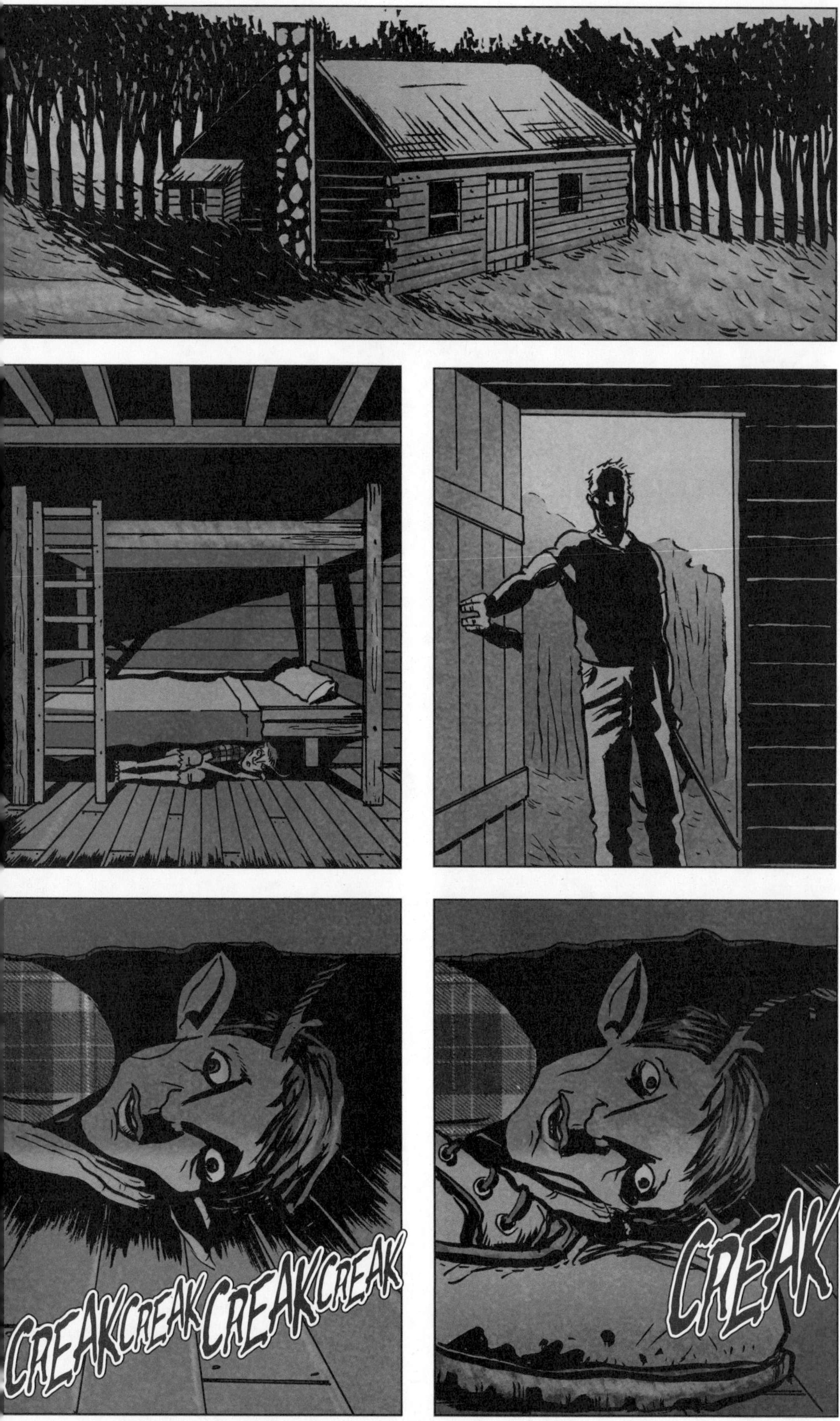
CREAK CREAK CREAK CREAK
CREAK

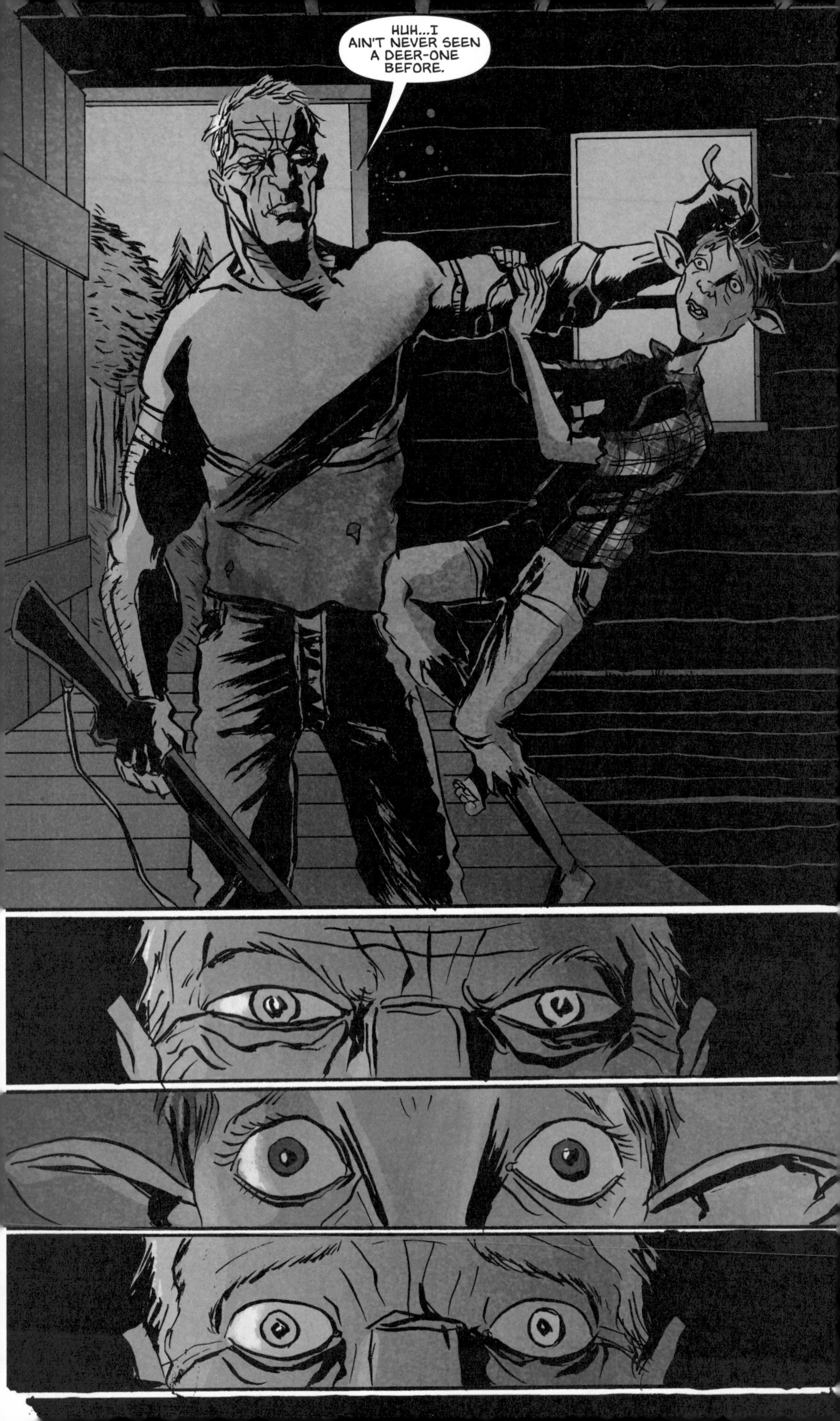
HUH...I AIN'T NEVER SEEN A DEER-ONE BEFORE.

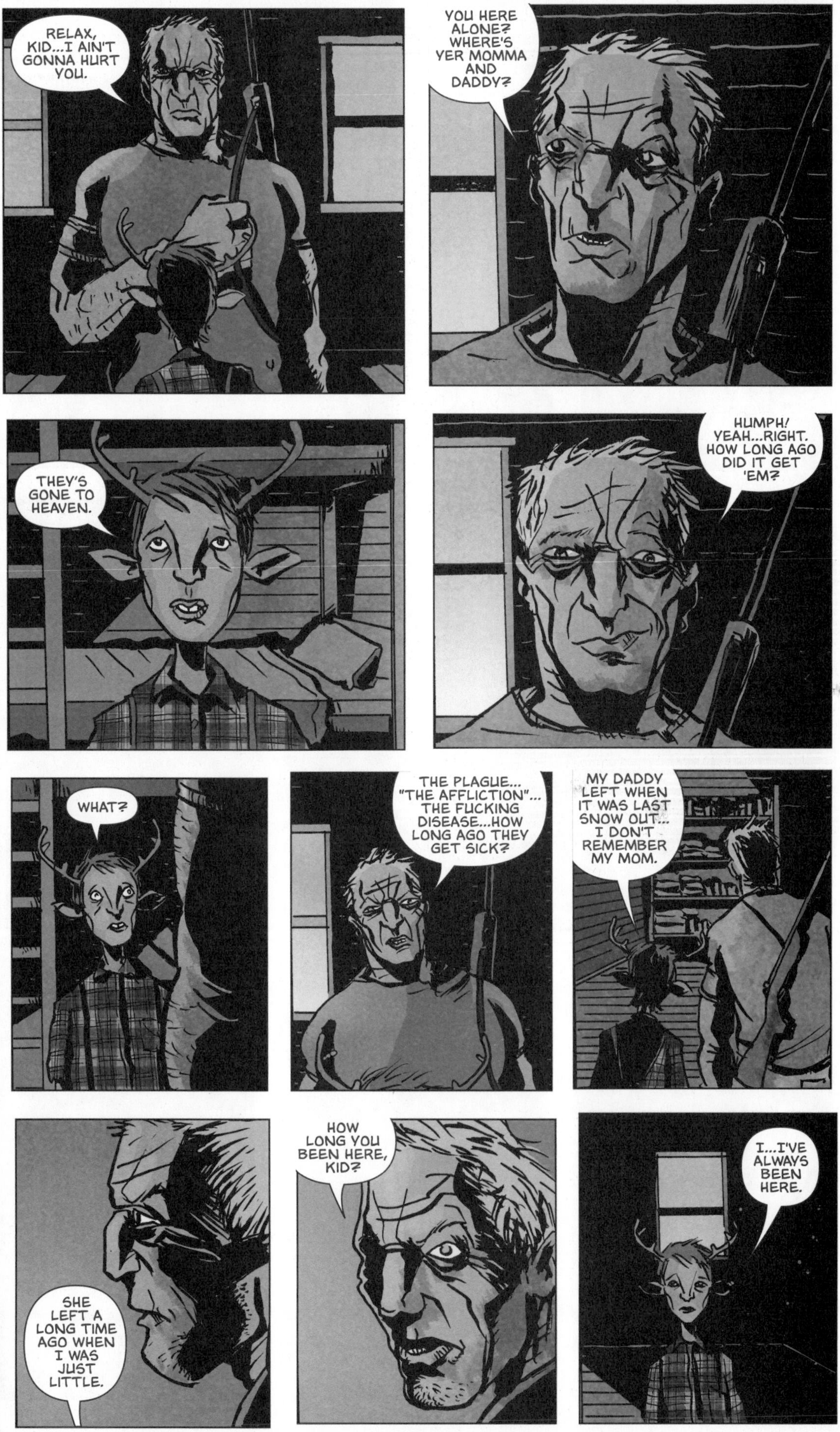
RELAX, KID...I AIN'T GONNA HURT YOU.
YOU HERE ALONE? WHERE'S YER MOMMA AND DADDY?
THEY'S GONE TO HEAVEN.
HUMPH! YEAH...RIGHT. HOW LONG AGO DID IT GET 'EM?
WHAT?
THE PLAGUE... "THE AFFLICTION"... THE FUCKING DISEASE...HOW LONG AGO THEY GET SICK?
MY DADDY LEFT WHEN IT WAS LAST SNOW OUT... I DON'T REMEMBER MY MOM.
SHE LEFT A LONG TIME AGO WHEN I WAS JUST LITTLE.
HOW LONG YOU BEEN HERE, KID?
I...I'VE ALWAYS BEEN HERE.

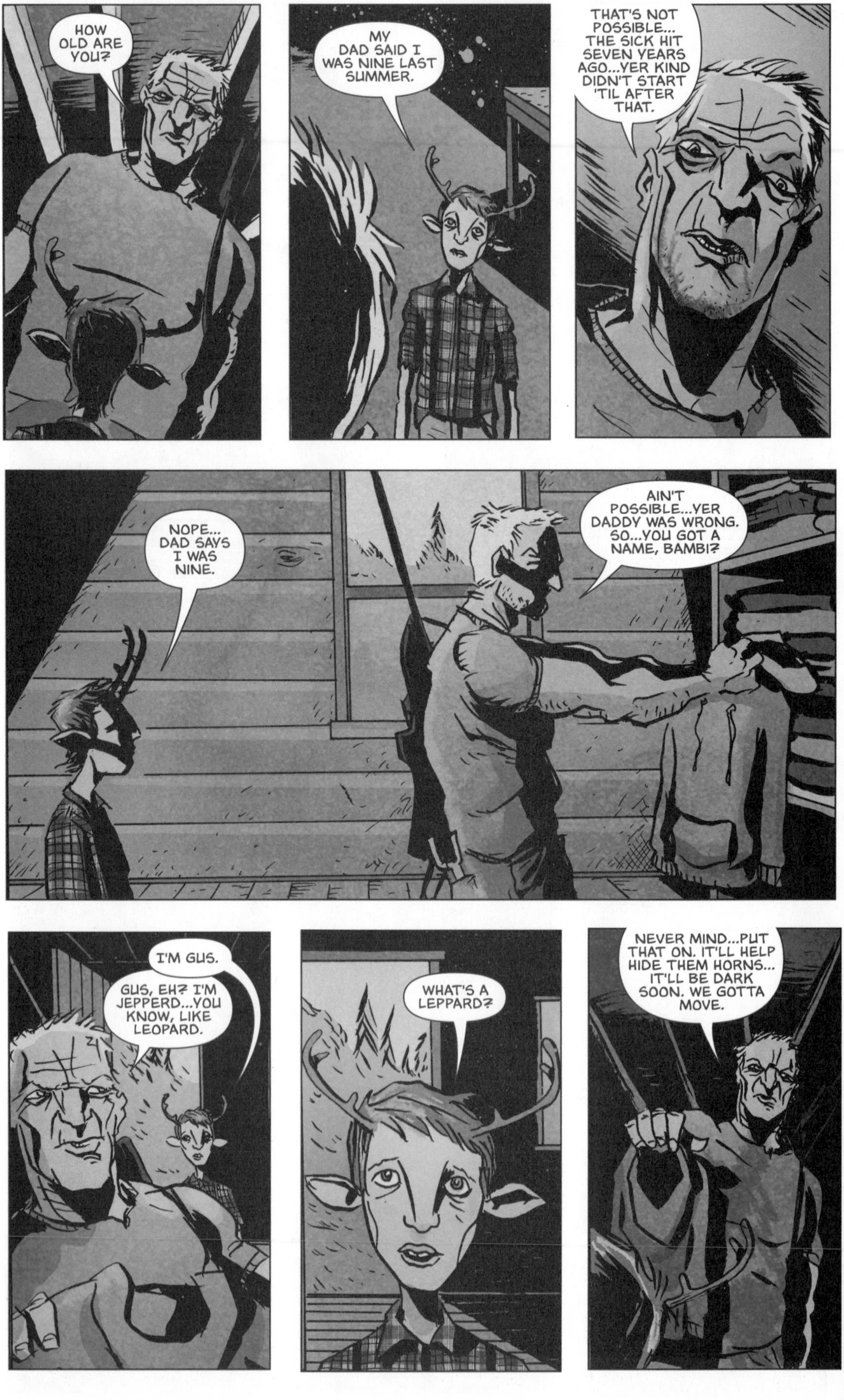
HOW OLD ARE YOU?
MY DAD SAID I WAS NINE LAST SUMMER.
THAT'S NOT POSSIBLE... THE SICK HIT SEVEN YEARS AGO...YER KIND DIDN'T START 'TIL AFTER THAT.
NOPE... DAD SAYS I WAS NINE.
AIN'T POSSIBLE...YER DADDY WAS WRONG. SO...YOU GOT A NAME, BAMBI?
I'M GUS.
GUS, EH? I'M JEPPERD...YOU KNOW, LIKE LEOPARD.
WHAT'S A LEPPARD?
NEVER MIND...PUT THAT ON. IT'LL HELP HIDE THEM HORNS... IT'LL BE DARK SOON. WE GOTTA MOVE.

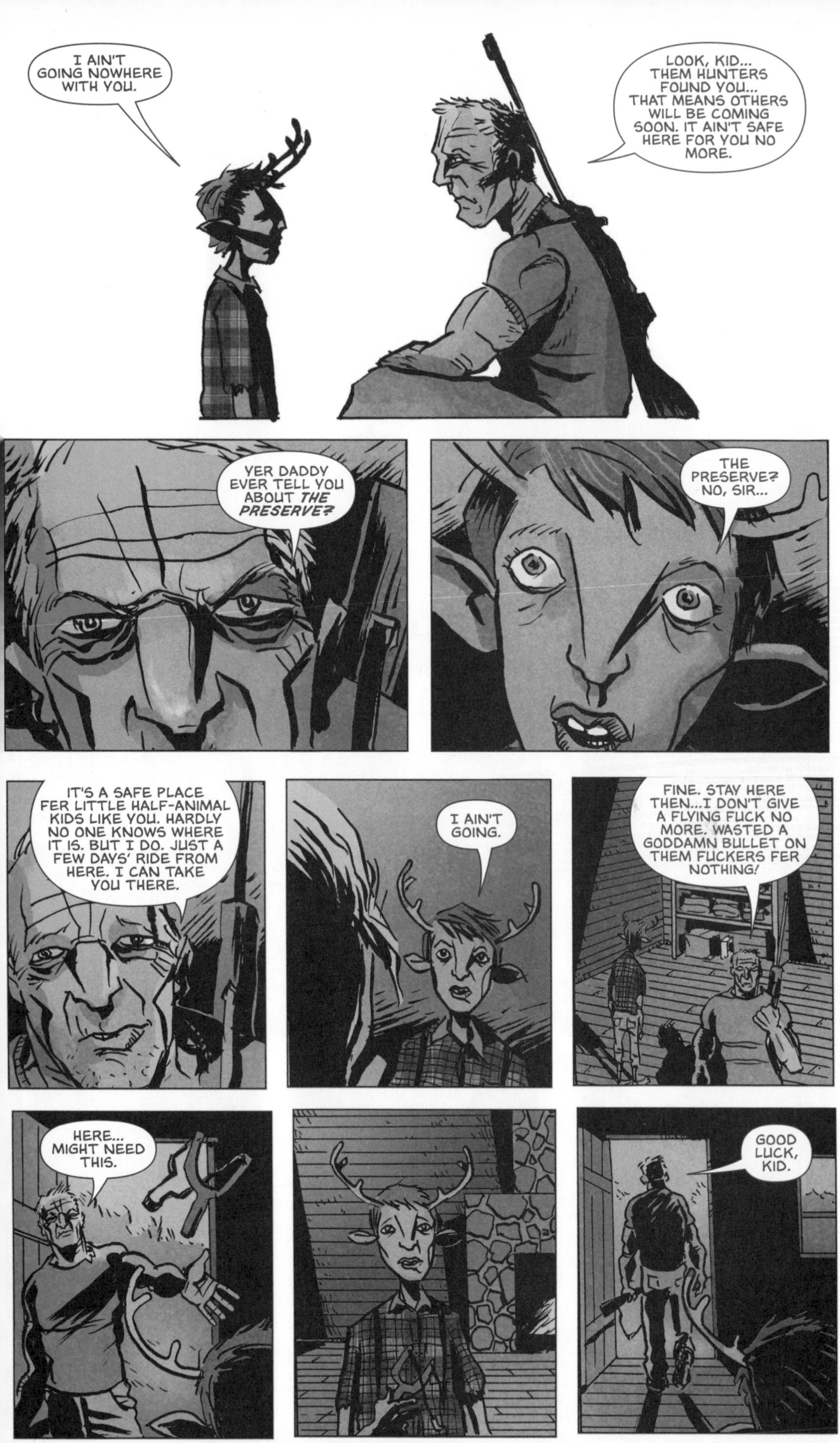
I AIN'T GOING NOWHERE WITH YOU.
LOOK, KID... THEM HUNTERS FOUND YOU... THAT MEANS OTHERS WILL BE COMING SOON. IT AIN'T SAFE HERE FOR YOU NO MORE.
YER DADDY EVER TELL YOU ABOUT *THE PRESERVE?*
THE PRESERVE? NO, SIR...
IT'S A SAFE PLACE FER LITTLE HALF-ANIMAL KIDS LIKE YOU. HARDLY NO ONE KNOWS WHERE IT IS. BUT I DO. JUST A FEW DAYS' RIDE FROM HERE. I CAN TAKE YOU THERE.
I AIN'T GOING.
FINE. STAY HERE THEN...I DON'T GIVE A FLYING FUCK NO MORE. WASTED A GODDAMN BULLET ON THEM FUCKERS FER NOTHING!
HERE... MIGHT NEED THIS.
GOOD LUCK, KID.

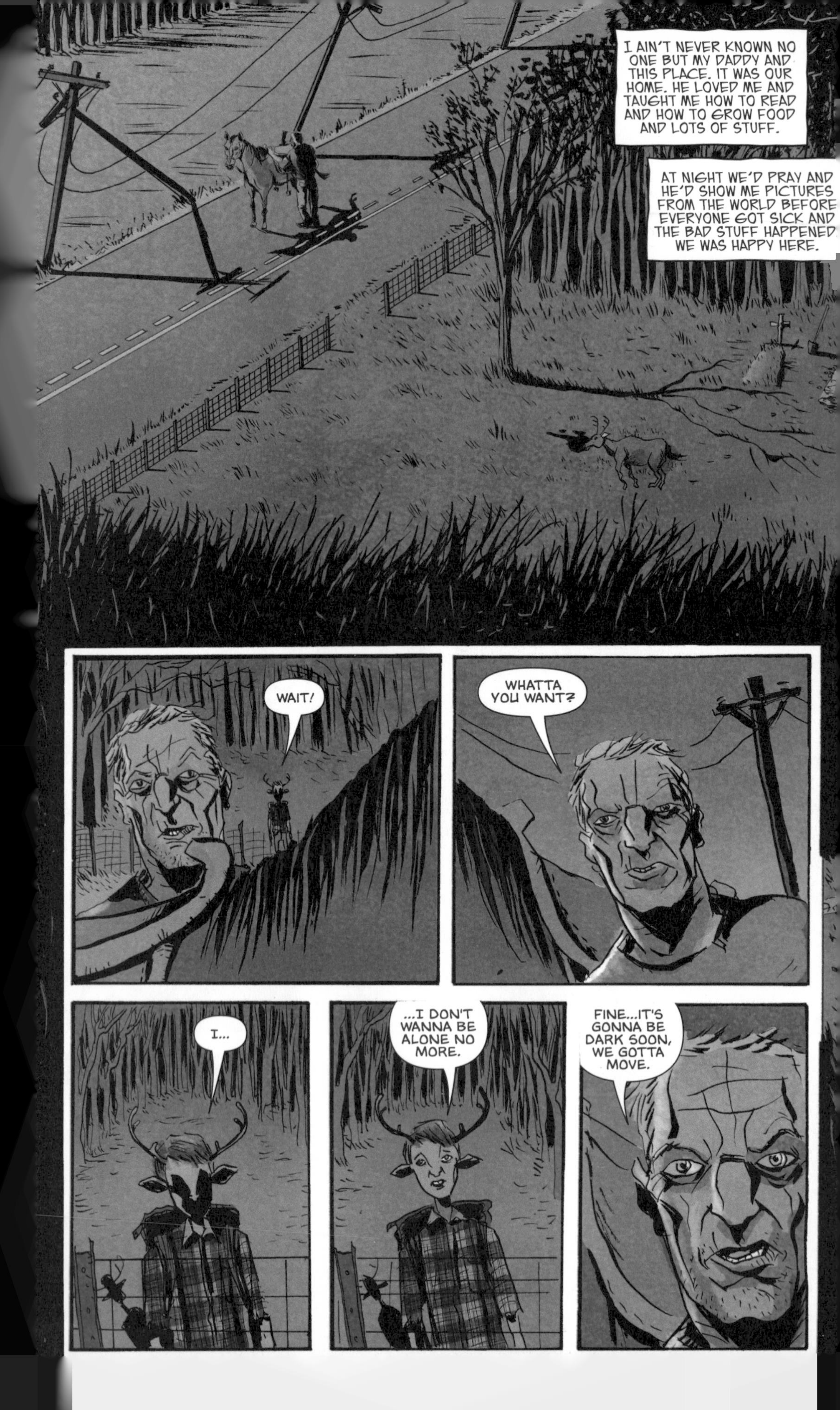
I AIN'T NEVER KNOWN NO ONE BUT MY DADDY AND THIS PLACE. IT WAS OUR HOME. HE LOVED ME AND TAUGHT ME HOW TO READ AND HOW TO GROW FOOD AND LOTS OF STUFF.
AT NIGHT WE'D PRAY AND HE'D SHOW ME PICTURES FROM THE WORLD BEFORE EVERYONE GOT SICK AND THE BAD STUFF HAPPENED WE WAS HAPPY HERE.
WAIT!
WHATTA YOU WANT?
I...
...I DON'T WANNA BE ALONE NO MORE.
FINE...IT'S GONNA BE DARK SOON, WE GOTTA MOVE.

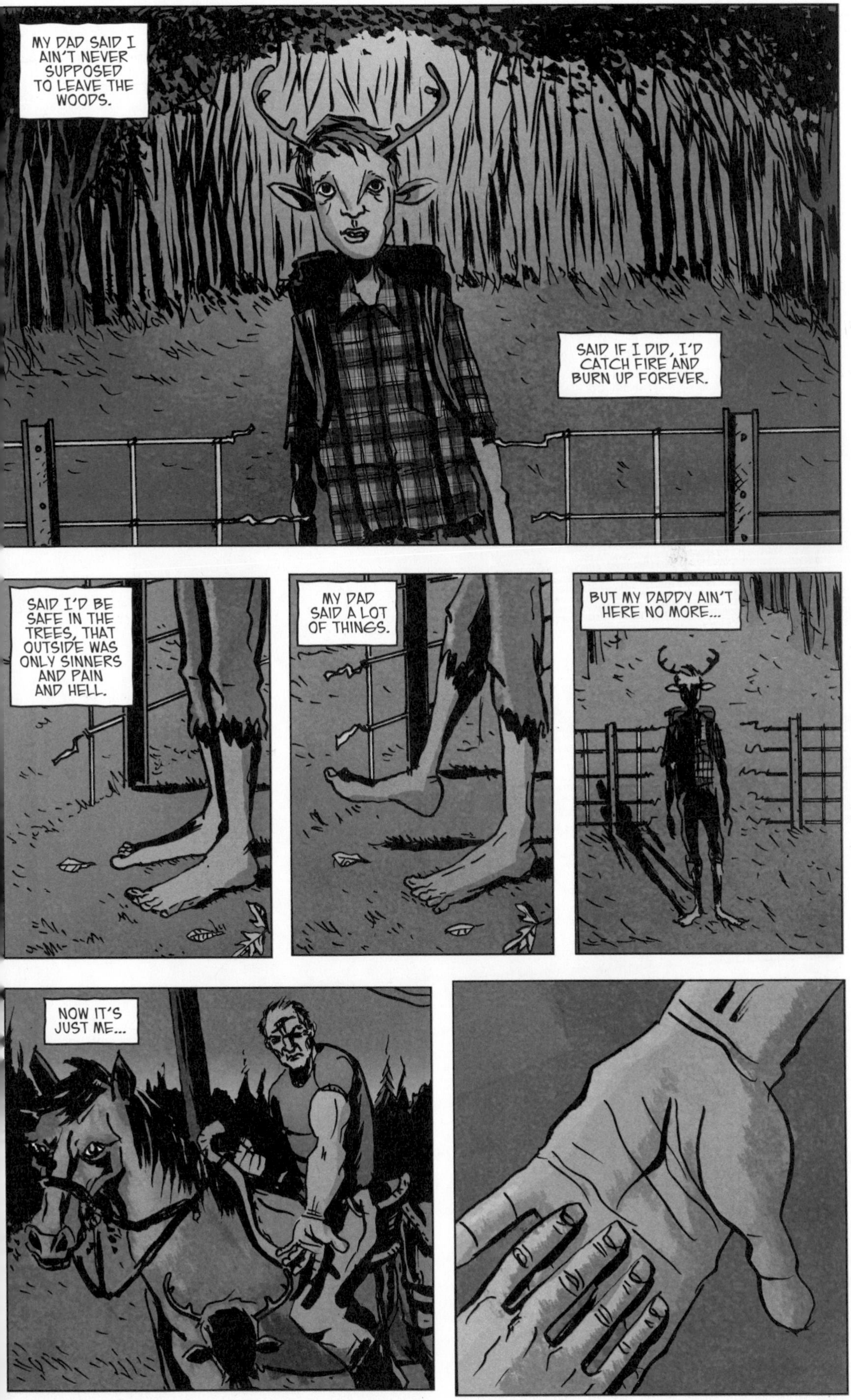
MY DAD SAID I AIN'T NEVER SUPPOSED TO LEAVE THE WOODS.
SAID IF I DID, I'D CATCH FIRE AND BURN UP FOREVER.
SAID I'D BE SAFE IN THE TREES, THAT OUTSIDE WAS ONLY SINNERS AND PAIN AND HELL.
MY DAD SAID A LOT OF THINGS.
BUT MY DADDY AIN'T HERE NO MORE...
NOW IT'S JUST ME...

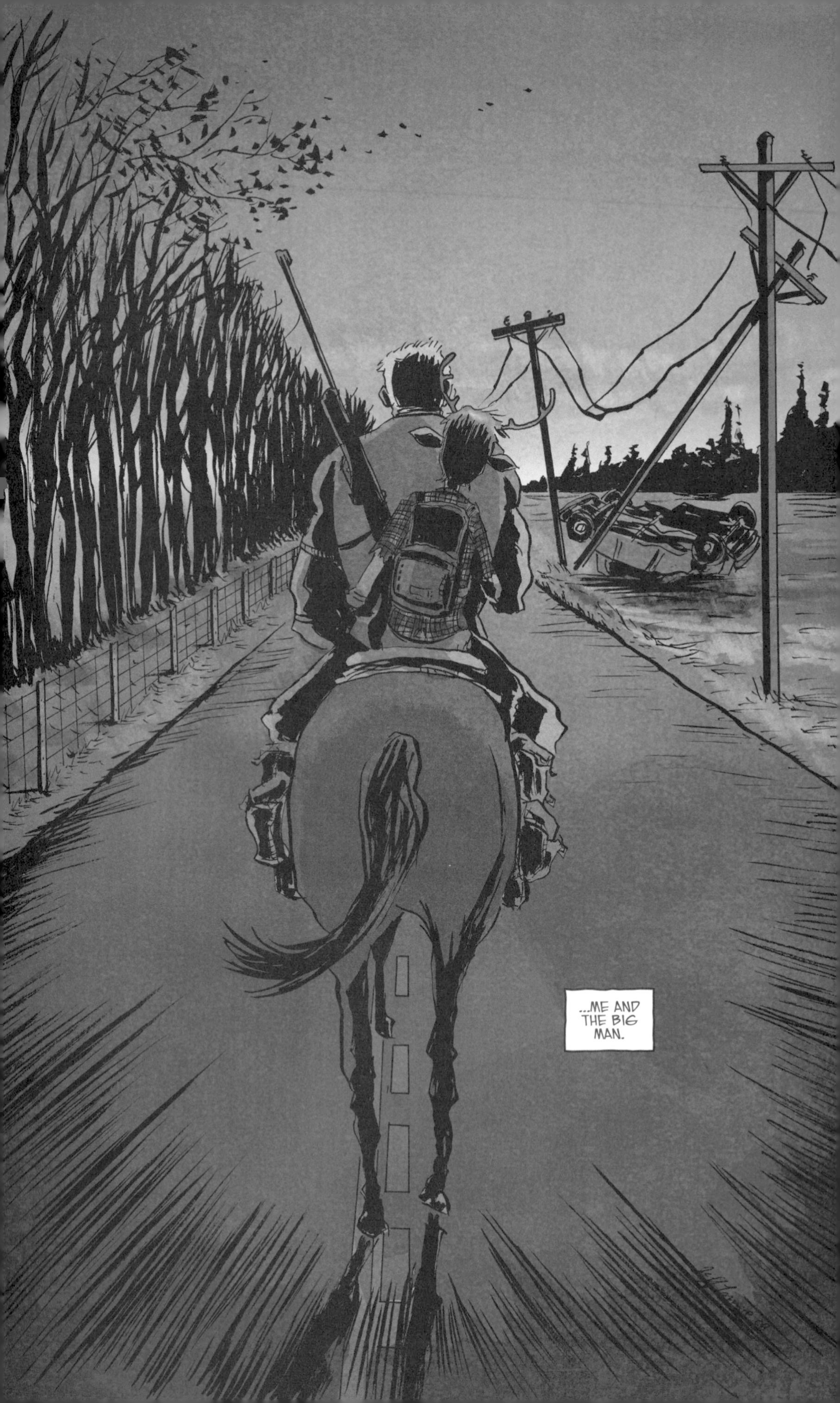
...ME AND THE BIG MAN.

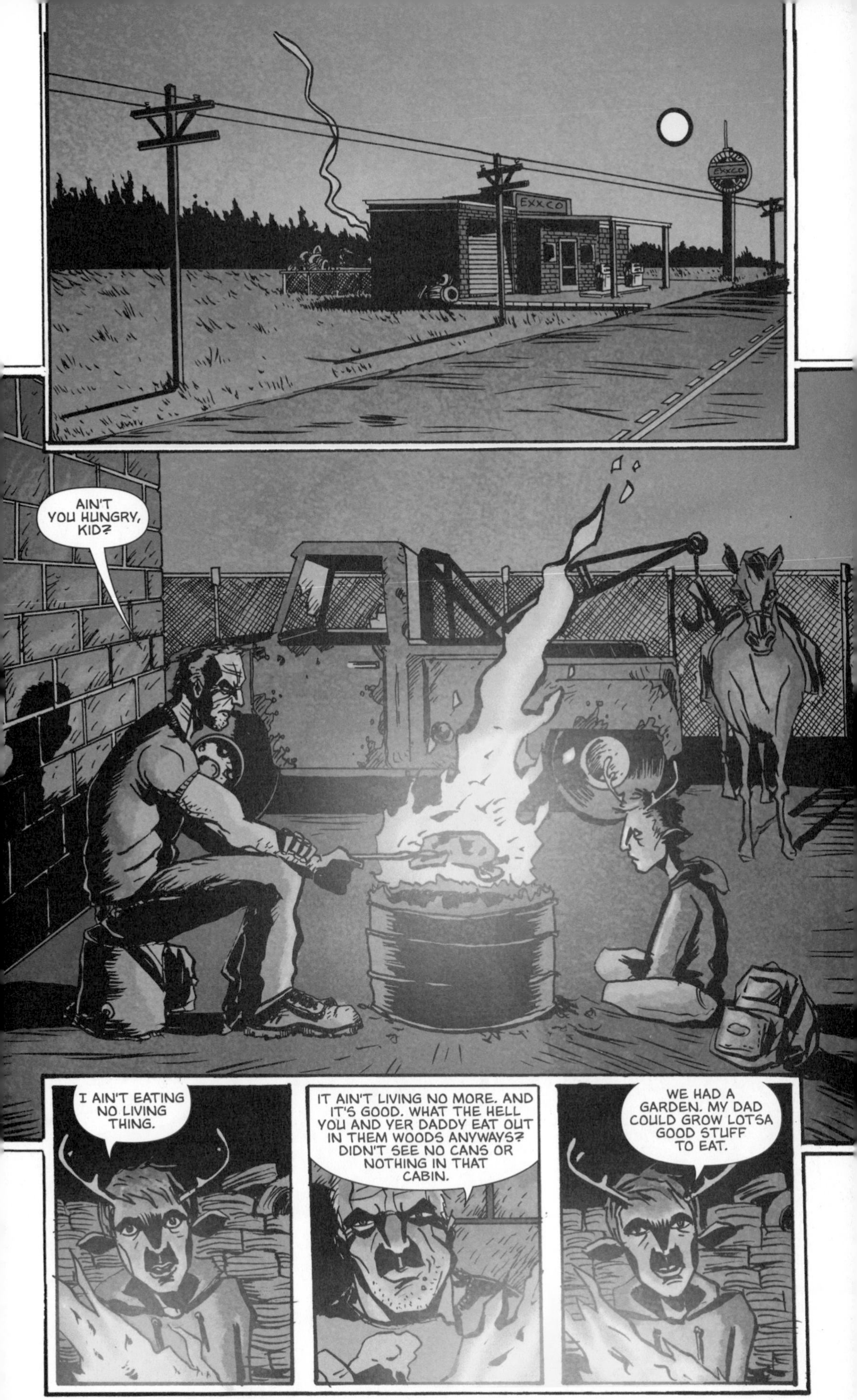
EXXCO
EXXCO
AIN'T YOU HUNGRY, KID?
I AIN'T EATING NO LIVING THING.
IT AIN'T LIVING NO MORE. AND IT'S GOOD. WHAT THE HELL YOU AND YER DADDY EAT OUT IN THEM WOODS ANYWAYS? DIDN'T SEE NO CANS OR NOTHING IN THAT CABIN.
WE HAD A GARDEN. MY DAD COULD GROW LOTSA GOOD STUFF TO EAT.

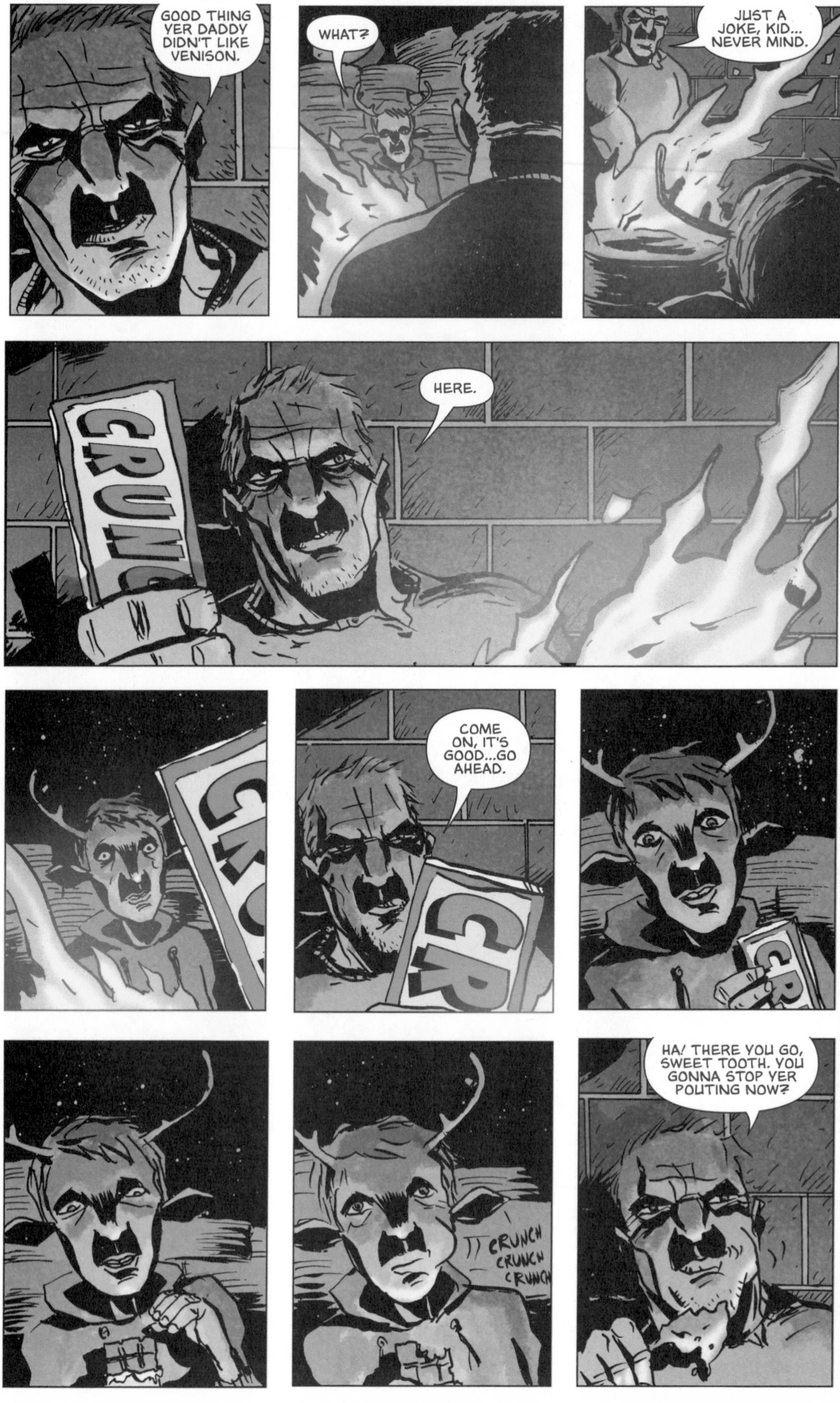
GOOD THING YER DADDY DIDN'T LIKE VENISON.
WHAT?
JUST A JOKE, KID... NEVER MIND.
CRUNC
HERE.
COME ON, IT'S GOOD...GO AHEAD.
CR
CRUNCH CRUNCH CRUNCH
HA! THERE YOU GO, SWEET TOOTH. YOU GONNA STOP YER POUTING NOW?

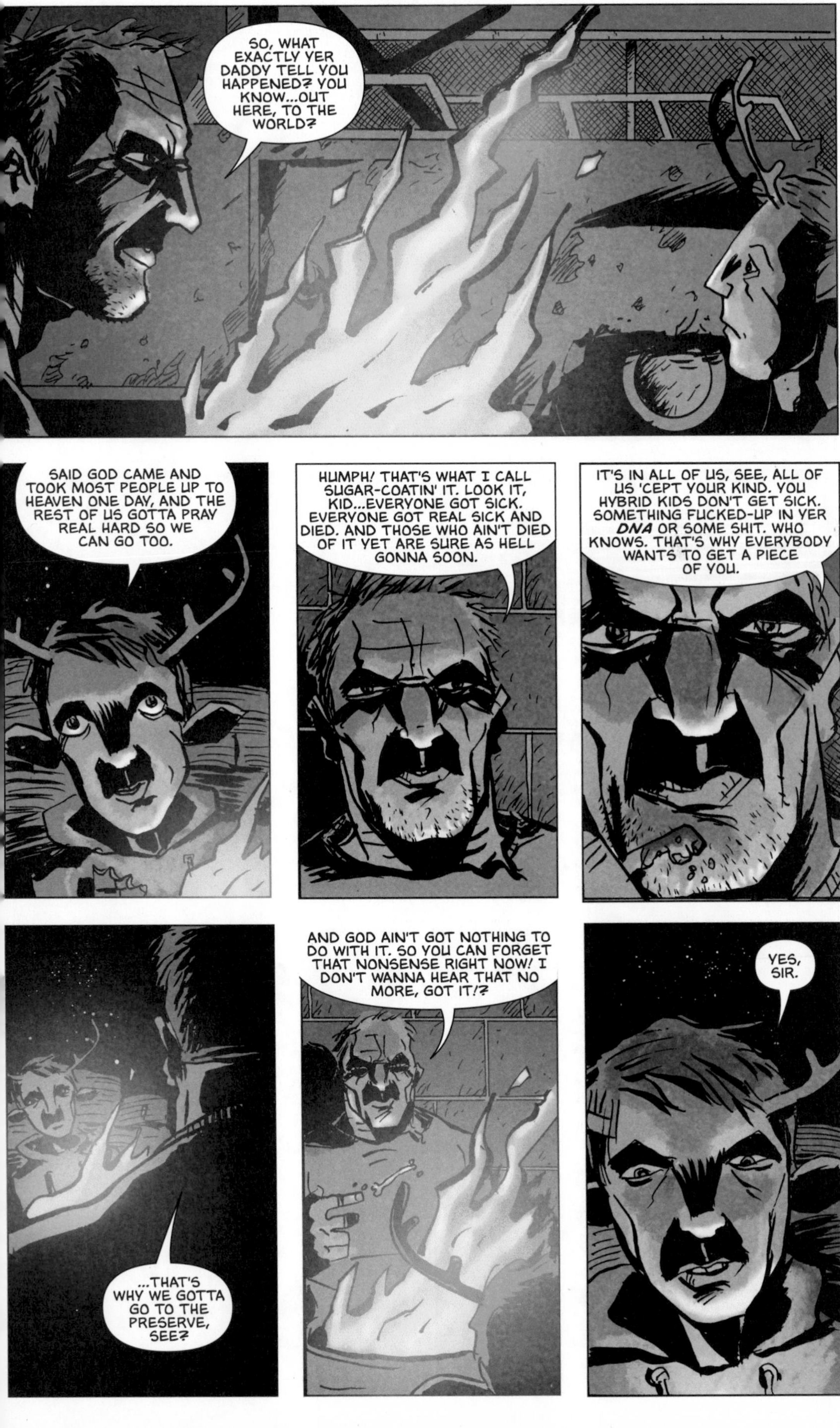
SO, WHAT EXACTLY YER DADDY TELL YOU HAPPENED? YOU KNOW...OUT HERE, TO THE WORLD?
SAID GOD CAME AND TOOK MOST PEOPLE UP TO HEAVEN ONE DAY, AND THE REST OF US GOTTA PRAY REAL HARD SO WE CAN GO TOO.
HUMPH! THAT'S WHAT I CALL SUGAR-COATIN' IT. LOOK IT, KID...EVERYONE GOT SICK. EVERYONE GOT REAL SICK AND DIED. AND THOSE WHO AIN'T DIED OF IT YET ARE SURE AS HELL GONNA SOON.
IT'S IN ALL OF US, SEE, ALL OF US 'CEPT YOUR KIND. YOU HYBRID KIDS DON'T GET SICK. SOMETHING FUCKED-UP IN YER *DNA* OR SOME SHIT. WHO KNOWS. THAT'S WHY EVERYBODY WANTS TO GET A PIECE OF YOU.
...THAT'S WHY WE GOTTA GO TO THE PRESERVE, SEE?
AND GOD AIN'T GOT NOTHING TO DO WITH IT. SO YOU CAN FORGET THAT NONSENSE RIGHT NOW! I DON'T WANNA HEAR THAT NO MORE, GOT IT!?
YES, SIR.

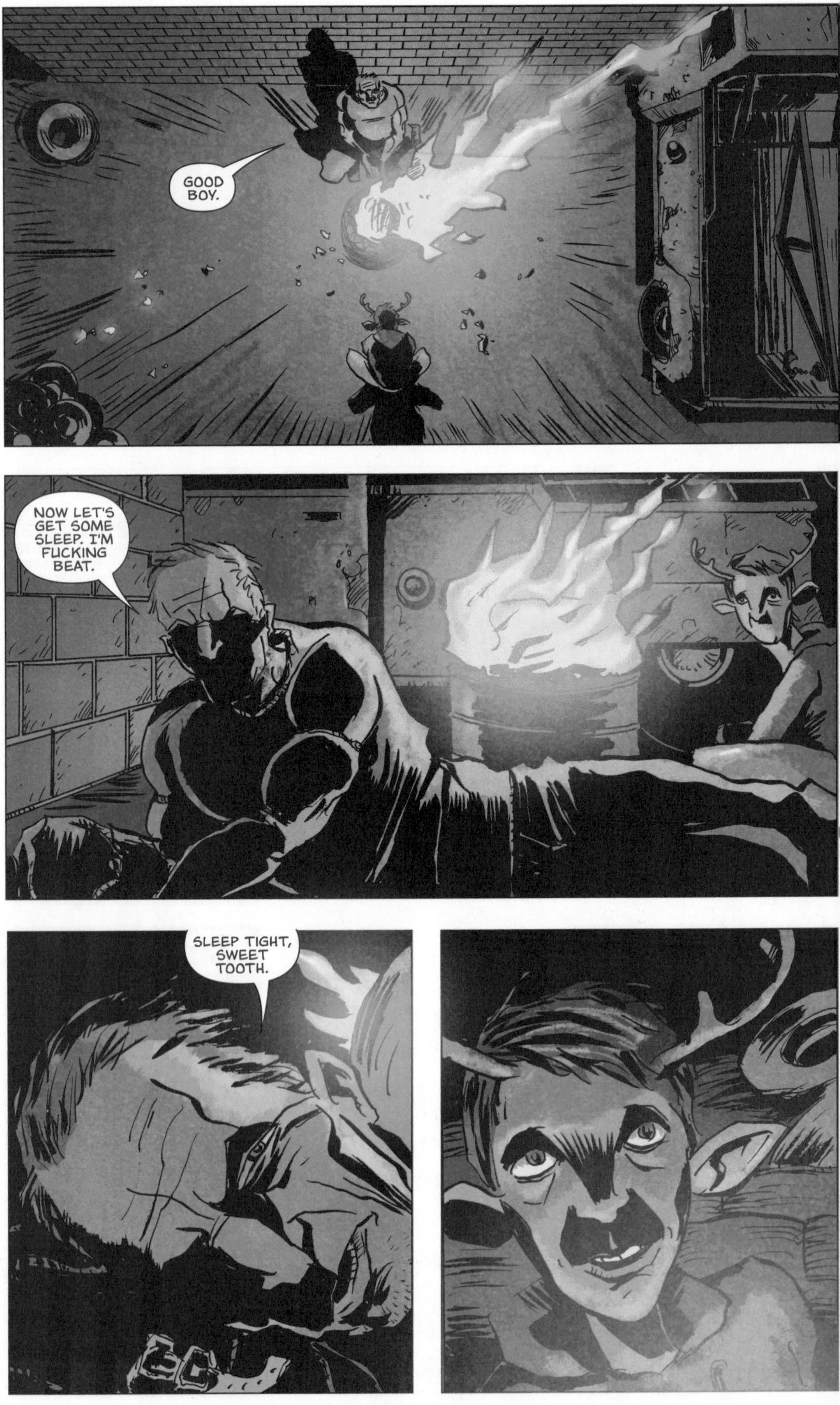
GOOD BOY.
NOW LET'S GET SOME SLEEP. I'M FUCKING BEAT.
SLEEP TIGHT, SWEET TOOTH.

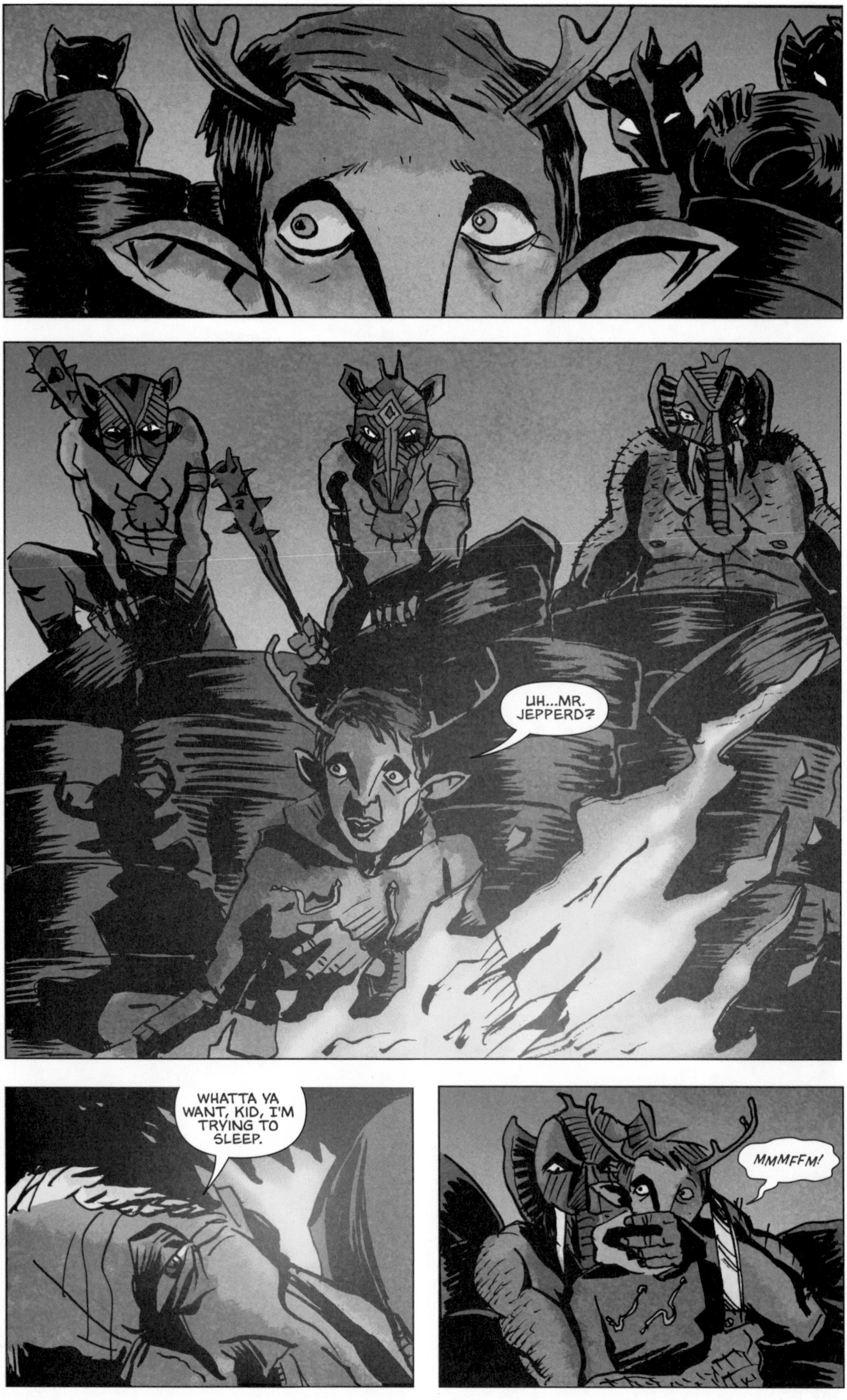
UH...MR. JEPPERD?
WHATTA YA WANT, KID, I'M TRYING TO SLEEP.
MMMFFM!

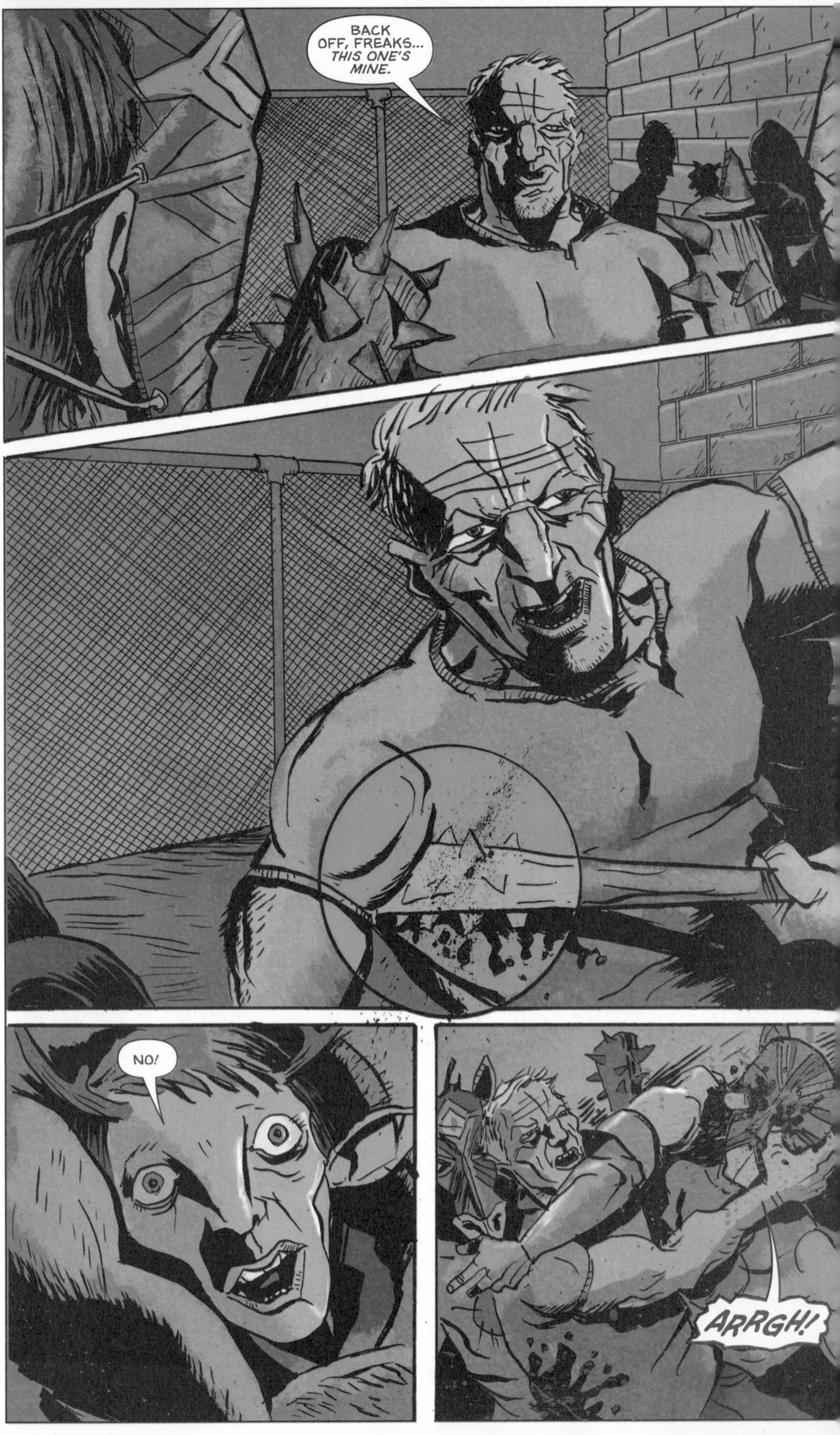
BACK OFF, FREAKS... THIS ONE'S MINE.
NO!
ARRGH!

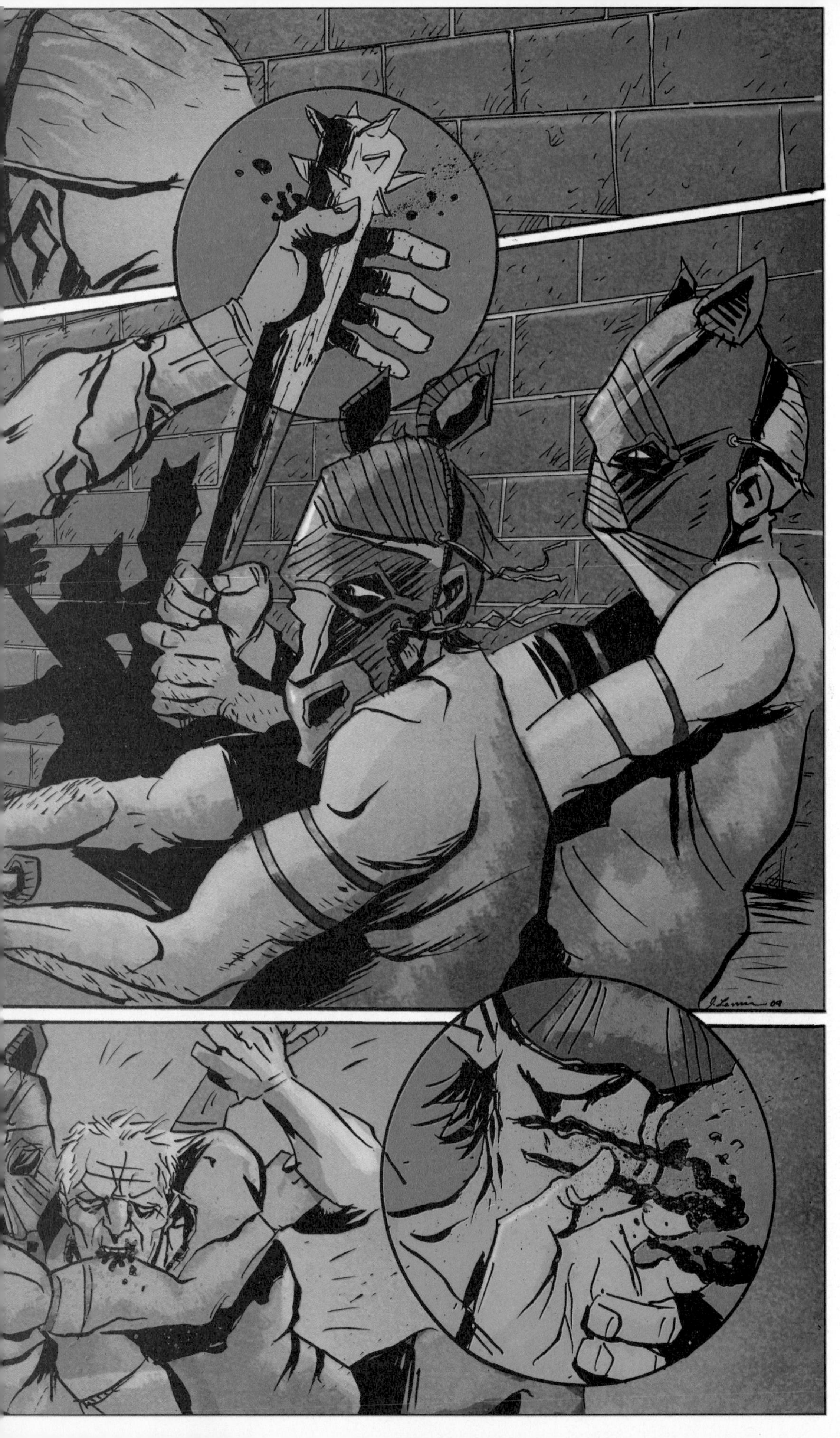

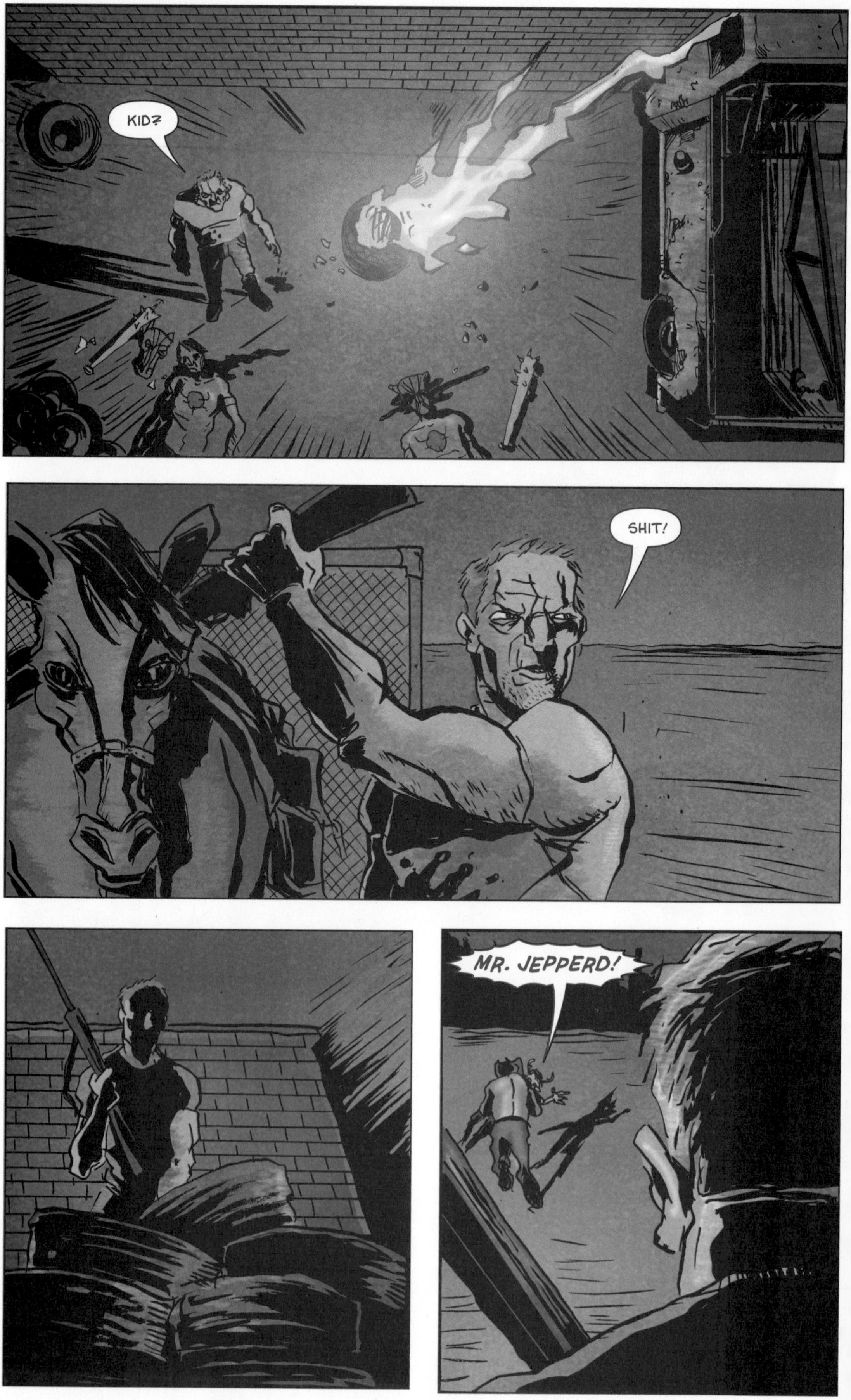
KID?
SHIT!
MR. JEPPERD!

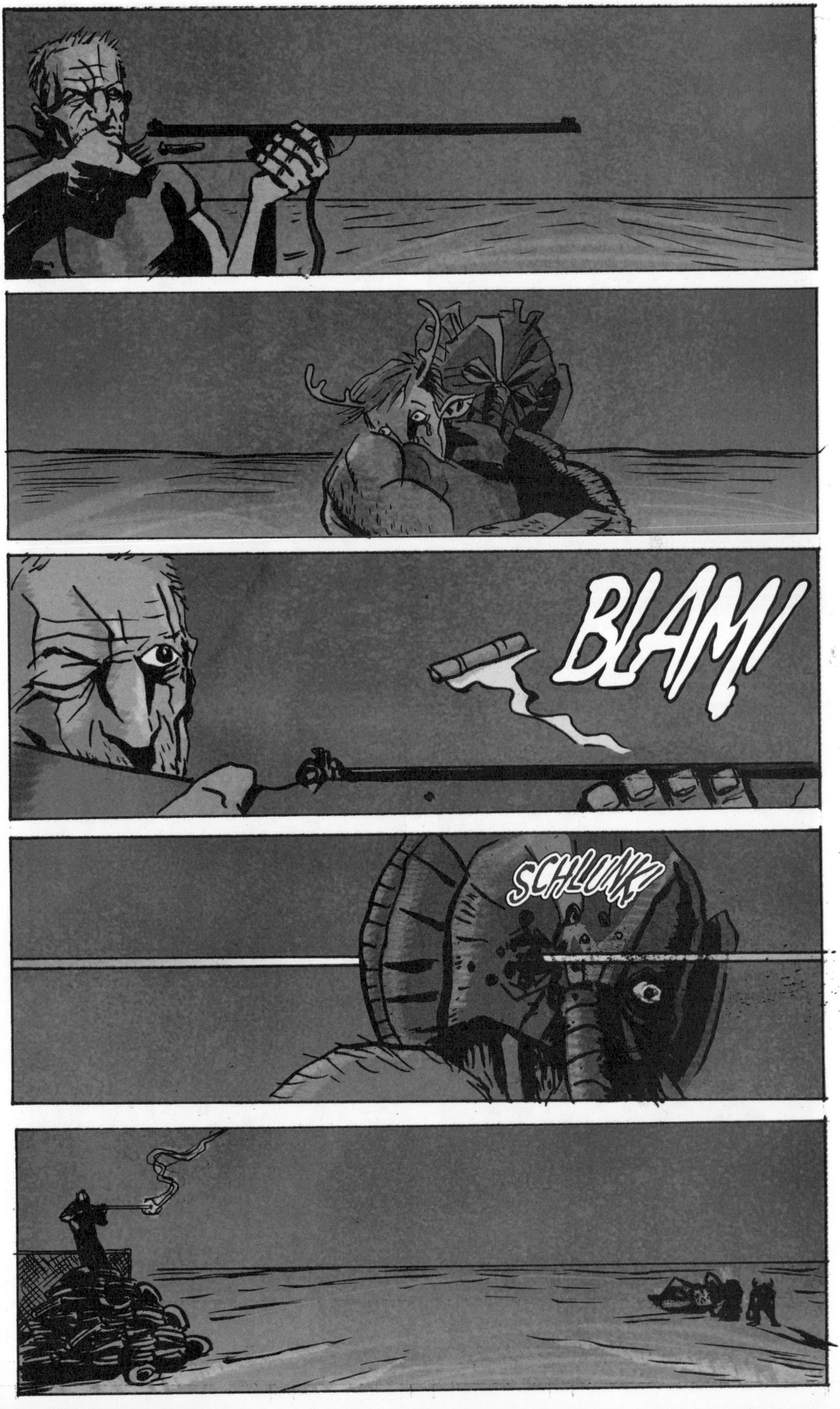
BLAM!
SCHLUNK!

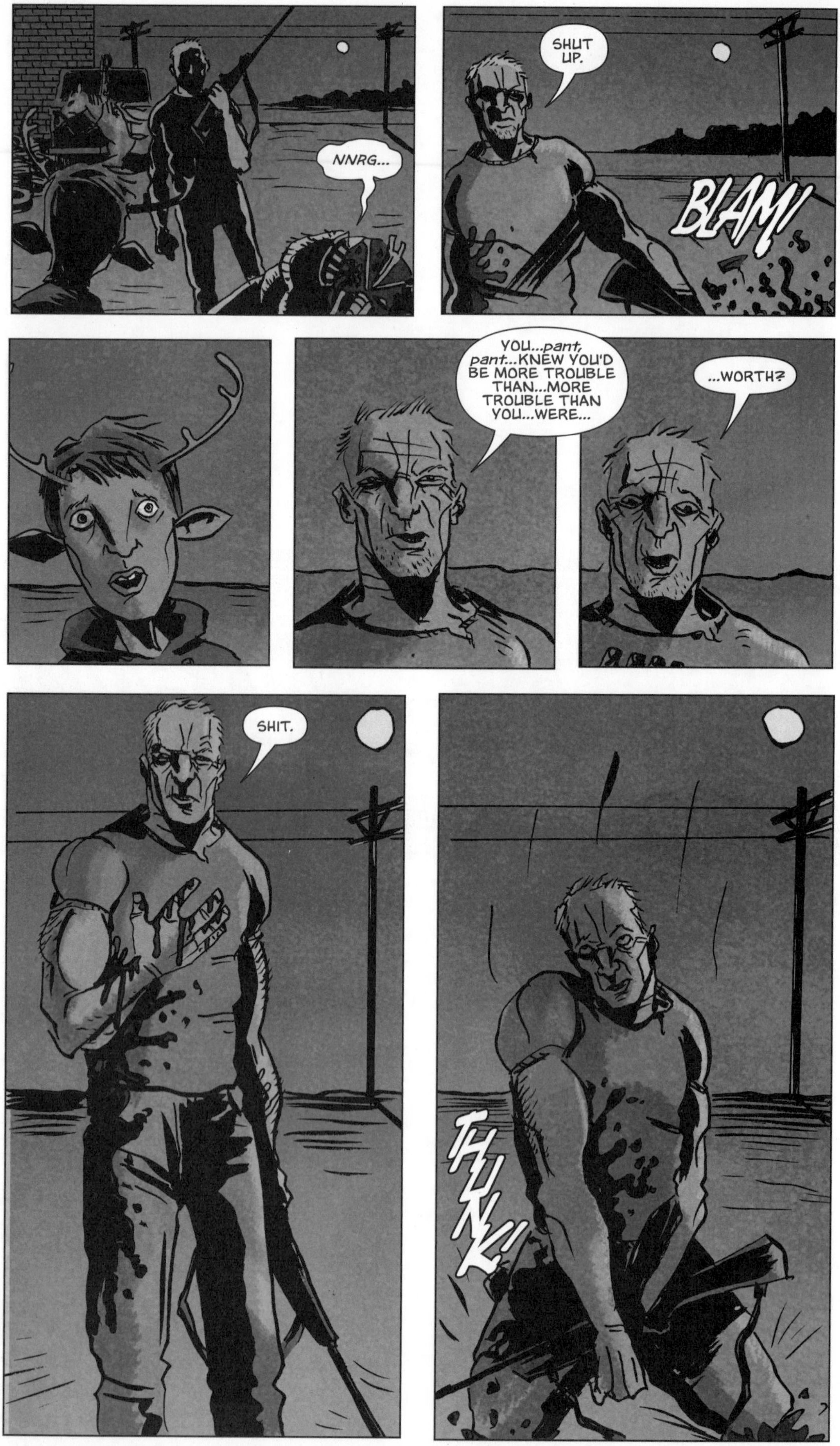
NNRG...
SHUT UP.
BLAM!
YOU...pant, pant...KNEW YOU'D BE MORE TROUBLE THAN...MORE TROUBLE THAN YOU...WERE...
...WORTH?
SHIT.
THUNK!

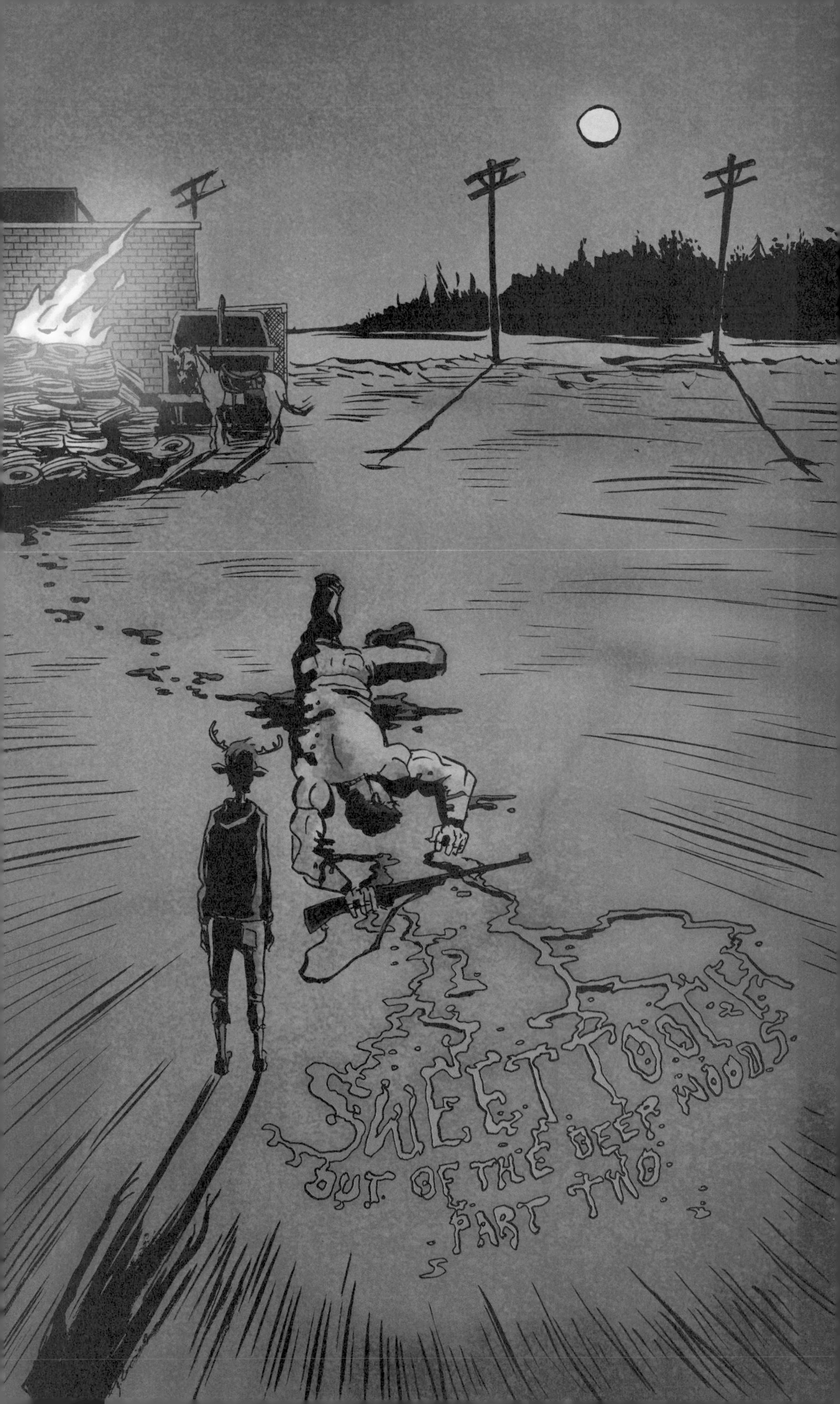
SWEET TOOTH
OUT OF THE DEEP WOODS
PART TWO

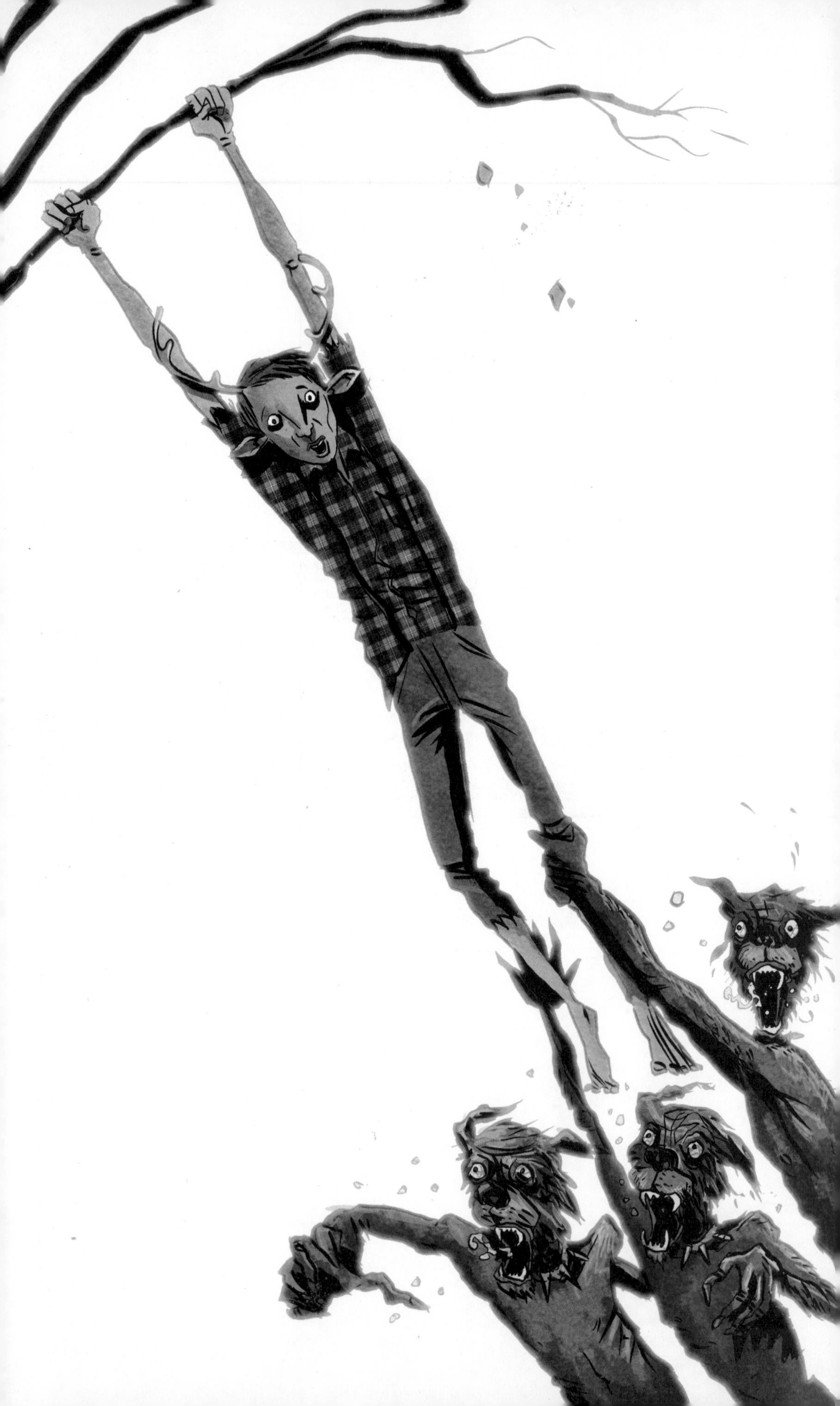

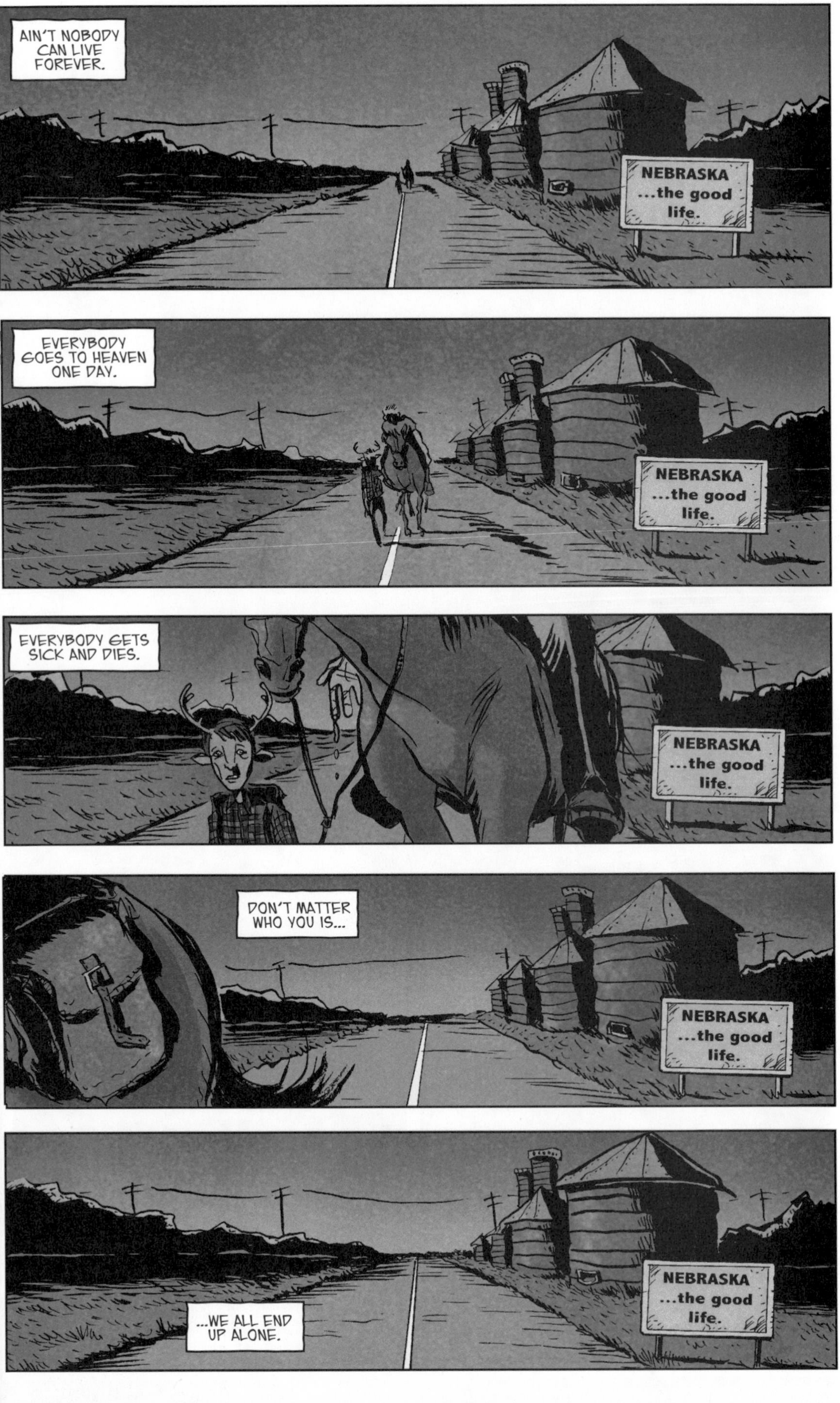
AIN'T NOBODY CAN LIVE FOREVER.
NEBRASKA ...the good life.
EVERYBODY GOES TO HEAVEN ONE DAY.
NEBRASKA ...the good life.
EVERYBODY GETS SICK AND DIES.
NEBRASKA ...the good life.
DON'T MATTER WHO YOU IS...
NEBRASKA ...the good life.
NEBRASKA ...the good life.
...WE ALL END UP ALONE.

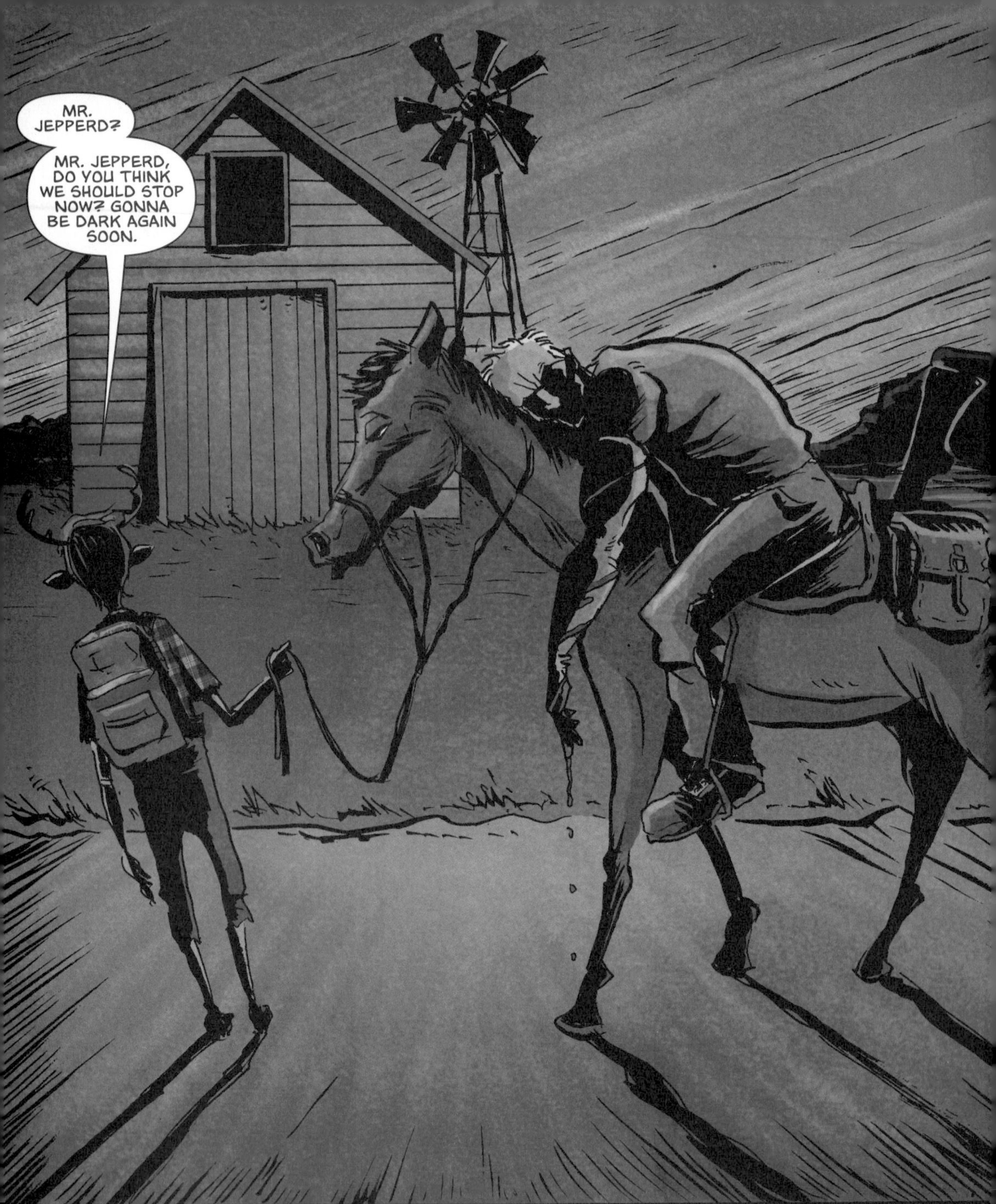
MR. JEPPERD?
MR. JEPPERD, DO YOU THINK WE SHOULD STOP NOW? GONNA BE DARK AGAIN SOON.

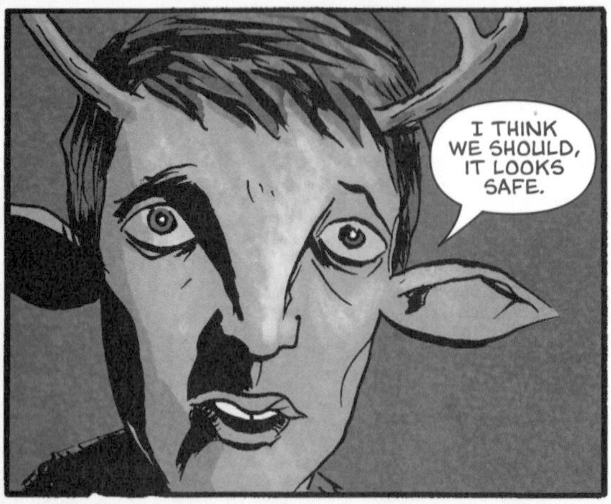
I THINK WE SHOULD, IT LOOKS SAFE.

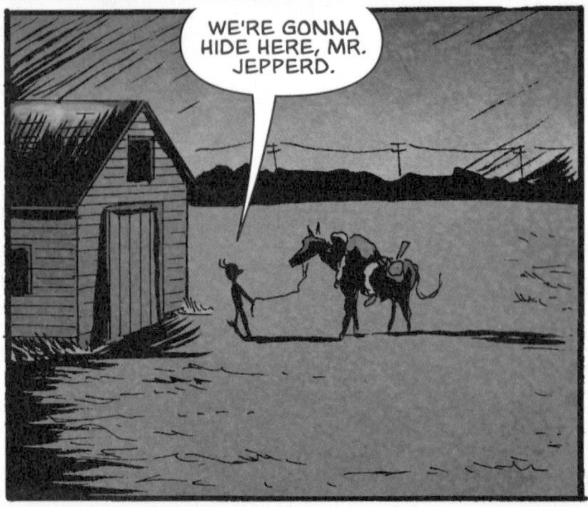
WE'RE GONNA HIDE HERE, MR. JEPPERD.

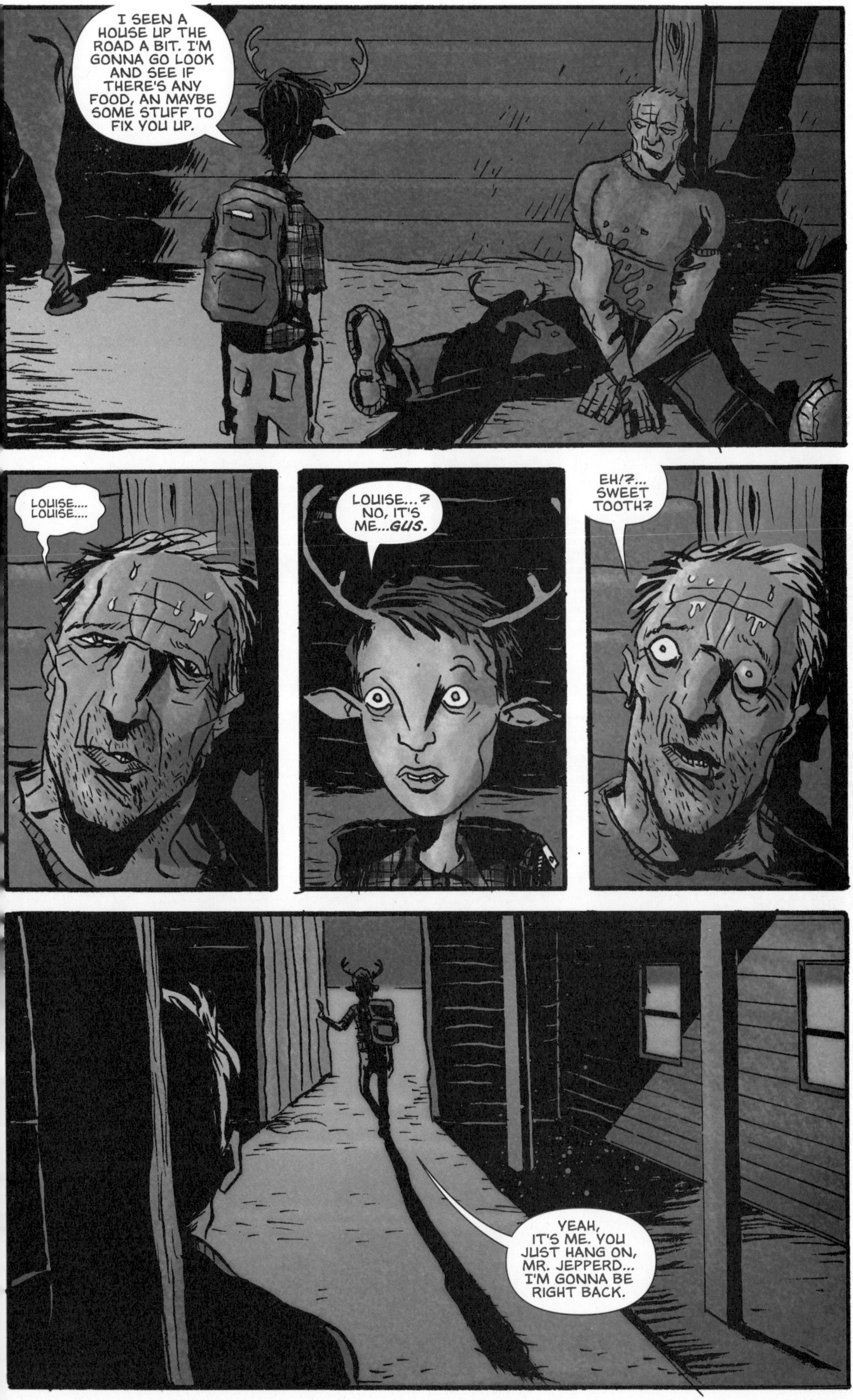
I SEEN A HOUSE UP THE ROAD A BIT. I'M GONNA GO LOOK AND SEE IF THERE'S ANY FOOD, AN MAYBE SOME STUFF TO FIX YOU UP.
LOUISE.... LOUISE....
LOUISE...? NO, IT'S ME...GUS.
EH!?... SWEET TOOTH?
YEAH, IT'S ME. YOU JUST HANG ON, MR. JEPPERD... I'M GONNA BE RIGHT BACK.

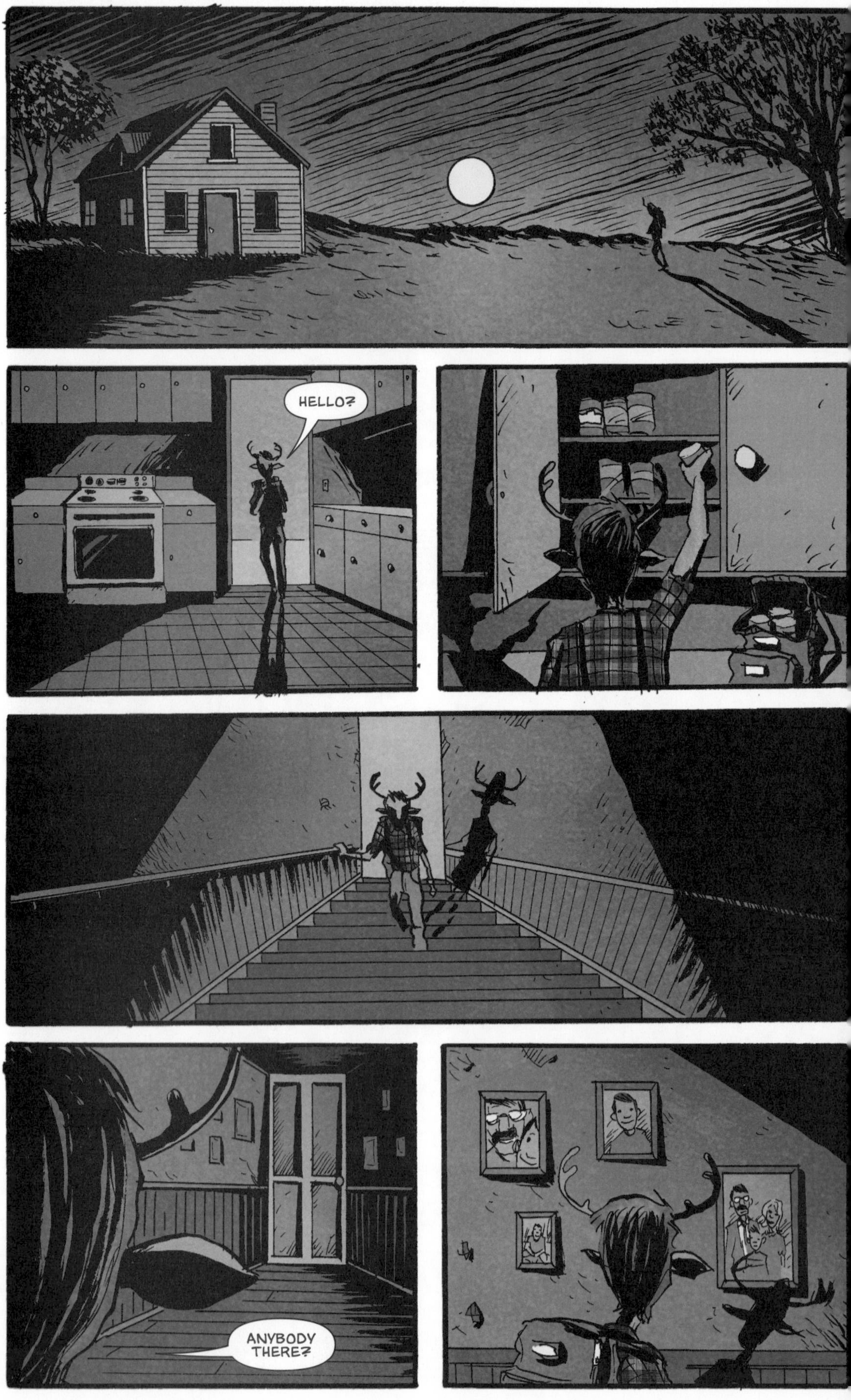
HELLO?
ANYBODY THERE?

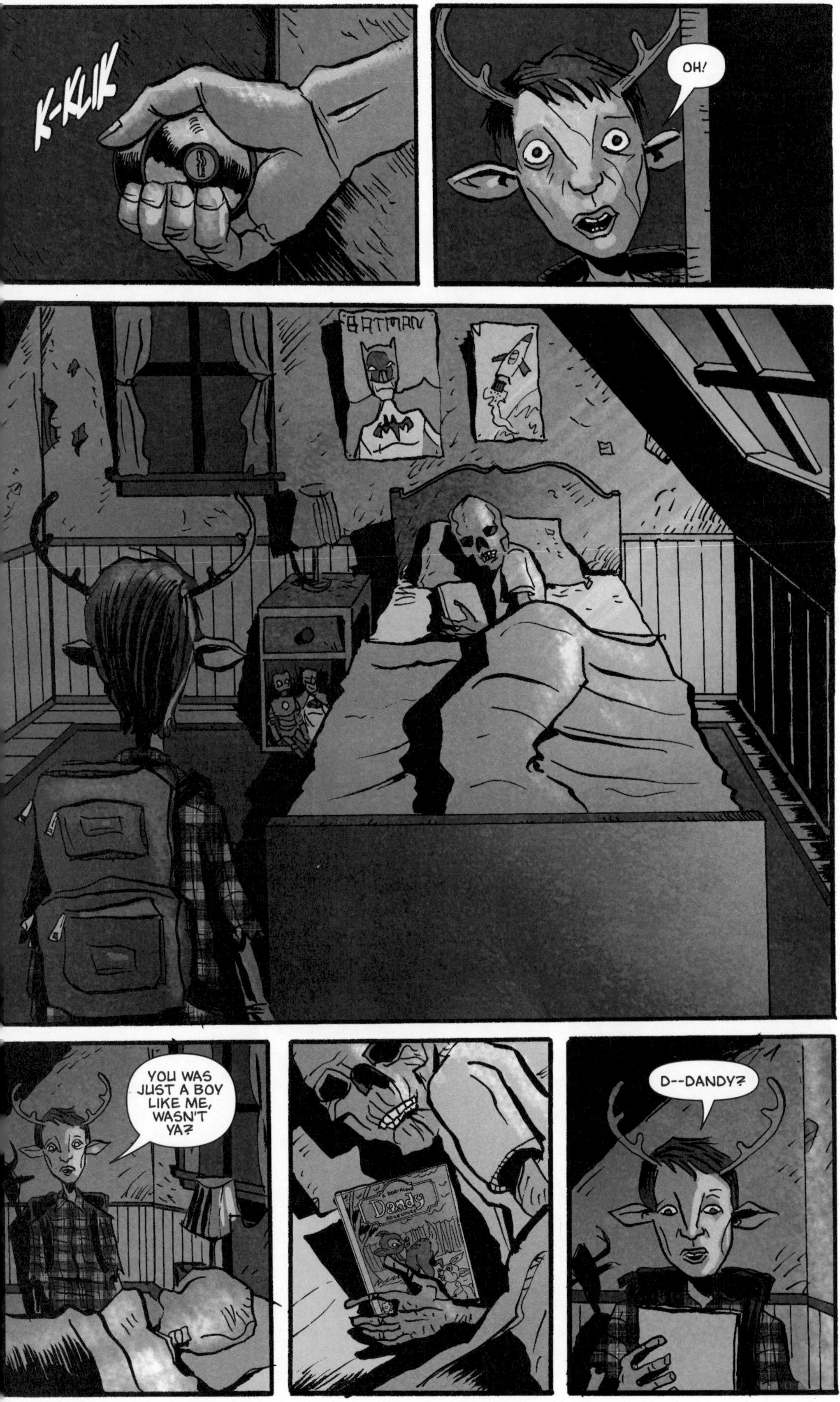
K-KLIK
OH!
BATMAN
YOU WAS JUST A BOY LIKE ME, WASN'T YA?
Dandy
D--DANDY?

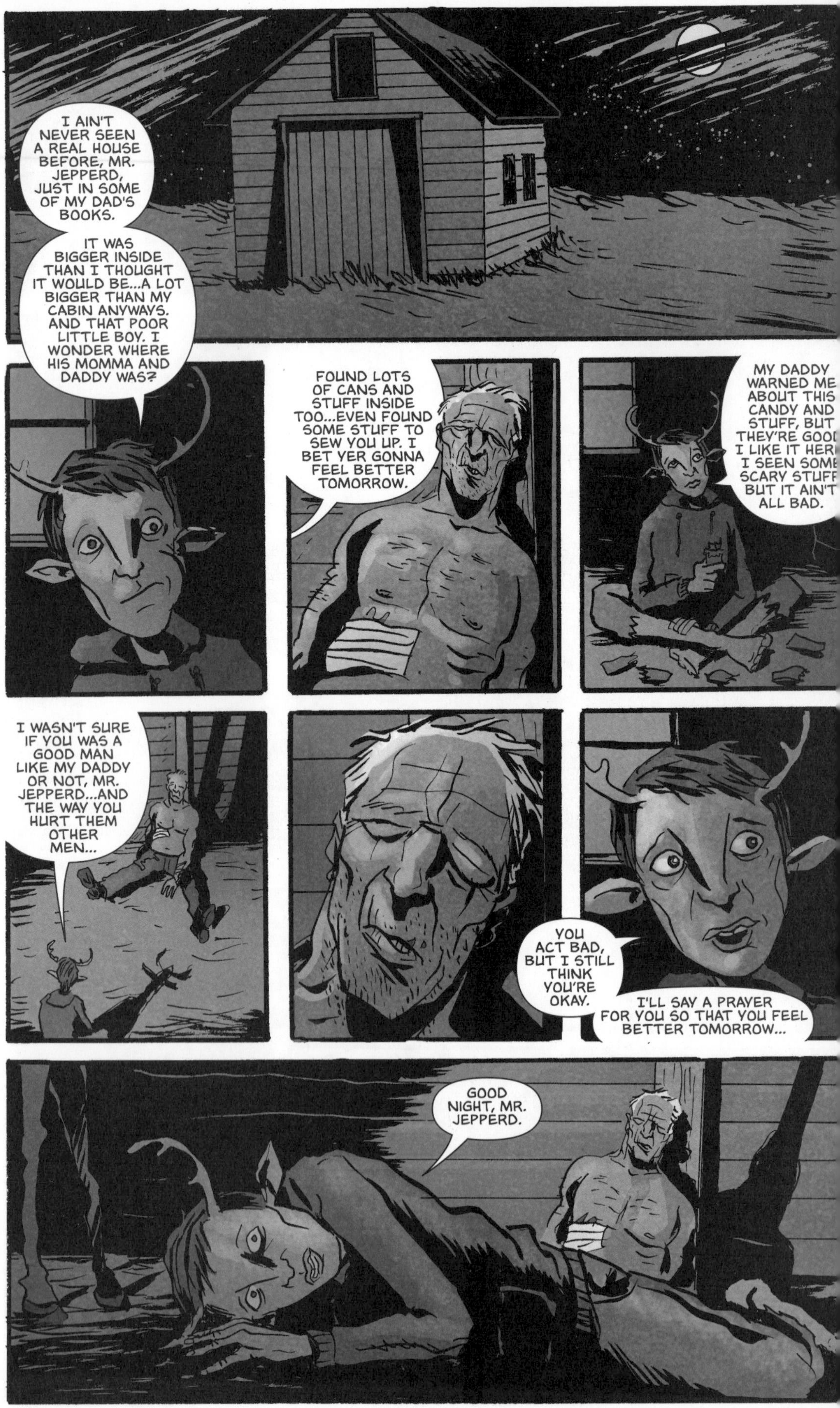

I AIN'T NEVER SEEN A REAL HOUSE BEFORE, MR. JEPPERD, JUST IN SOME OF MY DAD'S BOOKS.
IT WAS BIGGER INSIDE THAN I THOUGHT IT WOULD BE...A LOT BIGGER THAN MY CABIN ANYWAYS. AND THAT POOR LITTLE BOY. I WONDER WHERE HIS MOMMA AND DADDY WAS?
FOUND LOTS OF CANS AND STUFF INSIDE TOO...EVEN FOUND SOME STUFF TO SEW YOU UP. I BET YER GONNA FEEL BETTER TOMORROW.
MY DADDY WARNED ME ABOUT THIS CANDY AND STUFF, BUT THEY'RE GOOD I LIKE IT HERE I SEEN SOME SCARY STUFF BUT IT AIN'T ALL BAD.
I WASN'T SURE IF YOU WAS A GOOD MAN LIKE MY DADDY OR NOT, MR. JEPPERD...AND THE WAY YOU HURT THEM OTHER MEN...
YOU ACT BAD, BUT I STILL THINK YOU'RE OKAY.
I'LL SAY A PRAYER FOR YOU SO THAT YOU FEEL BETTER TOMORROW...
GOOD NIGHT, MR. JEPPERD.

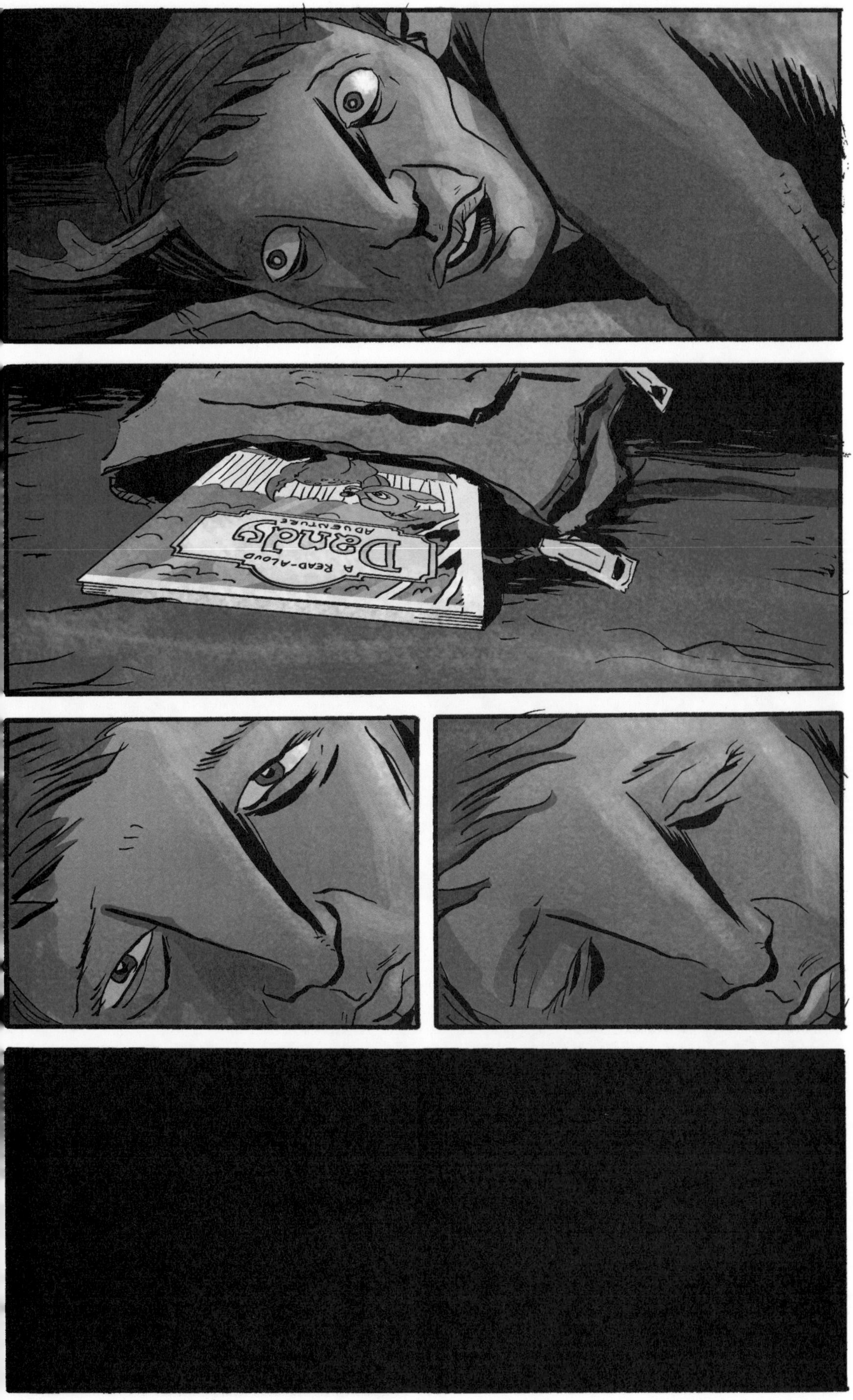
A READ-ALOUD
Dandy
ADVENTURE

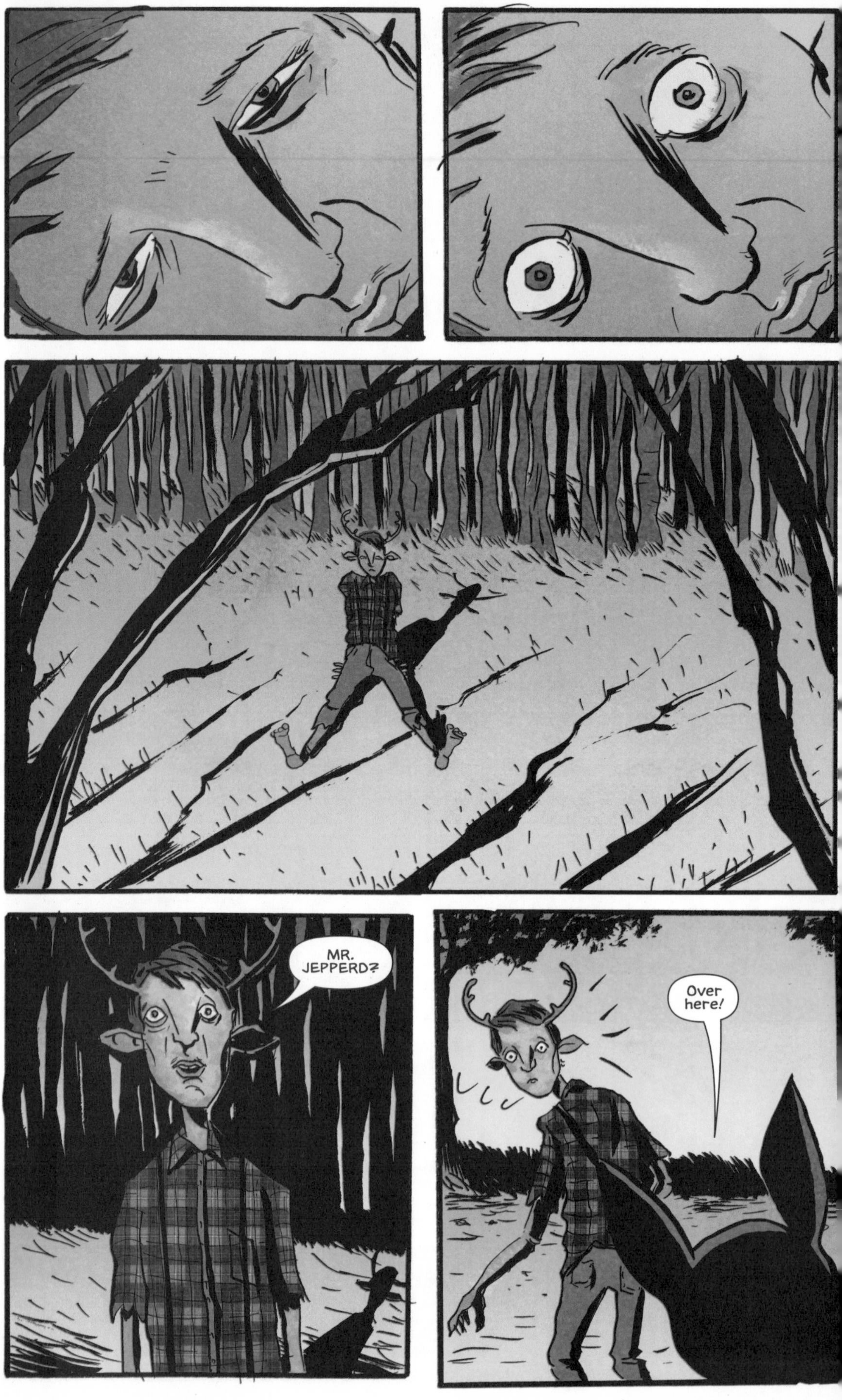
MR. JEPPERD?
Over here!

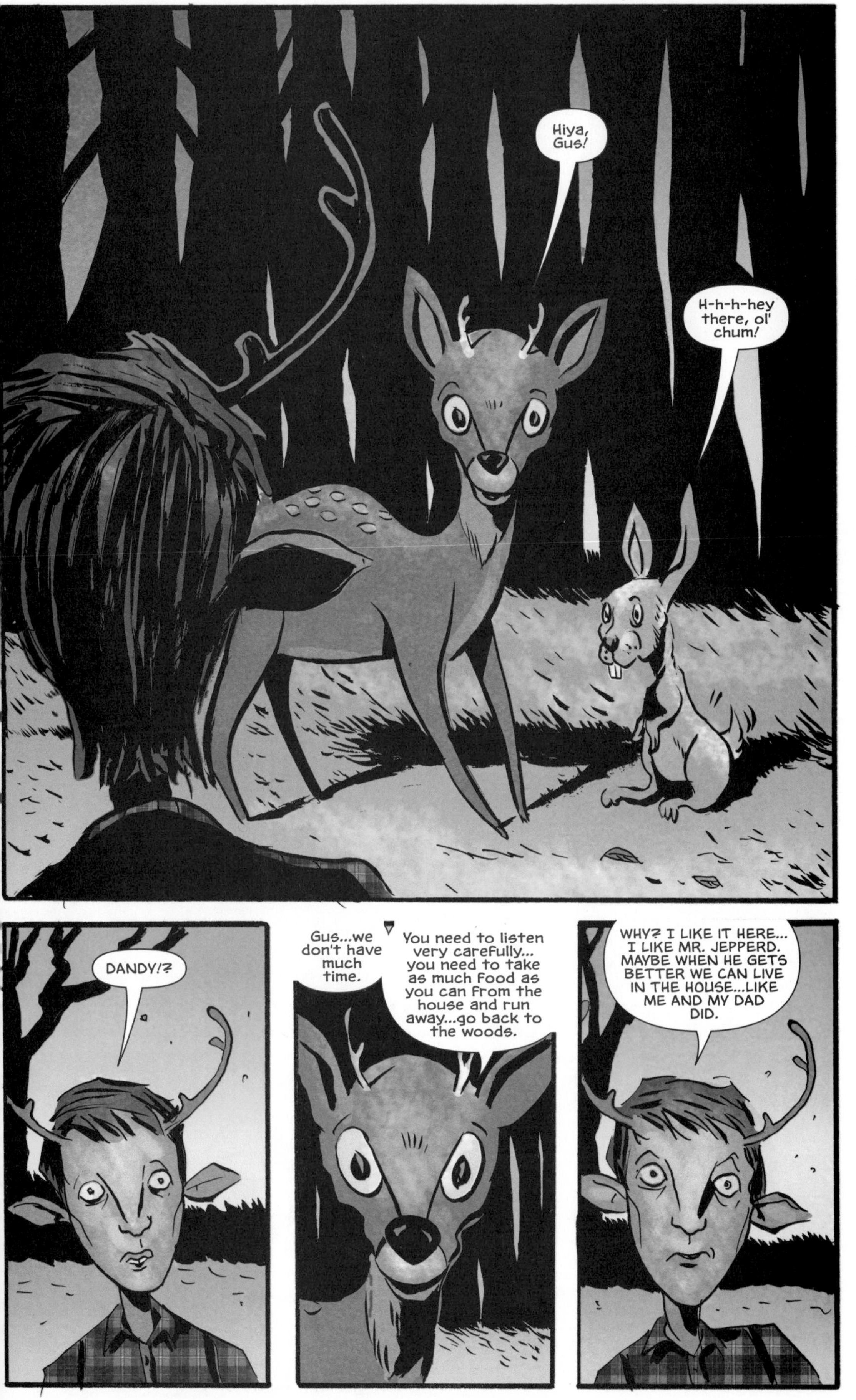
Hiya, Gus!
H-h-h-hey there, ol' chum!
DANDY!?
Gus...we don't have much time.
You need to listen very carefully... you need to take as much food as you can from the house and run away...go back to the woods.
WHY? I LIKE IT HERE... I LIKE MR. JEPPERD. MAYBE WHEN HE GETS BETTER WE CAN LIVE IN THE HOUSE...LIKE ME AND MY DAD DID.

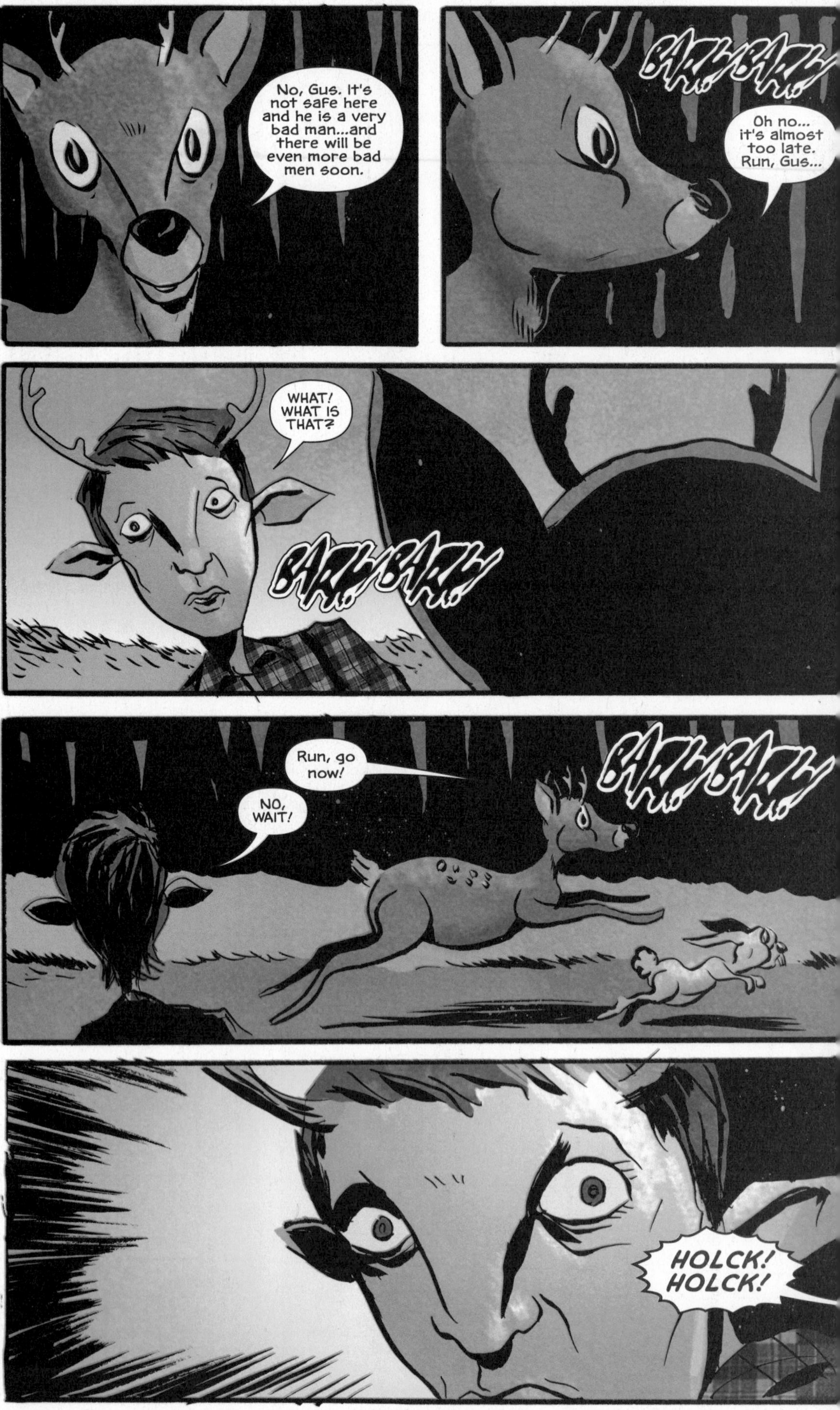

No, Gus. It's not safe here and he is a very bad man...and there will be even more bad men soon.
Oh no... it's almost too late. Run, Gus...
WHAT! WHAT IS THAT?
Run, go now!
NO, WAIT!
HOLCK! HOLCK!

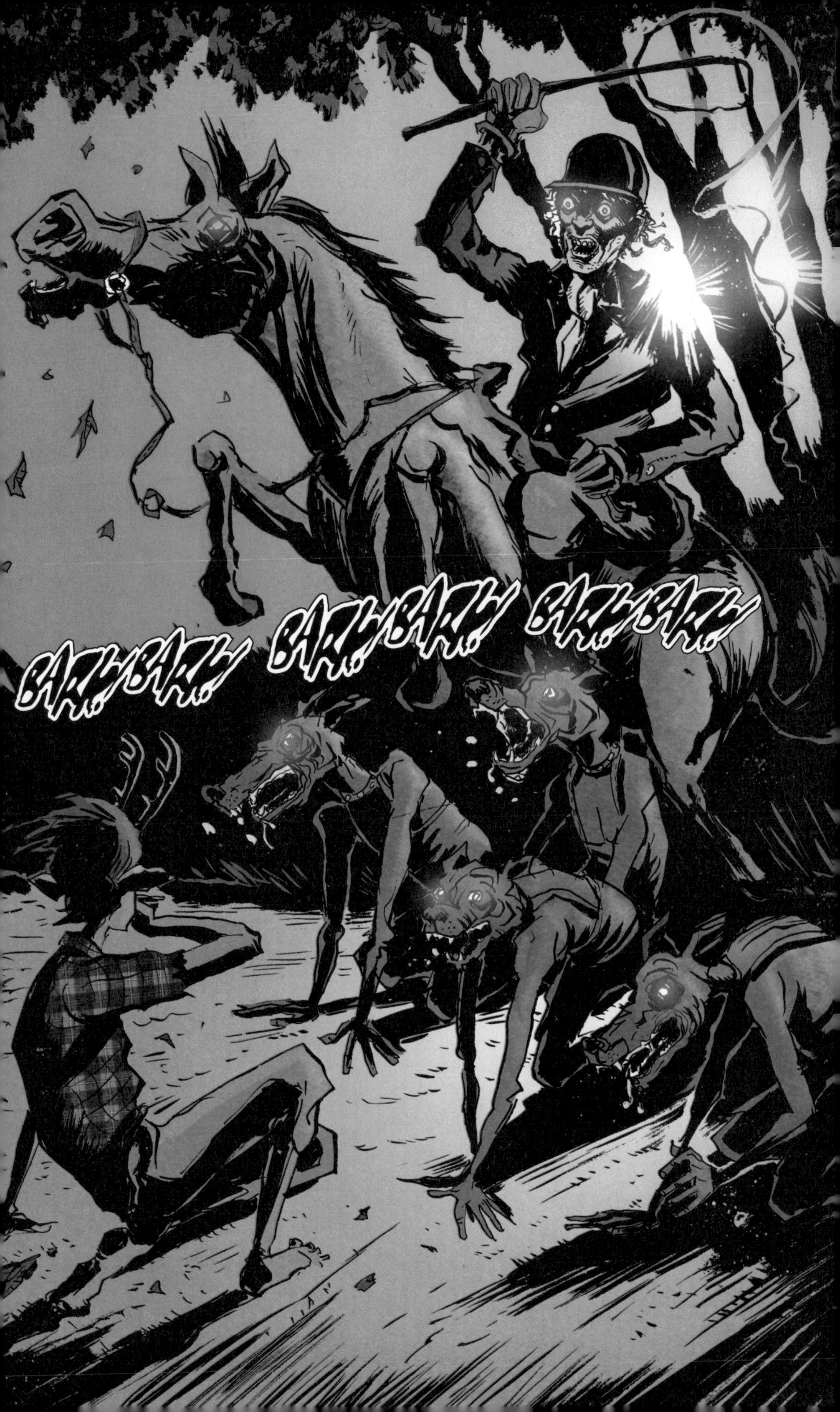
BARK BARK
BARK BARK
BARK BARK

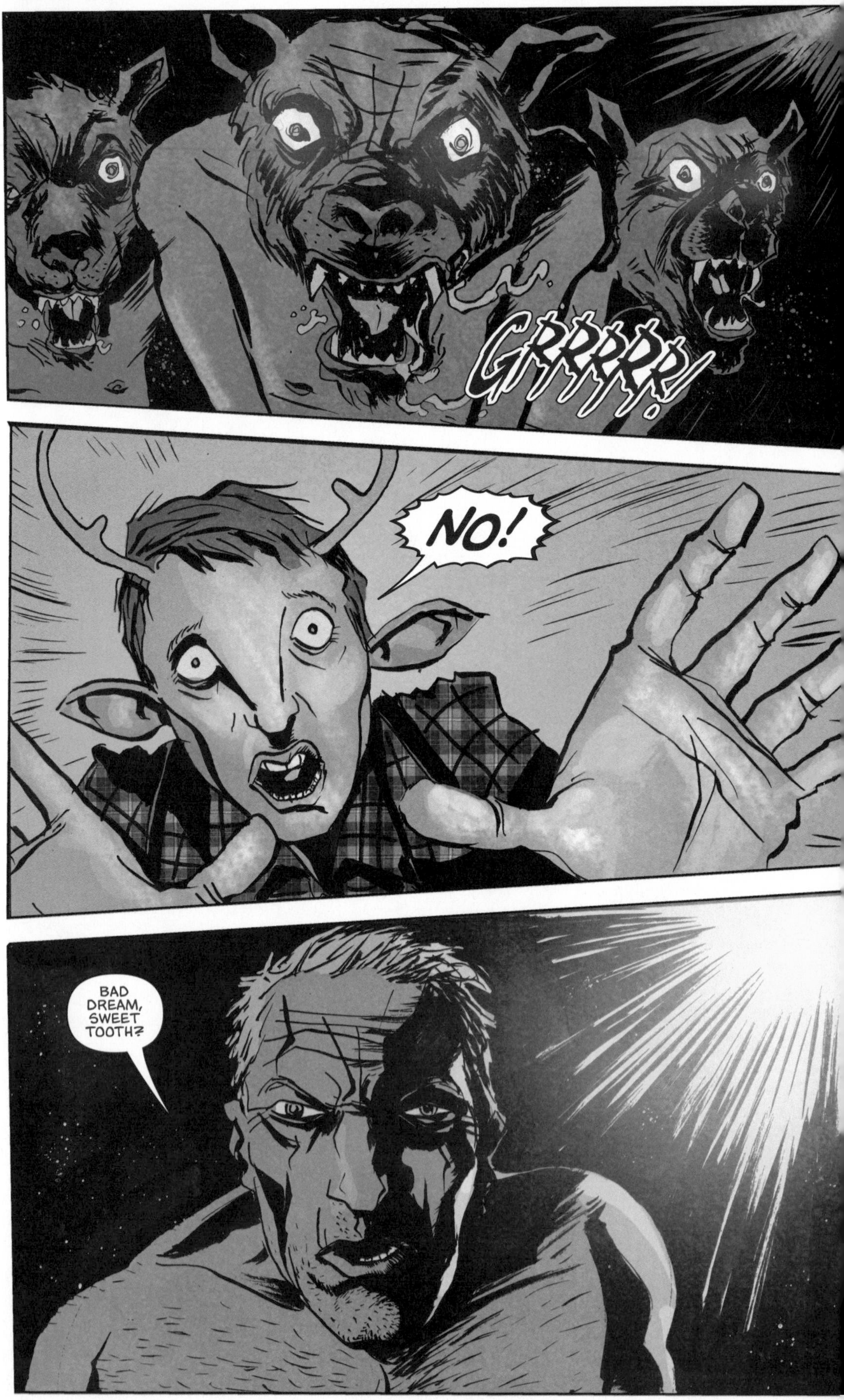
GRRRRR!
NO!
BAD DREAM, SWEET TOOTH?

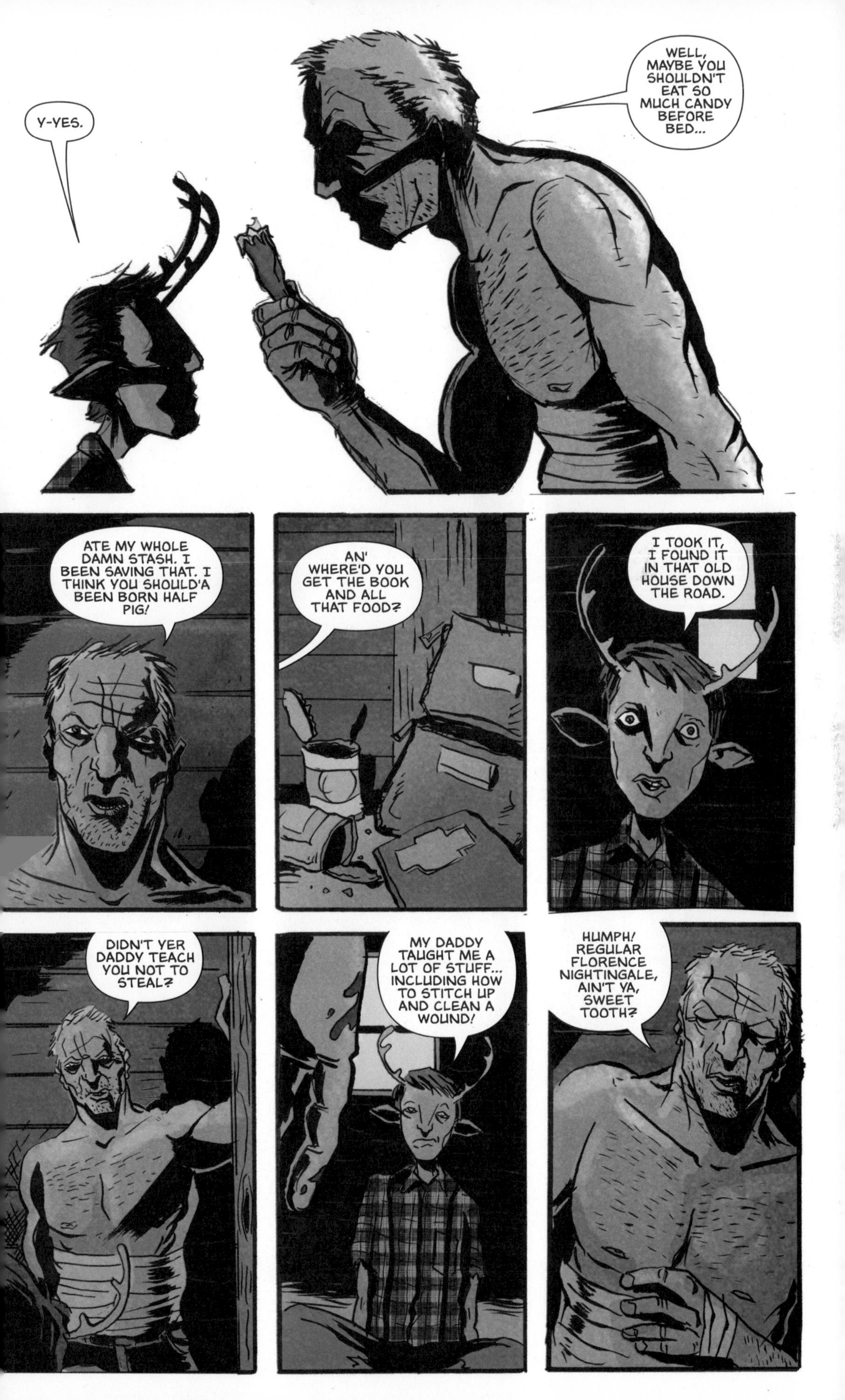
Y-YES.
WELL, MAYBE YOU SHOULDN'T EAT SO MUCH CANDY BEFORE BED...
ATE MY WHOLE DAMN STASH. I BEEN SAVING THAT. I THINK YOU SHOULD'A BEEN BORN HALF PIG!
AN' WHERE'D YOU GET THE BOOK AND ALL THAT FOOD?
I TOOK IT, I FOUND IT IN THAT OLD HOUSE DOWN THE ROAD.
DIDN'T YER DADDY TEACH YOU NOT TO STEAL?
MY DADDY TAUGHT ME A LOT OF STUFF... INCLUDING HOW TO STITCH UP AND CLEAN A WOUND!
HUMPH! REGULAR FLORENCE NIGHTINGALE, AIN'T YA, SWEET TOOTH?

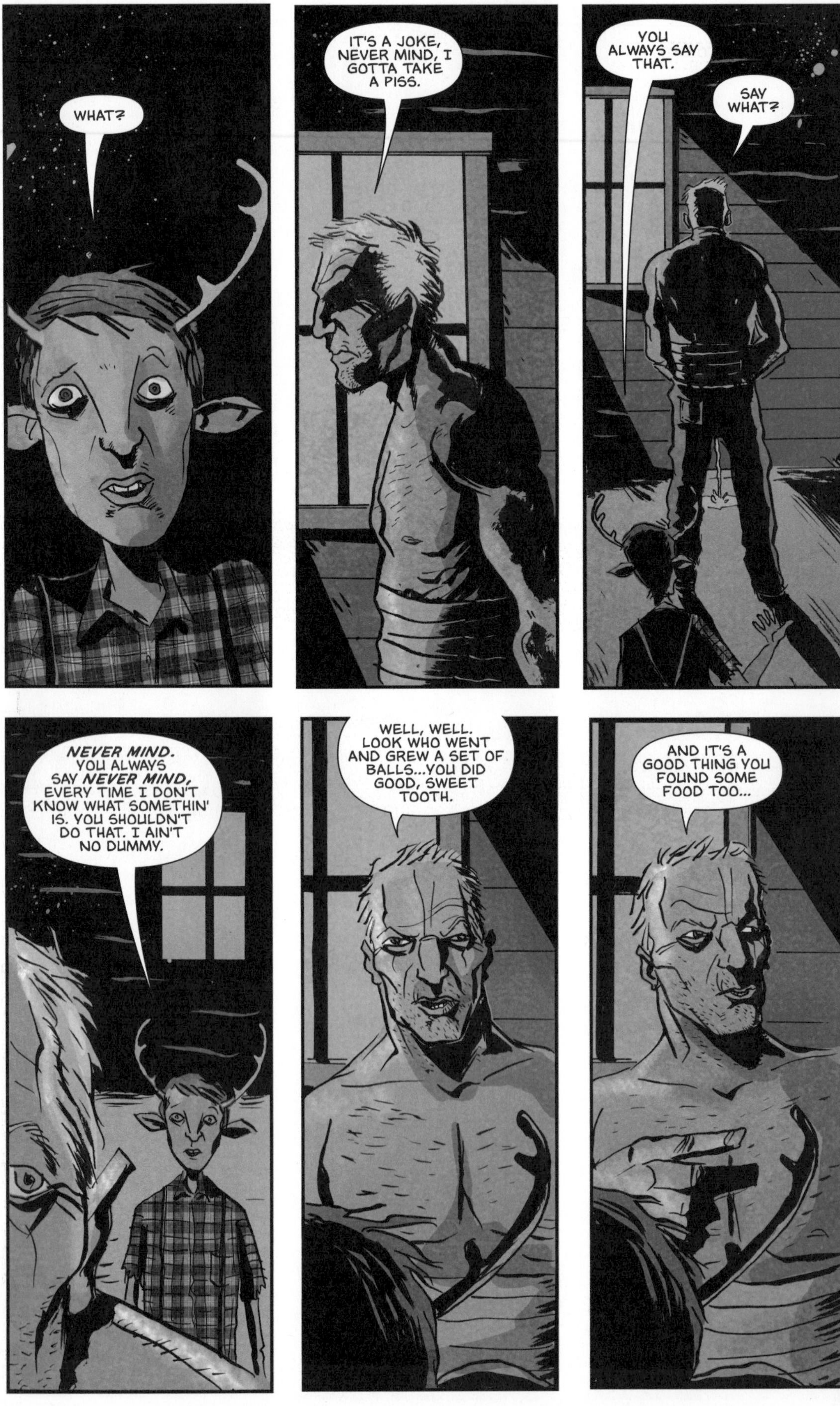
WHAT?
IT'S A JOKE, NEVER MIND, I GOTTA TAKE A PISS.
YOU ALWAYS SAY THAT.
SAY WHAT?
NEVER MIND. YOU ALWAYS SAY NEVER MIND, EVERY TIME I DON'T KNOW WHAT SOMETHIN' IS. YOU SHOULDN'T DO THAT. I AIN'T NO DUMMY.
WELL, WELL. LOOK WHO WENT AND GREW A SET OF BALLS...YOU DID GOOD, SWEET TOOTH.
AND IT'S A GOOD THING YOU FOUND SOME FOOD TOO...

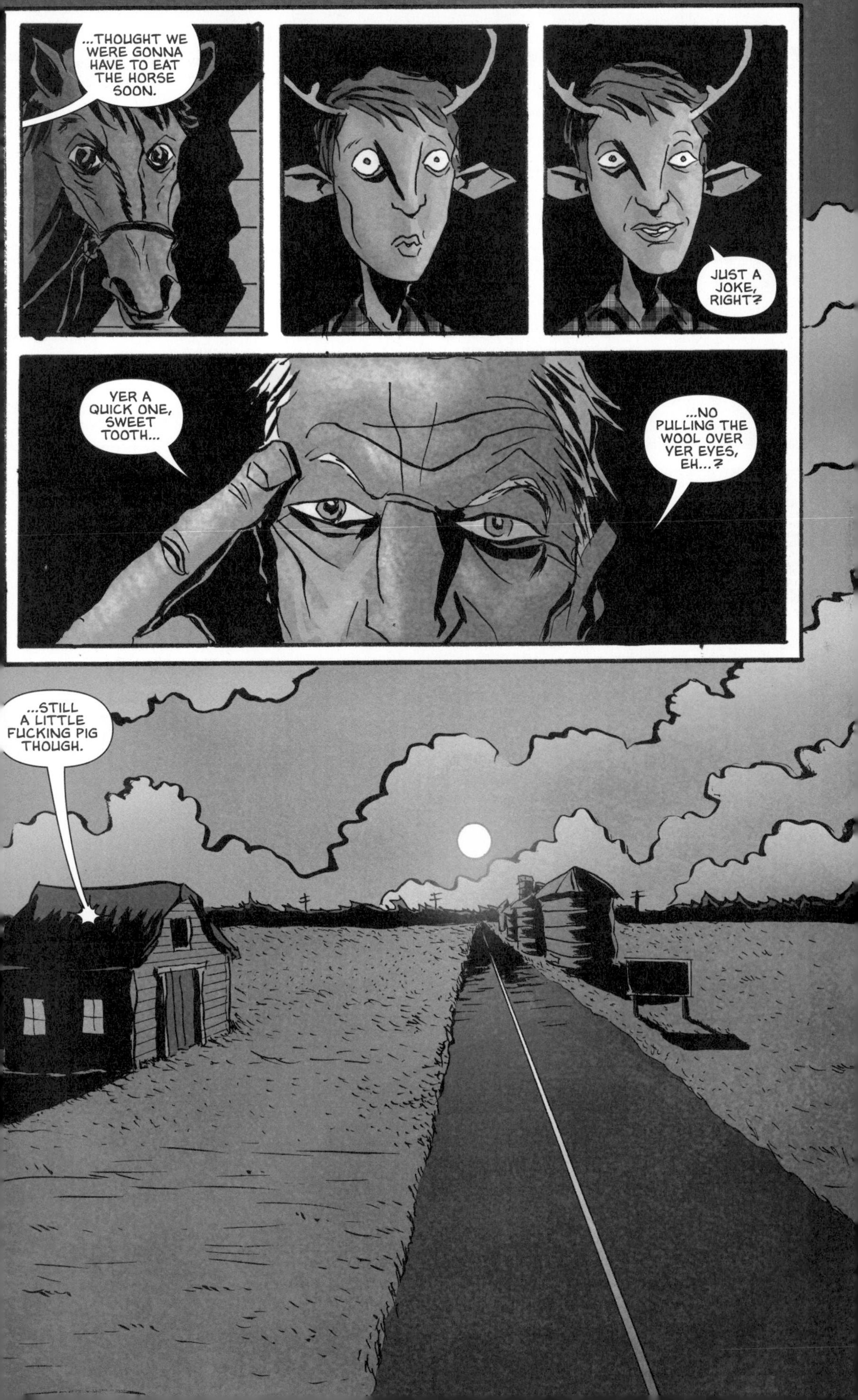
...THOUGHT WE WERE GONNA HAVE TO EAT THE HORSE SOON.
JUST A JOKE, RIGHT?
YER A QUICK ONE, SWEET TOOTH...
...NO PULLING THE WOOL OVER YER EYES, EH...?
...STILL A LITTLE FUCKING PIG THOUGH.

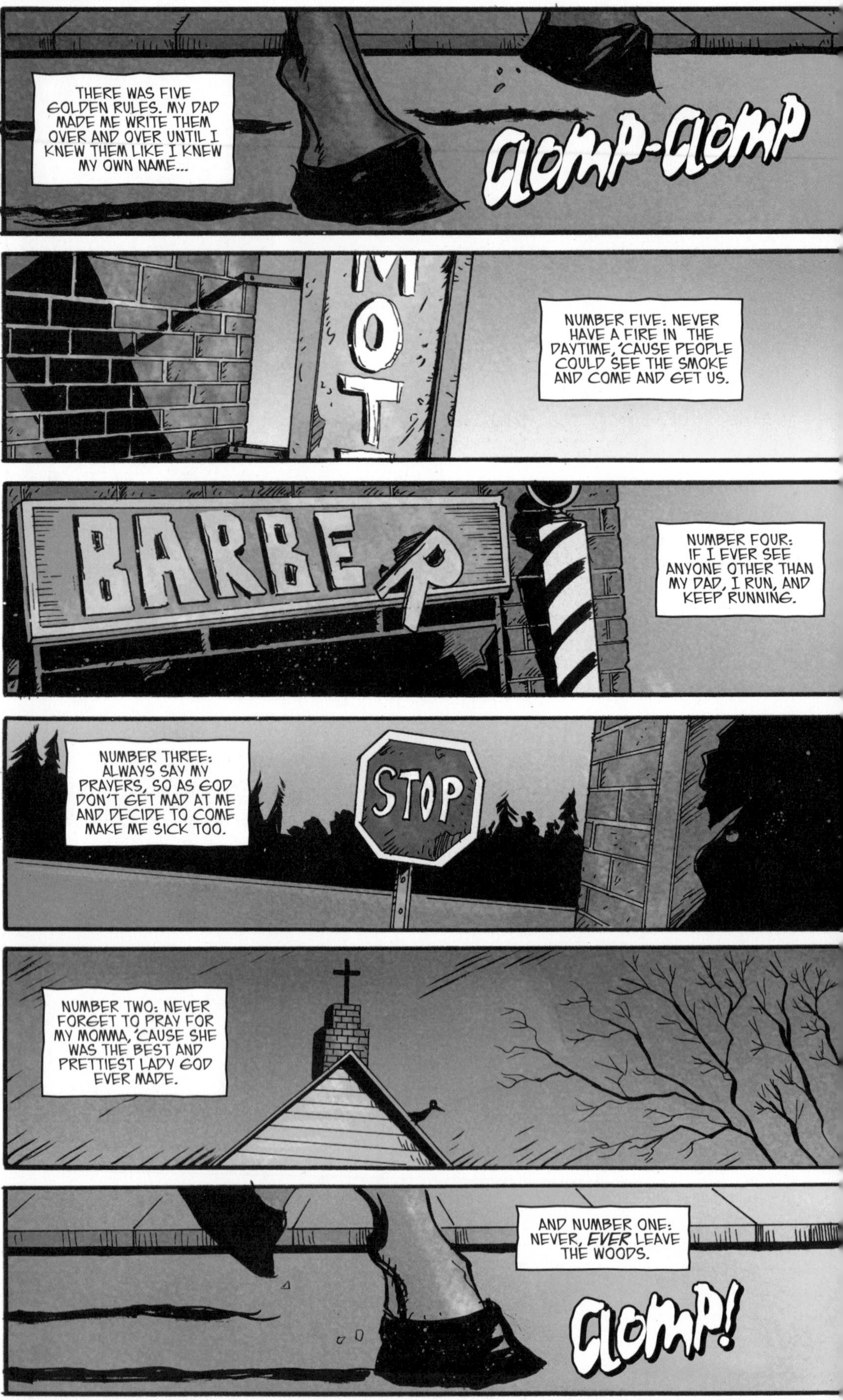
THERE WAS FIVE GOLDEN RULES. MY DAD MADE ME WRITE THEM OVER AND OVER UNTIL I KNEW THEM LIKE I KNEW MY OWN NAME...
CLOMP-CLOMP
MOT
NUMBER FIVE: NEVER HAVE A FIRE IN THE DAYTIME, 'CAUSE PEOPLE COULD SEE THE SMOKE AND COME AND GET US.
BARBER
NUMBER FOUR: IF I EVER SEE ANYONE OTHER THAN MY DAD, I RUN, AND KEEP RUNNING.
NUMBER THREE: ALWAYS SAY MY PRAYERS, SO AS GOD DON'T GET MAD AT ME AND DECIDE TO COME MAKE ME SICK TOO.
STOP
NUMBER TWO: NEVER FORGET TO PRAY FOR MY MOMMA, 'CAUSE SHE WAS THE BEST AND PRETTIEST LADY GOD EVER MADE.
AND NUMBER ONE: NEVER, EVER LEAVE THE WOODS.
CLOMP!

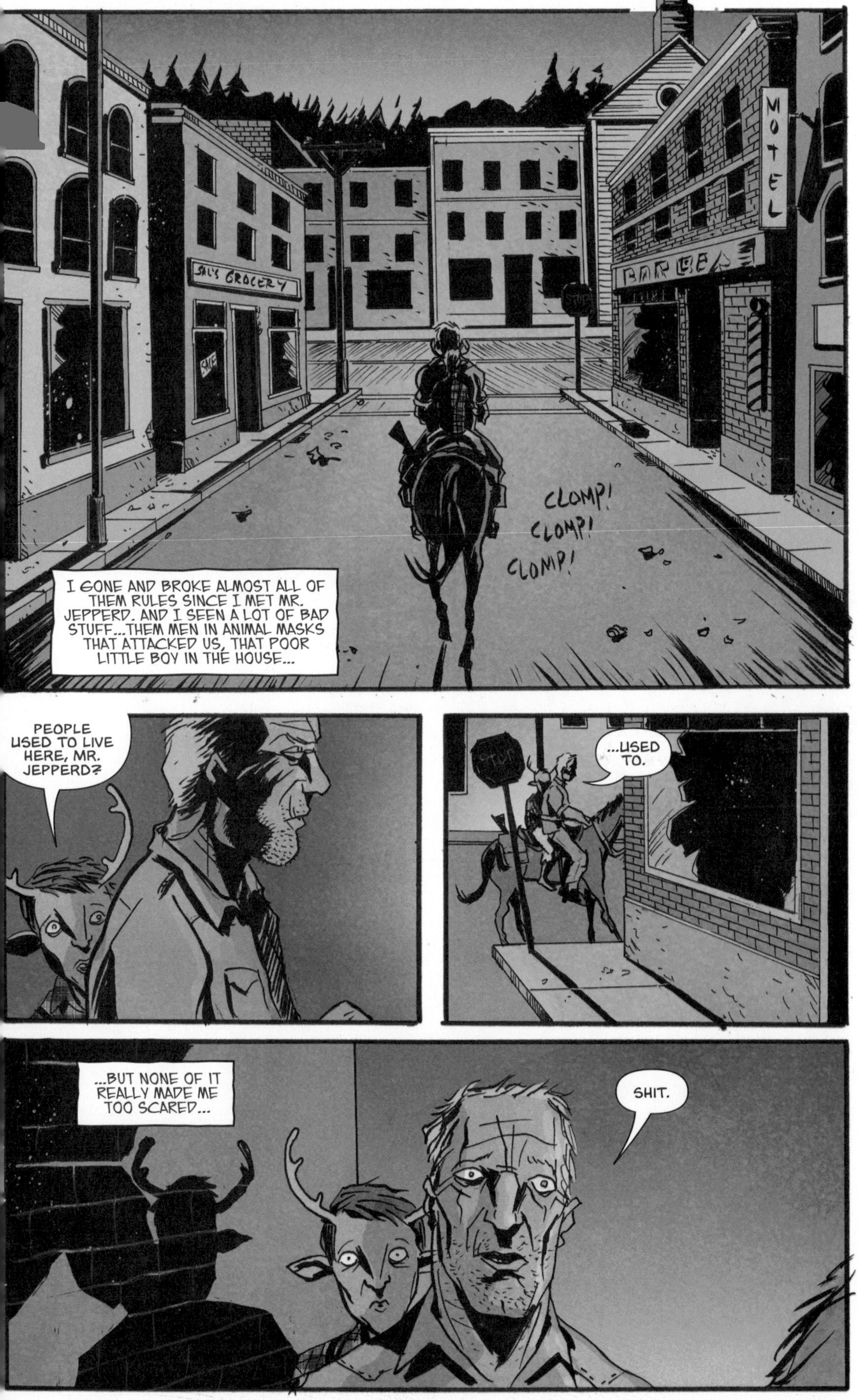
SAL'S GROCERY
SALE
STOP
MOTEL
BARBER
CLOMP!
CLOMP!
CLOMP!
I GONE AND BROKE ALMOST ALL OF THEM RULES SINCE I MET MR. JEPPERD. AND I SEEN A LOT OF BAD STUFF...THEM MEN IN ANIMAL MASKS THAT ATTACKED US, THAT POOR LITTLE BOY IN THE HOUSE...
PEOPLE USED TO LIVE HERE, MR. JEPPERD?
...USED TO.
...BUT NONE OF IT REALLY MADE ME TOO SCARED...
SHIT.

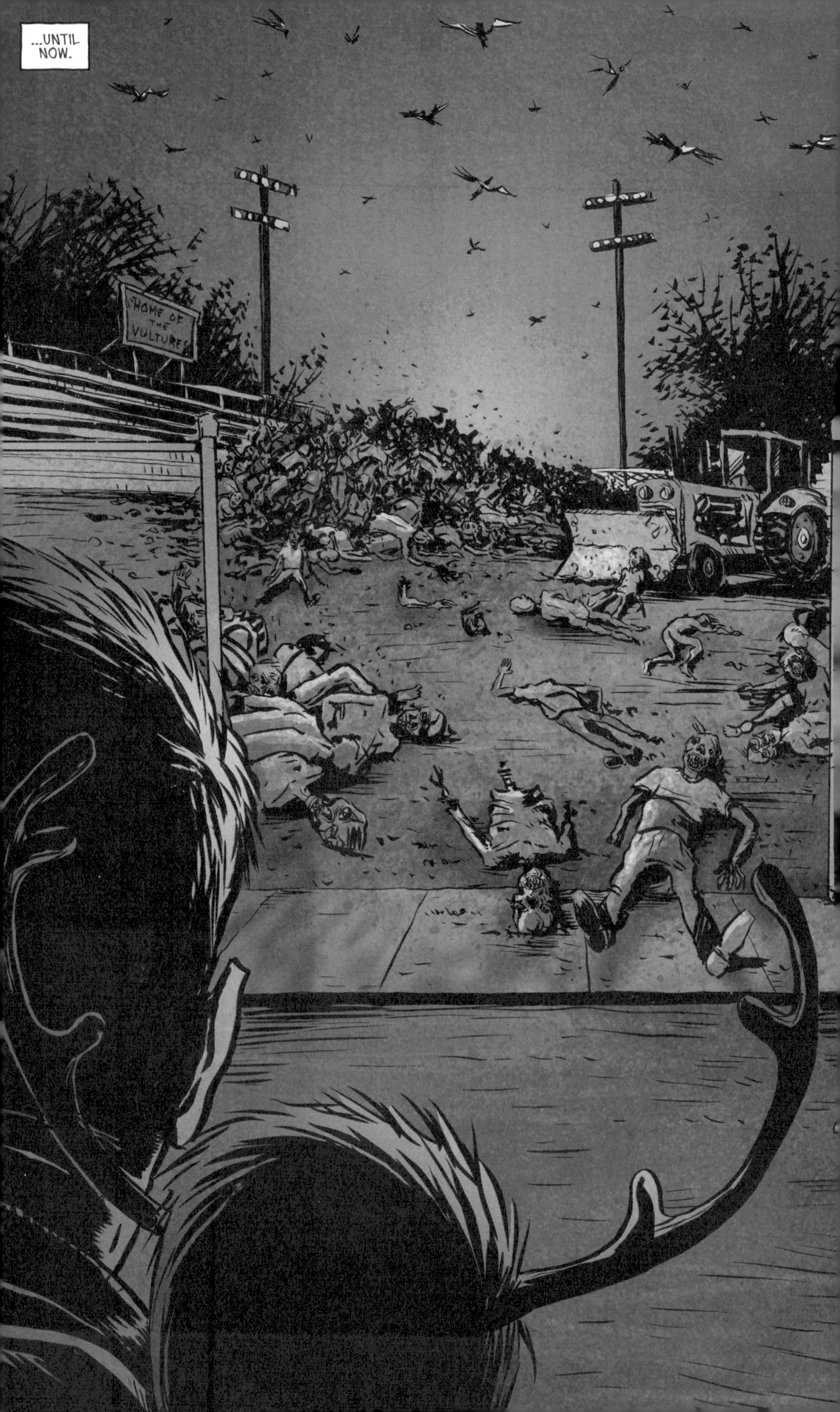
...UNTIL NOW.
HOME OF THE VULTURES

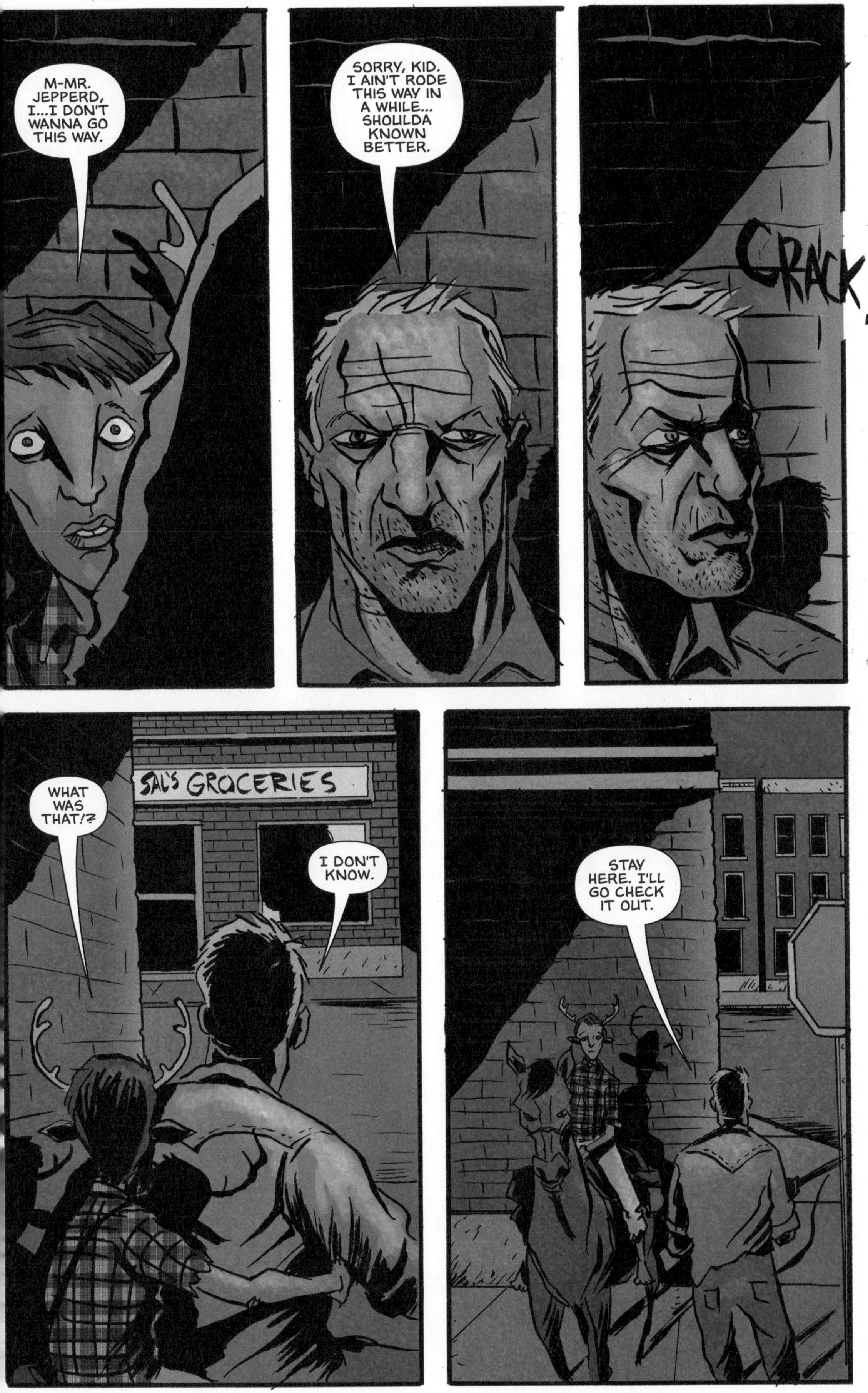
M-MR. JEPPERD, I...I DON'T WANNA GO THIS WAY.
SORRY, KID. I AIN'T RODE THIS WAY IN A WHILE... SHOULDA KNOWN BETTER.
CRACK!
SAL'S GROCERIES
WHAT WAS THAT!?
I DON'T KNOW.
STAY HERE. I'LL GO CHECK IT OUT.

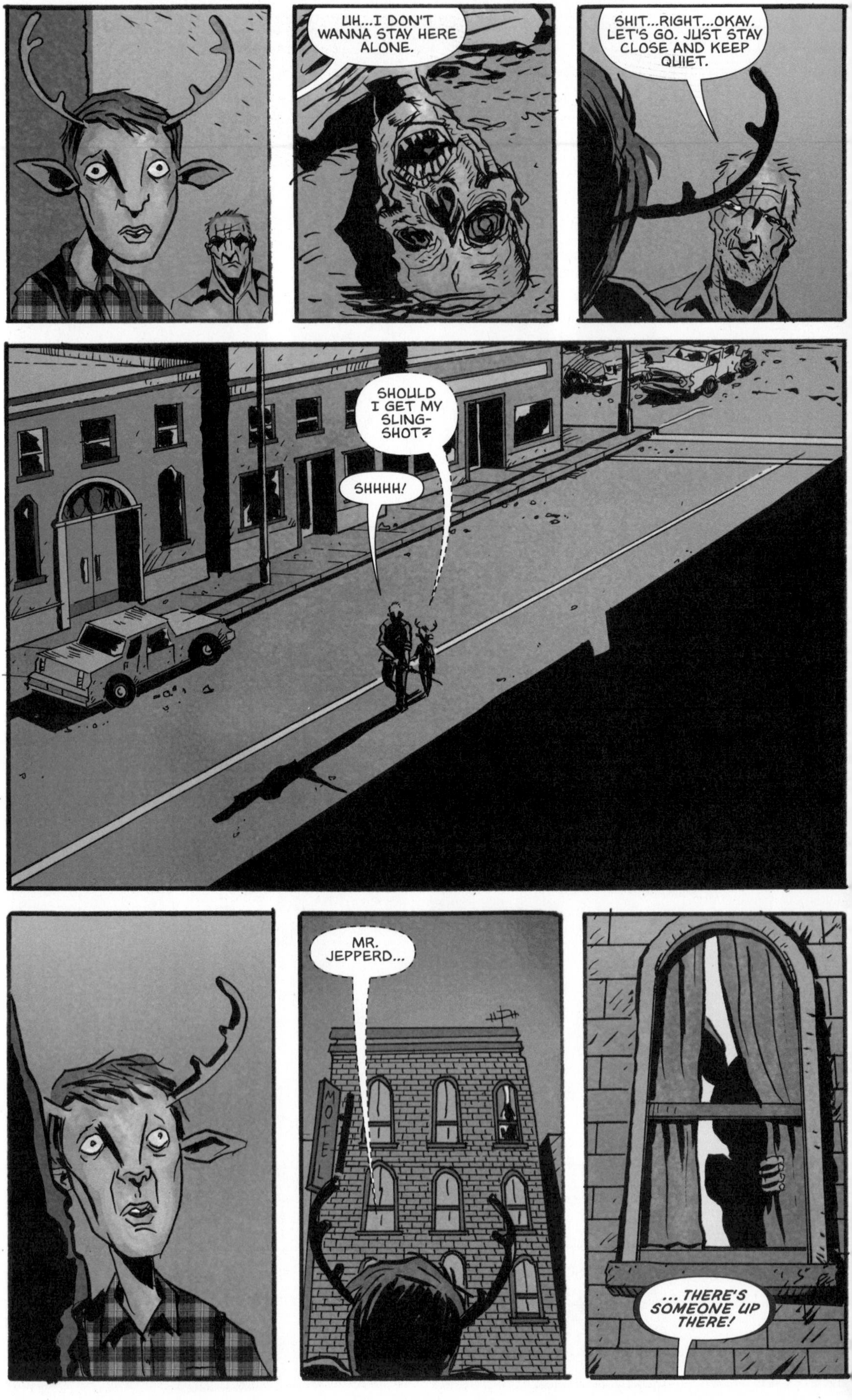
UH...I DON'T WANNA STAY HERE ALONE.
SHIT...RIGHT...OKAY. LET'S GO. JUST STAY CLOSE AND KEEP QUIET.
SHOULD I GET MY SLING-SHOT?
SHHHH!
MR. JEPPERD...
MOTEL
...THERE'S SOMEONE UP THERE!

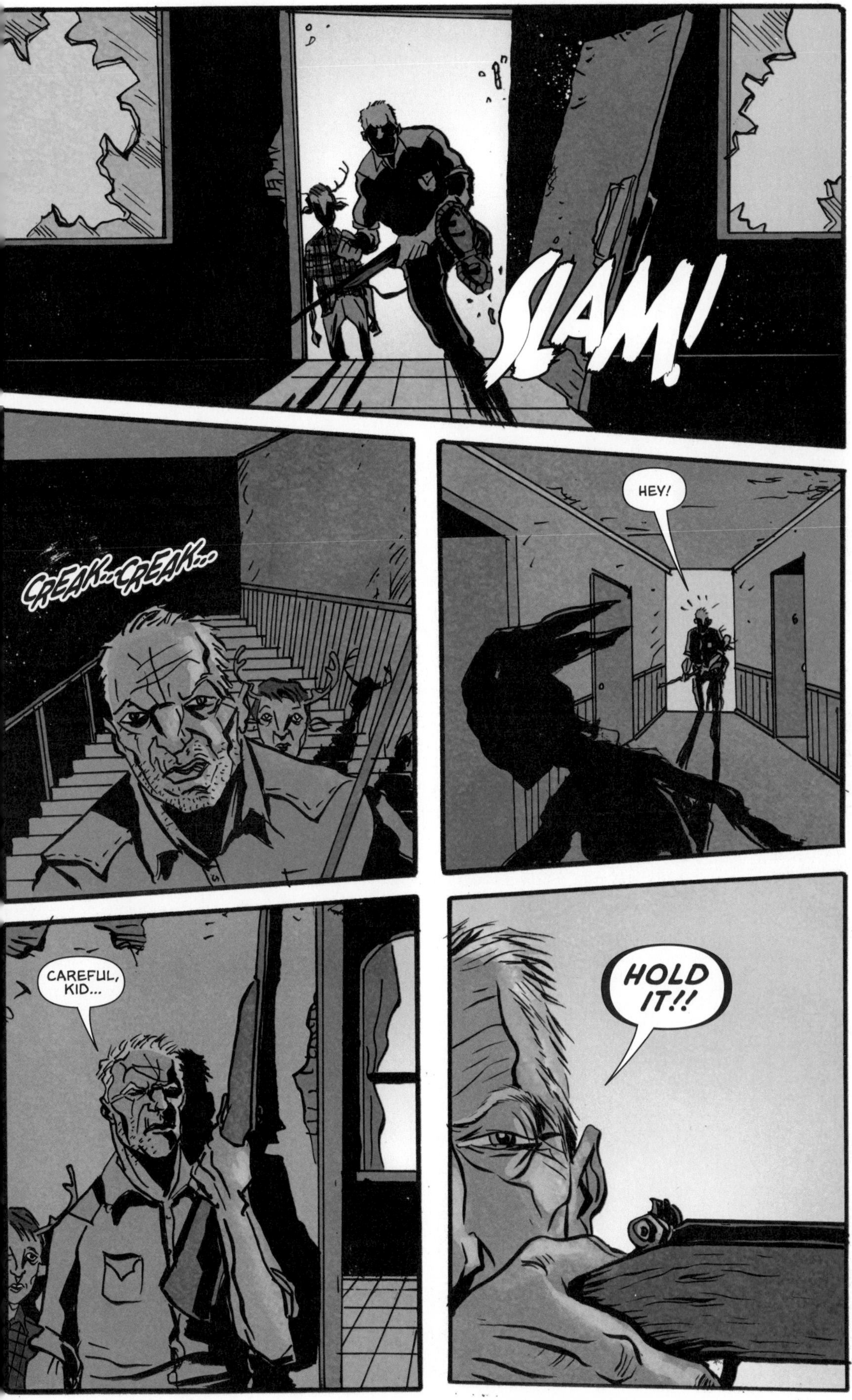
SLAM!
CREAK...CREAK...
HEY!
CAREFUL, KID...
HOLD IT!!

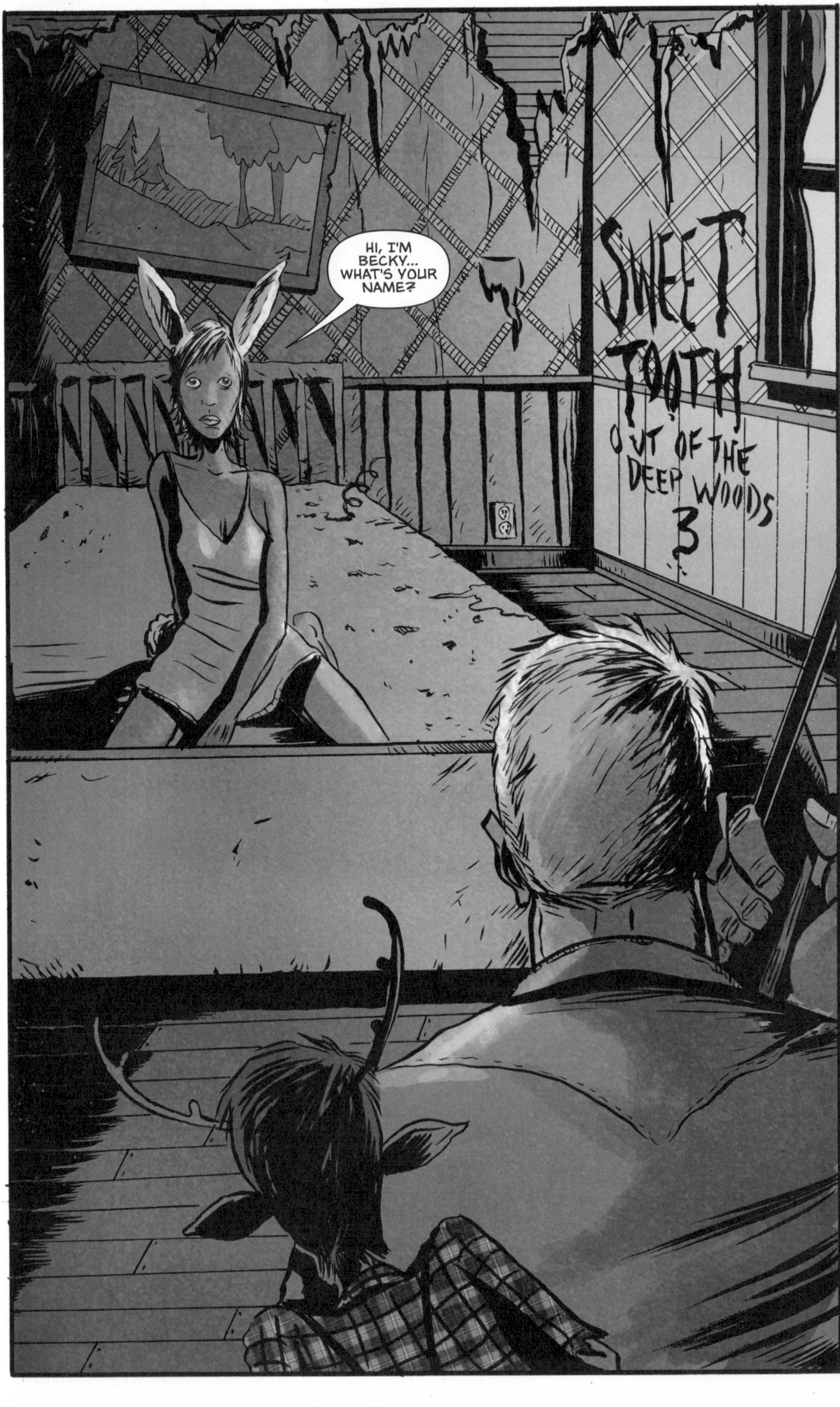
HI, I'M BECKY... WHAT'S YOUR NAME?
SWEET TOOTH
OUT OF THE DEEP WOODS
3

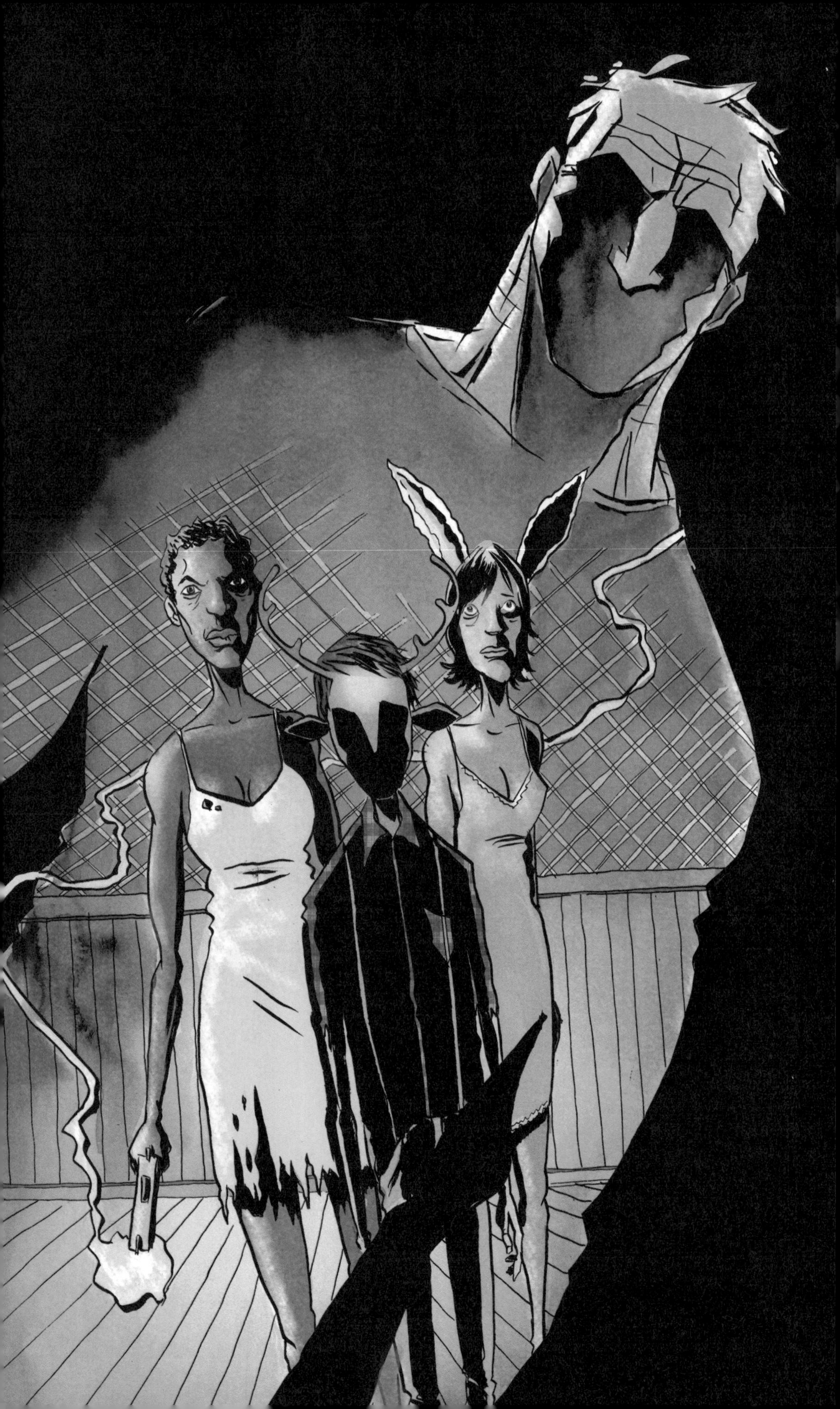

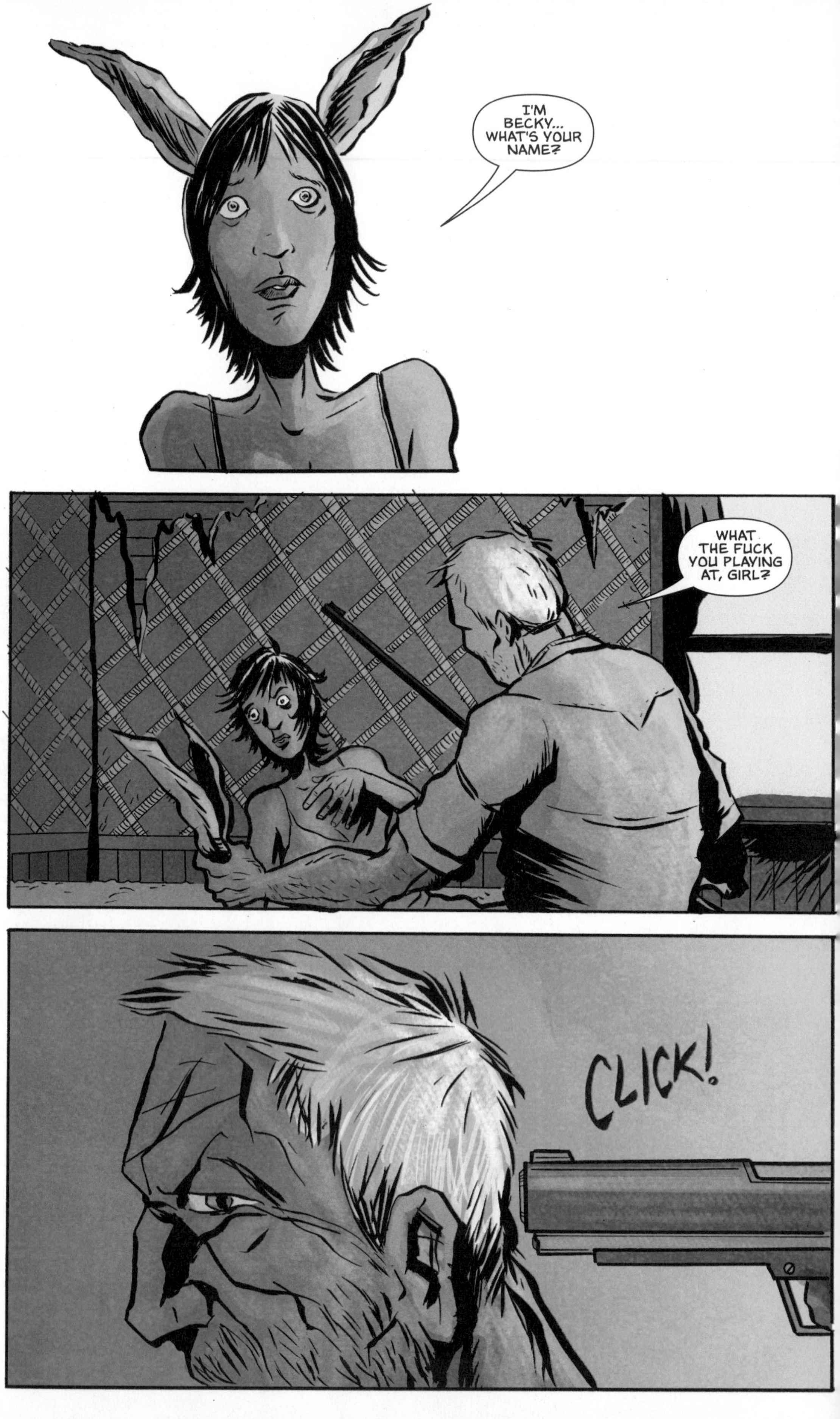
I'M BECKY... WHAT'S YOUR NAME?
WHAT THE FUCK YOU PLAYING AT, GIRL?
CLICK!

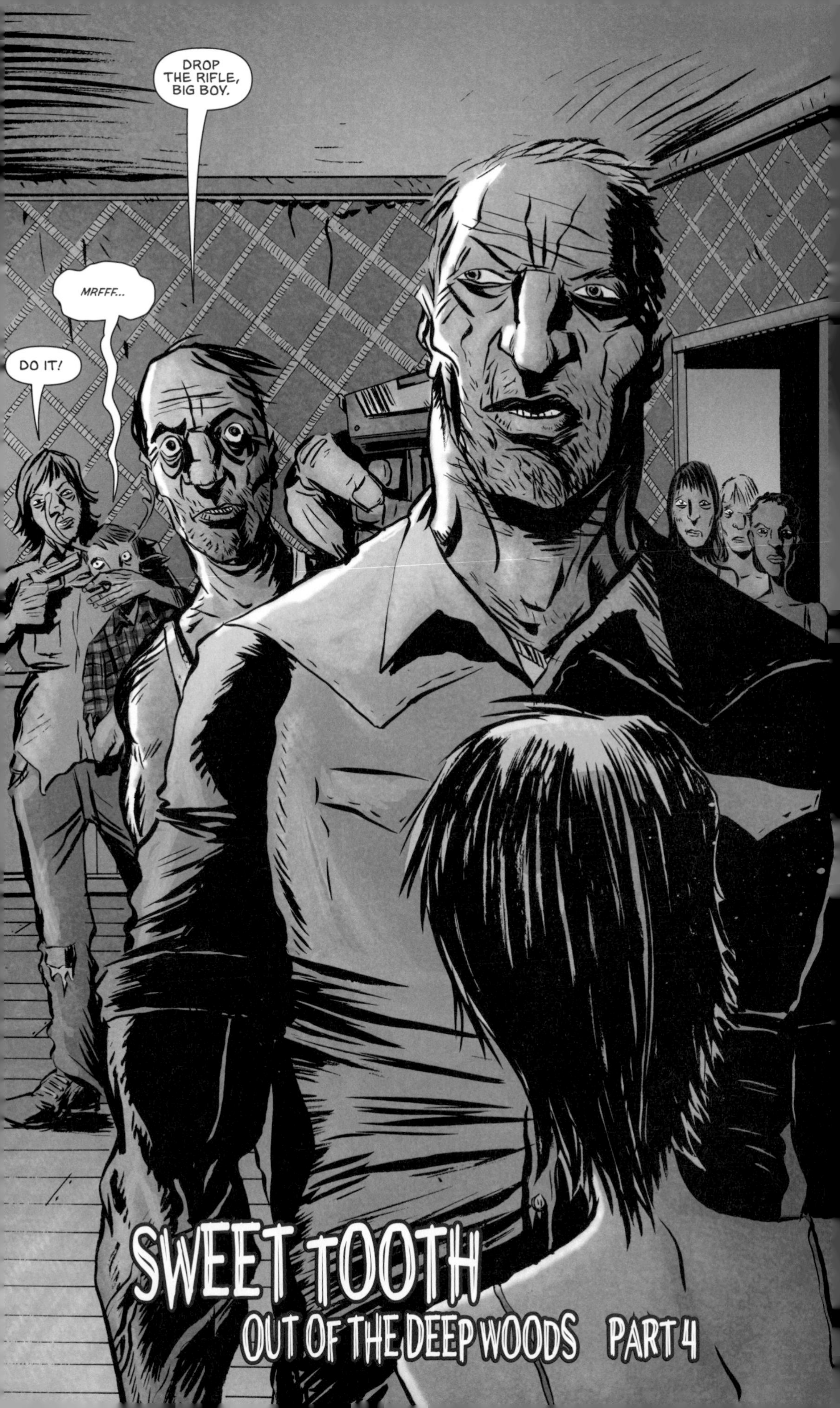
DO IT!
MRFFF...
DROP THE RIFLE, BIG BOY.
SWEET TOOTH
OUT OF THE DEEP WOODS PART 4

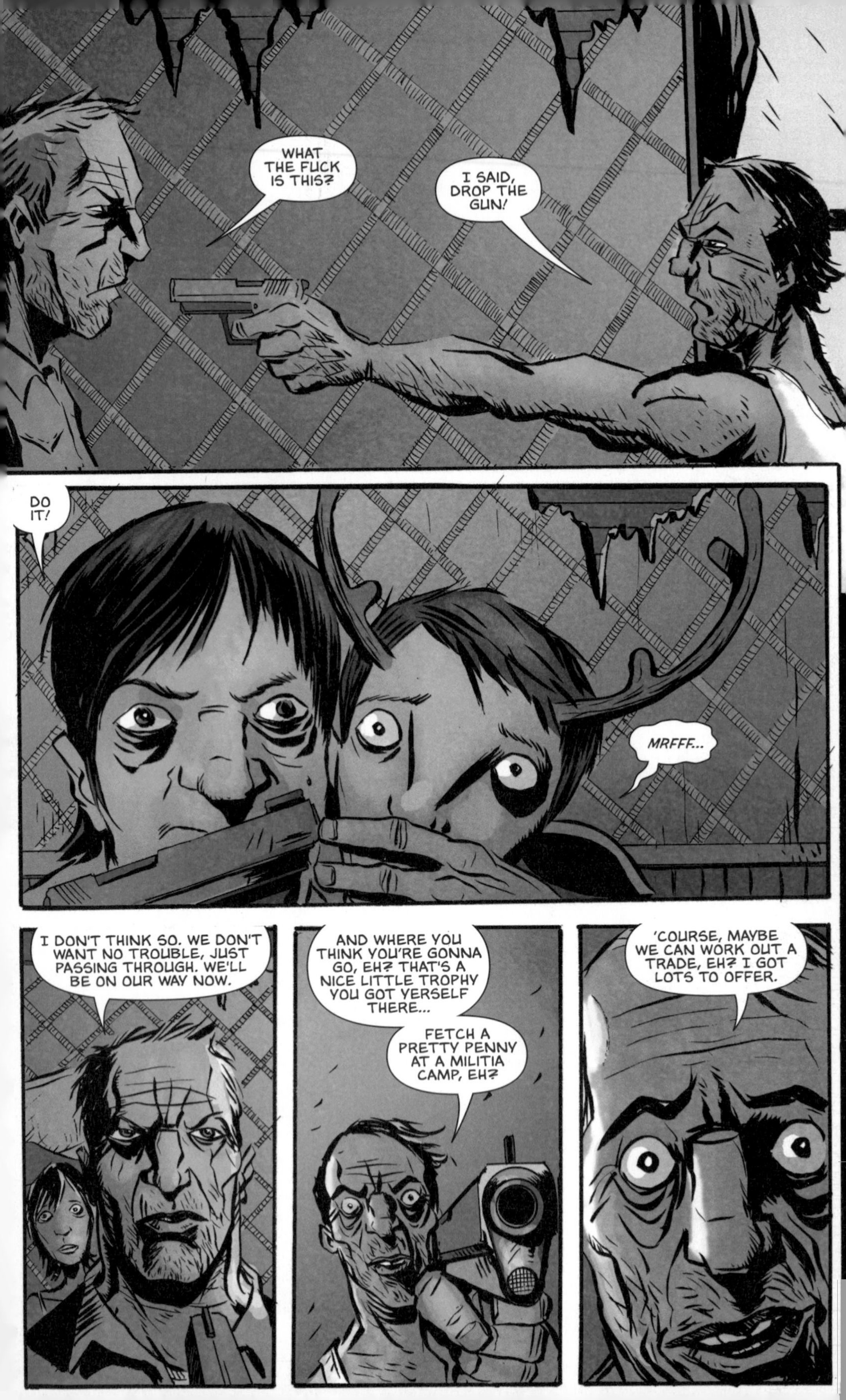
WHAT THE FUCK IS THIS?
I SAID, DROP THE GUN!
DO IT!
MRFFF...
I DON'T THINK SO. WE DON'T WANT NO TROUBLE, JUST PASSING THROUGH. WE'LL BE ON OUR WAY NOW.
AND WHERE YOU THINK YOU'RE GONNA GO, EH? THAT'S A NICE LITTLE TROPHY YOU GOT YERSELF THERE...
FETCH A PRETTY PENNY AT A MILITIA CAMP, EH?
'COURSE, MAYBE WE CAN WORK OUT A TRADE, EH? I GOT LOTS TO OFFER.

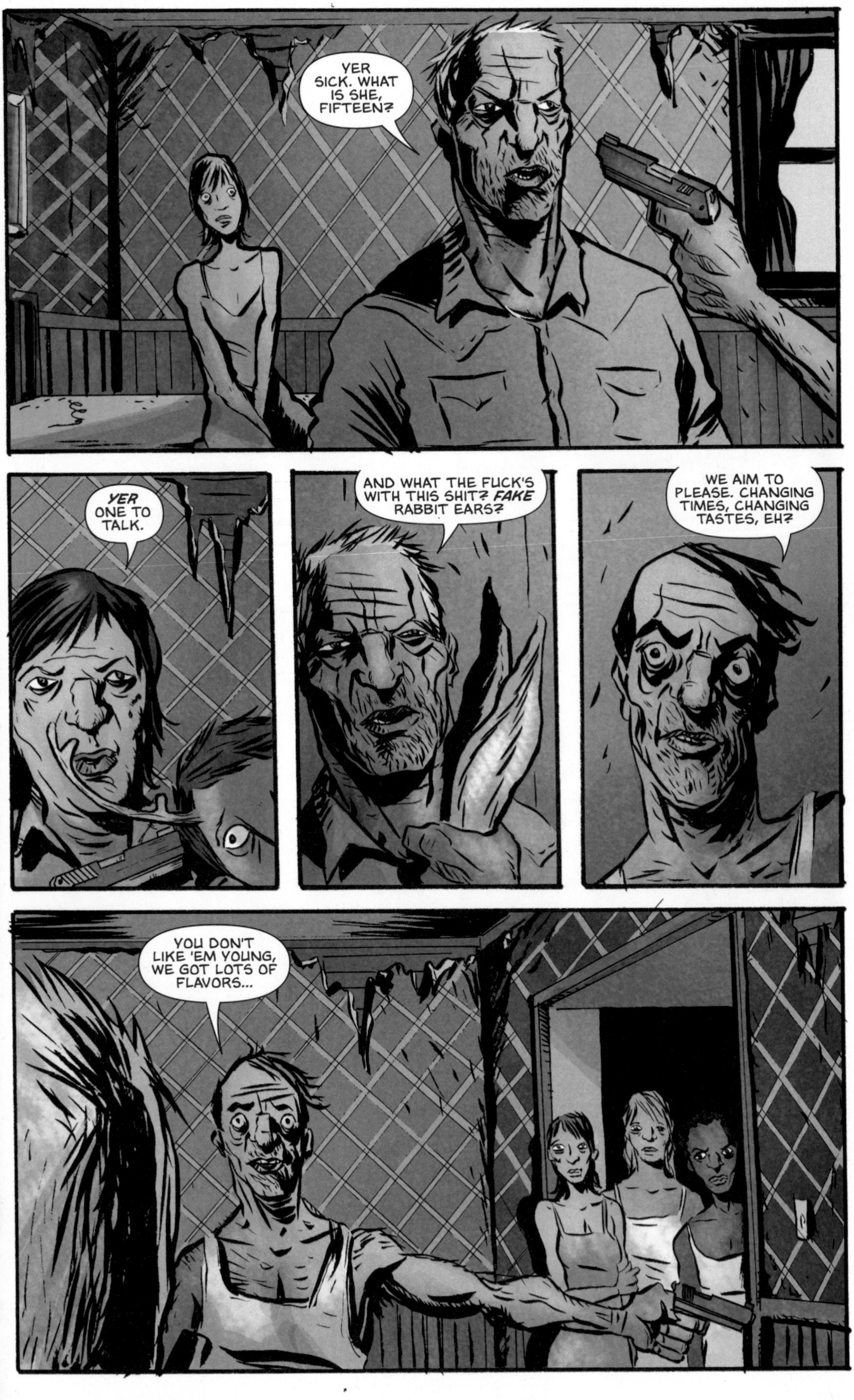
YER SICK. WHAT IS SHE, FIFTEEN?
YER ONE TO TALK.
AND WHAT THE FUCK'S WITH THIS SHIT? *FAKE* RABBIT EARS?
WE AIM TO PLEASE. CHANGING TIMES, CHANGING TASTES, EH?
YOU DON'T LIKE 'EM YOUNG, WE GOT LOTS OF FLAVORS...

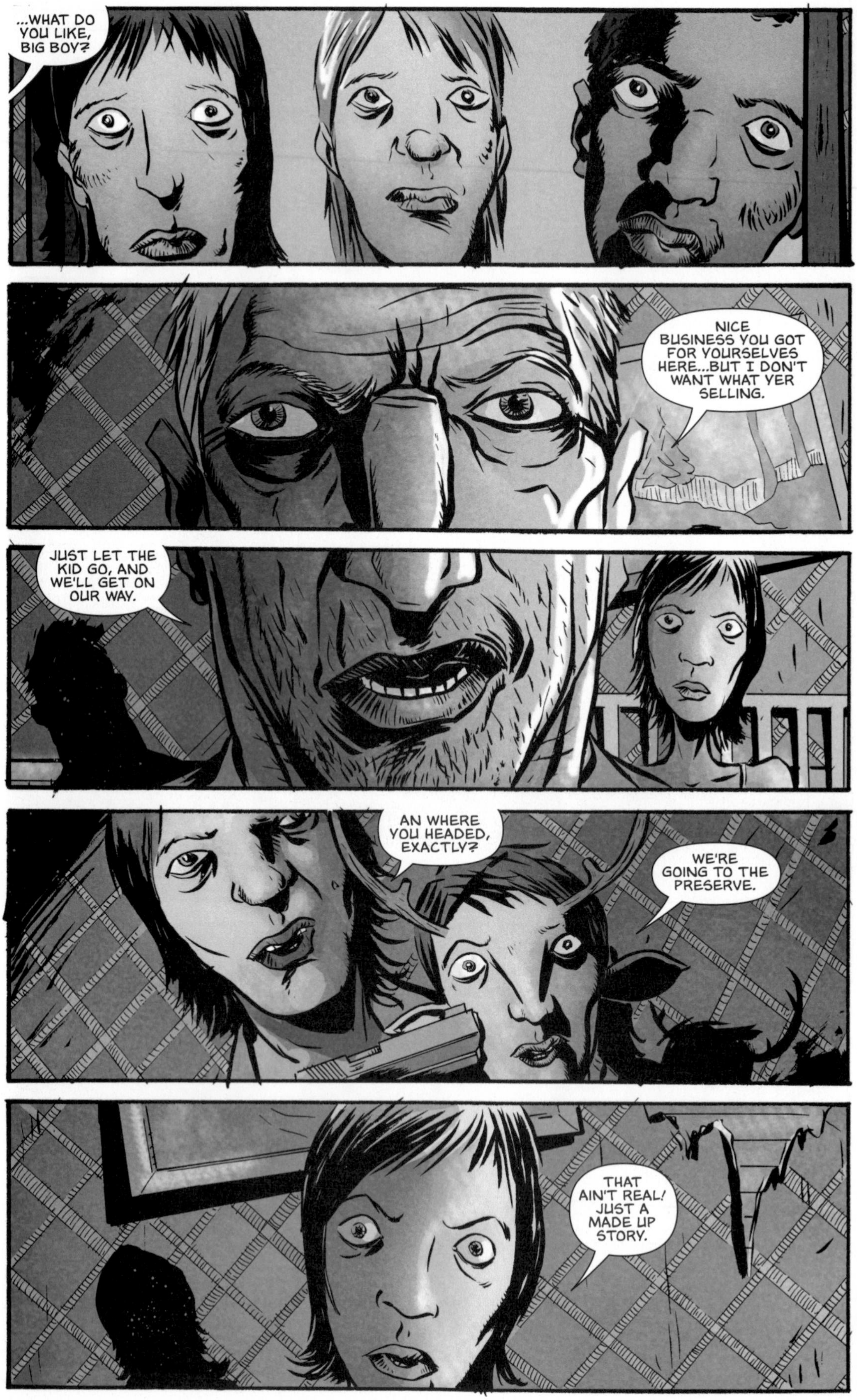
...WHAT DO YOU LIKE, BIG BOY?
NICE BUSINESS YOU GOT FOR YOURSELVES HERE...BUT I DON'T WANT WHAT YER SELLING.
JUST LET THE KID GO, AND WE'LL GET ON OUR WAY.
AN WHERE YOU HEADED, EXACTLY?
WE'RE GOING TO THE PRESERVE.
THAT AIN'T REAL! JUST A MADE UP STORY.

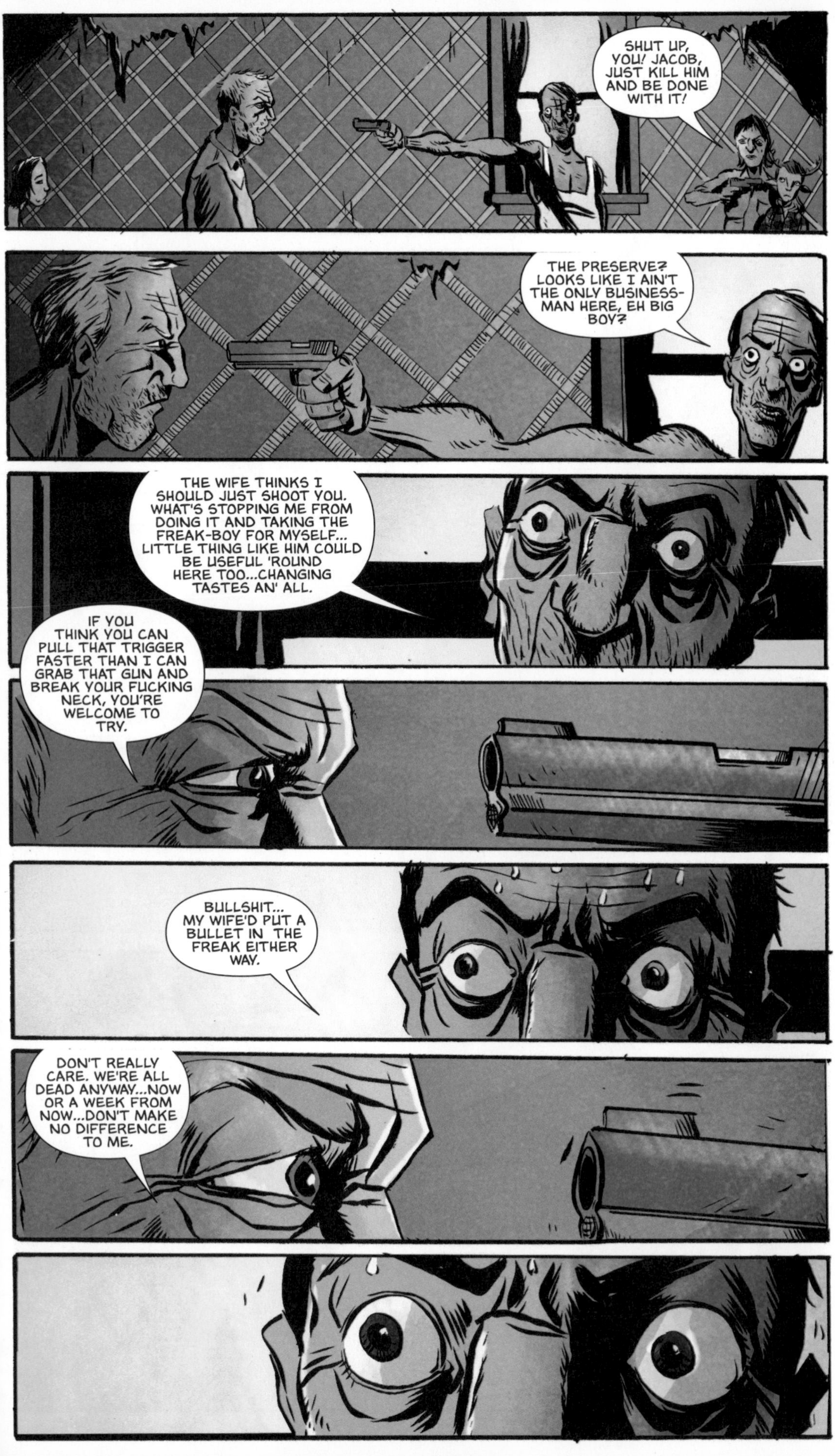
SHUT UP, YOU! JACOB, JUST KILL HIM AND BE DONE WITH IT!
THE PRESERVE? LOOKS LIKE I AIN'T THE ONLY BUSINESS-MAN HERE, EH BIG BOY?
THE WIFE THINKS I SHOULD JUST SHOOT YOU. WHAT'S STOPPING ME FROM DOING IT AND TAKING THE FREAK-BOY FOR MYSELF... LITTLE THING LIKE HIM COULD BE USEFUL 'ROUND HERE TOO...CHANGING TASTES AN' ALL.
IF YOU THINK YOU CAN PULL THAT TRIGGER FASTER THAN I CAN GRAB THAT GUN AND BREAK YOUR FUCKING NECK, YOU'RE WELCOME TO TRY.
BULLSHIT... MY WIFE'D PUT A BULLET IN THE FREAK EITHER WAY.
DON'T REALLY CARE. WE'RE ALL DEAD ANYWAY...NOW OR A WEEK FROM NOW...DON'T MAKE NO DIFFERENCE TO ME.

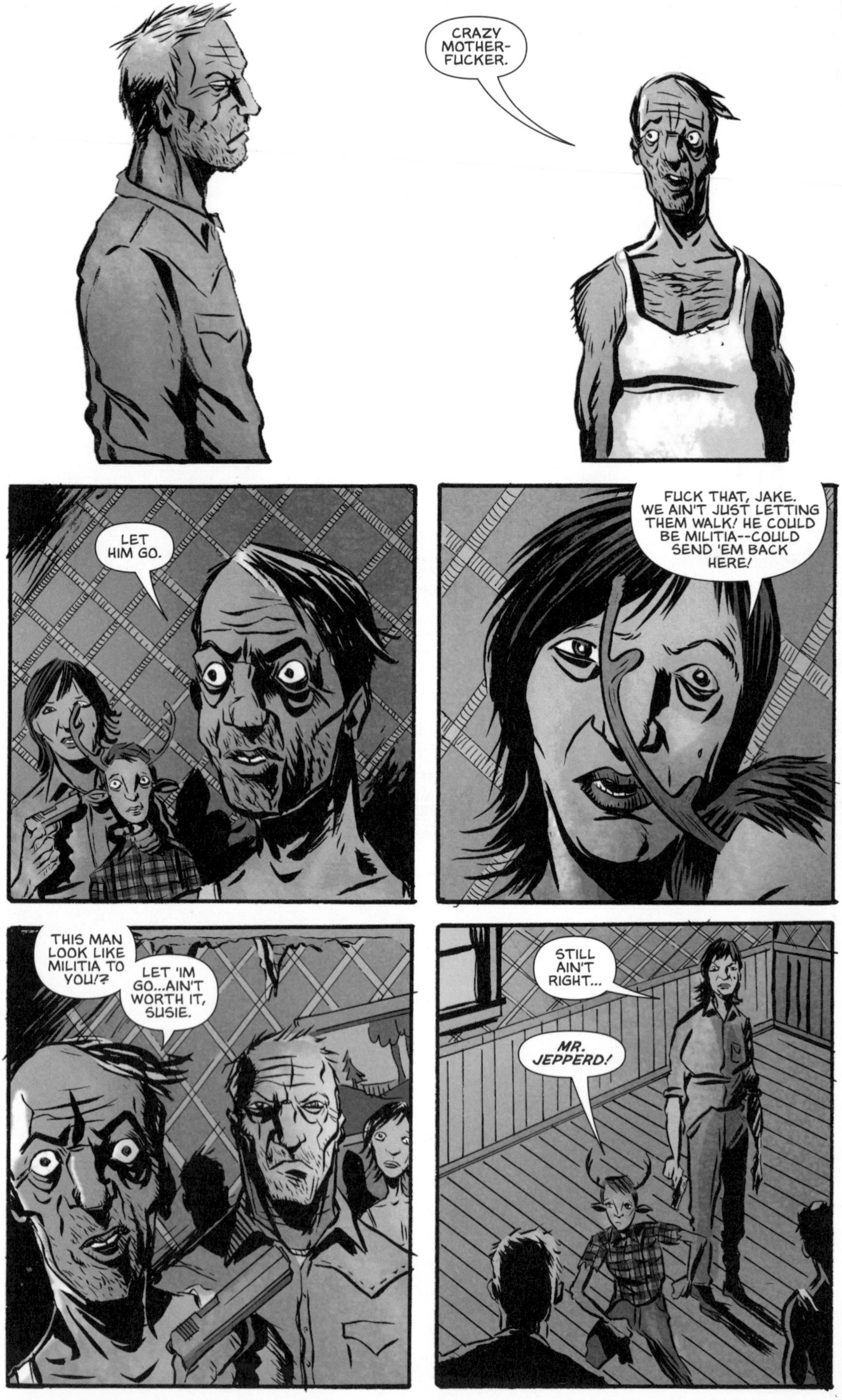
CRAZY MOTHER-FUCKER.
LET HIM GO.
FUCK THAT, JAKE. WE AIN'T JUST LETTING THEM WALK! HE COULD BE MILITIA--COULD SEND 'EM BACK HERE!
THIS MAN LOOK LIKE MILITIA TO YOU!?
LET 'IM GO...AIN'T WORTH IT, SUSIE.
STILL AIN'T RIGHT...
MR. JEPPERD!

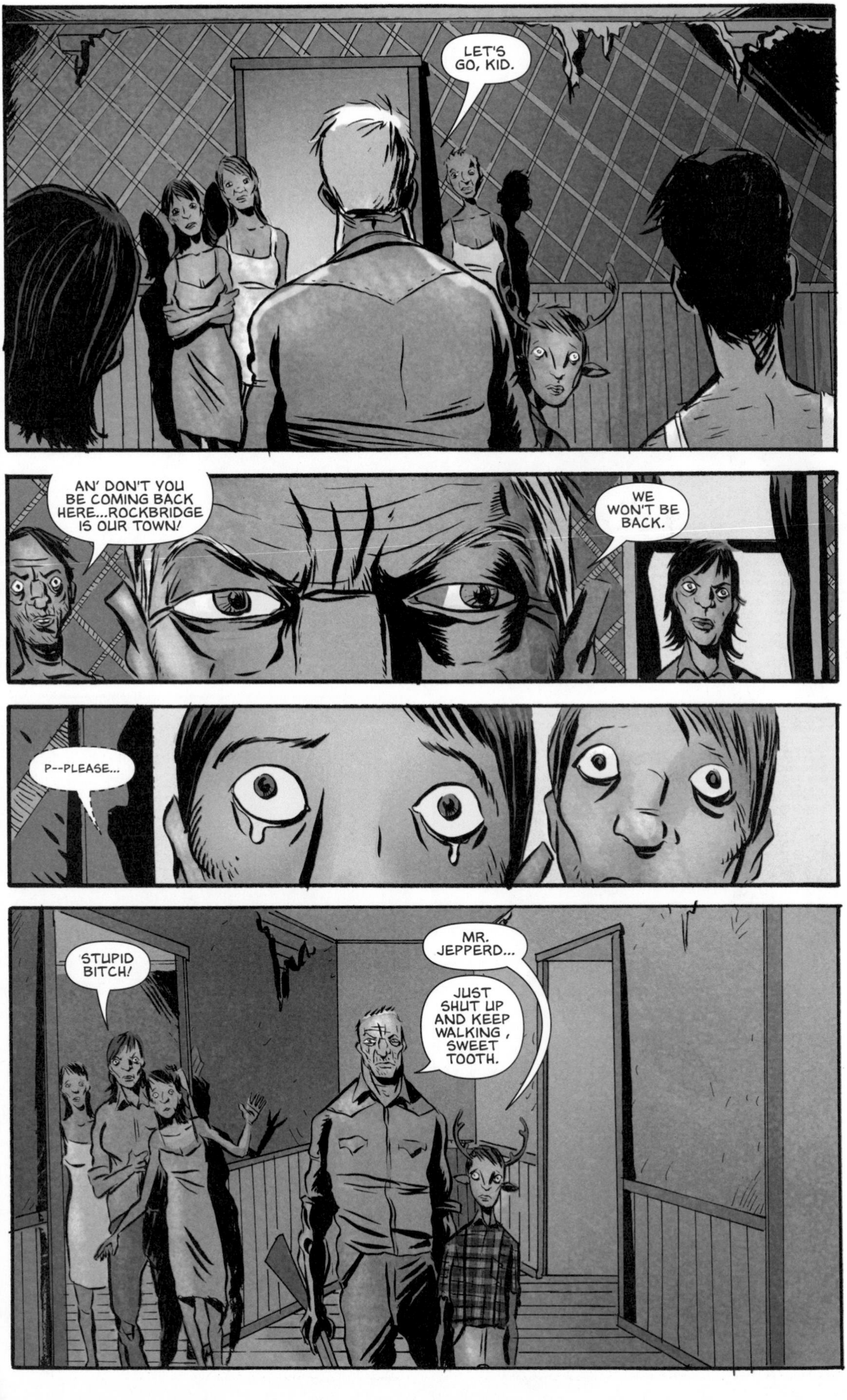

LET'S GO, KID.
AN' DON'T YOU BE COMING BACK HERE...ROCKBRIDGE IS OUR TOWN!
WE WON'T BE BACK.
P--PLEASE...
STUPID BITCH!
MR. JEPPERD...
JUST SHUT UP AND KEEP WALKING, SWEET TOOTH.

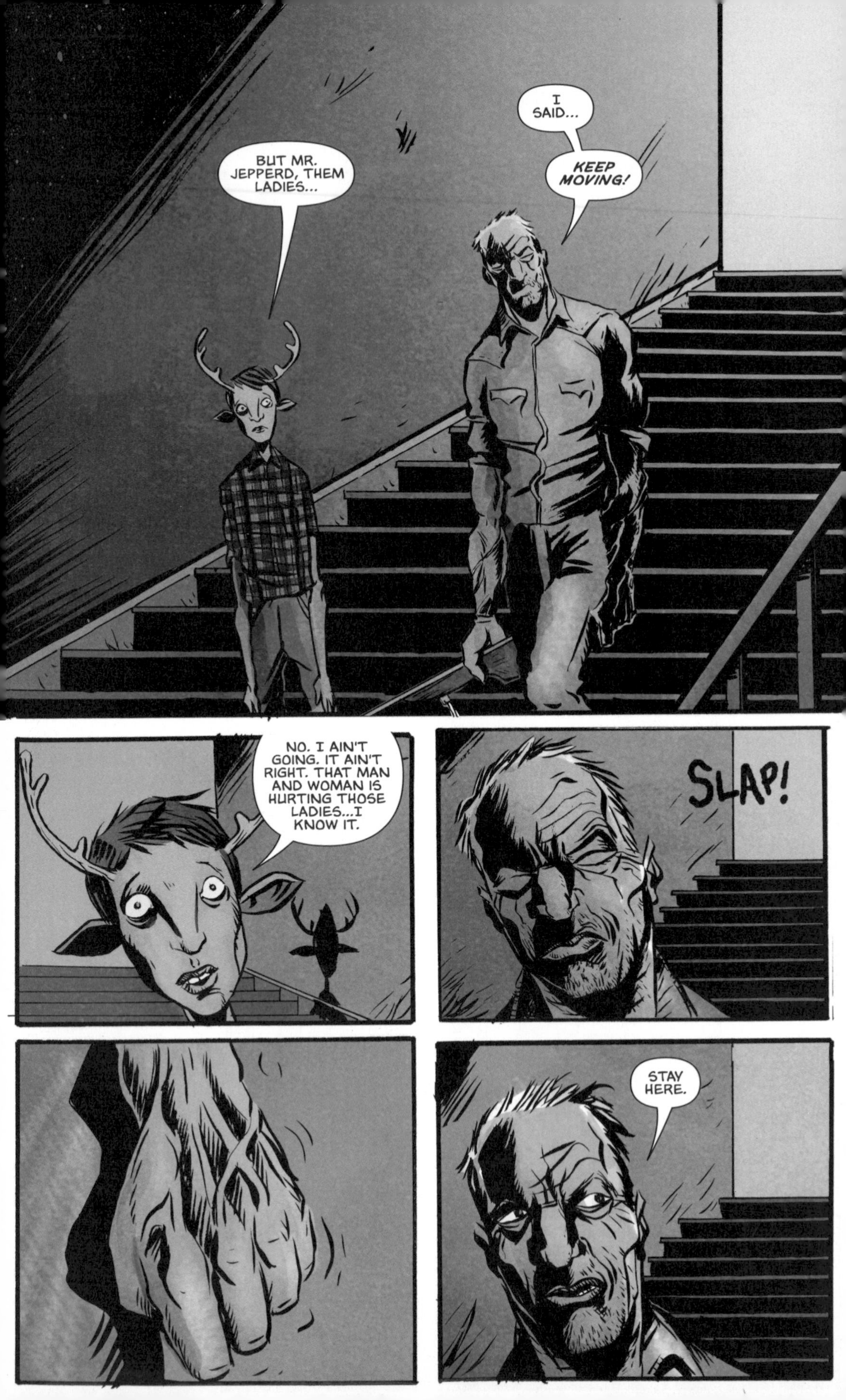
BUT MR. JEPPERD, THEM LADIES...
I SAID...
KEEP MOVING!
NO. I AIN'T GOING. IT AIN'T RIGHT. THAT MAN AND WOMAN IS HURTING THOSE LADIES...I KNOW IT.
SLAP!
STAY HERE.

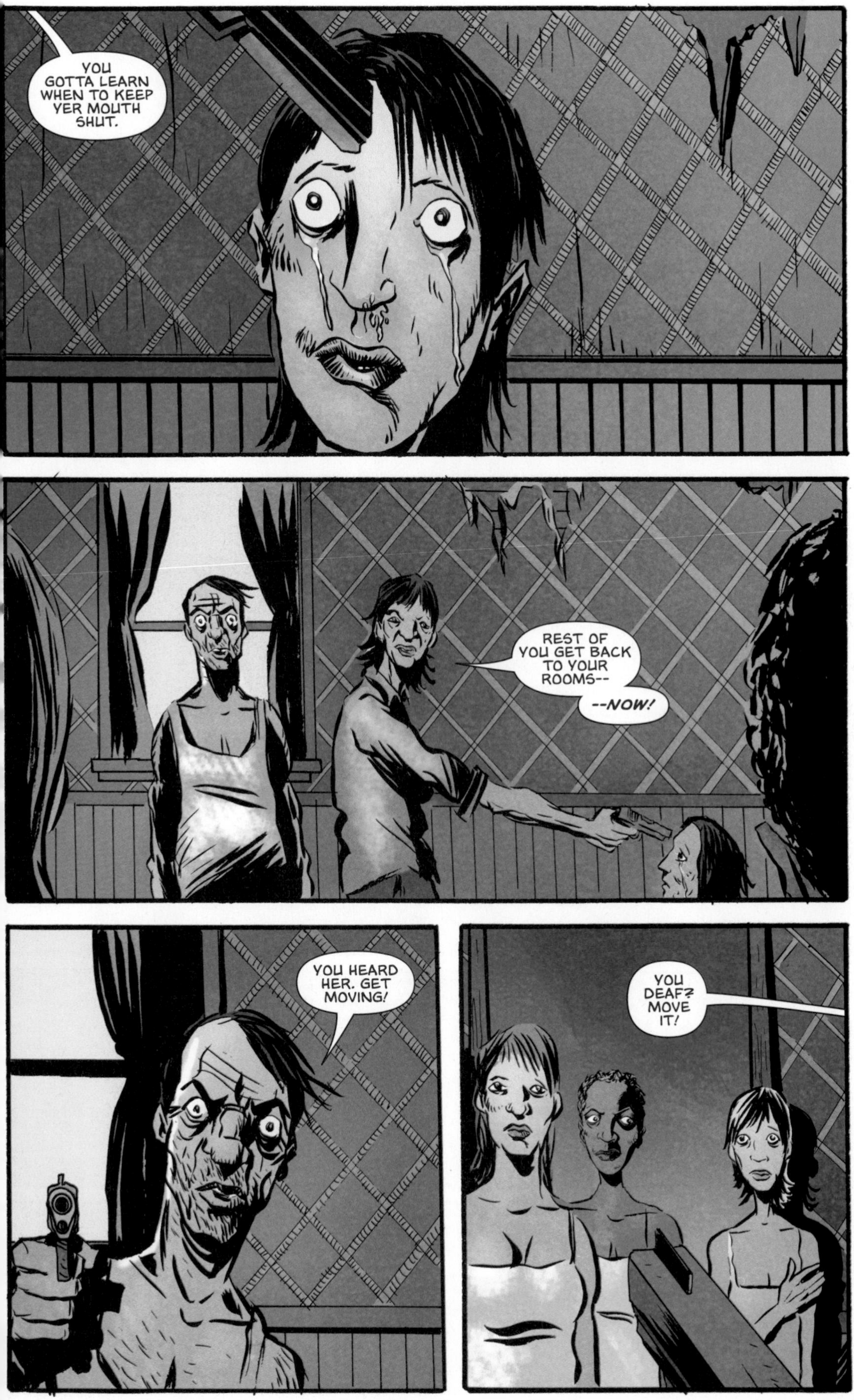
YOU GOTTA LEARN WHEN TO KEEP YER MOUTH SHUT.
REST OF YOU GET BACK TO YOUR ROOMS--
--NOW!
YOU HEARD HER. GET MOVING!
YOU DEAF? MOVE IT!

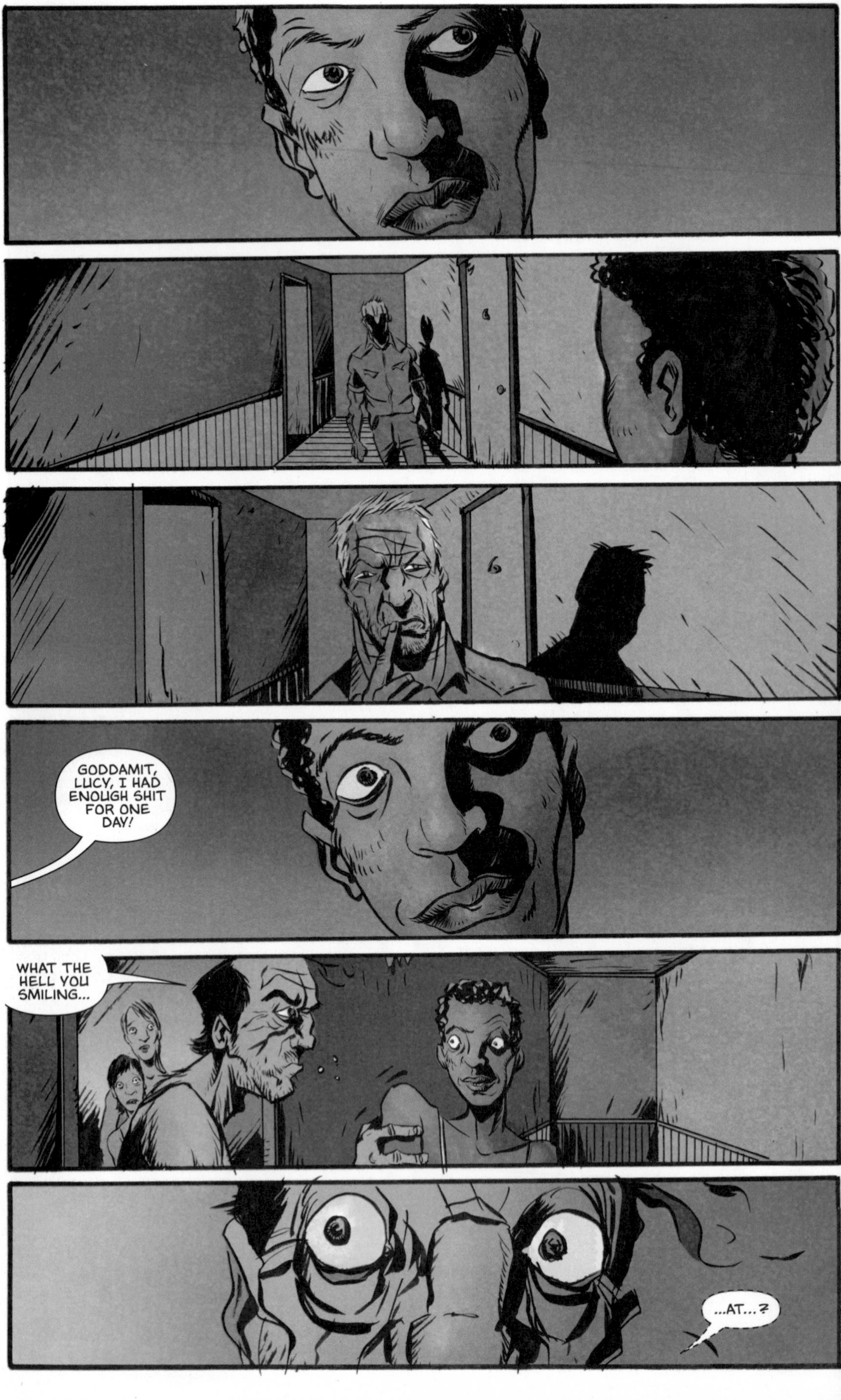
GODDAMIT, LUCY, I HAD ENOUGH SHIT FOR ONE DAY!
WHAT THE HELL YOU SMILING...
...AT...?

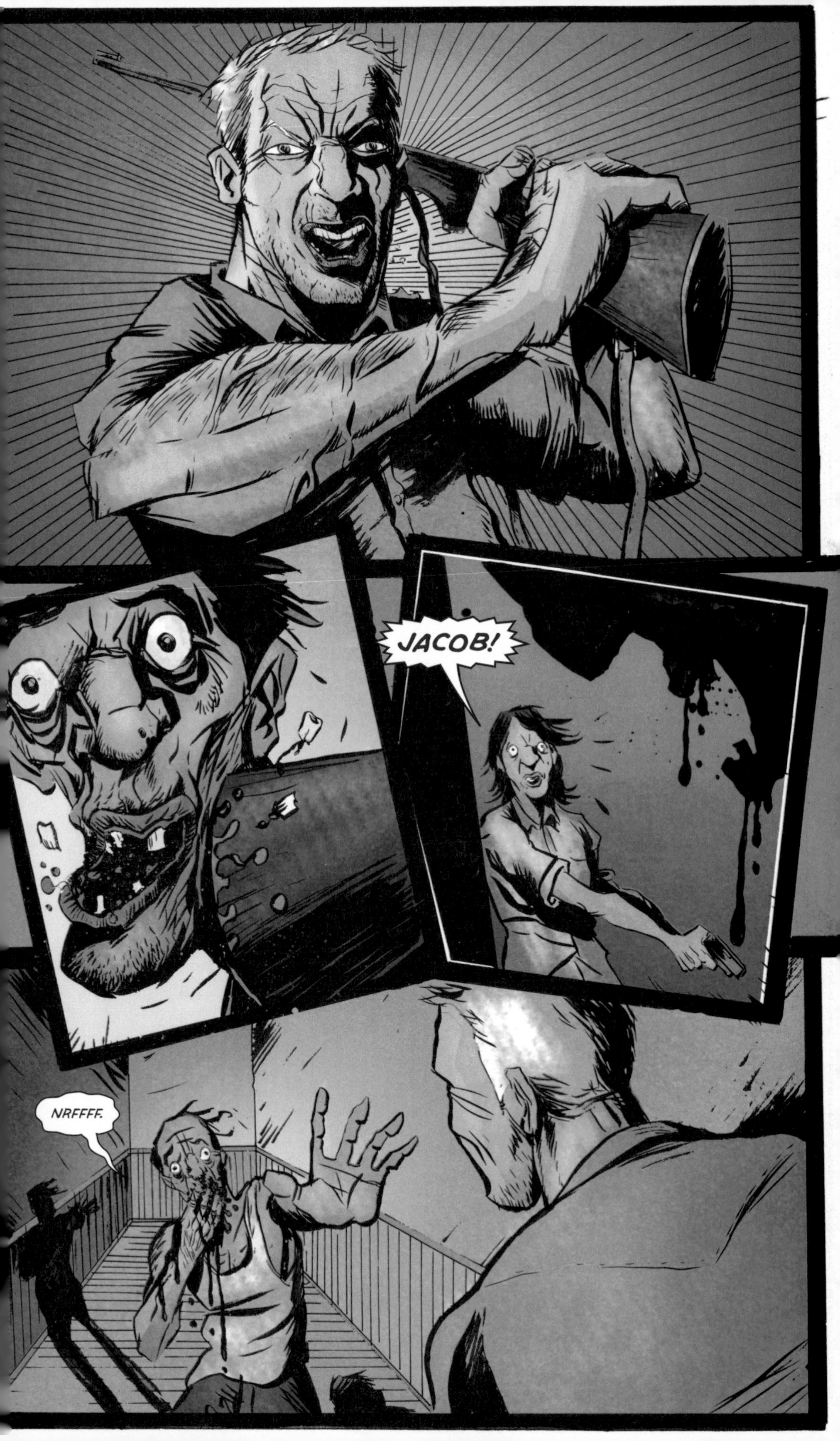
JACOB!
NRFFFF.

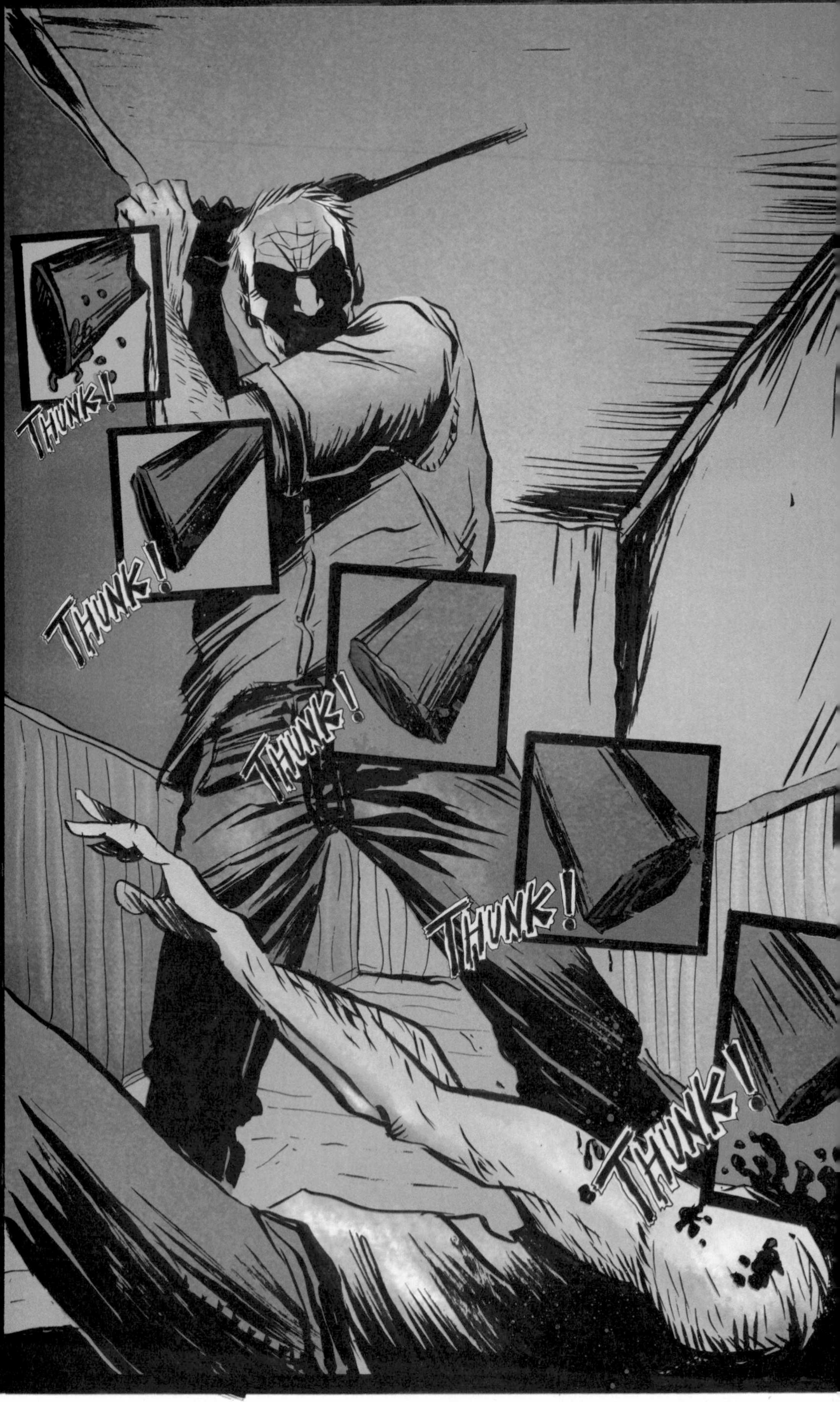
THUNK!
THUNK!
THUNK!
THUNK!
THUNK!

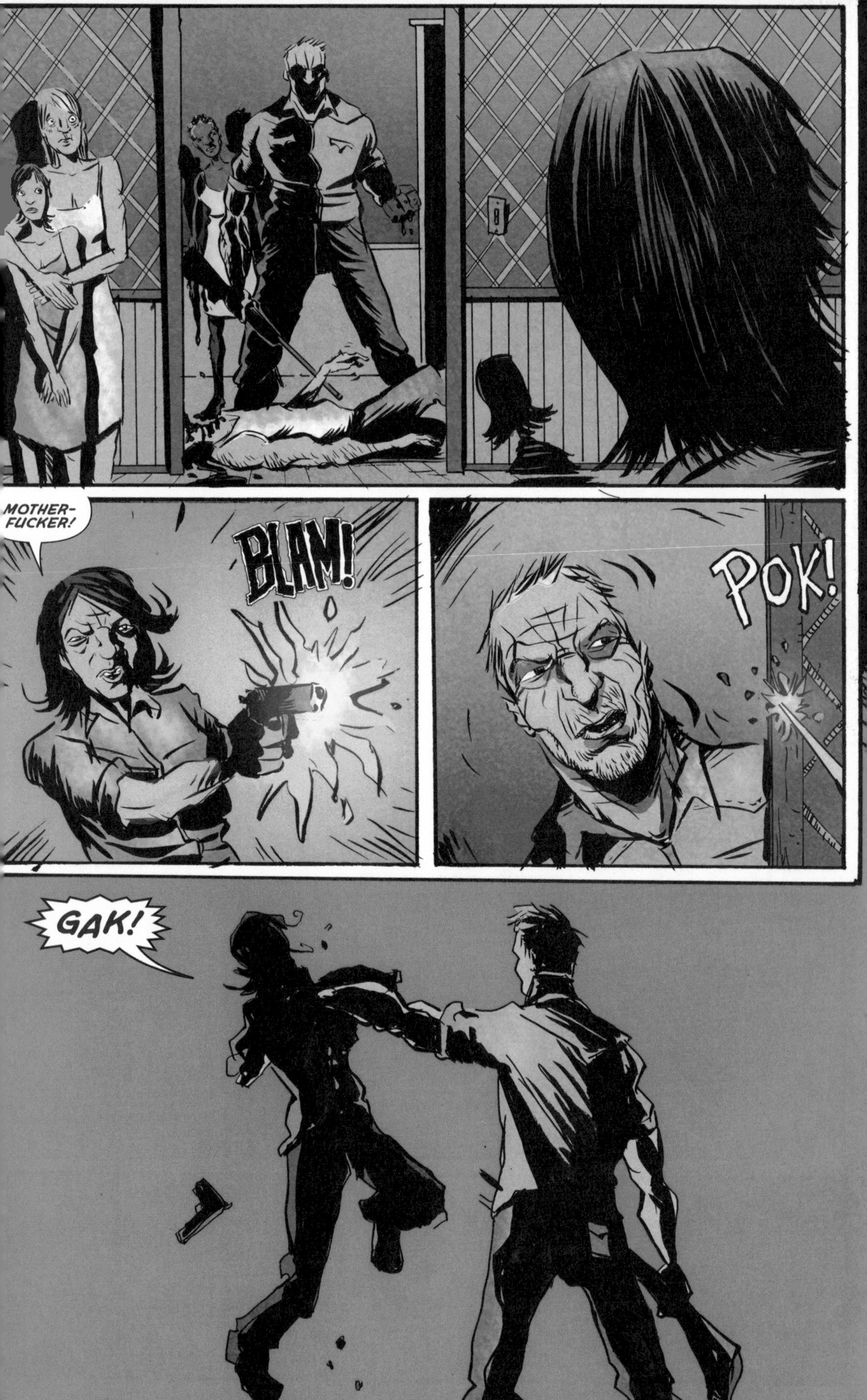
MOTHER-FUCKER!
BLAM!
POK!
GAK!

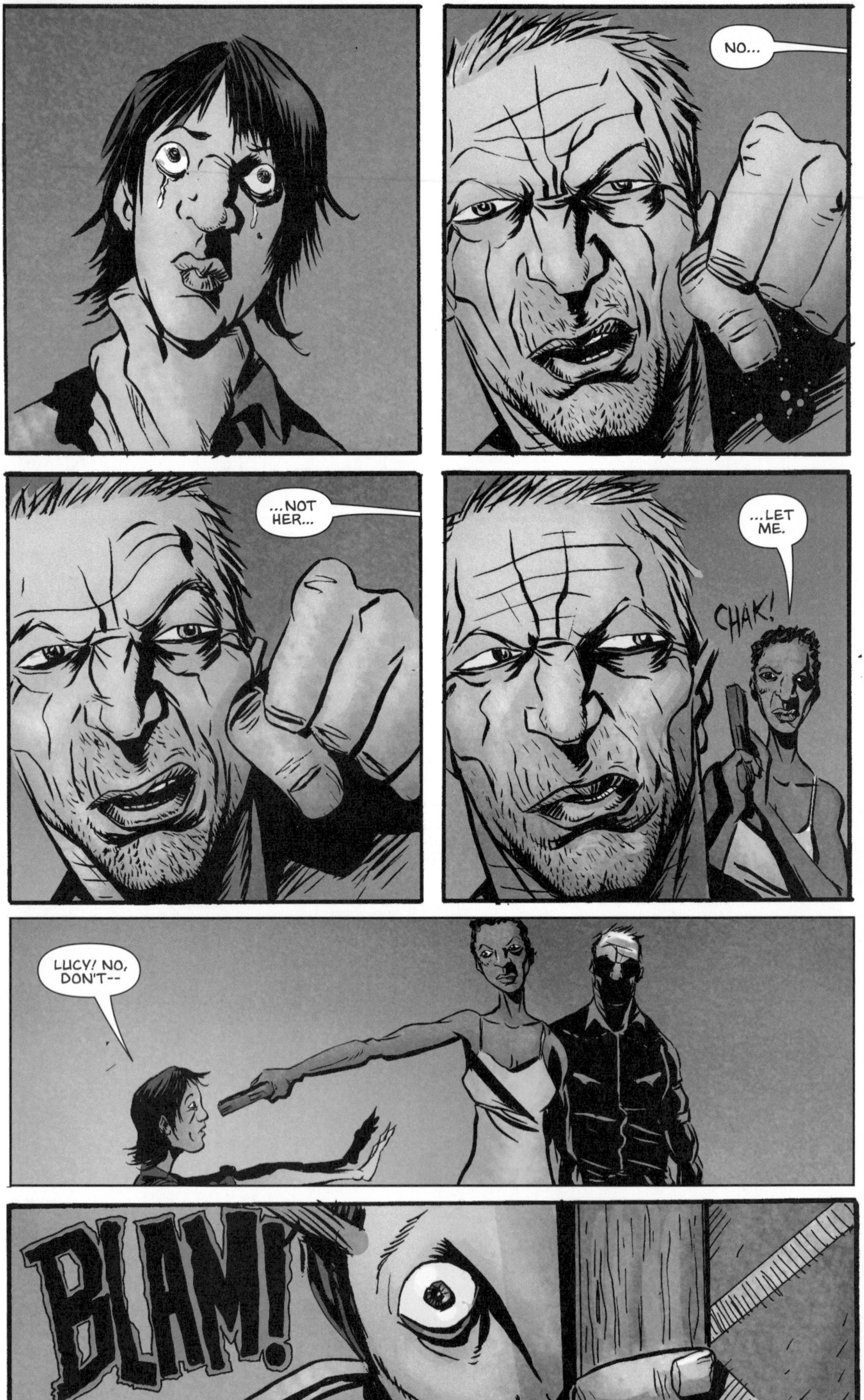
NO...
...NOT HER...
...LET ME.
CHAK!
LUCY! NO, DON'T--
BLAM!

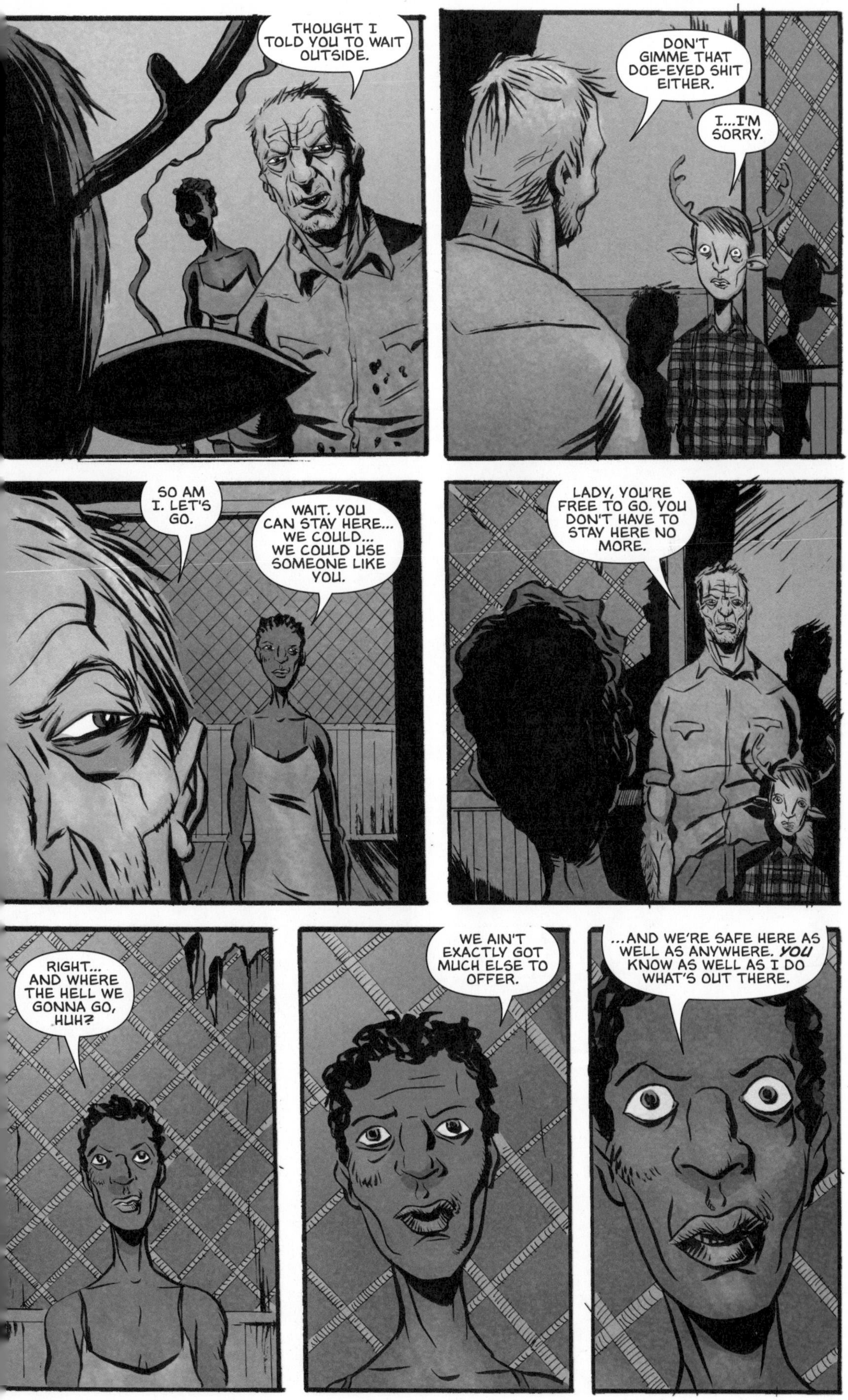
THOUGHT I TOLD YOU TO WAIT OUTSIDE.
DON'T GIMME THAT DOE-EYED SHIT EITHER.
I...I'M SORRY.
SO AM I. LET'S GO.
WAIT. YOU CAN STAY HERE... WE COULD... WE COULD USE SOMEONE LIKE YOU.
LADY, YOU'RE FREE TO GO. YOU DON'T HAVE TO STAY HERE NO MORE.
RIGHT... AND WHERE THE HELL WE GONNA GO, HUH?
WE AIN'T EXACTLY GOT MUCH ELSE TO OFFER.
...AND WE'RE SAFE HERE AS WELL AS ANYWHERE. *YOU* KNOW AS WELL AS I DO WHAT'S OUT THERE.

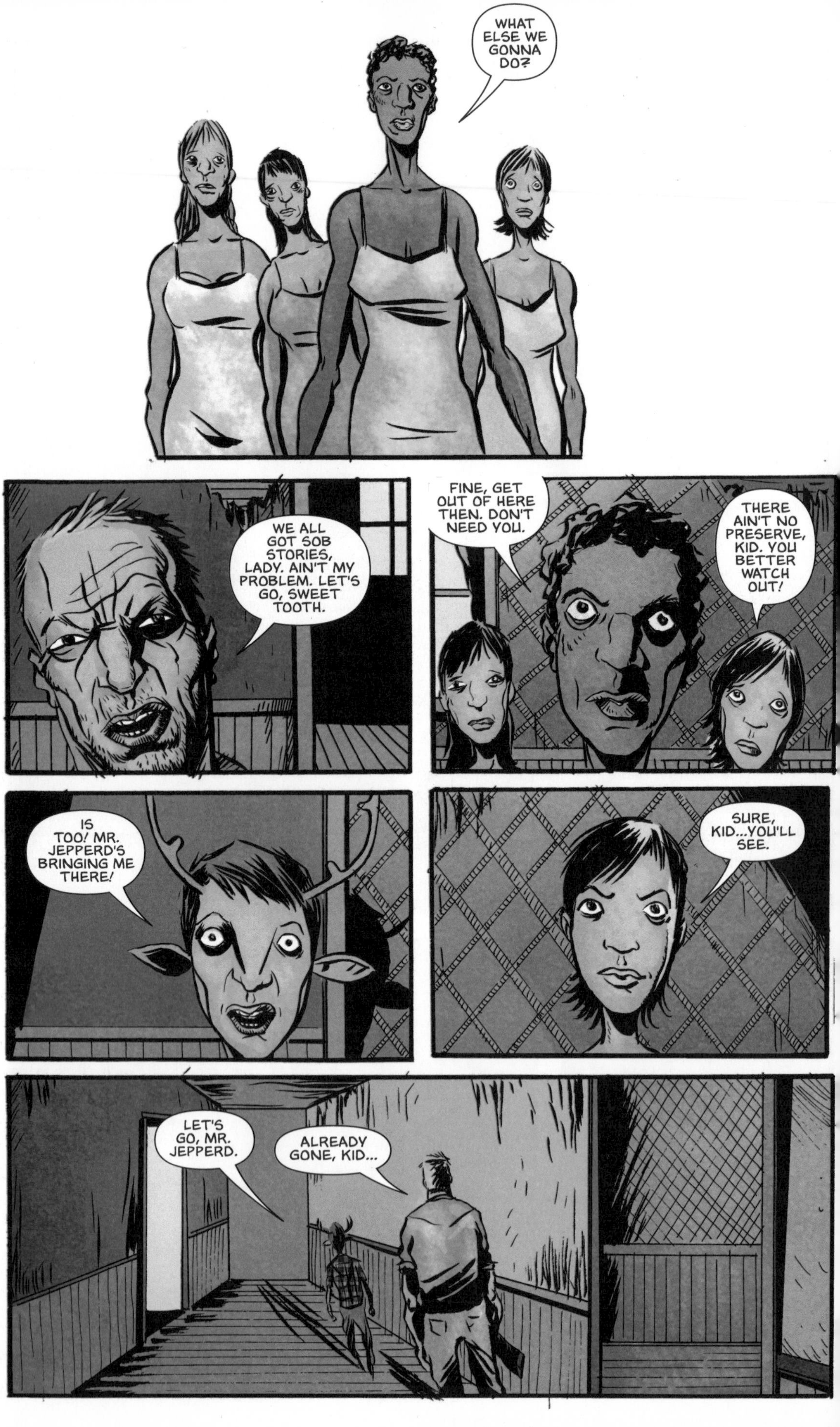
WHAT ELSE WE GONNA DO?
WE ALL GOT SOB STORIES, LADY. AIN'T MY PROBLEM. LET'S GO, SWEET TOOTH.
FINE, GET OUT OF HERE THEN. DON'T NEED YOU.
THERE AIN'T NO PRESERVE, KID. YOU BETTER WATCH OUT!
IS TOO! MR. JEPPERD'S BRINGING ME THERE!
SURE, KID...YOU'LL SEE.
LET'S GO, MR. JEPPERD.
ALREADY GONE, KID...

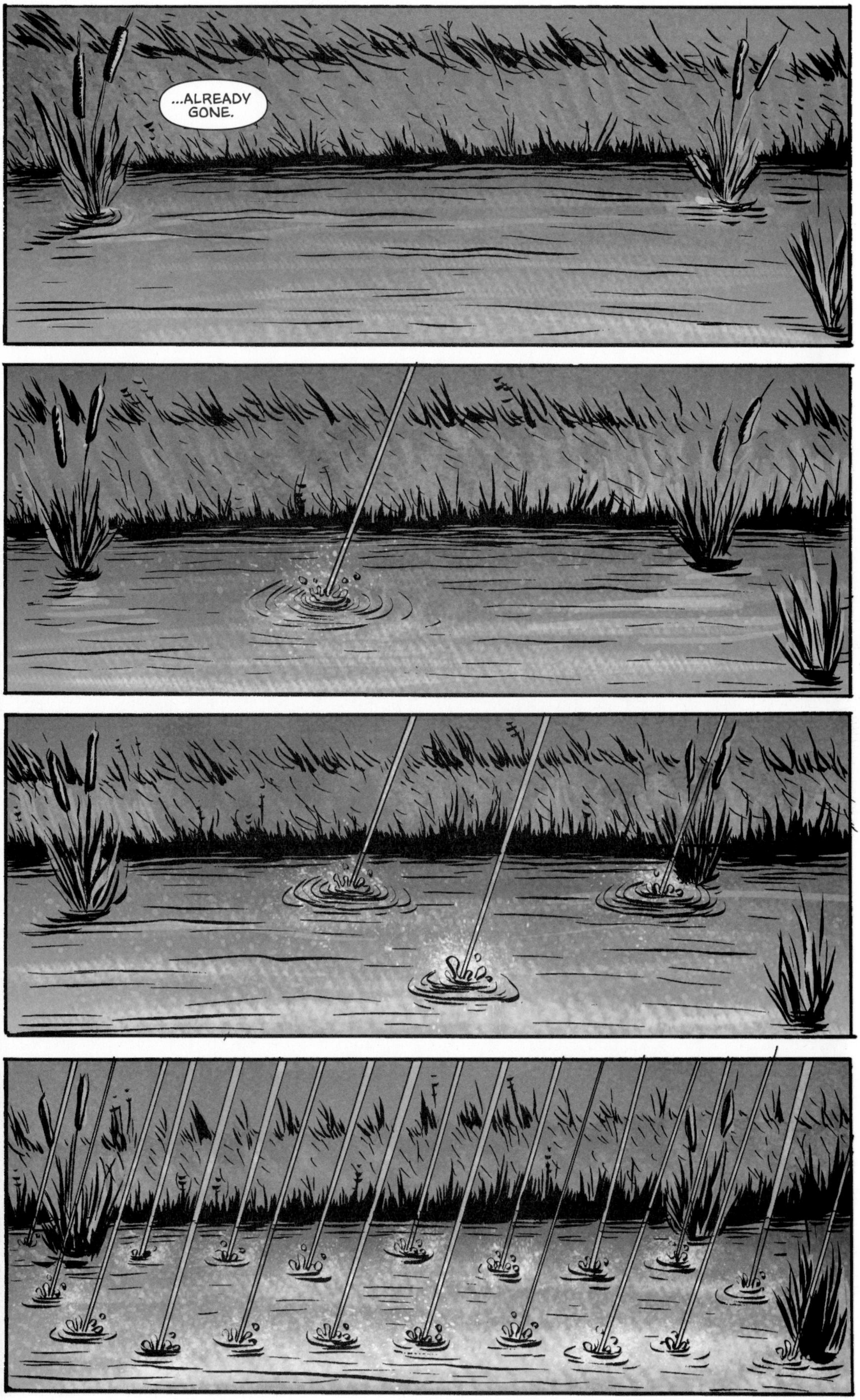
...ALREADY GONE.

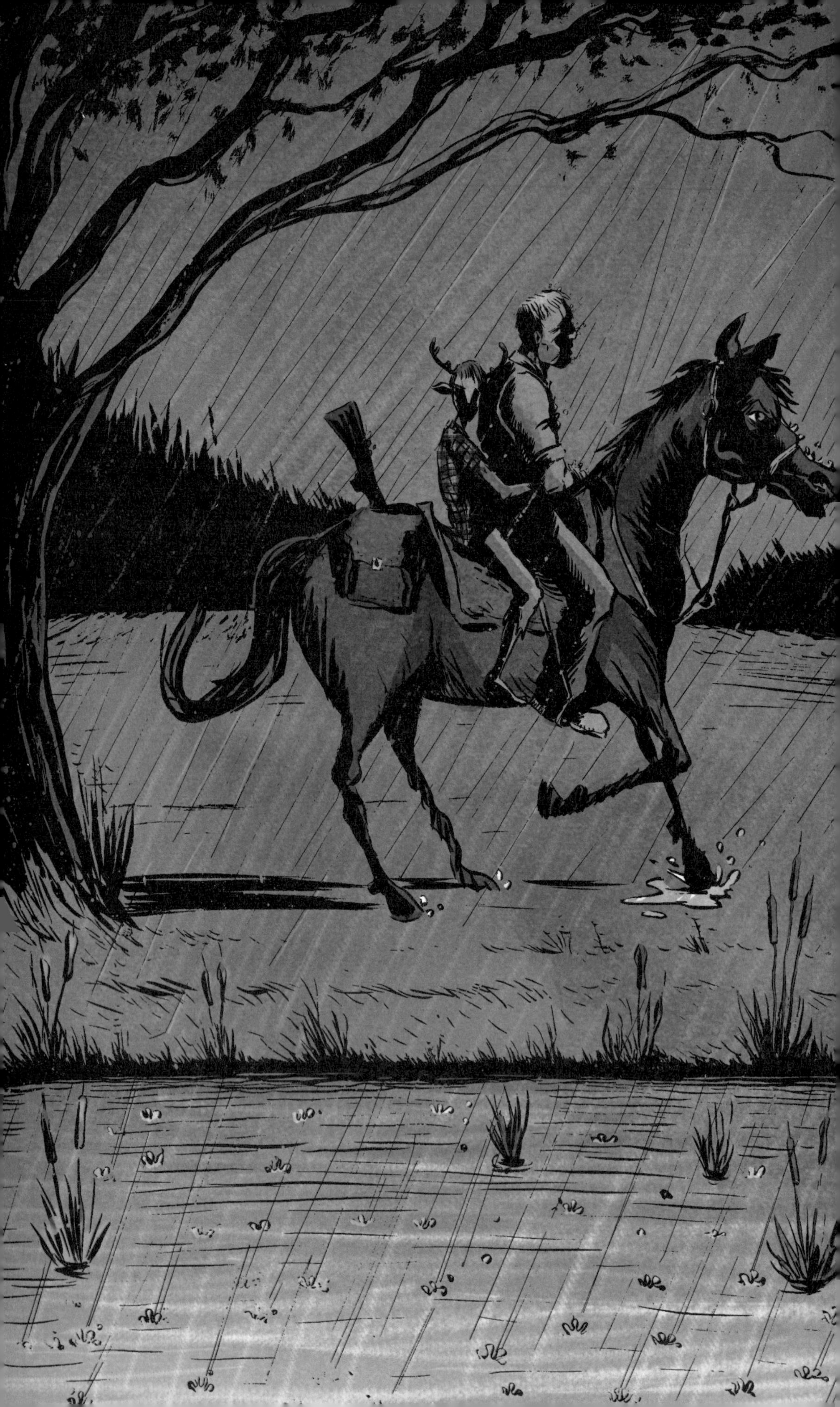

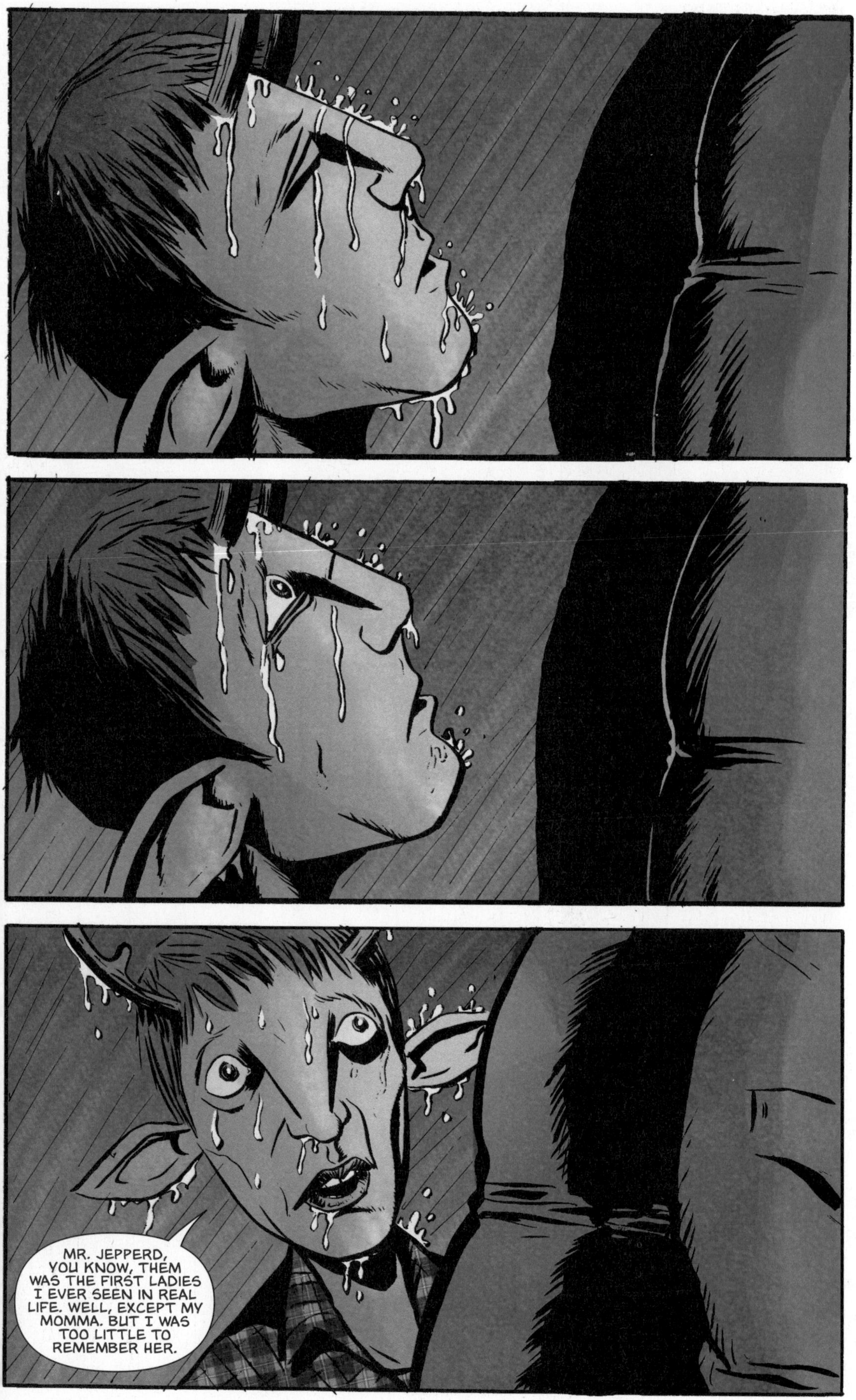
MR. JEPPERD, YOU KNOW, THEM WAS THE FIRST LADIES I EVER SEEN IN REAL LIFE. WELL, EXCEPT MY MOMMA. BUT I WAS TOO LITTLE TO REMEMBER HER.

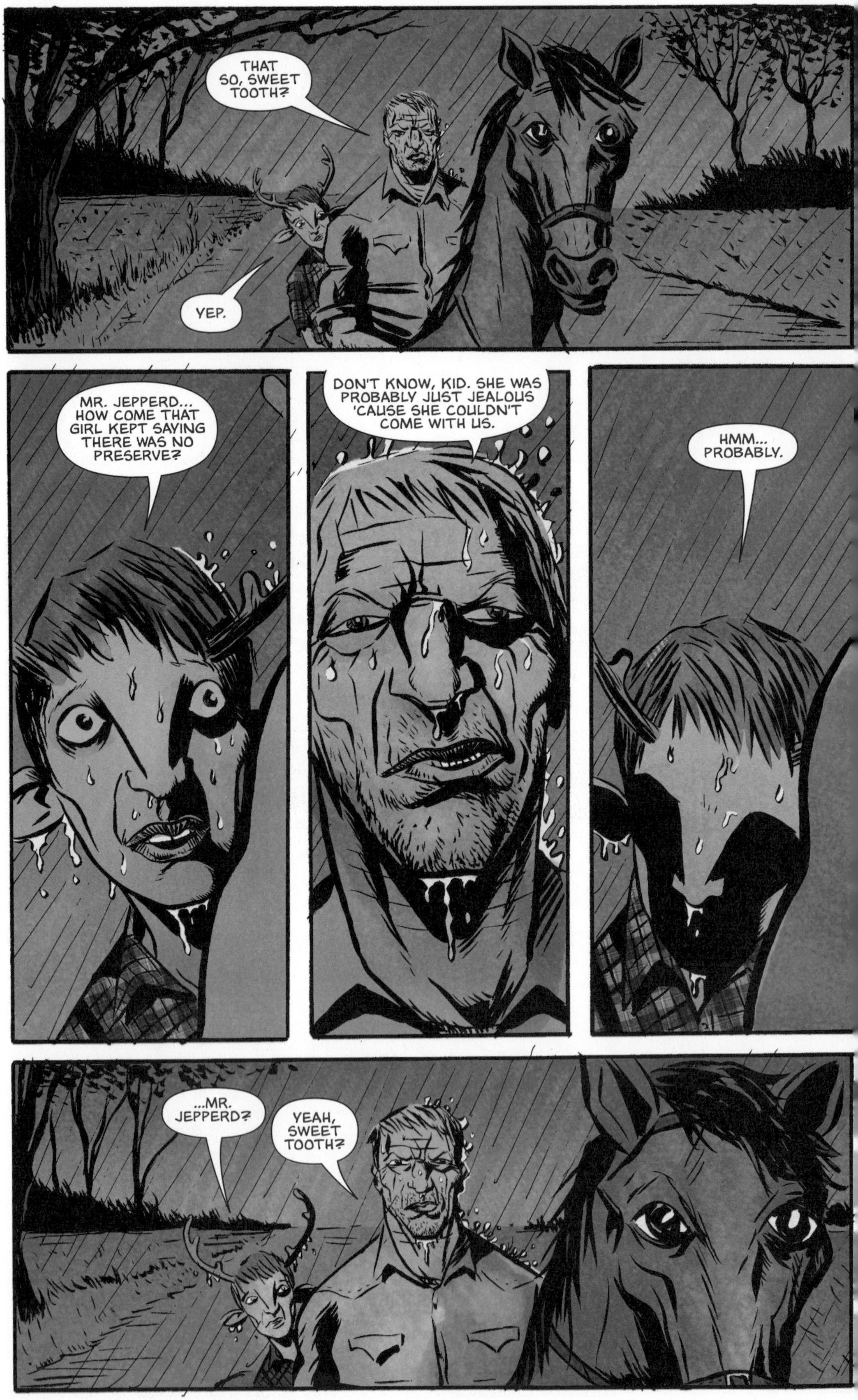
THAT SO, SWEET TOOTH?
YEP.
MR. JEPPERD... HOW COME THAT GIRL KEPT SAYING THERE WAS NO PRESERVE?
DON'T KNOW, KID. SHE WAS PROBABLY JUST JEALOUS 'CAUSE SHE COULDN'T COME WITH US.
HMM... PROBABLY.
...MR. JEPPERD?
YEAH, SWEET TOOTH?

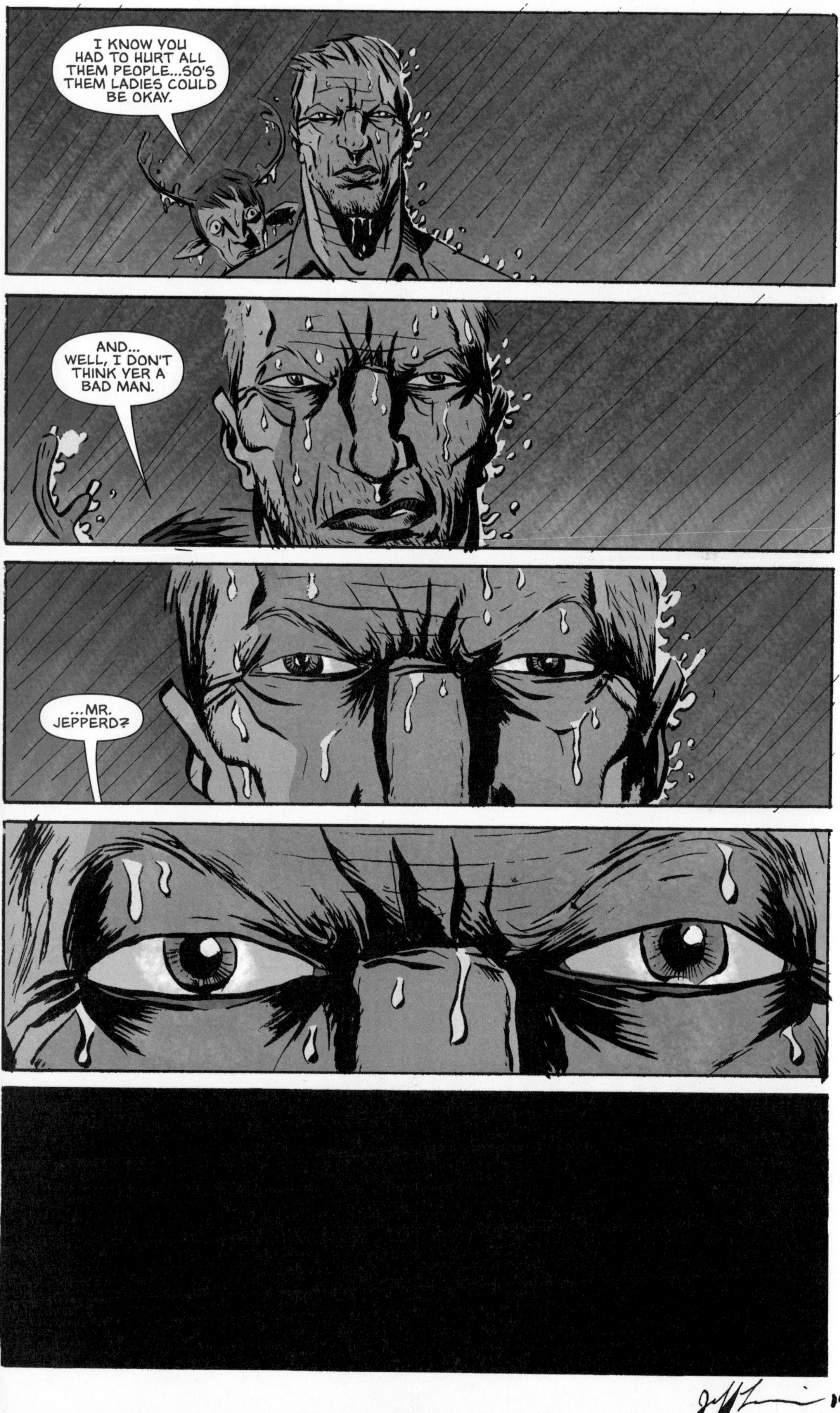
I KNOW YOU HAD TO HURT ALL THEM PEOPLE...SO'S THEM LADIES COULD BE OKAY.
AND... WELL, I DON'T THINK YER A BAD MAN.
...MR. JEPPERD?

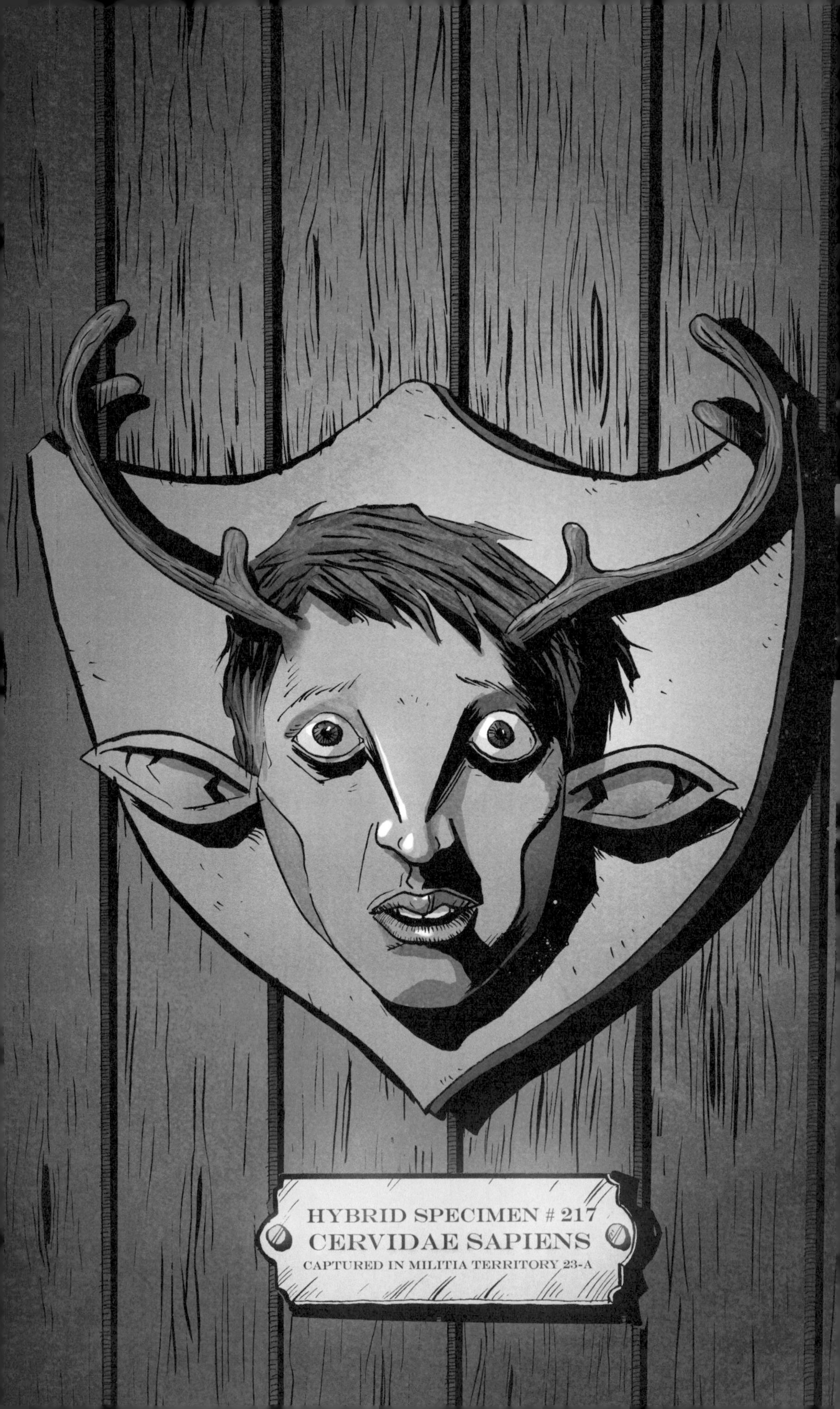
HYBRID SPECIMEN # 217
CERVIDAE SAPIENS
CAPTURED IN MILITIA TERRITORY 23-A

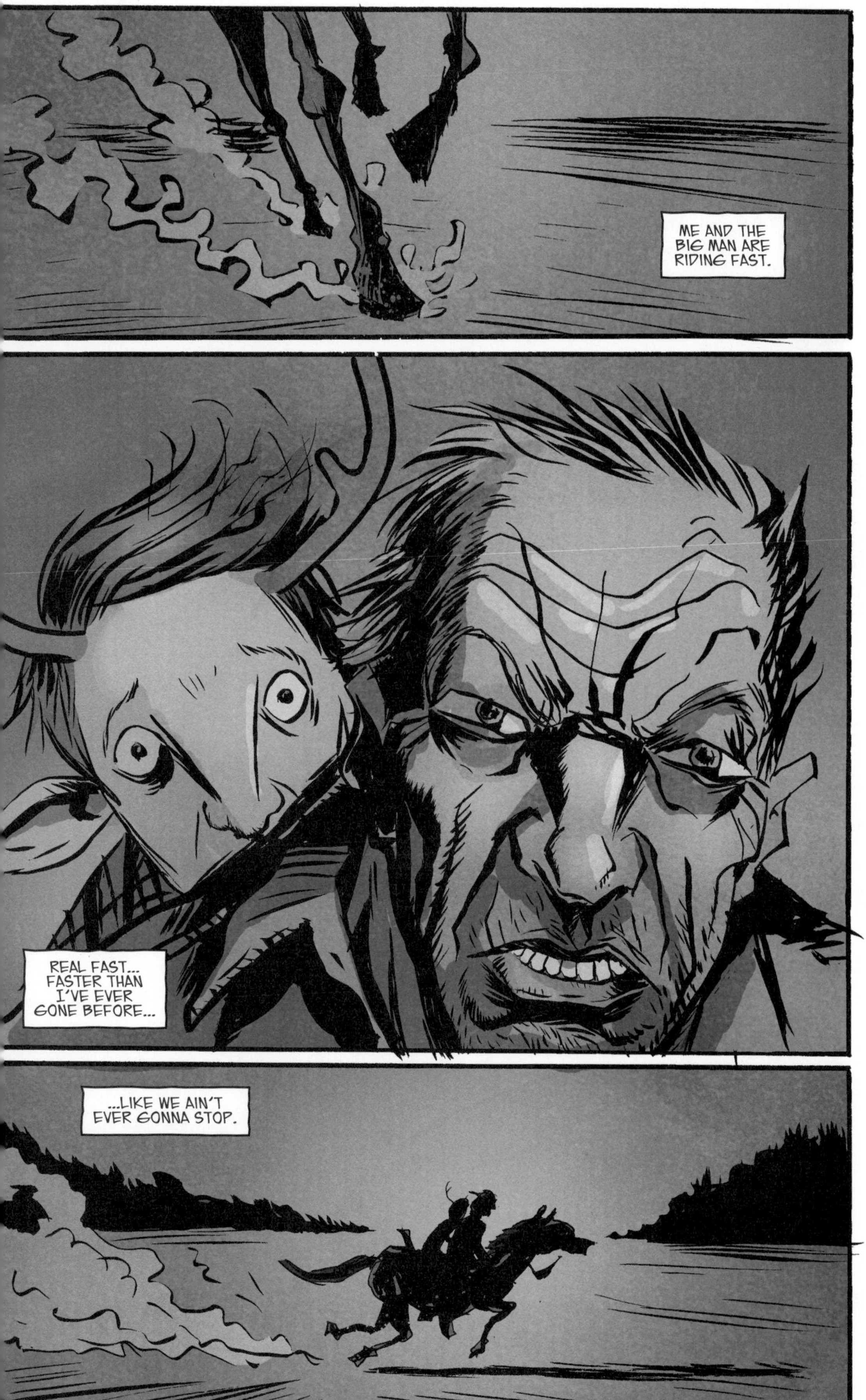
ME AND THE BIG MAN ARE RIDING FAST.
REAL FAST... FASTER THAN I'VE EVER GONE BEFORE...
...LIKE WE AIN'T EVER GONNA STOP.

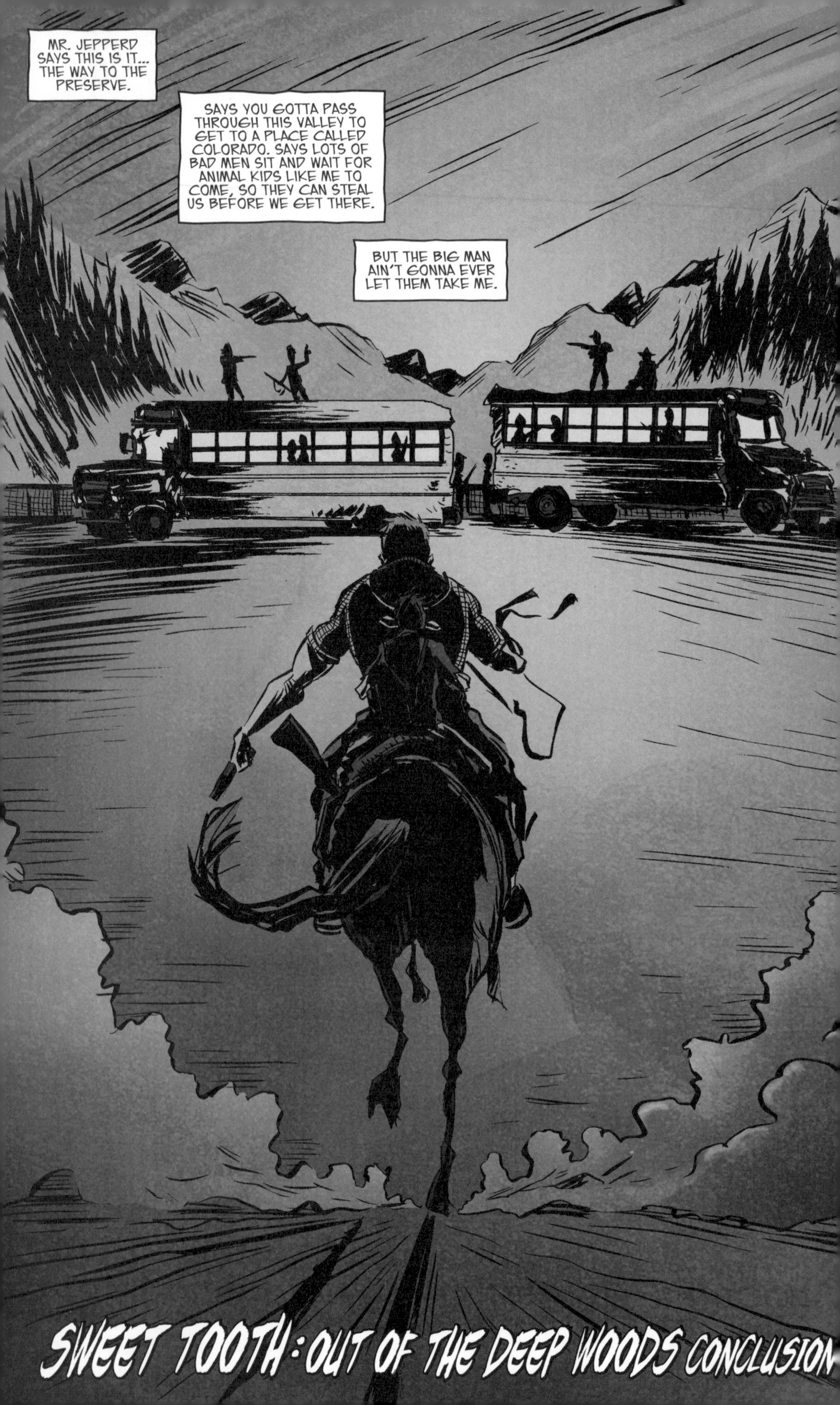
MR. JEPPERD SAYS THIS IS IT... THE WAY TO THE PRESERVE.
SAYS YOU GOTTA PASS THROUGH THIS VALLEY TO GET TO A PLACE CALLED COLORADO. SAYS LOTS OF BAD MEN SIT AND WAIT FOR ANIMAL KIDS LIKE ME TO COME, SO THEY CAN STEAL US BEFORE WE GET THERE.
BUT THE BIG MAN AIN'T GONNA EVER LET THEM TAKE ME.
SWEET TOOTH: OUT OF THE DEEP WOODS CONCLUSION

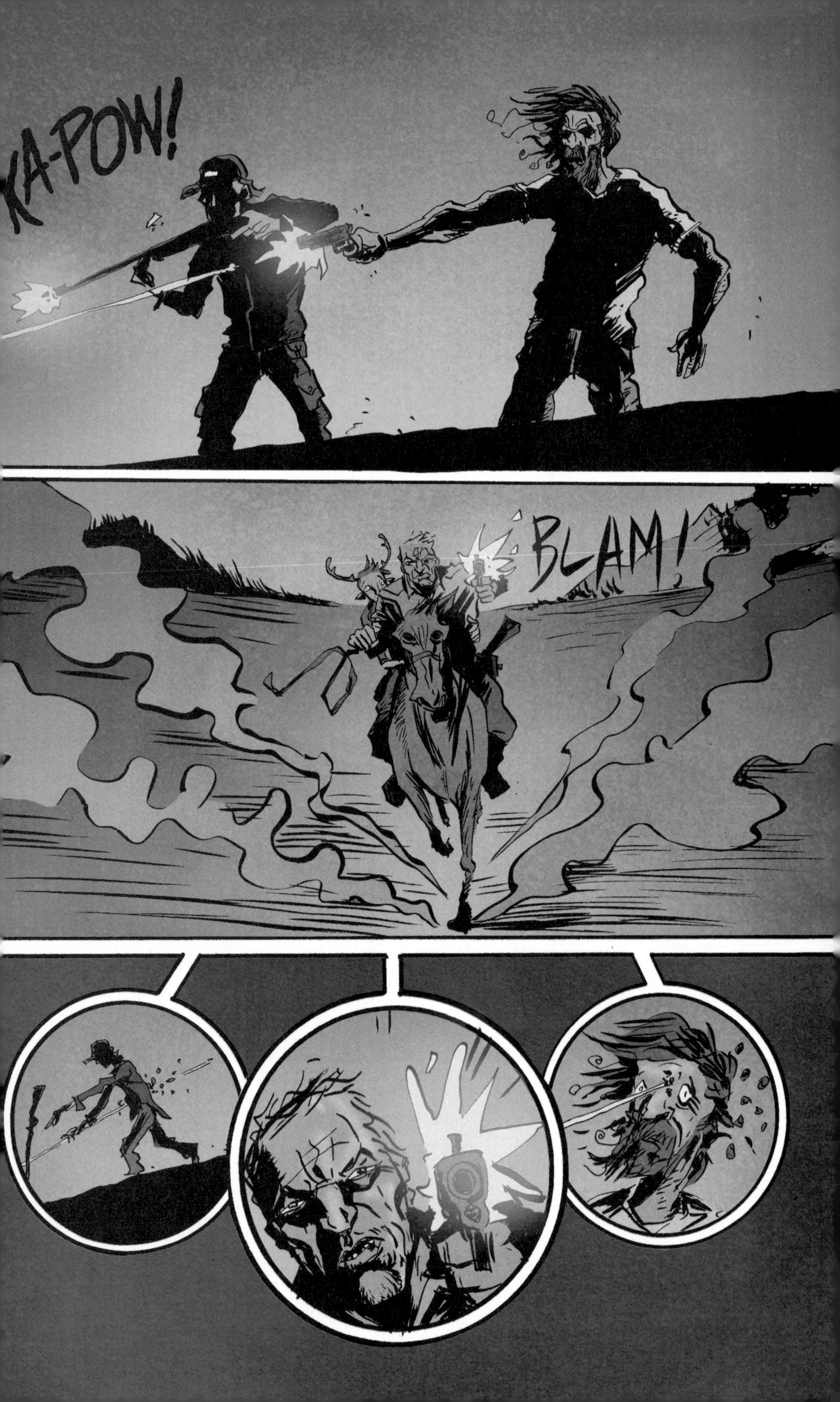
KA-POW!
BLAM!

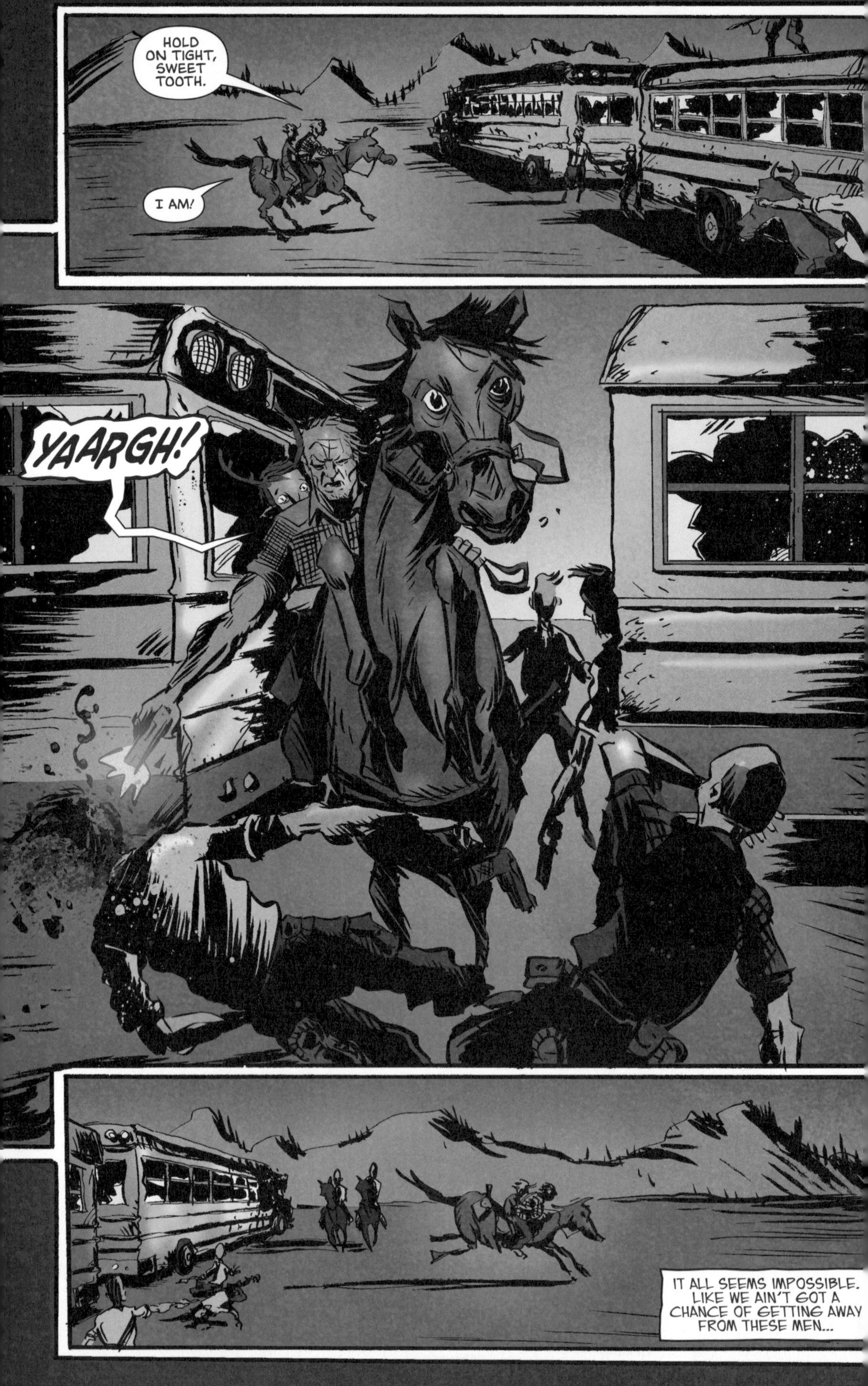
HOLD ON TIGHT, SWEET TOOTH.
I AM!
YAARGH!
IT ALL SEEMS IMPOSSIBLE. LIKE WE AIN'T GOT A CHANCE OF GETTING AWAY FROM THESE MEN...

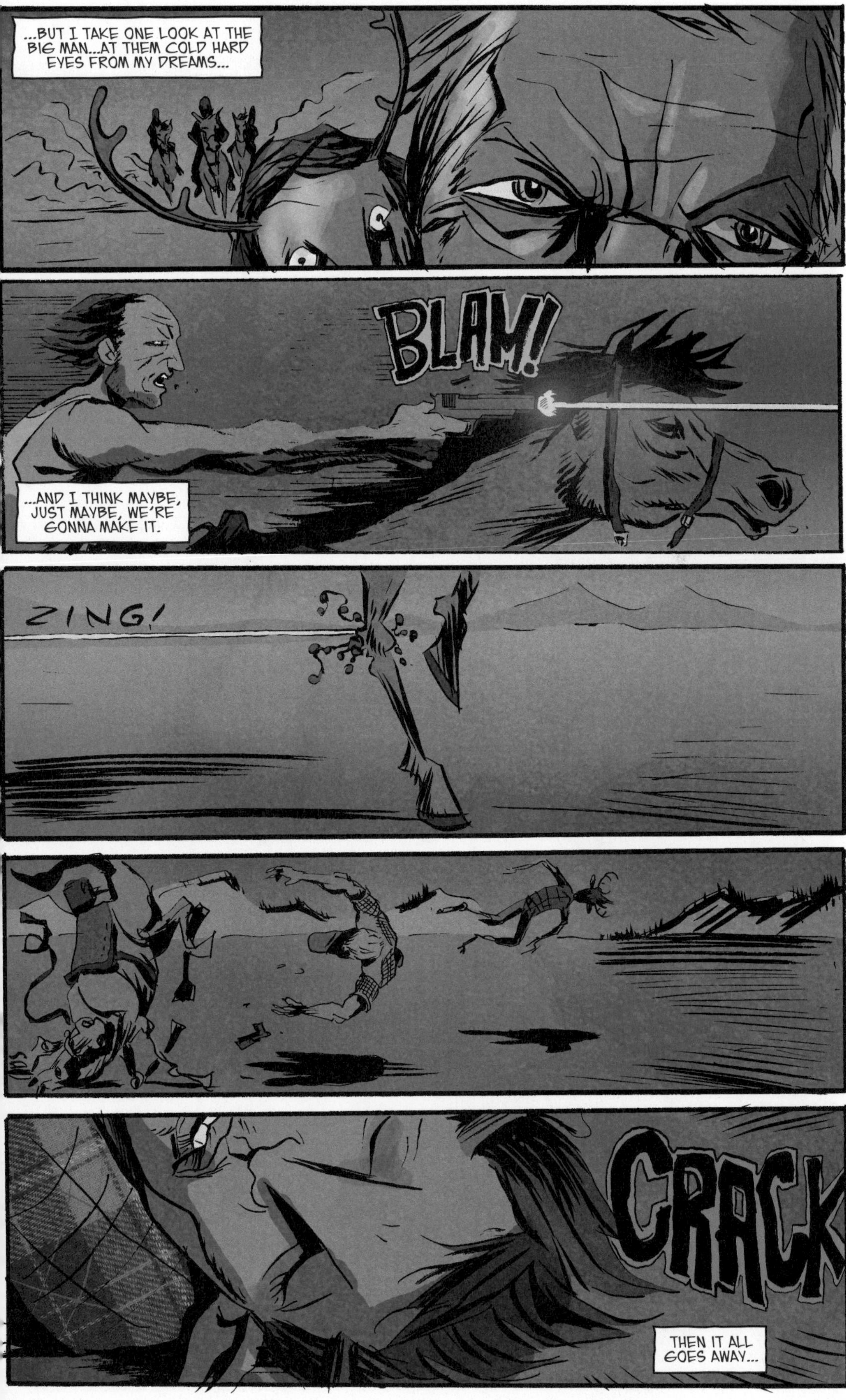
...BUT I TAKE ONE LOOK AT THE BIG MAN...AT THEM COLD HARD EYES FROM MY DREAMS...
BLAM!
...AND I THINK MAYBE, JUST MAYBE, WE'RE GONNA MAKE IT.
ZING!
CRACK
THEN IT ALL GOES AWAY...

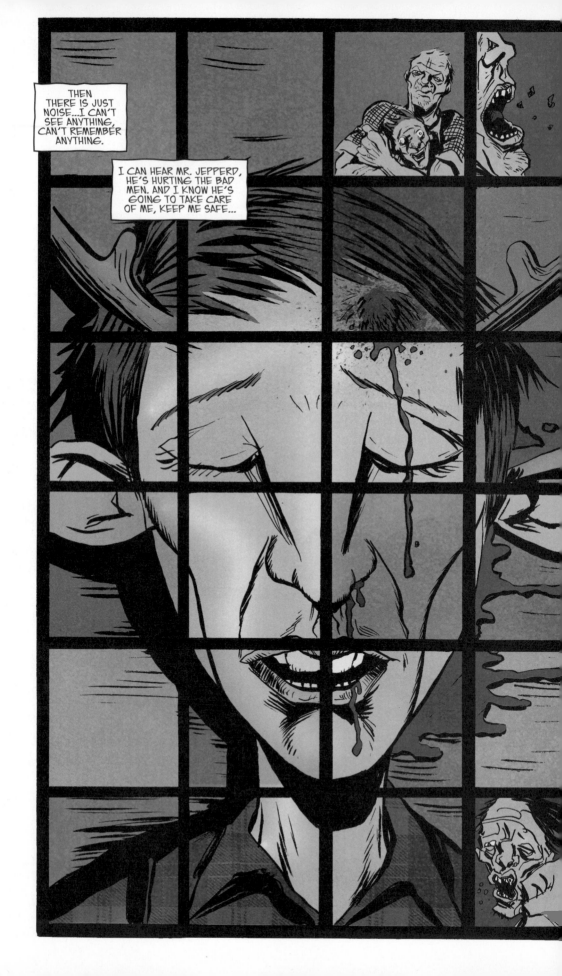

THEN THERE IS JUST NOISE...I CAN'T SEE ANYTHING, CAN'T REMEMBER ANYTHING.

I CAN HEAR MR. JEPPERD, HE'S HURTING THE BAD MEN. AND I KNOW HE'S GOING TO TAKE CARE OF ME, KEEP ME SAFE...

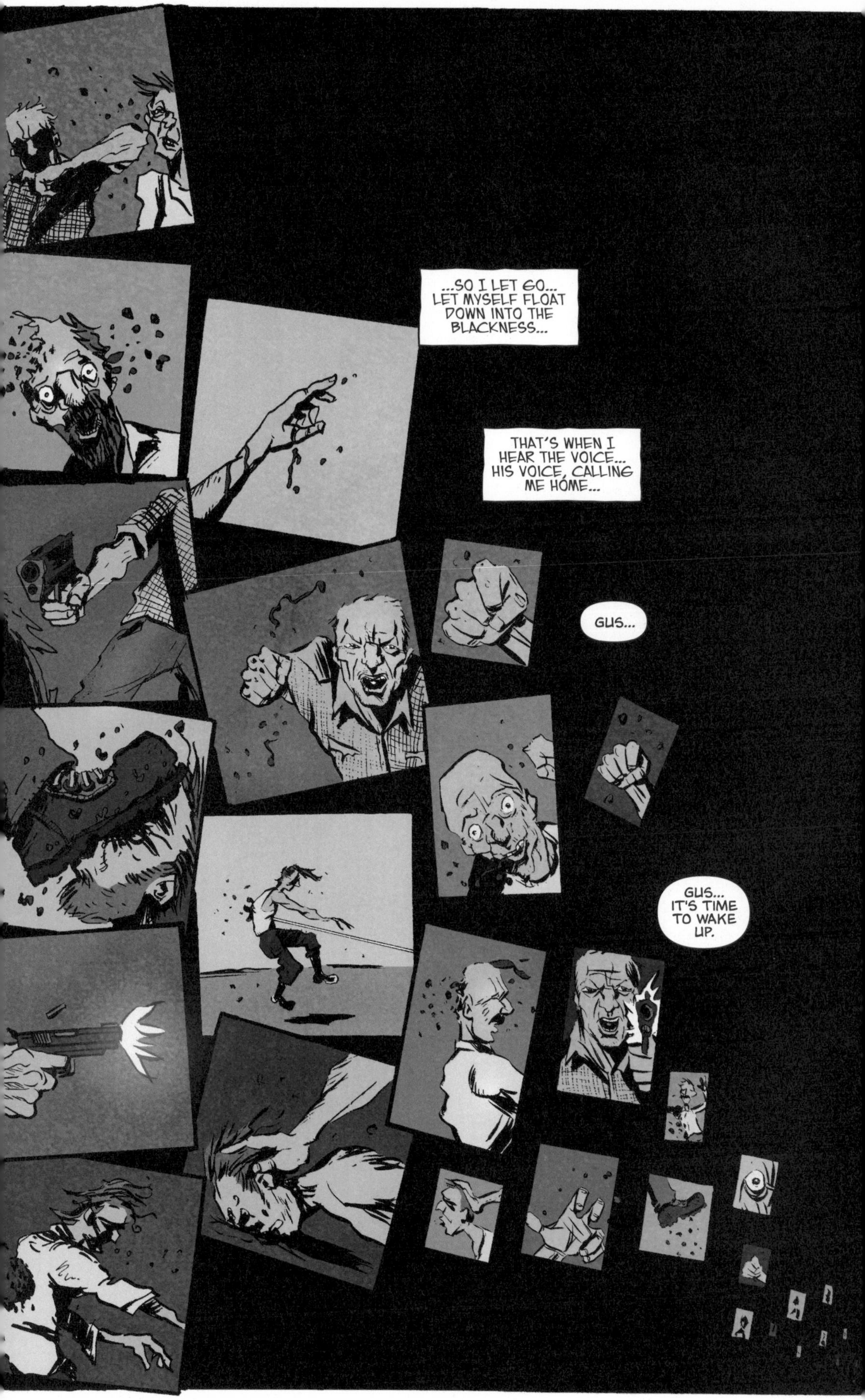
...SO I LET GO... LET MYSELF FLOAT DOWN INTO THE BLACKNESS...
THAT'S WHEN I HEAR THE VOICE... HIS VOICE, CALLING ME HOME...
GUS...
GUS... IT'S TIME TO WAKE UP.

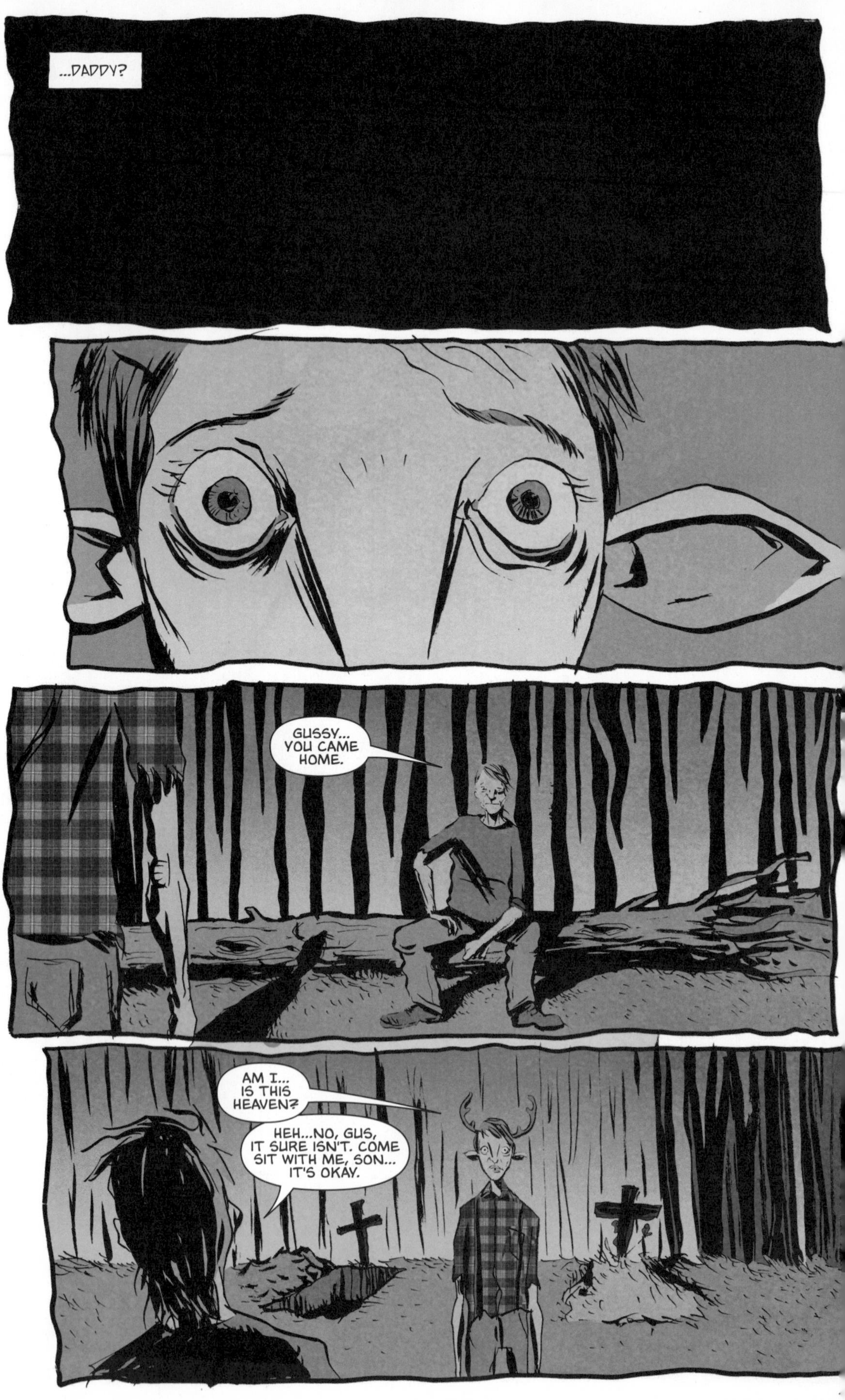
...DADDY?
GUSSY... YOU CAME HOME.
AM I... IS THIS HEAVEN?
HEH...NO, GUS, IT SURE ISN'T. COME SIT WITH ME, SON... IT'S OKAY.

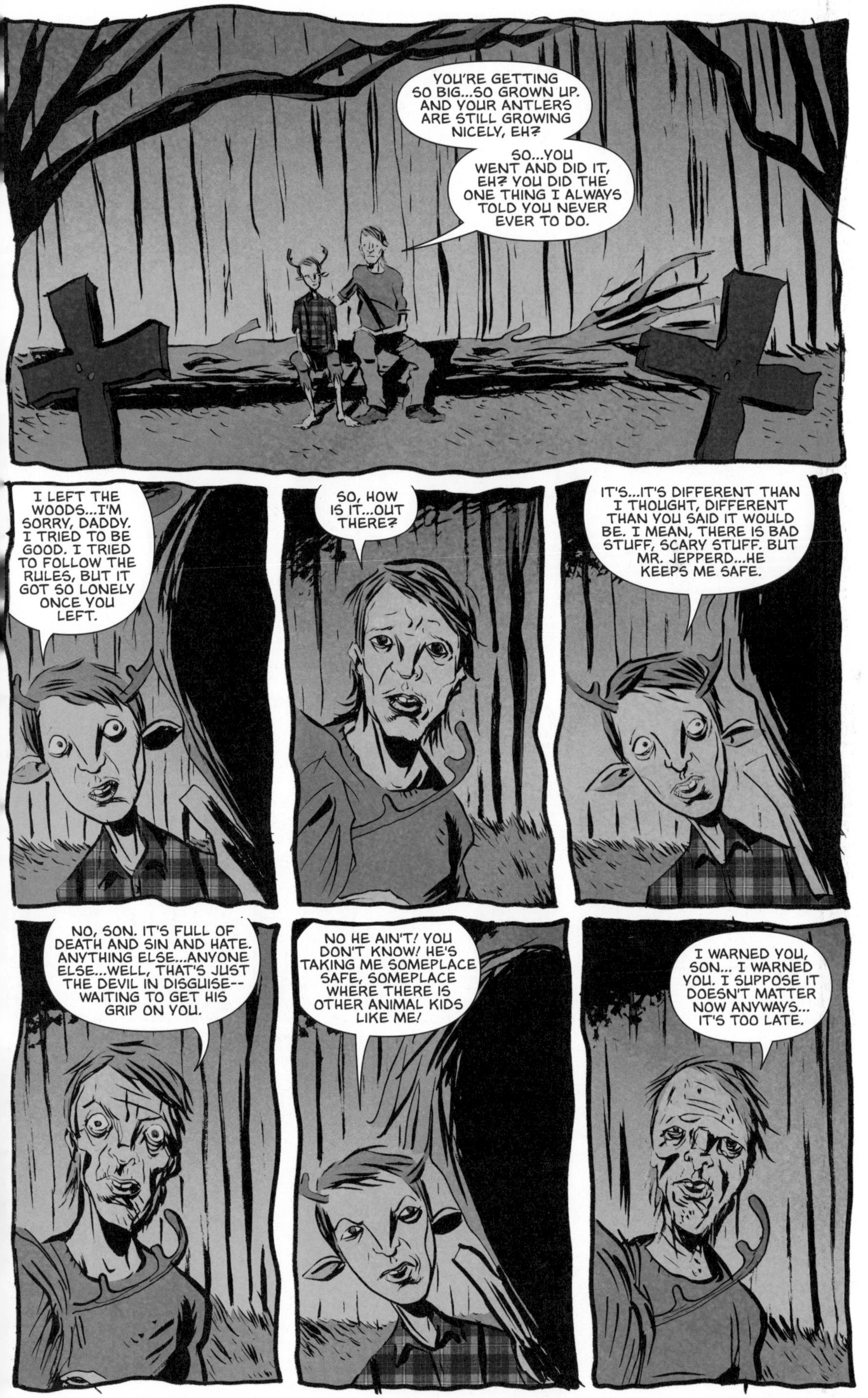
YOU'RE GETTING SO BIG...SO GROWN UP. AND YOUR ANTLERS ARE STILL GROWING NICELY, EH?
SO...YOU WENT AND DID IT, EH? YOU DID THE ONE THING I ALWAYS TOLD YOU NEVER EVER TO DO.
I LEFT THE WOODS...I'M SORRY, DADDY. I TRIED TO BE GOOD. I TRIED TO FOLLOW THE RULES, BUT IT GOT SO LONELY ONCE YOU LEFT.
SO, HOW IS IT...OUT THERE?
IT'S...IT'S DIFFERENT THAN I THOUGHT, DIFFERENT THAN YOU SAID IT WOULD BE. I MEAN, THERE IS BAD STUFF, SCARY STUFF. BUT MR. JEPPERD...HE KEEPS ME SAFE.
NO, SON. IT'S FULL OF DEATH AND SIN AND HATE. ANYTHING ELSE...ANYONE ELSE...WELL, THAT'S JUST THE DEVIL IN DISGUISE-- WAITING TO GET HIS GRIP ON YOU.
NO HE AIN'T! YOU DON'T KNOW! HE'S TAKING ME SOMEPLACE SAFE, SOMEPLACE WHERE THERE IS OTHER ANIMAL KIDS LIKE ME!
I WARNED YOU, SON... I WARNED YOU. I SUPPOSE IT DOESN'T MATTER NOW ANYWAYS... IT'S TOO LATE.

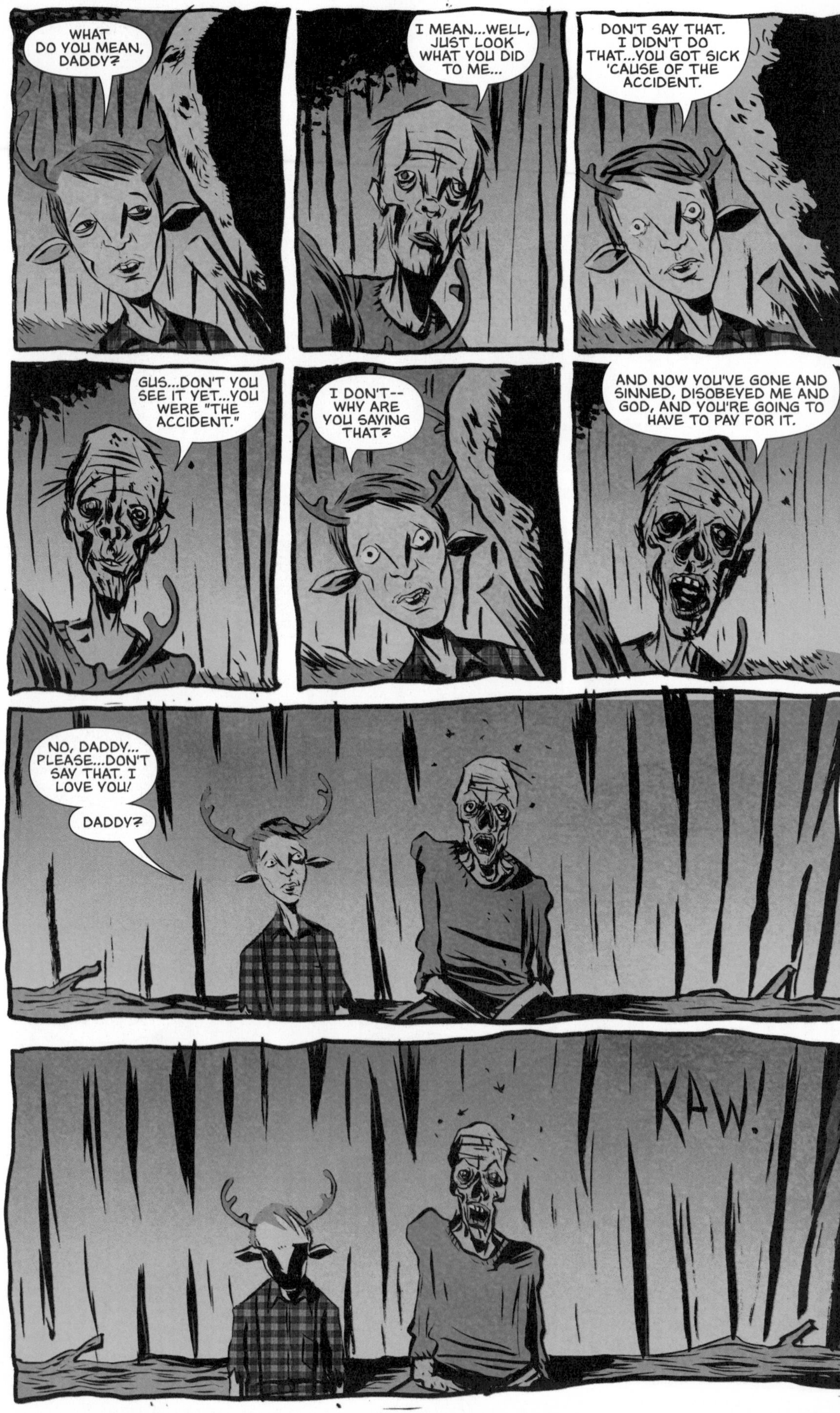
WHAT DO YOU MEAN, DADDY?
I MEAN...WELL, JUST LOOK WHAT YOU DID TO ME...
DON'T SAY THAT. I DIDN'T DO THAT...YOU GOT SICK 'CAUSE OF THE ACCIDENT.
GUS...DON'T YOU SEE IT YET...YOU WERE "THE ACCIDENT."
I DON'T-- WHY ARE YOU SAYING THAT?
AND NOW YOU'VE GONE AND SINNED, DISOBEYED ME AND GOD, AND YOU'RE GOING TO HAVE TO PAY FOR IT.
NO, DADDY... PLEASE...DON'T SAY THAT. I LOVE YOU!
DADDY?
KAW!

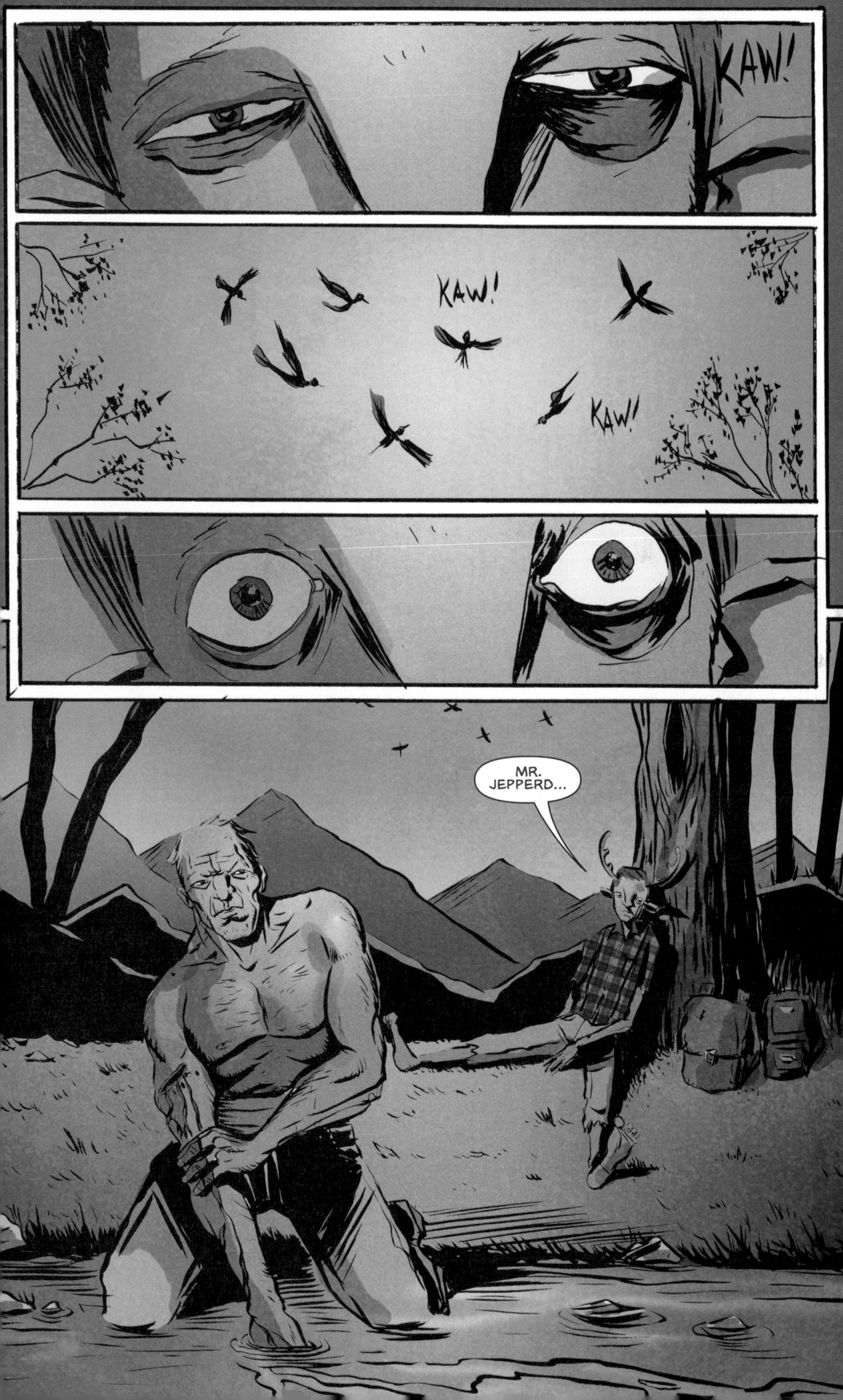
KAW!
KAW!
KAW!
MR. JEPPERD...

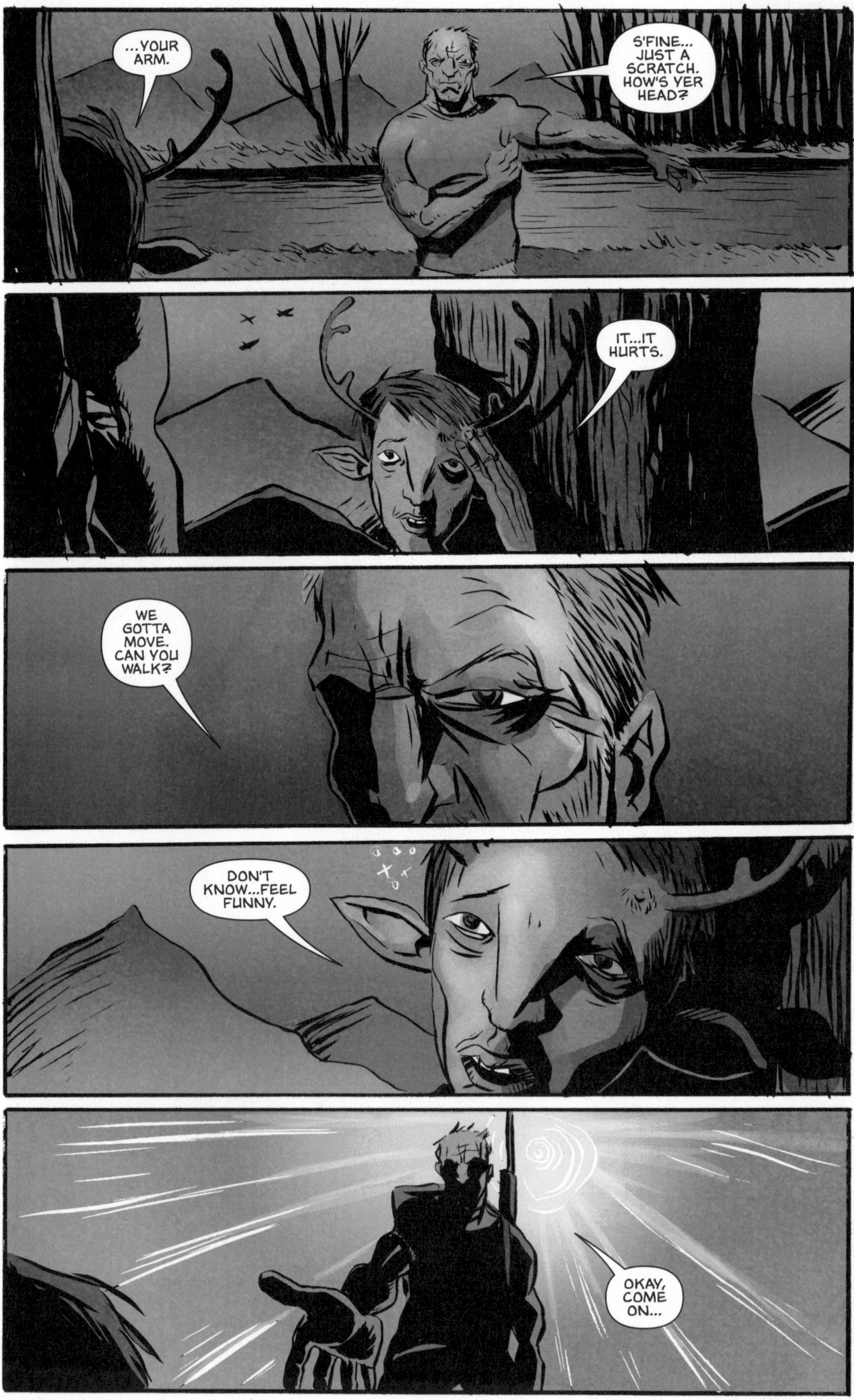
...YOUR ARM.
S'FINE... JUST A SCRATCH. HOW'S YER HEAD?
IT...IT HURTS.
WE GOTTA MOVE. CAN YOU WALK?
DON'T KNOW...FEEL FUNNY.
OKAY, COME ON...

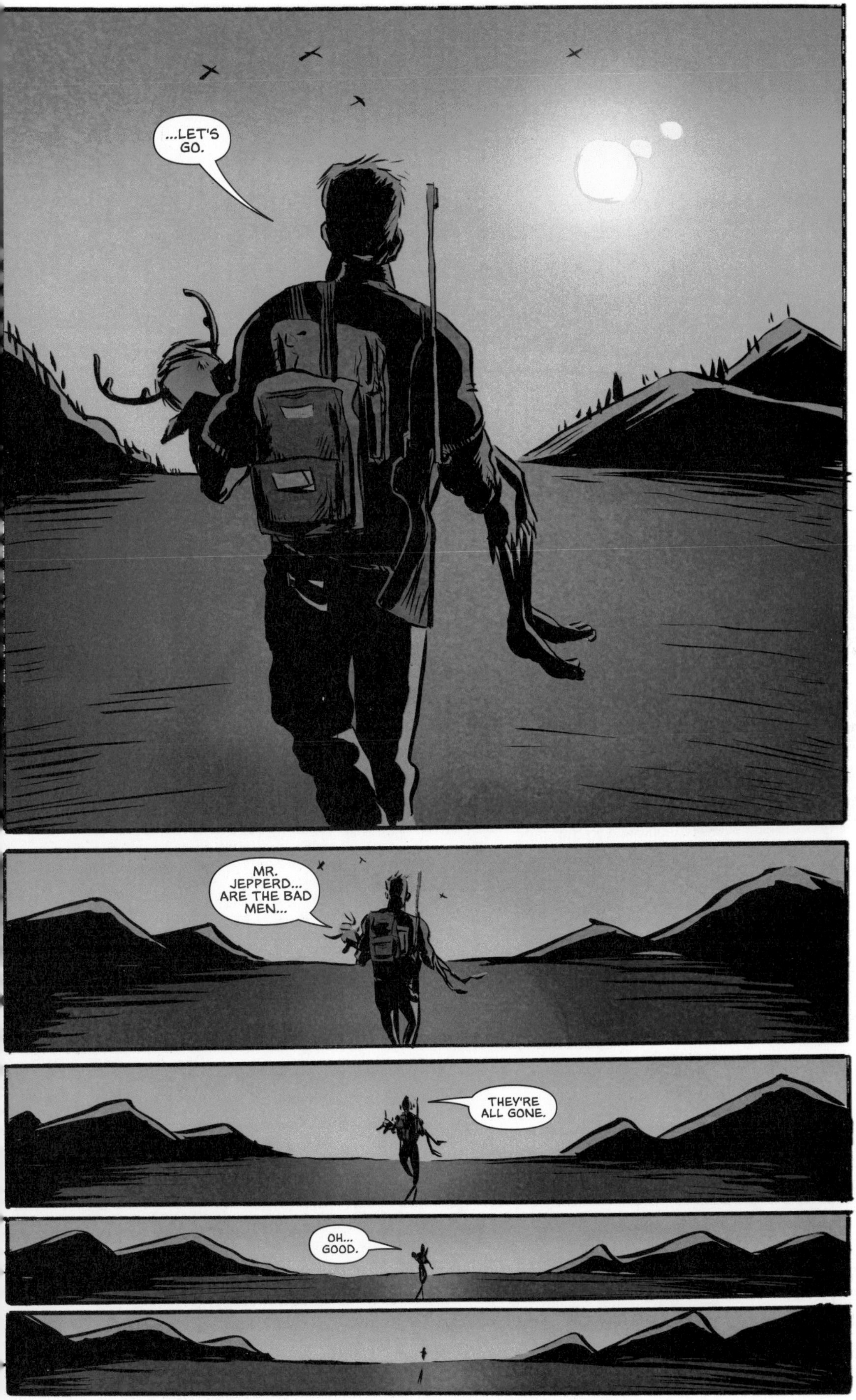
...LET'S GO.
MR. JEPPERD... ARE THE BAD MEN...
THEY'RE ALL GONE.
OH... GOOD.

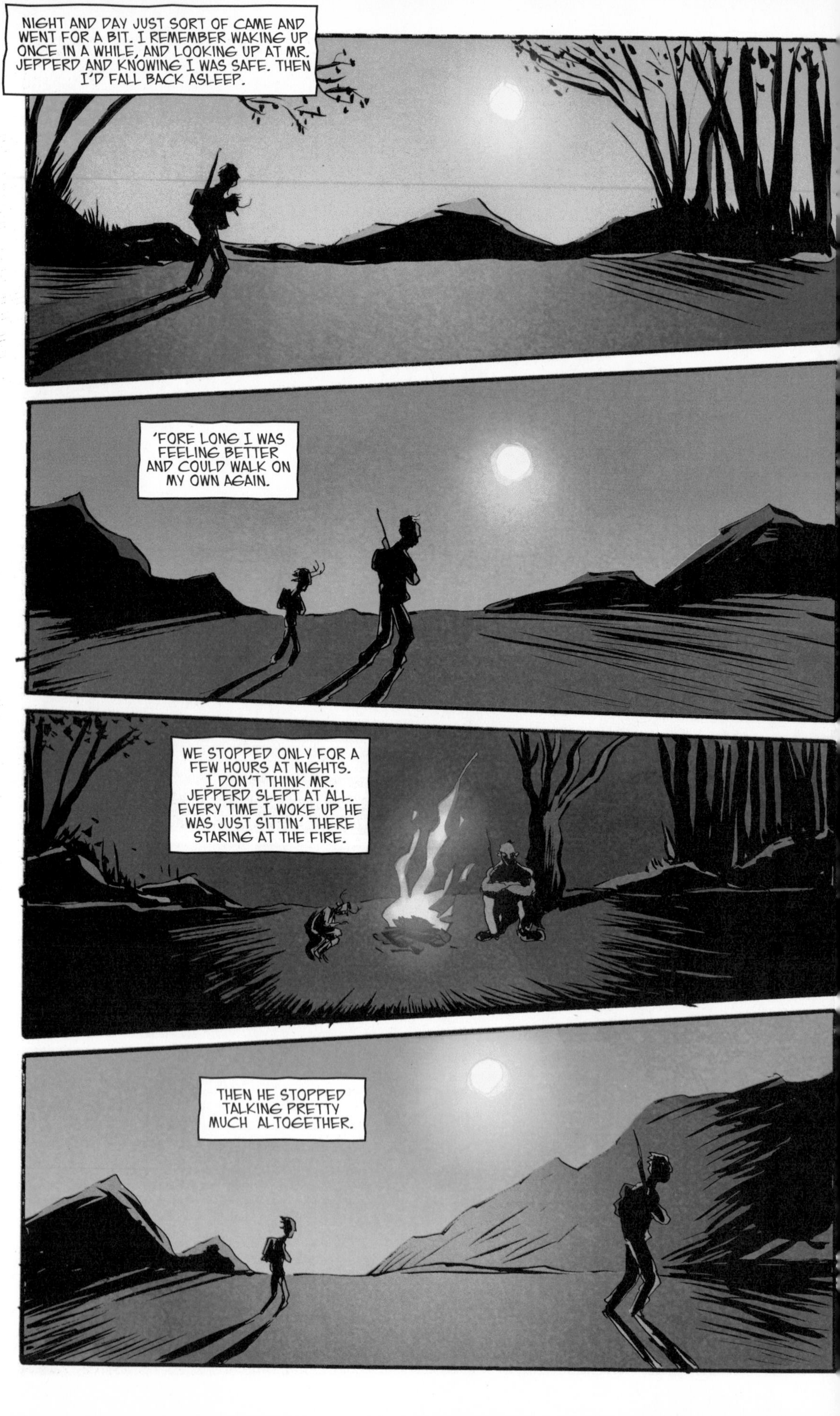
NIGHT AND DAY JUST SORT OF CAME AND WENT FOR A BIT. I REMEMBER WAKING UP ONCE IN A WHILE, AND LOOKING UP AT MR. JEPPERD AND KNOWING I WAS SAFE. THEN I'D FALL BACK ASLEEP.
'FORE LONG I WAS FEELING BETTER AND COULD WALK ON MY OWN AGAIN.
WE STOPPED ONLY FOR A FEW HOURS AT NIGHTS. I DON'T THINK MR. JEPPERD SLEPT AT ALL. EVERY TIME I WOKE UP HE WAS JUST SITTIN' THERE STARING AT THE FIRE.
THEN HE STOPPED TALKING PRETTY MUCH ALTOGETHER.

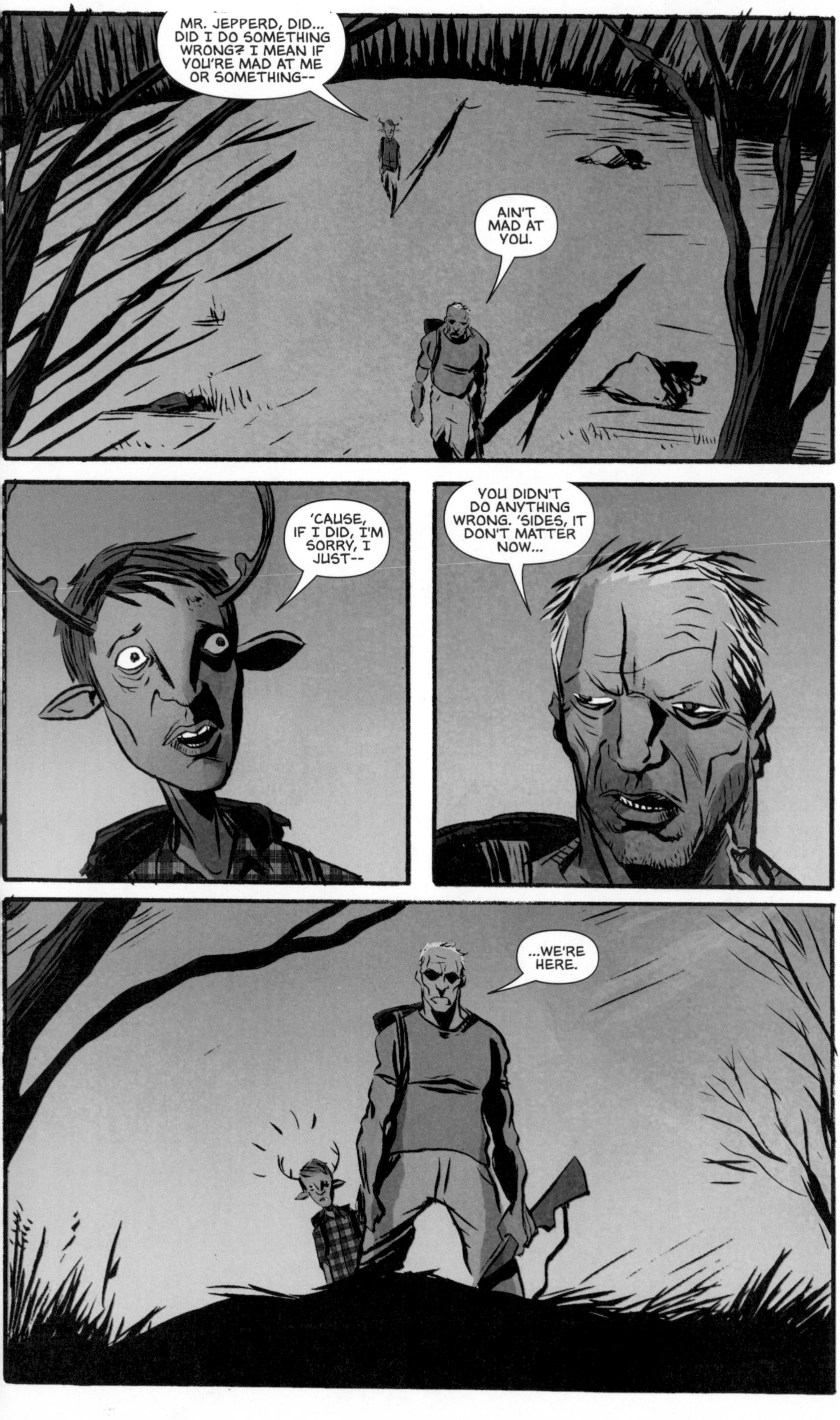

MR. JEPPERD, DID... DID I DO SOMETHING WRONG? I MEAN IF YOU'RE MAD AT ME OR SOMETHING--
AIN'T MAD AT YOU.
'CAUSE, IF I DID, I'M SORRY, I JUST--
YOU DIDN'T DO ANYTHING WRONG. 'SIDES, IT DON'T MATTER NOW...
...WE'RE HERE.

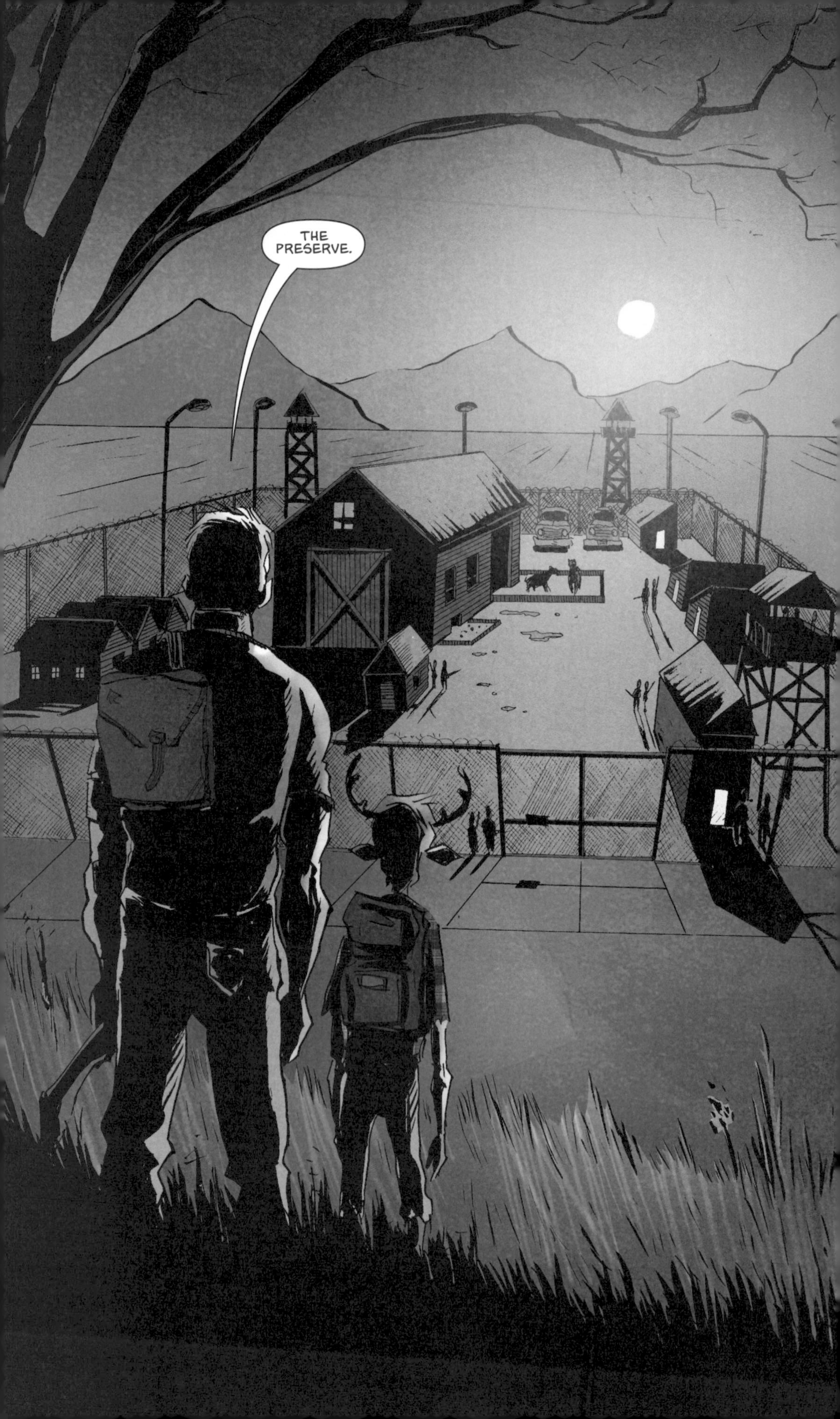
THE PRESERVE.

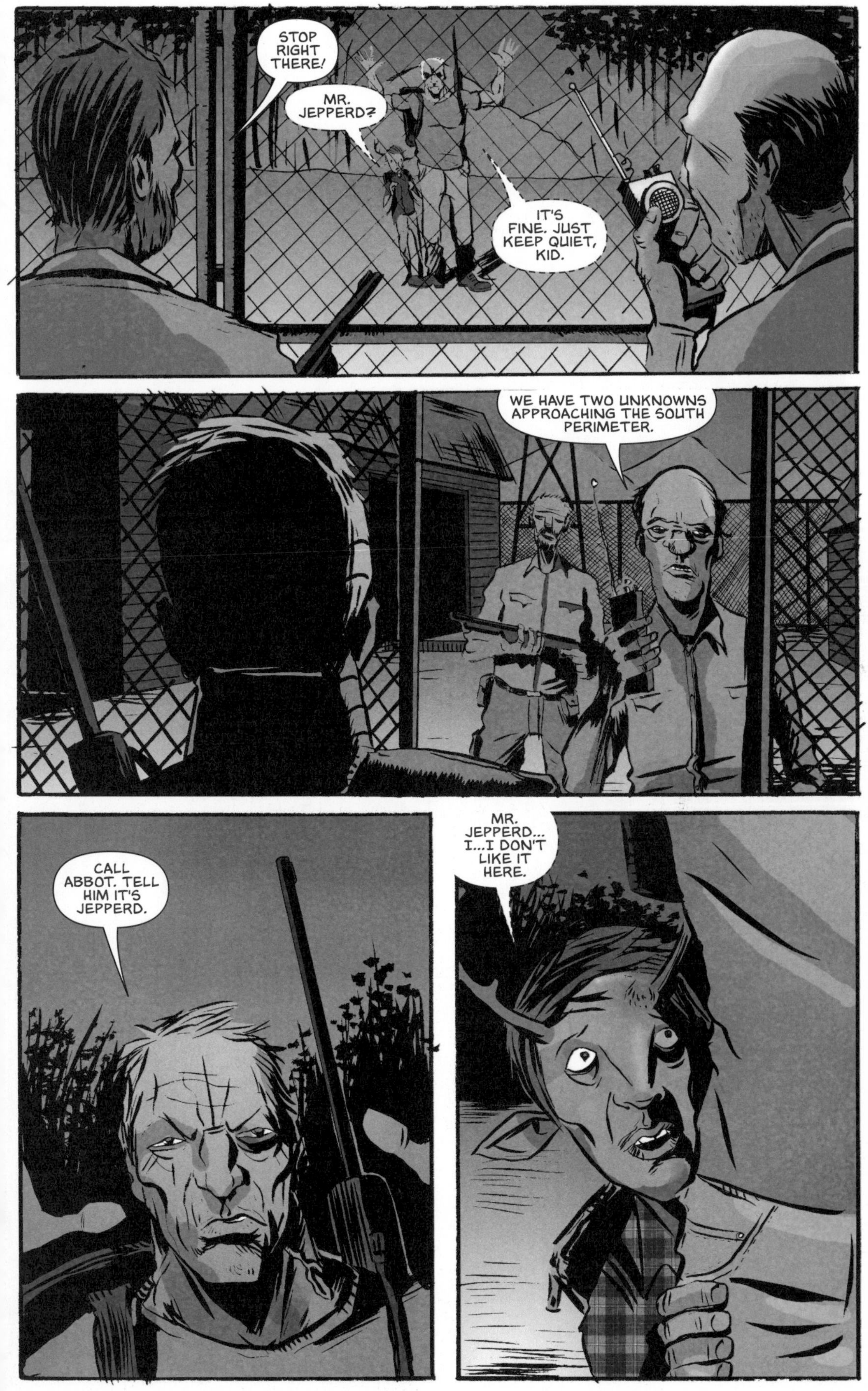
STOP RIGHT THERE!
MR. JEPPERD?
IT'S FINE. JUST KEEP QUIET, KID.
WE HAVE TWO UNKNOWNS APPROACHING THE SOUTH PERIMETER.
CALL ABBOT. TELL HIM IT'S JEPPERD.
MR. JEPPERD... I...I DON'T LIKE IT HERE.

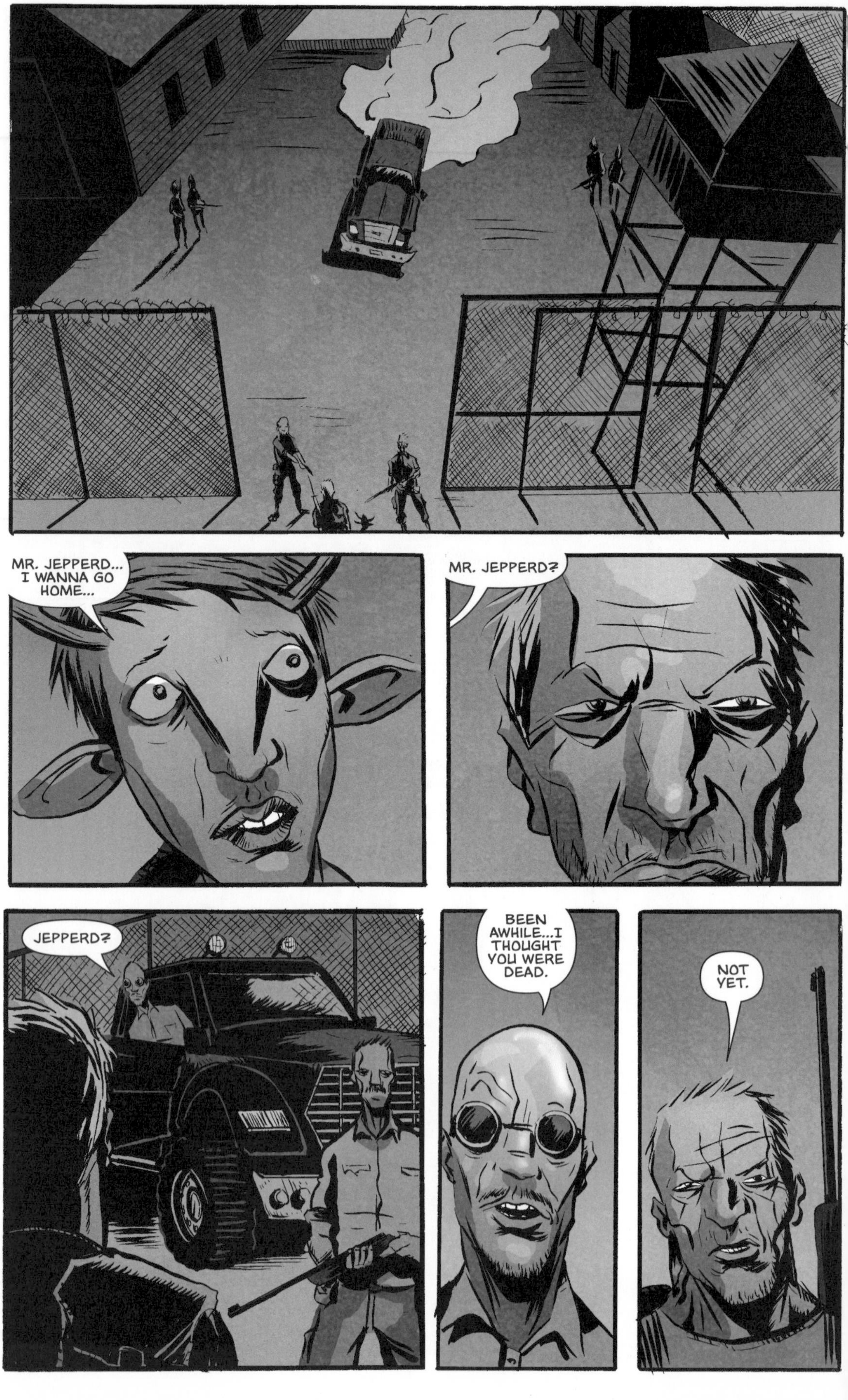
MR. JEPPERD... I WANNA GO HOME...
MR. JEPPERD?
JEPPERD?
BEEN AWHILE...I THOUGHT YOU WERE DEAD.
NOT YET.

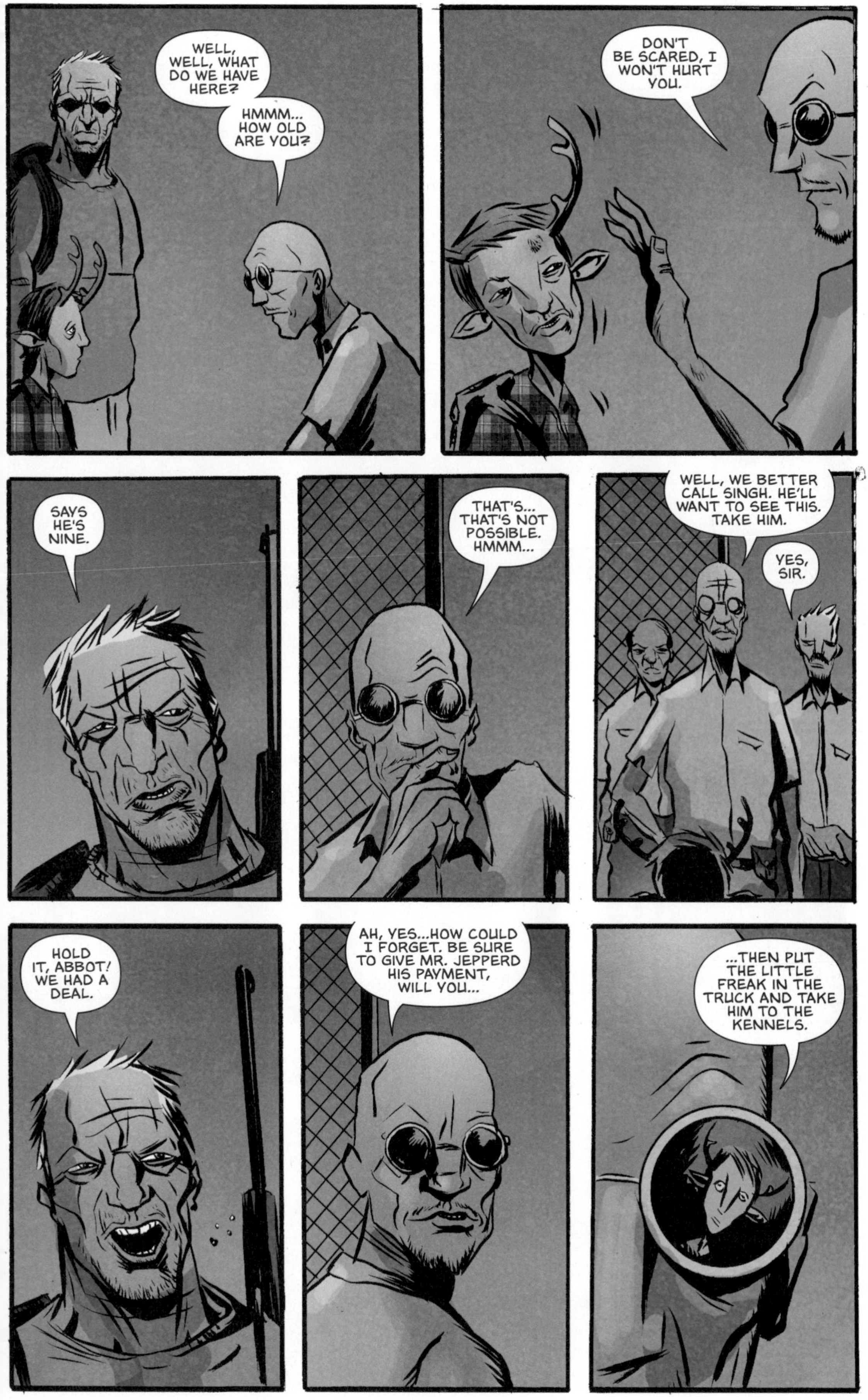
WELL, WELL, WHAT DO WE HAVE HERE?
HMMM... HOW OLD ARE YOU?
DON'T BE SCARED, I WON'T HURT YOU.
SAYS HE'S NINE.
THAT'S... THAT'S NOT POSSIBLE. HMMM...
WELL, WE BETTER CALL SINGH. HE'LL WANT TO SEE THIS. TAKE HIM.
YES, SIR.
HOLD IT, ABBOT! WE HAD A DEAL.
AH, YES...HOW COULD I FORGET. BE SURE TO GIVE MR. JEPPERD HIS PAYMENT, WILL YOU...
...THEN PUT THE LITTLE FREAK IN THE TRUCK AND TAKE HIM TO THE KENNELS.

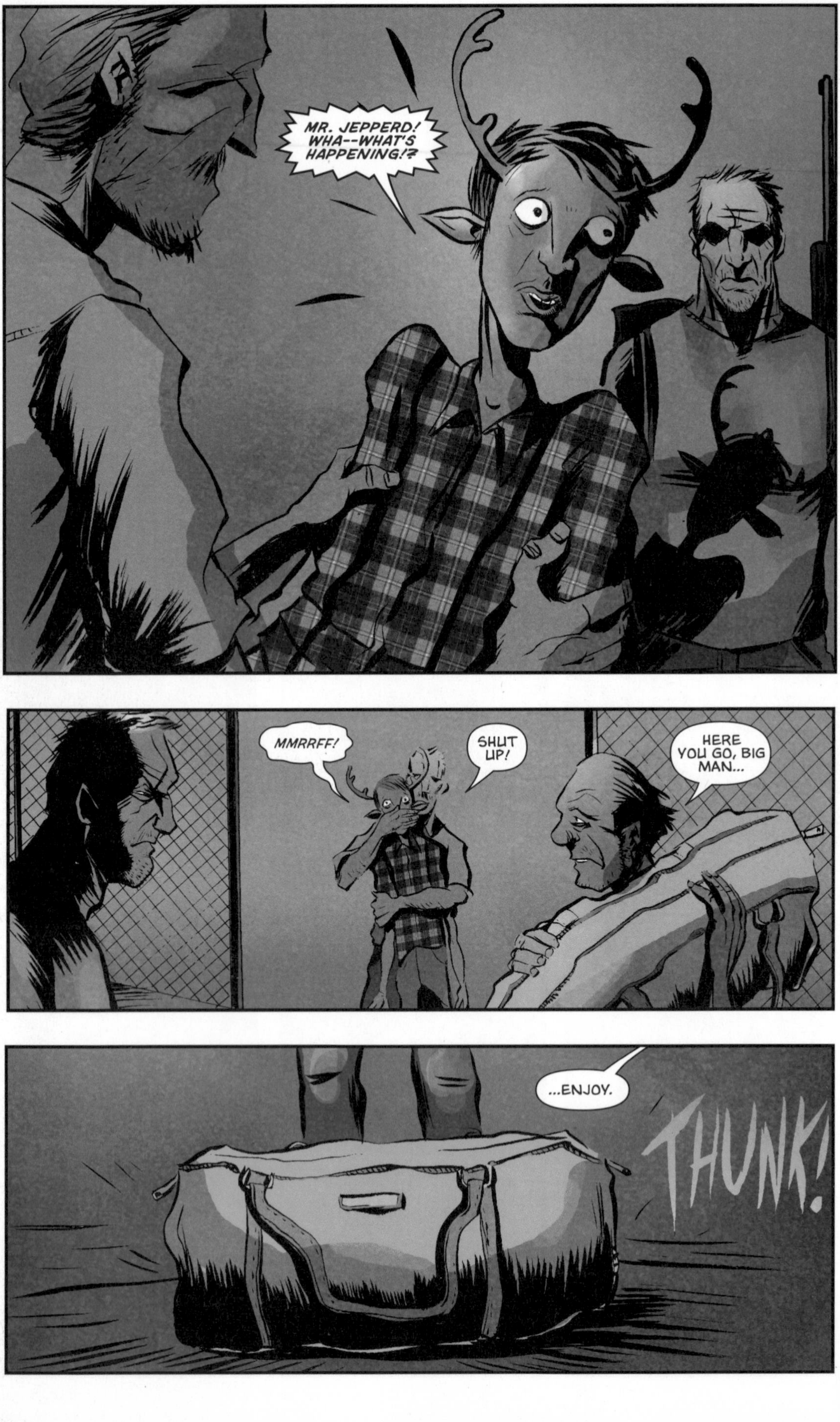
MR. JEPPERD! WHA--WHAT'S HAPPENING!?
MMRRFF!
SHUT UP!
HERE YOU GO, BIG MAN...
...ENJOY.
THUNK!

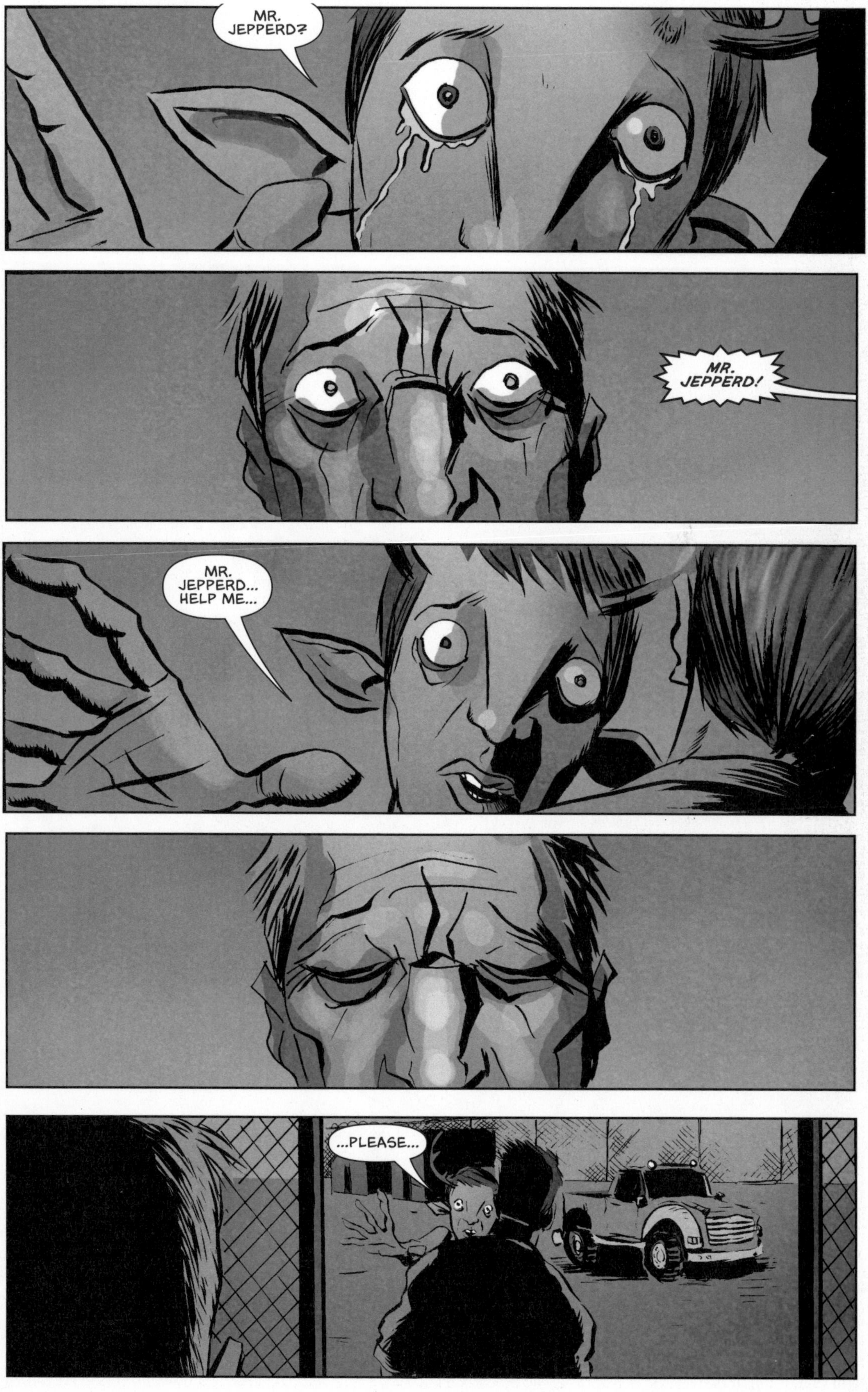
MR. JEPPERD?
MR. JEPPERD!
MR. JEPPERD... HELP ME...
...PLEASE...

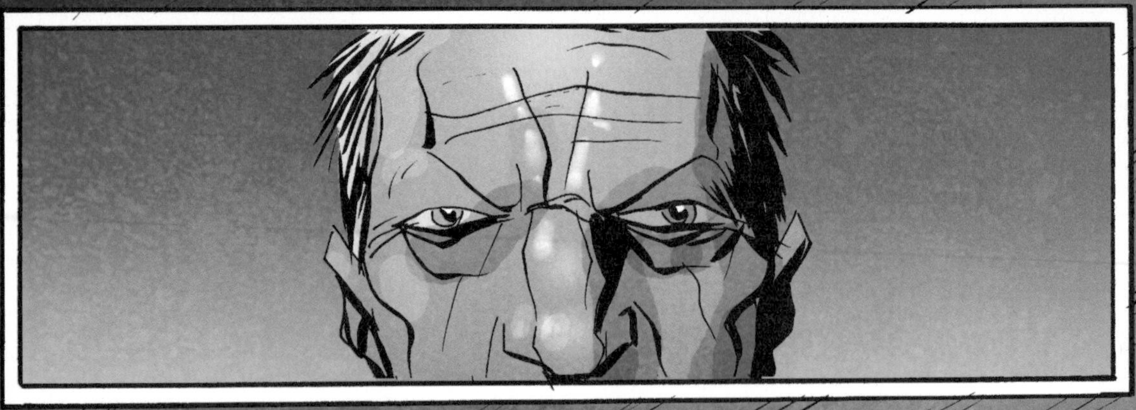

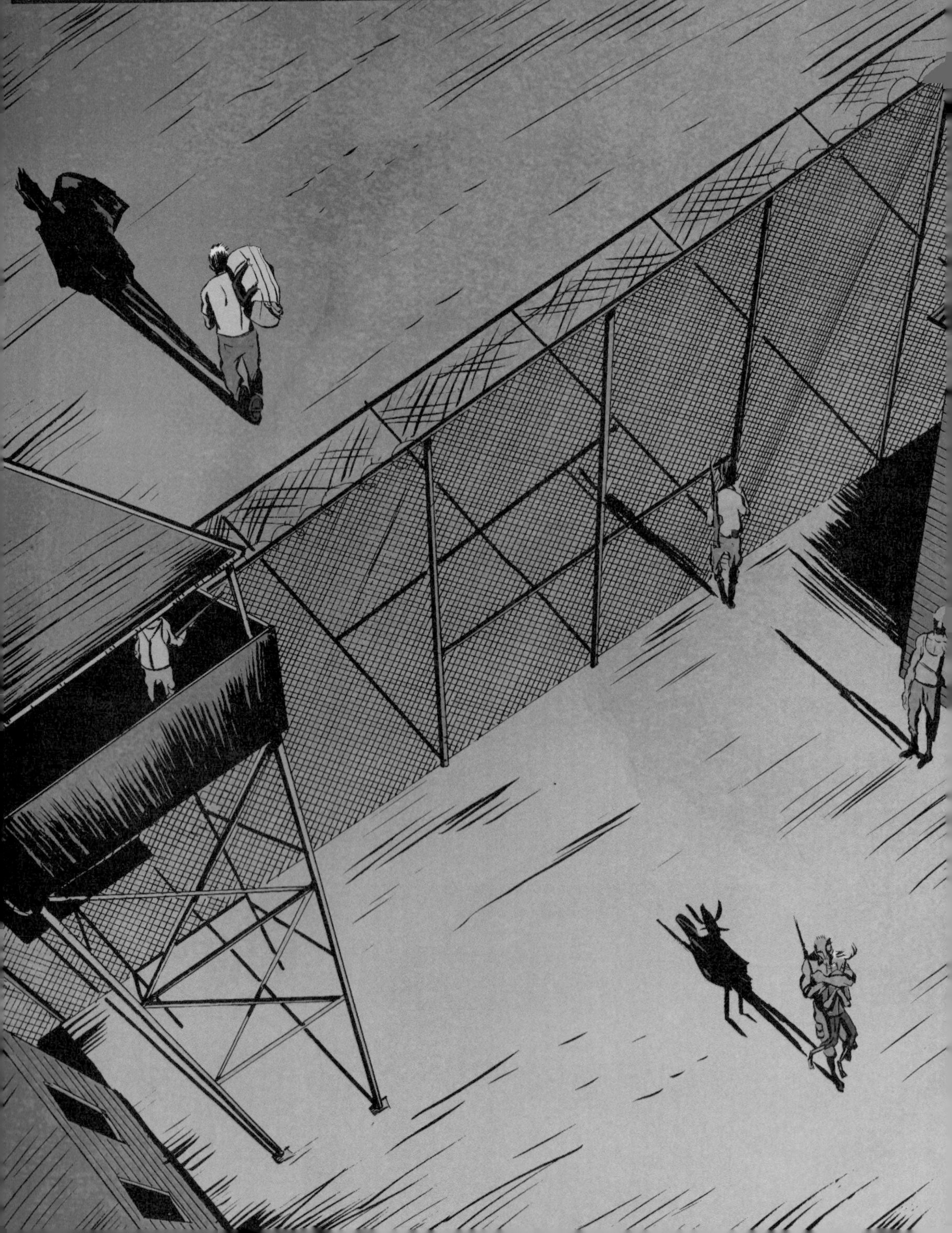

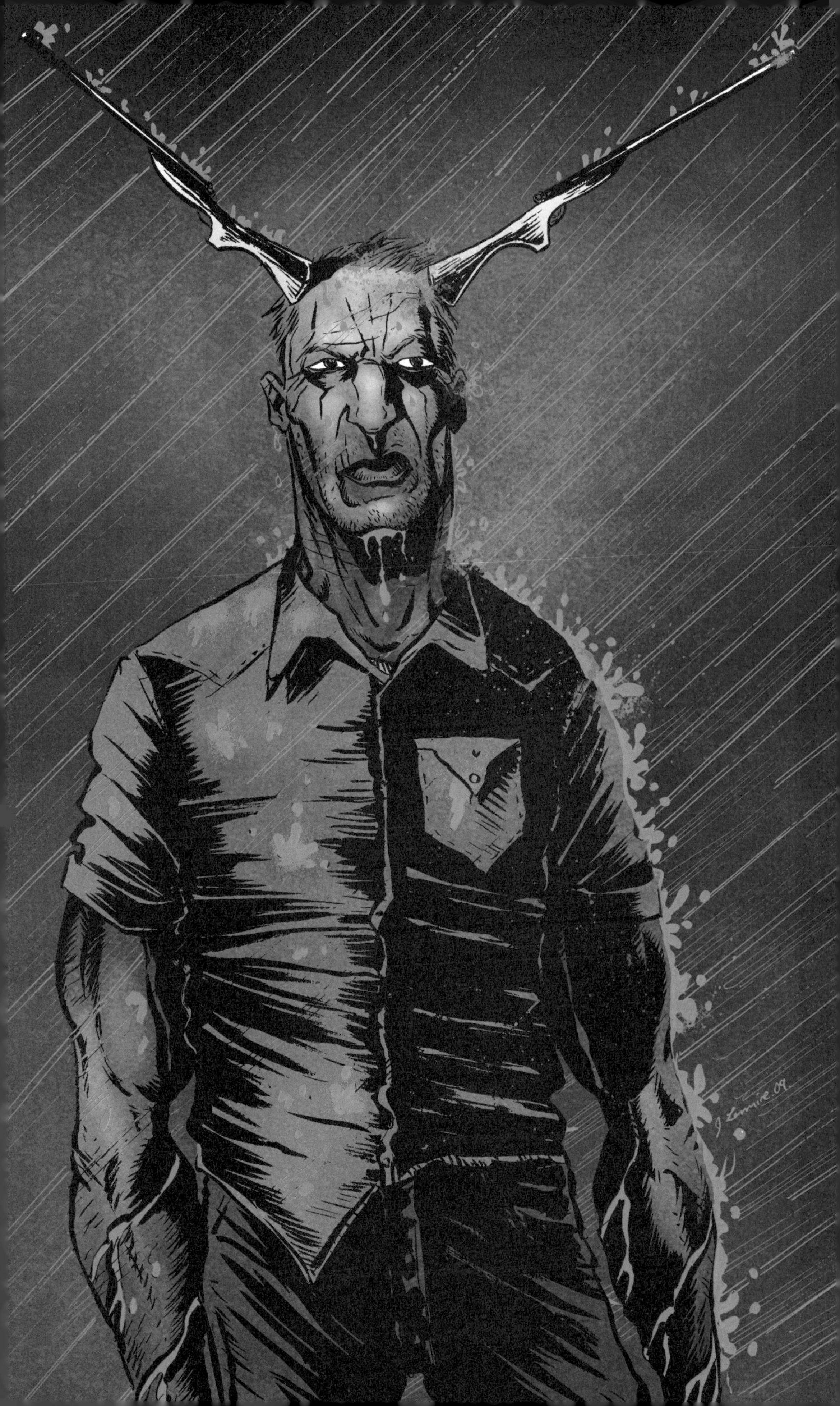

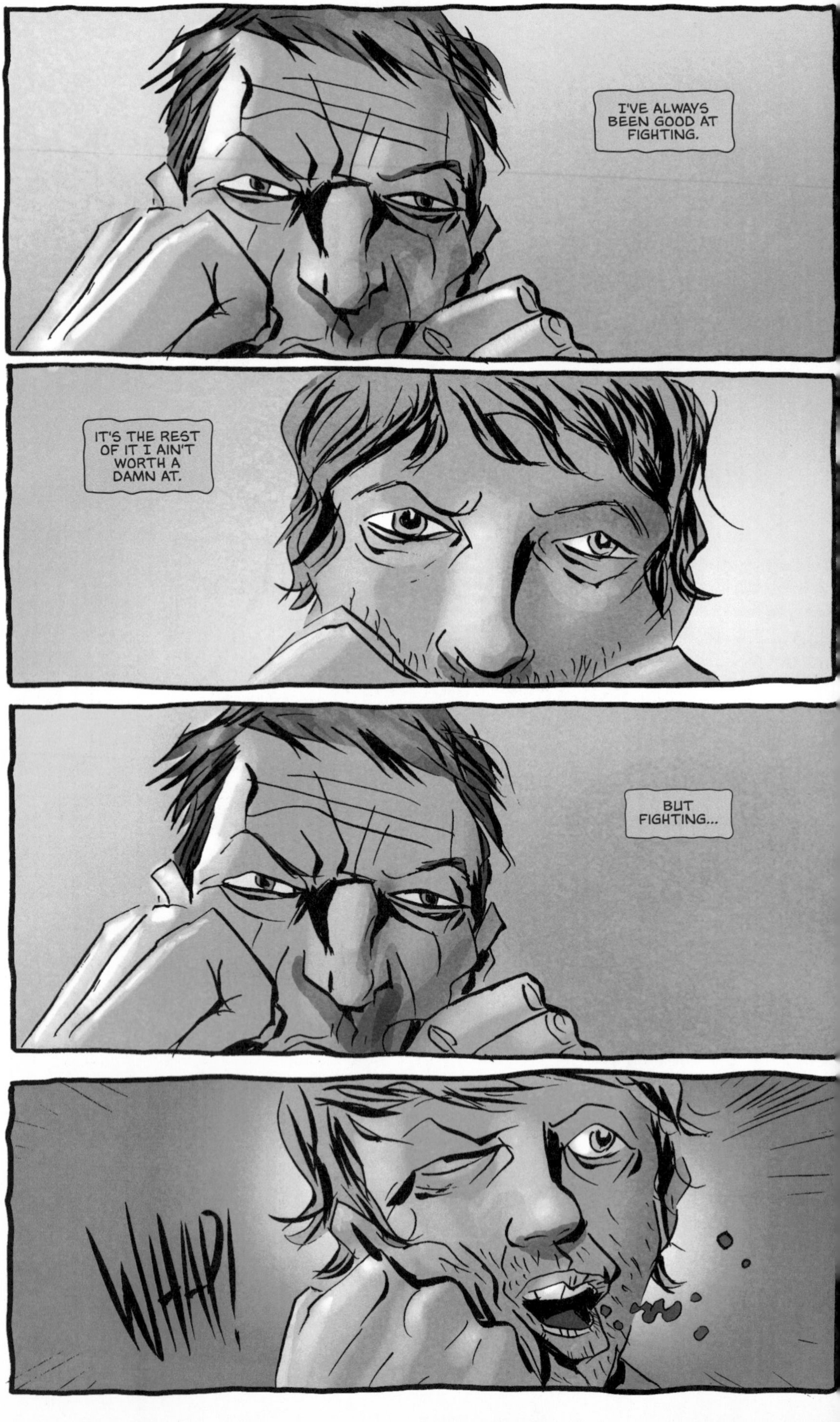
I'VE ALWAYS BEEN GOOD AT FIGHTING.
IT'S THE REST OF IT I AIN'T WORTH A DAMN AT.
BUT FIGHTING...
WHAP!

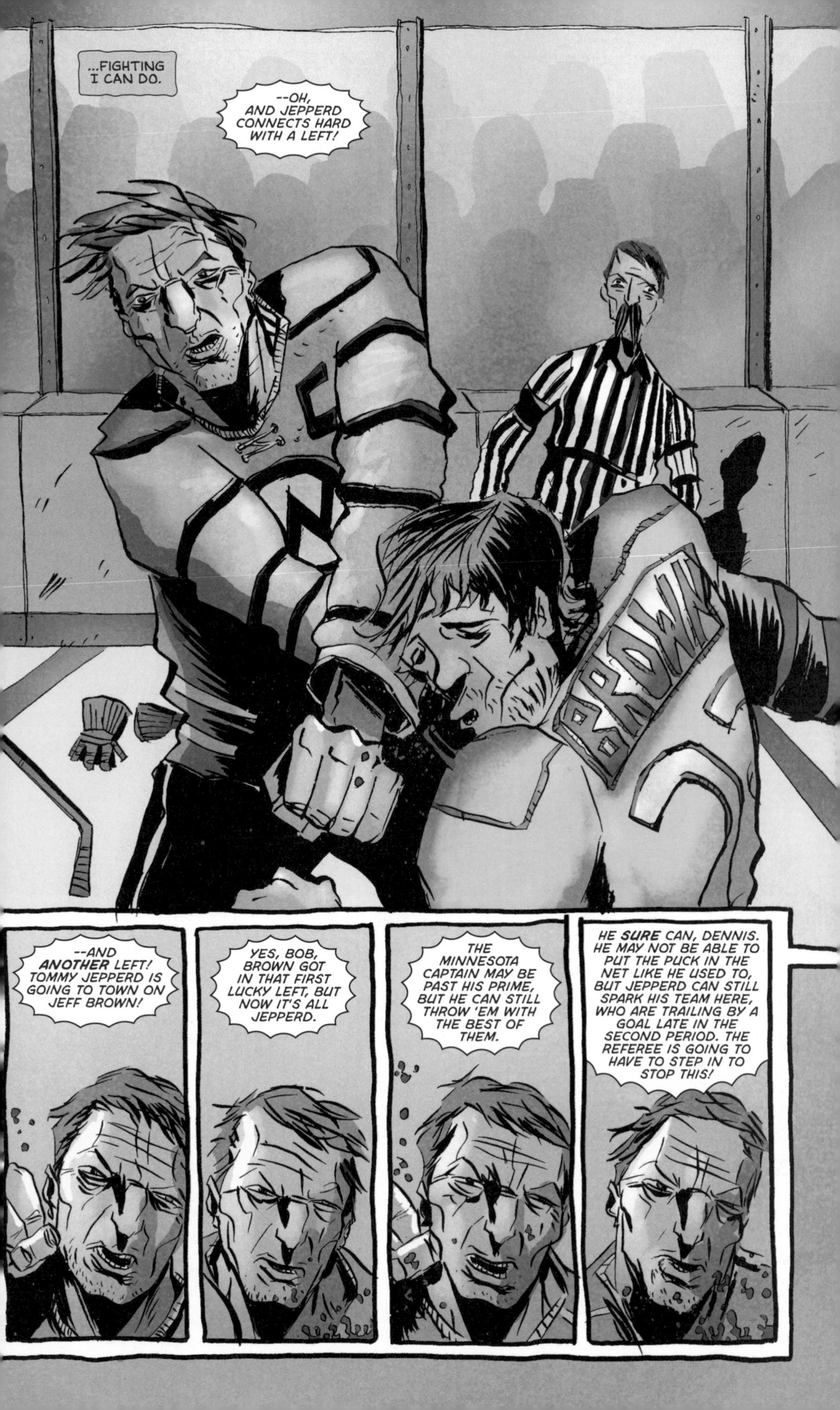
...FIGHTING I CAN DO.
--OH, AND JEPPERD CONNECTS HARD WITH A LEFT!
--AND ANOTHER LEFT! TOMMY JEPPERD IS GOING TO TOWN ON JEFF BROWN!
YES, BOB, BROWN GOT IN THAT FIRST LUCKY LEFT, BUT NOW IT'S ALL JEPPERD.
THE MINNESOTA CAPTAIN MAY BE PAST HIS PRIME, BUT HE CAN STILL THROW 'EM WITH THE BEST OF THEM.
HE SURE CAN, DENNIS. HE MAY NOT BE ABLE TO PUT THE PUCK IN THE NET LIKE HE USED TO, BUT JEPPERD CAN STILL SPARK HIS TEAM HERE, WHO ARE TRAILING BY A GOAL LATE IN THE SECOND PERIOD. THE REFEREE IS GOING TO HAVE TO STEP IN TO STOP THIS!

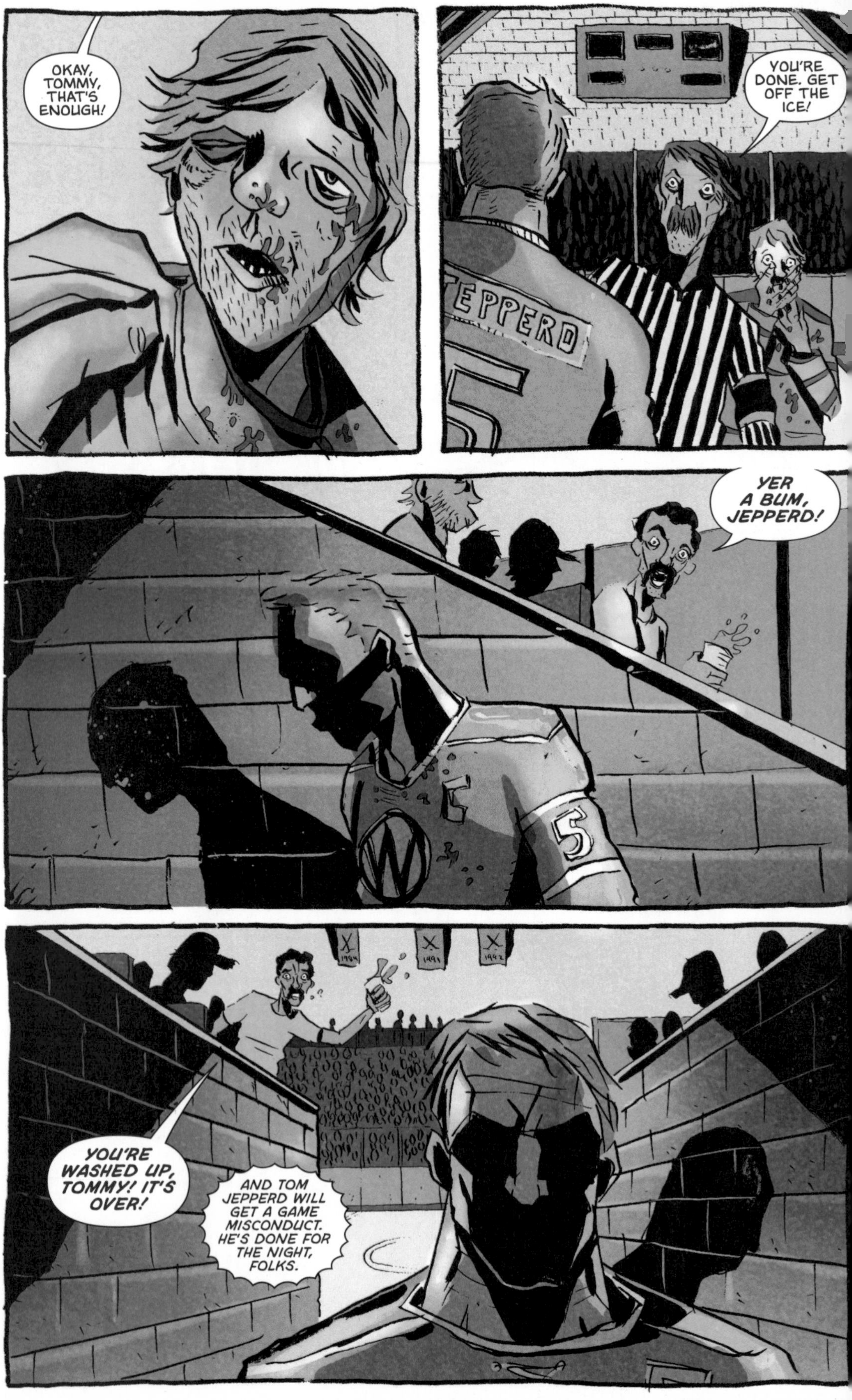
OKAY, TOMMY, THAT'S ENOUGH!
YOU'RE DONE. GET OFF THE ICE!
JEPPERD
5
YER A BUM, JEPPERD!
5
YOU'RE WASHED UP, TOMMY! IT'S OVER!
AND TOM JEPPERD WILL GET A GAME MISCONDUCT. HE'S DONE FOR THE NIGHT, FOLKS.

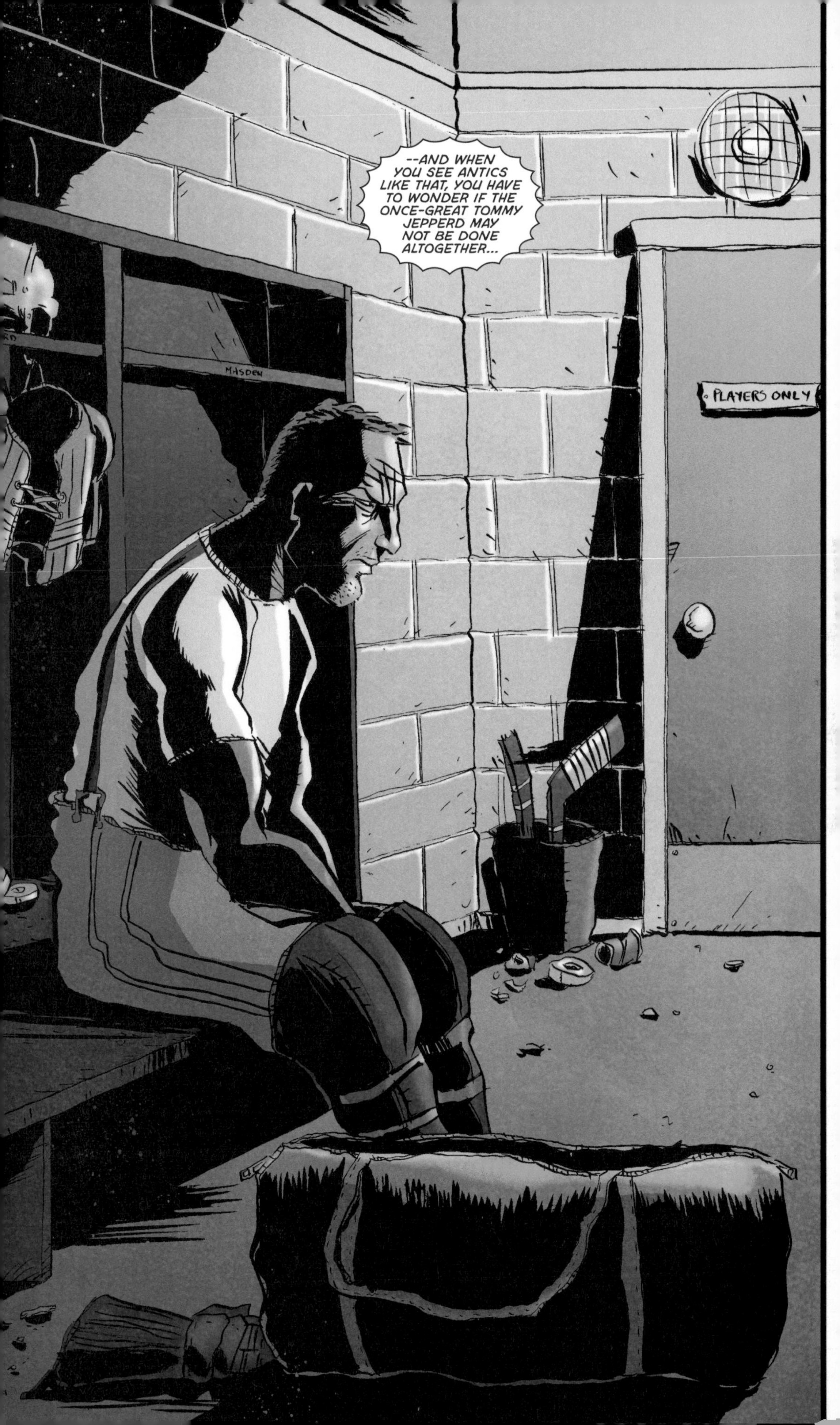
--AND WHEN YOU SEE ANTICS LIKE THAT, YOU HAVE TO WONDER IF THE ONCE-GREAT TOMMY JEPPERD MAY NOT BE DONE ALTOGETHER...
MASDEN
PLAYERS ONLY

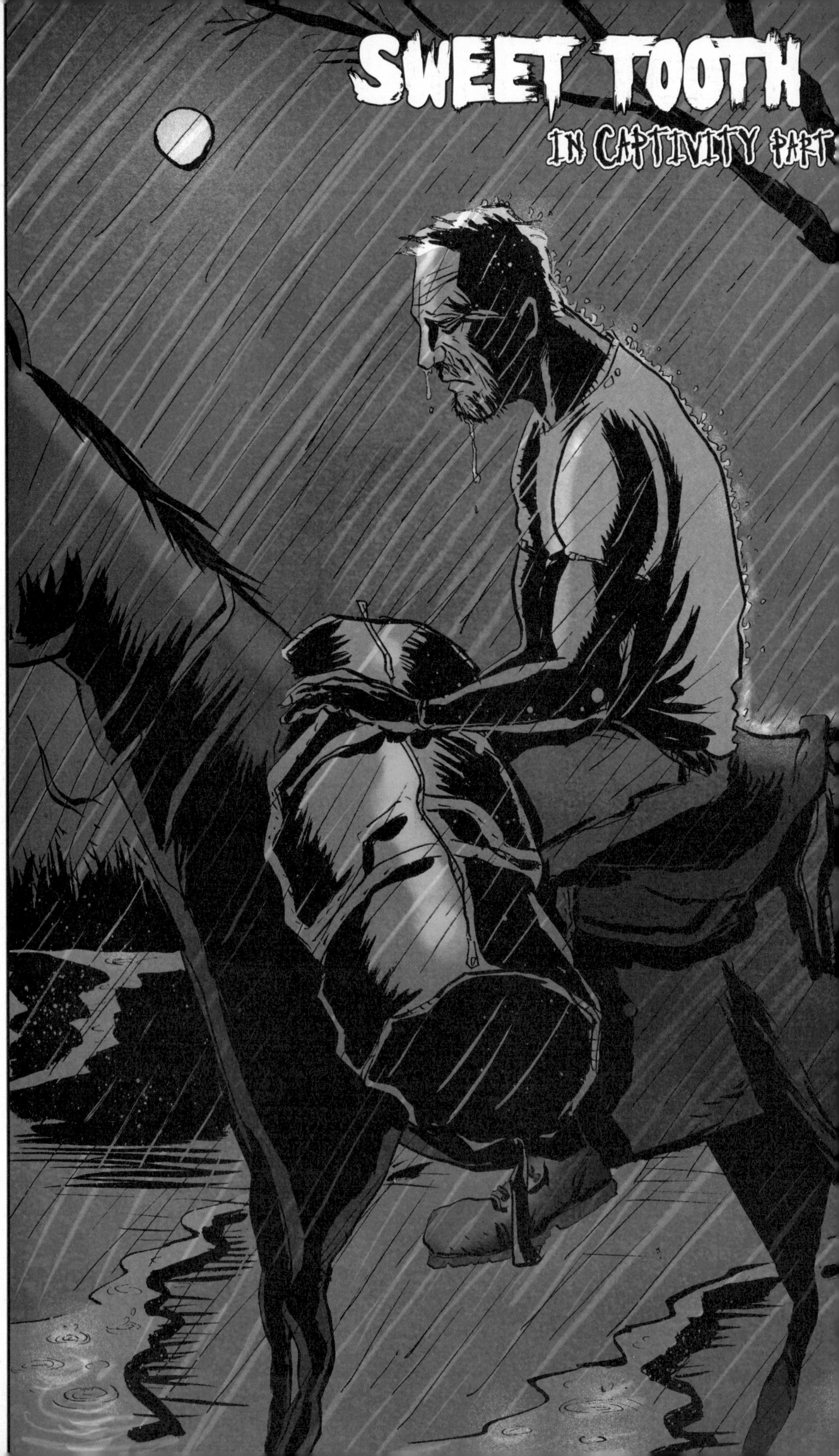
SWEET TOOTH
IN CAPTIVITY PART

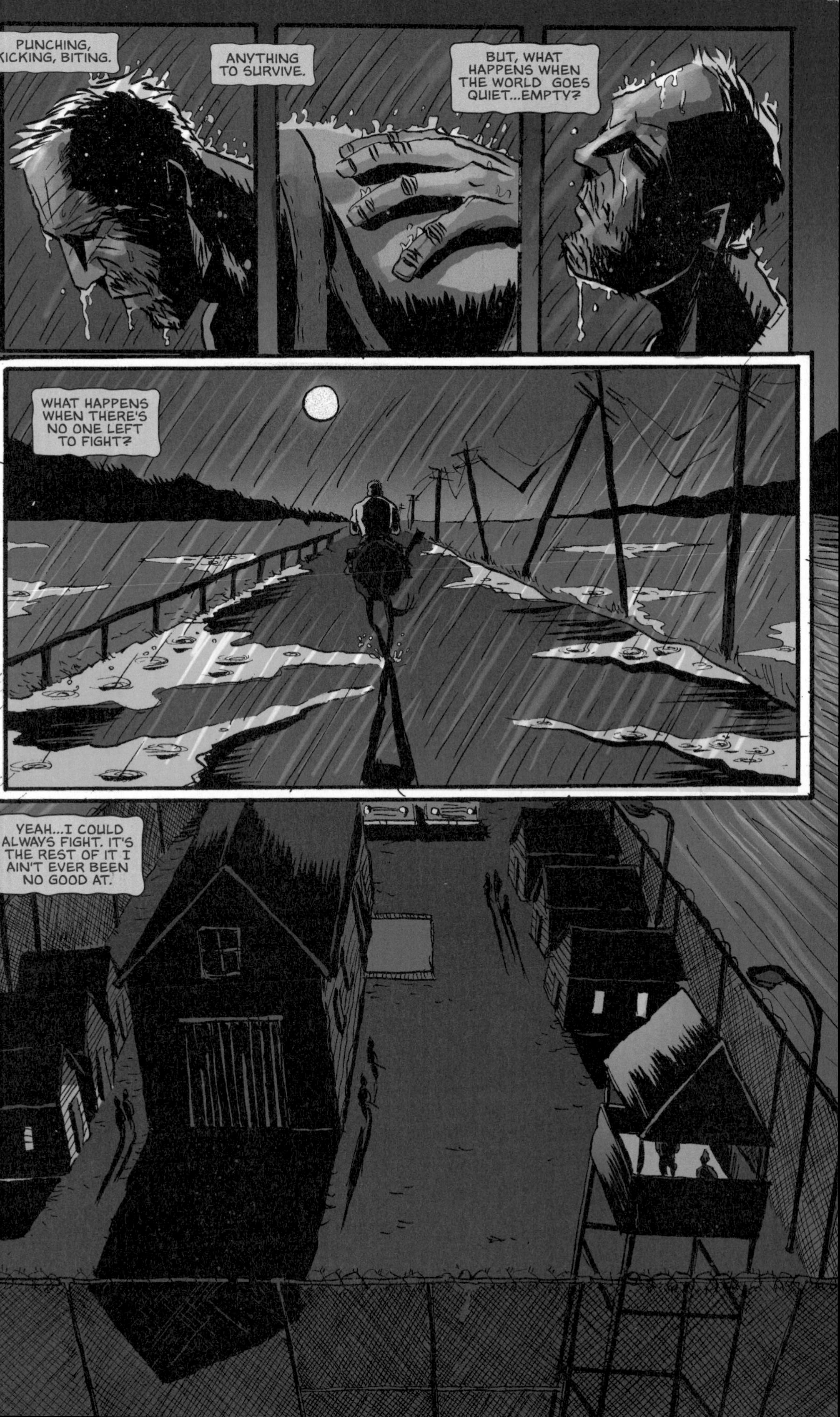
PUNCHING, KICKING, BITING.
ANYTHING TO SURVIVE.
BUT, WHAT HAPPENS WHEN THE WORLD GOES QUIET...EMPTY?
WHAT HAPPENS WHEN THERE'S NO ONE LEFT TO FIGHT?
YEAH...I COULD ALWAYS FIGHT. IT'S THE REST OF IT I AIN'T EVER BEEN NO GOOD AT.

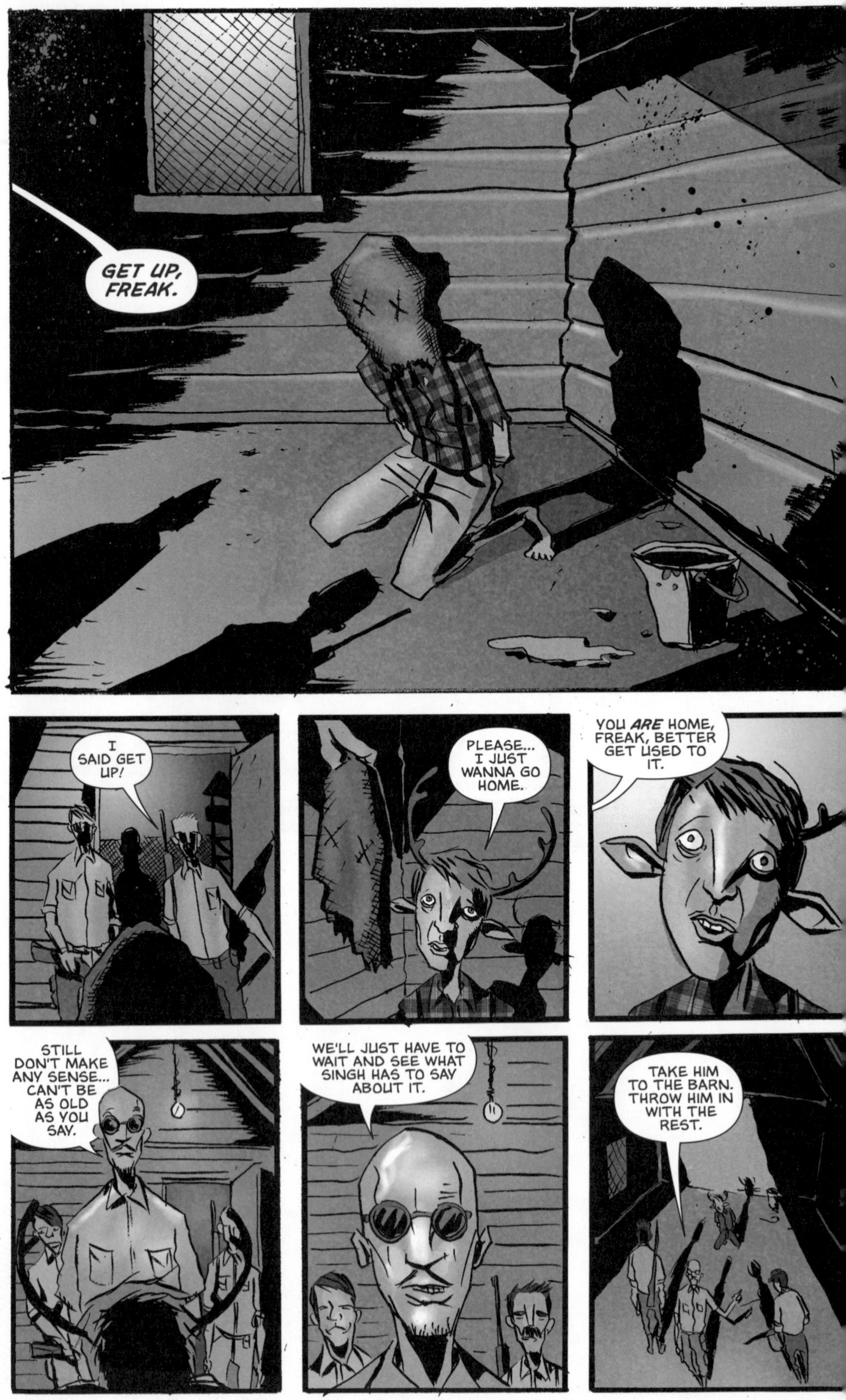
GET UP, FREAK.
I SAID GET UP!
PLEASE... I JUST WANNA GO HOME.
YOU ARE HOME, FREAK, BETTER GET USED TO IT.
STILL DON'T MAKE ANY SENSE... CAN'T BE AS OLD AS YOU SAY.
WE'LL JUST HAVE TO WAIT AND SEE WHAT SINGH HAS TO SAY ABOUT IT.
TAKE HIM TO THE BARN. THROW HIM IN WITH THE REST.

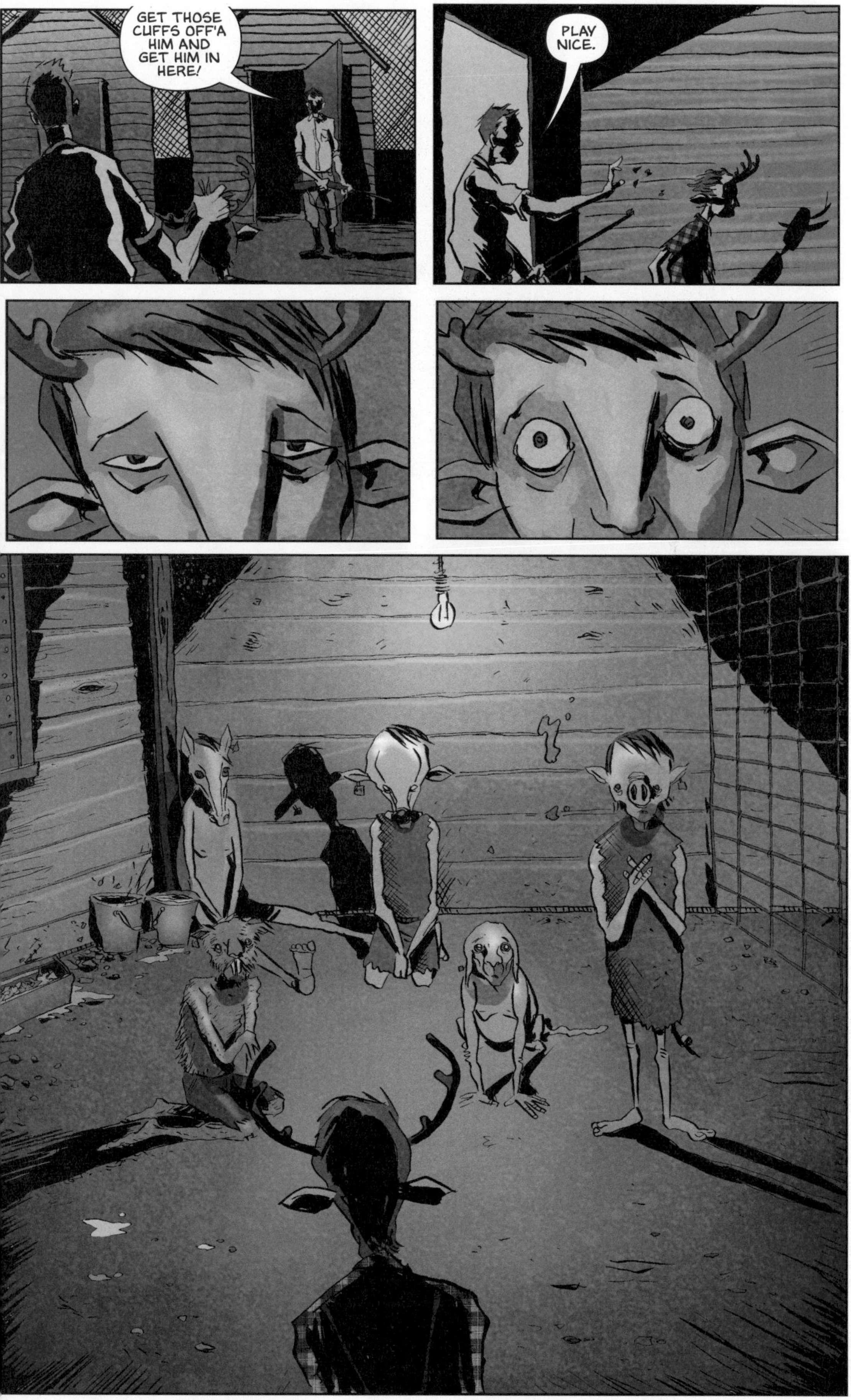
GET THOSE CUFFS OFF'A HIM AND GET HIM IN HERE!
PLAY NICE.

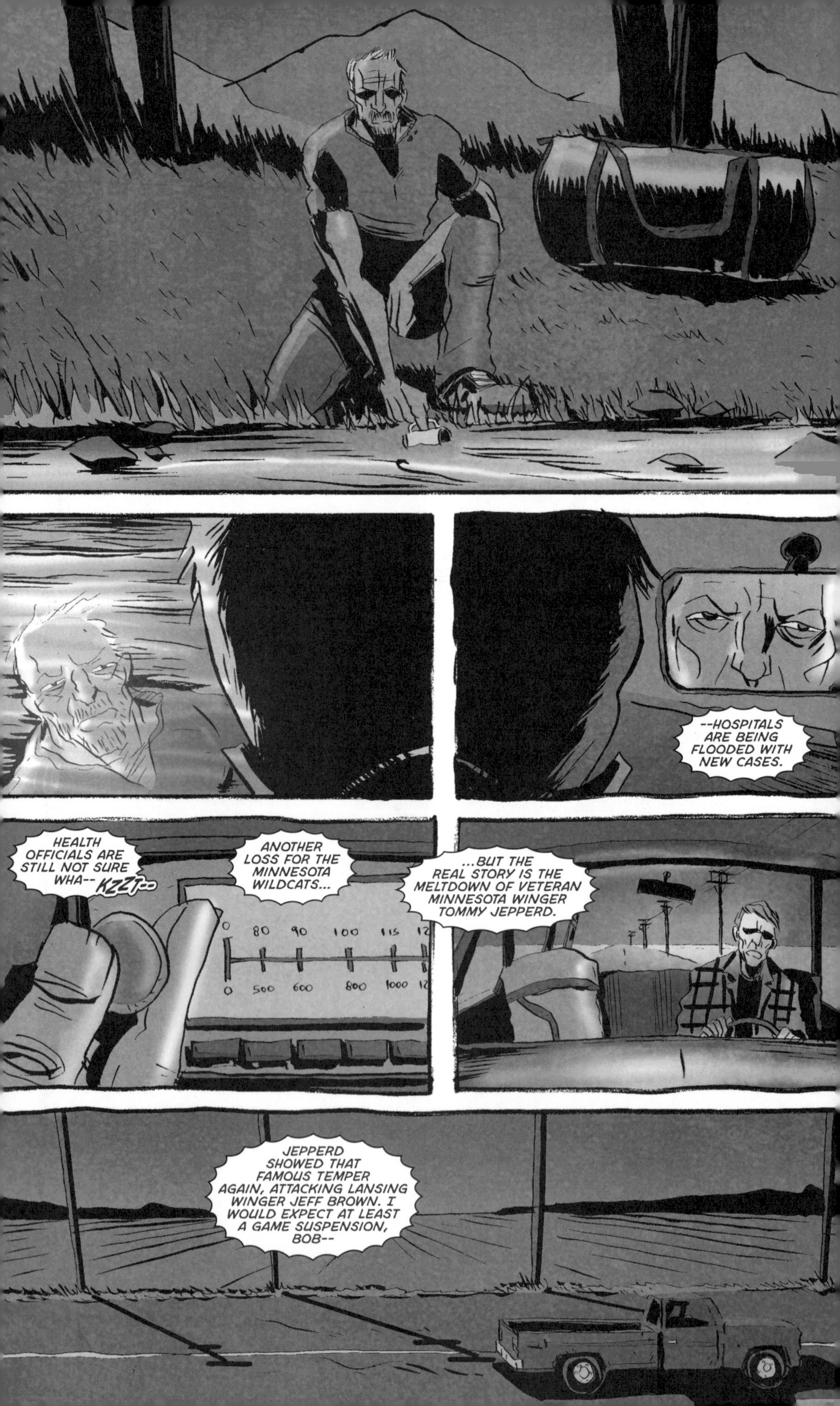
--HOSPITALS ARE BEING FLOODED WITH NEW CASES.
HEALTH OFFICIALS ARE STILL NOT SURE WHA-- KZZT--
0 80 90 100 115 12
0 500 600 800 1000 12
ANOTHER LOSS FOR THE MINNESOTA WILDCATS...
...BUT THE REAL STORY IS THE MELTDOWN OF VETERAN MINNESOTA WINGER TOMMY JEPPERD.
JEPPERD SHOWED THAT FAMOUS TEMPER AGAIN, ATTACKING LANSING WINGER JEFF BROWN. I WOULD EXPECT AT LEAST A GAME SUSPENSION, BOB--

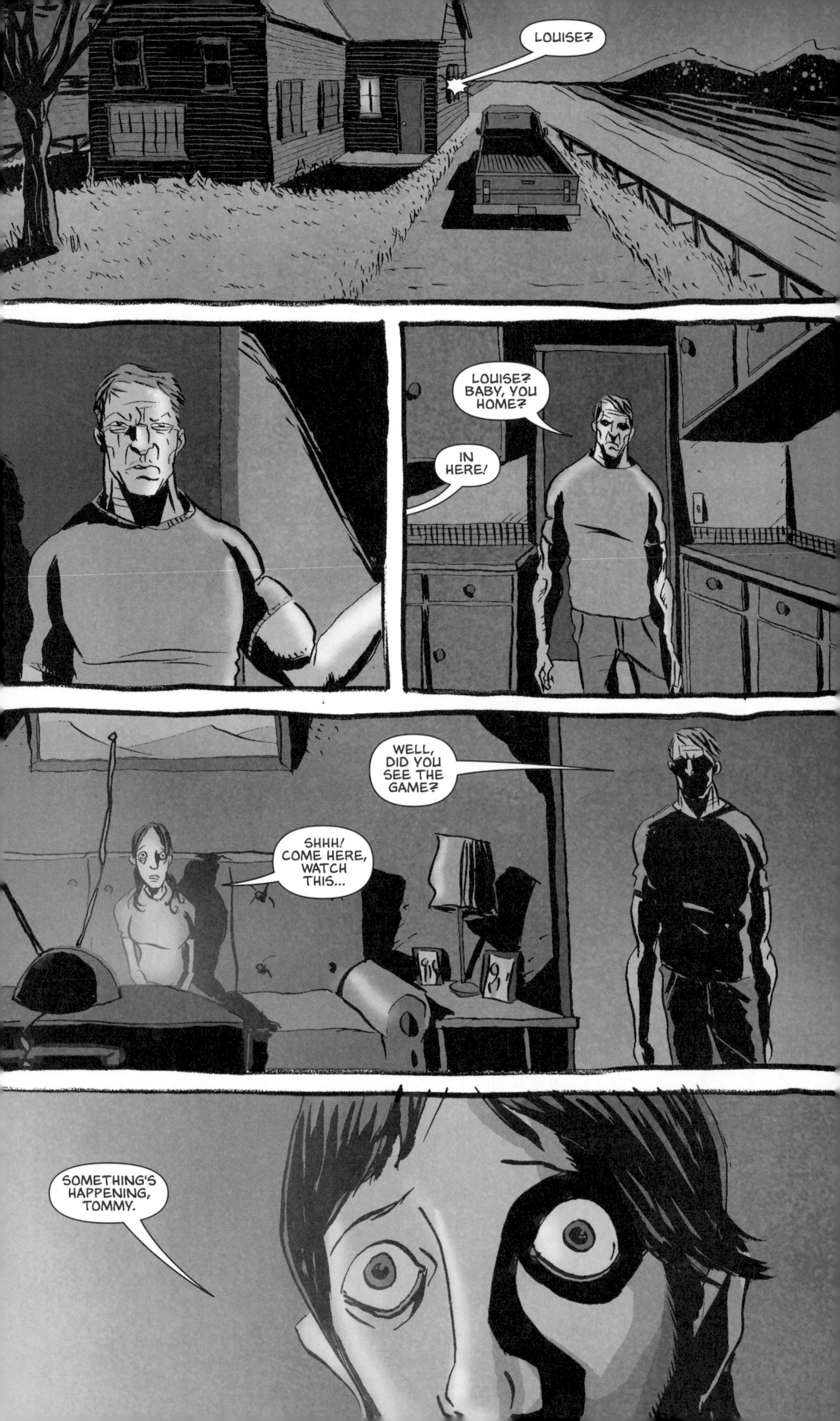
LOUISE?
LOUISE? BABY, YOU HOME?
IN HERE!
WELL, DID YOU SEE THE GAME?
SHHH! COME HERE, WATCH THIS...
SOMETHING'S HAPPENING, TOMMY.

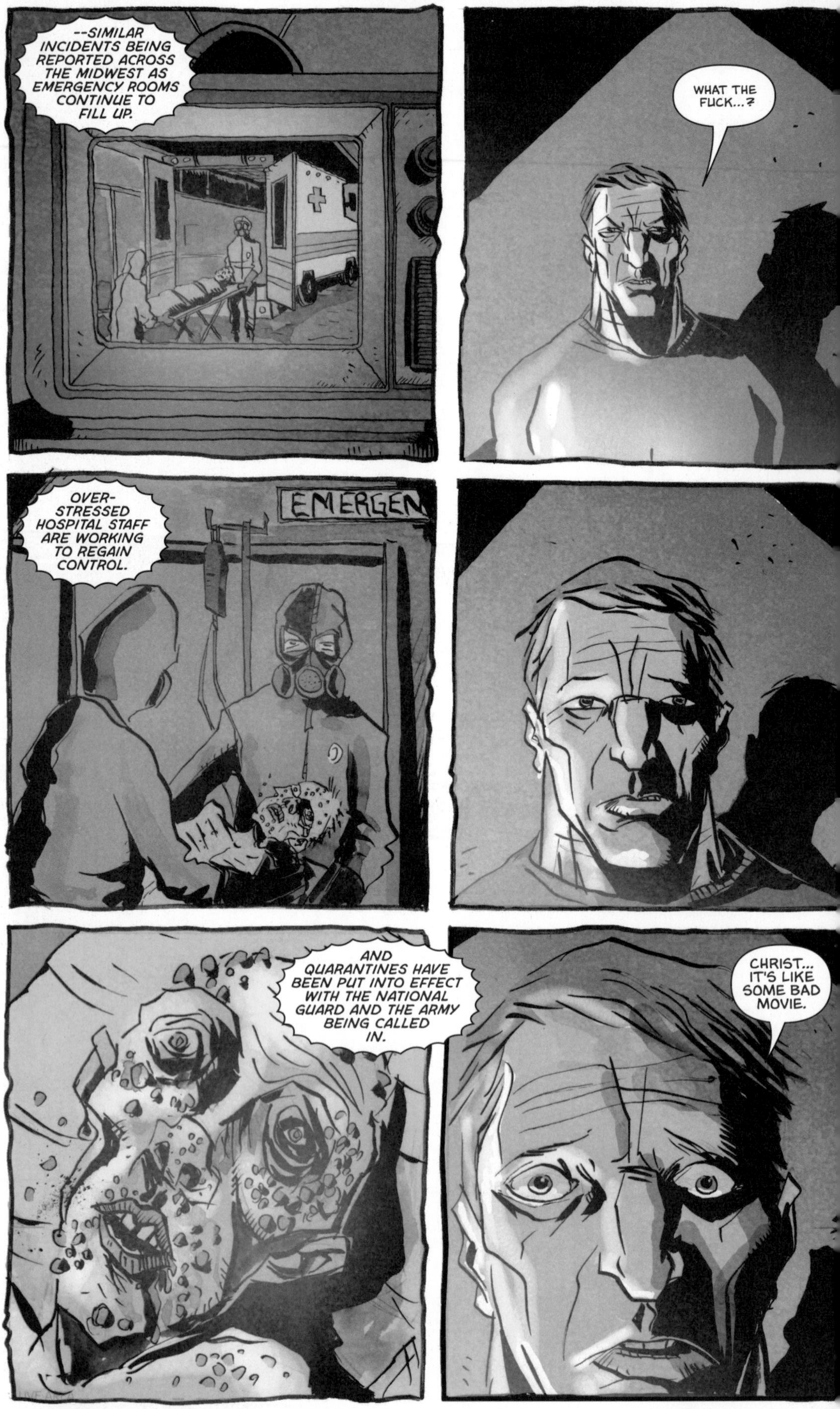
--SIMILAR INCIDENTS BEING REPORTED ACROSS THE MIDWEST AS EMERGENCY ROOMS CONTINUE TO FILL UP.
WHAT THE FUCK...?
EMERGEN
OVER-STRESSED HOSPITAL STAFF ARE WORKING TO REGAIN CONTROL.
AND QUARANTINES HAVE BEEN PUT INTO EFFECT WITH THE NATIONAL GUARD AND THE ARMY BEING CALLED IN.
CHRIST... IT'S LIKE SOME BAD MOVIE.

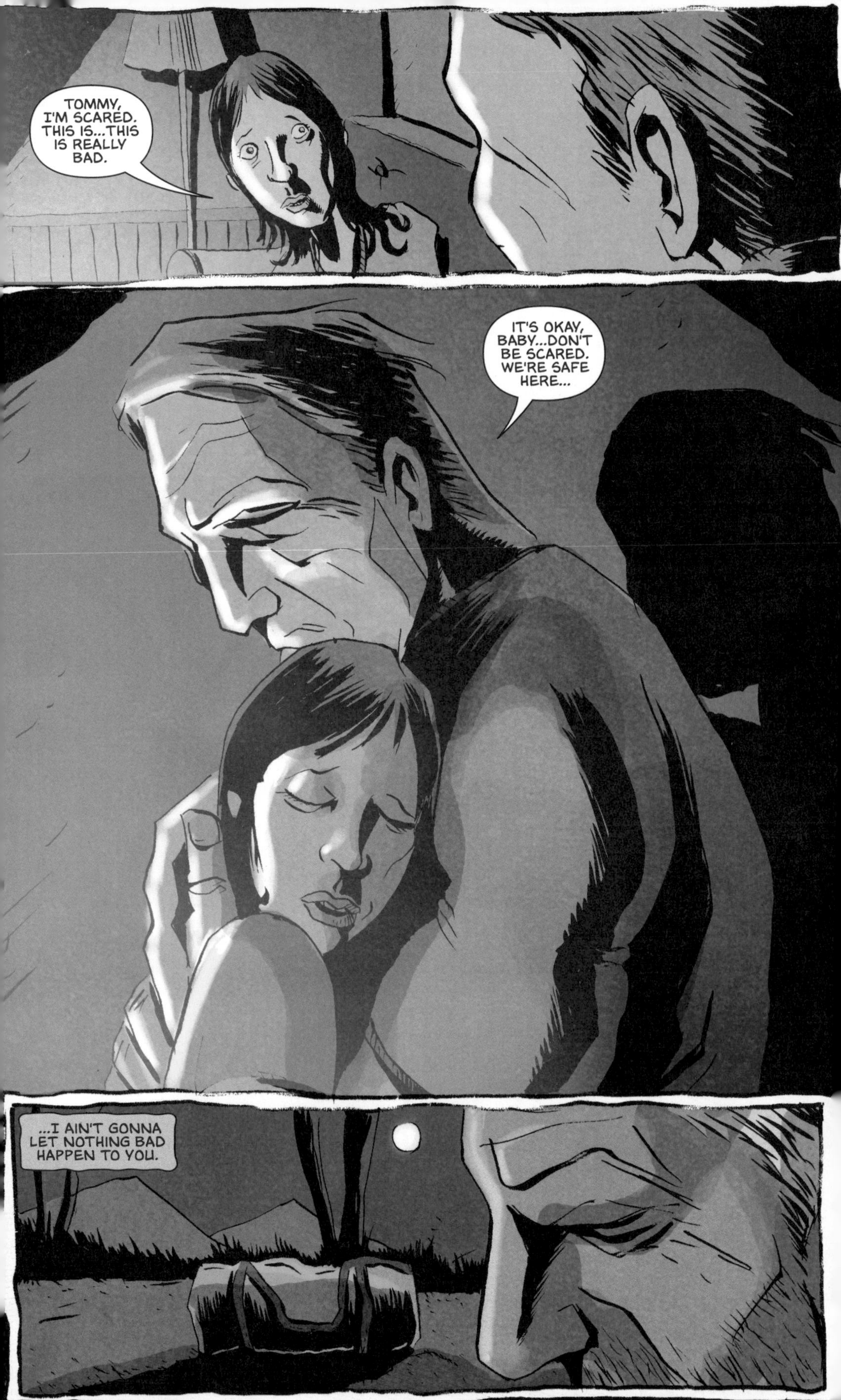
TOMMY, I'M SCARED. THIS IS...THIS IS REALLY BAD.
IT'S OKAY, BABY...DON'T BE SCARED. WE'RE SAFE HERE...
...I AIN'T GONNA LET NOTHING BAD HAPPEN TO YOU.

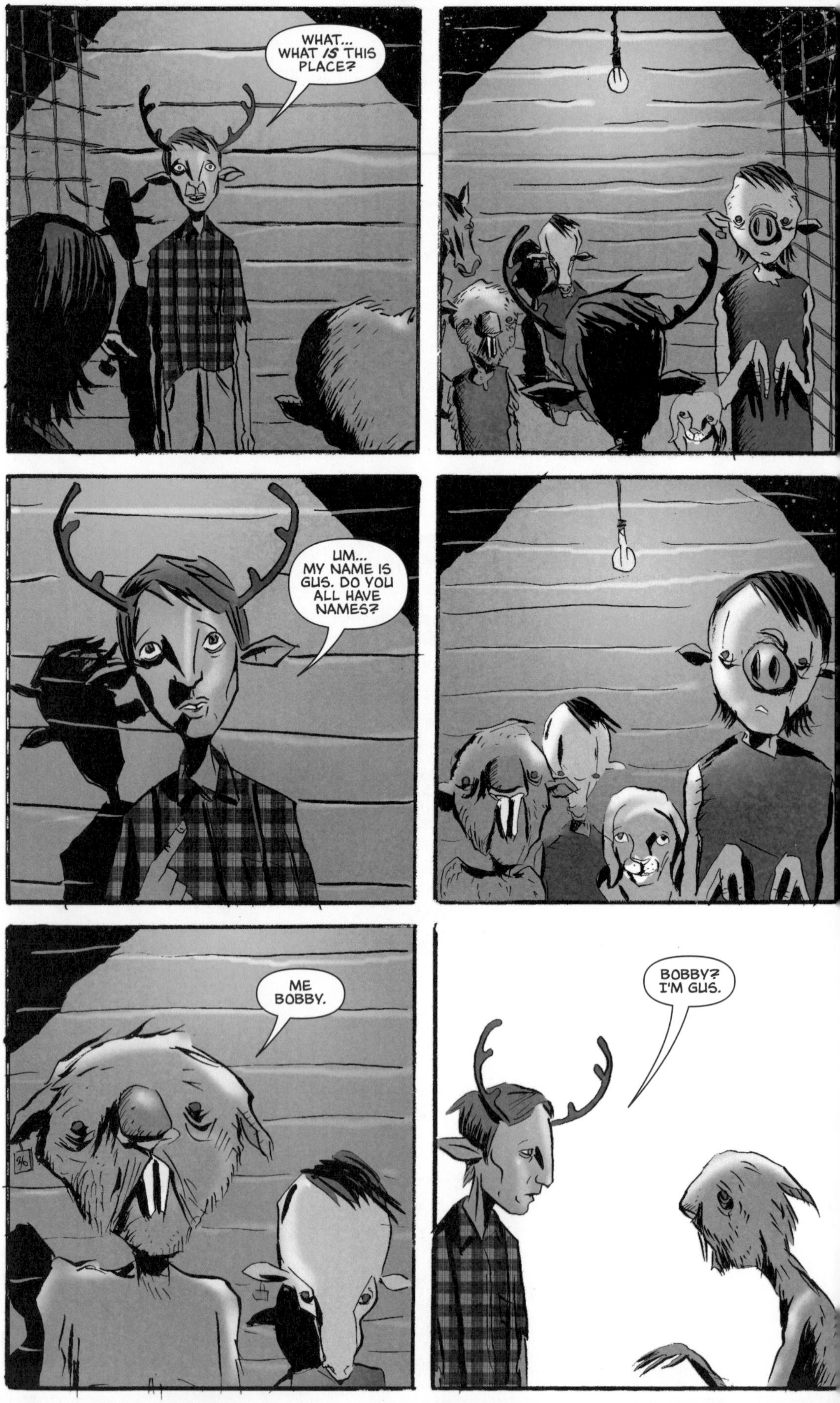
WHAT... WHAT *IS* THIS PLACE?
UM... MY NAME IS GUS. DO YOU ALL HAVE NAMES?
ME BOBBY.
BOBBY? I'M GUS.

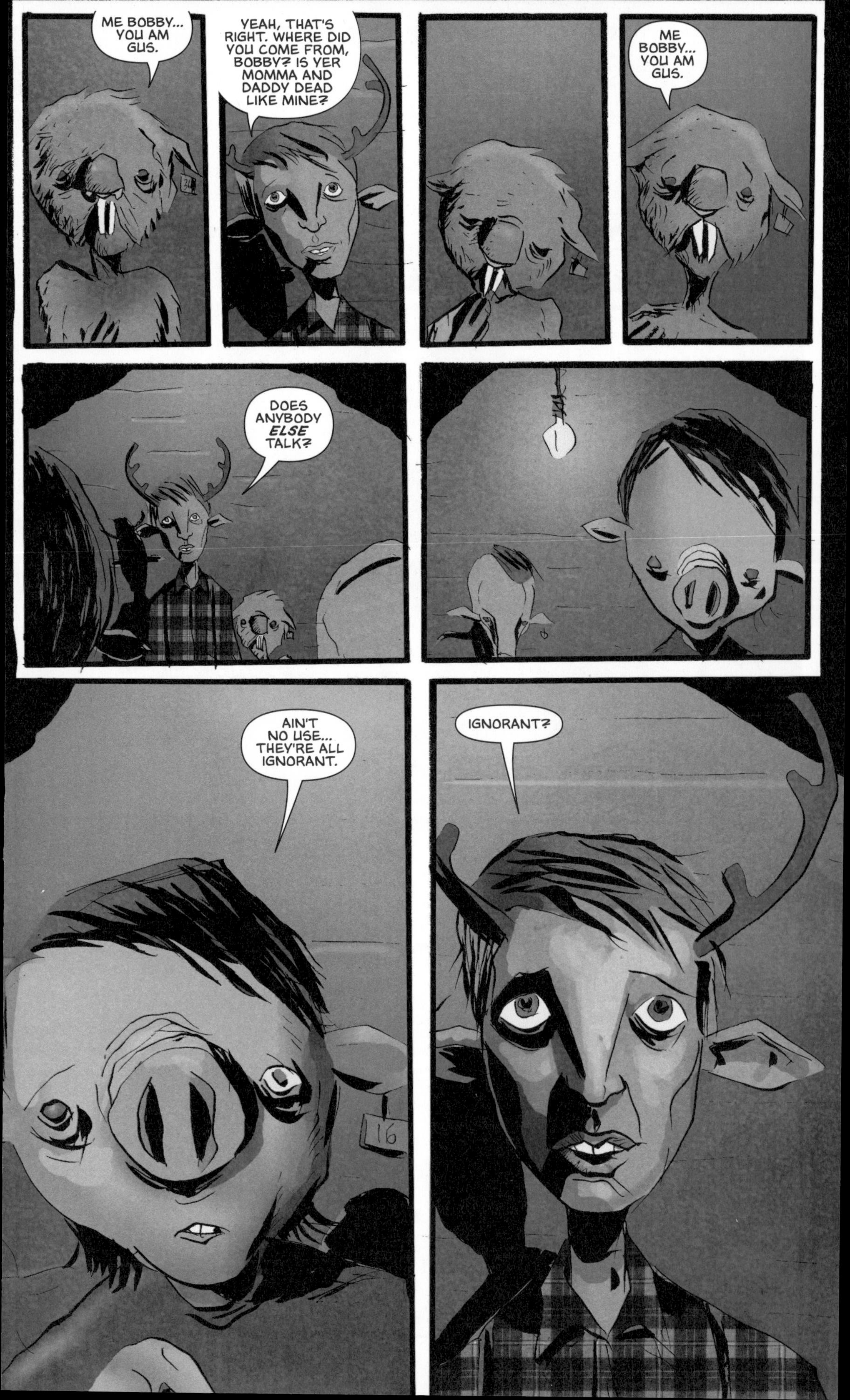
ME BOBBY... YOU AM GUS.
YEAH, THAT'S RIGHT. WHERE DID YOU COME FROM, BOBBY? IS YER MOMMA AND DADDY DEAD LIKE MINE?
ME BOBBY... YOU AM GUS.
DOES ANYBODY *ELSE* TALK?
AIN'T NO USE... THEY'RE ALL IGNORANT.
IGNORANT?

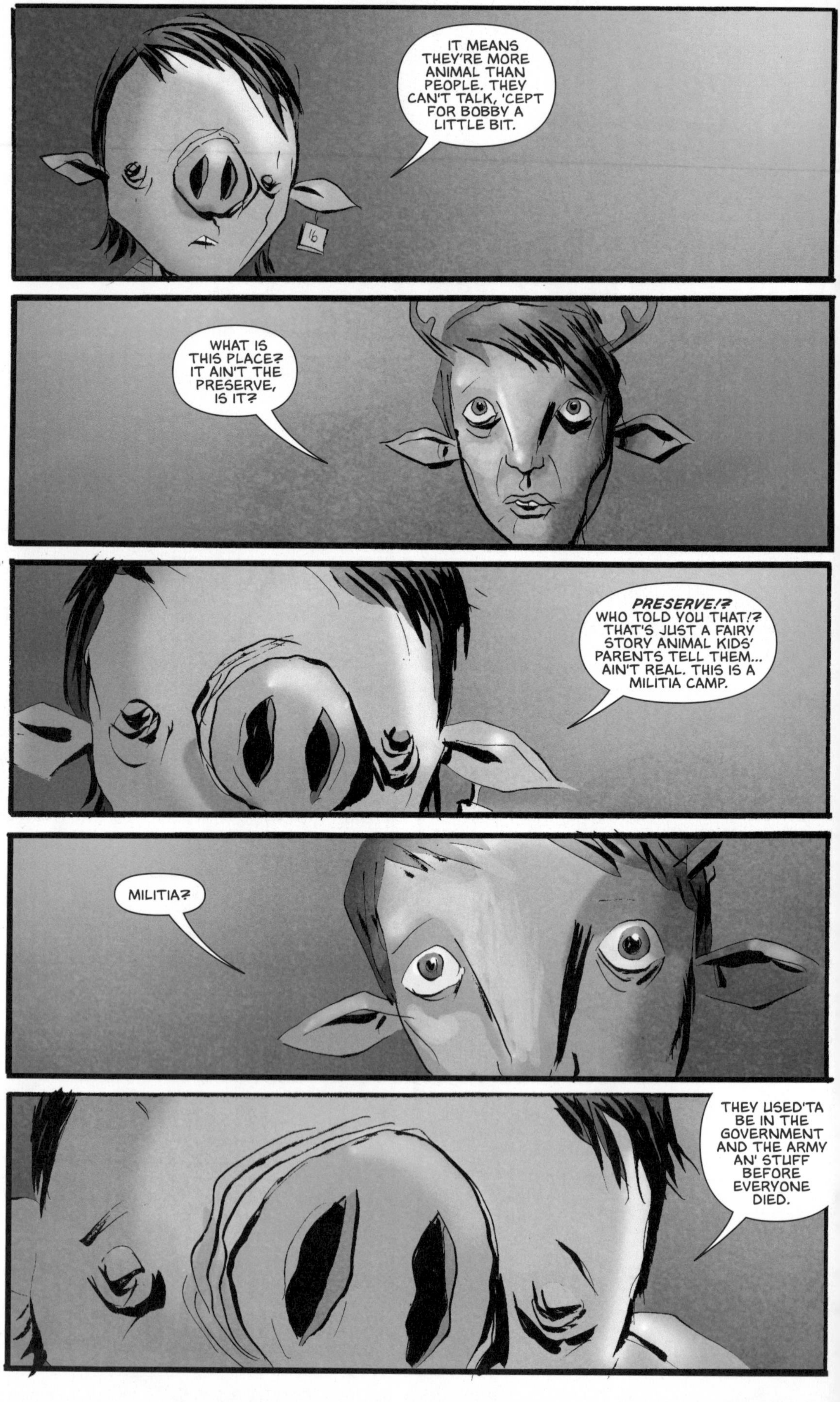
IT MEANS THEY'RE MORE ANIMAL THAN PEOPLE. THEY CAN'T TALK, 'CEPT FOR BOBBY A LITTLE BIT.
16
WHAT IS THIS PLACE? IT AIN'T THE PRESERVE, IS IT?
PRESERVE!? WHO TOLD YOU THAT!? THAT'S JUST A FAIRY STORY ANIMAL KIDS' PARENTS TELL THEM... AIN'T REAL. THIS IS A MILITIA CAMP.
MILITIA?
THEY USED'TA BE IN THE GOVERNMENT AND THE ARMY AN' STUFF BEFORE EVERYONE DIED.

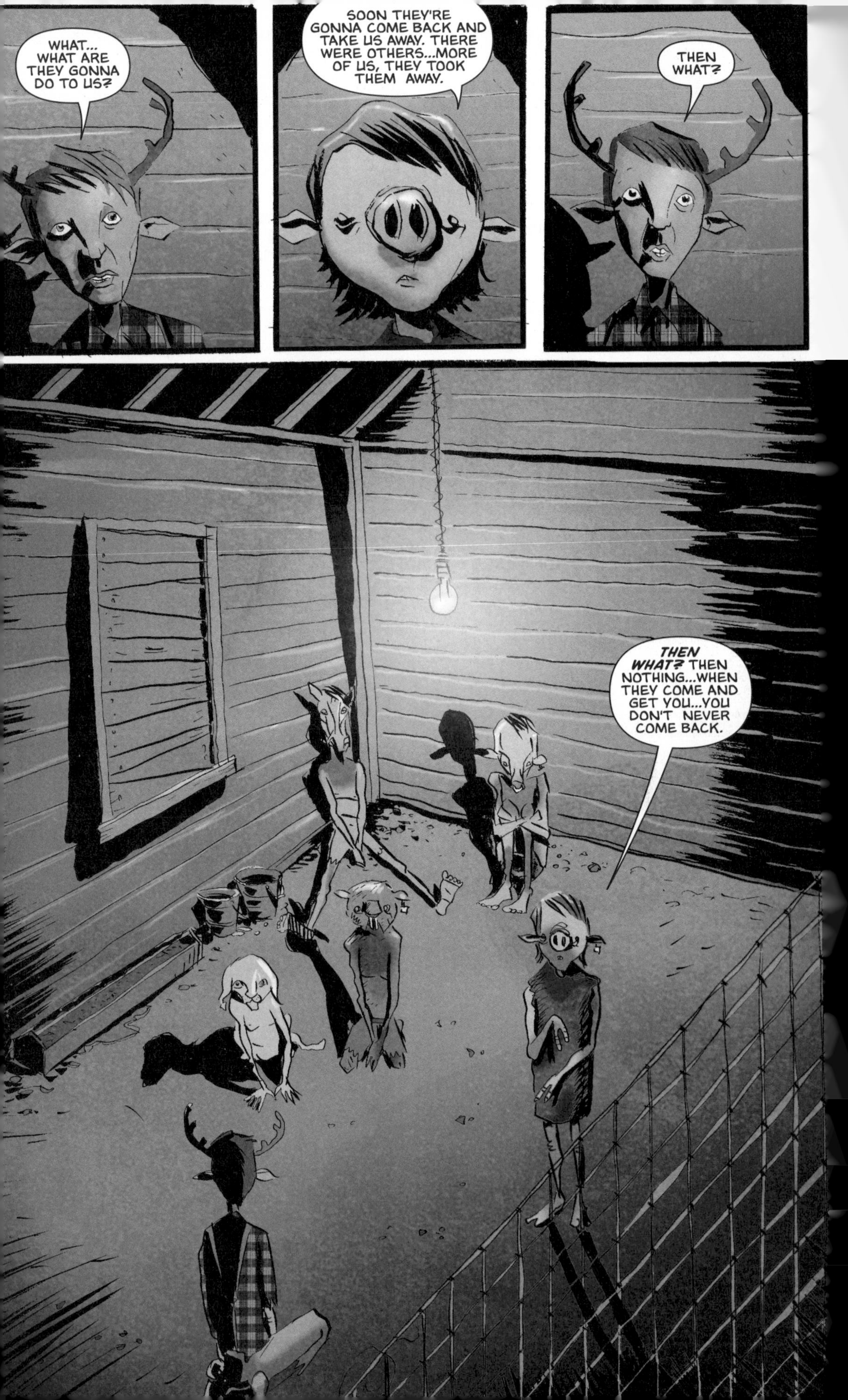
WHAT... WHAT ARE THEY GONNA DO TO US?
SOON THEY'RE GONNA COME BACK AND TAKE US AWAY. THERE WERE OTHERS...MORE OF US, THEY TOOK THEM AWAY.
THEN WHAT?
THEN WHAT? THEN NOTHING...WHEN THEY COME AND GET YOU...YOU DON'T NEVER COME BACK.

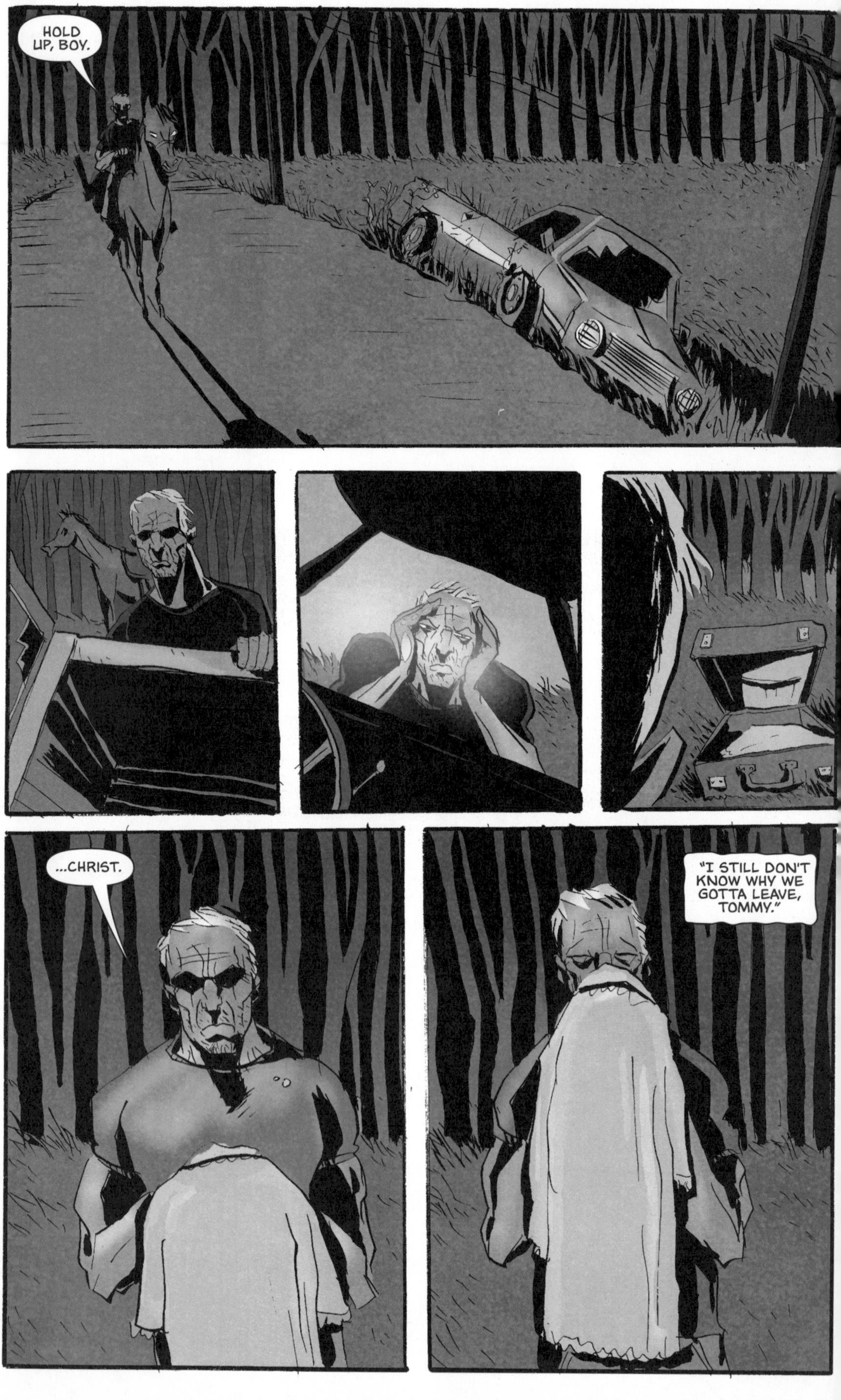
HOLD UP, BOY.
...CHRIST.
"I STILL DON'T KNOW WHY WE GOTTA LEAVE, TOMMY."

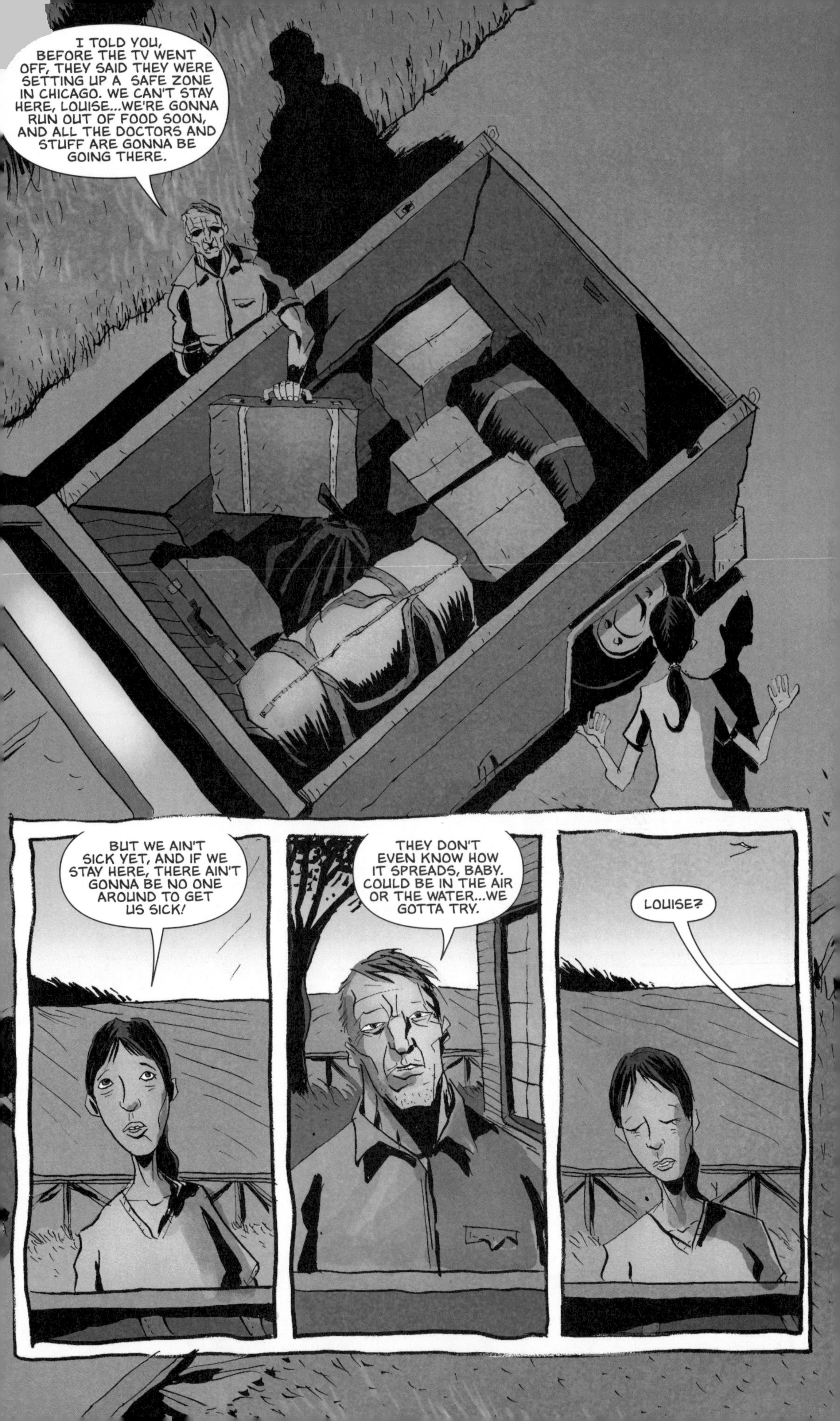
I TOLD YOU, BEFORE THE TV WENT OFF, THEY SAID THEY WERE SETTING UP A SAFE ZONE IN CHICAGO. WE CAN'T STAY HERE, LOUISE...WE'RE GONNA RUN OUT OF FOOD SOON, AND ALL THE DOCTORS AND STUFF ARE GONNA BE GOING THERE.
BUT WE AIN'T SICK YET, AND IF WE STAY HERE, THERE AIN'T GONNA BE NO ONE AROUND TO GET US SICK!
THEY DON'T EVEN KNOW HOW IT SPREADS, BABY. COULD BE IN THE AIR OR THE WATER...WE GOTTA TRY.
LOUISE?

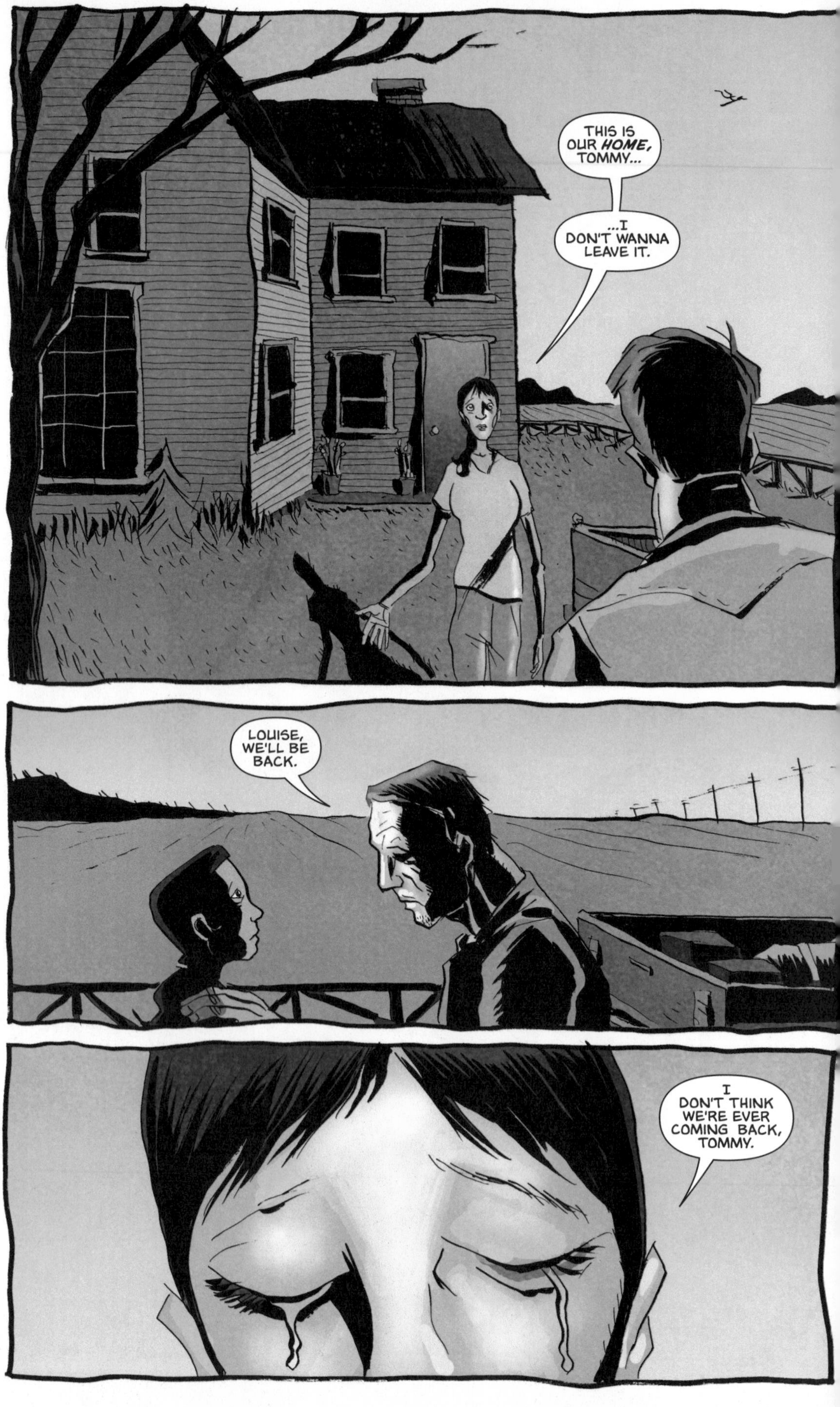
THIS IS OUR *HOME,* TOMMY...
...I DON'T WANNA LEAVE IT.
LOUISE, WE'LL BE BACK.
I DON'T THINK WE'RE EVER COMING BACK, TOMMY.

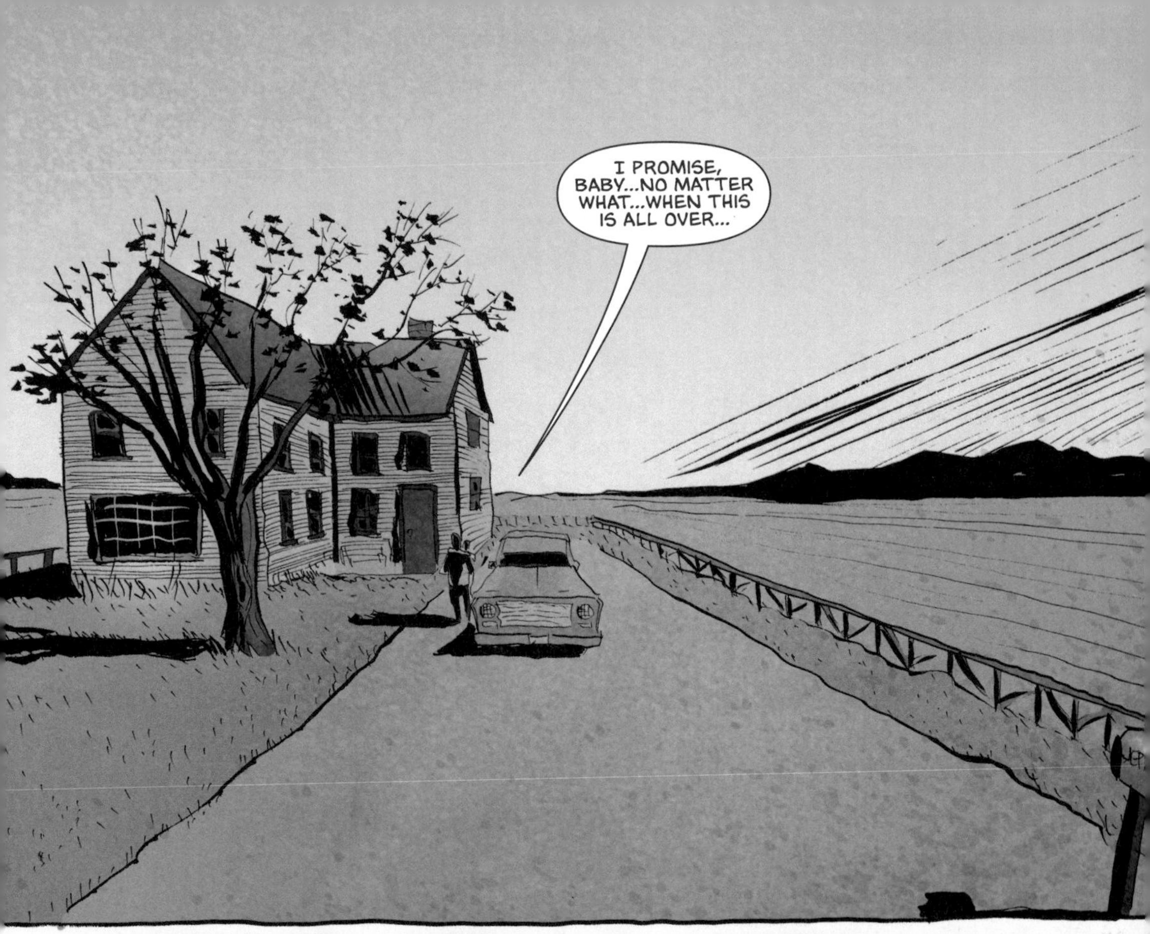
I PROMISE, BABY...NO MATTER WHAT...WHEN THIS IS ALL OVER...
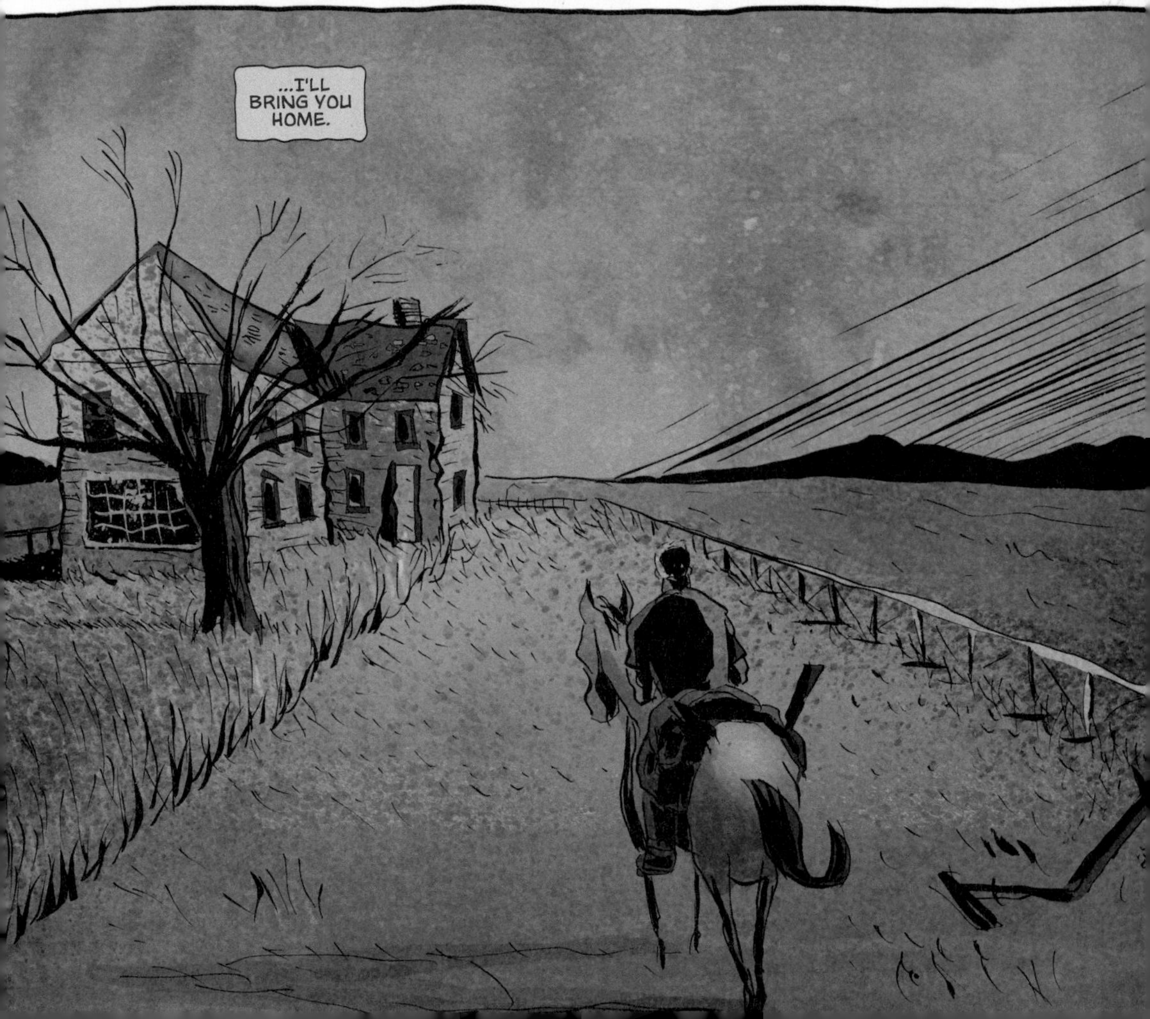
...I'LL BRING YOU HOME.

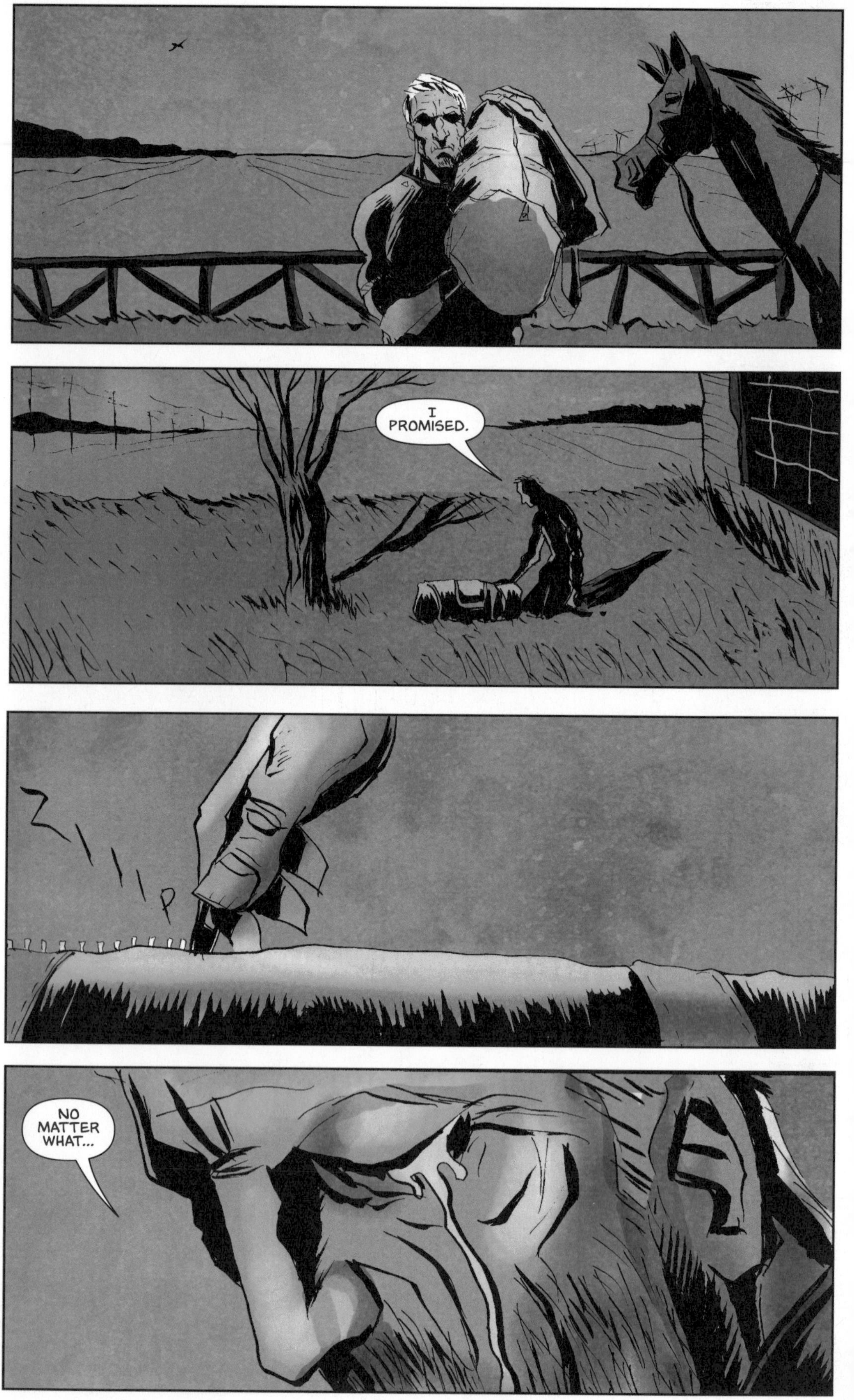
I PROMISED.
ZIIIP
NO MATTER WHAT...

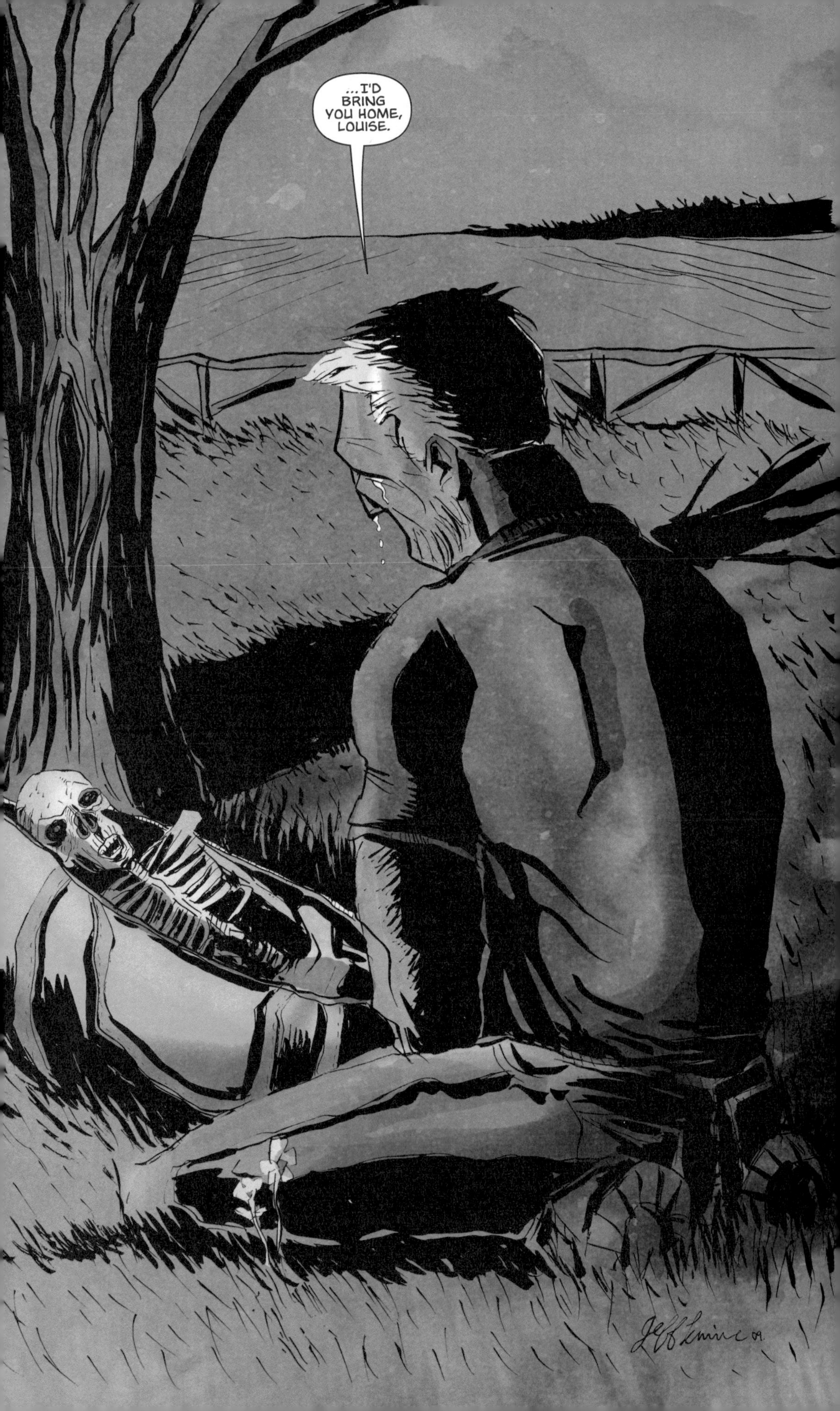
...I'D BRING YOU HOME, LOUISE.
Jeff Lemire 09.

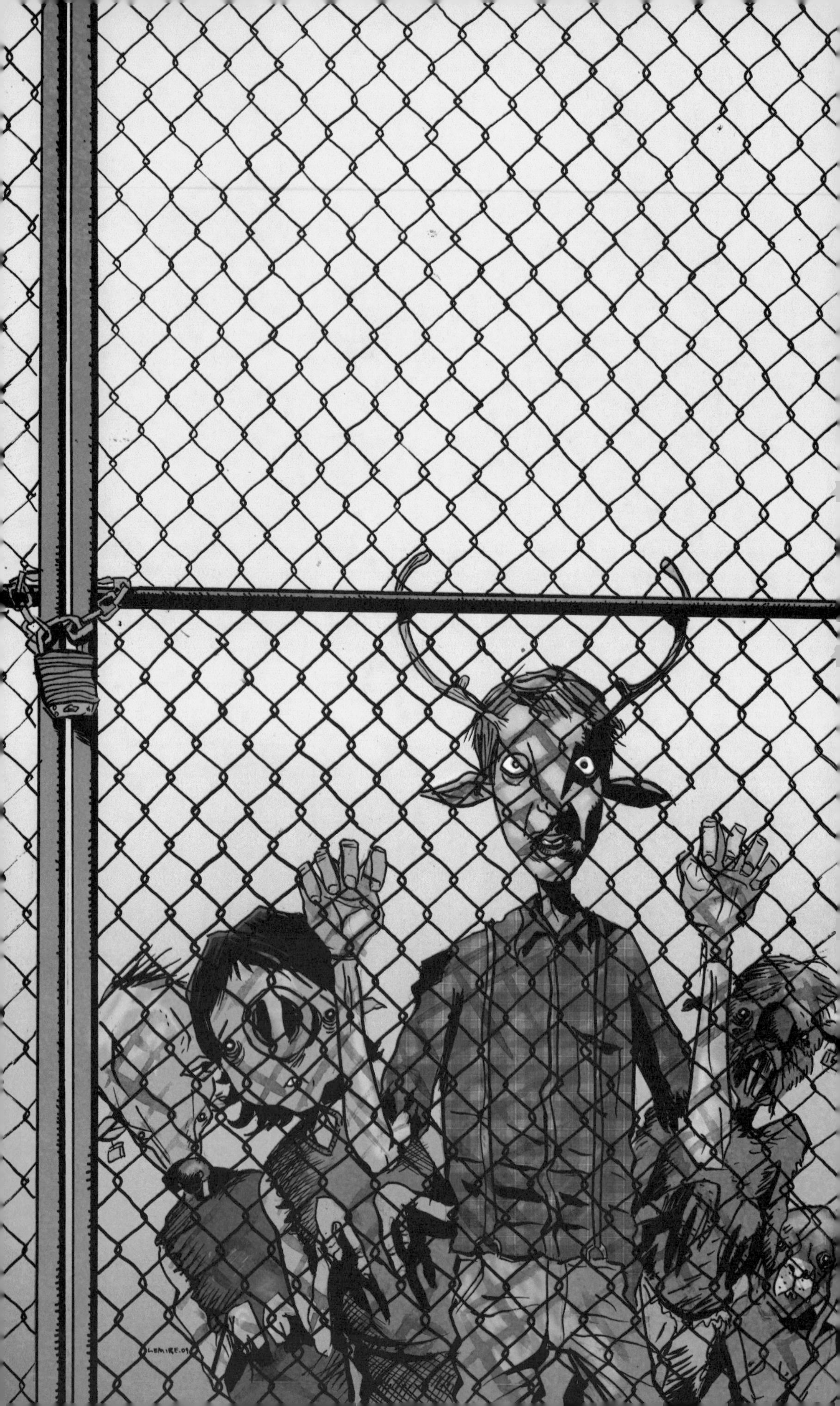
LEMIRE.09

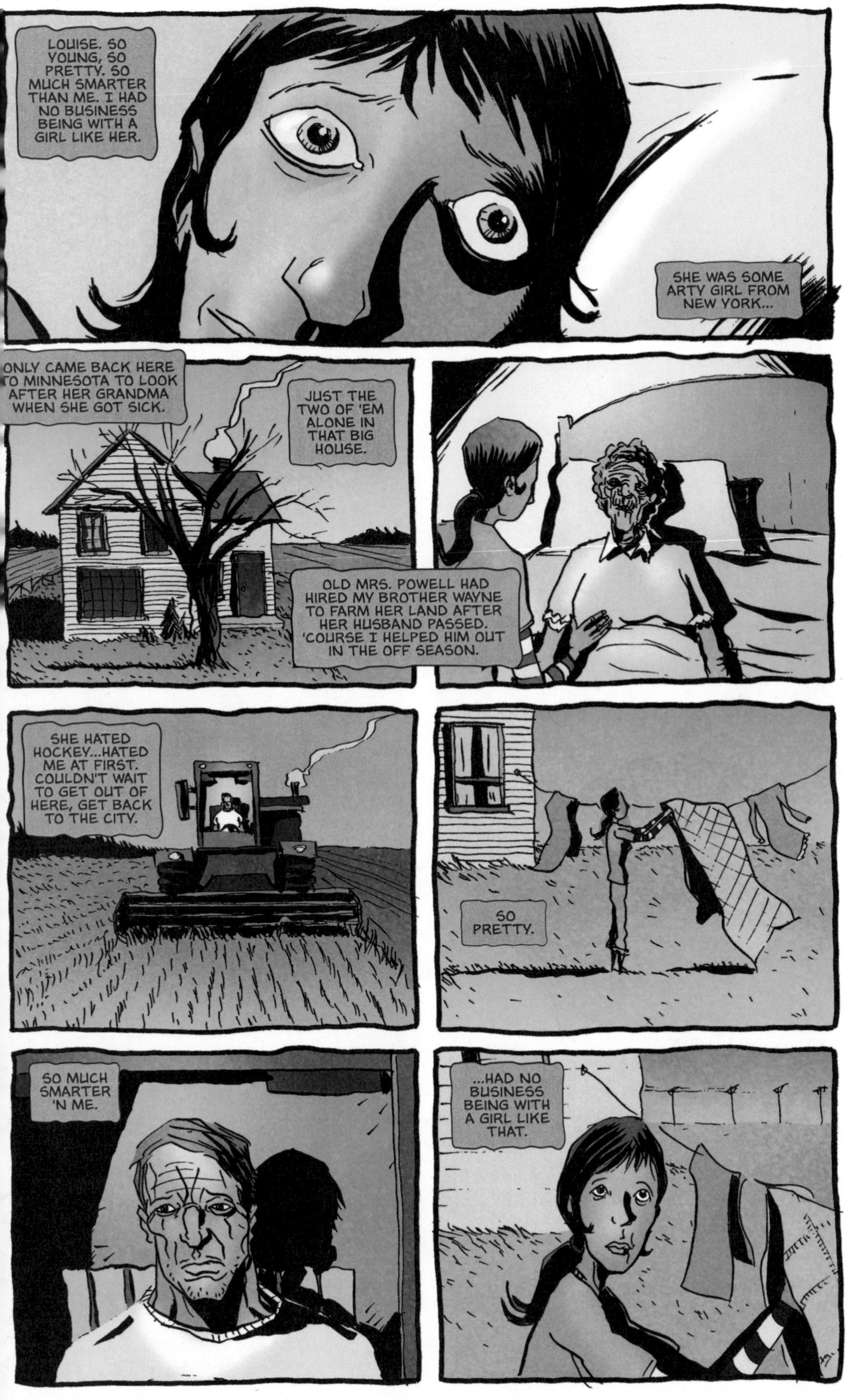
LOUISE. SO YOUNG, SO PRETTY. SO MUCH SMARTER THAN ME. I HAD NO BUSINESS BEING WITH A GIRL LIKE HER.
SHE WAS SOME ARTY GIRL FROM NEW YORK...
ONLY CAME BACK HERE TO MINNESOTA TO LOOK AFTER HER GRANDMA WHEN SHE GOT SICK.
JUST THE TWO OF 'EM ALONE IN THAT BIG HOUSE.
OLD MRS. POWELL HAD HIRED MY BROTHER WAYNE TO FARM HER LAND AFTER HER HUSBAND PASSED. 'COURSE I HELPED HIM OUT IN THE OFF SEASON.
SHE HATED HOCKEY...HATED ME AT FIRST. COULDN'T WAIT TO GET OUT OF HERE, GET BACK TO THE CITY.
SO PRETTY.
SO MUCH SMARTER 'N ME.
...HAD NO BUSINESS BEING WITH A GIRL LIKE THAT.

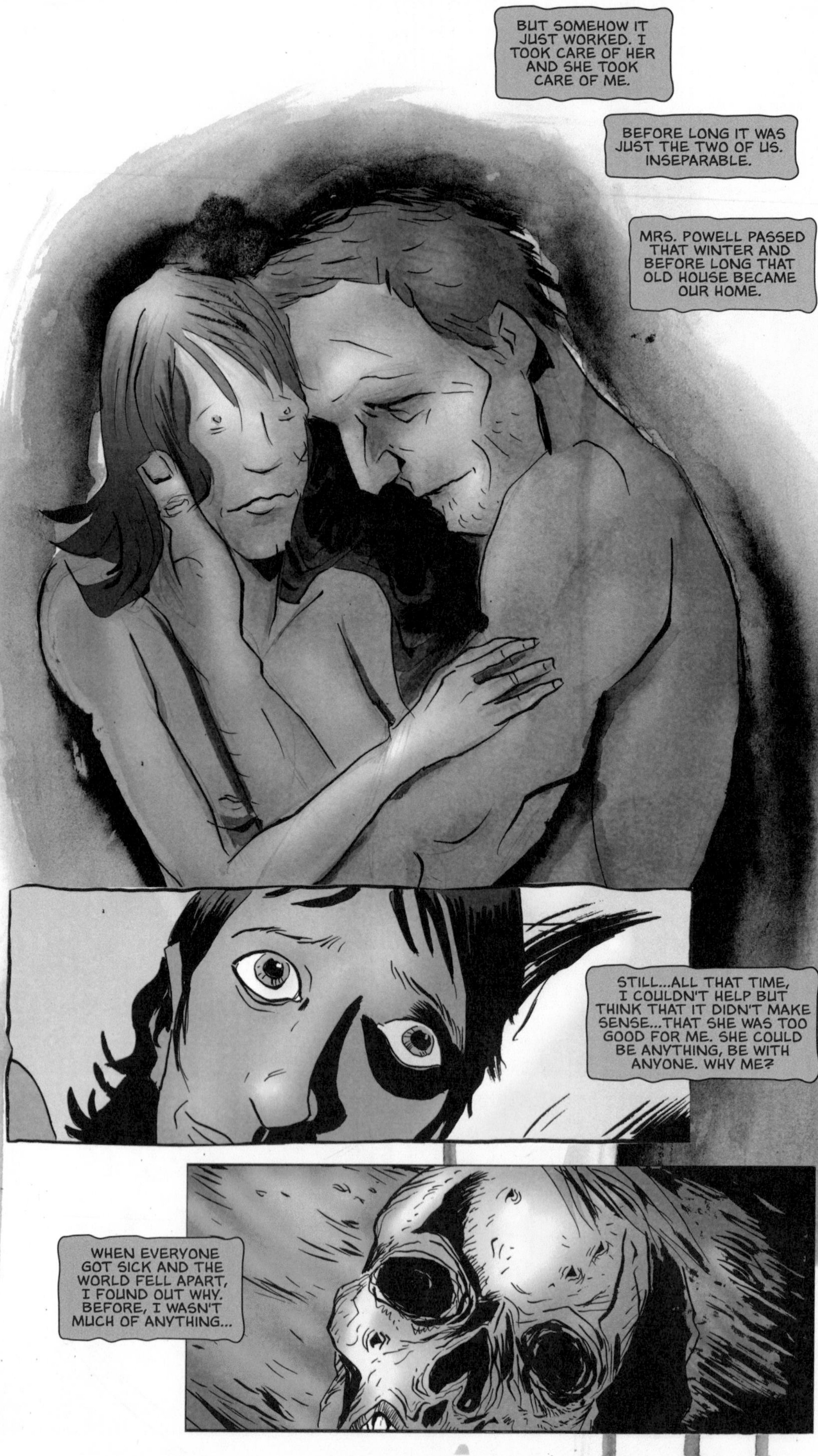
BUT SOMEHOW IT JUST WORKED. I TOOK CARE OF HER AND SHE TOOK CARE OF ME.
BEFORE LONG IT WAS JUST THE TWO OF US. INSEPARABLE.
MRS. POWELL PASSED THAT WINTER AND BEFORE LONG THAT OLD HOUSE BECAME OUR HOME.
STILL...ALL THAT TIME, I COULDN'T HELP BUT THINK THAT IT DIDN'T MAKE SENSE...THAT SHE WAS TOO GOOD FOR ME. SHE COULD BE ANYTHING, BE WITH ANYONE. WHY ME?
WHEN EVERYONE GOT SICK AND THE WORLD FELL APART, I FOUND OUT WHY. BEFORE, I WASN'T MUCH OF ANYTHING...

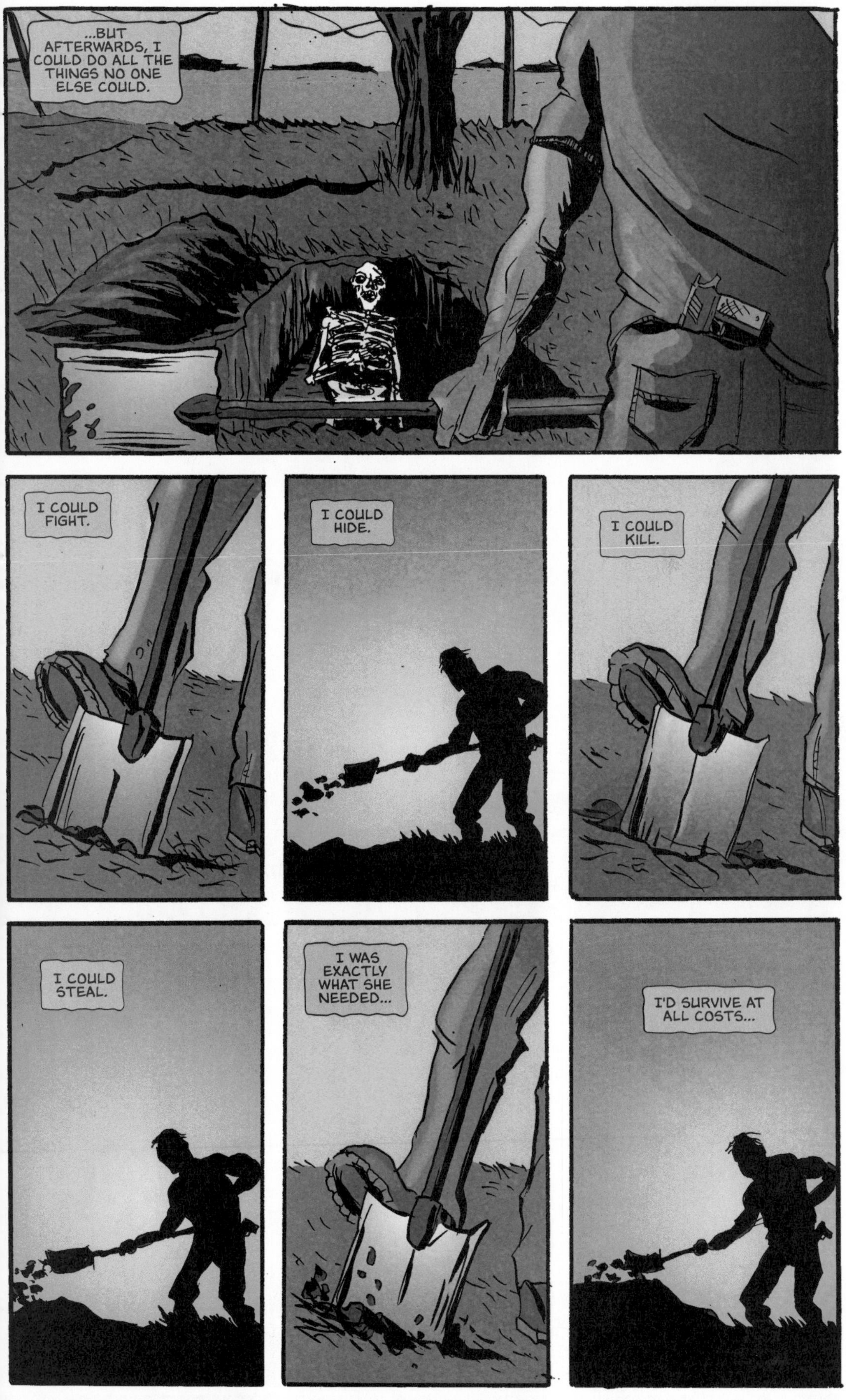
...BUT AFTERWARDS, I COULD DO ALL THE THINGS NO ONE ELSE COULD.
I COULD FIGHT.
I COULD HIDE.
I COULD KILL.
I COULD STEAL.
I WAS EXACTLY WHAT SHE NEEDED...
I'D SURVIVE AT ALL COSTS...

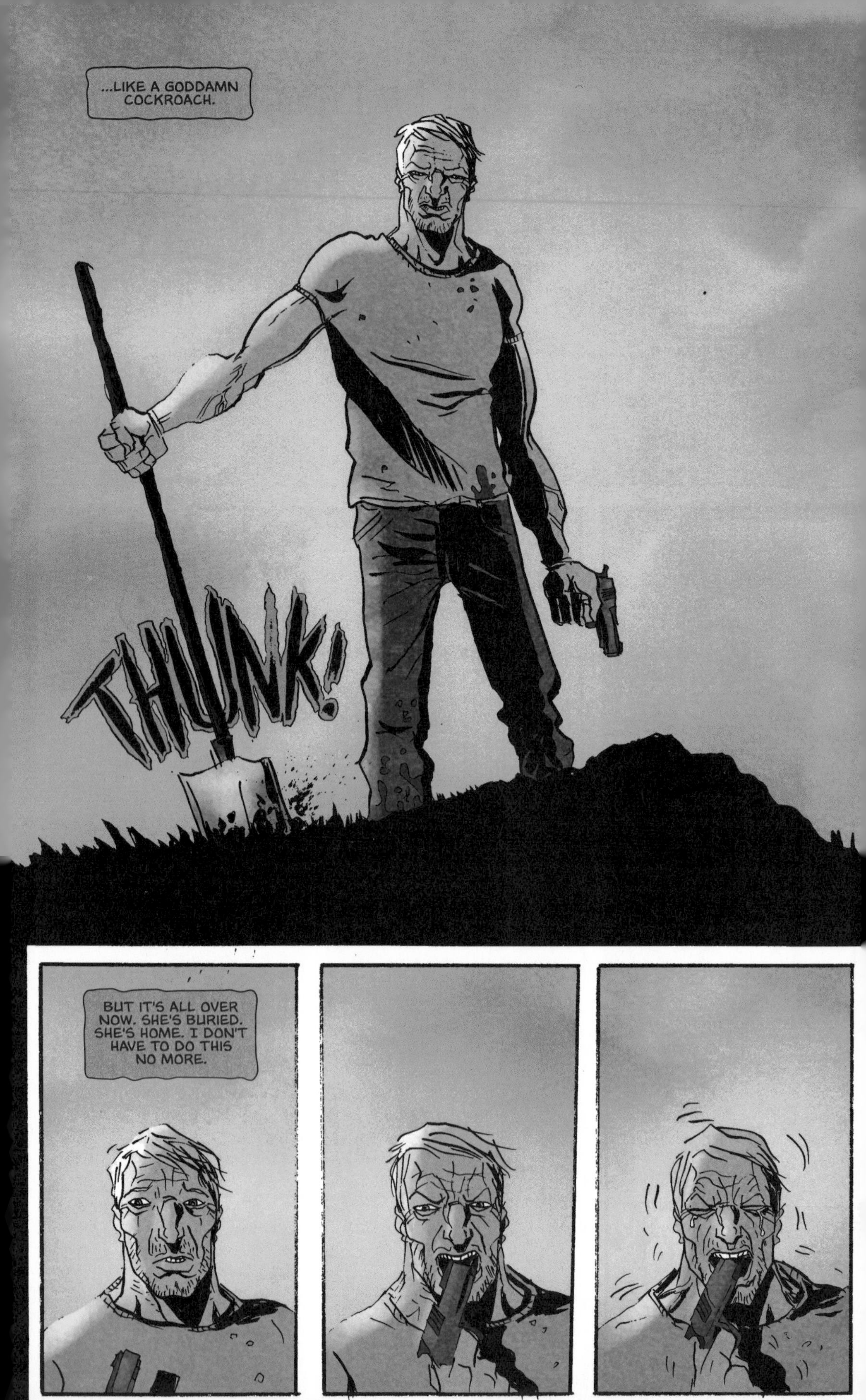
...LIKE A GODDAMN COCKROACH.
THUNK!
BUT IT'S ALL OVER NOW. SHE'S BURIED. SHE'S HOME. I DON'T HAVE TO DO THIS NO MORE.

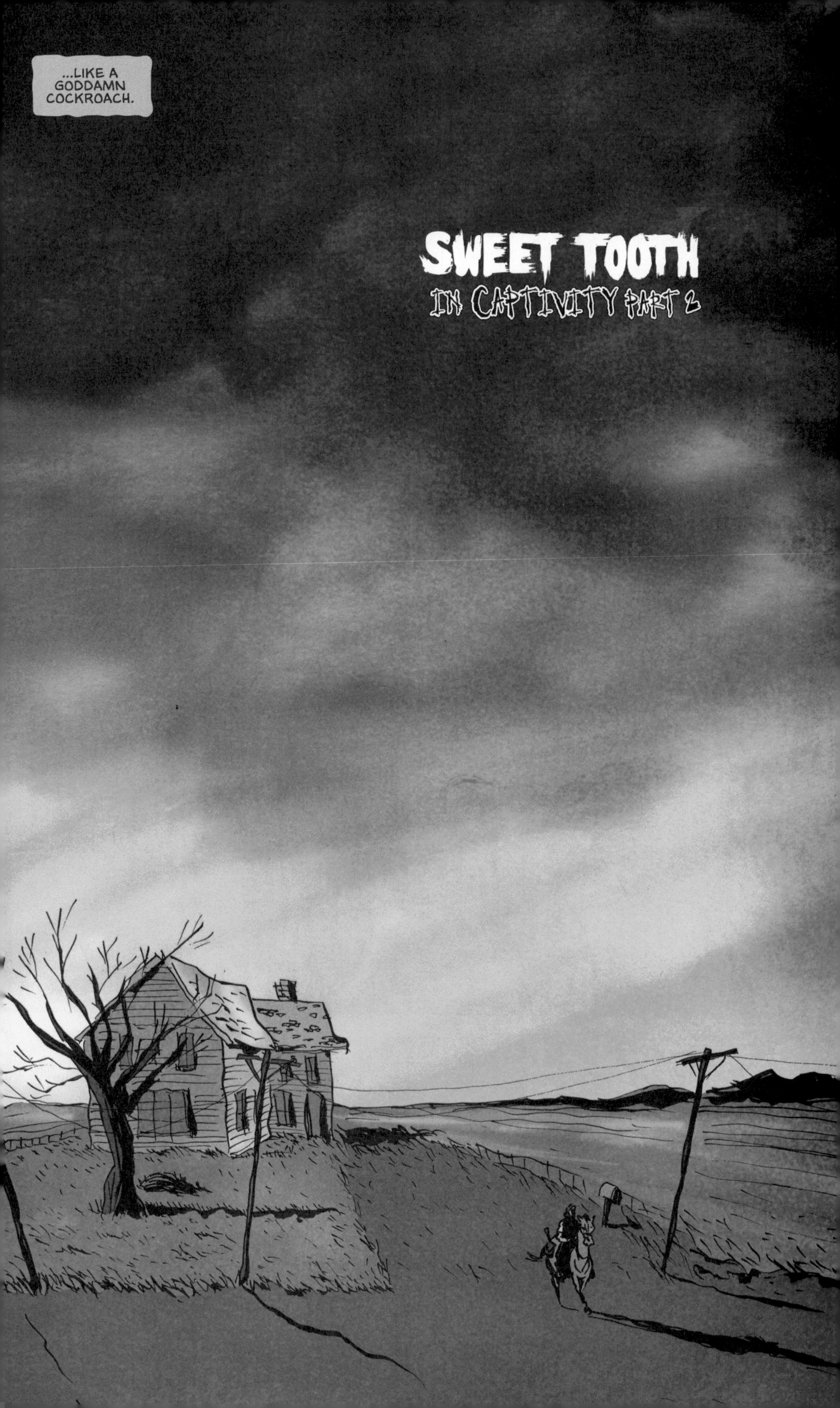
...LIKE A GODDAMN COCKROACH.
SWEET TOOTH
IN CAPTIVITY PART 2

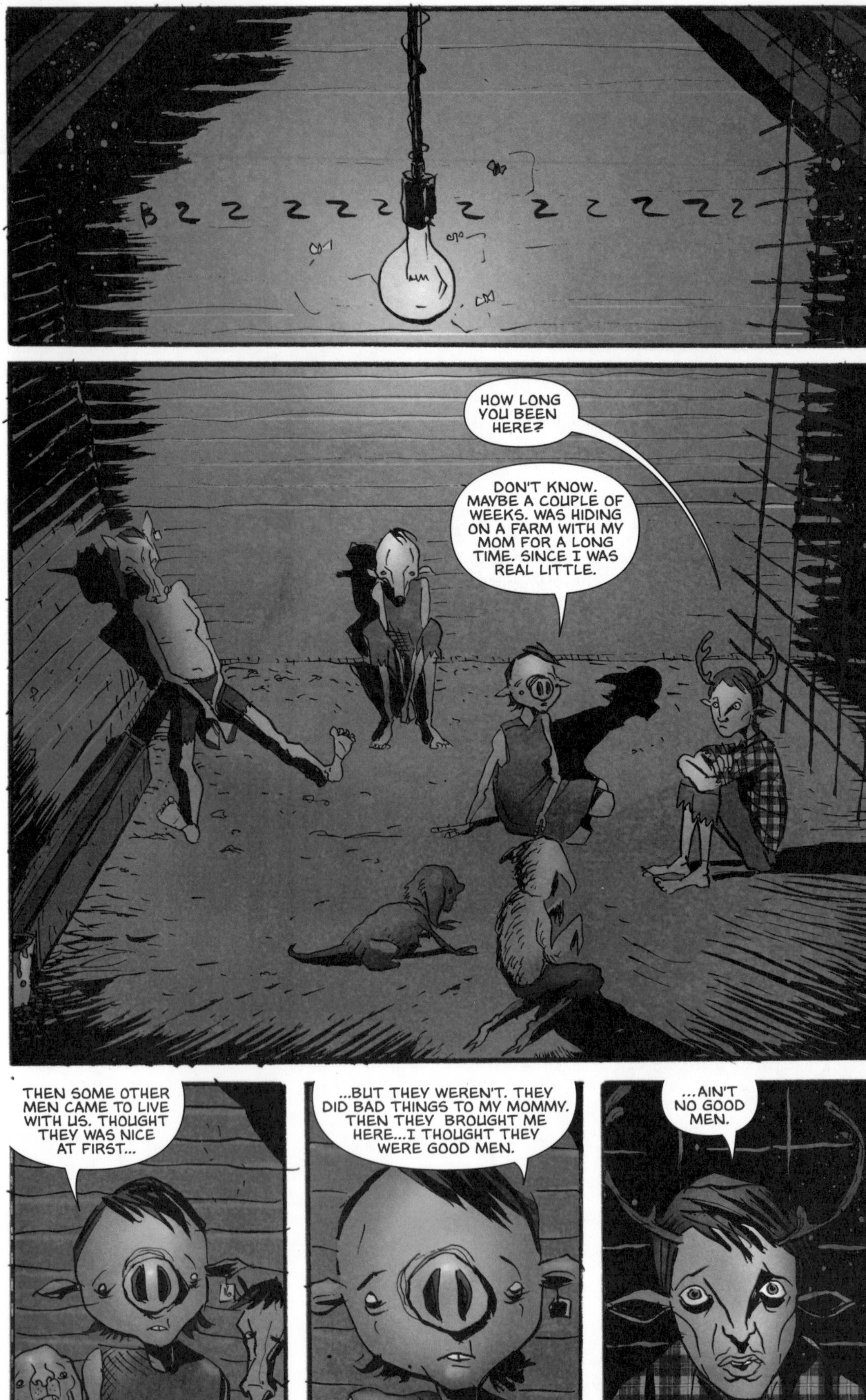
BZZZZZZZZZZZ
HOW LONG YOU BEEN HERE?
DON'T KNOW. MAYBE A COUPLE OF WEEKS. WAS HIDING ON A FARM WITH MY MOM FOR A LONG TIME. SINCE I WAS REAL LITTLE.
THEN SOME OTHER MEN CAME TO LIVE WITH US. THOUGHT THEY WAS NICE AT FIRST...
...BUT THEY WEREN'T. THEY DID BAD THINGS TO MY MOMMY. THEN THEY BROUGHT ME HERE...I THOUGHT THEY WERE GOOD MEN.
...AIN'T NO GOOD MEN.

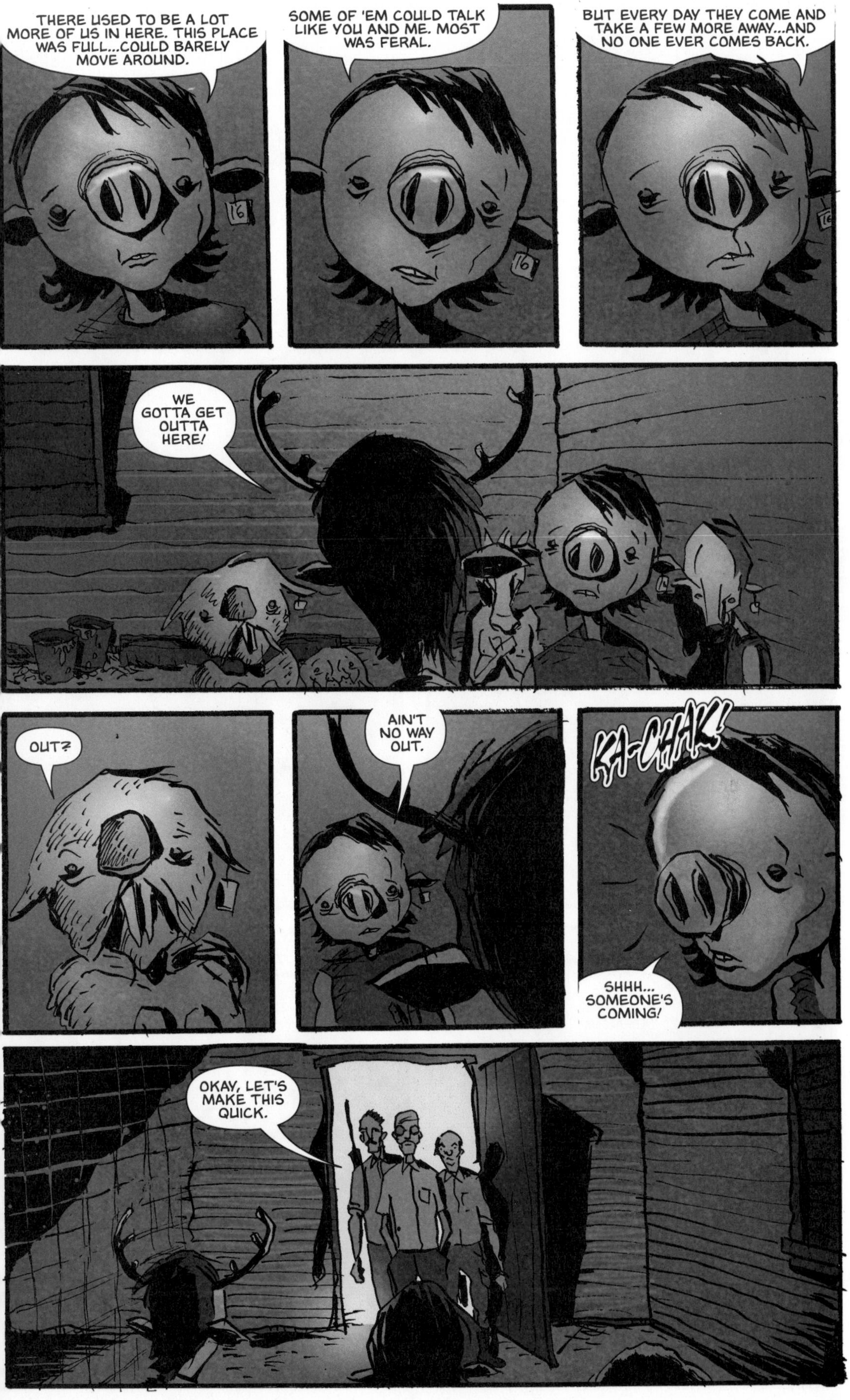
THERE USED TO BE A LOT MORE OF US IN HERE. THIS PLACE WAS FULL...COULD BARELY MOVE AROUND.
SOME OF 'EM COULD TALK LIKE YOU AND ME. MOST WAS FERAL.
BUT EVERY DAY THEY COME AND TAKE A FEW MORE AWAY...AND NO ONE EVER COMES BACK.
WE GOTTA GET OUTTA HERE!
OUT?
AIN'T NO WAY OUT.
KA-CHAK!
SHHH... SOMEONE'S COMING!
OKAY, LET'S MAKE THIS QUICK.

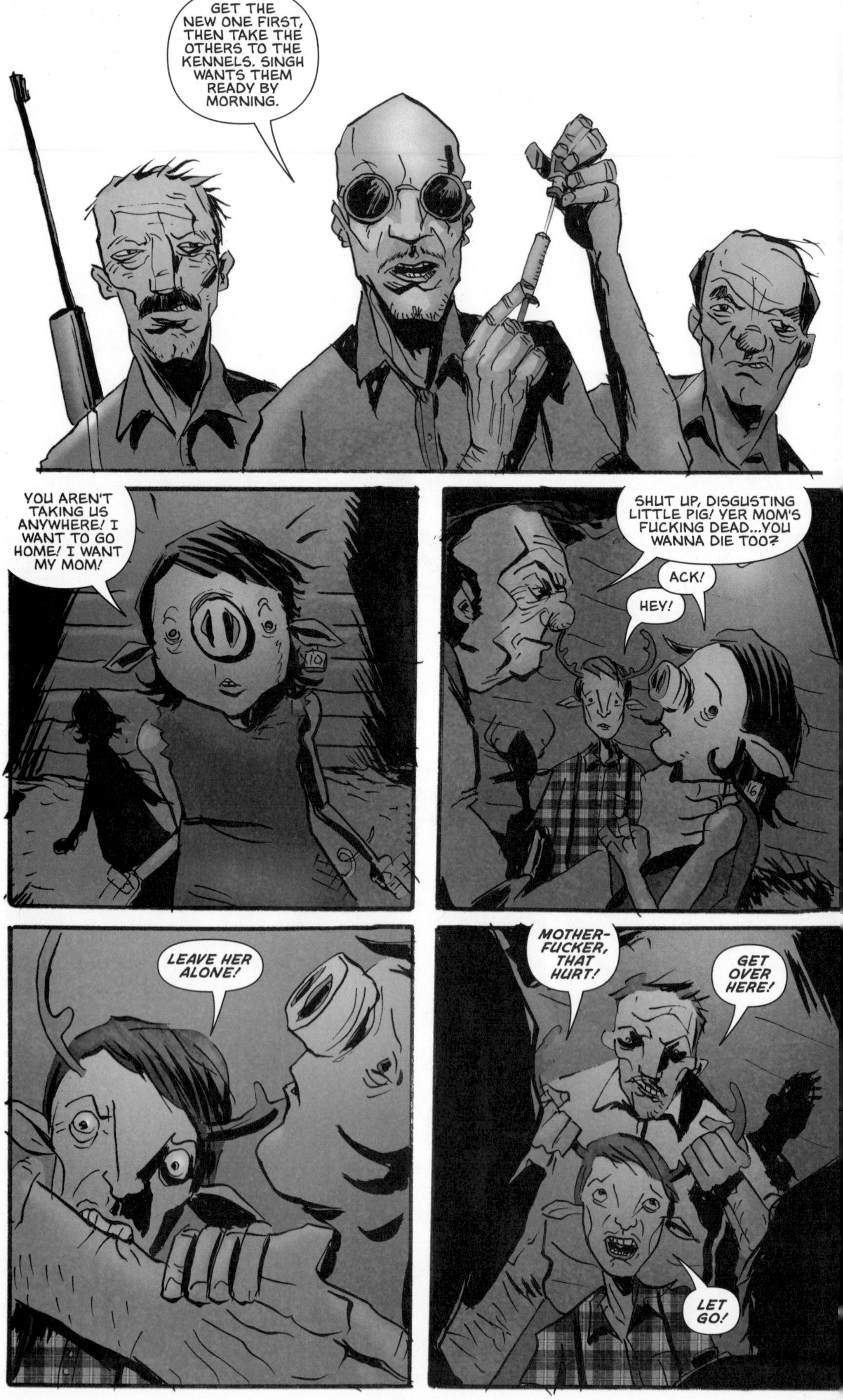

GET THE NEW ONE FIRST, THEN TAKE THE OTHERS TO THE KENNELS. SINGH WANTS THEM READY BY MORNING.
YOU AREN'T TAKING US ANYWHERE! I WANT TO GO HOME! I WANT MY MOM!
SHUT UP, DISGUSTING LITTLE PIG! YER MOM'S FUCKING DEAD...YOU WANNA DIE TOO?
HEY!
ACK!
LEAVE HER ALONE!
MOTHER-FUCKER, THAT HURT!
GET OVER HERE!
LET GO!

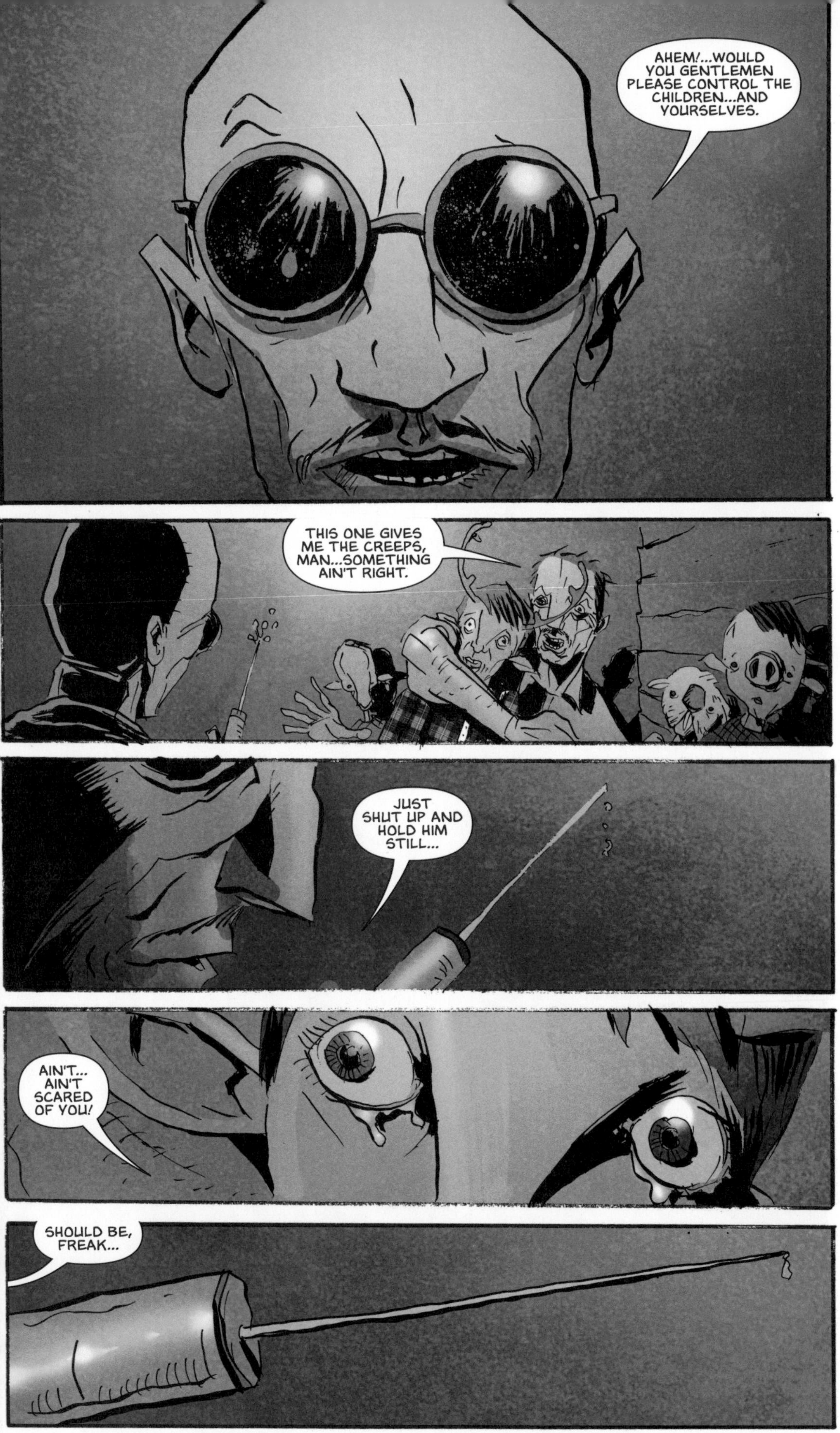
AHEM!...WOULD YOU GENTLEMEN PLEASE CONTROL THE CHILDREN...AND YOURSELVES.
THIS ONE GIVES ME THE CREEPS, MAN...SOMETHING AIN'T RIGHT.
JUST SHUT UP AND HOLD HIM STILL...
AIN'T... AIN'T SCARED OF YOU!
SHOULD BE, FREAK...

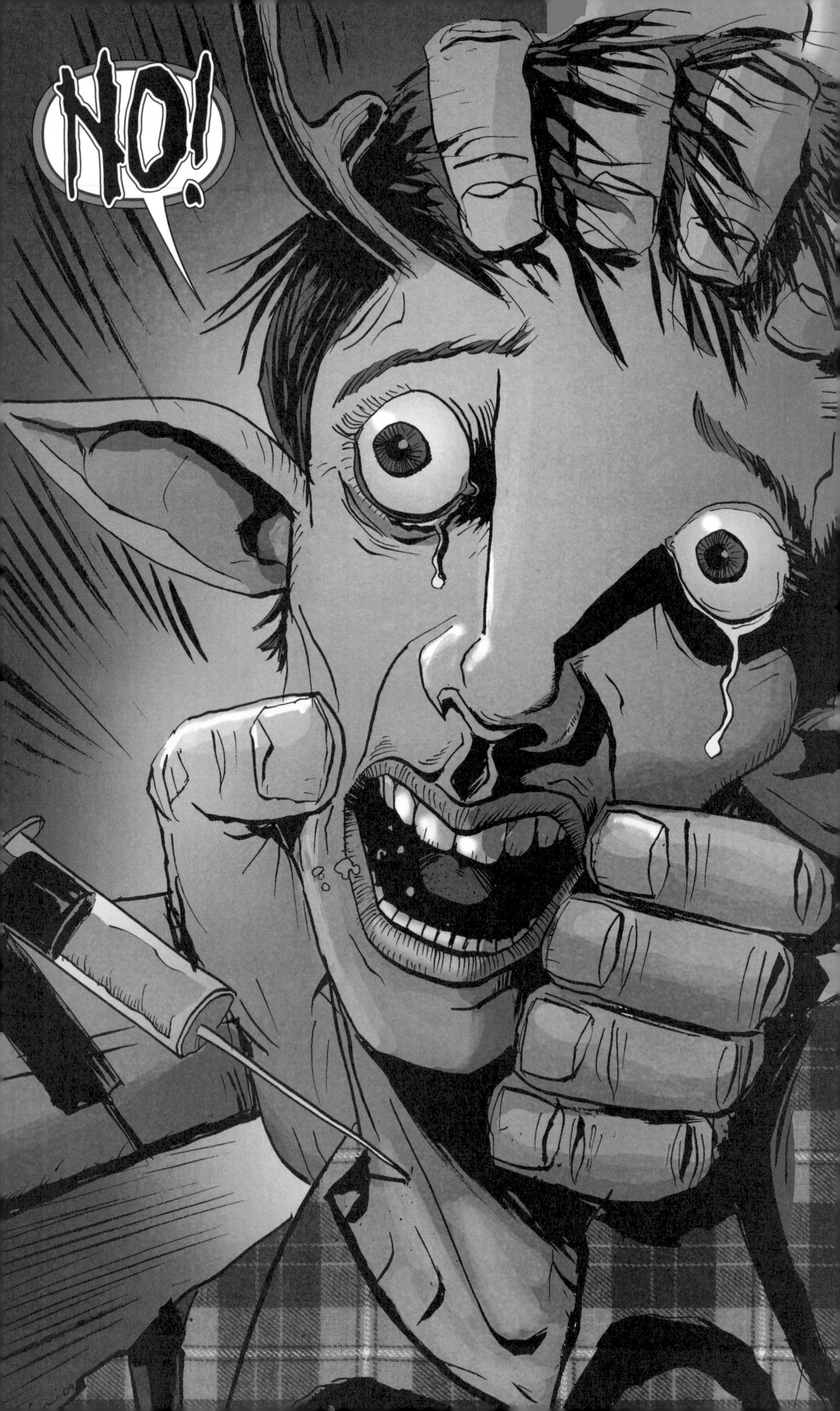
NO!

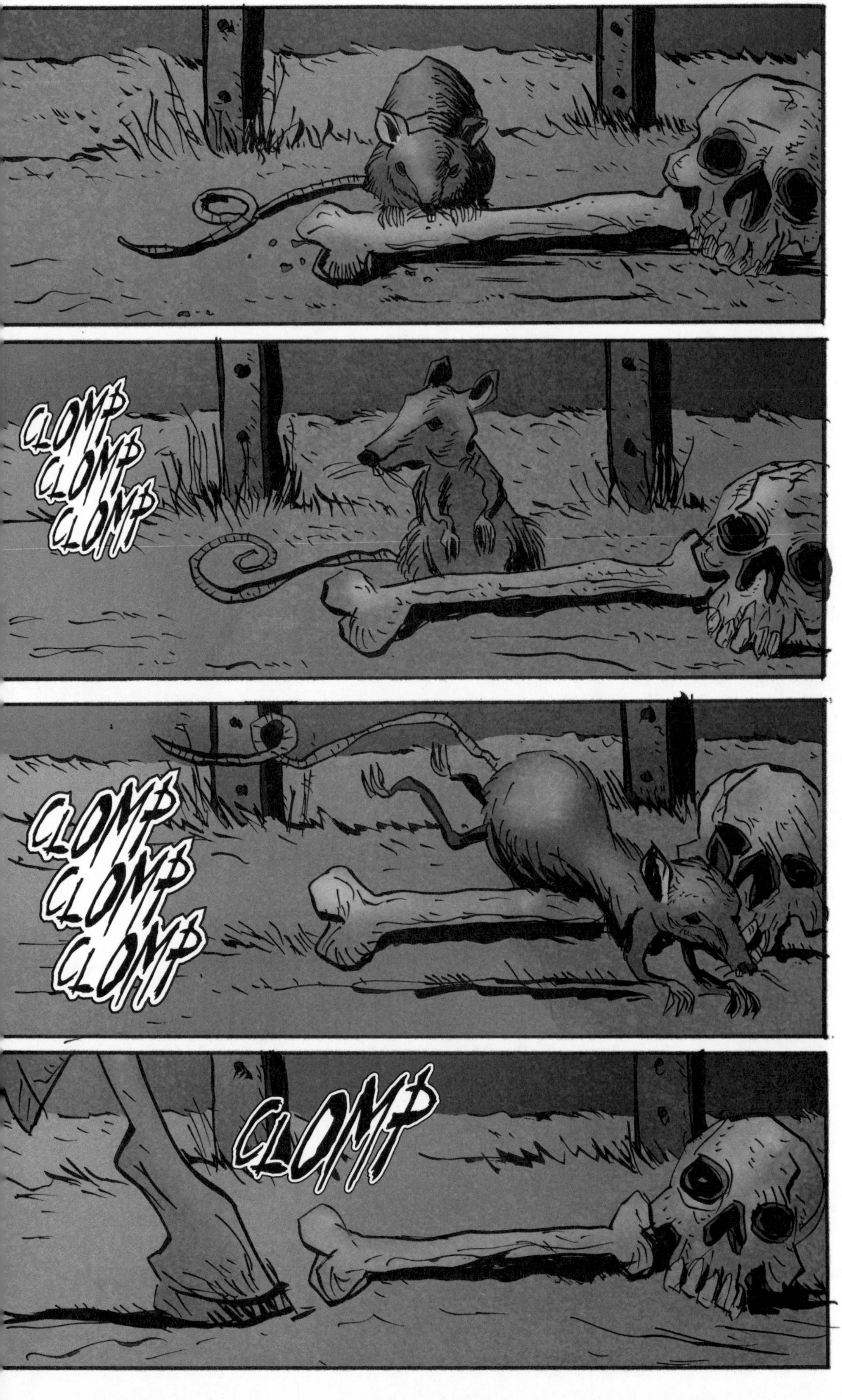
CLOMP
CLOMP
CLOMP
CLOMP
CLOMP
CLOMP
CLOMP

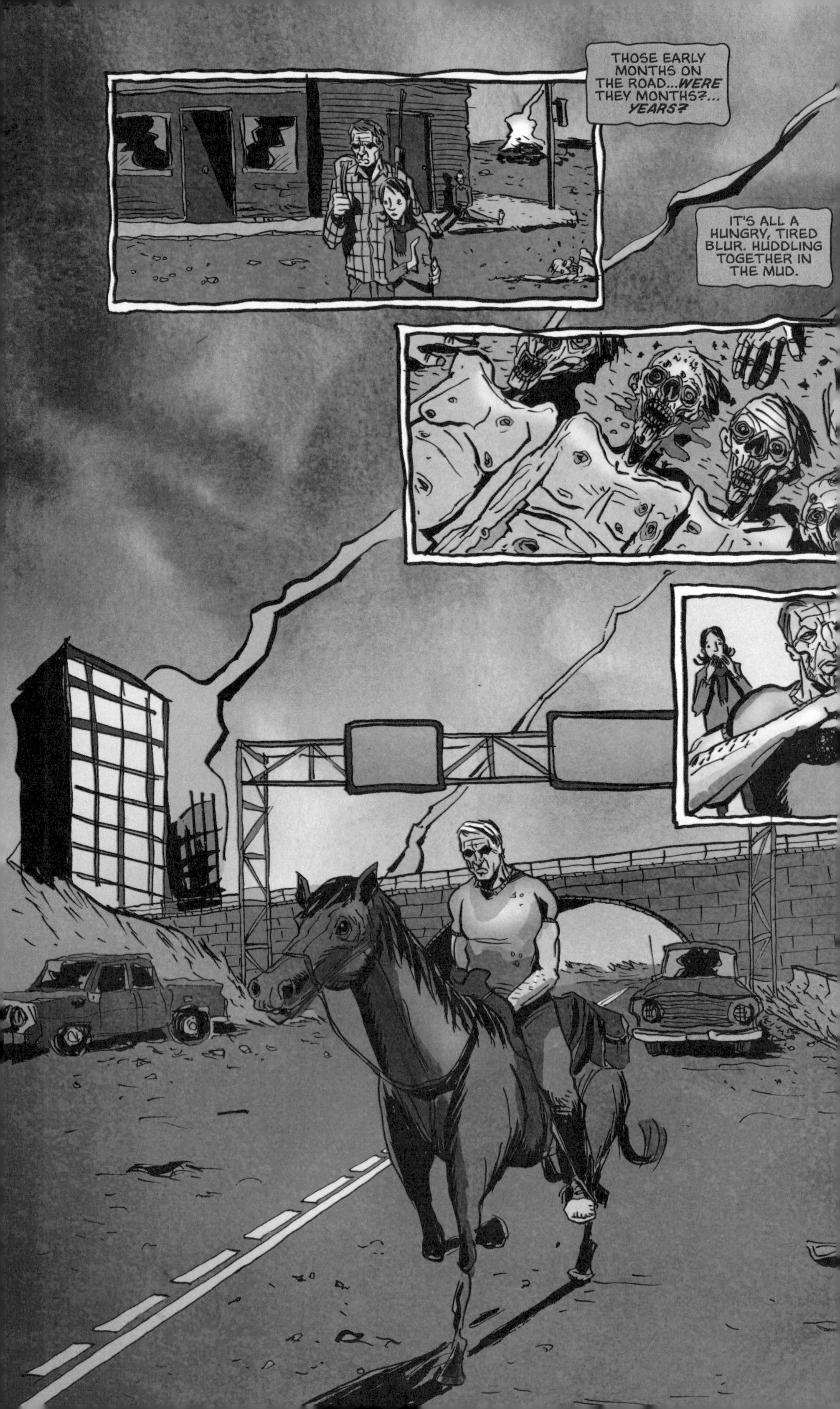
THOSE EARLY MONTHS ON THE ROAD...WERE THEY MONTHS?...YEARS?
IT'S ALL A HUNGRY, TIRED BLUR. HUDDLING TOGETHER IN THE MUD.

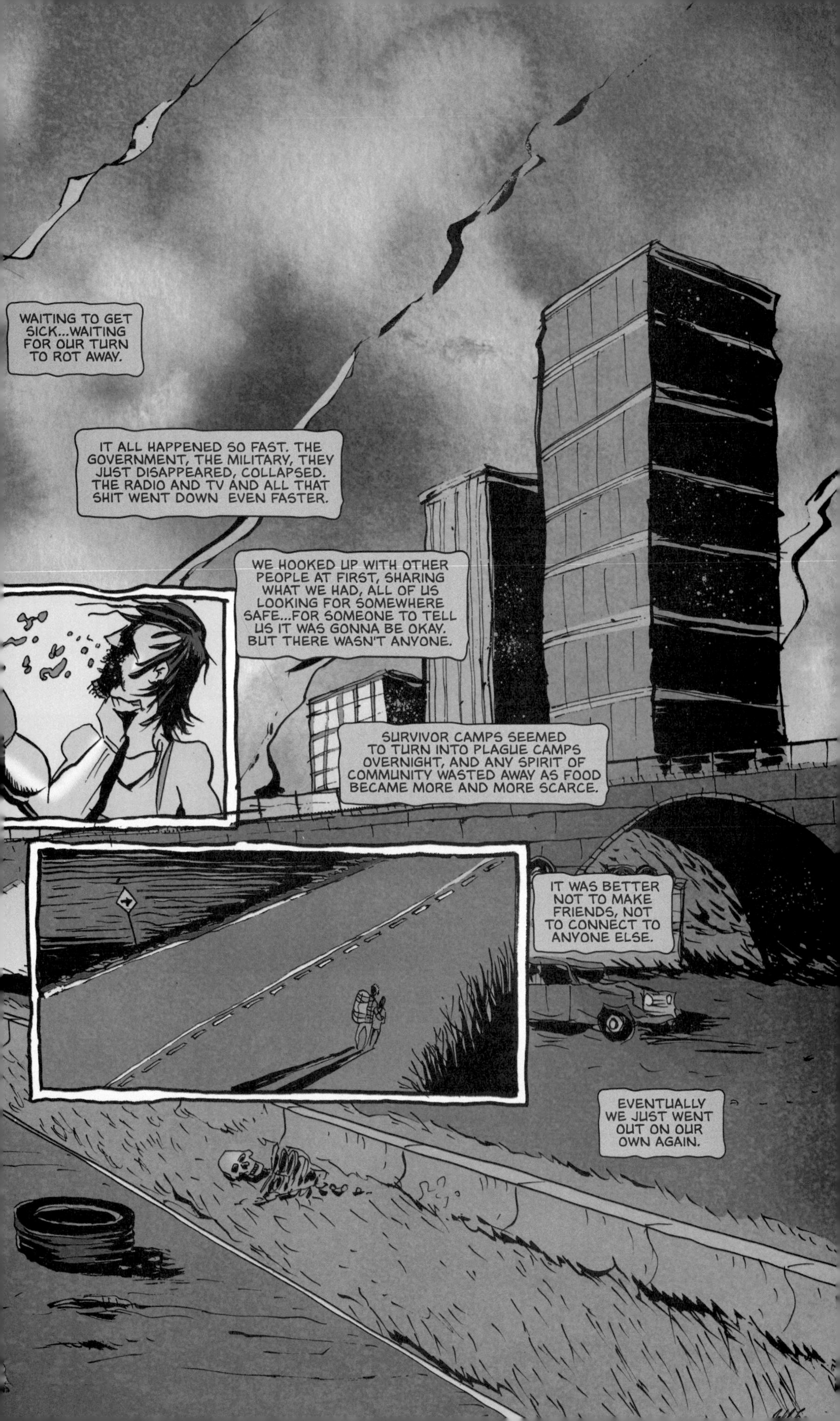
WAITING TO GET SICK...WAITING FOR OUR TURN TO ROT AWAY.
IT ALL HAPPENED SO FAST. THE GOVERNMENT, THE MILITARY, THEY JUST DISAPPEARED, COLLAPSED. THE RADIO AND TV AND ALL THAT SHIT WENT DOWN EVEN FASTER.
WE HOOKED UP WITH OTHER PEOPLE AT FIRST, SHARING WHAT WE HAD, ALL OF US LOOKING FOR SOMEWHERE SAFE...FOR SOMEONE TO TELL US IT WAS GONNA BE OKAY. BUT THERE WASN'T ANYONE.
SURVIVOR CAMPS SEEMED TO TURN INTO PLAGUE CAMPS OVERNIGHT, AND ANY SPIRIT OF COMMUNITY WASTED AWAY AS FOOD BECAME MORE AND MORE SCARCE.
IT WAS BETTER NOT TO MAKE FRIENDS, NOT TO CONNECT TO ANYONE ELSE.
EVENTUALLY WE JUST WENT OUT ON OUR OWN AGAIN.

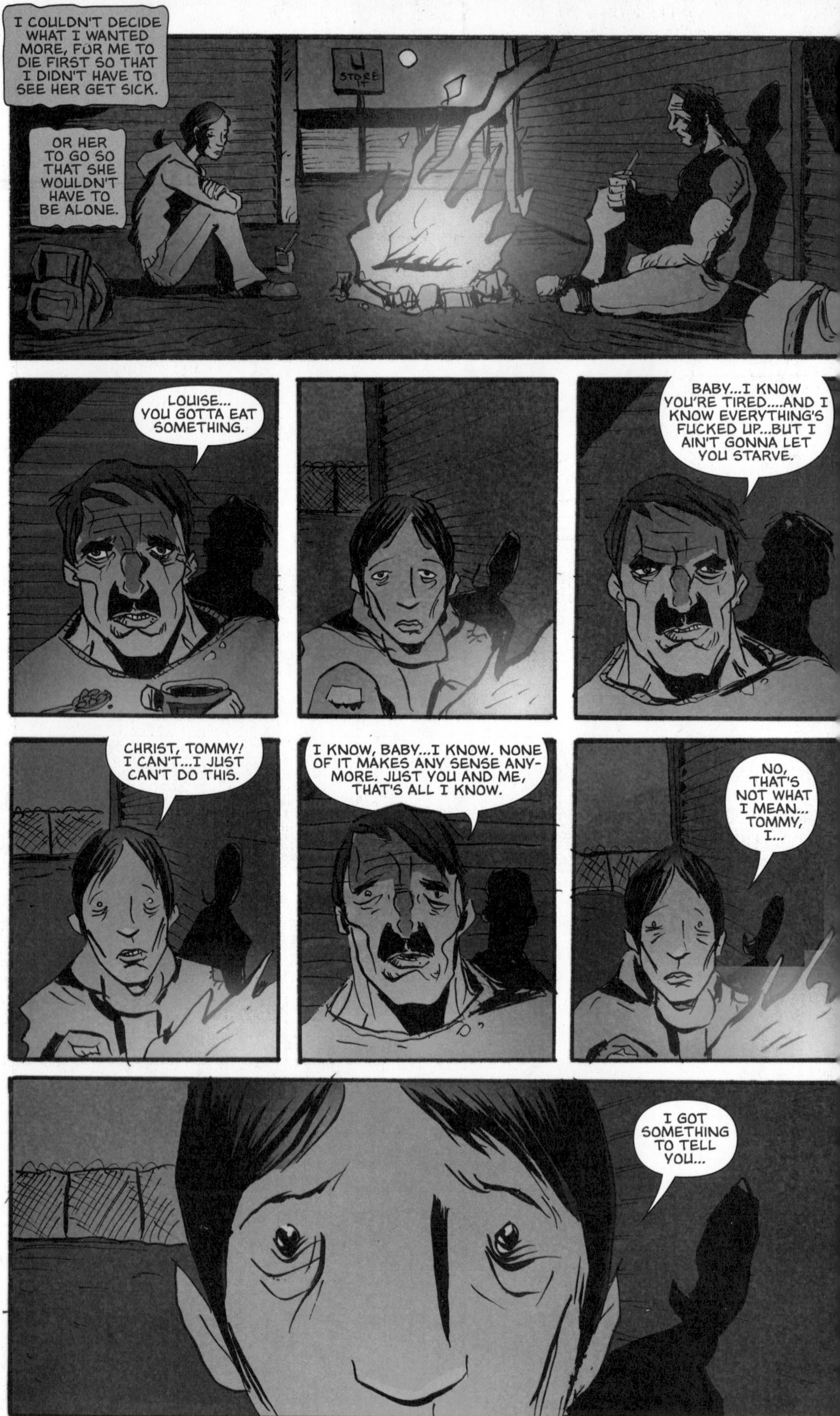

I COULDN'T DECIDE WHAT I WANTED MORE, FOR ME TO DIE FIRST SO THAT I DIDN'T HAVE TO SEE HER GET SICK.
OR HER TO GO SO THAT SHE WOULDN'T HAVE TO BE ALONE.
STORE IT
LOUISE... YOU GOTTA EAT SOMETHING.
BABY...I KNOW YOU'RE TIRED....AND I KNOW EVERYTHING'S FUCKED UP...BUT I AIN'T GONNA LET YOU STARVE.
CHRIST, TOMMY! I CAN'T...I JUST CAN'T DO THIS.
I KNOW, BABY...I KNOW. NONE OF IT MAKES ANY SENSE ANY-MORE. JUST YOU AND ME, THAT'S ALL I KNOW.
NO, THAT'S NOT WHAT I MEAN... TOMMY, I...
I GOT SOMETHING TO TELL YOU...

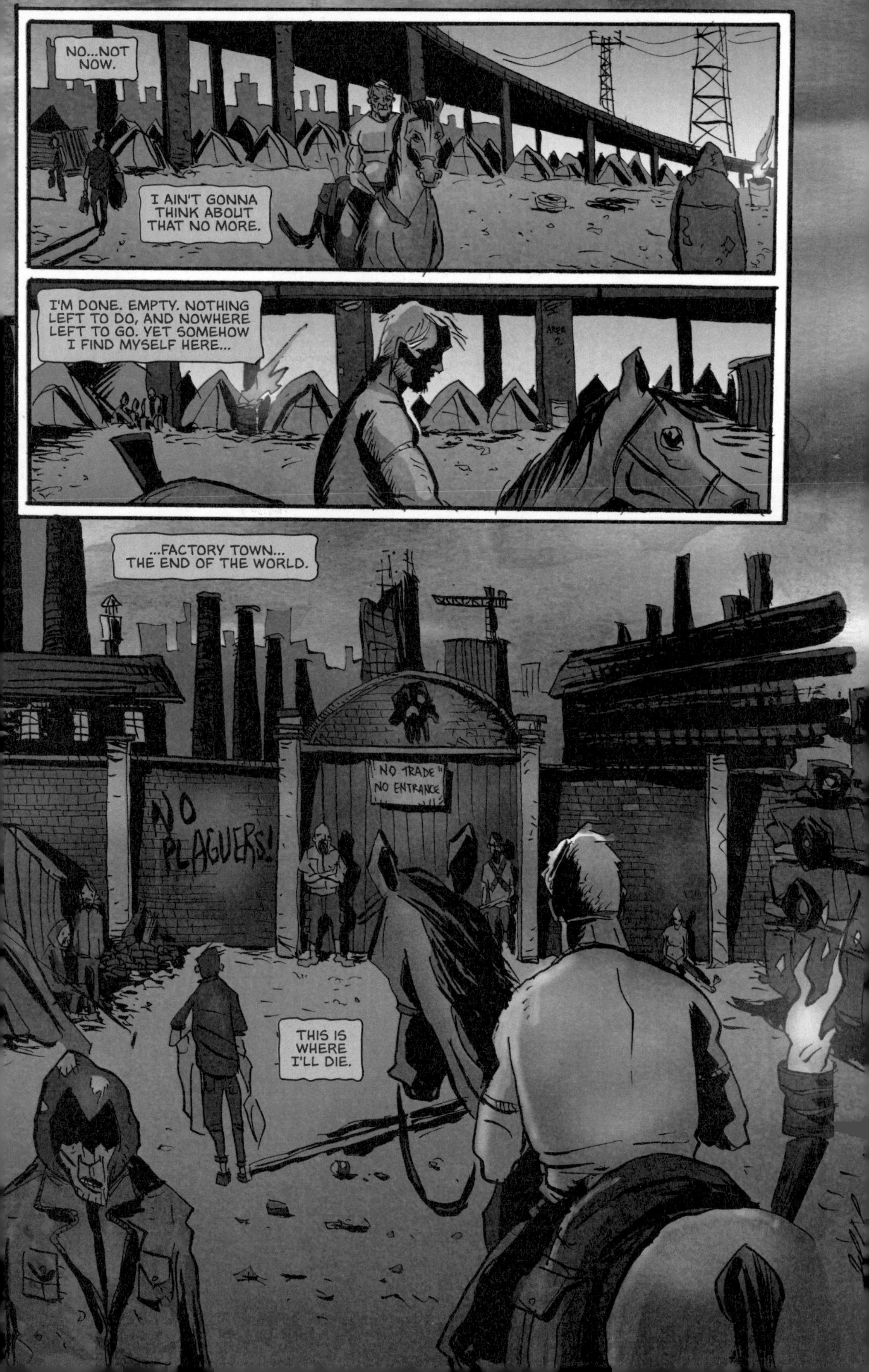
NO...NOT NOW.
I AIN'T GONNA THINK ABOUT THAT NO MORE.
I'M DONE. EMPTY. NOTHING LEFT TO DO, AND NOWHERE LEFT TO GO. YET SOMEHOW I FIND MYSELF HERE...
...FACTORY TOWN... THE END OF THE WORLD.
NO PLAGUERS!
NO TRADE NO ENTRANCE
THIS IS WHERE I'LL DIE.

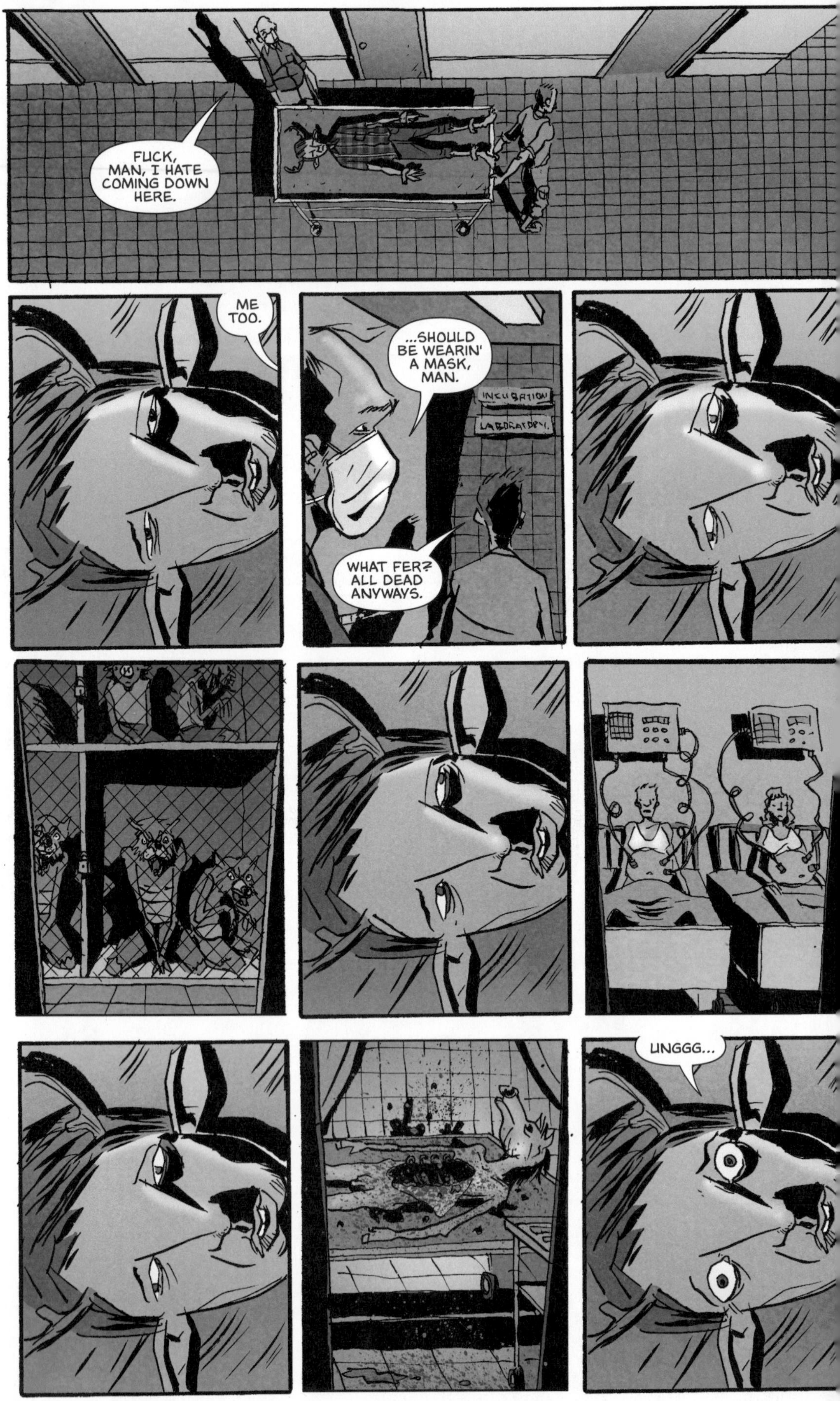
FUCK, MAN, I HATE COMING DOWN HERE.
ME TOO.
...SHOULD BE WEARIN' A MASK, MAN.
WHAT FER? ALL DEAD ANYWAYS.
UNGGG...

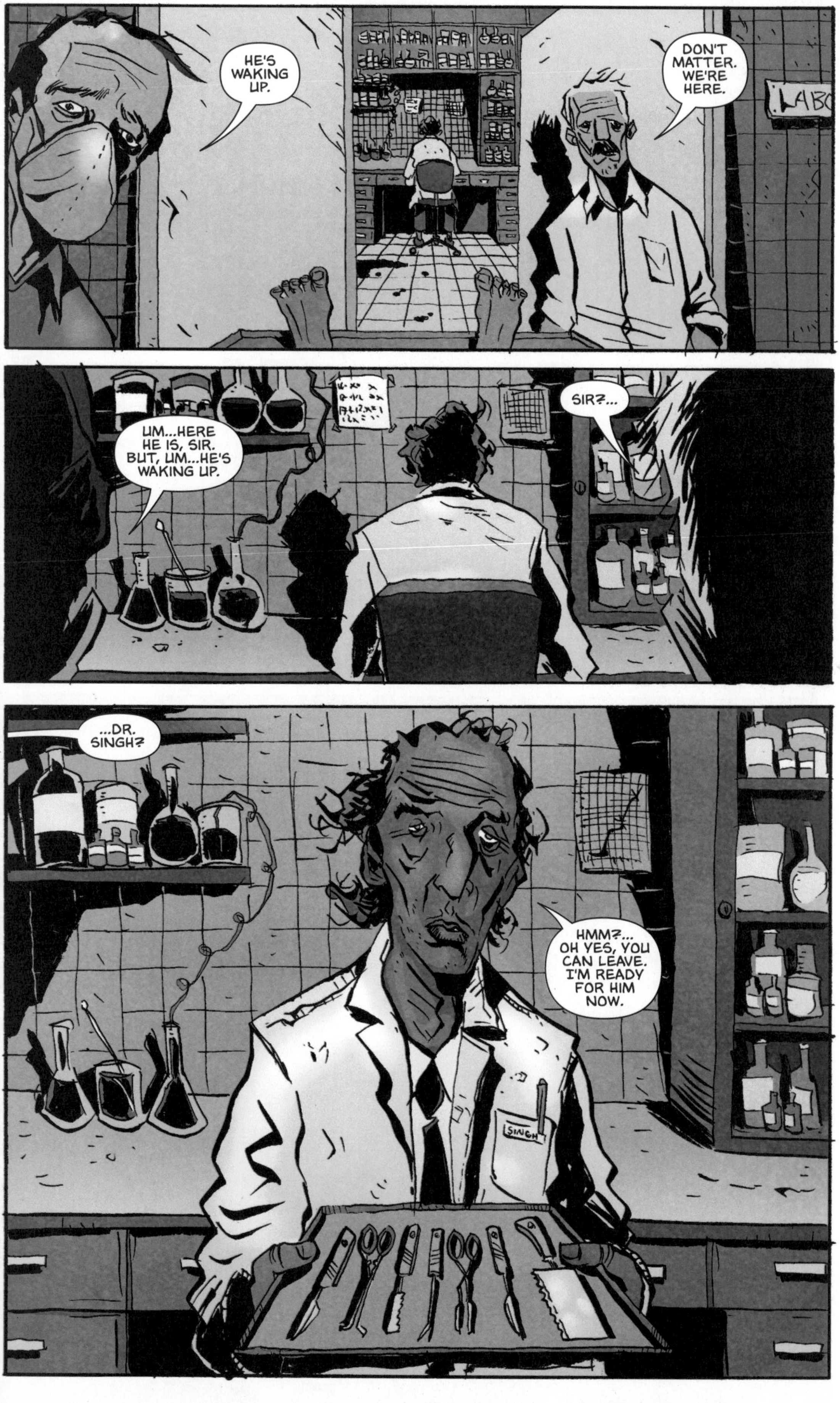
HE'S WAKING UP.
DON'T MATTER. WE'RE HERE.
LABO
UM...HERE HE IS, SIR. BUT, UM...HE'S WAKING UP.
SIR?...
...DR. SINGH?
HMM?... OH YES, YOU CAN LEAVE. I'M READY FOR HIM NOW.
SINGH

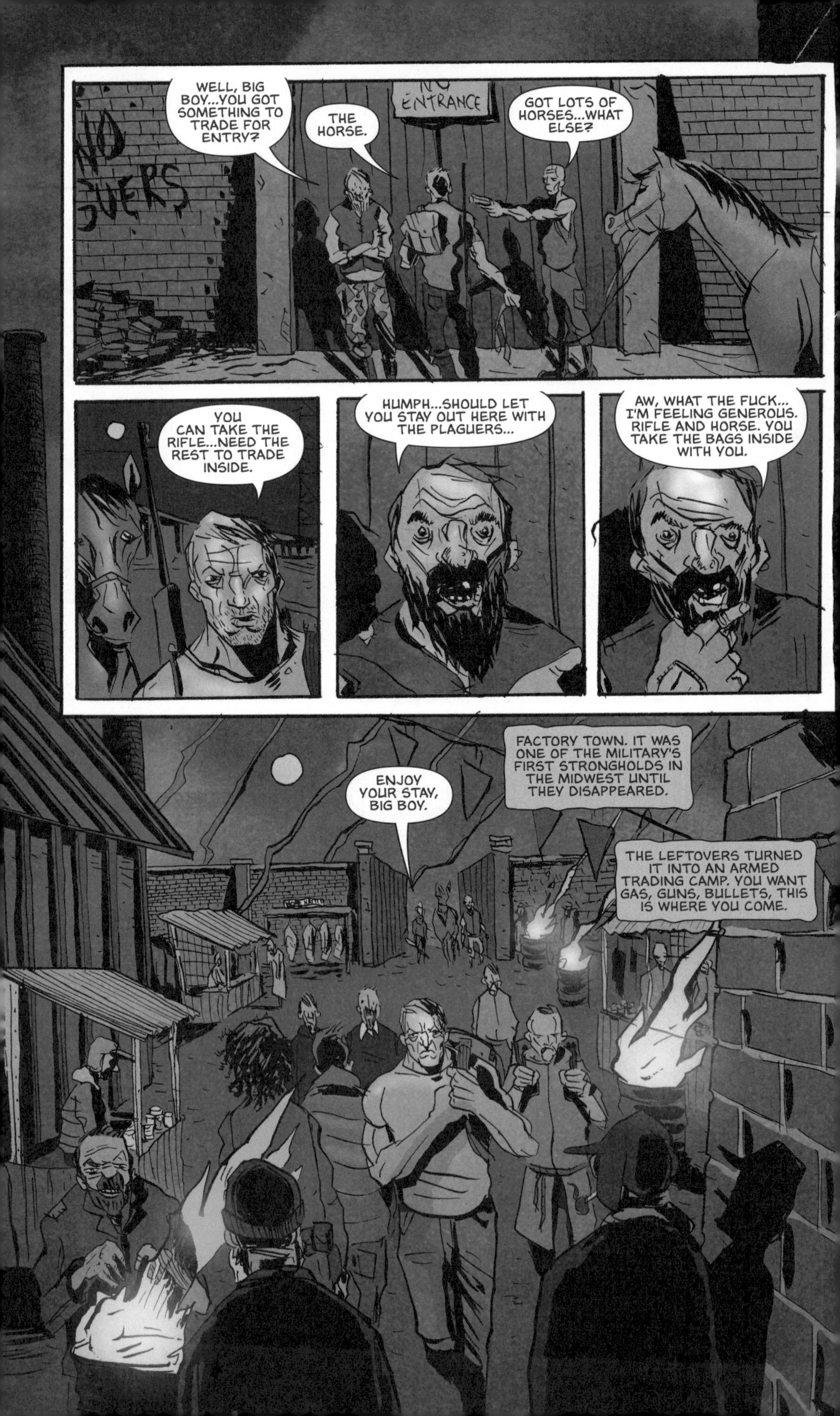
NO ENTRANCE
WELL, BIG BOY...YOU GOT SOMETHING TO TRADE FOR ENTRY?
THE HORSE.
GOT LOTS OF HORSES...WHAT ELSE?
YOU CAN TAKE THE RIFLE...NEED THE REST TO TRADE INSIDE.
HUMPH...SHOULD LET YOU STAY OUT HERE WITH THE PLAGUERS...
AW, WHAT THE FUCK... I'M FEELING GENEROUS. RIFLE AND HORSE. YOU TAKE THE BAGS INSIDE WITH YOU.
FACTORY TOWN. IT WAS ONE OF THE MILITARY'S FIRST STRONGHOLDS IN THE MIDWEST UNTIL THEY DISAPPEARED.
ENJOY YOUR STAY, BIG BOY.
THE LEFTOVERS TURNED IT INTO AN ARMED TRADING CAMP. YOU WANT GAS, GUNS, BULLETS, THIS IS WHERE YOU COME.

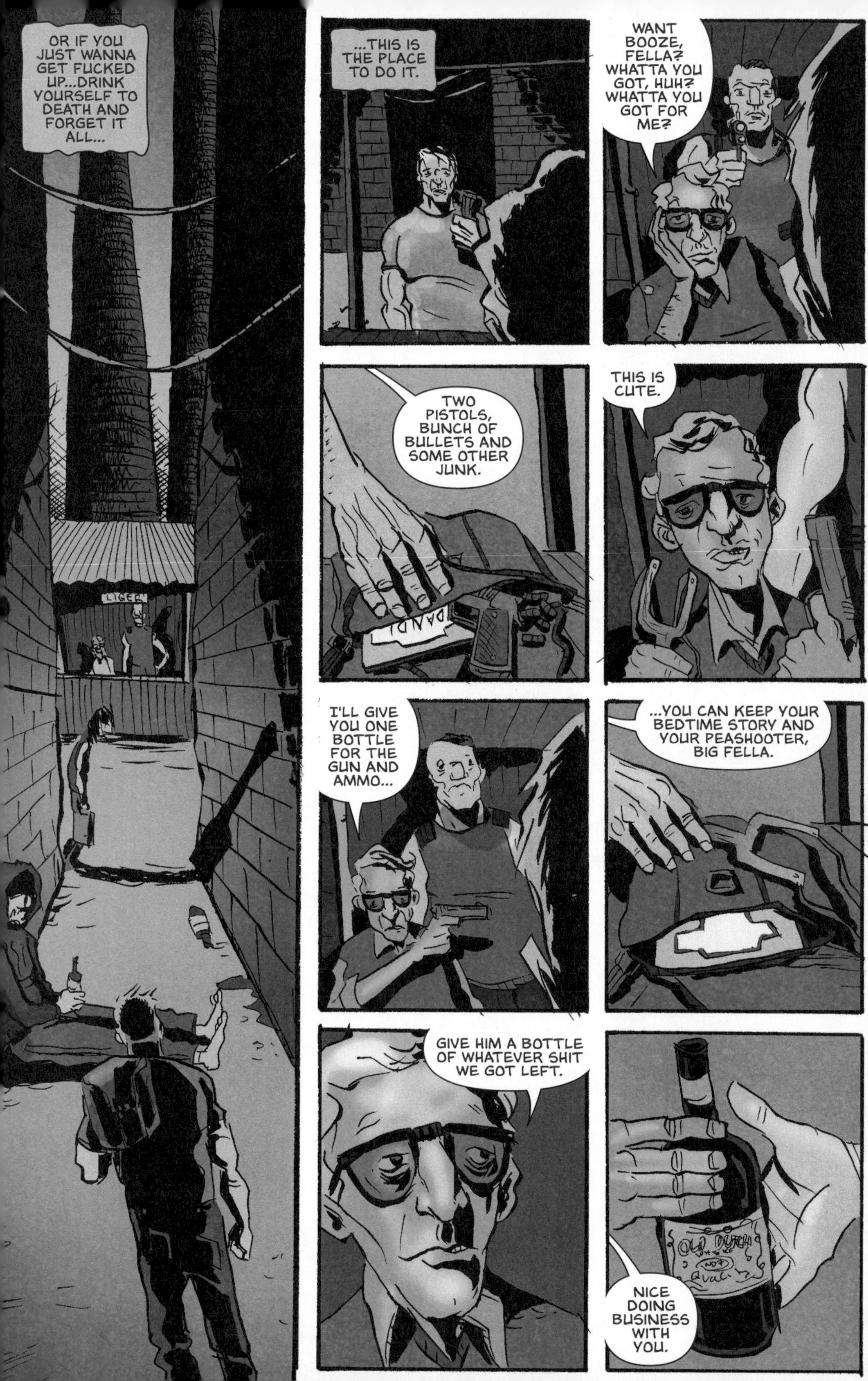
OR IF YOU JUST WANNA GET FUCKED UP...DRINK YOURSELF TO DEATH AND FORGET IT ALL...
...THIS IS THE PLACE TO DO IT.
WANT BOOZE, FELLA? WHATTA YOU GOT, HUH? WHATTA YOU GOT FOR ME?
TWO PISTOLS, BUNCH OF BULLETS AND SOME OTHER JUNK.
THIS IS CUTE.
I'LL GIVE YOU ONE BOTTLE FOR THE GUN AND AMMO...
...YOU CAN KEEP YOUR BEDTIME STORY AND YOUR PEASHOOTER, BIG FELLA.
GIVE HIM A BOTTLE OF WHATEVER SHIT WE GOT LEFT.
NICE DOING BUSINESS WITH YOU.

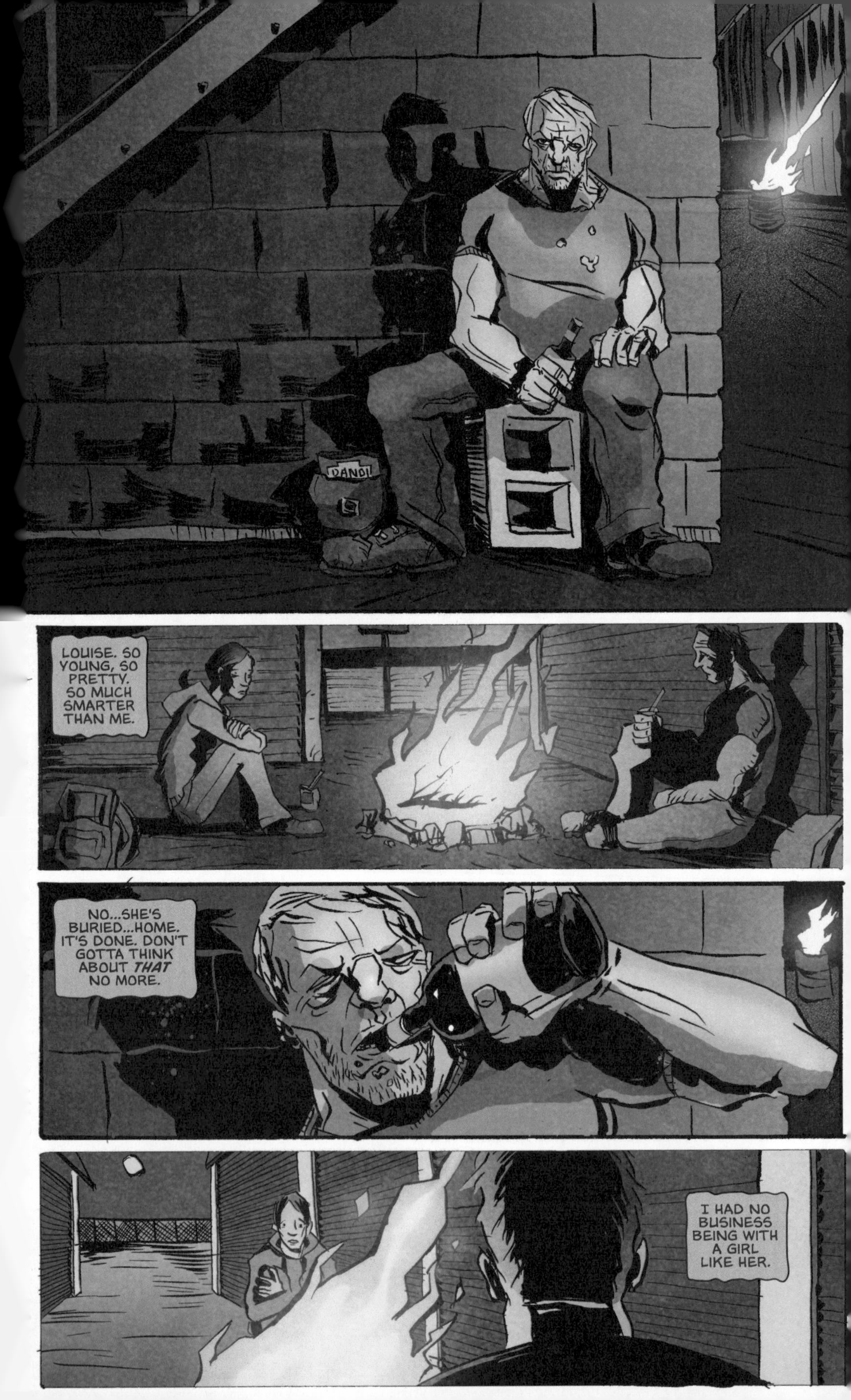
DANDI
LOUISE. SO YOUNG, SO PRETTY. SO MUCH SMARTER THAN ME.
NO...SHE'S BURIED...HOME. IT'S DONE. DON'T GOTTA THINK ABOUT *THAT* NO MORE.
I HAD NO BUSINESS BEING WITH A GIRL LIKE HER.

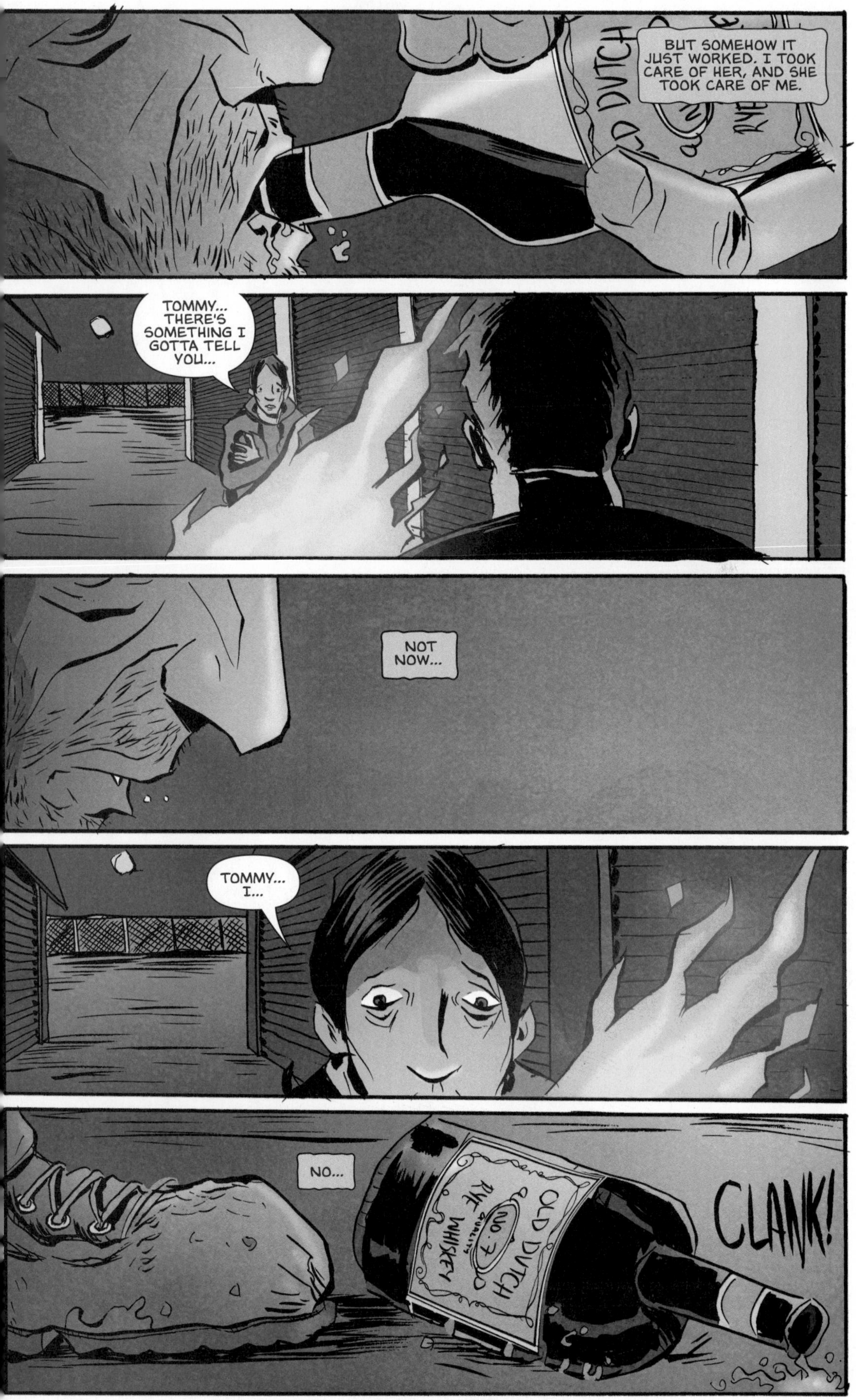
BUT SOMEHOW IT JUST WORKED. I TOOK CARE OF HER, AND SHE TOOK CARE OF ME.
OLD DUTCH
TOMMY... THERE'S SOMETHING I GOTTA TELL YOU...
NOT NOW...
TOMMY... I...
NO...
OLD DUTCH
NO. 7
QUALITY
RYE
WHISKEY
CLANK!

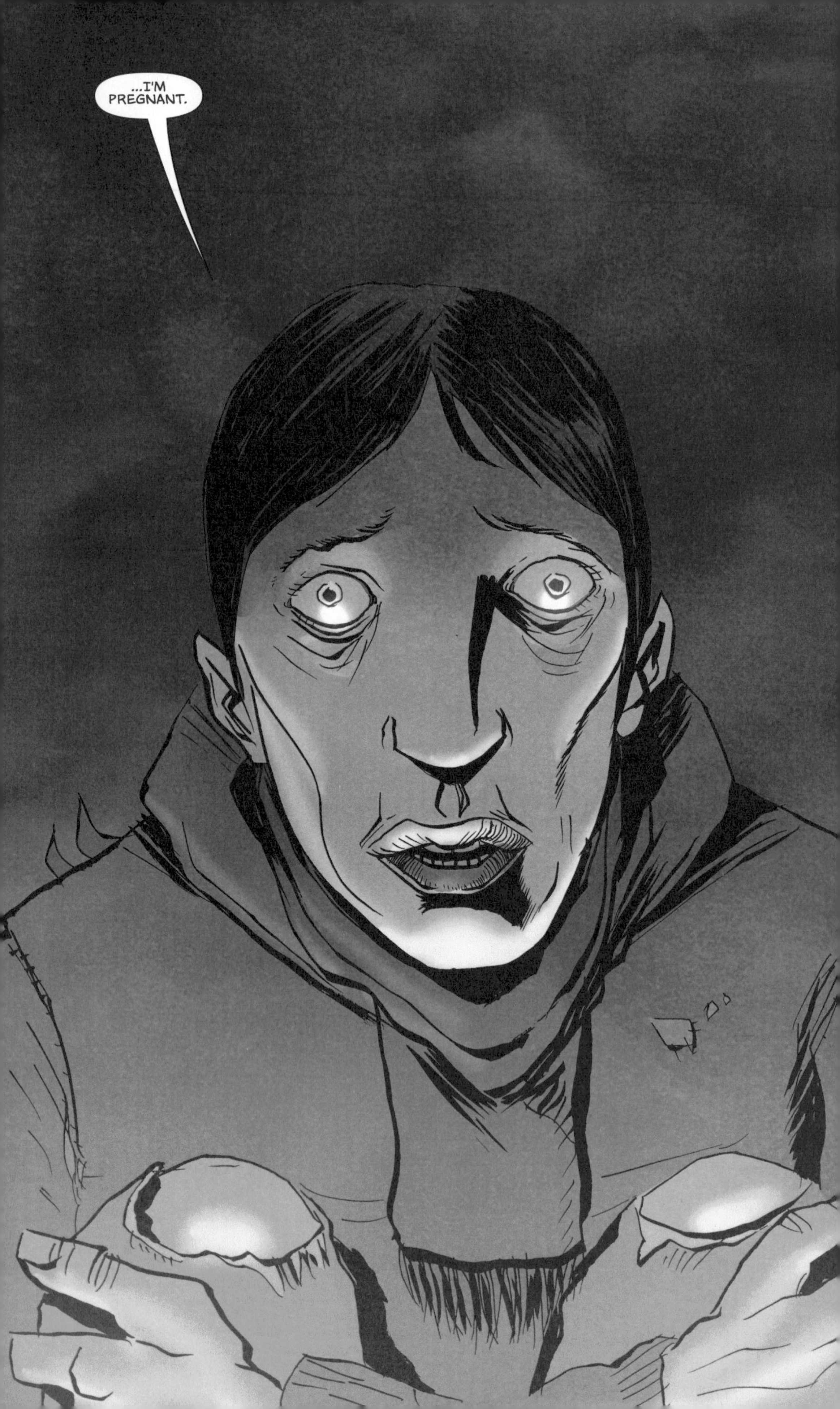
...I'M PREGNANT.

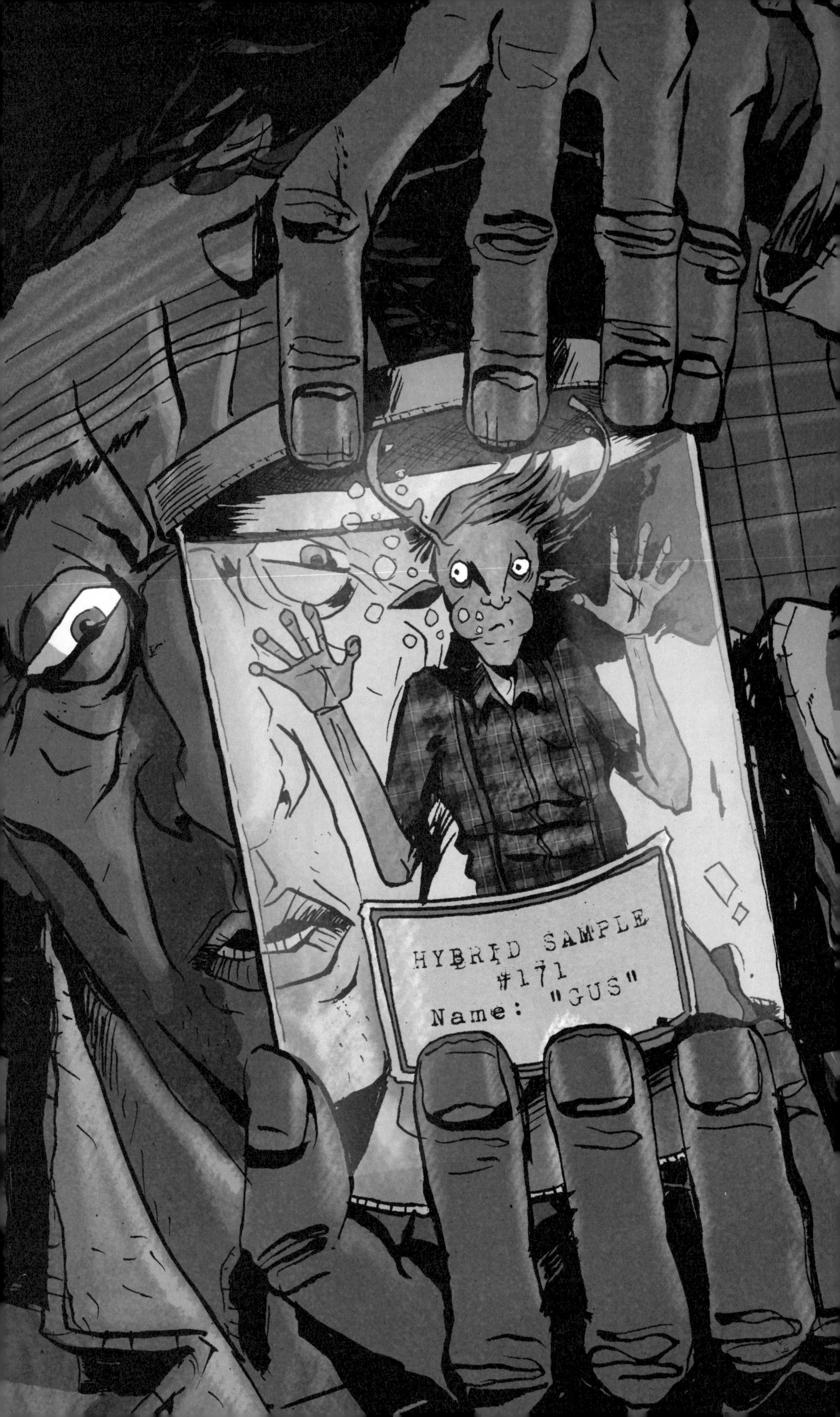
HYBRID SAMPLE
#171
Name: "GUS"

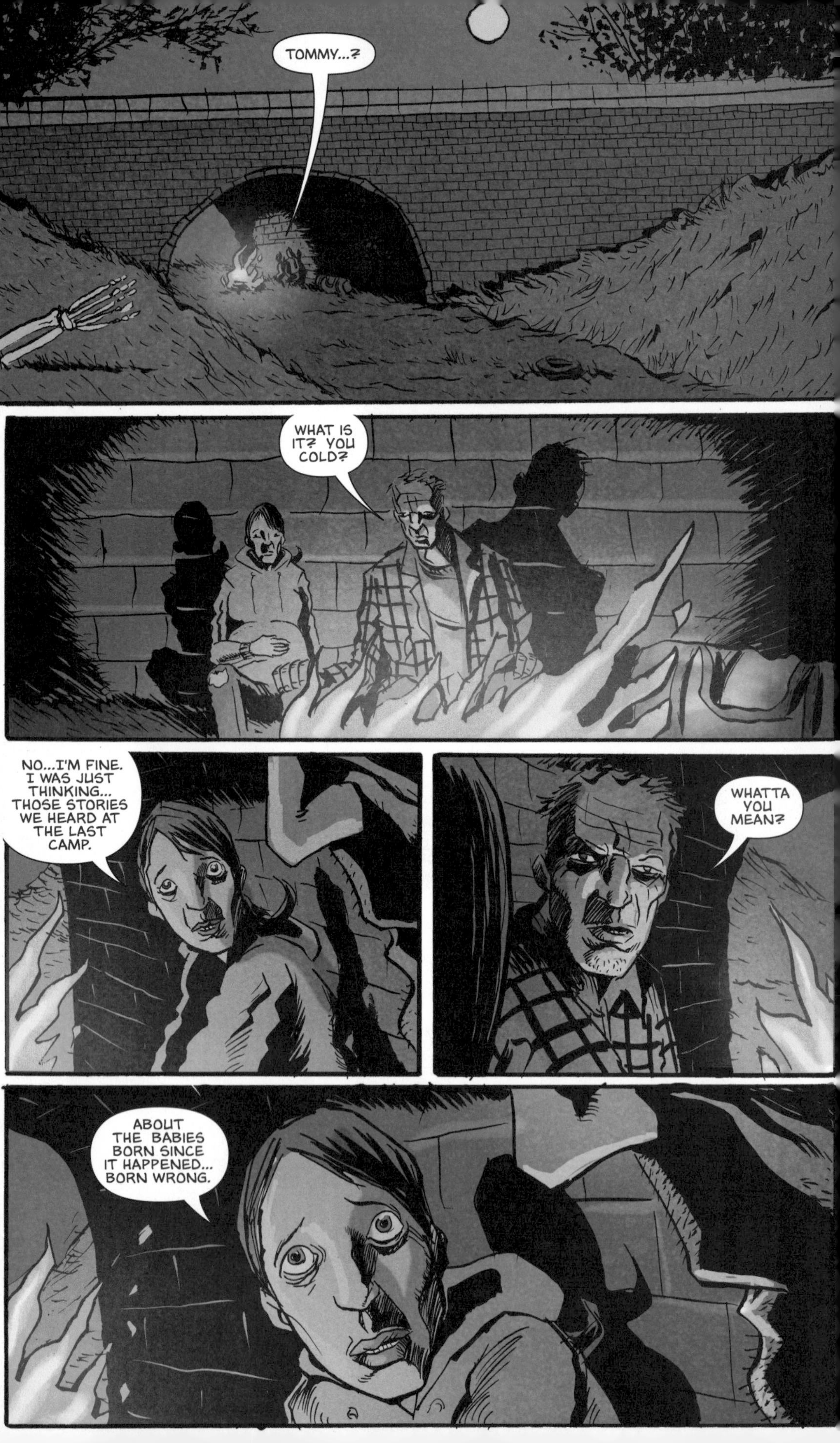
TOMMY...?
WHAT IS IT? YOU COLD?
NO...I'M FINE. I WAS JUST THINKING... THOSE STORIES WE HEARD AT THE LAST CAMP.
WHATTA YOU MEAN?
ABOUT THE BABIES BORN SINCE IT HAPPENED... BORN WRONG.

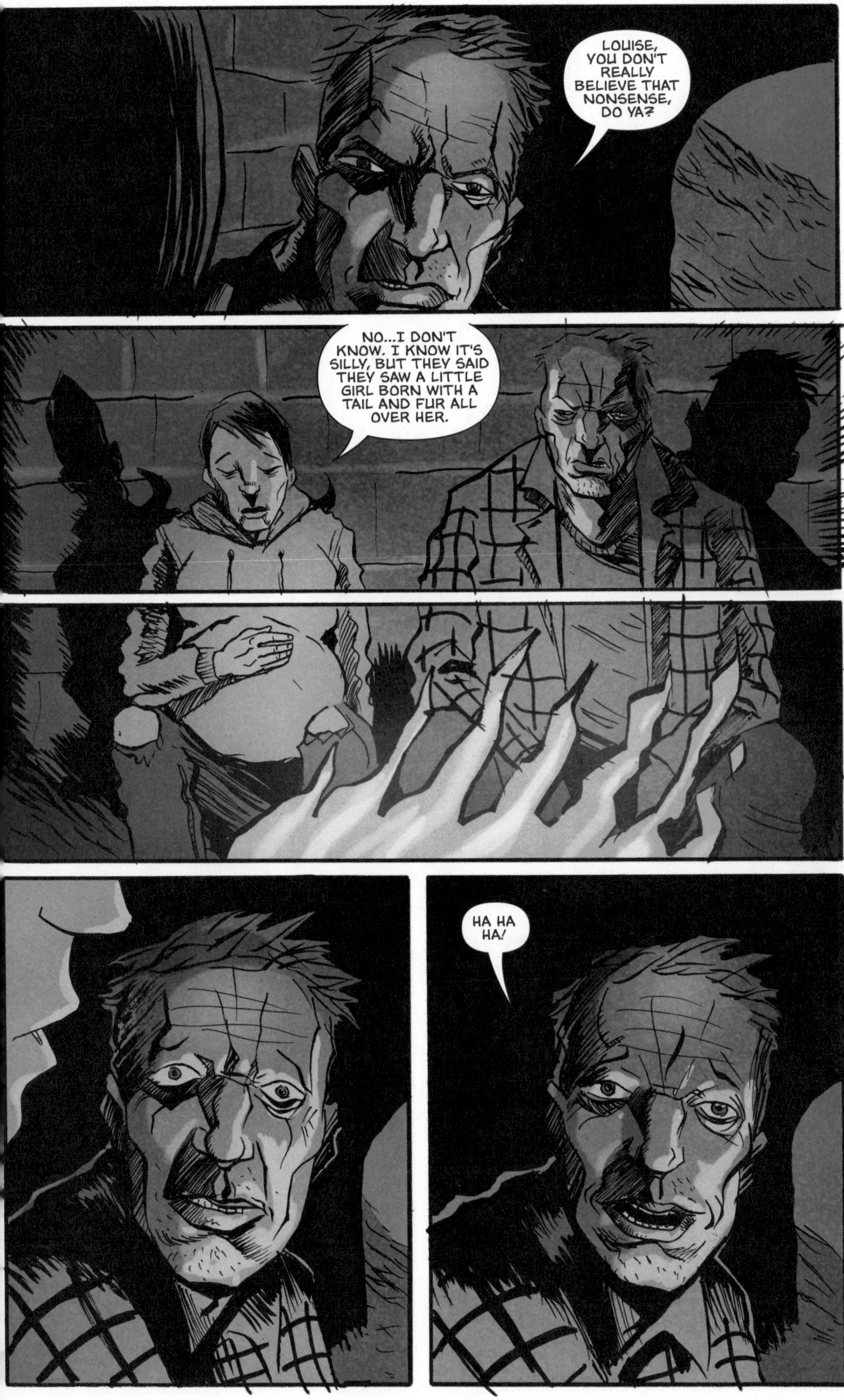
LOUISE, YOU DON'T REALLY BELIEVE THAT NONSENSE, DO YA?
NO...I DON'T KNOW. I KNOW IT'S SILLY, BUT THEY SAID THEY SAW A LITTLE GIRL BORN WITH A TAIL AND FUR ALL OVER HER.
HA HA HA!

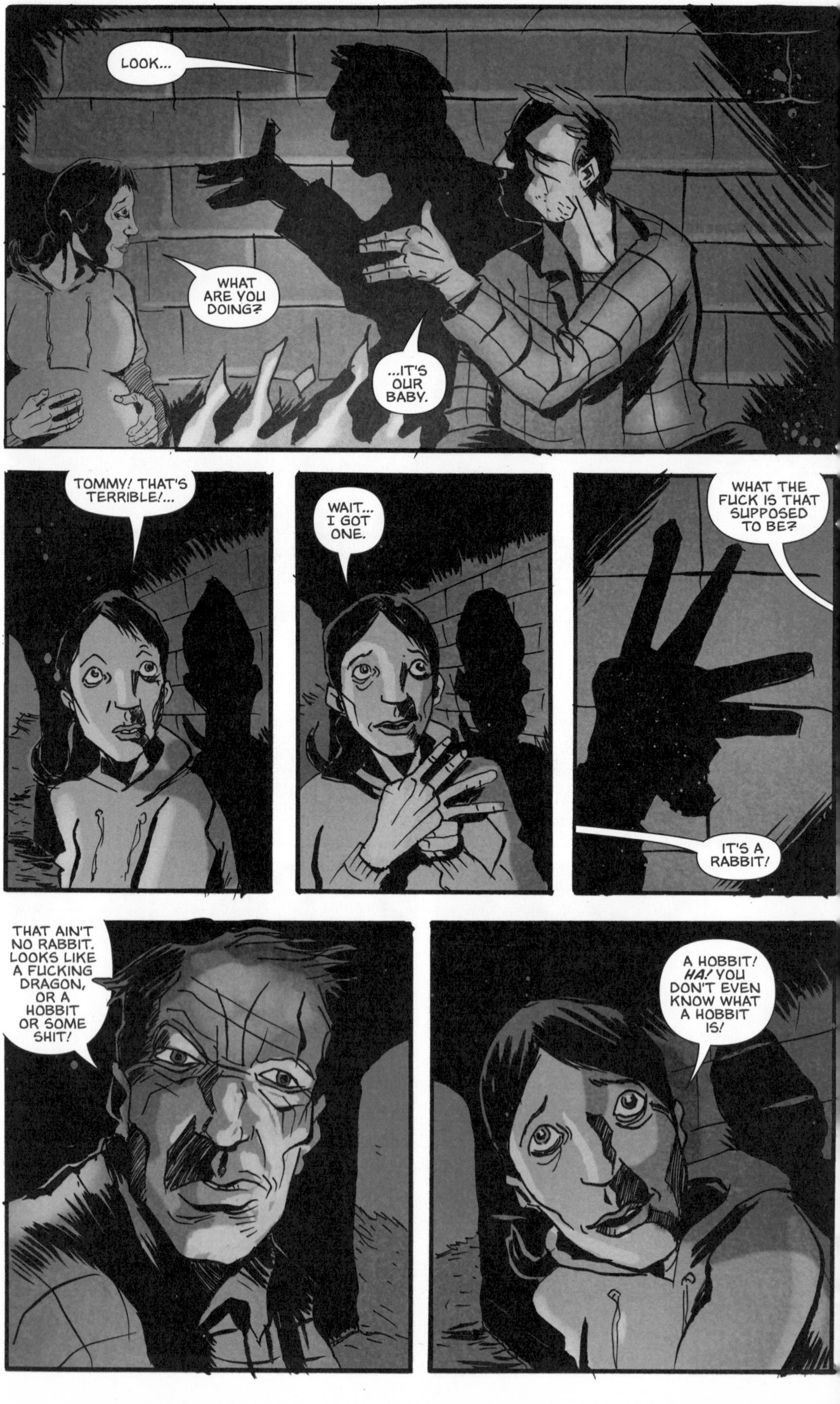
LOOK...
WHAT ARE YOU DOING?
...IT'S OUR BABY.
TOMMY! THAT'S TERRIBLE!...
WAIT... I GOT ONE.
WHAT THE FUCK IS THAT SUPPOSED TO BE?
IT'S A RABBIT!
THAT AIN'T NO RABBIT. LOOKS LIKE A FUCKING DRAGON, OR A HOBBIT OR SOME SHIT!
A HOBBIT! HA! YOU DON'T EVEN KNOW WHAT A HOBBIT IS!

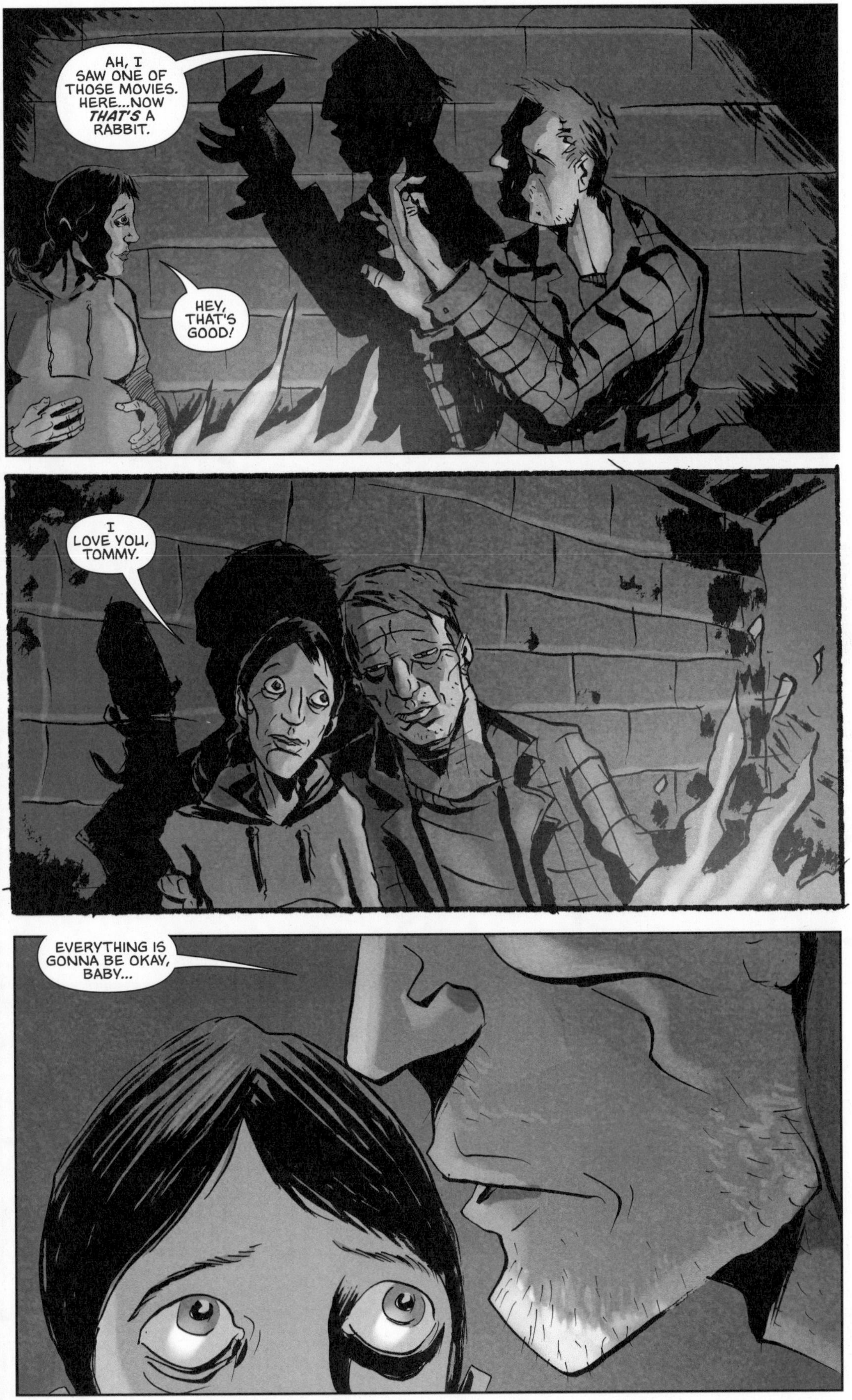
AH, I SAW ONE OF THOSE MOVIES. HERE...NOW *THAT'S* A RABBIT.
HEY, THAT'S GOOD!
I LOVE YOU, TOMMY.
EVERYTHING IS GONNA BE OKAY, BABY...

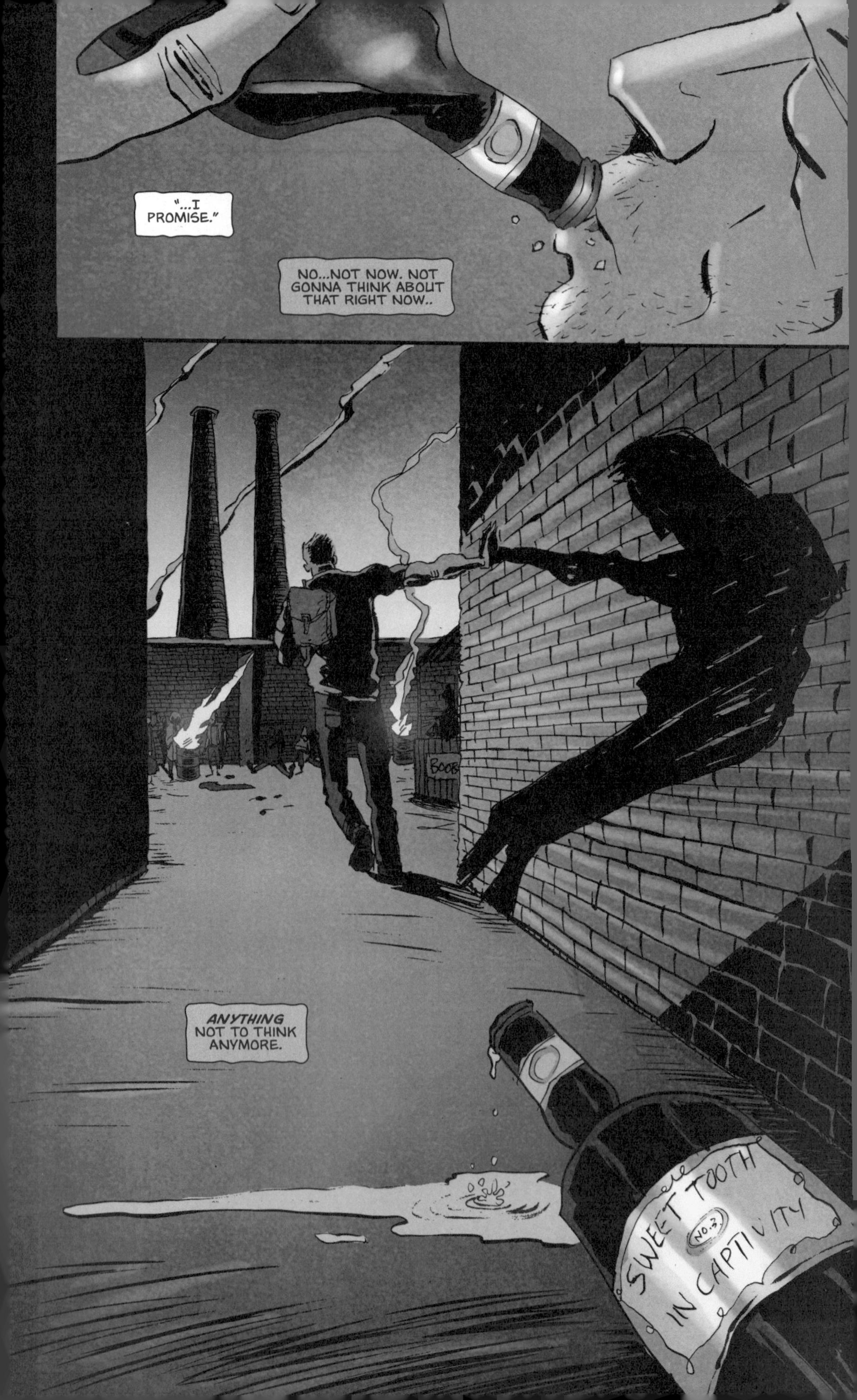
"...I PROMISE."
NO...NOT NOW. NOT GONNA THINK ABOUT THAT RIGHT NOW..
ANYTHING NOT TO THINK ANYMORE.
SWEET TOOTH
NO.3
IN CAPTIVITY

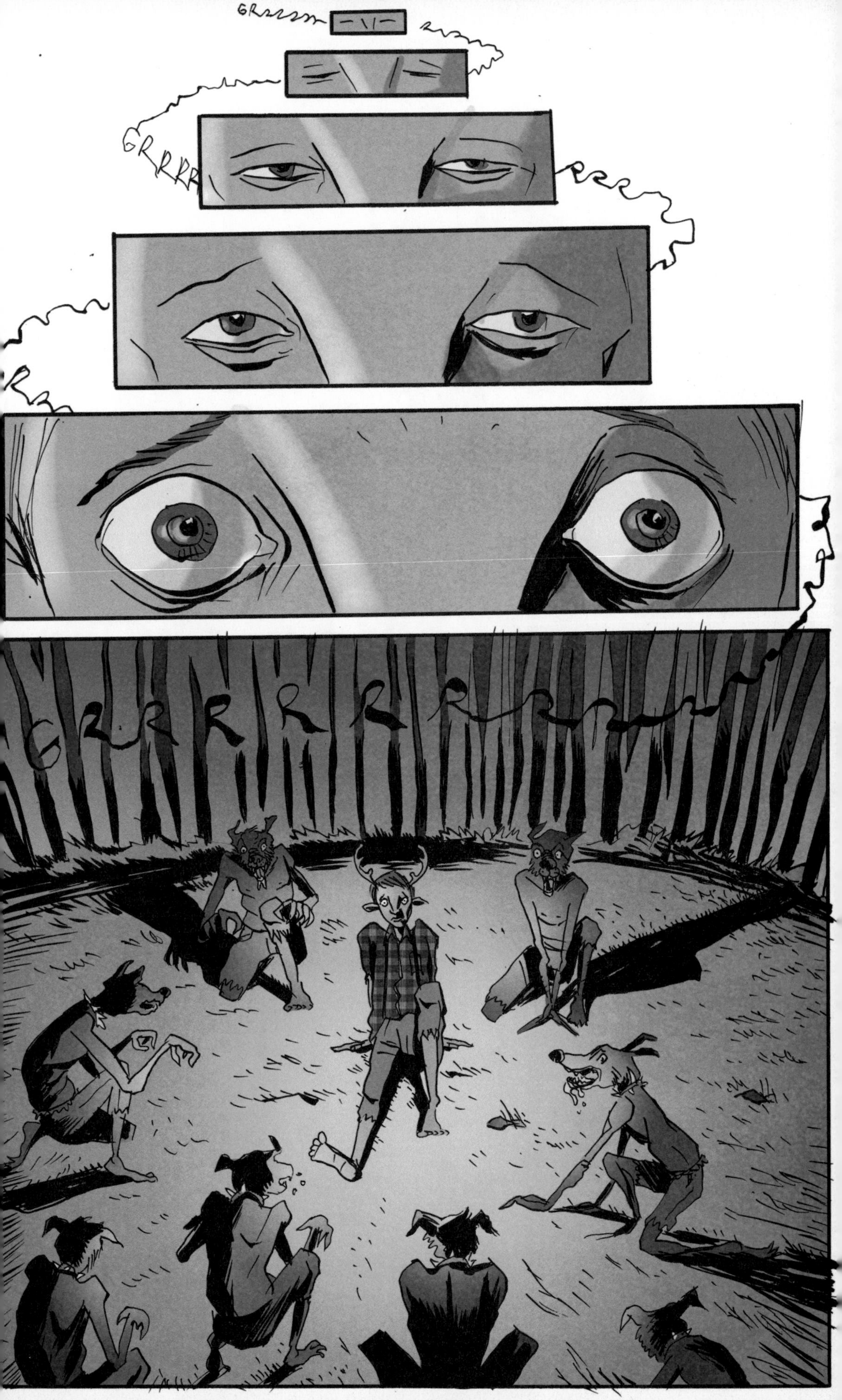
GRRRRRR
GRRRRR
GRRRRRRRRRR

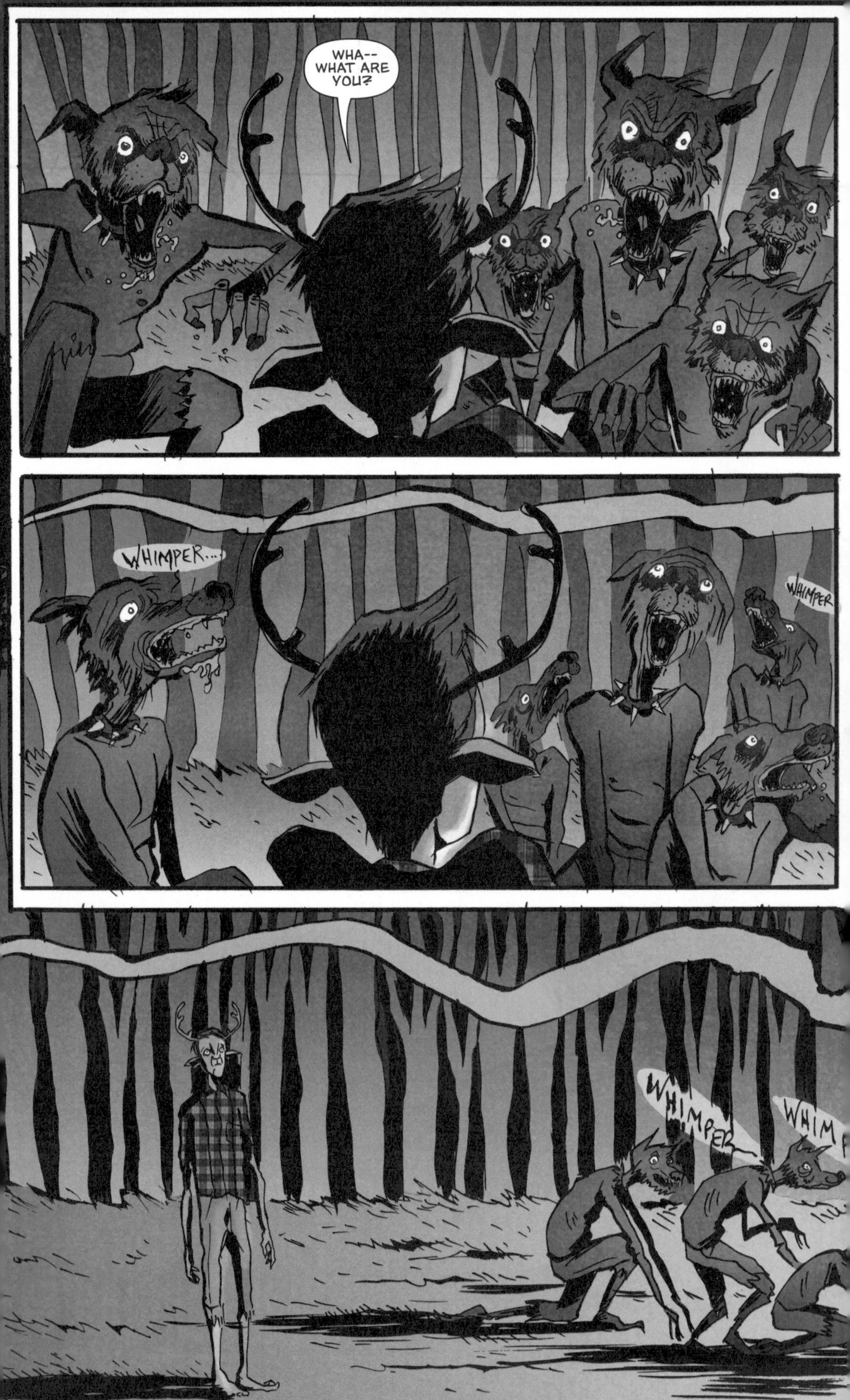
WHA--
WHAT ARE
YOU?
WHIMPER...
WHIMPER
WHIMPER--
WHIM

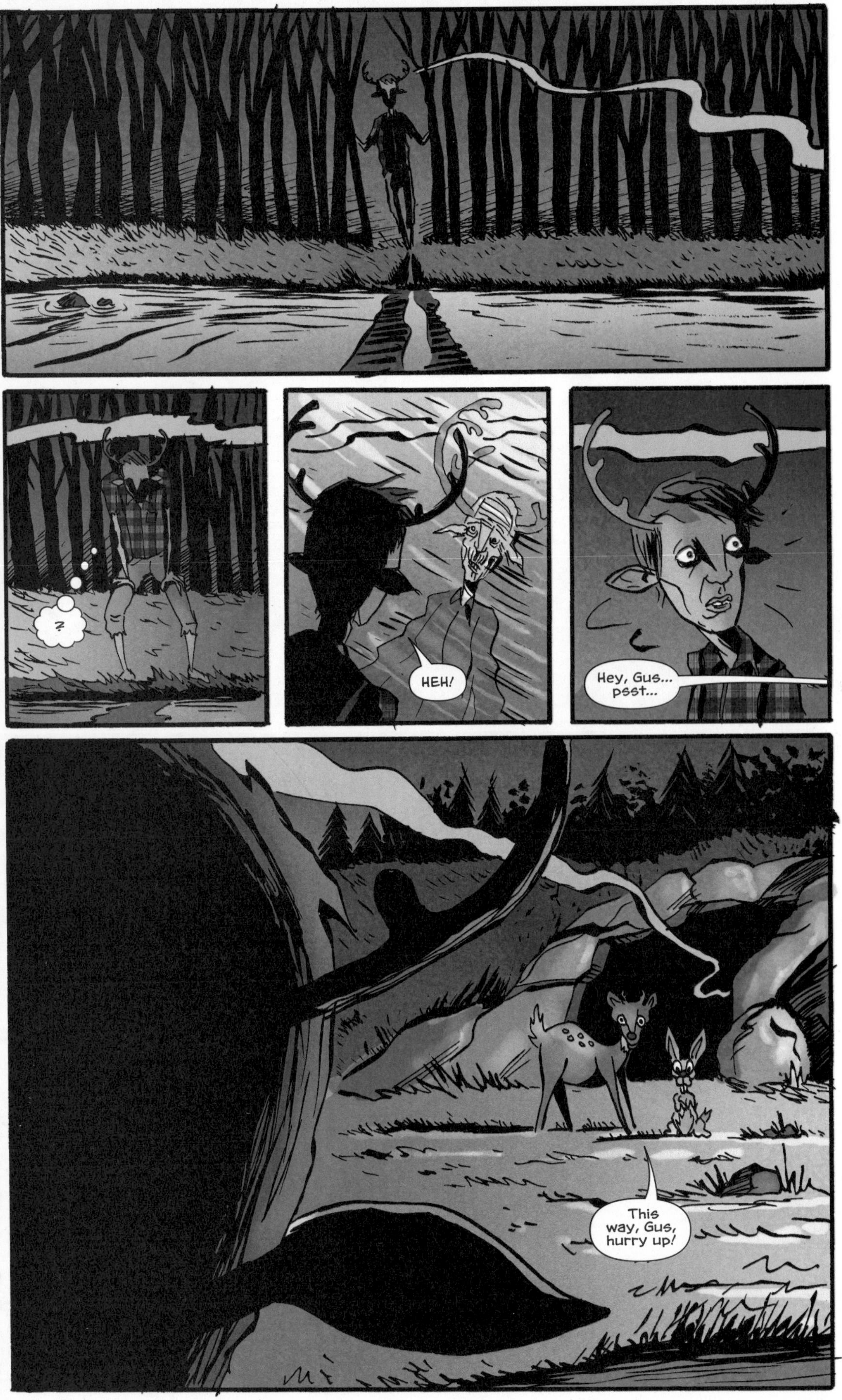
?
HEH!
Hey, Gus... psst...
This way, Gus, hurry up!

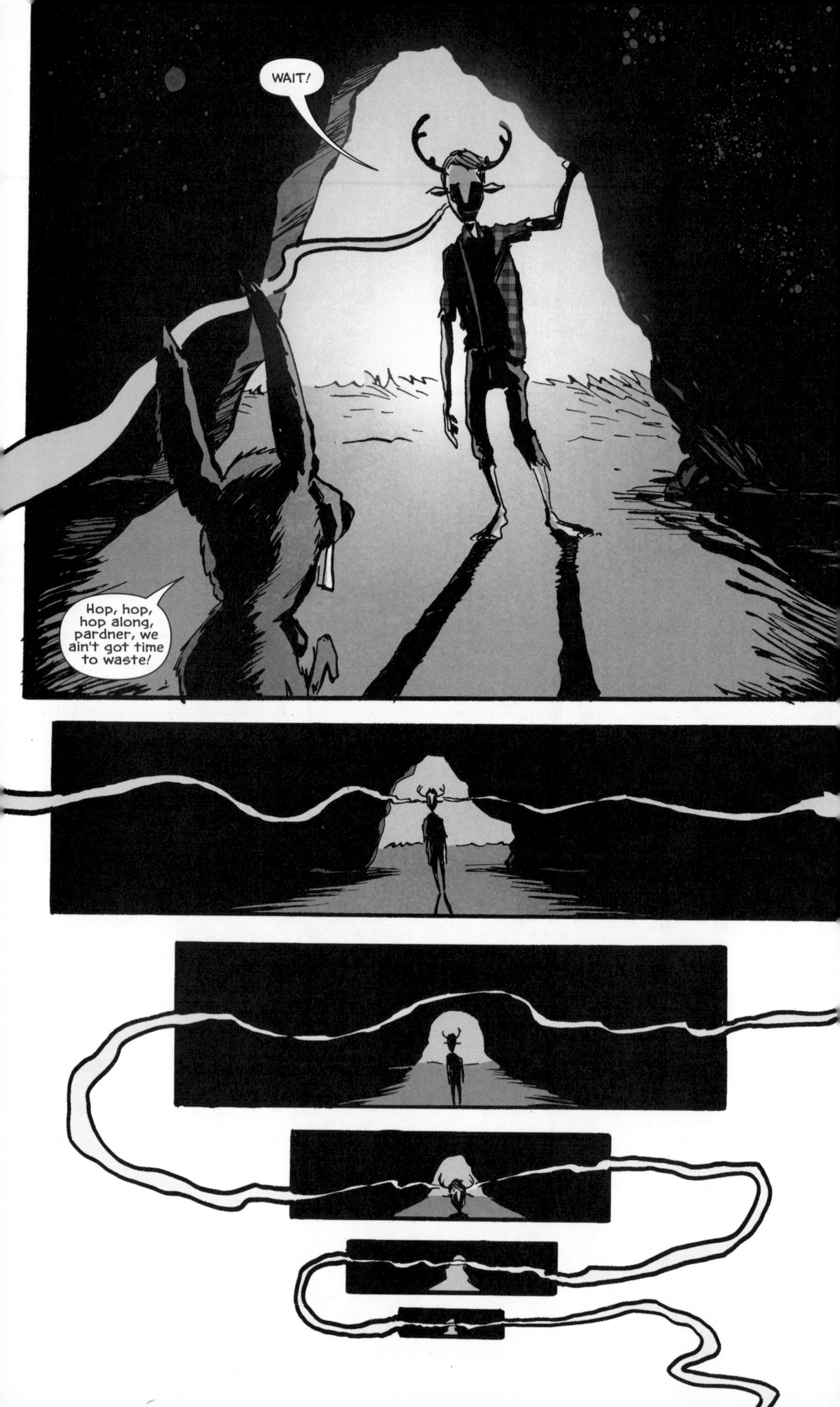
WAIT!
Hop, hop, hop along, pardner, we ain't got time to waste!

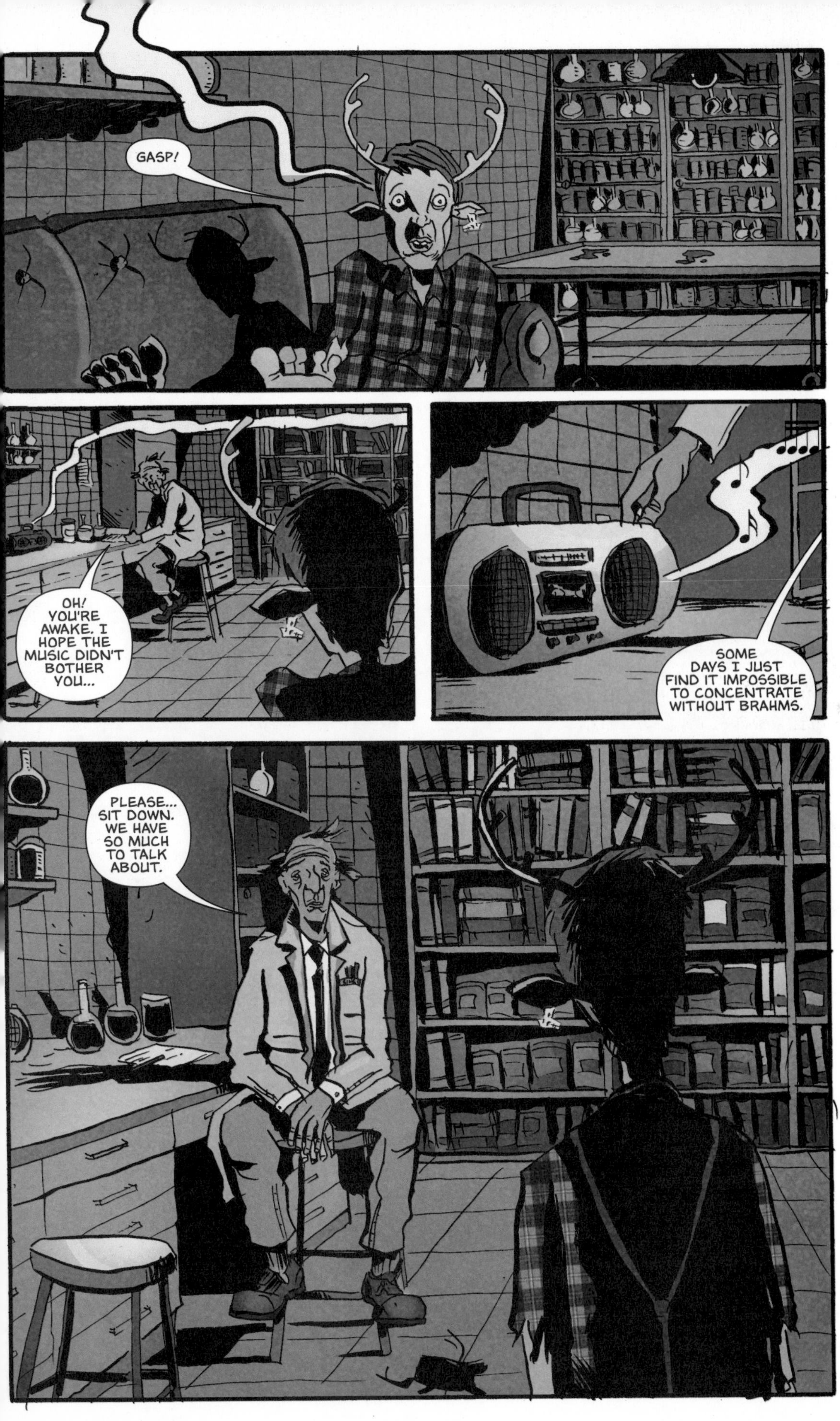
GASP!
OH! YOU'RE AWAKE. I HOPE THE MUSIC DIDN'T BOTHER YOU...
SOME DAYS I JUST FIND IT IMPOSSIBLE TO CONCENTRATE WITHOUT BRAHMS.
PLEASE... SIT DOWN. WE HAVE SO MUCH TO TALK ABOUT.

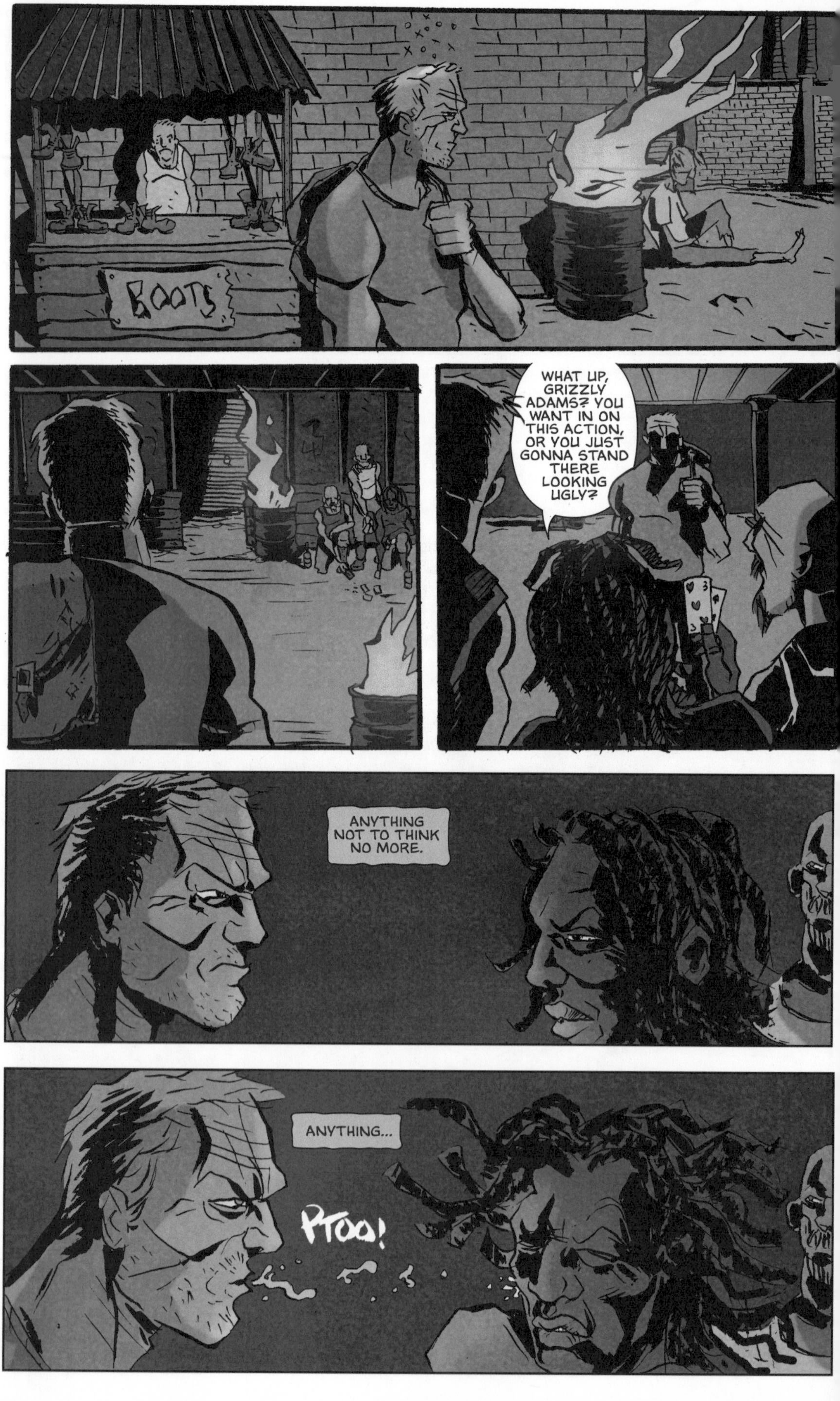
BOOTS
WHAT UP, GRIZZLY ADAMS? YOU WANT IN ON THIS ACTION, OR YOU JUST GONNA STAND THERE LOOKING UGLY?
ANYTHING NOT TO THINK NO MORE.
ANYTHING...
PTOO!

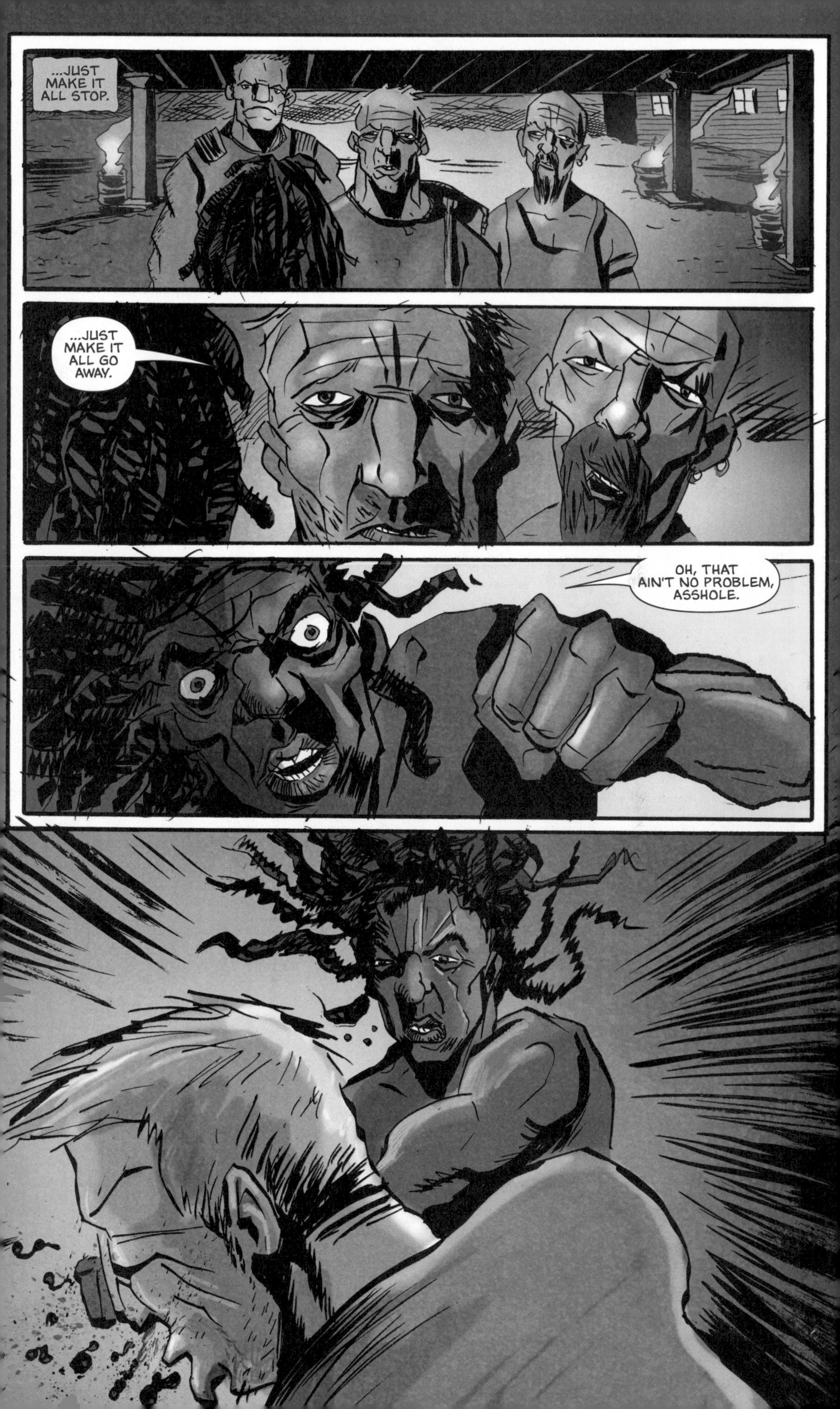
...JUST MAKE IT ALL STOP.
...JUST MAKE IT ALL GO AWAY.
OH, THAT AIN'T NO PROBLEM, ASSHOLE.

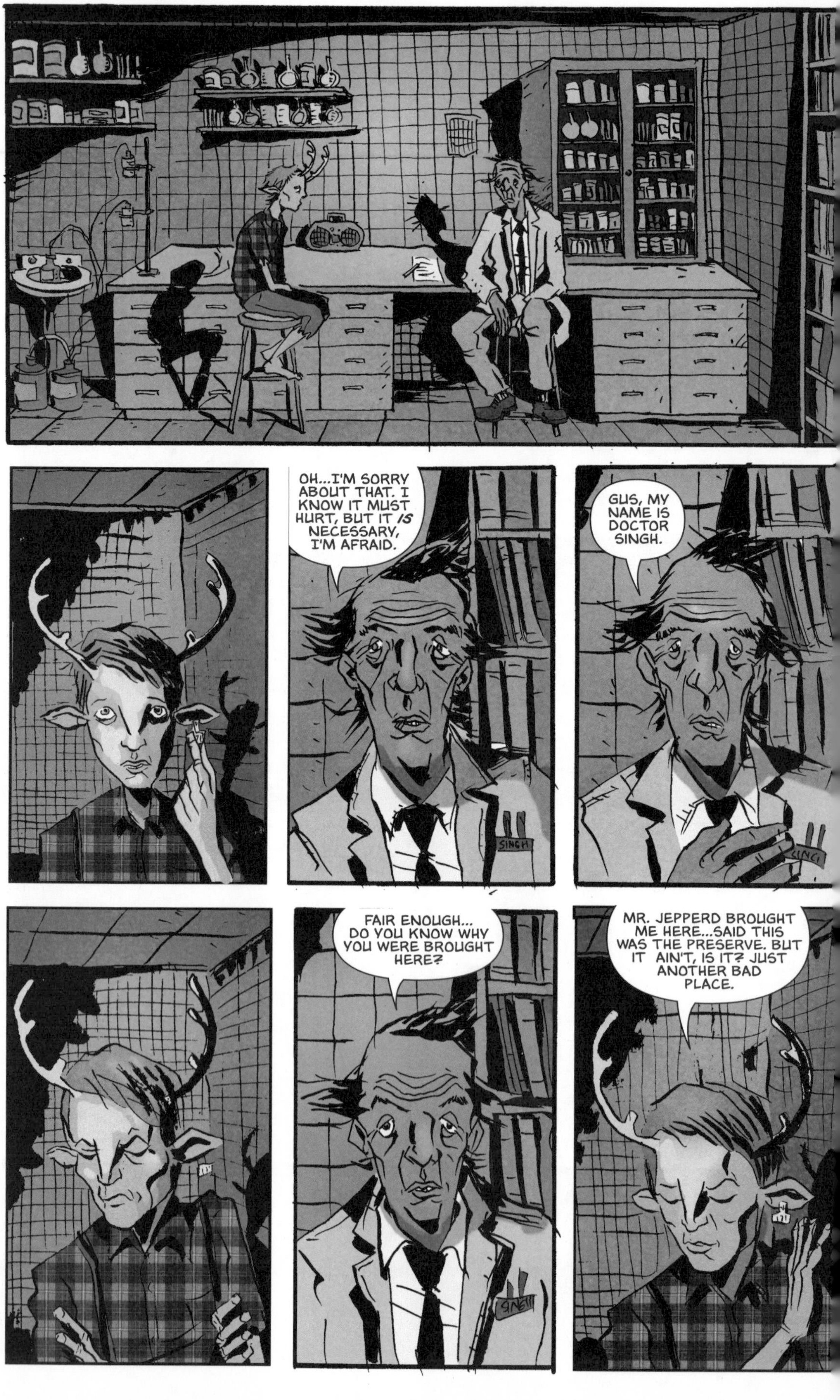

OH...I'M SORRY ABOUT THAT. I KNOW IT MUST HURT, BUT IT *IS* NECESSARY, I'M AFRAID.
SINGH
GUS, MY NAME IS DOCTOR SINGH.
FAIR ENOUGH... DO YOU KNOW WHY YOU WERE BROUGHT HERE?
MR. JEPPERD BROUGHT ME HERE...SAID THIS WAS THE PRESERVE. BUT IT AIN'T, IS IT? JUST ANOTHER BAD PLACE.

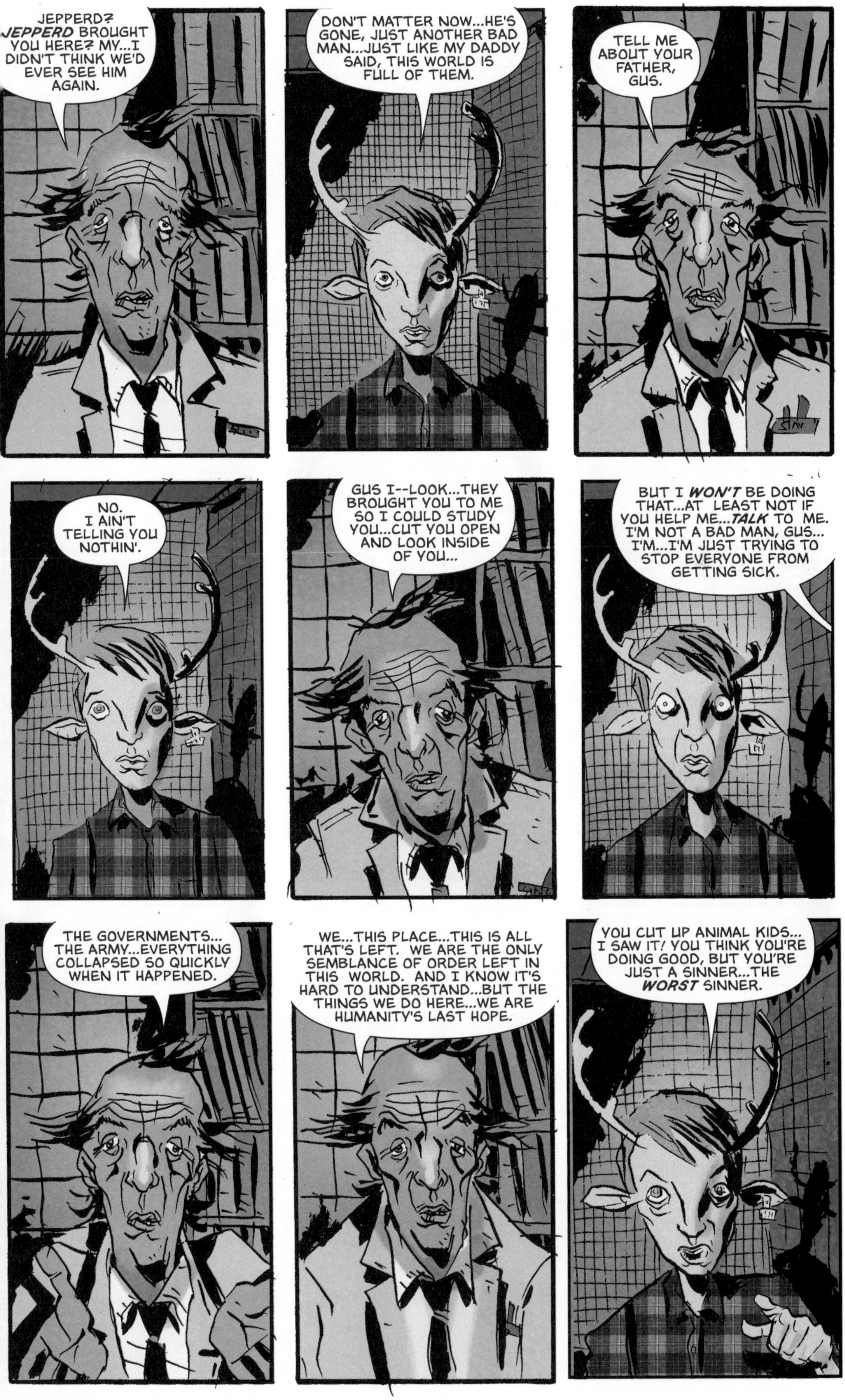
JEPPERD? JEPPERD BROUGHT YOU HERE? MY...I DIDN'T THINK WE'D EVER SEE HIM AGAIN.
DON'T MATTER NOW...HE'S GONE, JUST ANOTHER BAD MAN...JUST LIKE MY DADDY SAID, THIS WORLD IS FULL OF THEM.
TELL ME ABOUT YOUR FATHER, GUS.
NO. I AIN'T TELLING YOU NOTHIN'.
GUS I--LOOK...THEY BROUGHT YOU TO ME SO I COULD STUDY YOU...CUT YOU OPEN AND LOOK INSIDE OF YOU...
BUT I WON'T BE DOING THAT...AT LEAST NOT IF YOU HELP ME...TALK TO ME. I'M NOT A BAD MAN, GUS... I'M...I'M JUST TRYING TO STOP EVERYONE FROM GETTING SICK.
THE GOVERNMENTS... THE ARMY...EVERYTHING COLLAPSED SO QUICKLY WHEN IT HAPPENED.
WE...THIS PLACE...THIS IS ALL THAT'S LEFT. WE ARE THE ONLY SEMBLANCE OF ORDER LEFT IN THIS WORLD. AND I KNOW IT'S HARD TO UNDERSTAND...BUT THE THINGS WE DO HERE...WE ARE HUMANITY'S LAST HOPE.
YOU CUT UP ANIMAL KIDS... I SAW IT! YOU THINK YOU'RE DOING GOOD, BUT YOU'RE JUST A SINNER...THE WORST SINNER.

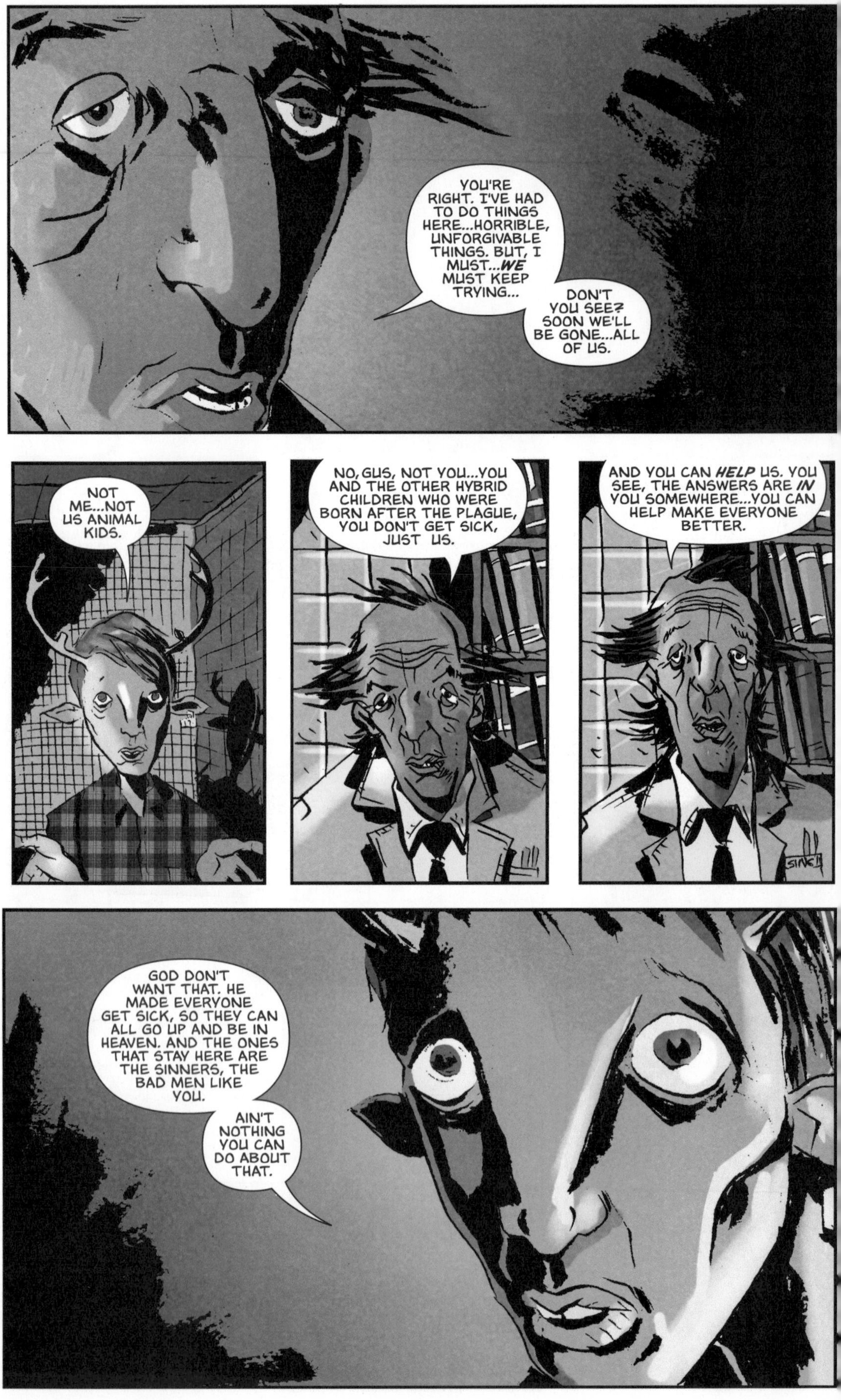
YOU'RE RIGHT. I'VE HAD TO DO THINGS HERE...HORRIBLE, UNFORGIVABLE THINGS. BUT, I MUST...*WE* MUST KEEP TRYING...
DON'T YOU SEE? SOON WE'LL BE GONE...ALL OF US.
NOT ME...NOT US ANIMAL KIDS.
NO, GUS, NOT YOU...YOU AND THE OTHER HYBRID CHILDREN WHO WERE BORN AFTER THE PLAGUE, YOU DON'T GET SICK, JUST US.
AND YOU CAN *HELP* US. YOU SEE, THE ANSWERS ARE *IN* YOU SOMEWHERE...YOU CAN HELP MAKE EVERYONE BETTER.
GOD DON'T WANT THAT. HE MADE EVERYONE GET SICK, SO THEY CAN ALL GO UP AND BE IN HEAVEN. AND THE ONES THAT STAY HERE ARE THE SINNERS, THE BAD MEN LIKE YOU.
AIN'T NOTHING YOU CAN DO ABOUT THAT.

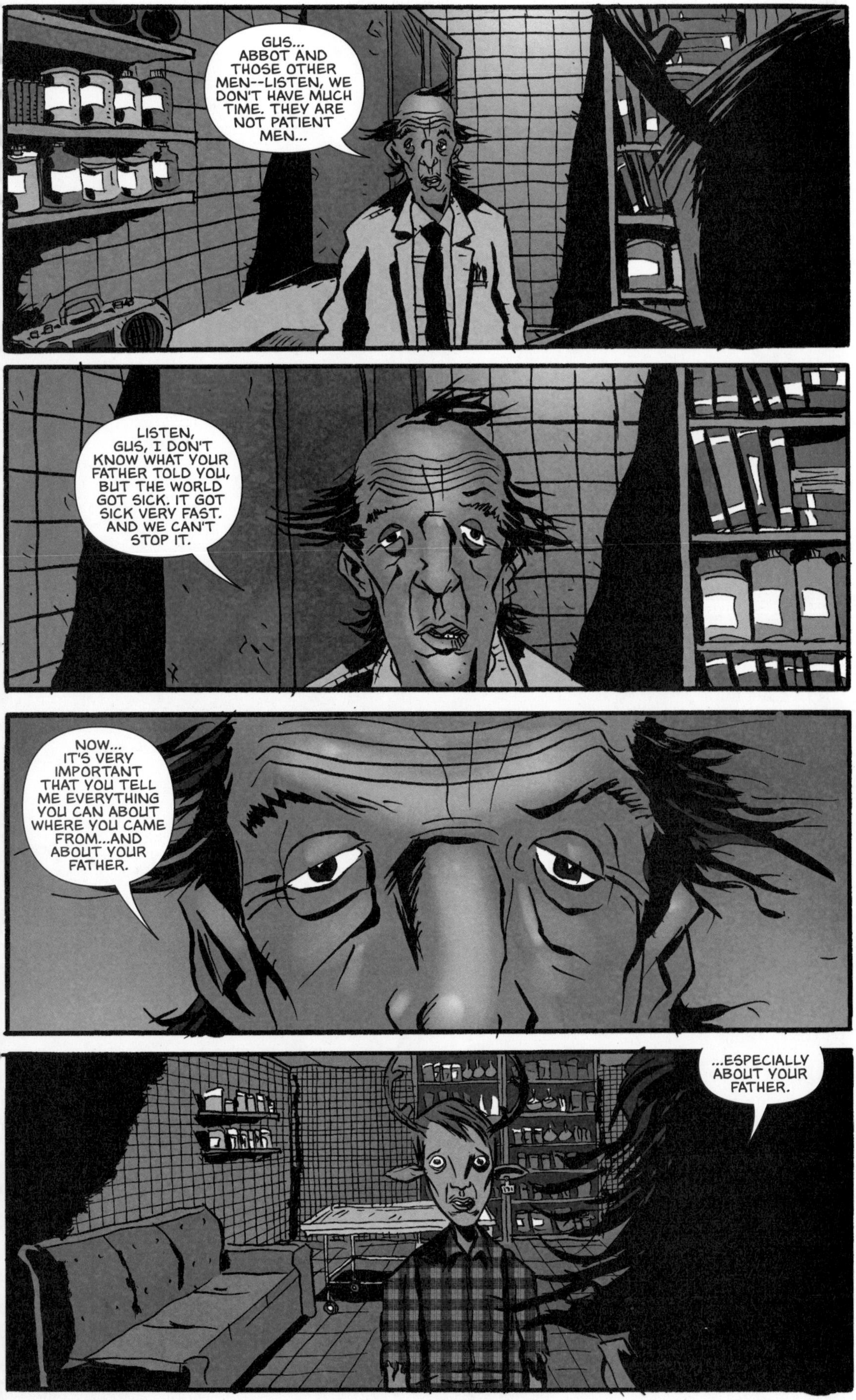
GUS... ABBOT AND THOSE OTHER MEN--LISTEN, WE DON'T HAVE MUCH TIME. THEY ARE NOT PATIENT MEN...
LISTEN, GUS, I DON'T KNOW WHAT YOUR FATHER TOLD YOU, BUT THE WORLD GOT SICK. IT GOT SICK VERY FAST. AND WE CAN'T STOP IT.
NOW... IT'S VERY IMPORTANT THAT YOU TELL ME EVERYTHING YOU CAN ABOUT WHERE YOU CAME FROM...AND ABOUT YOUR FATHER.
...ESPECIALLY ABOUT YOUR FATHER.

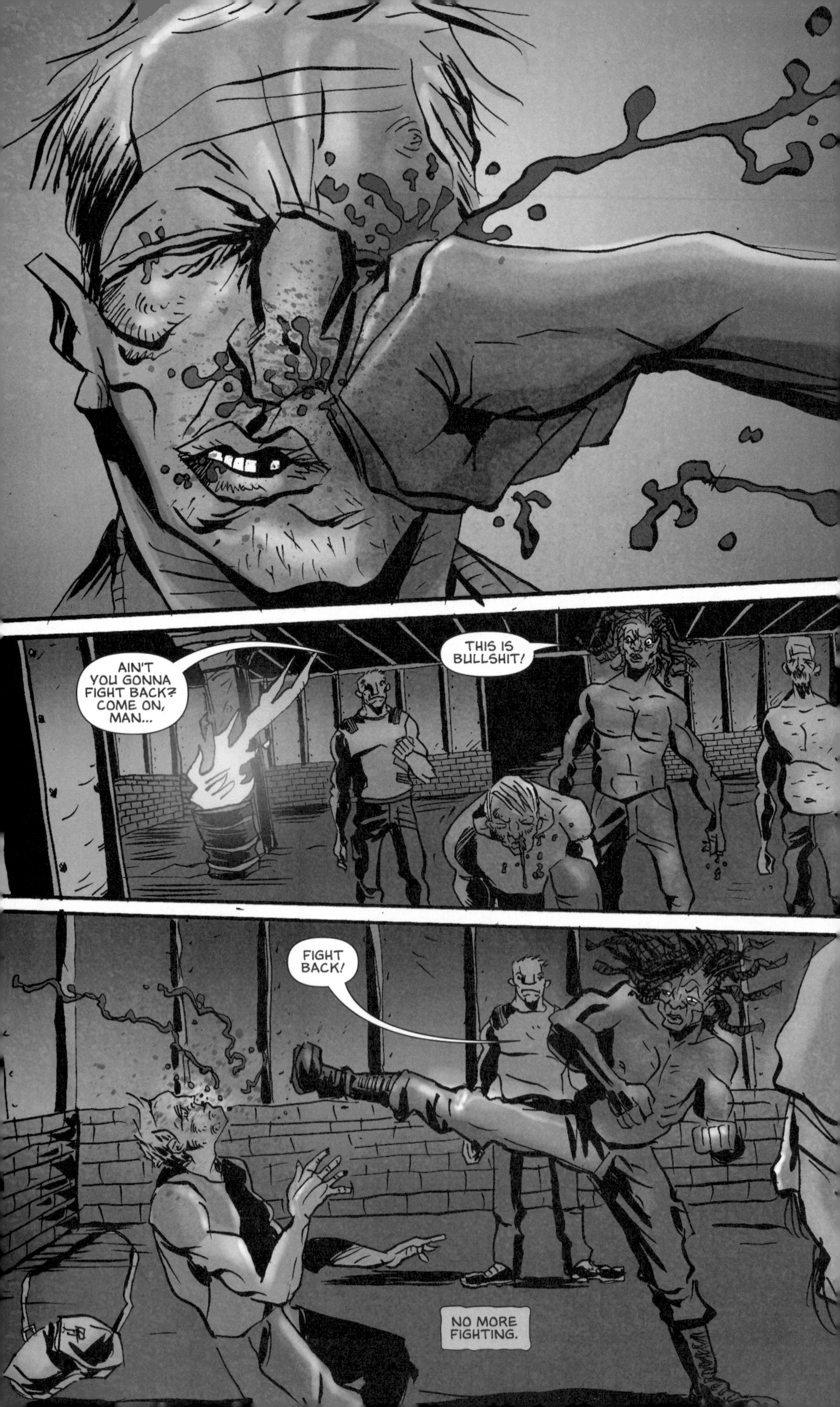
AIN'T YOU GONNA FIGHT BACK? COME ON, MAN...
THIS IS BULLSHIT!
FIGHT BACK!
NO MORE FIGHTING.

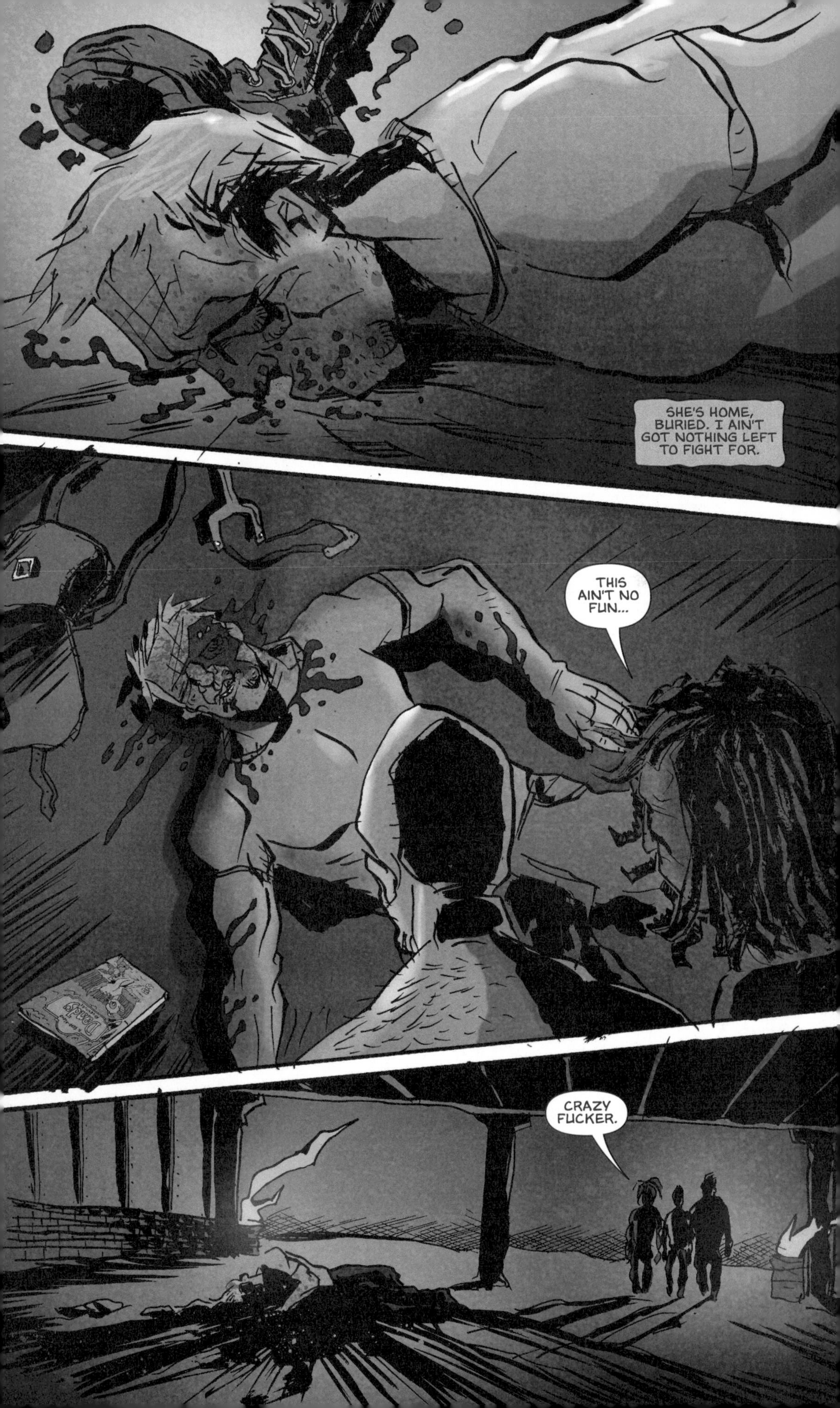
SHE'S HOME, BURIED. I AIN'T GOT NOTHING LEFT TO FIGHT FOR.
THIS AIN'T NO FUN...
CRAZY FUCKER.

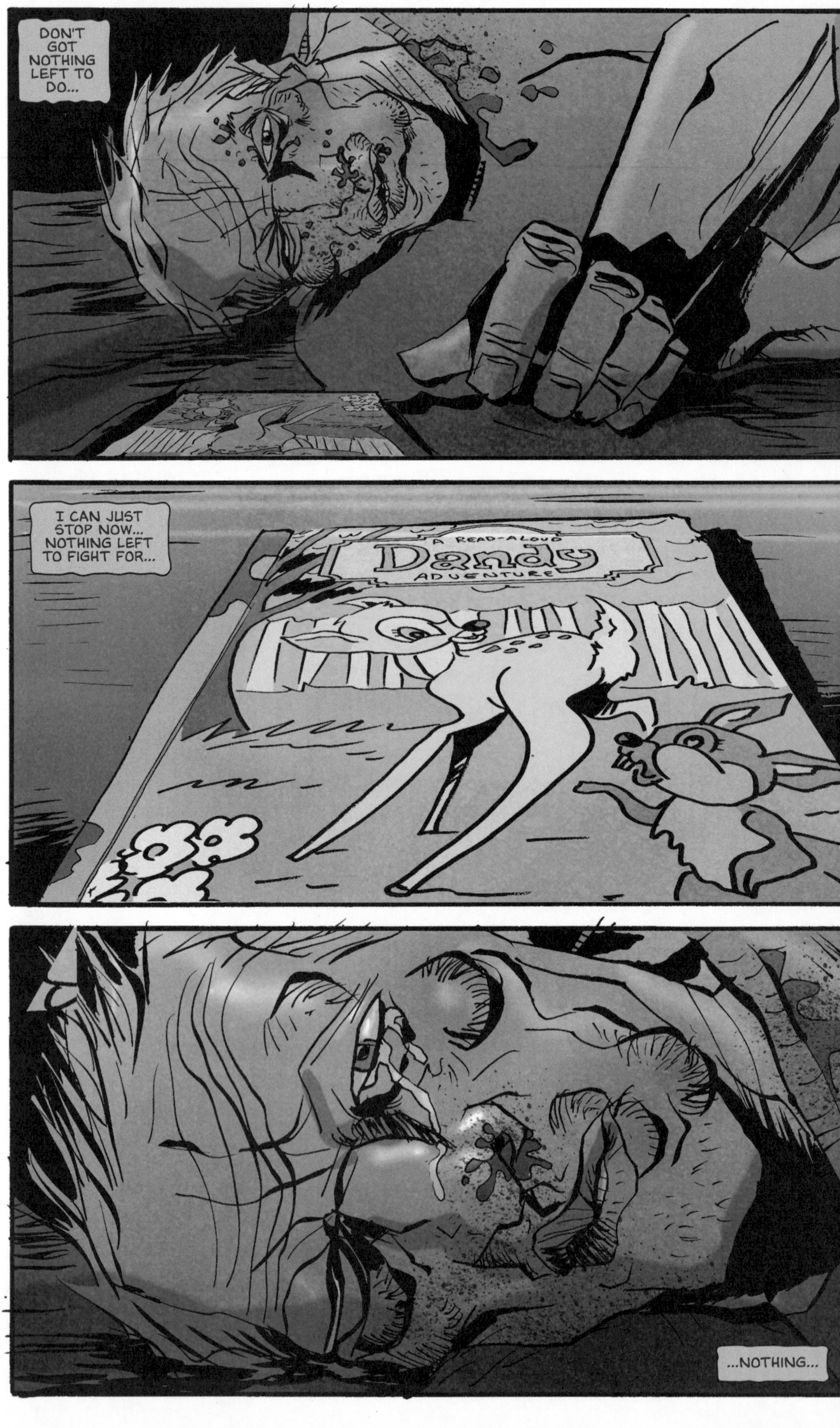

DON'T GOT NOTHING LEFT TO DO...
I CAN JUST STOP NOW... NOTHING LEFT TO FIGHT FOR...
A READ-ALOUD
Dandy
ADVENTURE
...NOTHING...

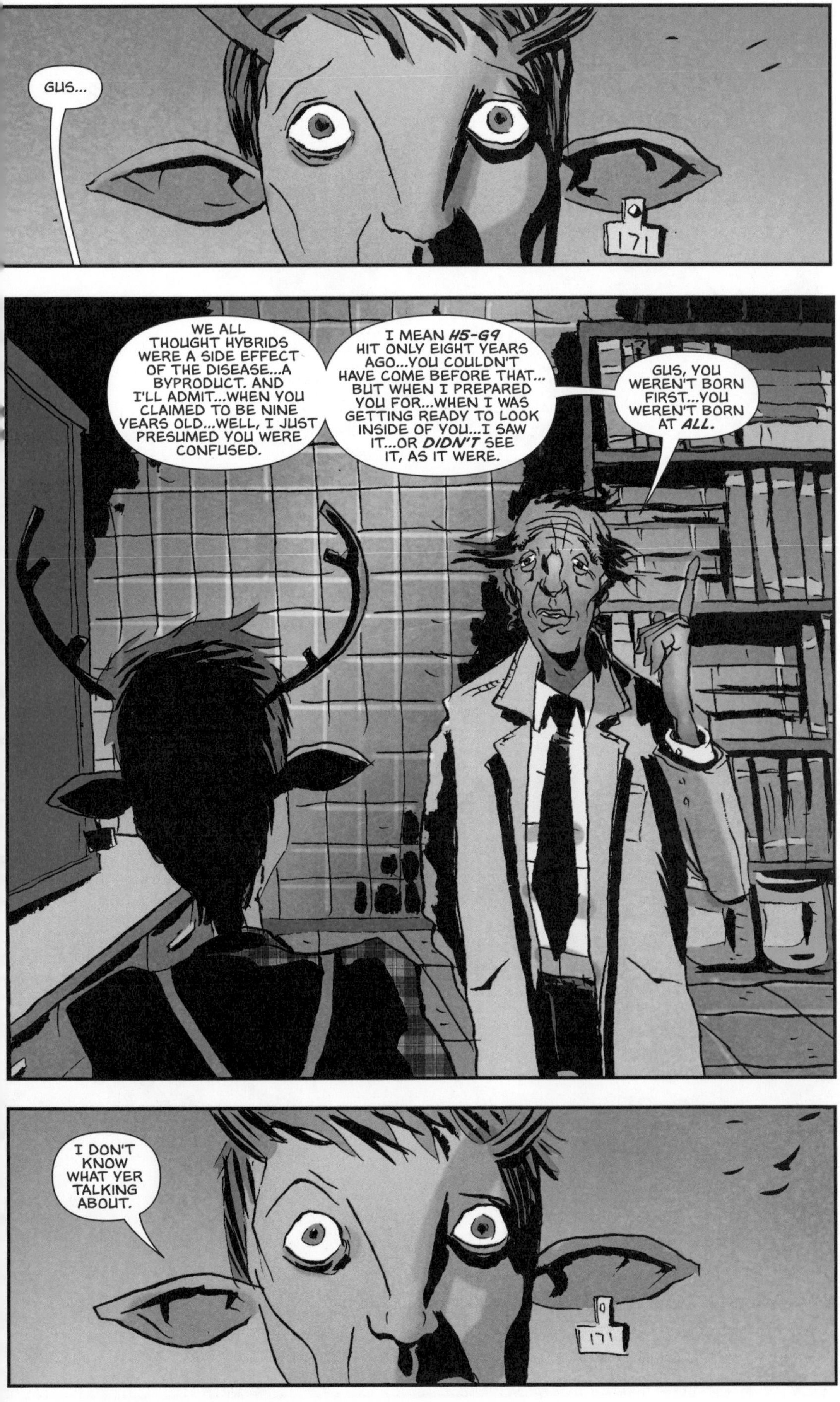
GUS...
171
WE ALL THOUGHT HYBRIDS WERE A SIDE EFFECT OF THE DISEASE...A BYPRODUCT. AND I'LL ADMIT...WHEN YOU CLAIMED TO BE NINE YEARS OLD...WELL, I JUST PRESUMED YOU WERE CONFUSED.
I MEAN *H5-G9* HIT ONLY EIGHT YEARS AGO...YOU COULDN'T HAVE COME BEFORE THAT... BUT WHEN I PREPARED YOU FOR...WHEN I WAS GETTING READY TO LOOK INSIDE OF YOU...I SAW IT...OR *DIDN'T* SEE IT, AS IT WERE.
GUS, YOU WEREN'T BORN FIRST...YOU WEREN'T BORN AT *ALL*.
I DON'T KNOW WHAT YER TALKING ABOUT.
171

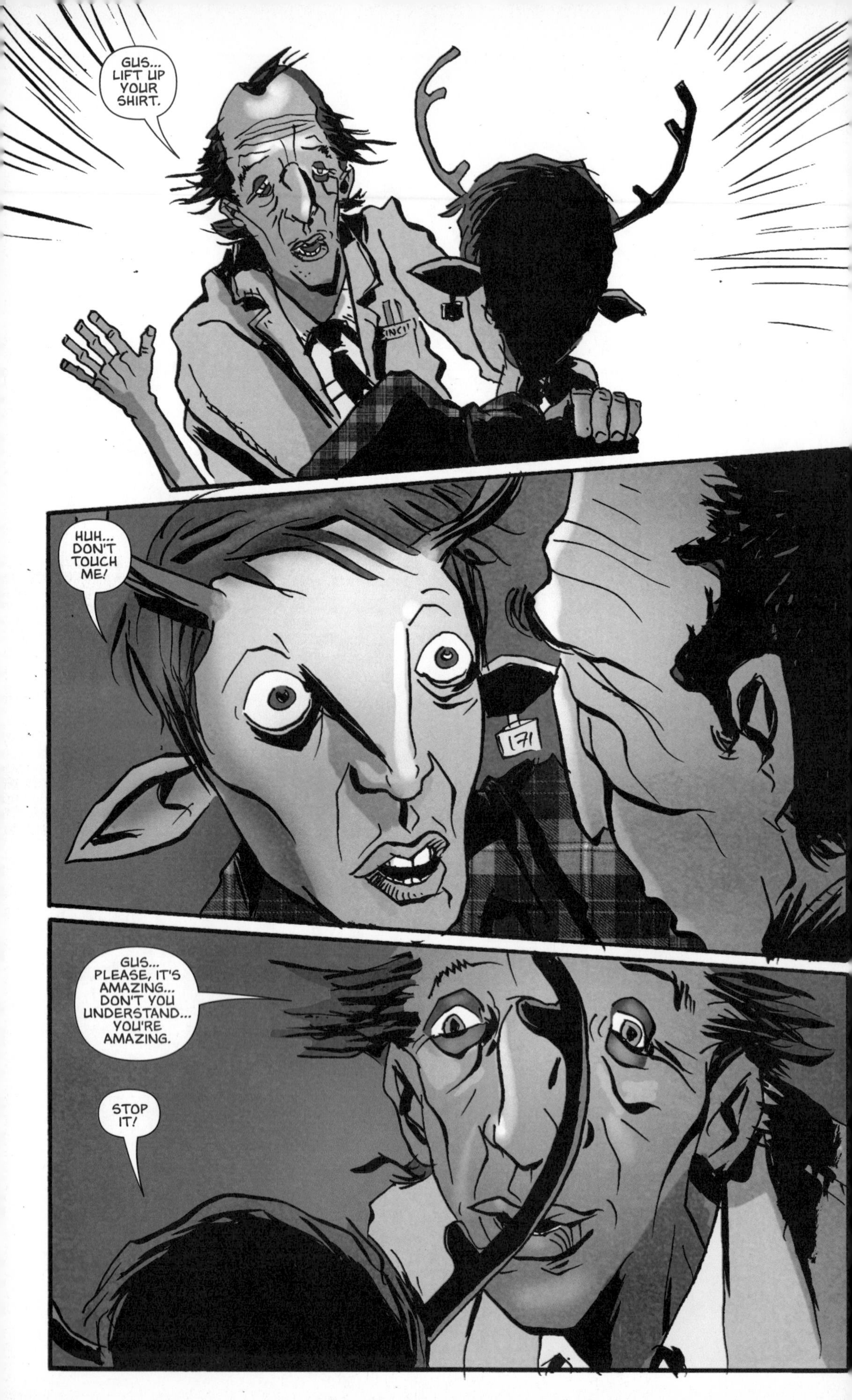
GUS... LIFT UP YOUR SHIRT.
HUH... DON'T TOUCH ME!
171
GUS... PLEASE, IT'S AMAZING... DON'T YOU UNDERSTAND... YOU'RE AMAZING.
STOP IT!

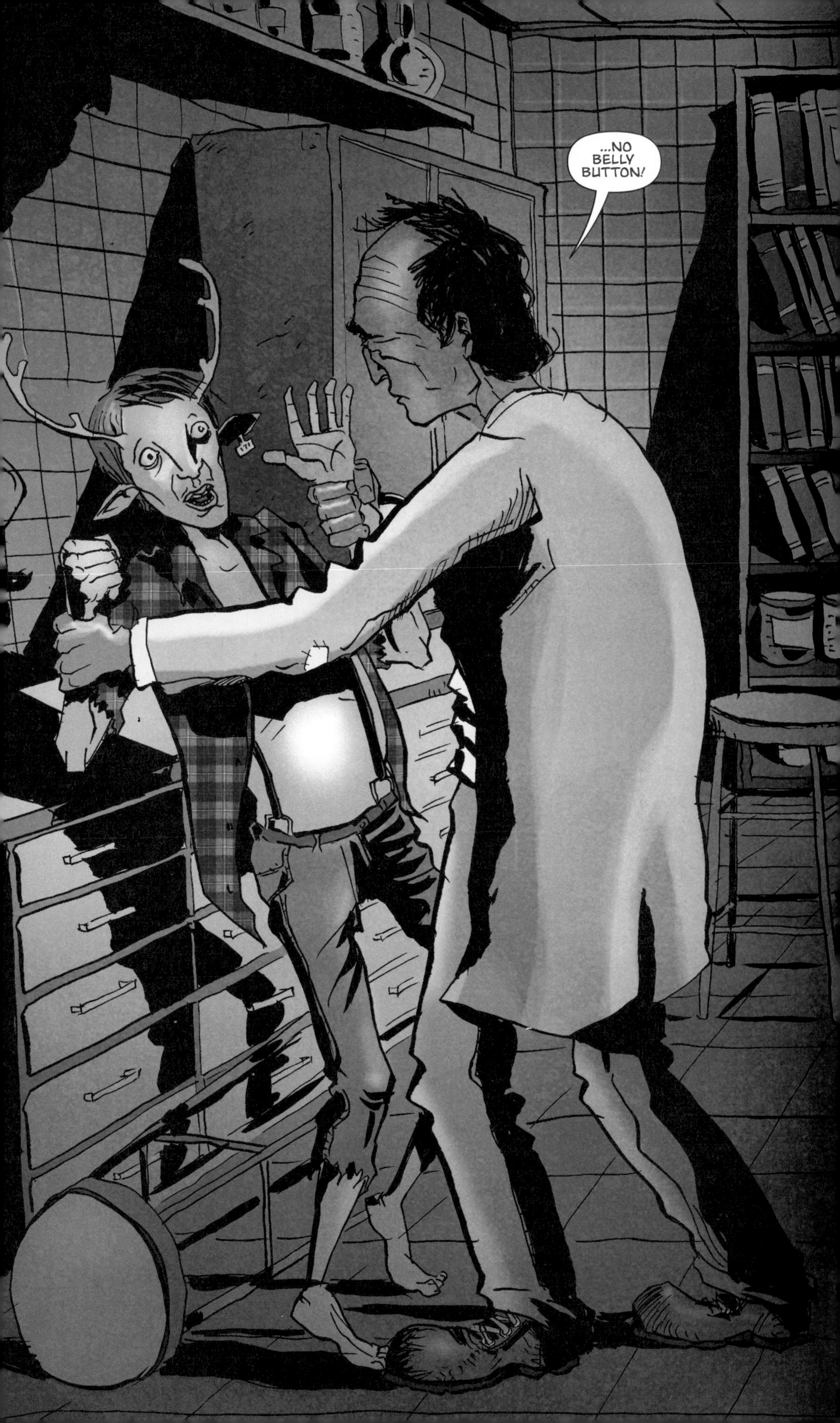
...NO BELLY BUTTON!

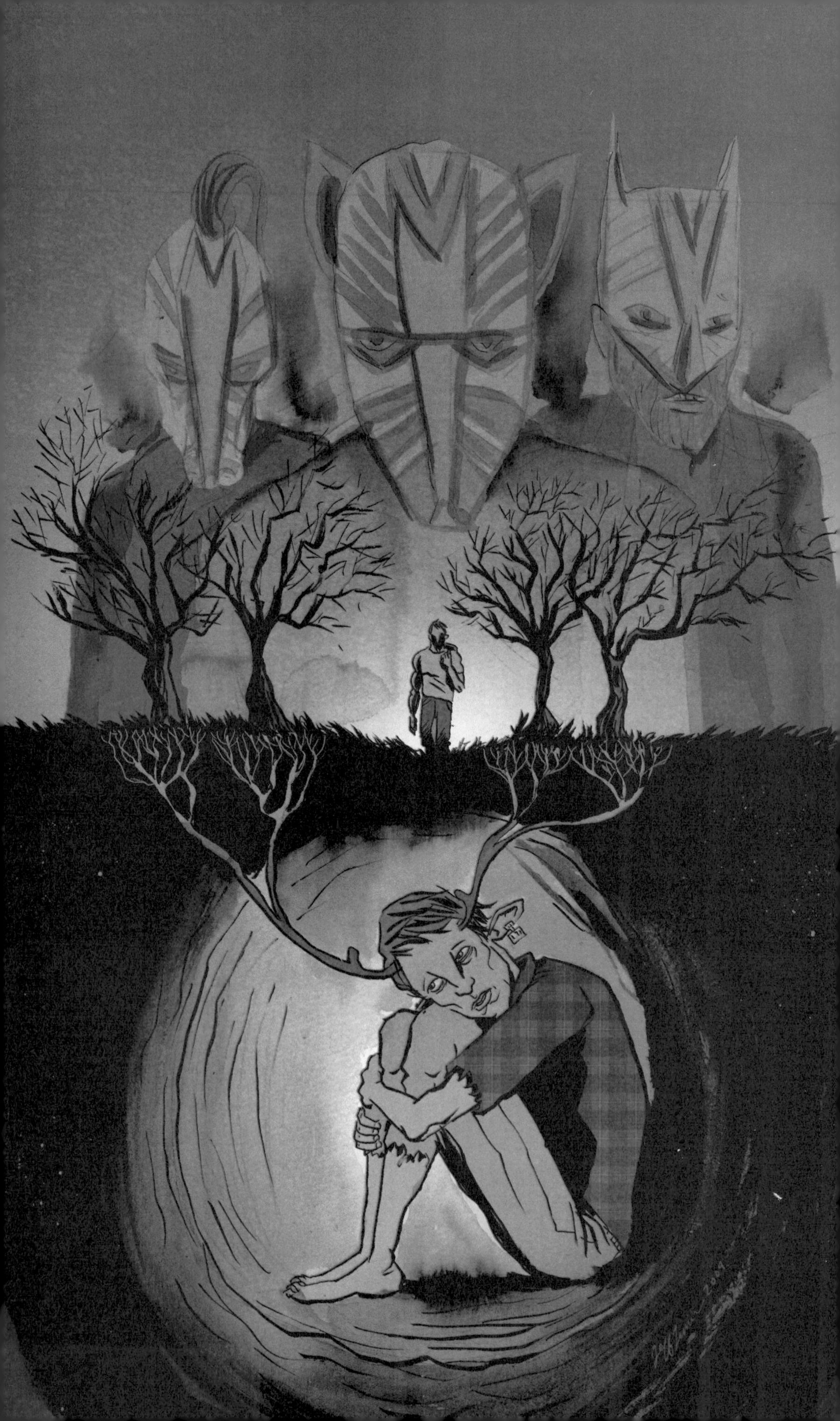

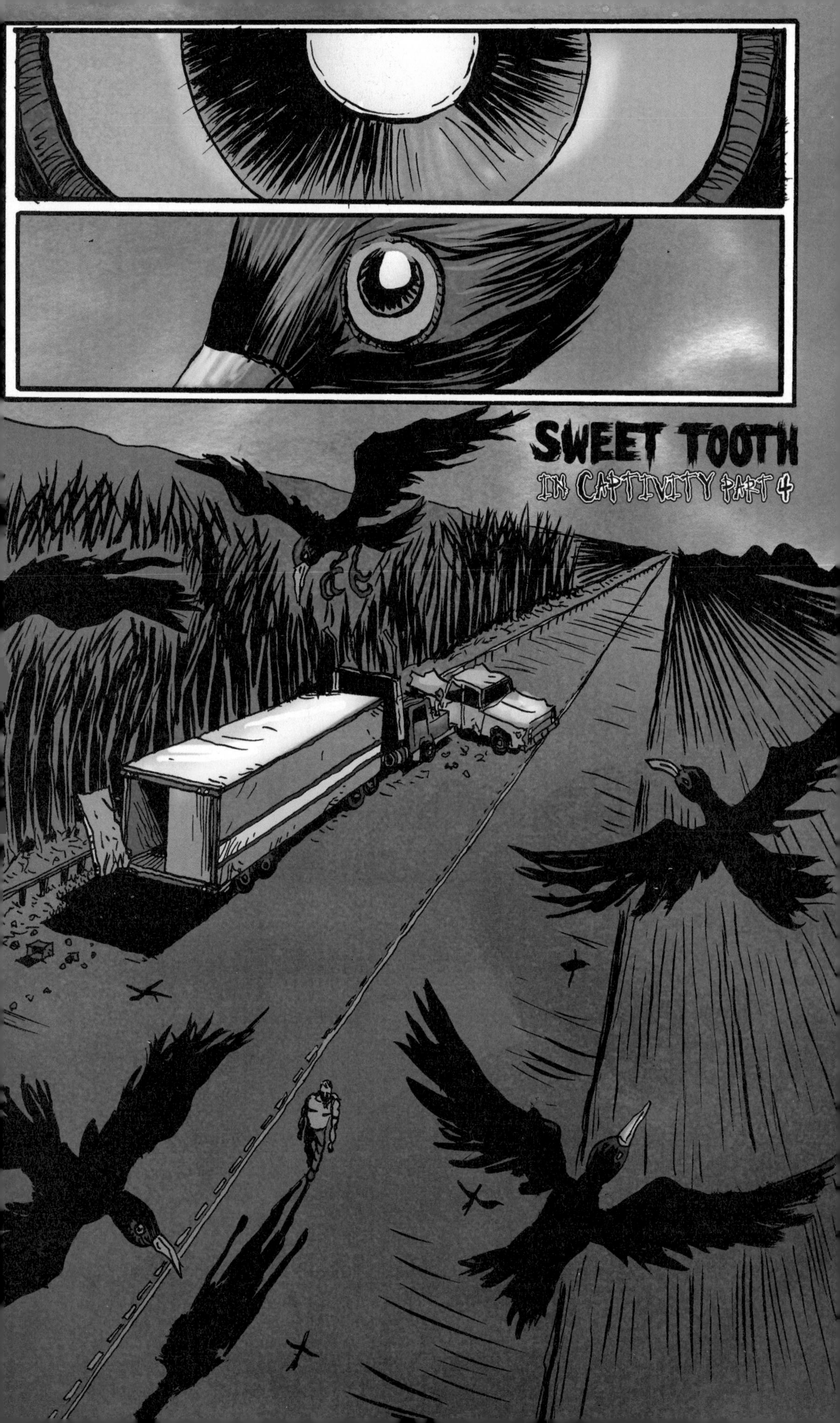
SWEET TOOTH
IN CAPTIVITY PART 4

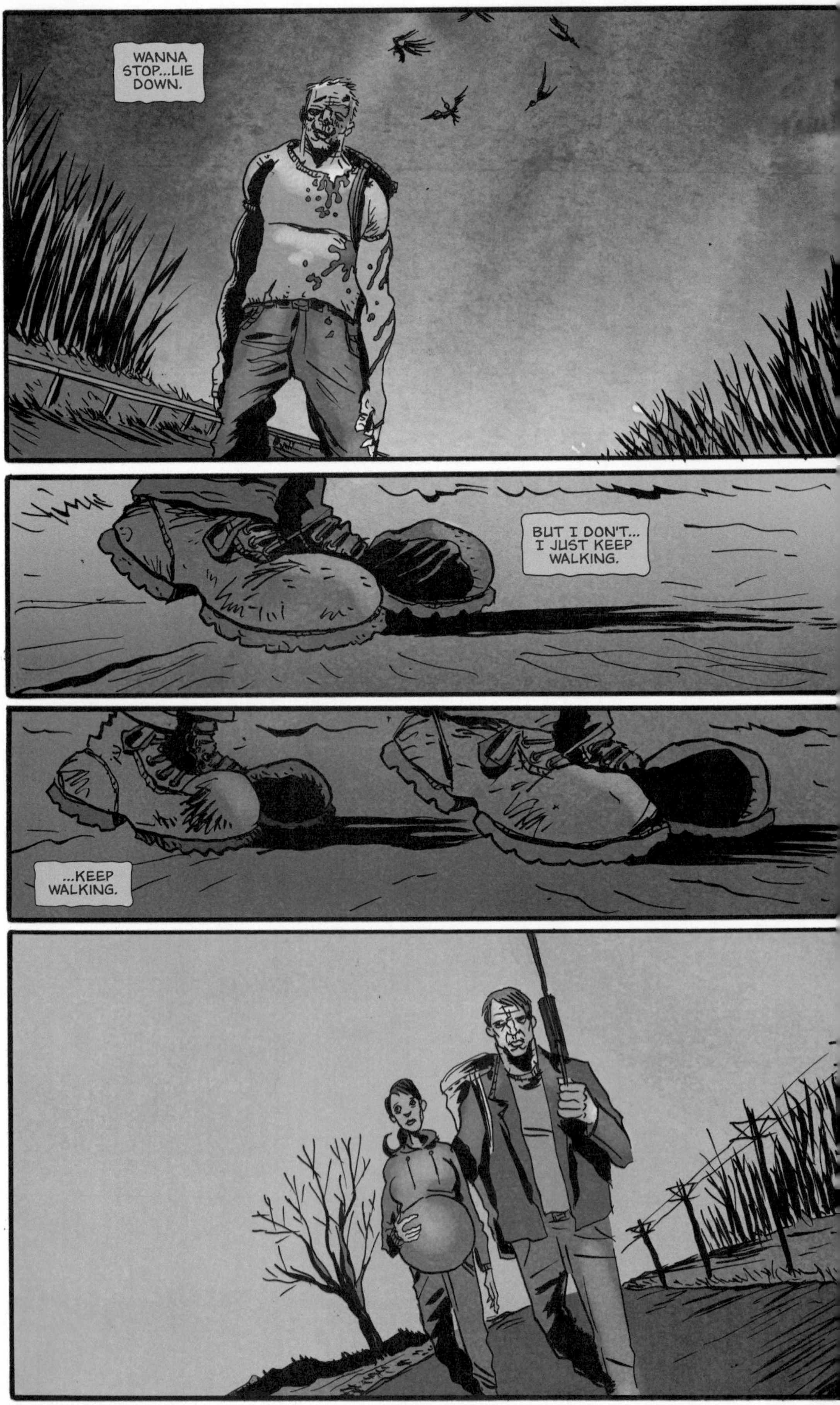
WANNA STOP...LIE DOWN.
BUT I DON'T... I JUST KEEP WALKING.
...KEEP WALKING.

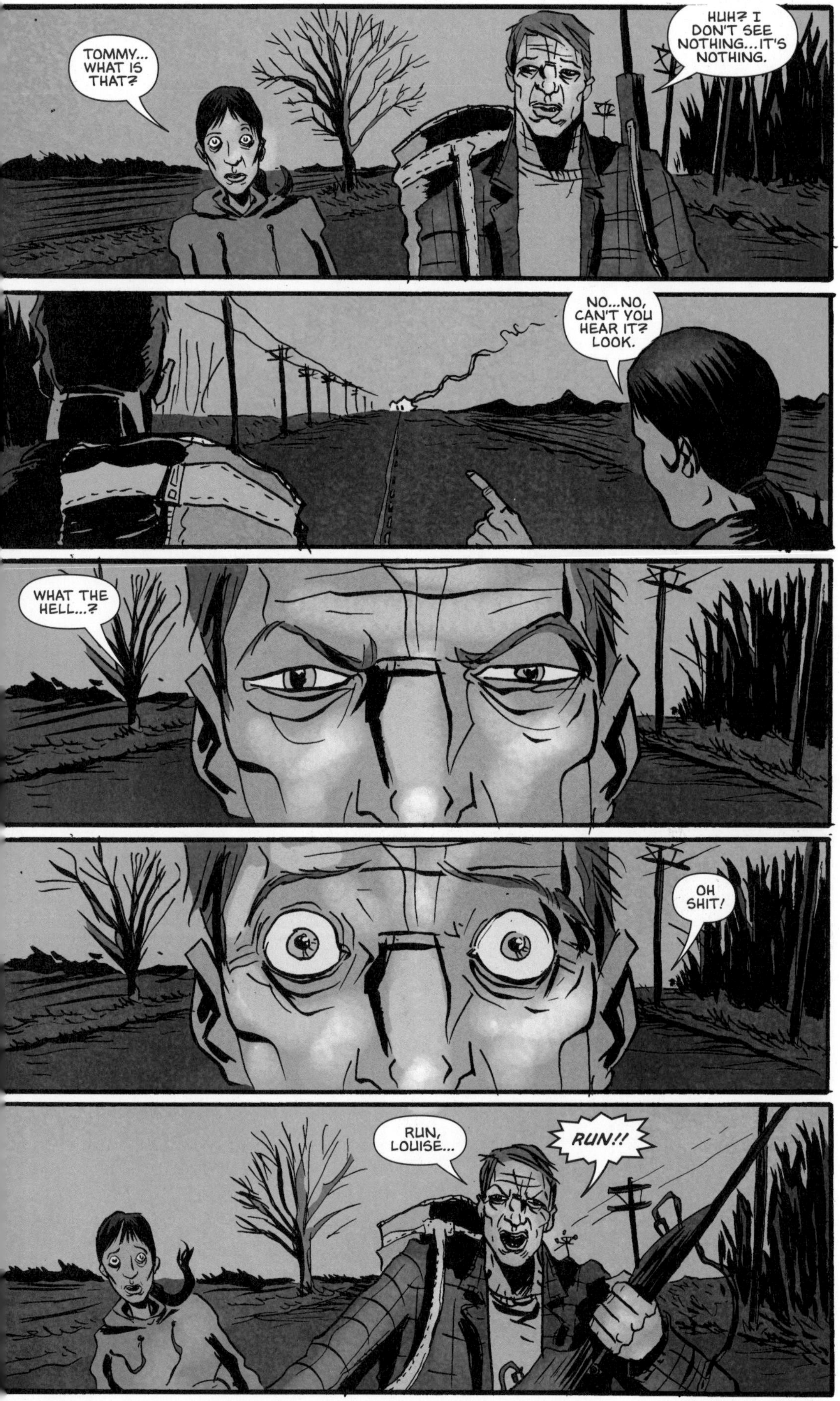
TOMMY... WHAT IS THAT?
HUH? I DON'T SEE NOTHING...IT'S NOTHING.
NO...NO, CAN'T YOU HEAR IT? LOOK.
WHAT THE HELL...?
OH SHIT!
RUN, LOUISE...
RUN!!

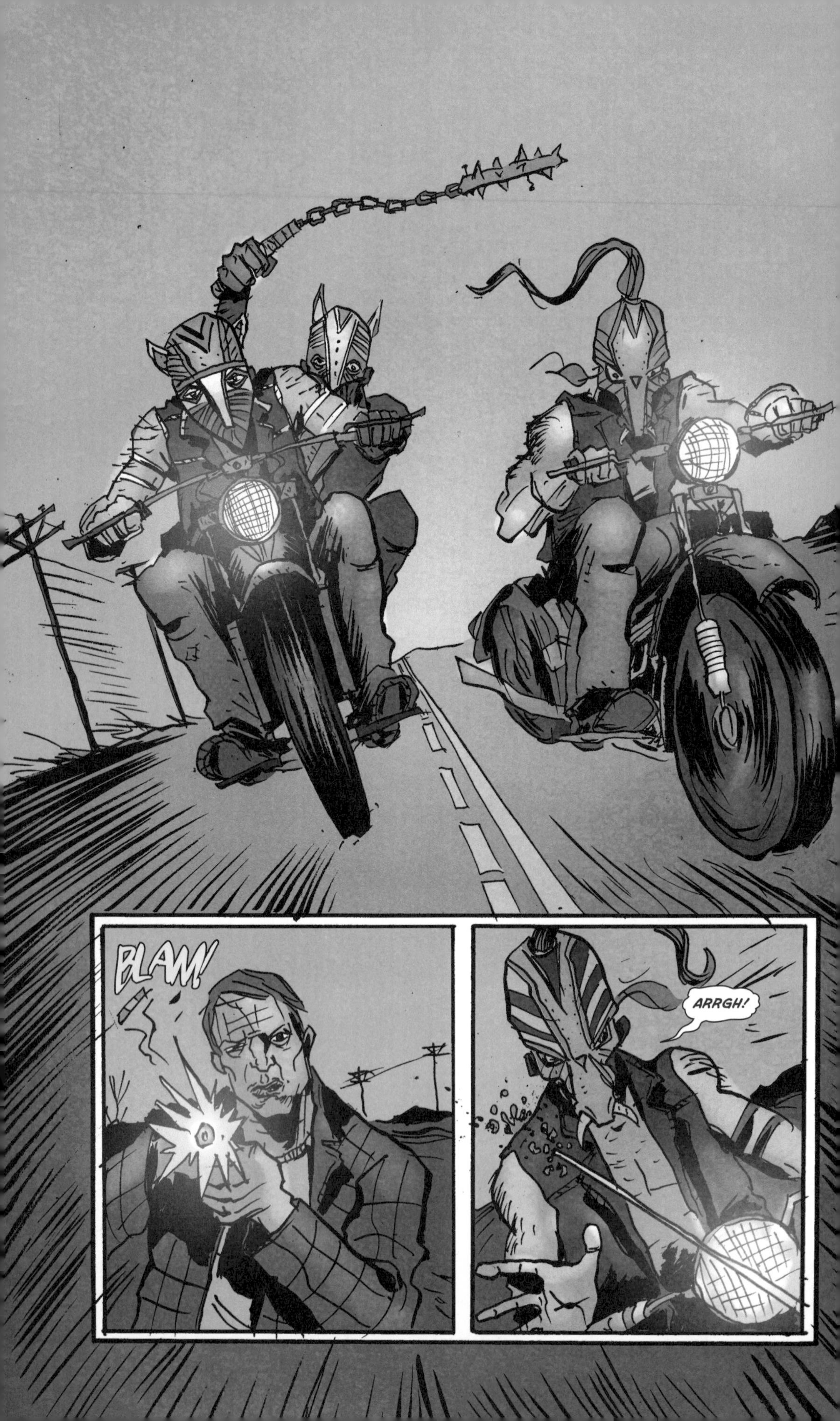
BLAM!
ARRGH!

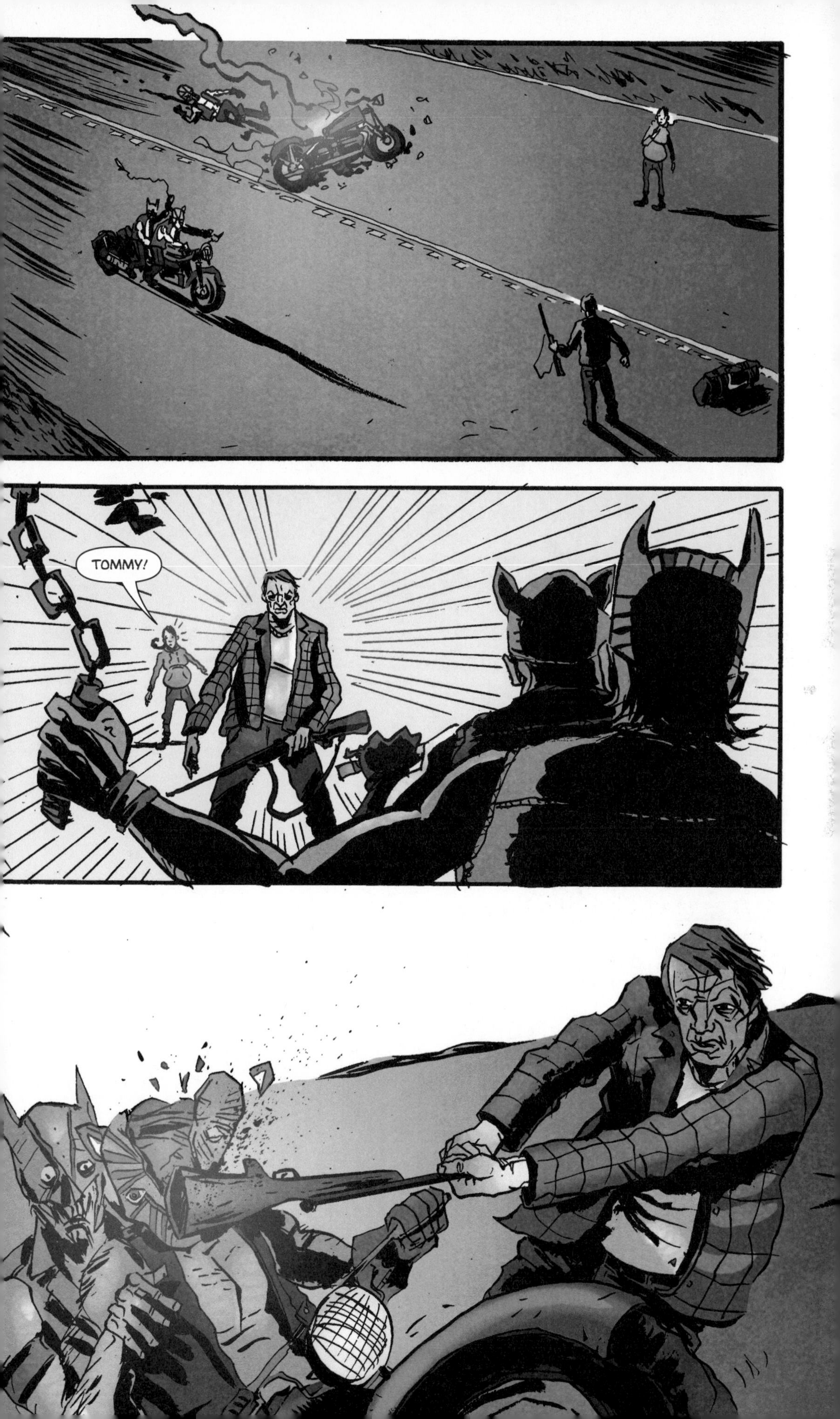
TOMMY!

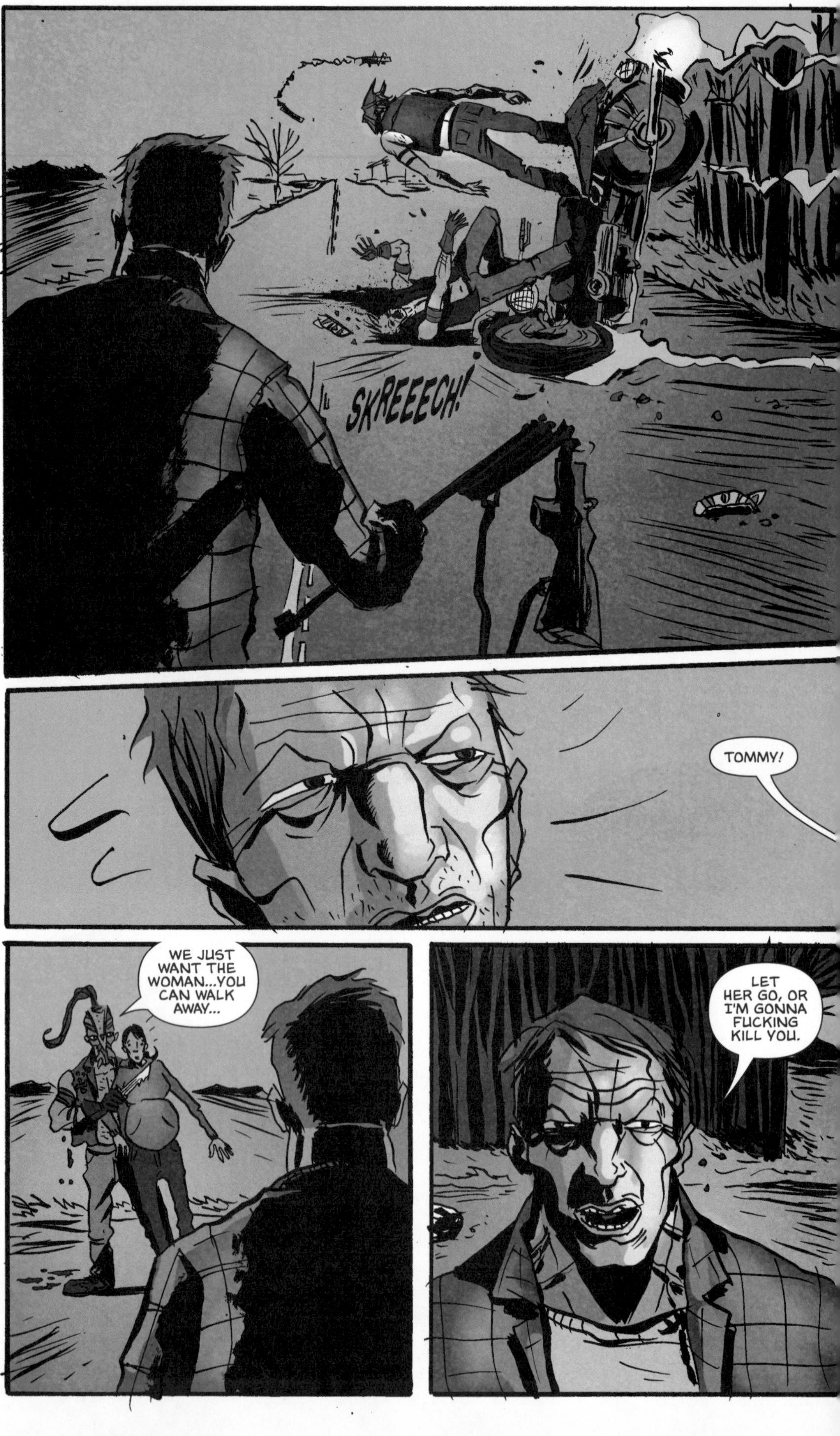
SKREEECH!
TOMMY!
WE JUST WANT THE WOMAN...YOU CAN WALK AWAY...
LET HER GO, OR I'M GONNA FUCKING KILL YOU.

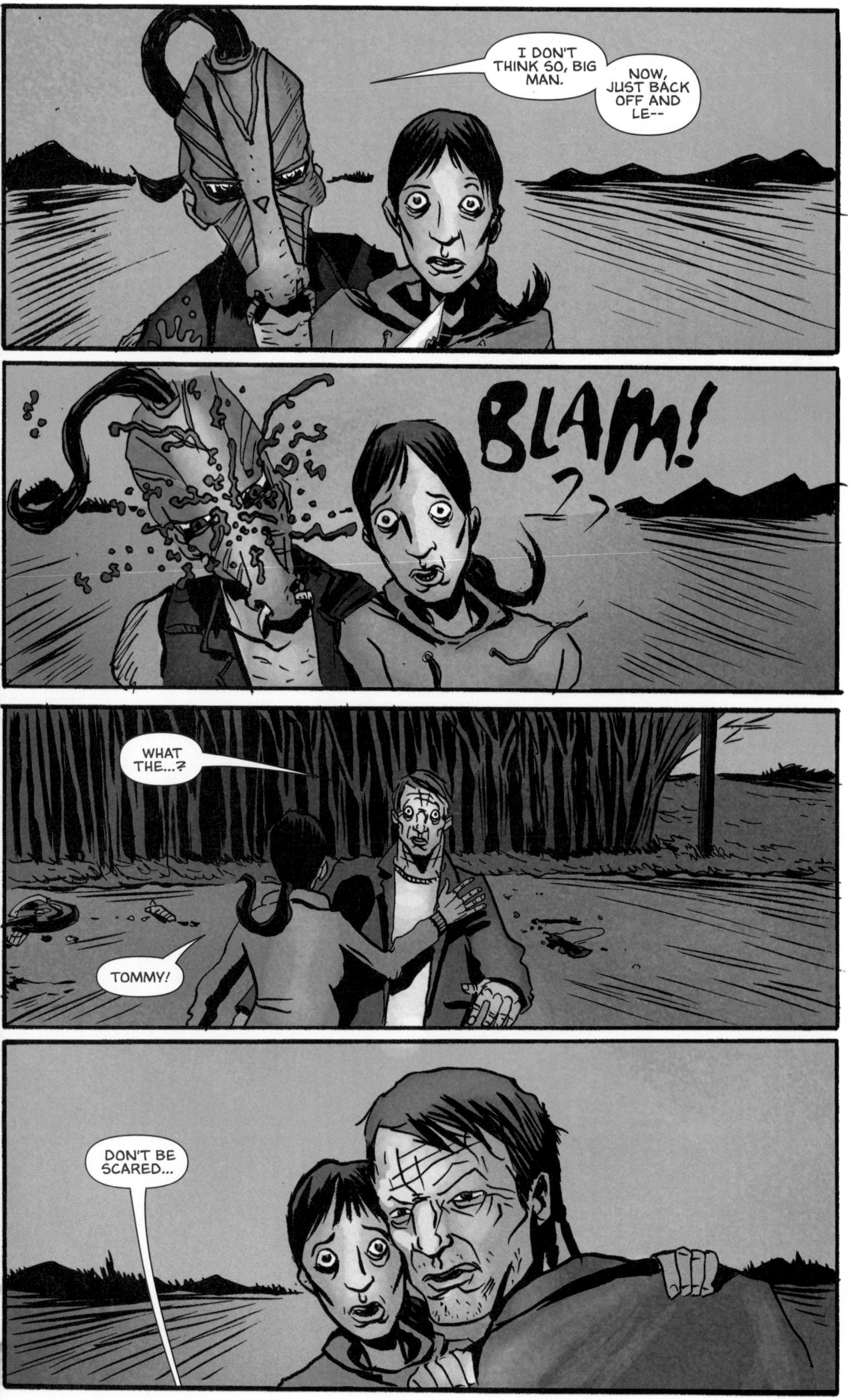
I DON'T THINK SO, BIG MAN.
NOW, JUST BACK OFF AND LE--
BLAM!
WHAT THE...?
TOMMY!
DON'T BE SCARED...

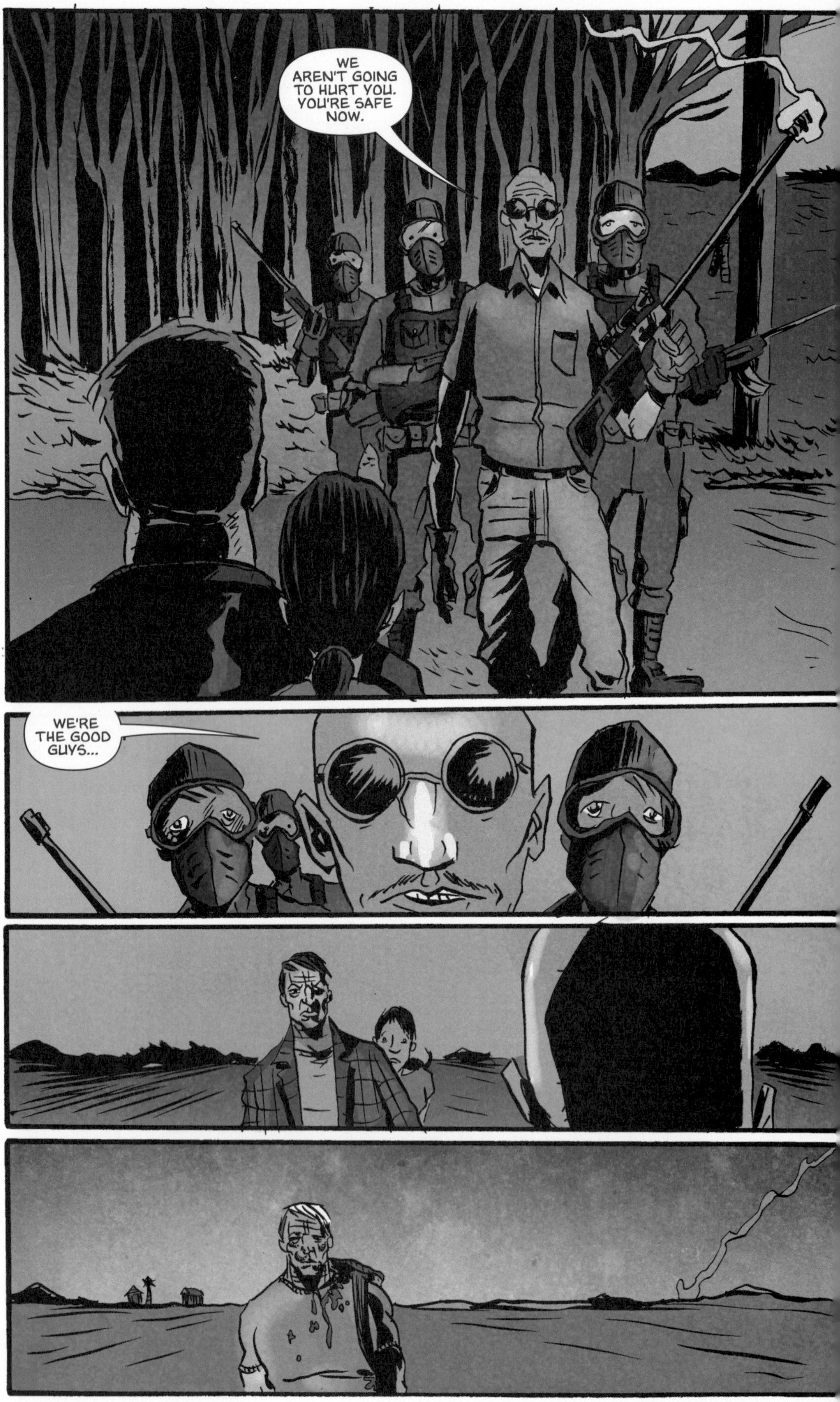
WE AREN'T GOING TO HURT YOU. YOU'RE SAFE NOW.
WE'RE THE GOOD GUYS...

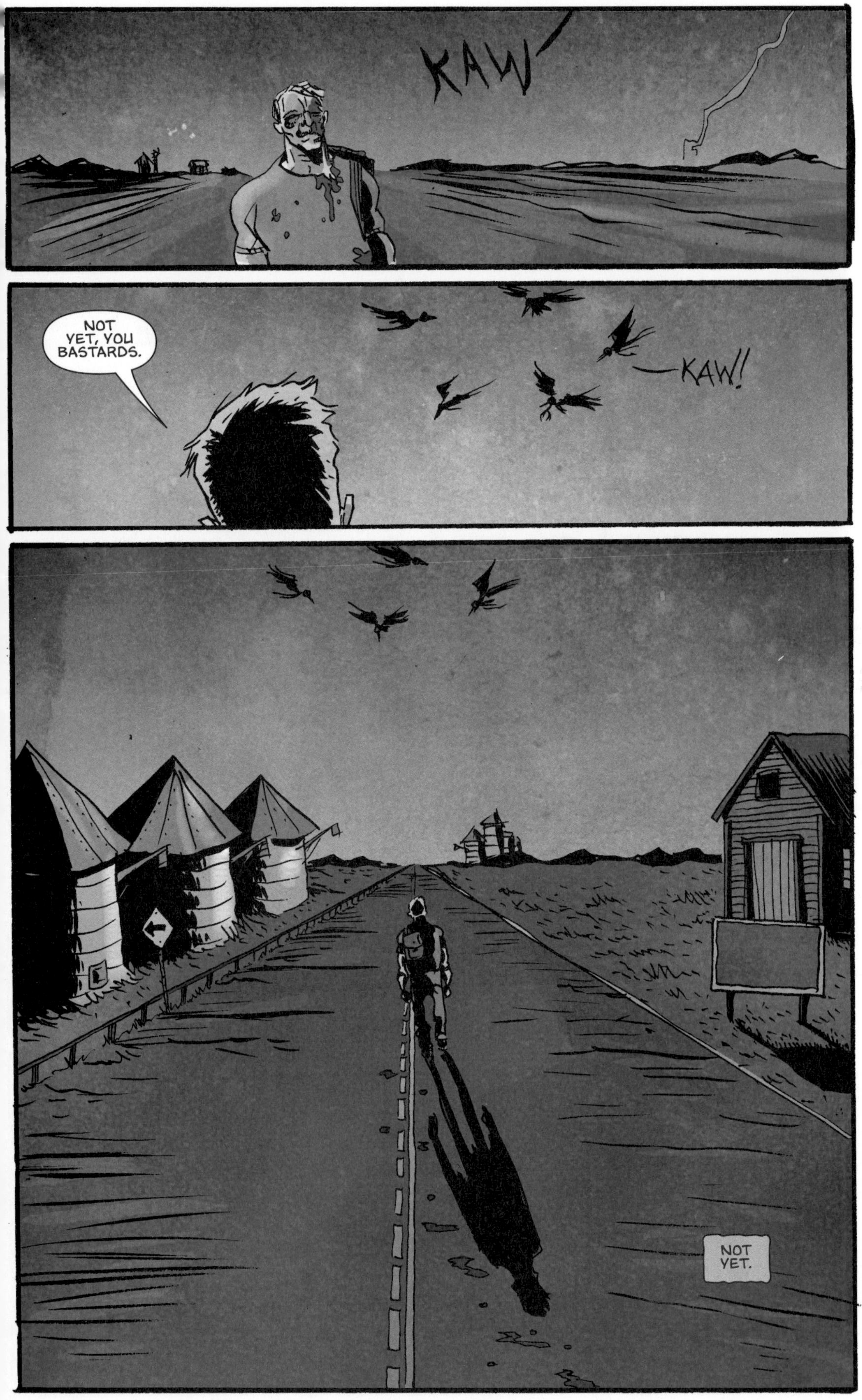
KAW
NOT YET, YOU BASTARDS.
KAW!
NOT YET.

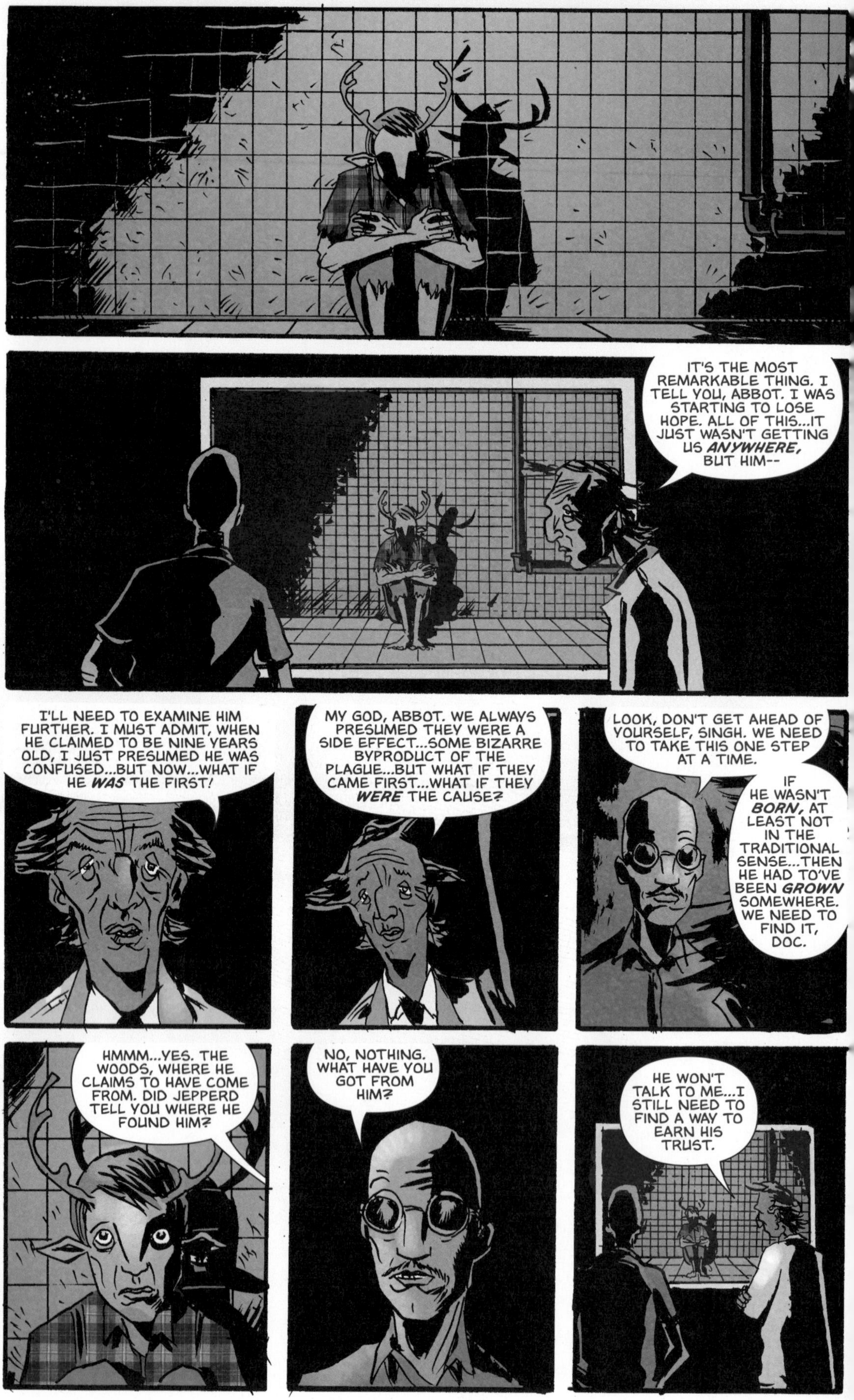

IT'S THE MOST REMARKABLE THING. I TELL YOU, ABBOT. I WAS STARTING TO LOSE HOPE. ALL OF THIS...IT JUST WASN'T GETTING US *ANYWHERE,* BUT HIM--
I'LL NEED TO EXAMINE HIM FURTHER. I MUST ADMIT, WHEN HE CLAIMED TO BE NINE YEARS OLD, I JUST PRESUMED HE WAS CONFUSED...BUT NOW...WHAT IF HE *WAS* THE FIRST!
MY GOD, ABBOT. WE ALWAYS PRESUMED THEY WERE A SIDE EFFECT...SOME BIZARRE BYPRODUCT OF THE PLAGUE...BUT WHAT IF THEY CAME FIRST...WHAT IF THEY *WERE* THE CAUSE?
LOOK, DON'T GET AHEAD OF YOURSELF, SINGH. WE NEED TO TAKE THIS ONE STEP AT A TIME.
IF HE WASN'T *BORN,* AT LEAST NOT IN THE TRADITIONAL SENSE...THEN HE HAD TO'VE BEEN *GROWN* SOMEWHERE. WE NEED TO FIND IT, DOC.
HMMM...YES. THE WOODS, WHERE HE CLAIMS TO HAVE COME FROM. DID JEPPERD TELL YOU WHERE HE FOUND HIM?
NO, NOTHING. WHAT HAVE YOU GOT FROM HIM?
HE WON'T TALK TO ME...I STILL NEED TO FIND A WAY TO EARN HIS TRUST.

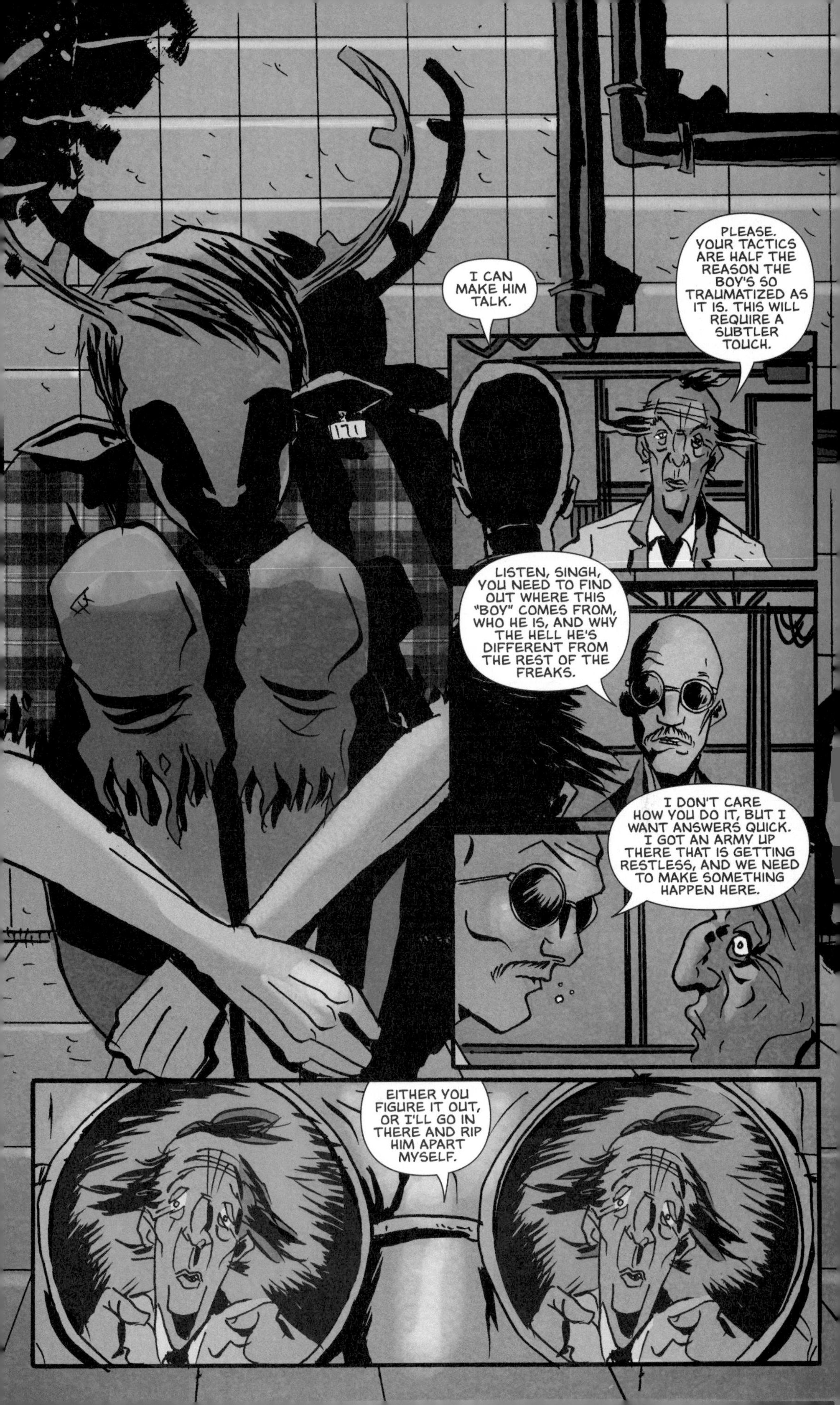
I CAN MAKE HIM TALK.
PLEASE. YOUR TACTICS ARE HALF THE REASON THE BOY'S SO TRAUMATIZED AS IT IS. THIS WILL REQUIRE A SUBTLER TOUCH.
LISTEN, SINGH, YOU NEED TO FIND OUT WHERE THIS "BOY" COMES FROM, WHO HE IS, AND WHY THE HELL HE'S DIFFERENT FROM THE REST OF THE FREAKS.
I DON'T CARE HOW YOU DO IT, BUT I WANT ANSWERS QUICK. I GOT AN ARMY UP THERE THAT IS GETTING RESTLESS, AND WE NEED TO MAKE SOMETHING HAPPEN HERE.
EITHER YOU FIGURE IT OUT, OR I'LL GO IN THERE AND RIP HIM APART MYSELF.

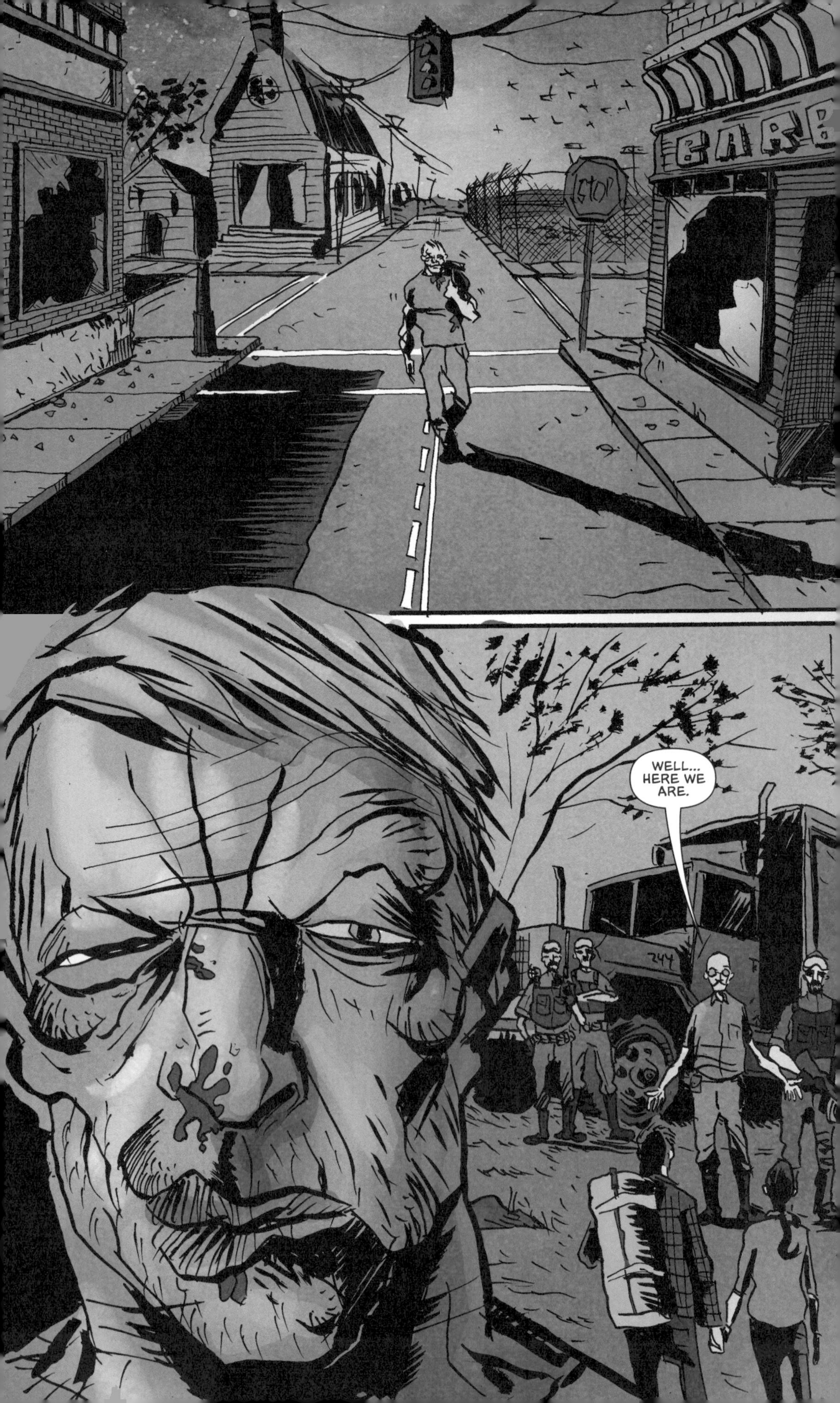

BARB
STOP
WELL... HERE WE ARE.

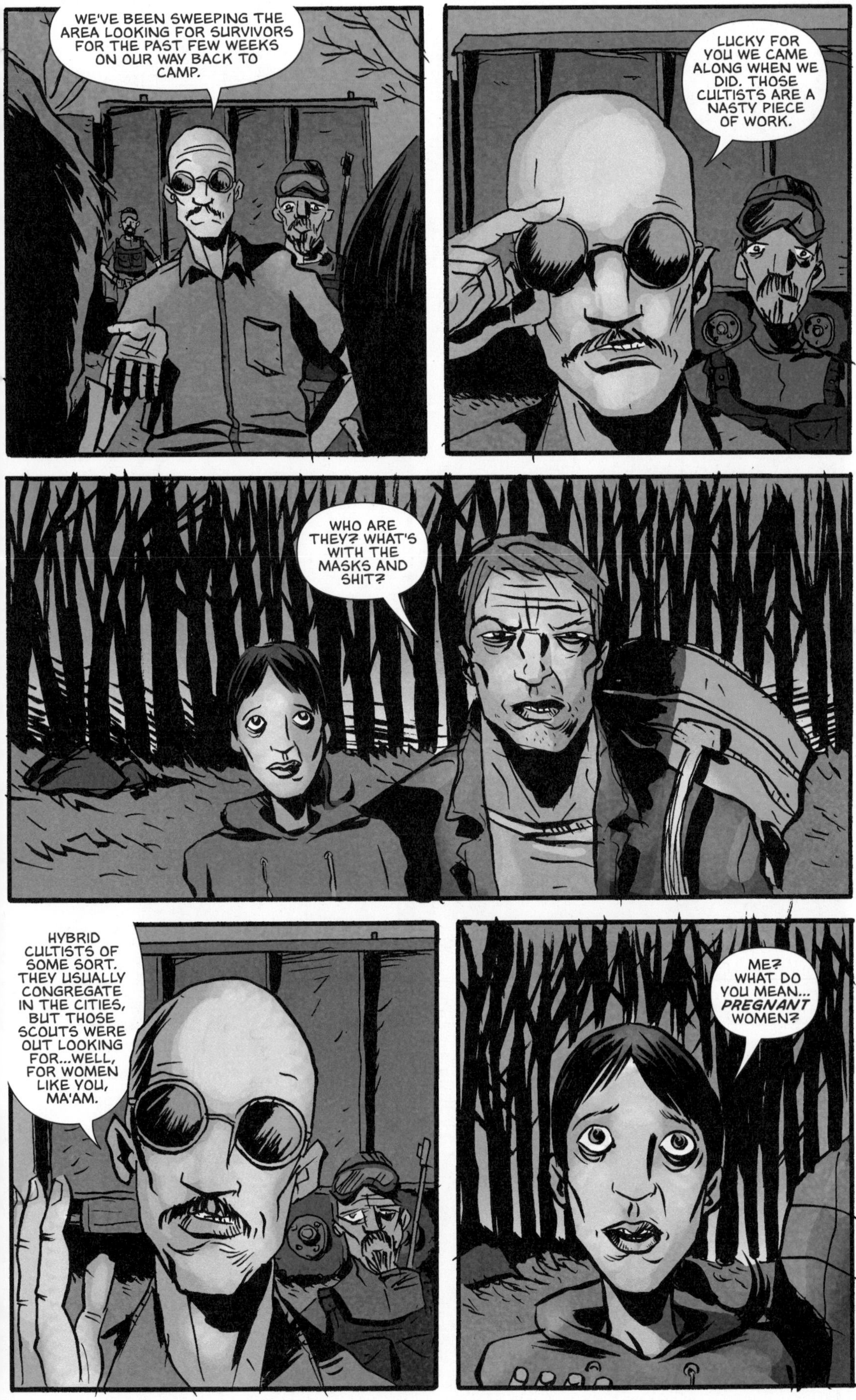
WE'VE BEEN SWEEPING THE AREA LOOKING FOR SURVIVORS FOR THE PAST FEW WEEKS ON OUR WAY BACK TO CAMP.
LUCKY FOR YOU WE CAME ALONG WHEN WE DID. THOSE CULTISTS ARE A NASTY PIECE OF WORK.
WHO ARE THEY? WHAT'S WITH THE MASKS AND SHIT?
HYBRID CULTISTS OF SOME SORT. THEY USUALLY CONGREGATE IN THE CITIES, BUT THOSE SCOUTS WERE OUT LOOKING FOR...WELL, FOR WOMEN LIKE YOU, MA'AM.
ME? WHAT DO YOU MEAN... *PREGNANT* WOMEN?

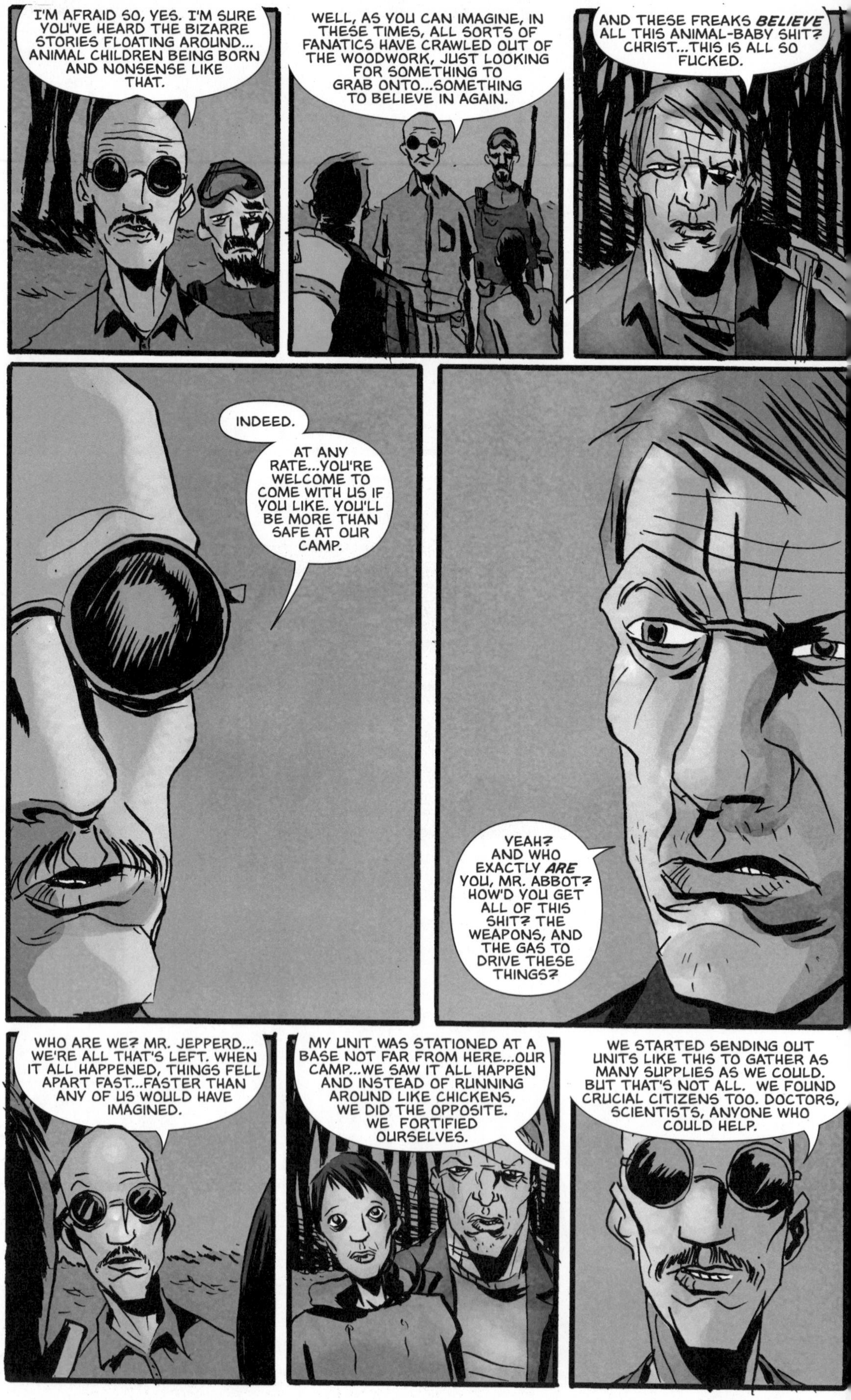

I'M AFRAID SO, YES. I'M SURE YOU'VE HEARD THE BIZARRE STORIES FLOATING AROUND... ANIMAL CHILDREN BEING BORN AND NONSENSE LIKE THAT.
WELL, AS YOU CAN IMAGINE, IN THESE TIMES, ALL SORTS OF FANATICS HAVE CRAWLED OUT OF THE WOODWORK, JUST LOOKING FOR SOMETHING TO GRAB ONTO...SOMETHING TO BELIEVE IN AGAIN.
AND THESE FREAKS *BELIEVE* ALL THIS ANIMAL-BABY SHIT? CHRIST...THIS IS ALL SO FUCKED.
INDEED.
AT ANY RATE...YOU'RE WELCOME TO COME WITH US IF YOU LIKE. YOU'LL BE MORE THAN SAFE AT OUR CAMP.
YEAH? AND WHO EXACTLY *ARE* YOU, MR. ABBOT? HOW'D YOU GET ALL OF THIS SHIT? THE WEAPONS, AND THE GAS TO DRIVE THESE THINGS?
WHO ARE WE? MR. JEPPERD... WE'RE ALL THAT'S LEFT. WHEN IT ALL HAPPENED, THINGS FELL APART FAST...FASTER THAN ANY OF US WOULD HAVE IMAGINED.
MY UNIT WAS STATIONED AT A BASE NOT FAR FROM HERE...OUR CAMP...WE SAW IT ALL HAPPEN AND INSTEAD OF RUNNING AROUND LIKE CHICKENS, WE DID THE OPPOSITE. WE FORTIFIED OURSELVES.
WE STARTED SENDING OUT UNITS LIKE THIS TO GATHER AS MANY SUPPLIES AS WE COULD. BUT THAT'S NOT ALL. WE FOUND CRUCIAL CITIZENS TOO. DOCTORS, SCIENTISTS, ANYONE WHO COULD HELP.

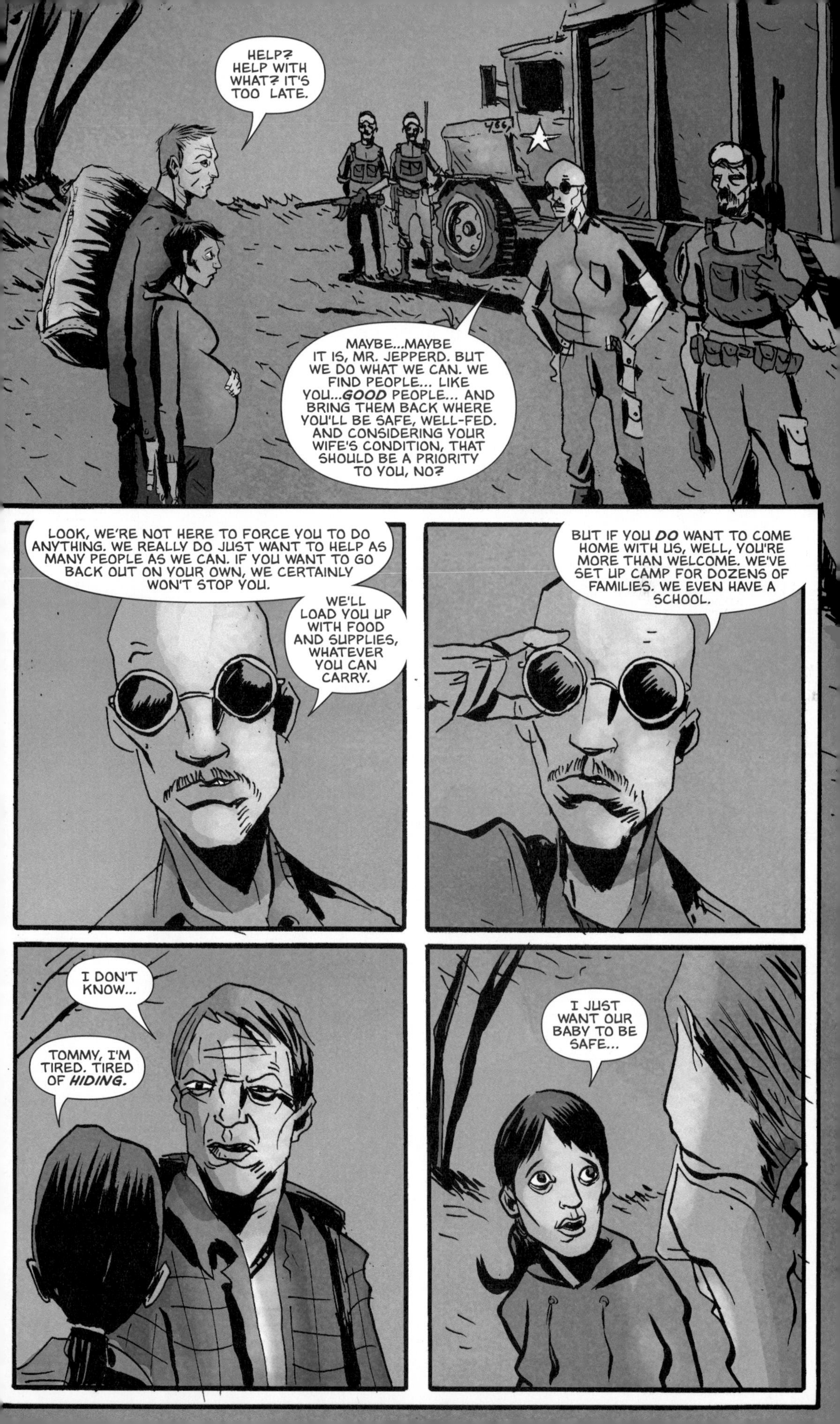
HELP? HELP WITH WHAT? IT'S TOO LATE.
MAYBE...MAYBE IT IS, MR. JEPPERD. BUT WE DO WHAT WE CAN. WE FIND PEOPLE... LIKE YOU...**GOOD** PEOPLE... AND BRING THEM BACK WHERE YOU'LL BE SAFE, WELL-FED. AND CONSIDERING YOUR WIFE'S CONDITION, THAT SHOULD BE A PRIORITY TO YOU, NO?
LOOK, WE'RE NOT HERE TO FORCE YOU TO DO ANYTHING. WE REALLY DO JUST WANT TO HELP AS MANY PEOPLE AS WE CAN. IF YOU WANT TO GO BACK OUT ON YOUR OWN, WE CERTAINLY WON'T STOP YOU.
WE'LL LOAD YOU UP WITH FOOD AND SUPPLIES, WHATEVER YOU CAN CARRY.
BUT IF YOU **DO** WANT TO COME HOME WITH US, WELL, YOU'RE MORE THAN WELCOME. WE'VE SET UP CAMP FOR DOZENS OF FAMILIES. WE EVEN HAVE A SCHOOL.
I DON'T KNOW...
TOMMY, I'M TIRED. TIRED OF ***HIDING***.
I JUST WANT OUR BABY TO BE SAFE...

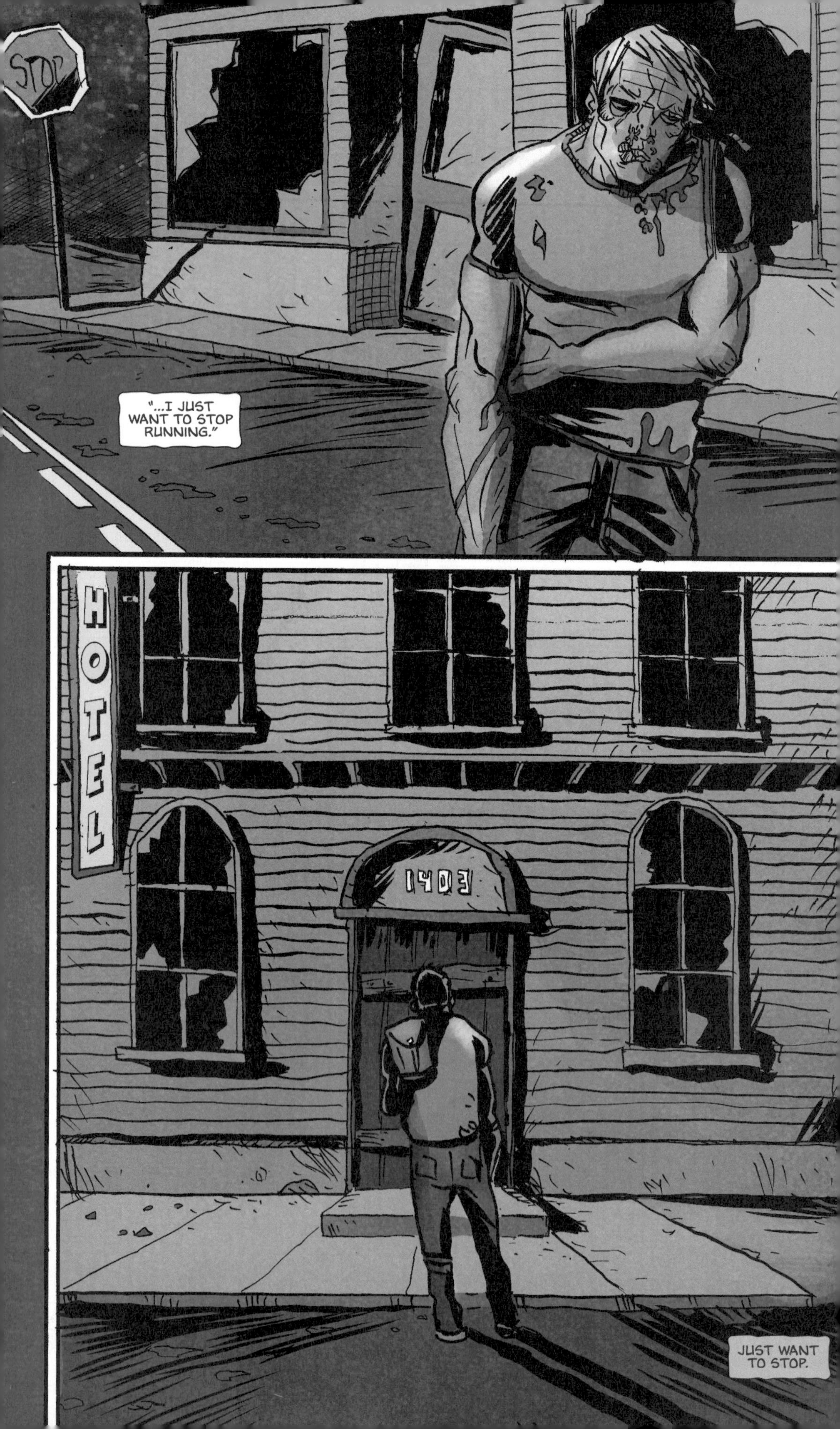
STOP
"...I JUST WANT TO STOP RUNNING."
HOTEL
1403
JUST WANT TO STOP.

IT'S OKAY, GUS... DON'T BE SCARED.

I WON'T TOUCH YOU AGAIN, I PROMISE.

I JUST WANNA GO HOME. PLEASE...CAN'T YOU JUST LEAVE ME ALONE?

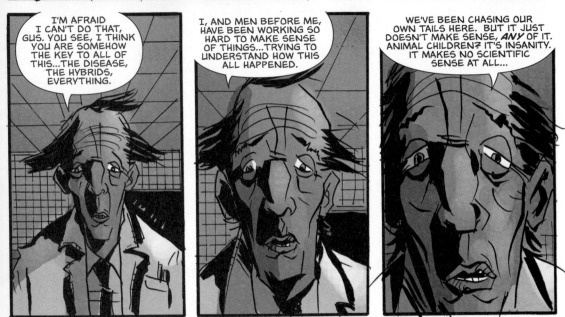

I'M AFRAID I CAN'T DO THAT, GUS. YOU SEE, I THINK YOU ARE SOMEHOW THE KEY TO ALL OF THIS...THE DISEASE, THE HYBRIDS, EVERYTHING.

I, AND MEN BEFORE ME, HAVE BEEN WORKING SO HARD TO MAKE SENSE OF THINGS...TRYING TO UNDERSTAND HOW THIS ALL HAPPENED.

WE'VE BEEN CHASING OUR OWN TAILS HERE. BUT IT JUST DOESN'T MAKE SENSE, *ANY* OF IT. ANIMAL CHILDREN? IT'S INSANITY. IT MAKES NO SCIENTIFIC SENSE AT ALL...

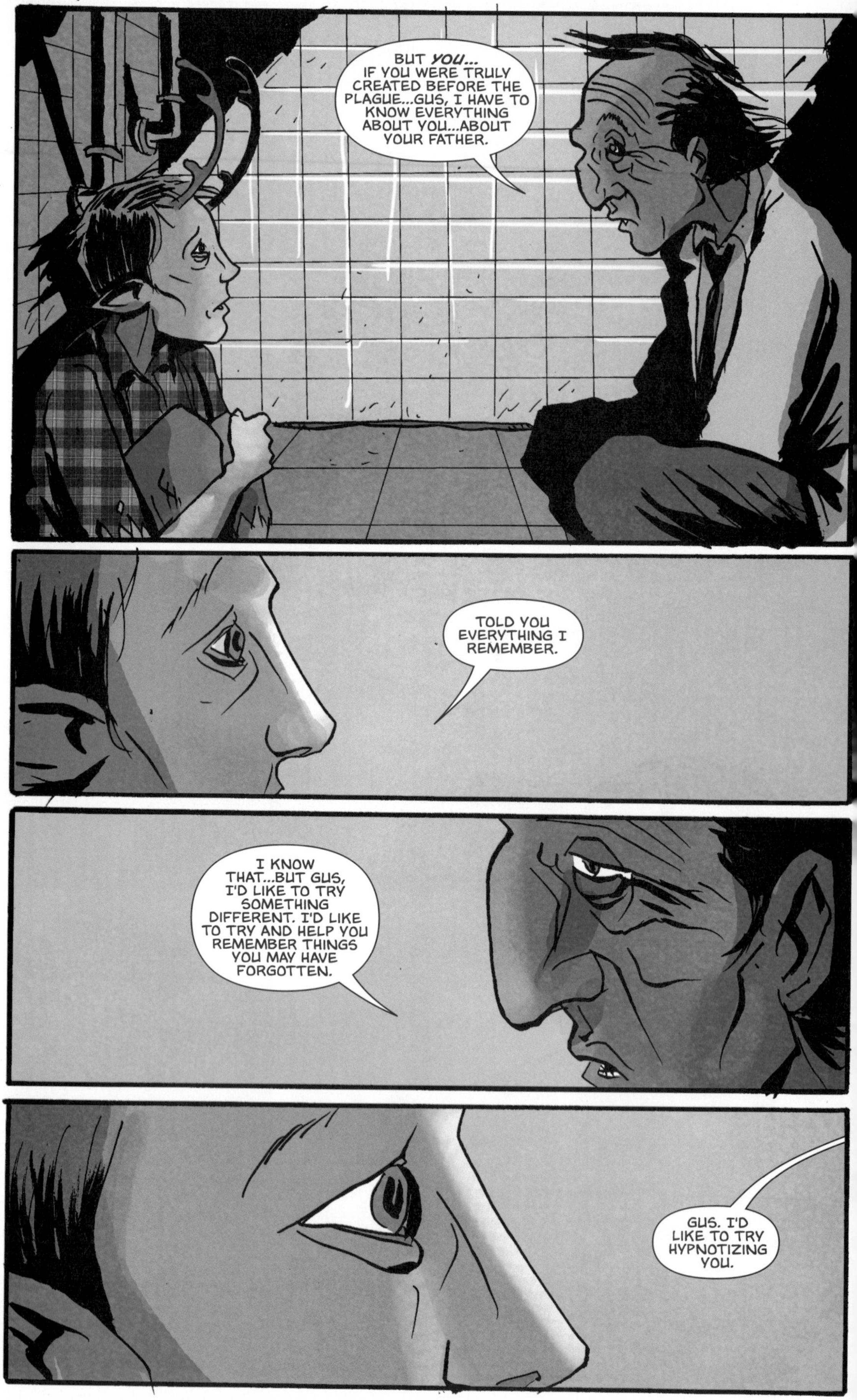
BUT *YOU*... IF YOU WERE TRULY CREATED BEFORE THE PLAGUE...GUS, I HAVE TO KNOW EVERYTHING ABOUT YOU...ABOUT YOUR FATHER.
TOLD YOU EVERYTHING I REMEMBER.
I KNOW THAT...BUT GUS, I'D LIKE TO TRY SOMETHING DIFFERENT. I'D LIKE TO TRY AND HELP YOU REMEMBER THINGS YOU MAY HAVE FORGOTTEN.
GUS. I'D LIKE TO TRY HYPNOTIZING YOU.

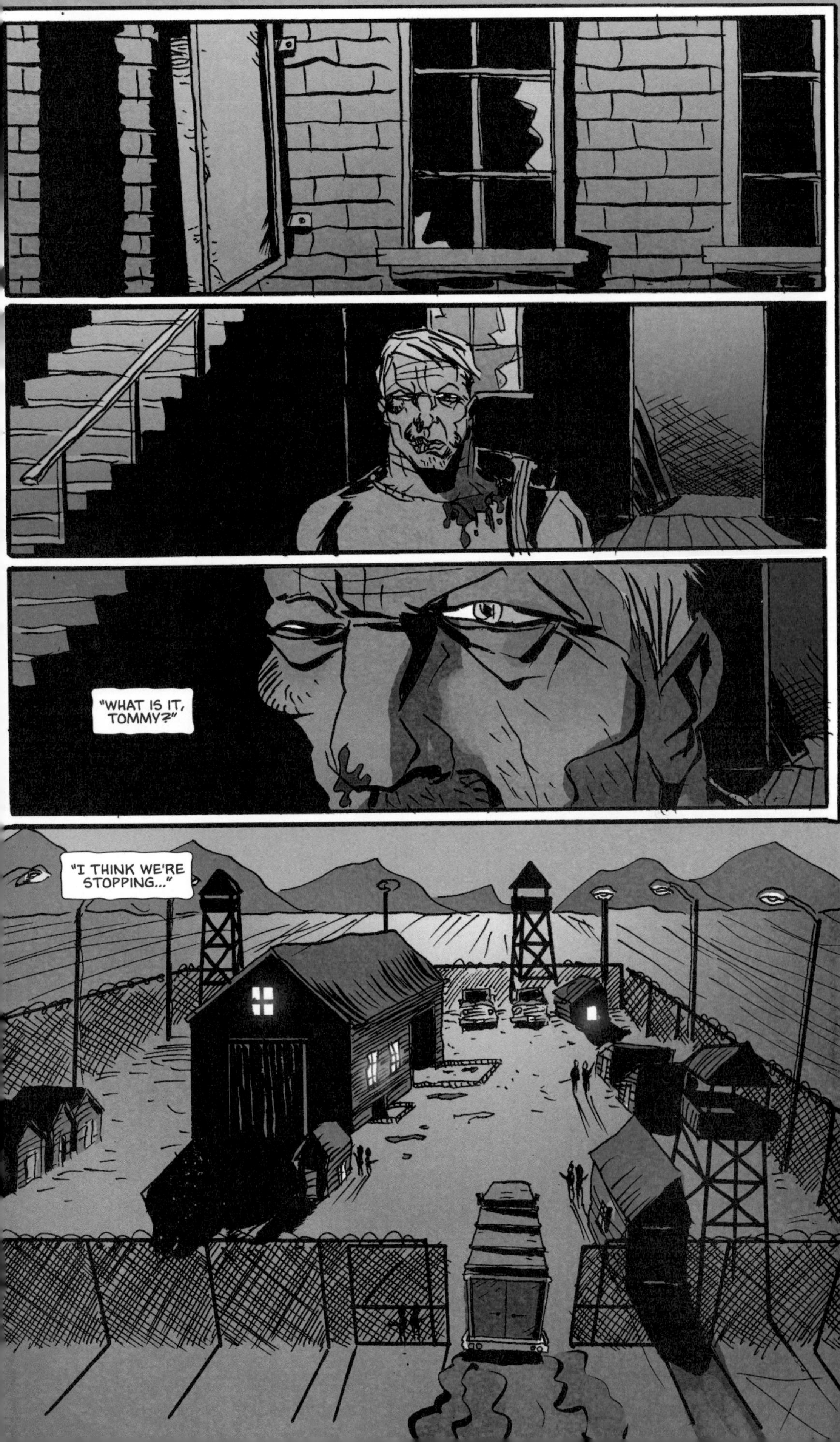
"WHAT IS IT, TOMMY?"
"I THINK WE'RE STOPPING..."

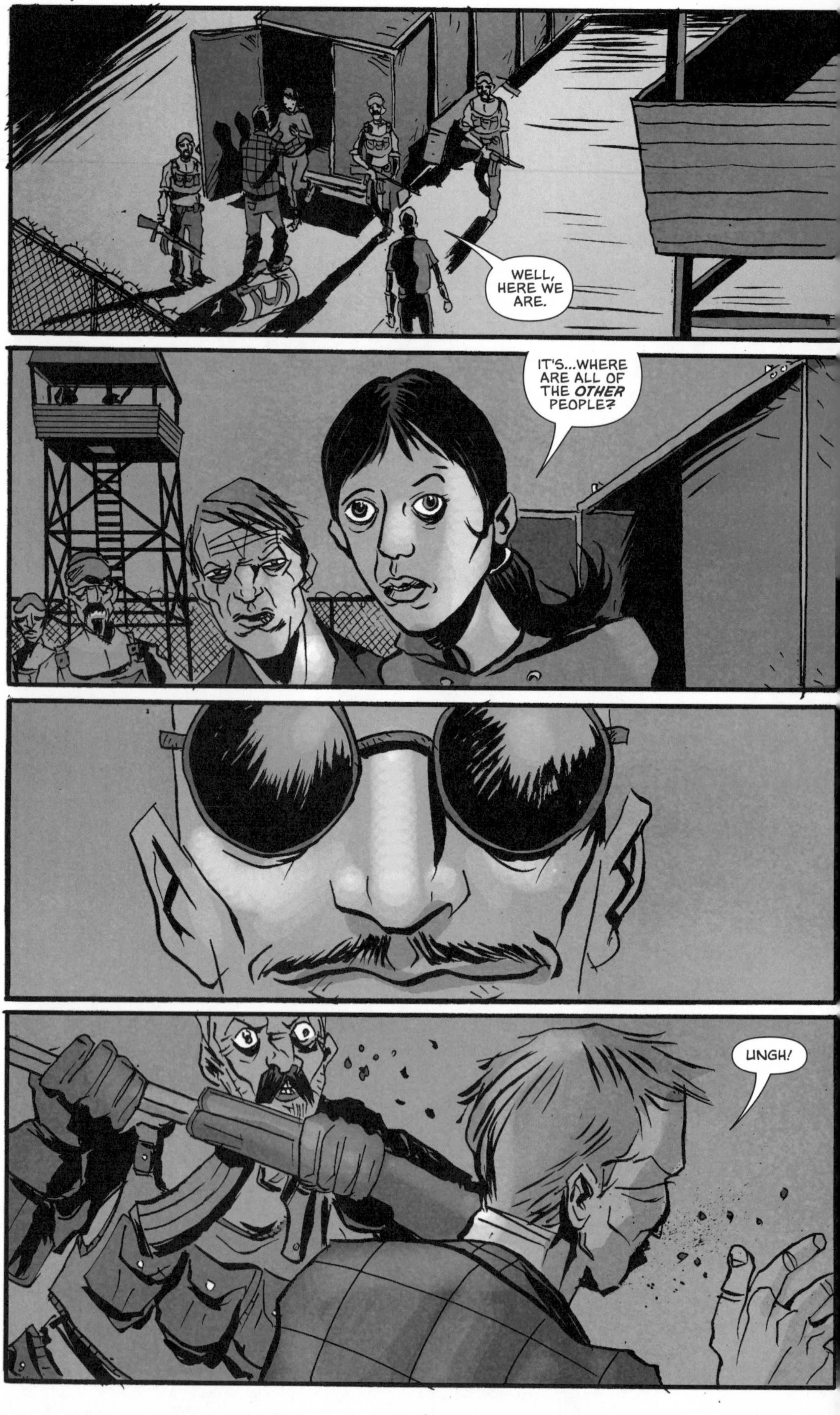
WELL, HERE WE ARE.
IT'S...WHERE ARE ALL OF THE *OTHER* PEOPLE?
UNGH!

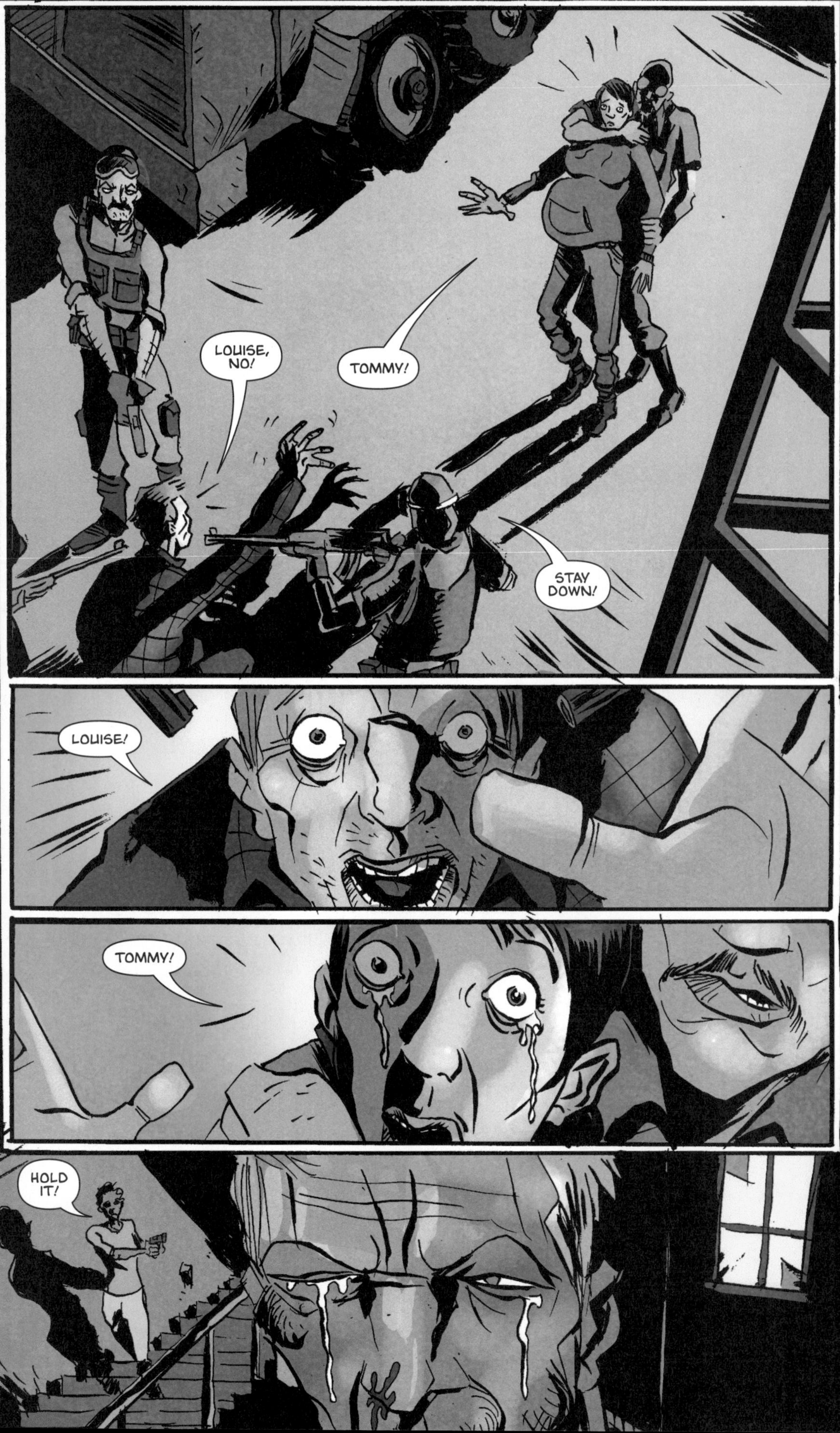
TOMMY!
LOUISE, NO!
STAY DOWN!
LOUISE!
TOMMY!
HOLD IT!

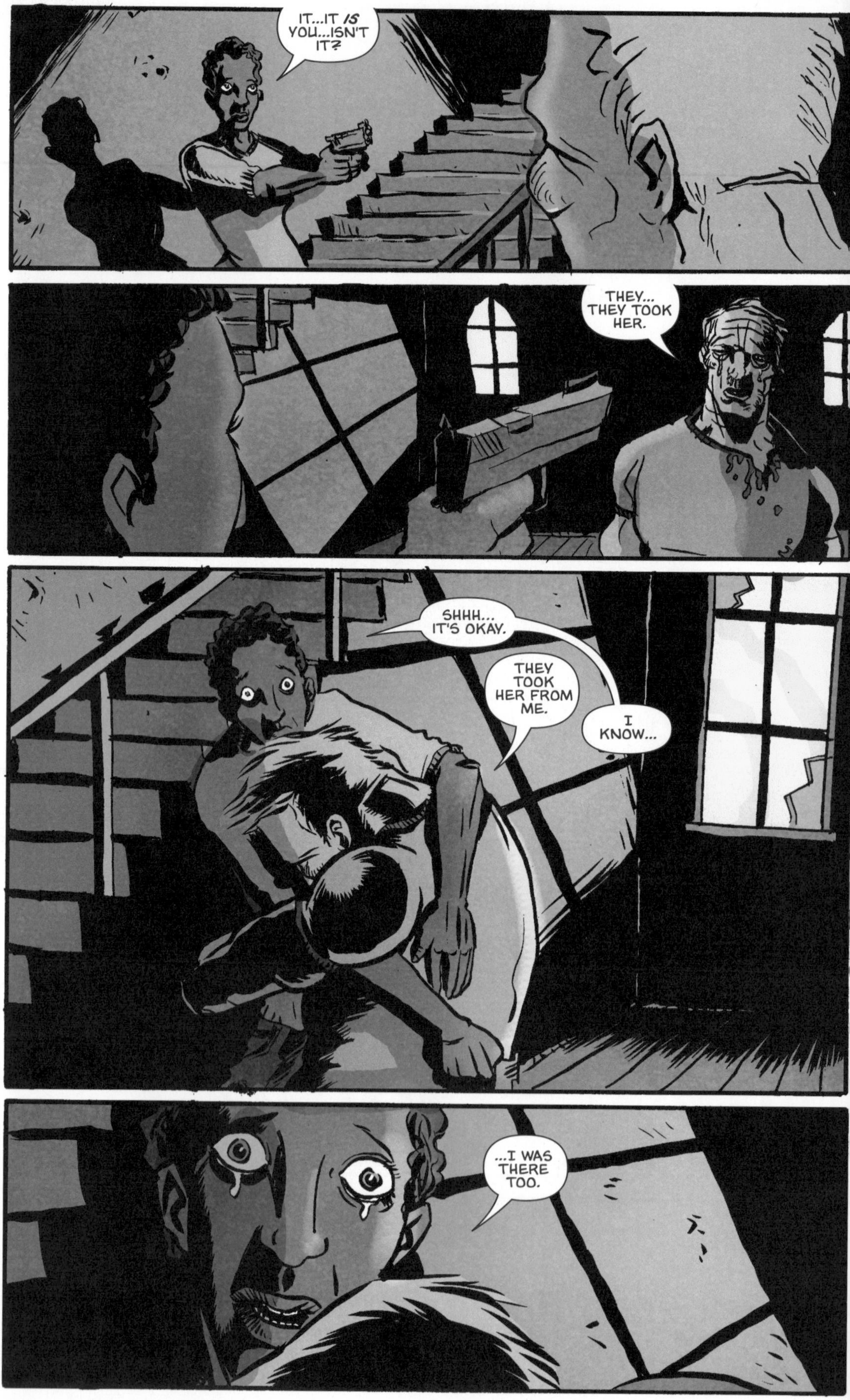
IT...IT *IS* YOU...ISN'T IT?
THEY... THEY TOOK HER.
SHHH... IT'S OKAY.
THEY TOOK HER FROM ME.
I KNOW...
...I WAS THERE TOO.

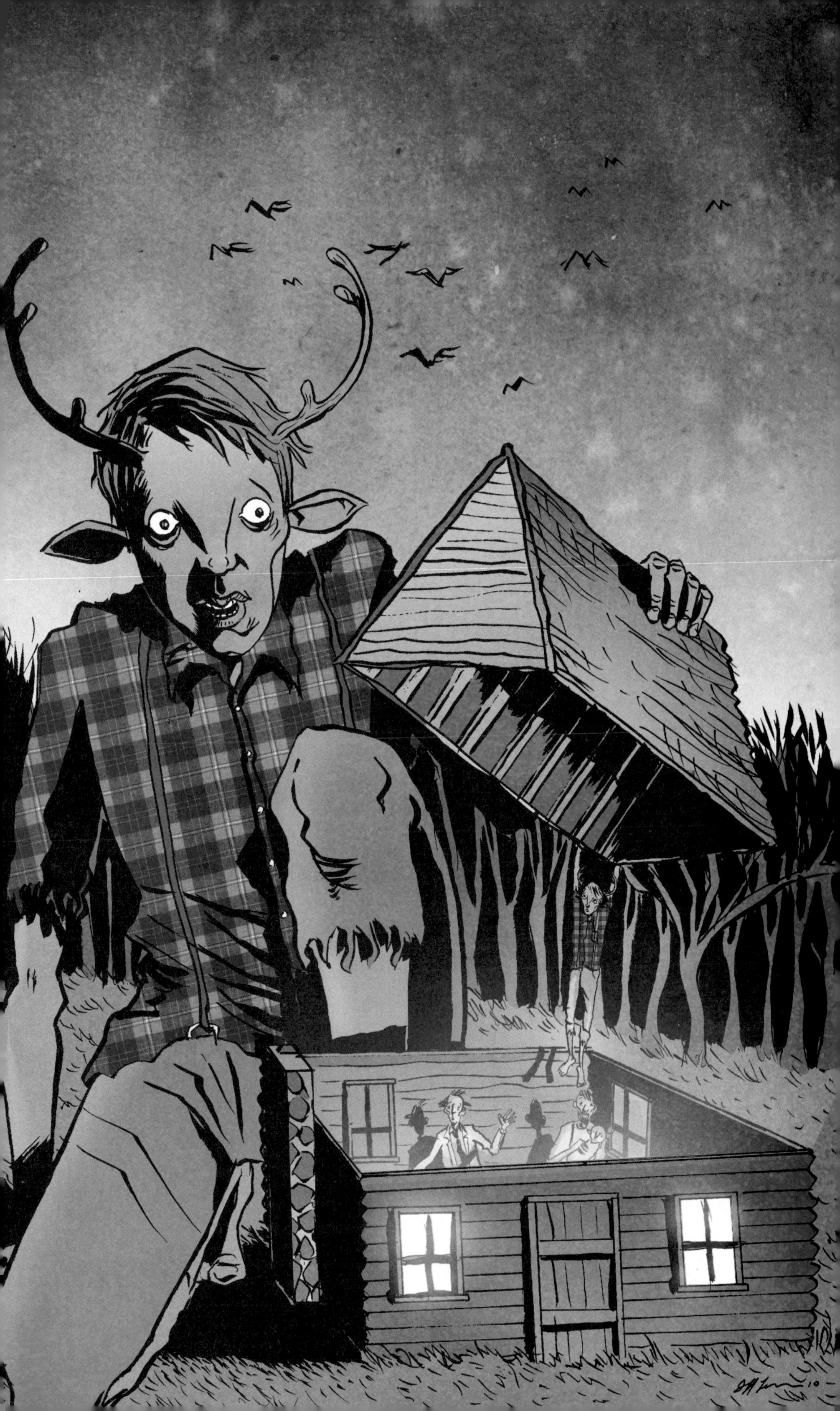

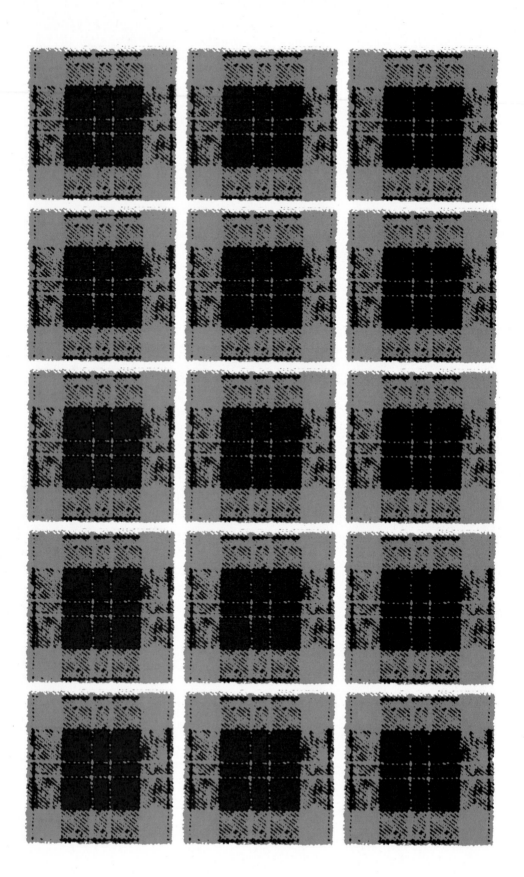

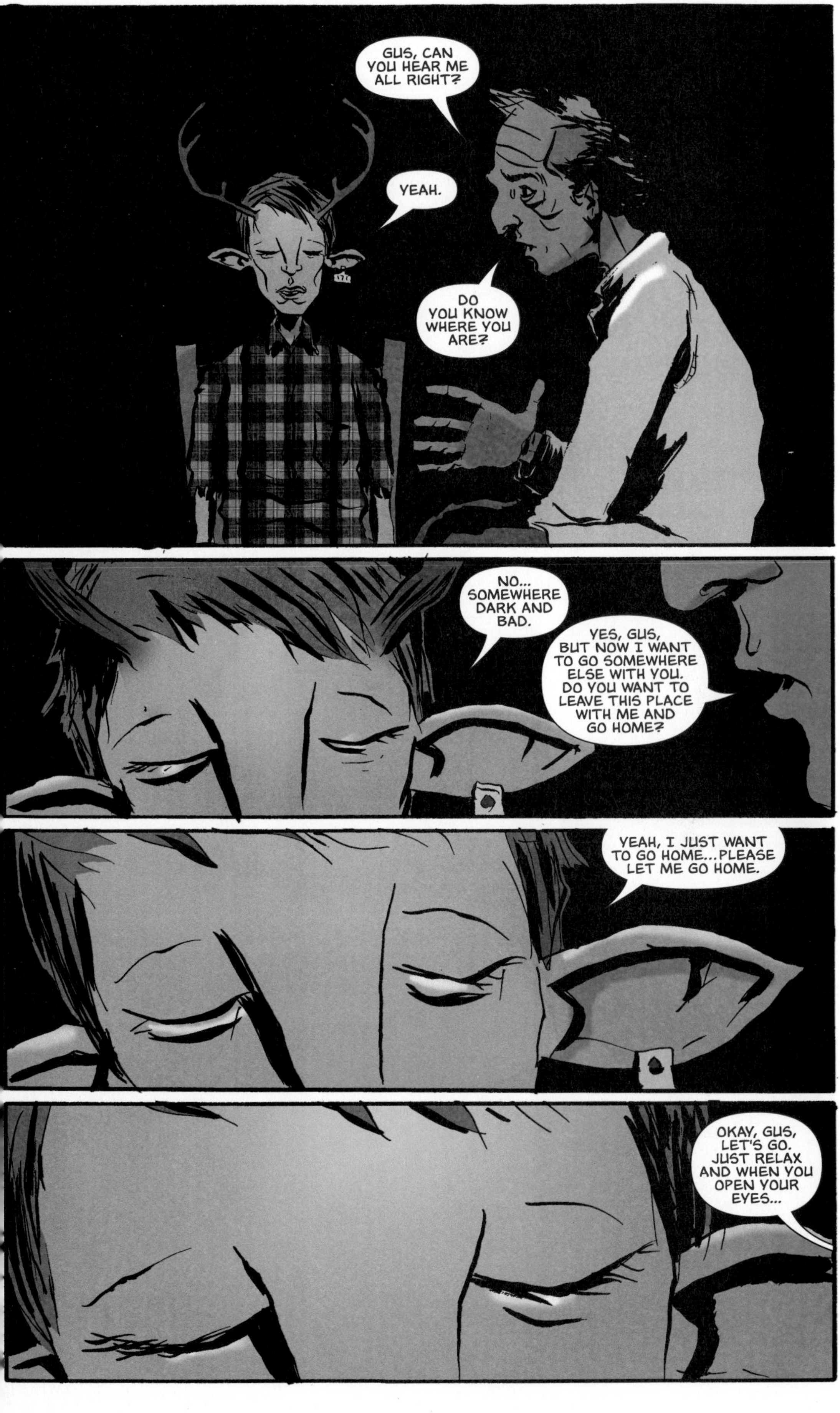
GUS, CAN YOU HEAR ME ALL RIGHT?
YEAH.
DO YOU KNOW WHERE YOU ARE?
NO... SOMEWHERE DARK AND BAD.
YES, GUS, BUT NOW I WANT TO GO SOMEWHERE ELSE WITH YOU. DO YOU WANT TO LEAVE THIS PLACE WITH ME AND GO HOME?
YEAH, I JUST WANT TO GO HOME...PLEASE LET ME GO HOME.
OKAY, GUS, LET'S GO. JUST RELAX AND WHEN YOU OPEN YOUR EYES...

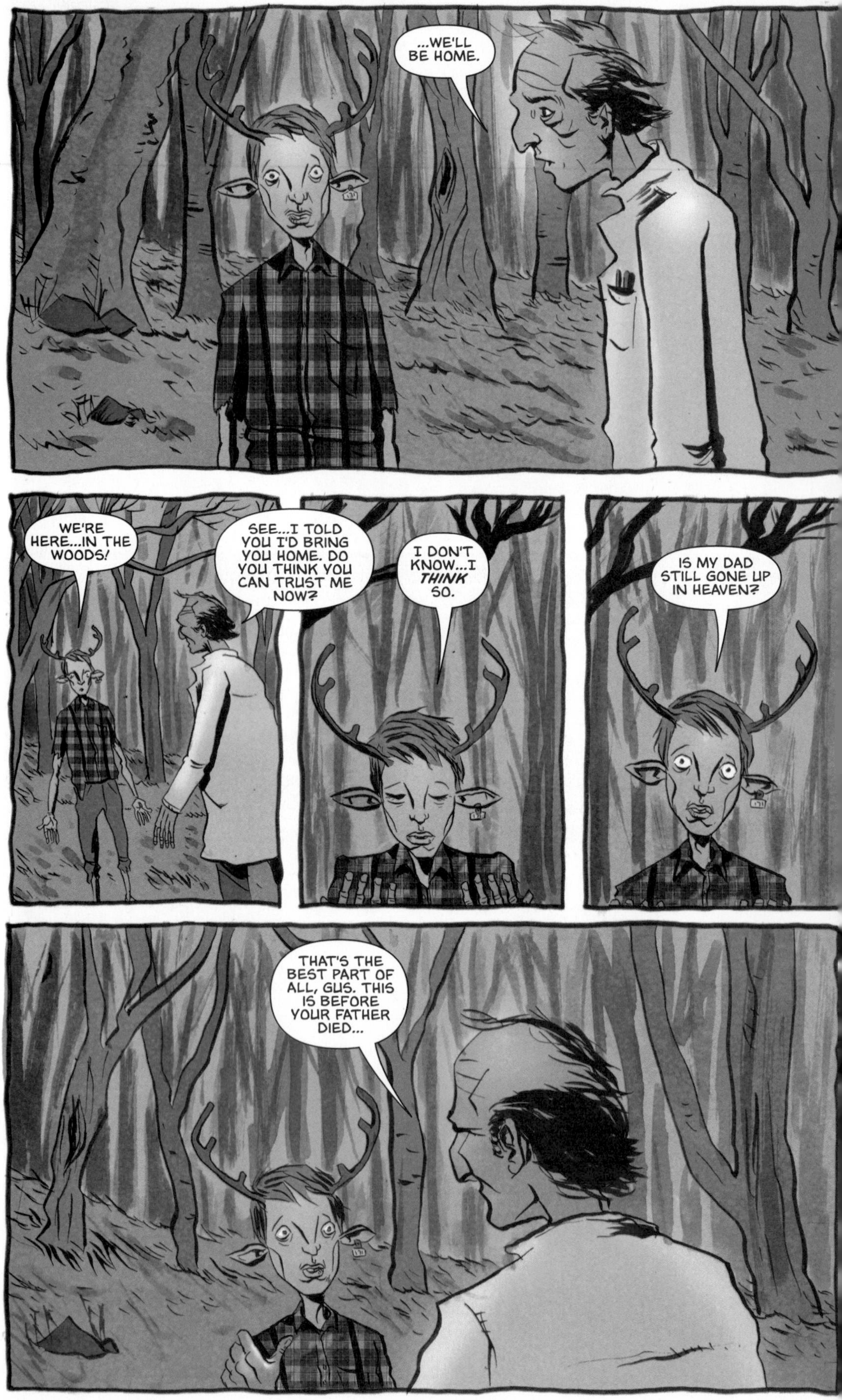
...WE'LL BE HOME.
WE'RE HERE...IN THE WOODS!
SEE...I TOLD YOU I'D BRING YOU HOME. DO YOU THINK YOU CAN TRUST ME NOW?
I DON'T KNOW...I *THINK* SO.
IS MY DAD STILL GONE UP IN HEAVEN?
THAT'S THE BEST PART OF ALL, GUS. THIS IS BEFORE YOUR FATHER DIED...

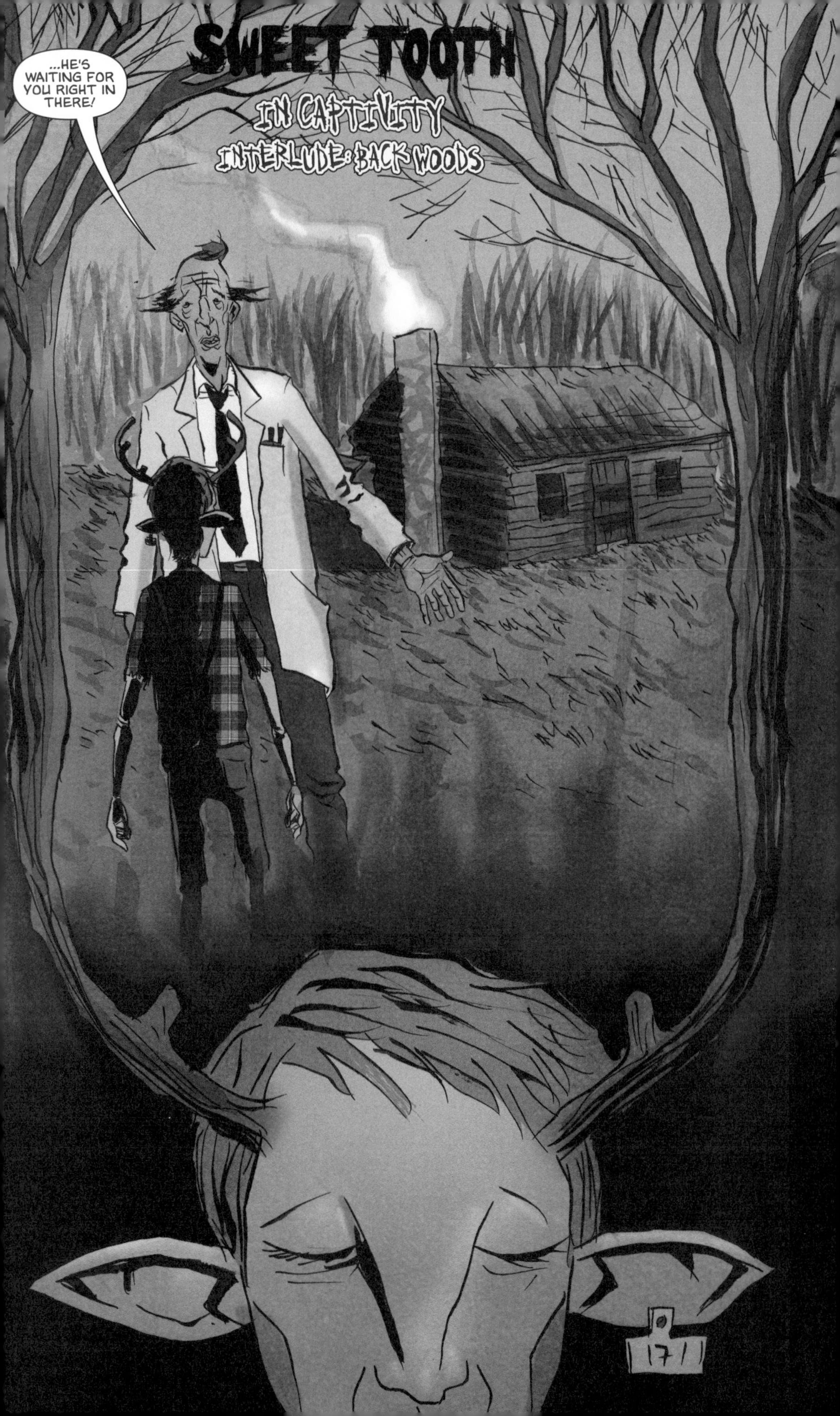

SWEET TOOTH
...HE'S WAITING FOR YOU RIGHT IN THERE!
IN CAPTIVITY
INTERLUDE: BACK WOODS
171

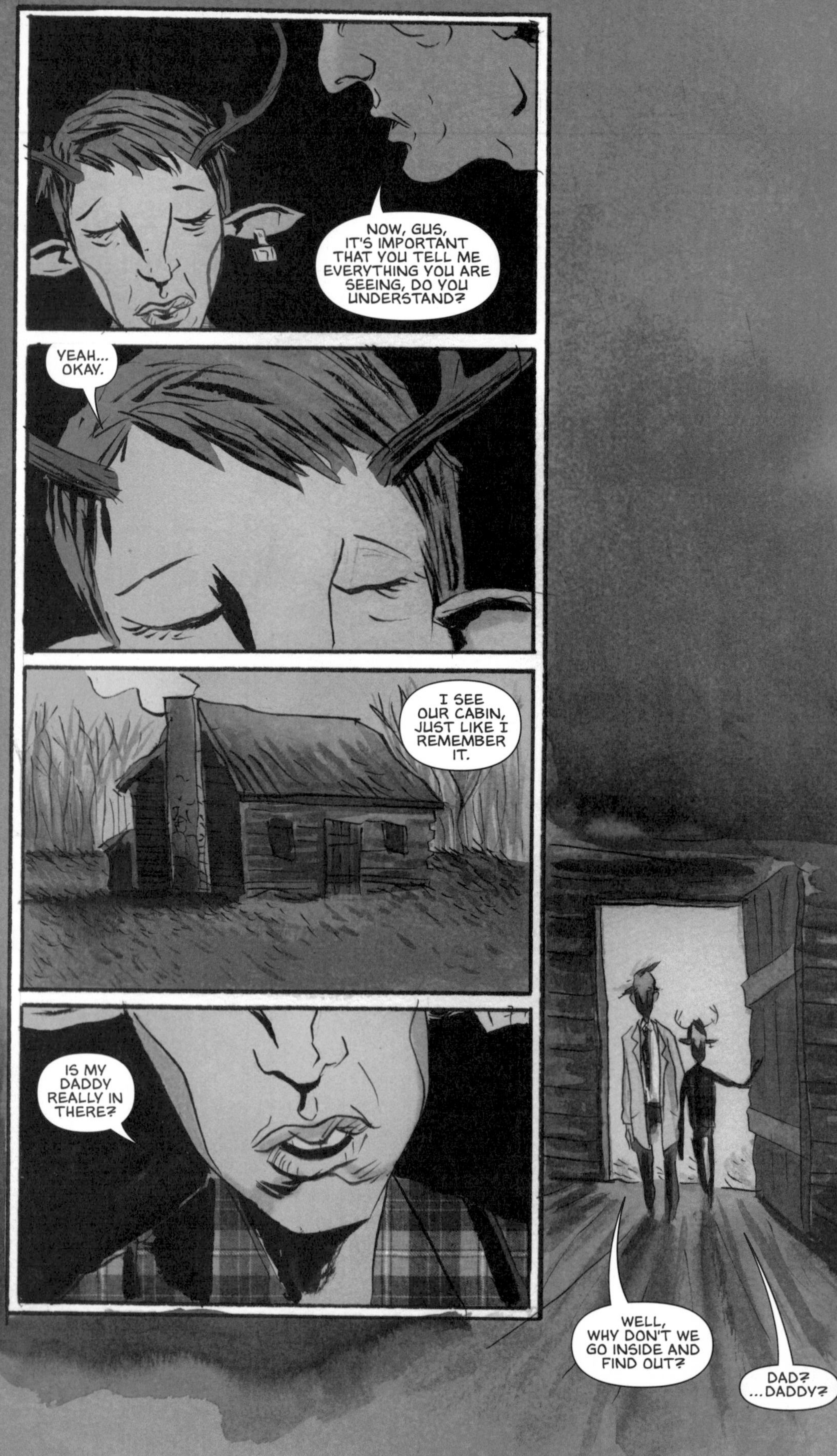
NOW, GUS, IT'S IMPORTANT THAT YOU TELL ME EVERYTHING YOU ARE SEEING, DO YOU UNDERSTAND?
YEAH... OKAY.
I SEE OUR CABIN, JUST LIKE I REMEMBER IT.
IS MY DADDY REALLY IN THERE?
WELL, WHY DON'T WE GO INSIDE AND FIND OUT?
DAD? ...DADDY?

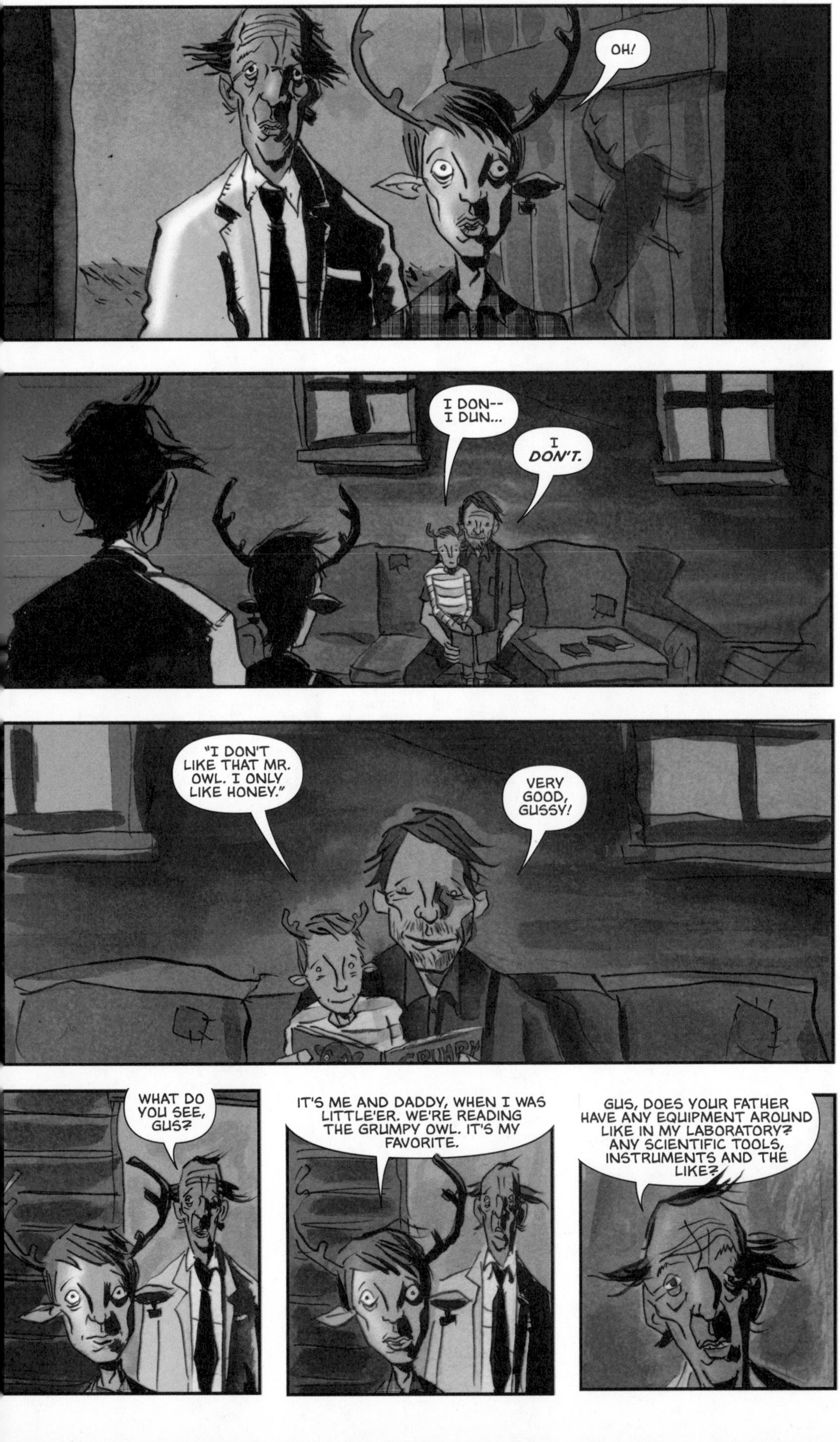

OH!
I DON--
I DUN...
I *DON'T.*
"I DON'T LIKE THAT MR. OWL. I ONLY LIKE HONEY."
VERY GOOD, GUSSY!
WHAT DO YOU SEE, GUS?
IT'S ME AND DADDY, WHEN I WAS LITTLE'ER. WE'RE READING THE GRUMPY OWL. IT'S MY FAVORITE.
GUS, DOES YOUR FATHER HAVE ANY EQUIPMENT AROUND LIKE IN MY LABORATORY? ANY SCIENTIFIC TOOLS, INSTRUMENTS AND THE LIKE?

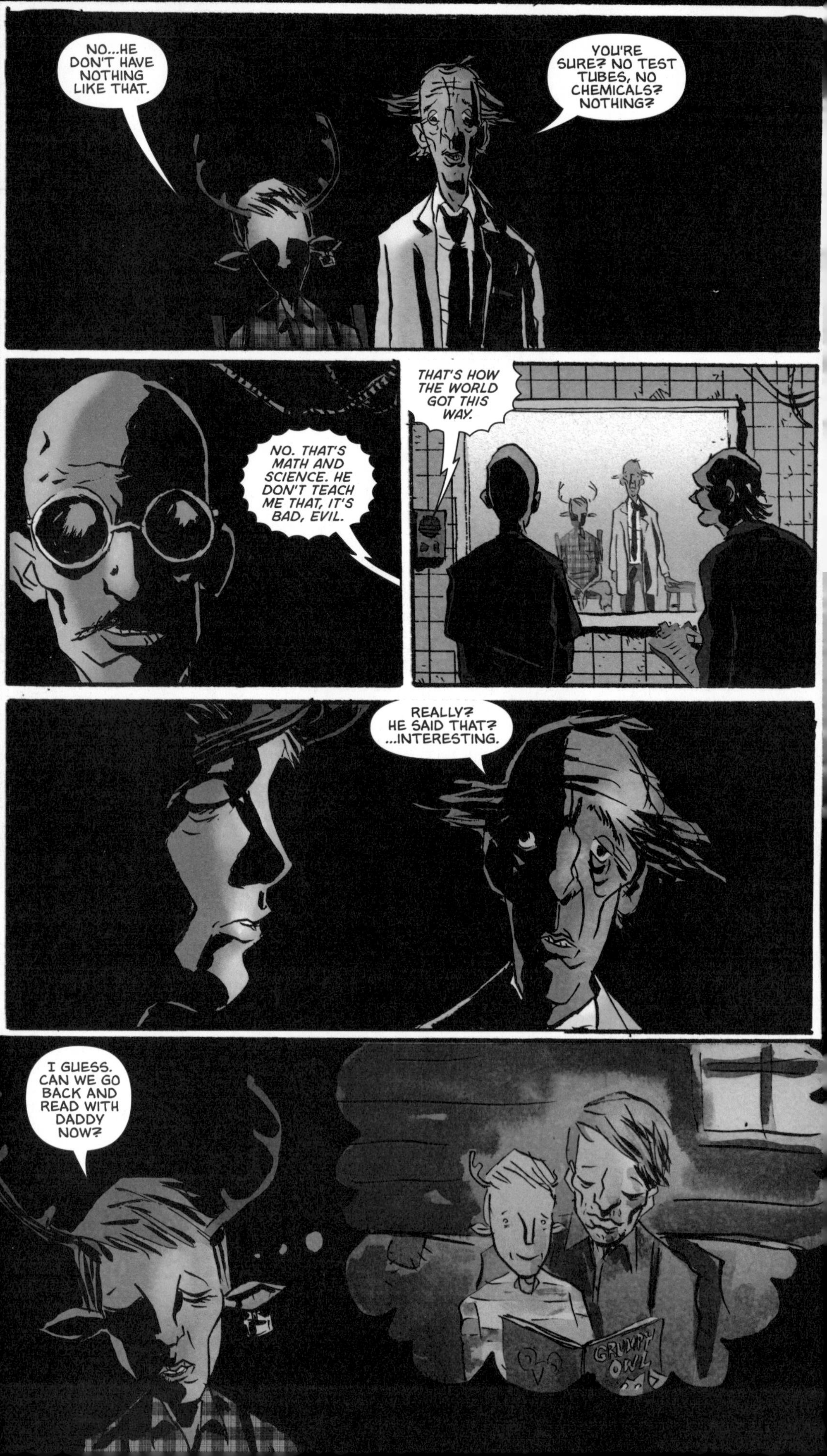
NO...HE DON'T HAVE NOTHING LIKE THAT.
YOU'RE SURE? NO TEST TUBES, NO CHEMICALS? NOTHING?
NO. THAT'S MATH AND SCIENCE. HE DON'T TEACH ME THAT, IT'S BAD, EVIL.
THAT'S HOW THE WORLD GOT THIS WAY.
REALLY? HE SAID THAT? ...INTERESTING.
I GUESS. CAN WE GO BACK AND READ WITH DADDY NOW?
GRUMPY OWL

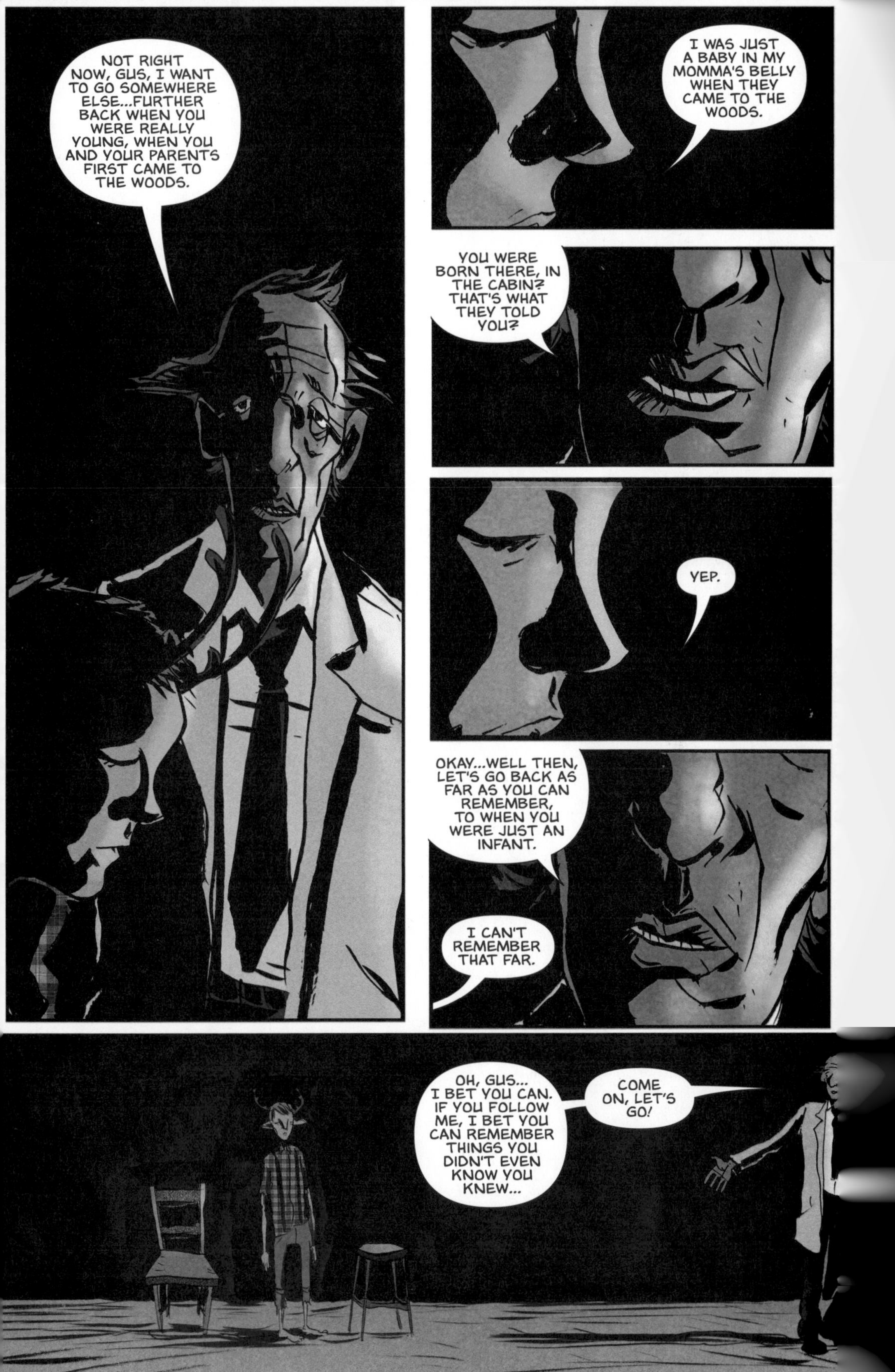
NOT RIGHT NOW, GUS, I WANT TO GO SOMEWHERE ELSE...FURTHER BACK WHEN YOU WERE REALLY YOUNG, WHEN YOU AND YOUR PARENTS FIRST CAME TO THE WOODS.
I WAS JUST A BABY IN MY MOMMA'S BELLY WHEN THEY CAME TO THE WOODS.
YOU WERE BORN THERE, IN THE CABIN? THAT'S WHAT THEY TOLD YOU?
YEP.
OKAY...WELL THEN, LET'S GO BACK AS FAR AS YOU CAN REMEMBER, TO WHEN YOU WERE JUST AN INFANT.
I CAN'T REMEMBER THAT FAR.
OH, GUS... I BET YOU CAN. IF YOU FOLLOW ME, I BET YOU CAN REMEMBER THINGS YOU DIDN'T EVEN KNOW YOU KNEW...
COME ON, LET'S GO!

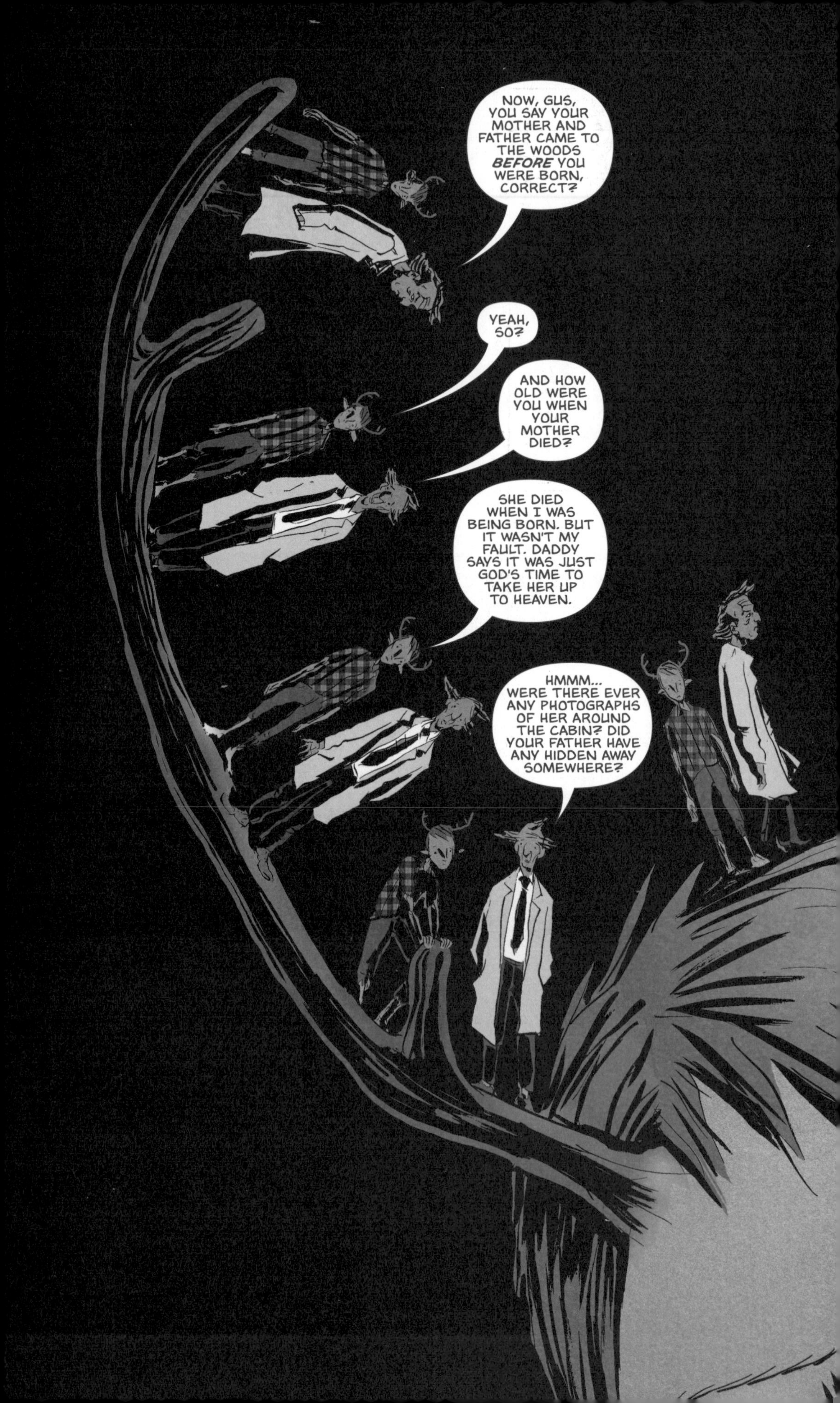
NOW, GUS, YOU SAY YOUR MOTHER AND FATHER CAME TO THE WOODS *BEFORE* YOU WERE BORN, CORRECT?
YEAH, SO?
AND HOW OLD WERE YOU WHEN YOUR MOTHER DIED?
SHE DIED WHEN I WAS BEING BORN. BUT IT WASN'T MY FAULT. DADDY SAYS IT WAS JUST GOD'S TIME TO TAKE HER UP TO HEAVEN.
HMMM... WERE THERE EVER ANY PHOTOGRAPHS OF HER AROUND THE CABIN? DID YOUR FATHER HAVE ANY HIDDEN AWAY SOMEWHERE?

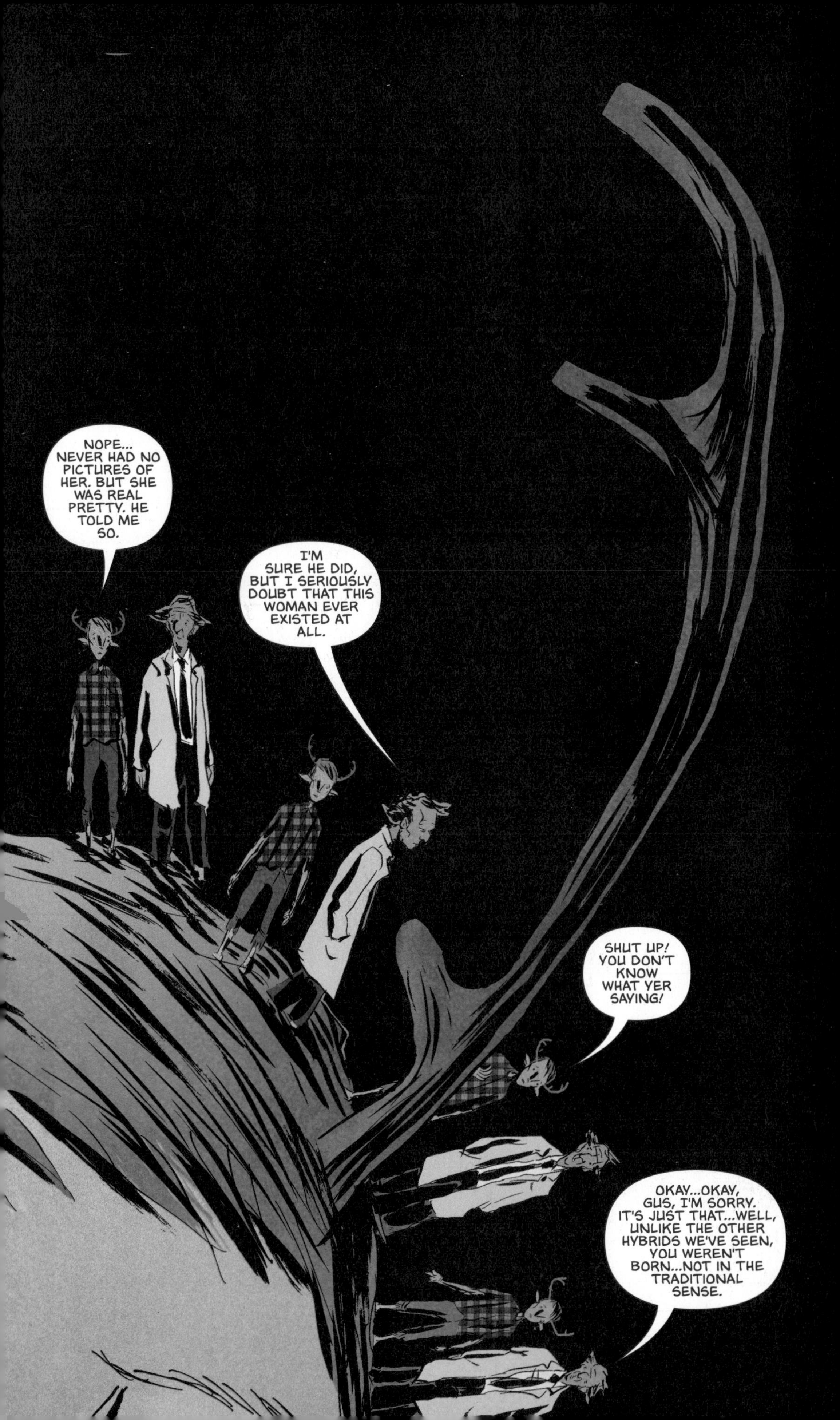
NOPE... NEVER HAD NO PICTURES OF HER. BUT SHE WAS REAL PRETTY. HE TOLD ME SO.
I'M SURE HE DID, BUT I SERIOUSLY DOUBT THAT THIS WOMAN EVER EXISTED AT ALL.
SHUT UP! YOU DON'T KNOW WHAT YER SAYING!
OKAY...OKAY, GUS, I'M SORRY. IT'S JUST THAT...WELL, UNLIKE THE OTHER HYBRIDS WE'VE SEEN, YOU WEREN'T BORN...NOT IN THE TRADITIONAL SENSE.

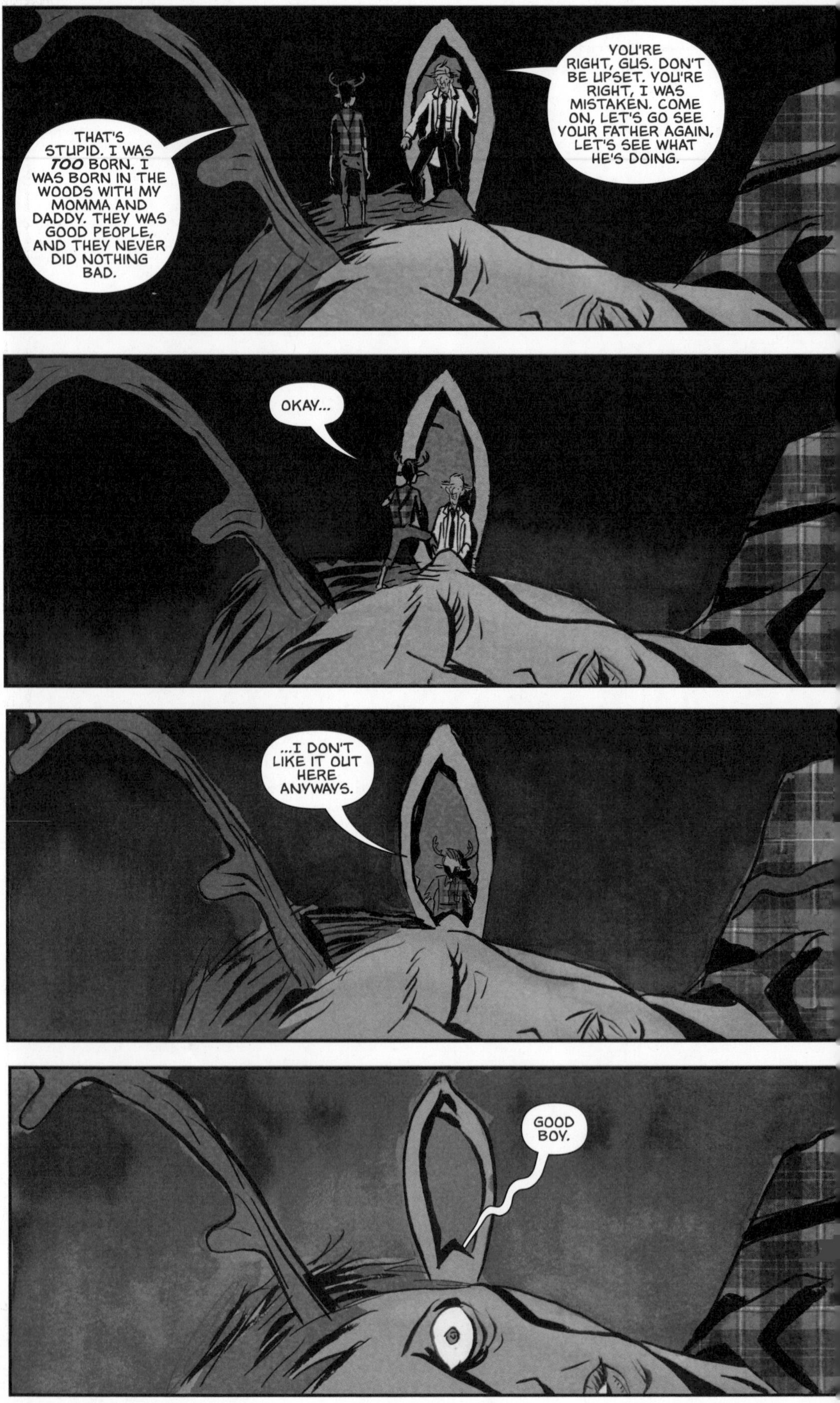
YOU'RE RIGHT, GUS. DON'T BE UPSET. YOU'RE RIGHT, I WAS MISTAKEN. COME ON, LET'S GO SEE YOUR FATHER AGAIN, LET'S SEE WHAT HE'S DOING.
THAT'S STUPID. I WAS *TOO* BORN. I WAS BORN IN THE WOODS WITH MY MOMMA AND DADDY. THEY WAS GOOD PEOPLE, AND THEY NEVER DID NOTHING BAD.
OKAY...
...I DON'T LIKE IT OUT HERE ANYWAYS.
GOOD BOY.

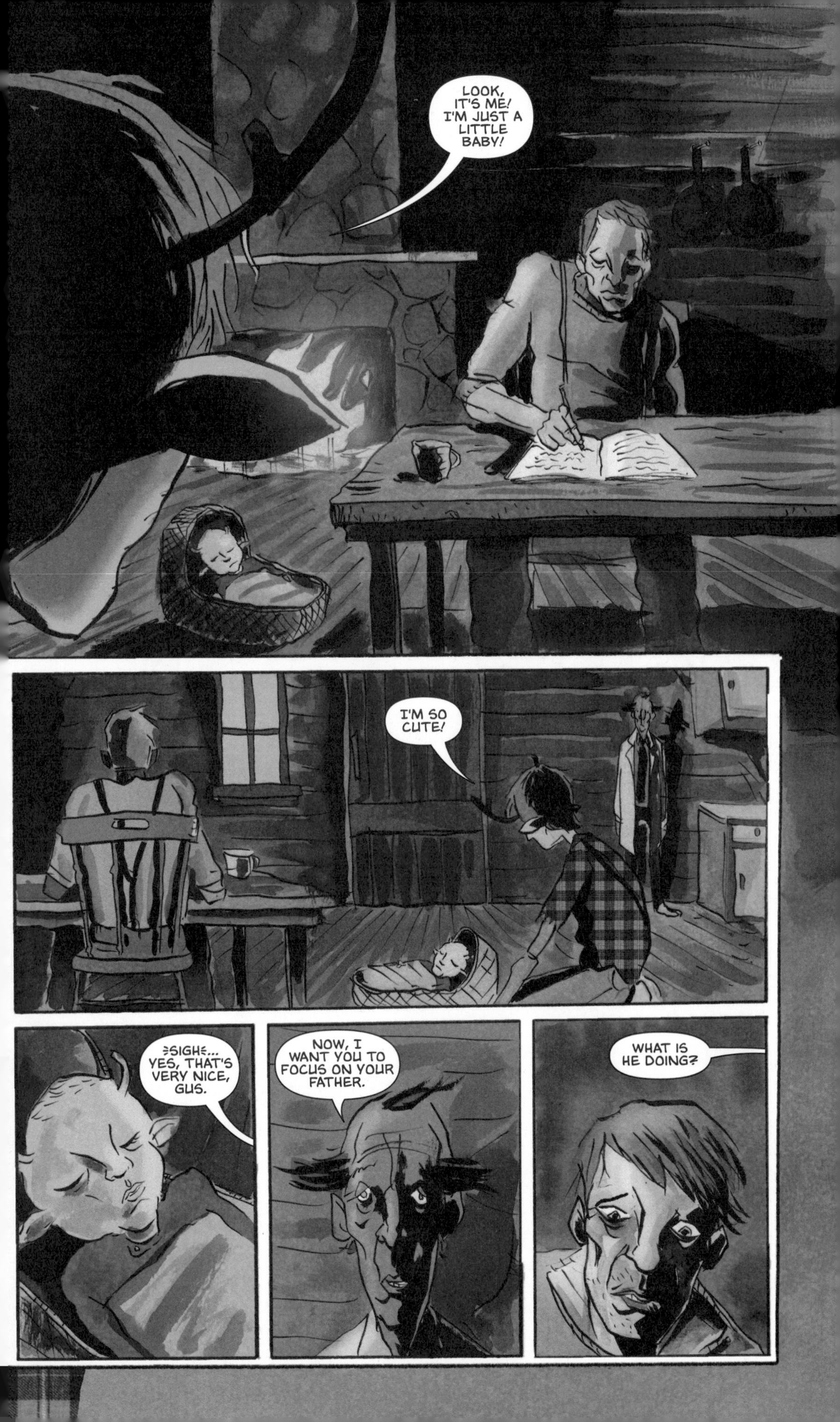
LOOK, IT'S ME! I'M JUST A LITTLE BABY!
I'M SO CUTE!
≈SIGH≈... YES, THAT'S VERY NICE, GUS.
NOW, I WANT YOU TO FOCUS ON YOUR FATHER.
WHAT IS HE DOING?

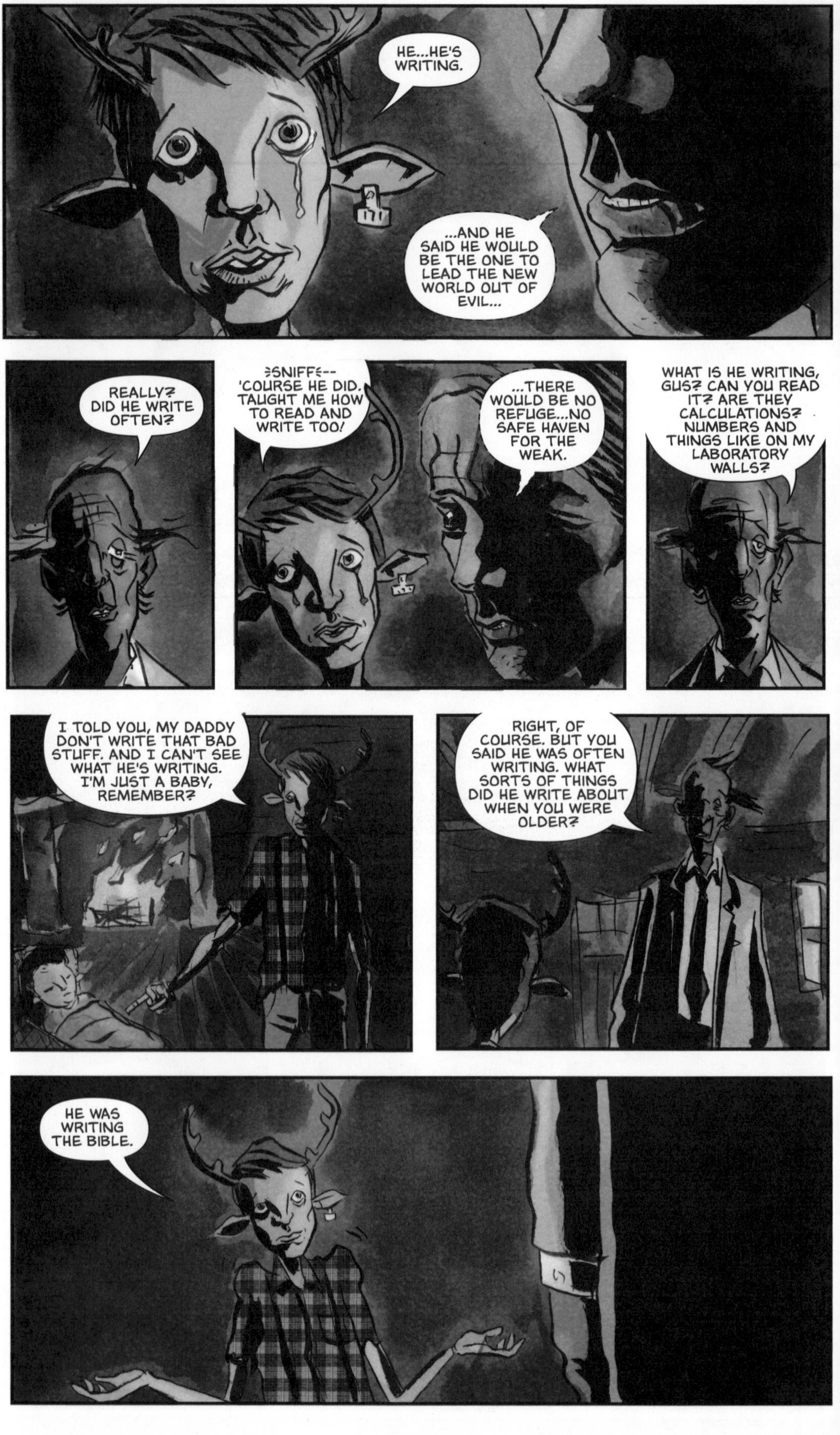
HE...HE'S WRITING.
...AND HE SAID HE WOULD BE THE ONE TO LEAD THE NEW WORLD OUT OF EVIL...
REALLY? DID HE WRITE OFTEN?
SNIFF-- 'COURSE HE DID. TAUGHT ME HOW TO READ AND WRITE TOO!
...THERE WOULD BE NO REFUGE...NO SAFE HAVEN FOR THE WEAK.
WHAT IS HE WRITING, GUS? CAN YOU READ IT? ARE THEY CALCULATIONS? NUMBERS AND THINGS LIKE ON MY LABORATORY WALLS?
I TOLD YOU, MY DADDY DON'T WRITE THAT BAD STUFF. AND I CAN'T SEE WHAT HE'S WRITING. I'M JUST A BABY, REMEMBER?
RIGHT, OF COURSE. BUT YOU SAID HE WAS OFTEN WRITING. WHAT SORTS OF THINGS DID HE WRITE ABOUT WHEN YOU WERE OLDER?
HE WAS WRITING THE BIBLE.

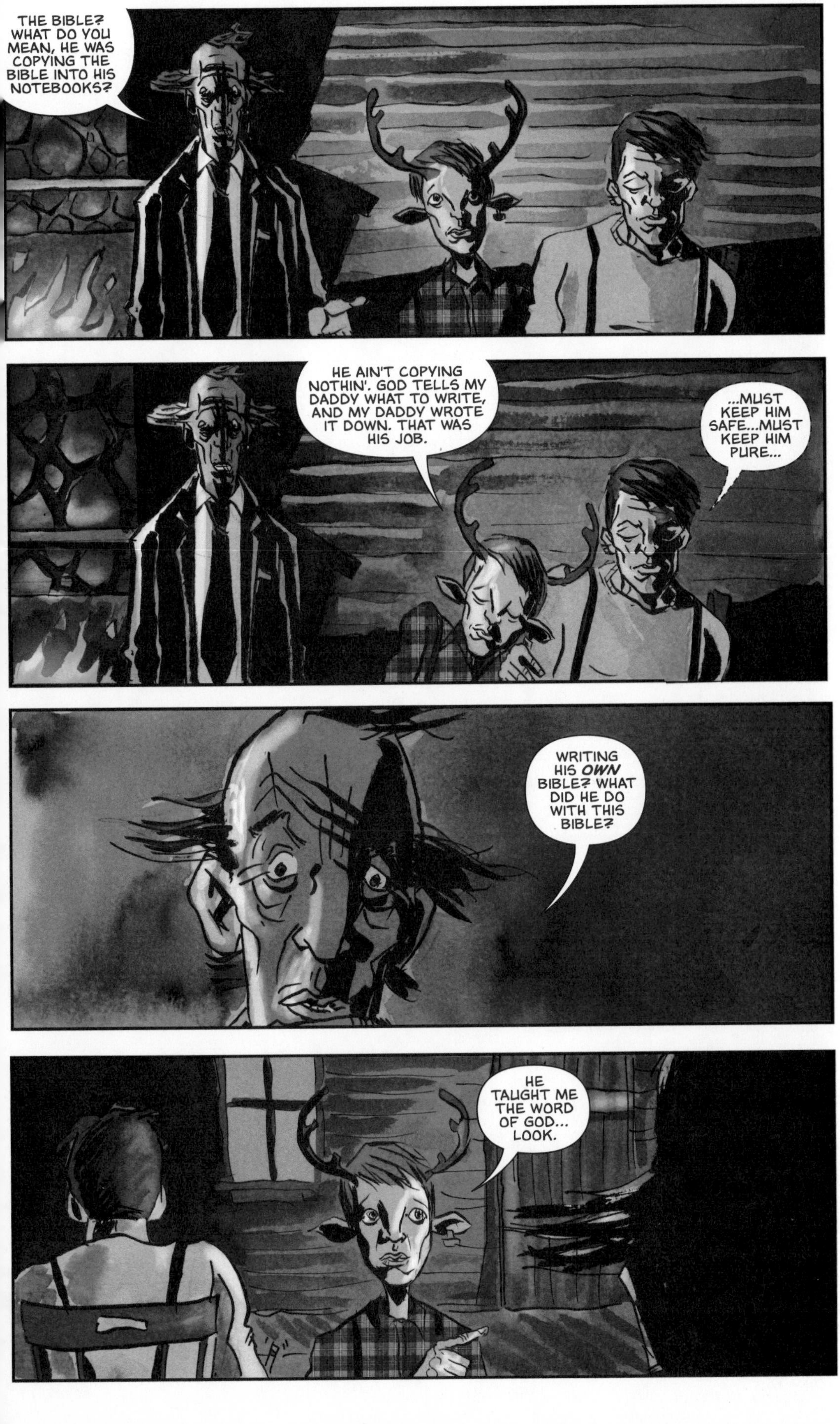
THE BIBLE? WHAT DO YOU MEAN, HE WAS COPYING THE BIBLE INTO HIS NOTEBOOKS?
HE AIN'T COPYING NOTHIN'. GOD TELLS MY DADDY WHAT TO WRITE, AND MY DADDY WROTE IT DOWN. THAT WAS HIS JOB.
...MUST KEEP HIM SAFE...MUST KEEP HIM PURE...
WRITING HIS *OWN* BIBLE? WHAT DID HE DO WITH THIS BIBLE?
HE TAUGHT ME THE WORD OF GOD... LOOK.

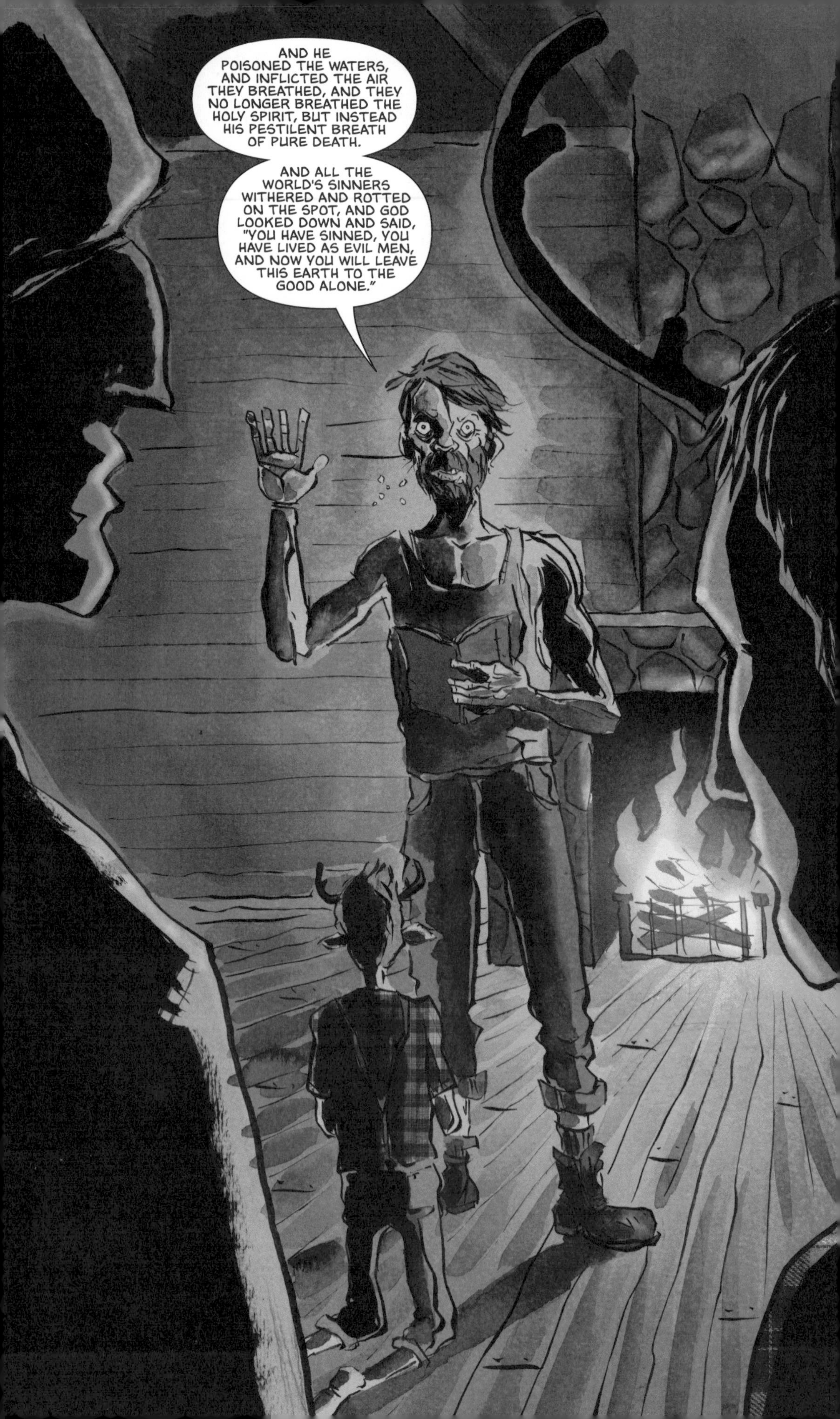
AND HE POISONED THE WATERS, AND INFLICTED THE AIR THEY BREATHED, AND THEY NO LONGER BREATHED THE HOLY SPIRIT, BUT INSTEAD HIS PESTILENT BREATH OF PURE DEATH.
AND ALL THE WORLD'S SINNERS WITHERED AND ROTTED ON THE SPOT, AND GOD LOOKED DOWN AND SAID, "YOU HAVE SINNED, YOU HAVE LIVED AS EVIL MEN, AND NOW YOU WILL LEAVE THIS EARTH TO THE GOOD ALONE."

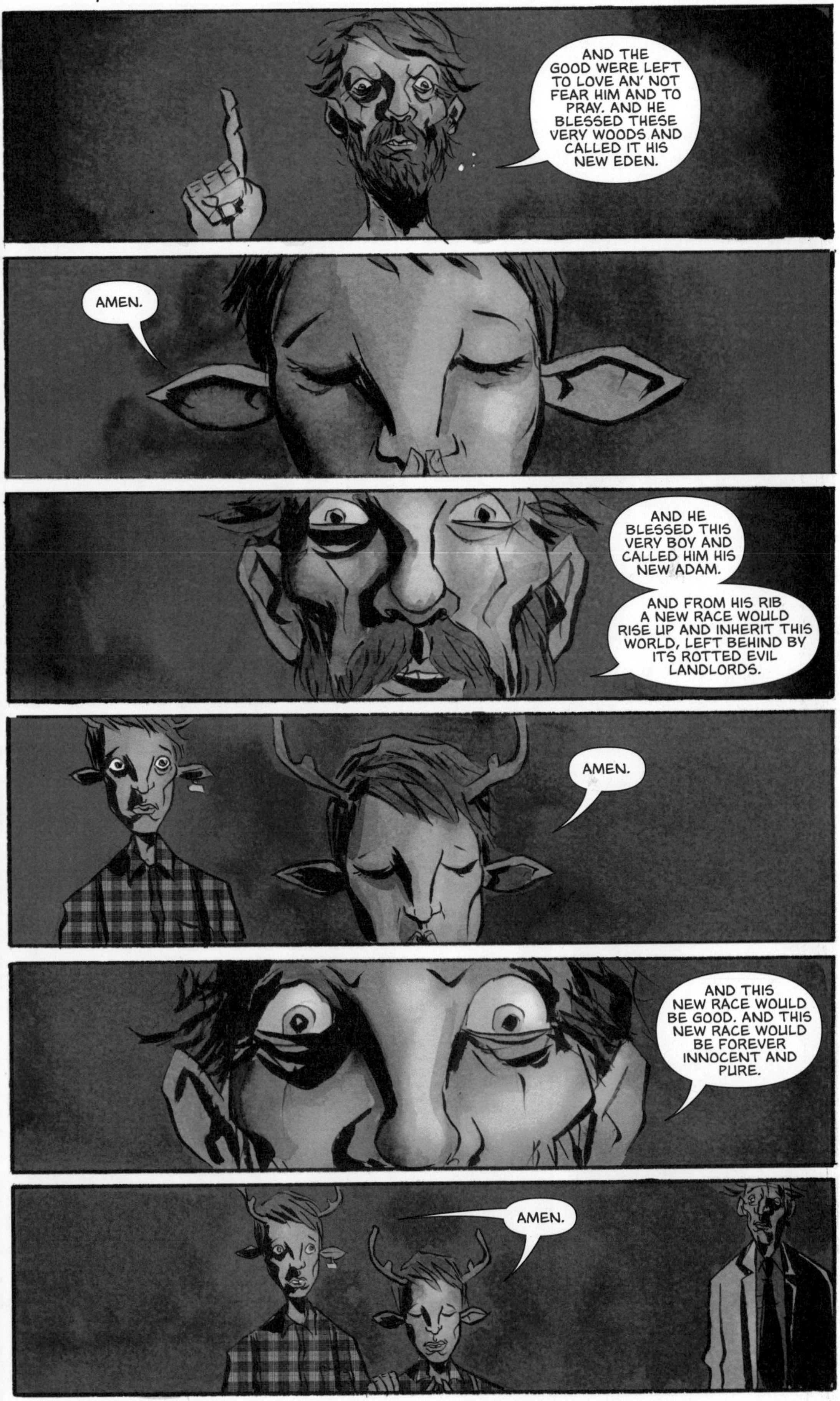
AND THE GOOD WERE LEFT TO LOVE AN' NOT FEAR HIM AND TO PRAY. AND HE BLESSED THESE VERY WOODS AND CALLED IT HIS NEW EDEN.
AMEN.
AND HE BLESSED THIS VERY BOY AND CALLED HIM HIS NEW ADAM.
AND FROM HIS RIB A NEW RACE WOULD RISE UP AND INHERIT THIS WORLD, LEFT BEHIND BY ITS ROTTED EVIL LANDLORDS.
AMEN.
AND THIS NEW RACE WOULD BE GOOD. AND THIS NEW RACE WOULD BE FOREVER INNOCENT AND PURE.
AMEN.

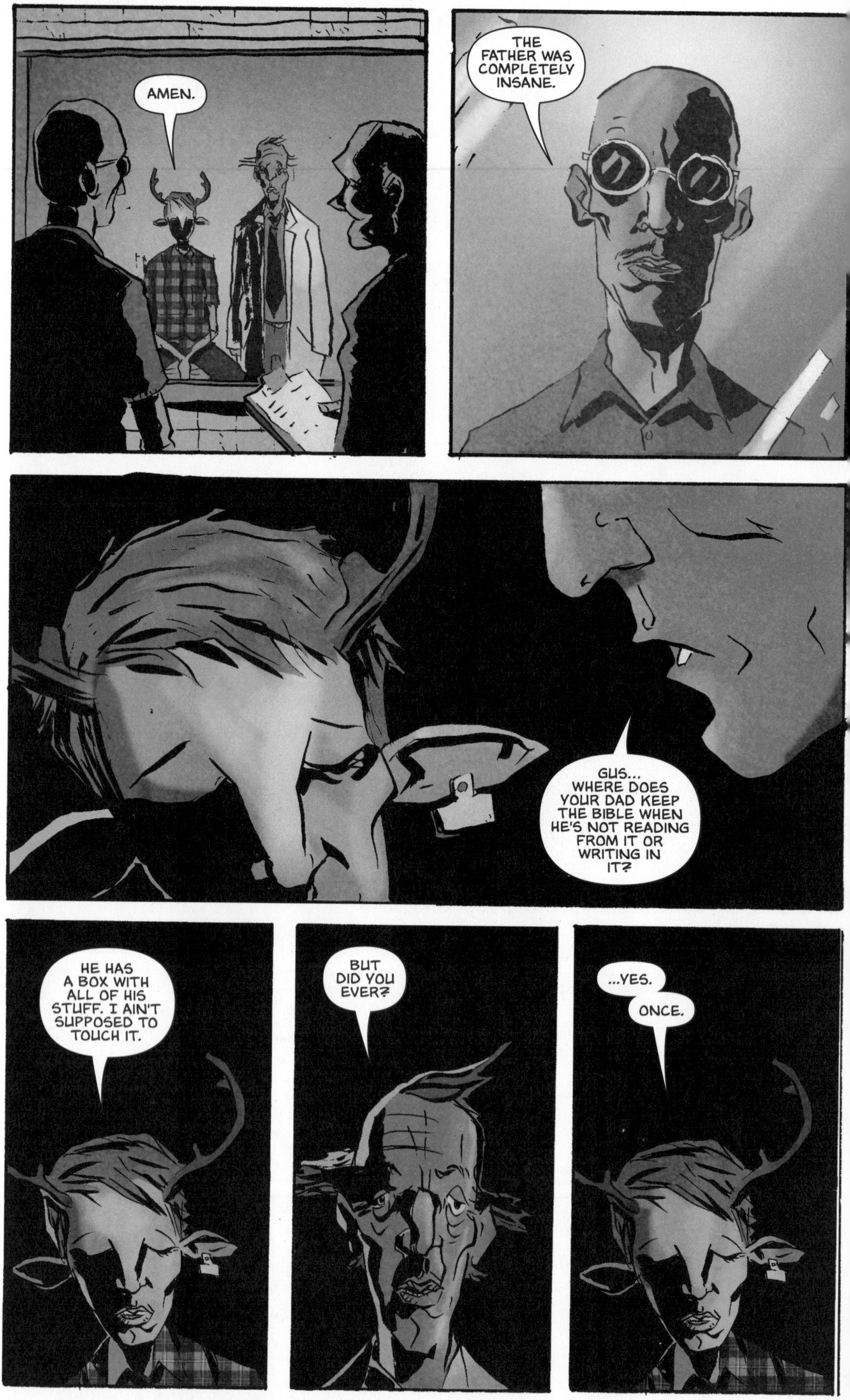
AMEN.
THE FATHER WAS COMPLETELY INSANE.
GUS... WHERE DOES YOUR DAD KEEP THE BIBLE WHEN HE'S NOT READING FROM IT OR WRITING IN IT?
HE HAS A BOX WITH ALL OF HIS STUFF. I AIN'T SUPPOSED TO TOUCH IT.
BUT DID YOU EVER?
...YES.
ONCE.

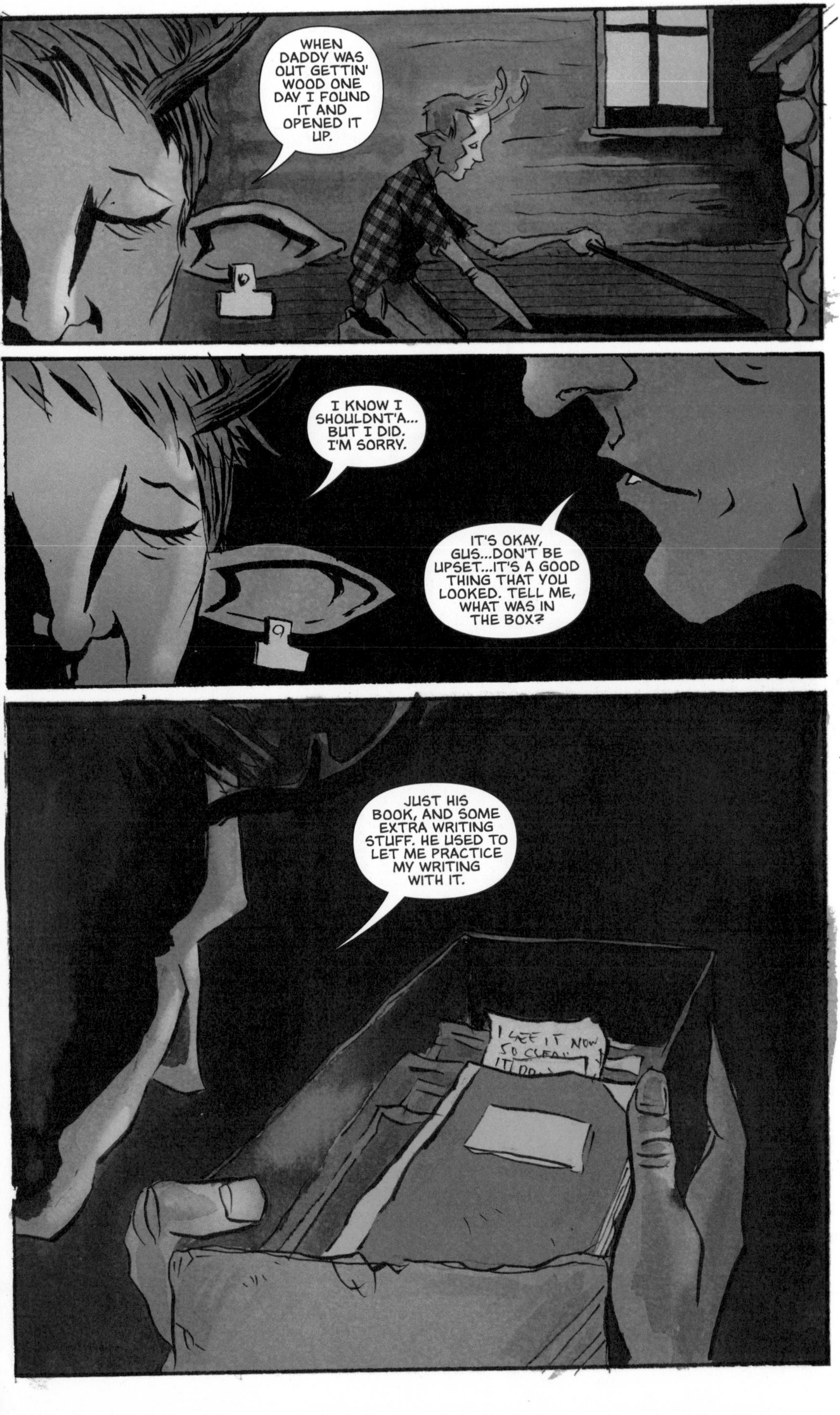
WHEN DADDY WAS OUT GETTIN' WOOD ONE DAY I FOUND IT AND OPENED IT UP.
I KNOW I SHOULDNT'A... BUT I DID. I'M SORRY.
IT'S OKAY, GUS...DON'T BE UPSET...IT'S A GOOD THING THAT YOU LOOKED. TELL ME, WHAT WAS IN THE BOX?
JUST HIS BOOK, AND SOME EXTRA WRITING STUFF. HE USED TO LET ME PRACTICE MY WRITING WITH IT.
I SEE IT NOW

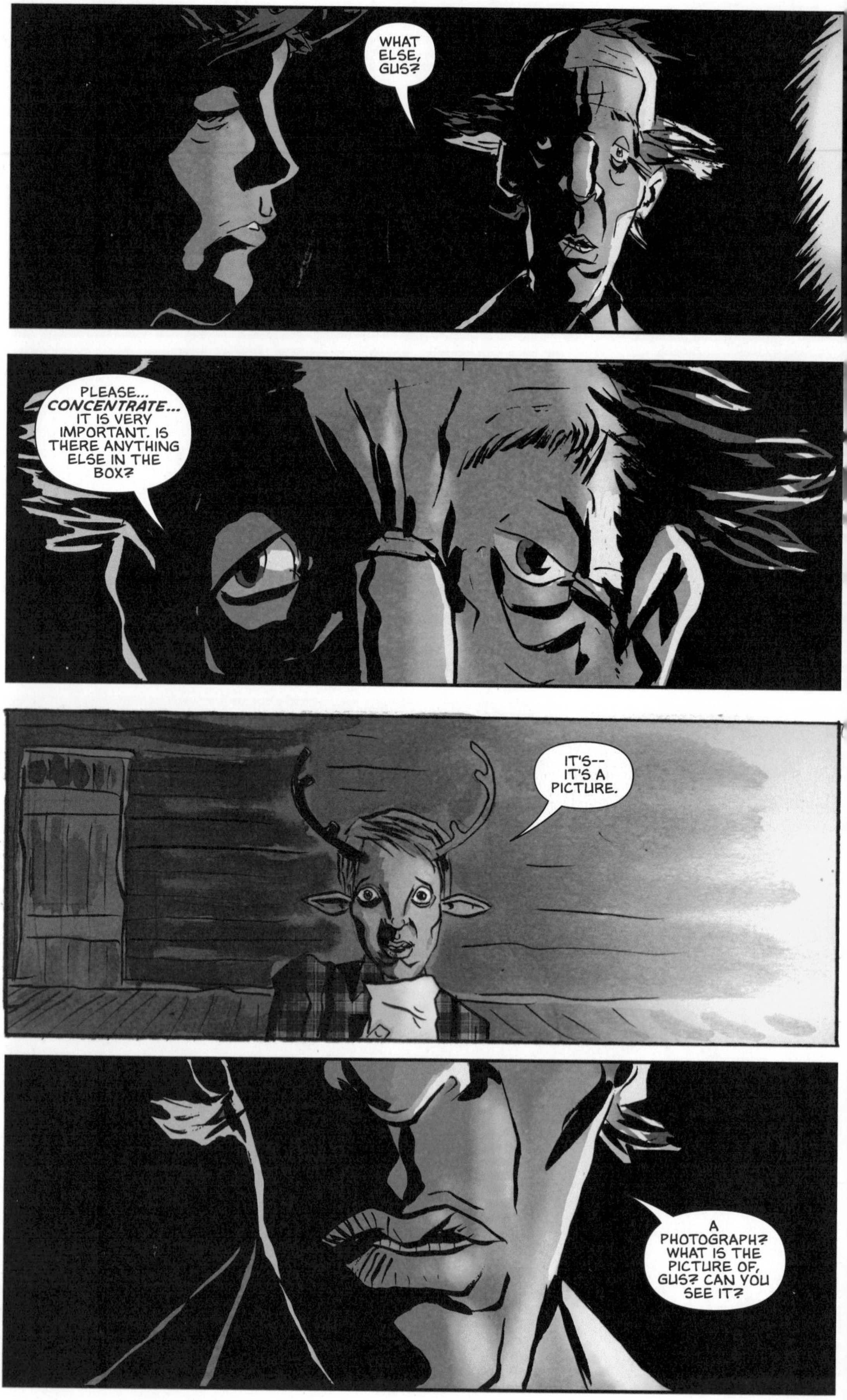

WHAT ELSE, GUS?
PLEASE... ***CONCENTRATE...*** IT IS VERY IMPORTANT. IS THERE ANYTHING ELSE IN THE BOX?
IT'S-- IT'S A PICTURE.
A PHOTOGRAPH? WHAT IS THE PICTURE OF, GUS? CAN YOU SEE IT?

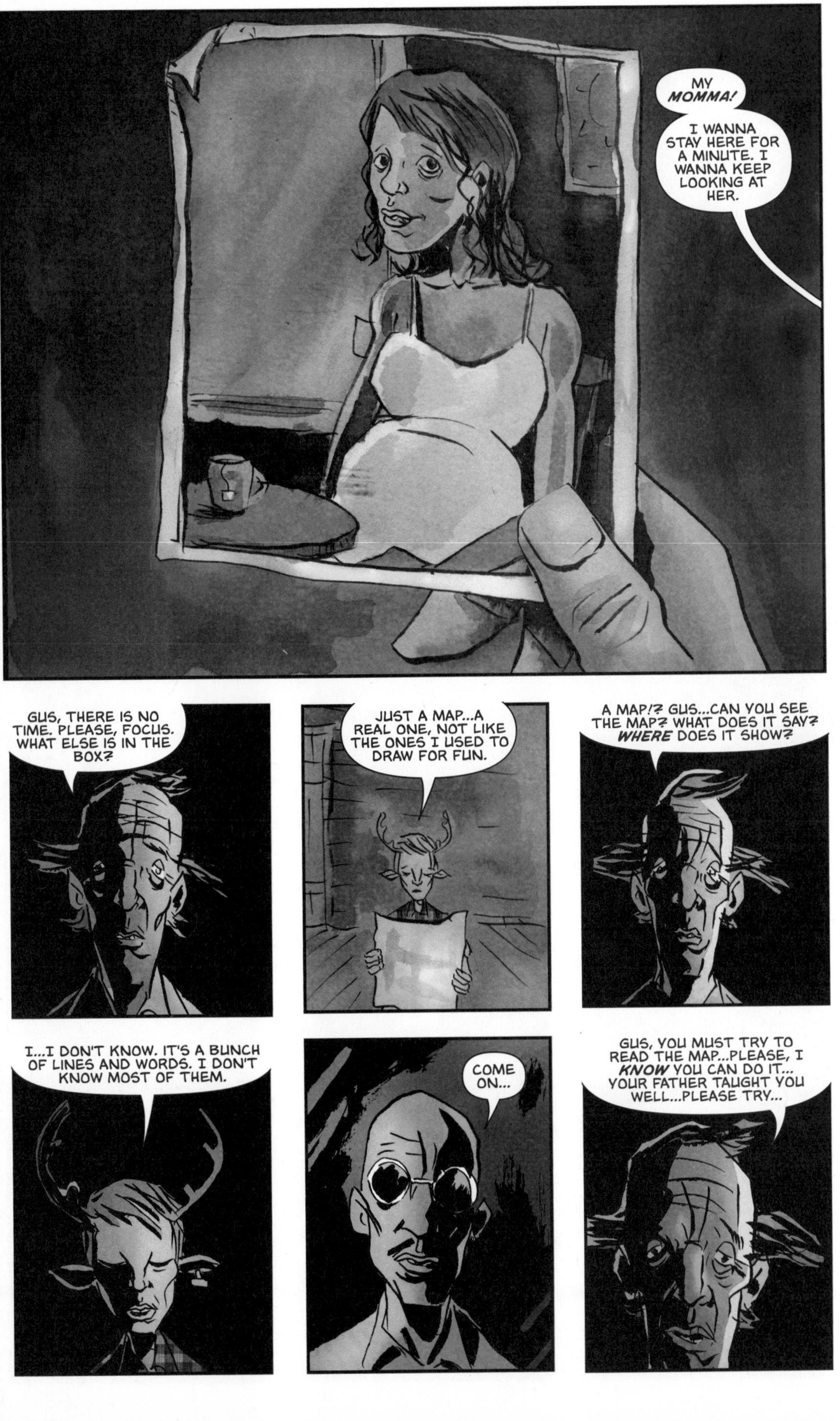
MY MOMMA!
I WANNA STAY HERE FOR A MINUTE. I WANNA KEEP LOOKING AT HER.
GUS, THERE IS NO TIME. PLEASE, FOCUS. WHAT ELSE IS IN THE BOX?
JUST A MAP...A REAL ONE, NOT LIKE THE ONES I USED TO DRAW FOR FUN.
A MAP!? GUS...CAN YOU SEE THE MAP? WHAT DOES IT SAY? WHERE DOES IT SHOW?
I...I DON'T KNOW. IT'S A BUNCH OF LINES AND WORDS. I DON'T KNOW MOST OF THEM.
COME ON...
GUS, YOU MUST TRY TO READ THE MAP...PLEASE, I KNOW YOU CAN DO IT... YOUR FATHER TAUGHT YOU WELL...PLEASE TRY...

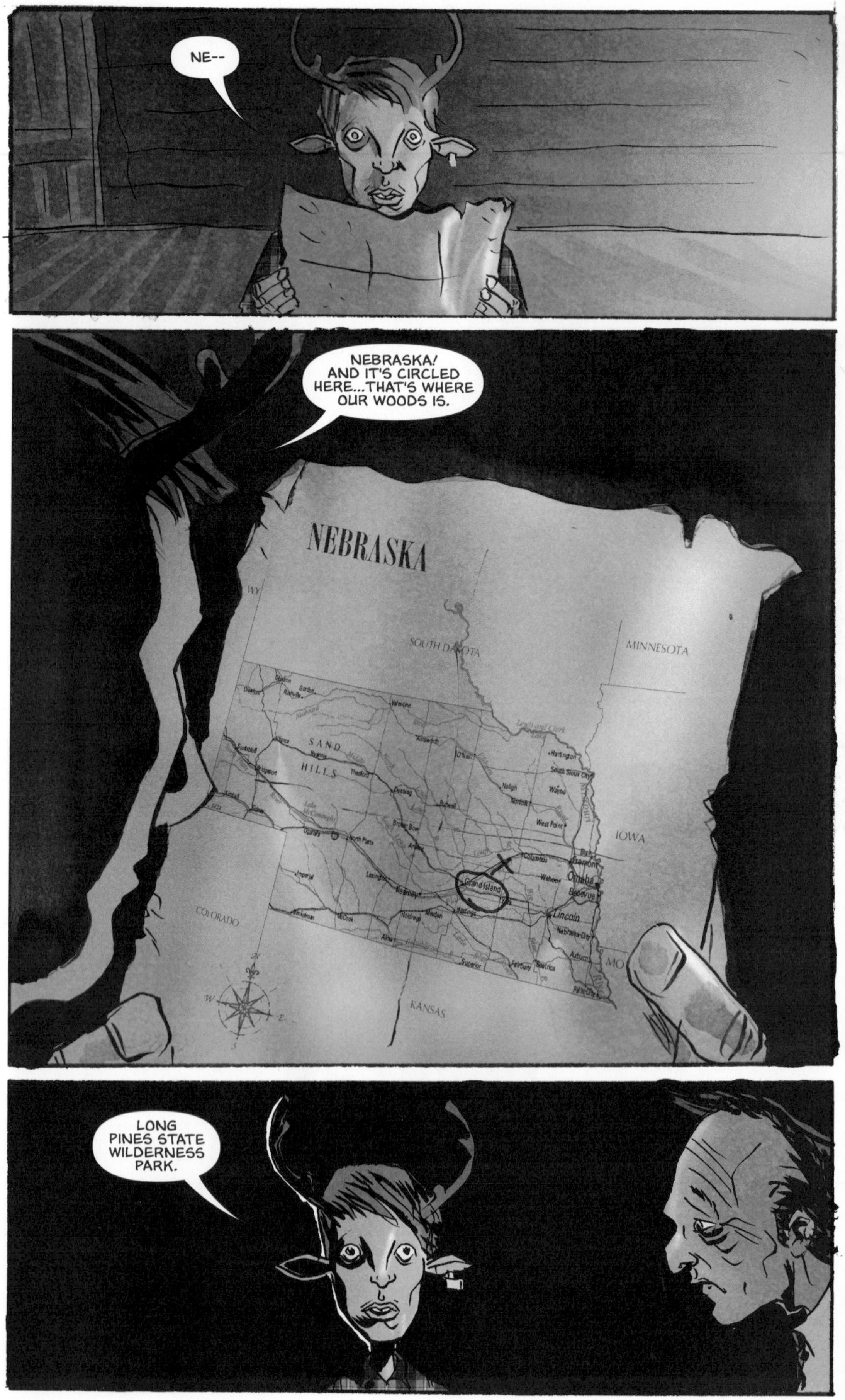
NE--
NEBRASKA! AND IT'S CIRCLED HERE...THAT'S WHERE OUR WOODS IS.
NEBRASKA
WY
SOUTH DAKOTA
MINNESOTA
SAND HILLS
IOWA
Grand Island
Lincoln
COLORADO
KANSAS
MO
LONG PINES STATE WILDERNESS PARK.

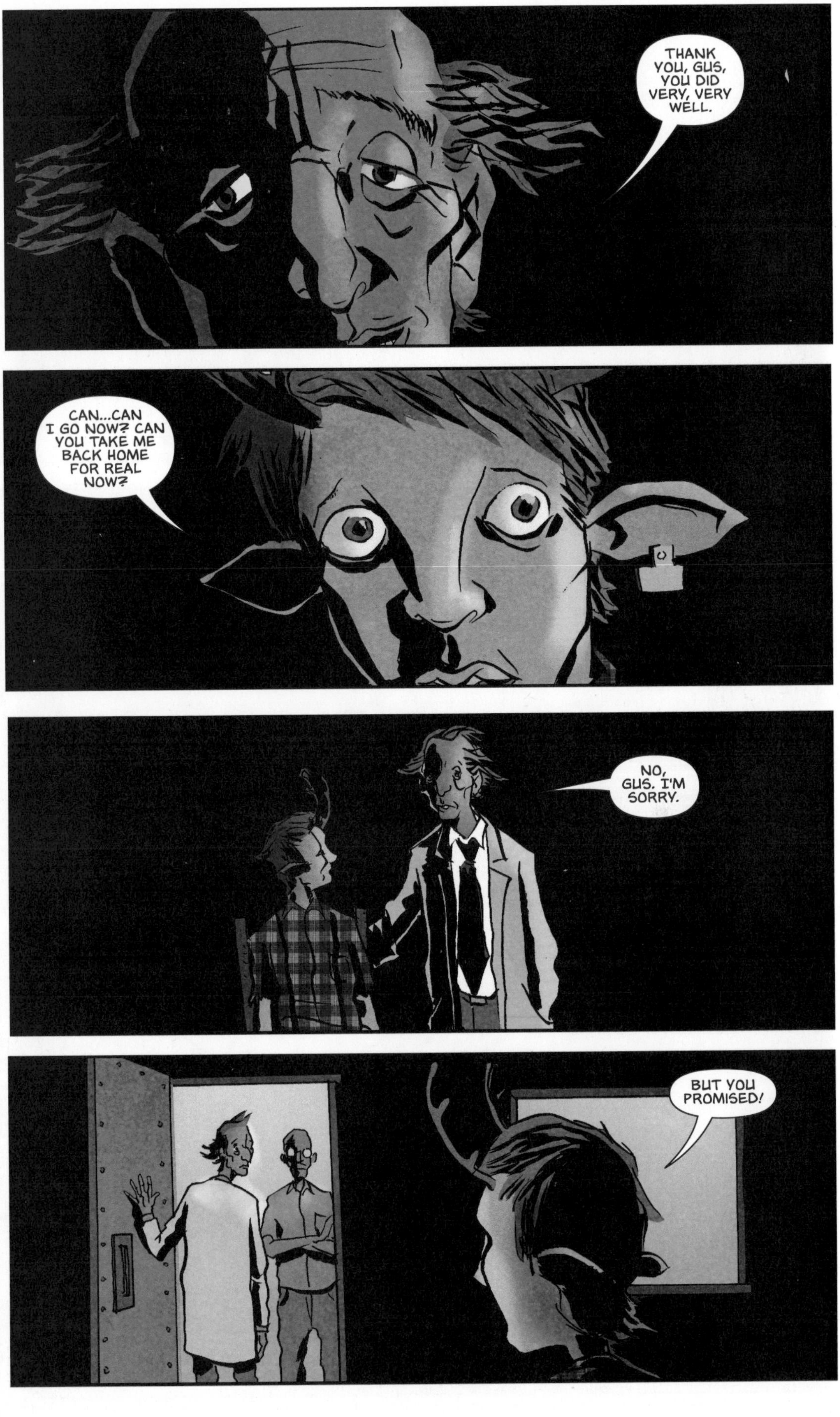
THANK YOU, GUS, YOU DID VERY, VERY WELL.
CAN...CAN I GO NOW? CAN YOU TAKE ME BACK HOME FOR REAL NOW?
NO, GUS. I'M SORRY.
BUT YOU PROMISED!

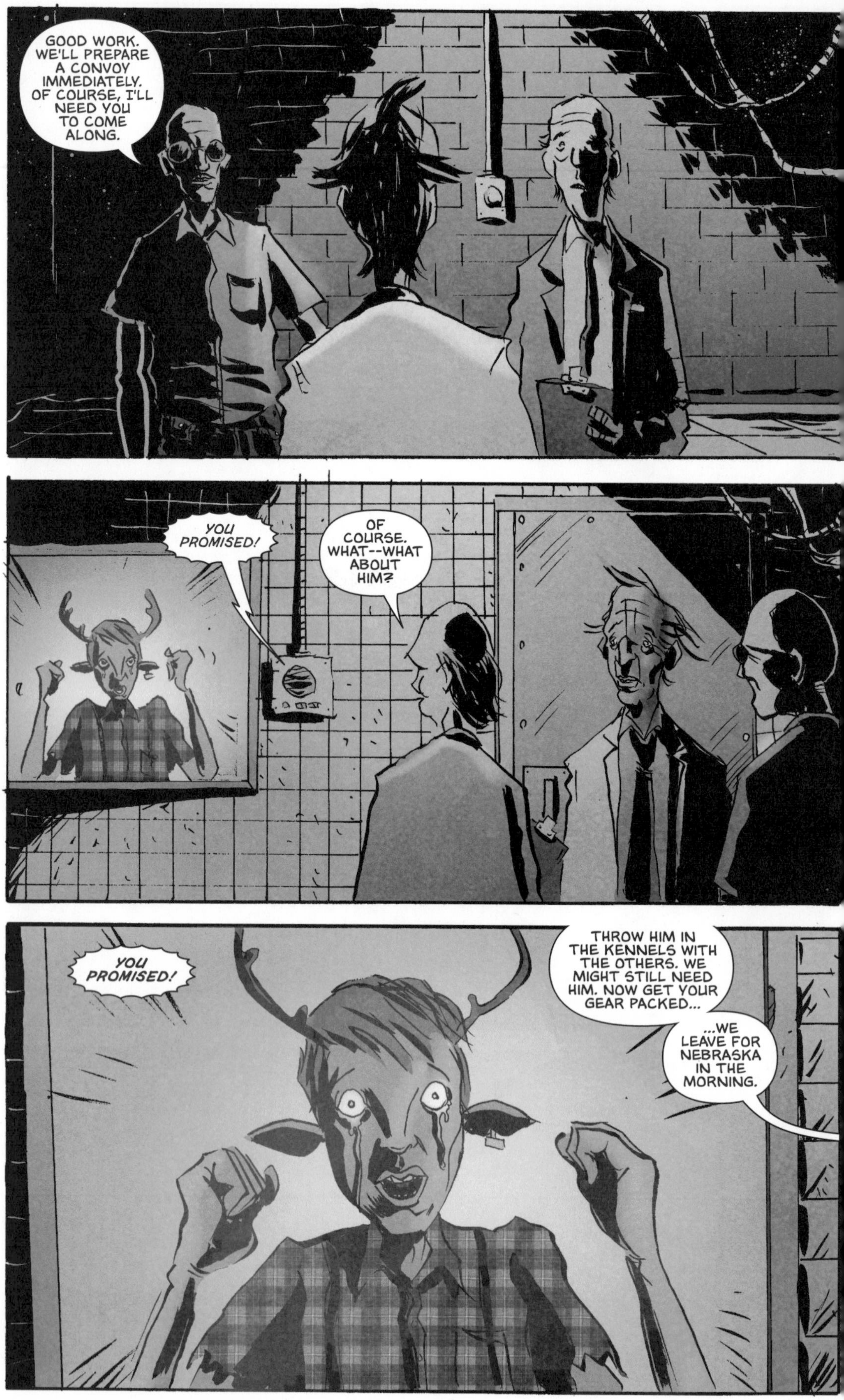
GOOD WORK. WE'LL PREPARE A CONVOY IMMEDIATELY. OF COURSE, I'LL NEED YOU TO COME ALONG.
YOU PROMISED!
OF COURSE. WHAT--WHAT ABOUT HIM?
YOU PROMISED!
THROW HIM IN THE KENNELS WITH THE OTHERS. WE MIGHT STILL NEED HIM. NOW GET YOUR GEAR PACKED...
...WE LEAVE FOR NEBRASKA IN THE MORNING.

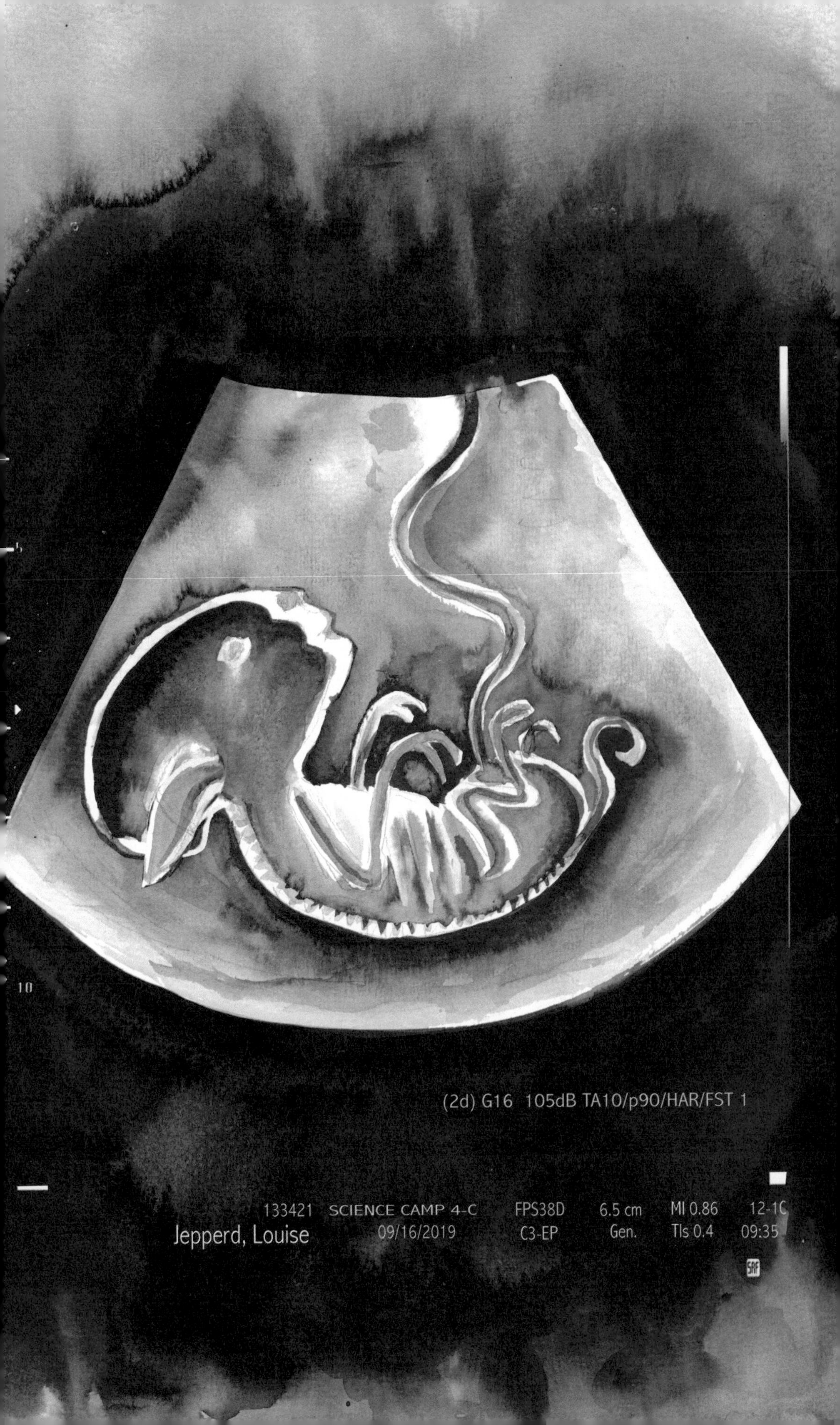
5
10
(2d) G16 105dB TA10/p90/HAR/FST 1
133421 SCIENCE CAMP 4-C FPS38D 6.5 cm MI 0.86 12-1C
Jepperd, Louise 09/16/2019 C3-EP Gen. TIs 0.4 09:35

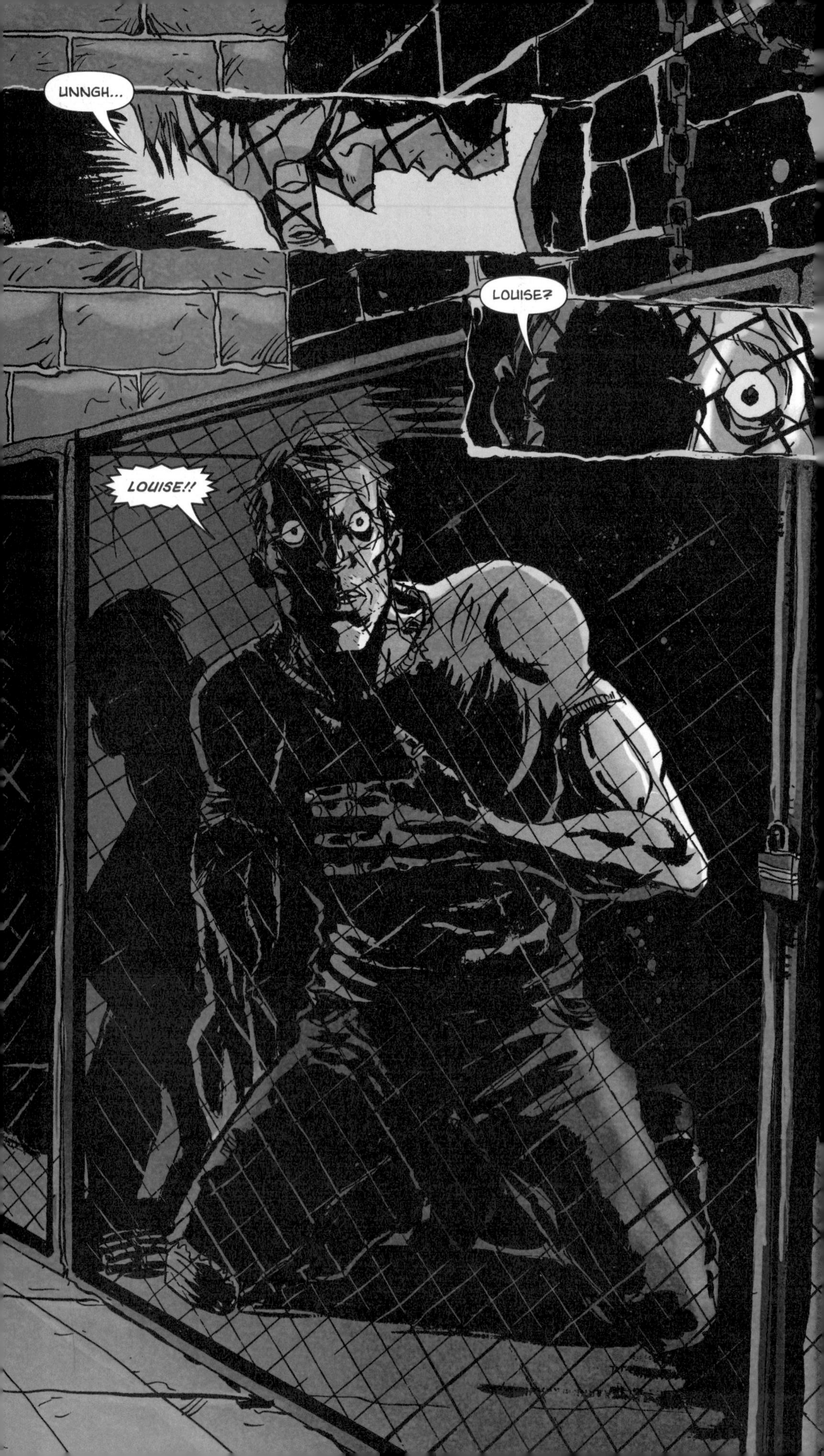
UNNGH...
LOUISE?
LOUISE!!

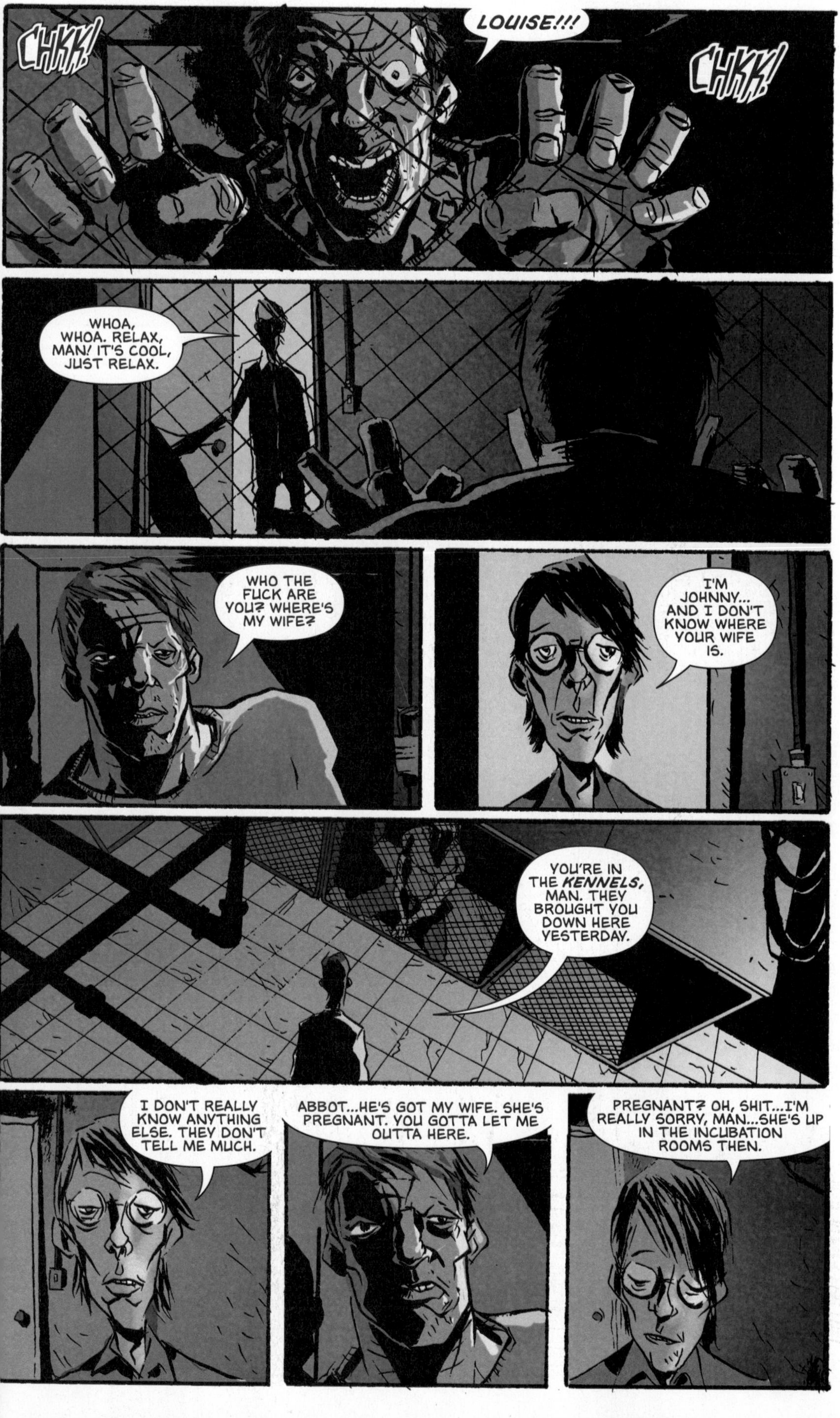
CHKK!
LOUISE!!!
CHKK!
WHOA, WHOA. RELAX, MAN! IT'S COOL, JUST RELAX.
WHO THE FUCK ARE YOU? WHERE'S MY WIFE?
I'M JOHNNY... AND I DON'T KNOW WHERE YOUR WIFE IS.
YOU'RE IN THE *KENNELS,* MAN. THEY BROUGHT YOU DOWN HERE YESTERDAY.
I DON'T REALLY KNOW ANYTHING ELSE. THEY DON'T TELL ME MUCH.
ABBOT...HE'S GOT MY WIFE. SHE'S PREGNANT. YOU GOTTA LET ME OUTTA HERE.
PREGNANT? OH, SHIT...I'M REALLY SORRY, MAN...SHE'S UP IN THE INCUBATION ROOMS THEN.

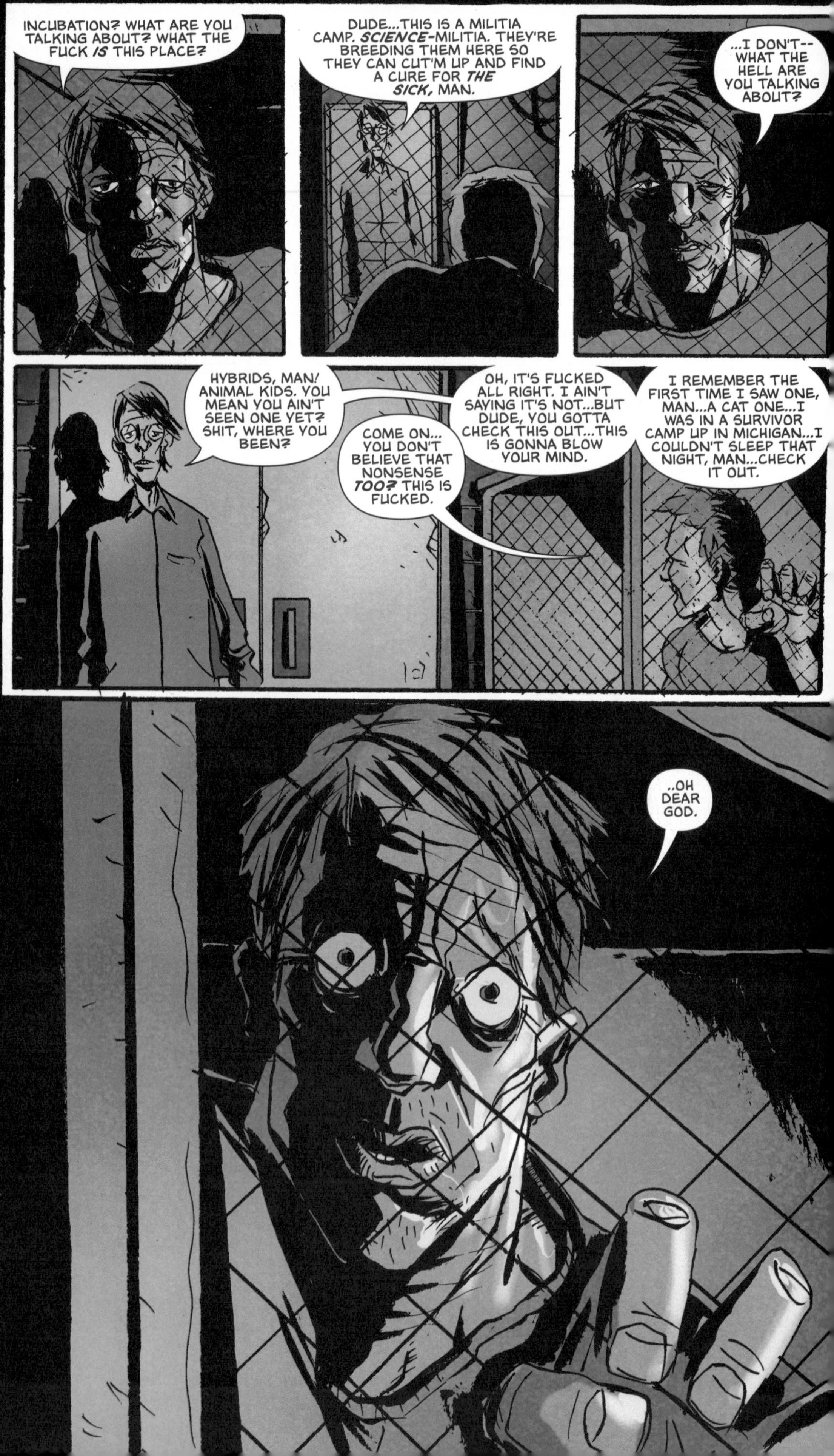
INCUBATION? WHAT ARE YOU TALKING ABOUT? WHAT THE FUCK *IS* THIS PLACE?
DUDE...THIS IS A MILITIA CAMP. *SCIENCE*-MILITIA. THEY'RE BREEDING THEM HERE SO THEY CAN CUT'M UP AND FIND A CURE FOR *THE SICK,* MAN.
...I DON'T-- WHAT THE HELL ARE YOU TALKING ABOUT?
HYBRIDS, MAN! ANIMAL KIDS. YOU MEAN YOU AIN'T SEEN ONE YET? SHIT, WHERE YOU BEEN?
COME ON... YOU DON'T BELIEVE THAT NONSENSE *TOO?* THIS IS FUCKED.
OH, IT'S FUCKED ALL RIGHT. I AIN'T SAYING IT'S NOT...BUT DUDE, YOU GOTTA CHECK THIS OUT...THIS IS GONNA BLOW YOUR MIND.
I REMEMBER THE FIRST TIME I SAW ONE, MAN...A CAT ONE...I WAS IN A SURVIVOR CAMP UP IN MICHIGAN...I COULDN'T SLEEP THAT NIGHT, MAN...CHECK IT OUT.
..OH DEAR GOD.

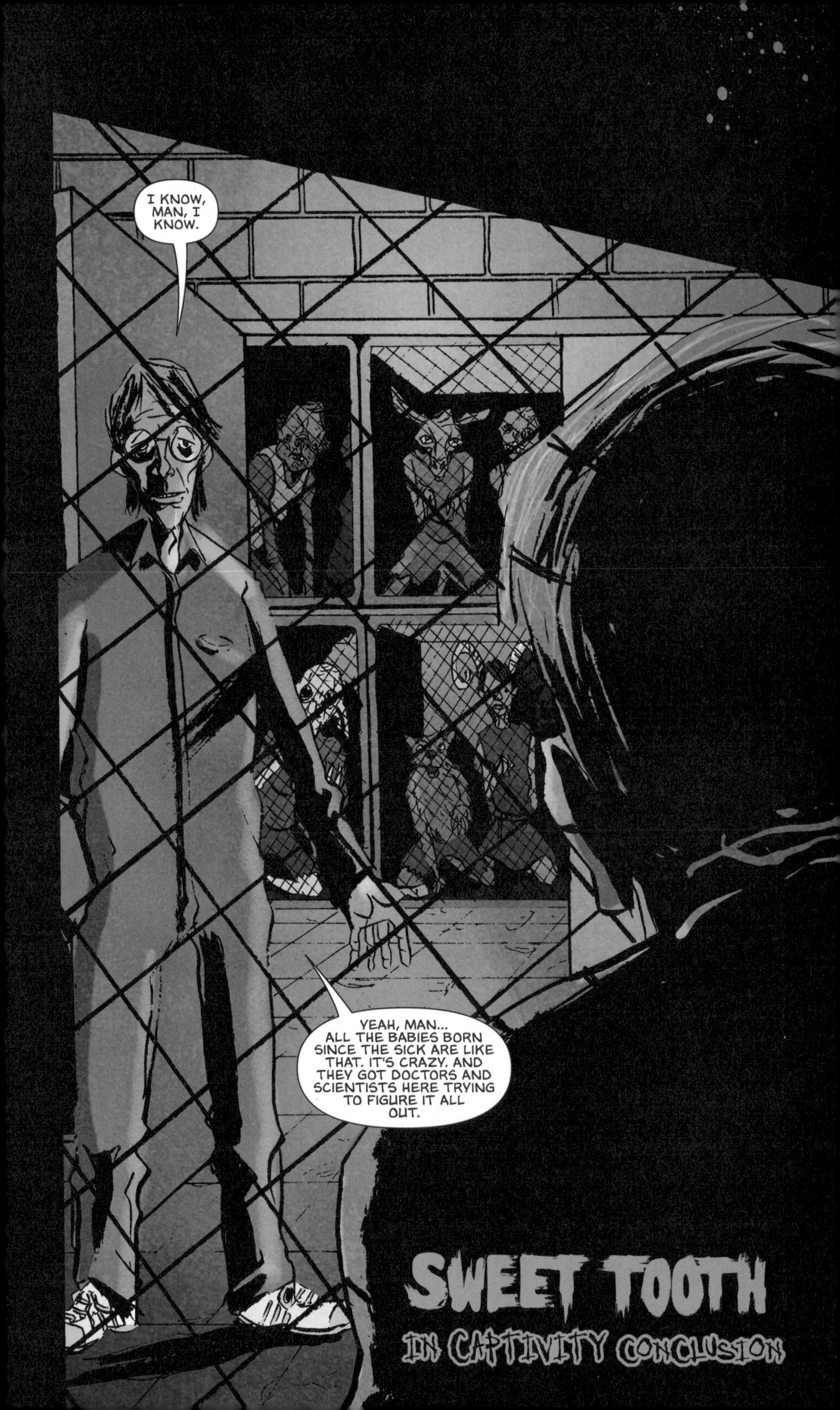
I KNOW, MAN, I KNOW.
YEAH, MAN... ALL THE BABIES BORN SINCE THE SICK ARE LIKE THAT. IT'S CRAZY. AND THEY GOT DOCTORS AND SCIENTISTS HERE TRYING TO FIGURE IT ALL OUT.
SWEET TOOTH
IN CAPTIVITY CONCLUSION

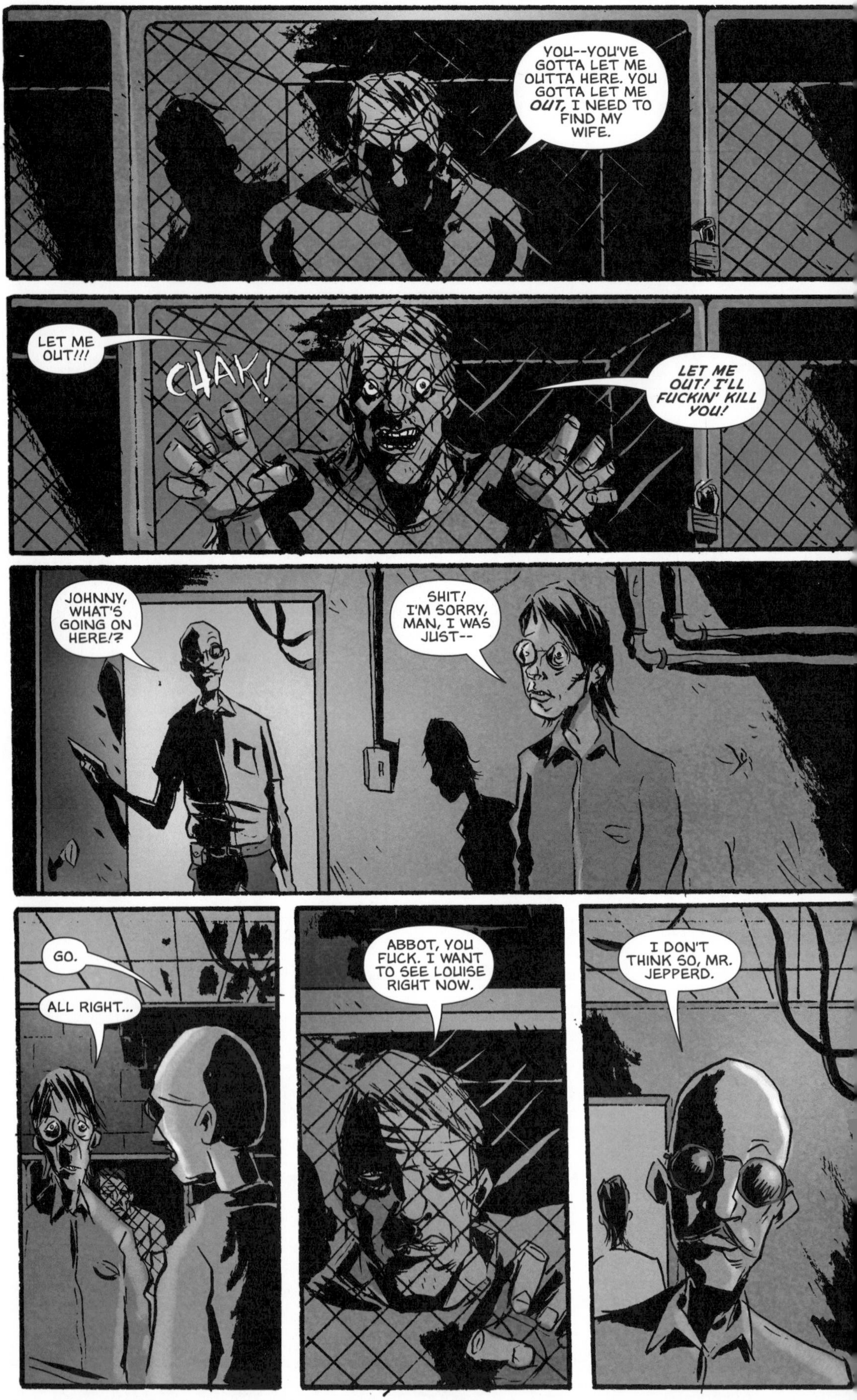
YOU--YOU'VE GOTTA LET ME OUTTA HERE. YOU GOTTA LET ME *OUT,* I NEED TO FIND MY WIFE.
LET ME OUT!!!
CHAK!
LET ME OUT! I'LL FUCKIN' KILL YOU!
JOHNNY, WHAT'S GOING ON HERE!?
SHIT! I'M SORRY, MAN, I WAS JUST--
GO.
ALL RIGHT...
ABBOT, YOU FUCK. I WANT TO SEE LOUISE RIGHT NOW.
I DON'T THINK SO, MR. JEPPERD.

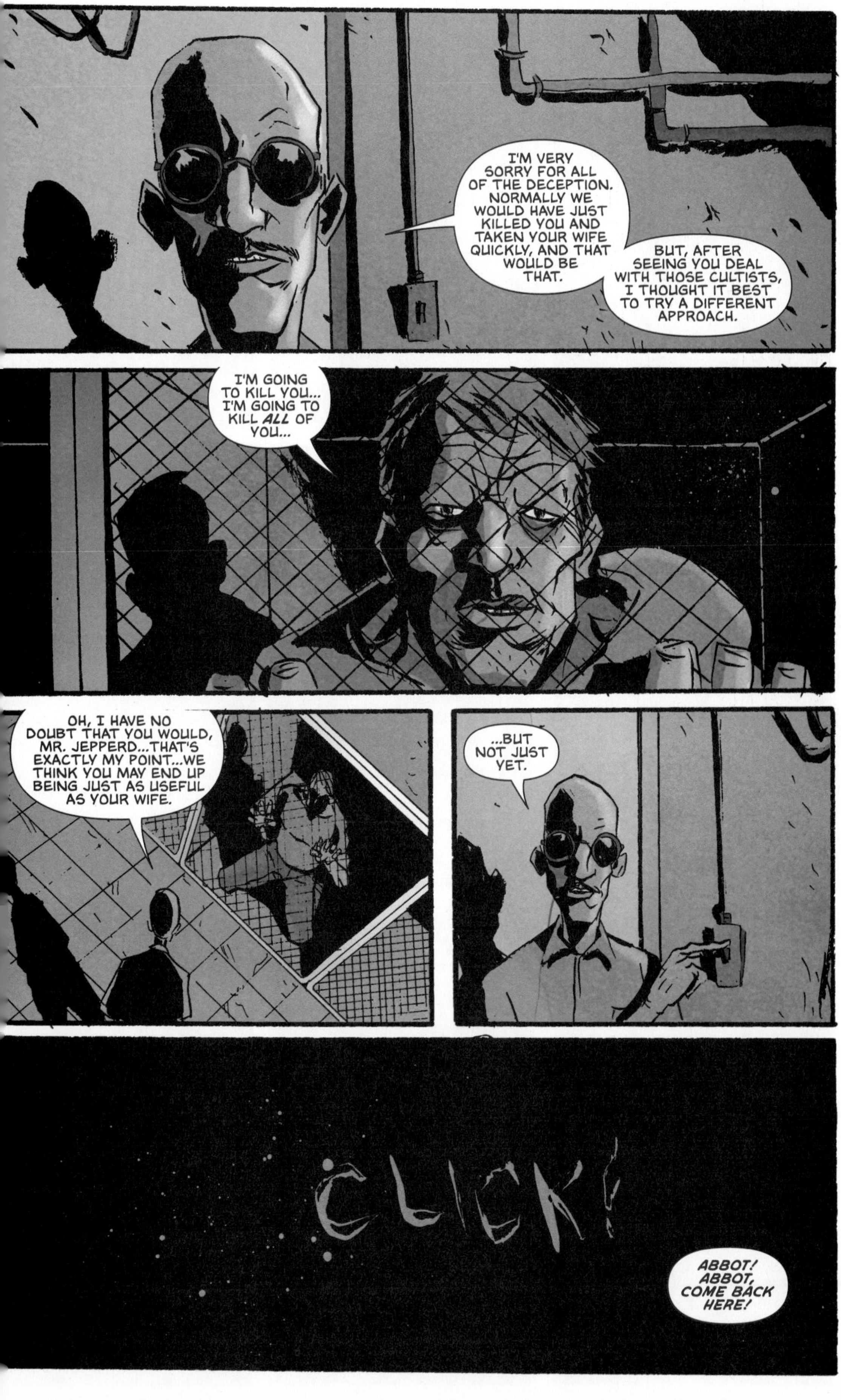
I'M VERY SORRY FOR ALL OF THE DECEPTION. NORMALLY WE WOULD HAVE JUST KILLED YOU AND TAKEN YOUR WIFE QUICKLY, AND THAT WOULD BE THAT.
BUT, AFTER SEEING YOU DEAL WITH THOSE CULTISTS, I THOUGHT IT BEST TO TRY A DIFFERENT APPROACH.
I'M GOING TO KILL YOU... I'M GOING TO KILL *ALL* OF YOU...
OH, I HAVE NO DOUBT THAT YOU WOULD, MR. JEPPERD...THAT'S EXACTLY MY POINT...WE THINK YOU MAY END UP BEING JUST AS USEFUL AS YOUR WIFE.
...BUT NOT JUST YET.
CLICK!
ABBOT! ABBOT, COME BACK HERE!

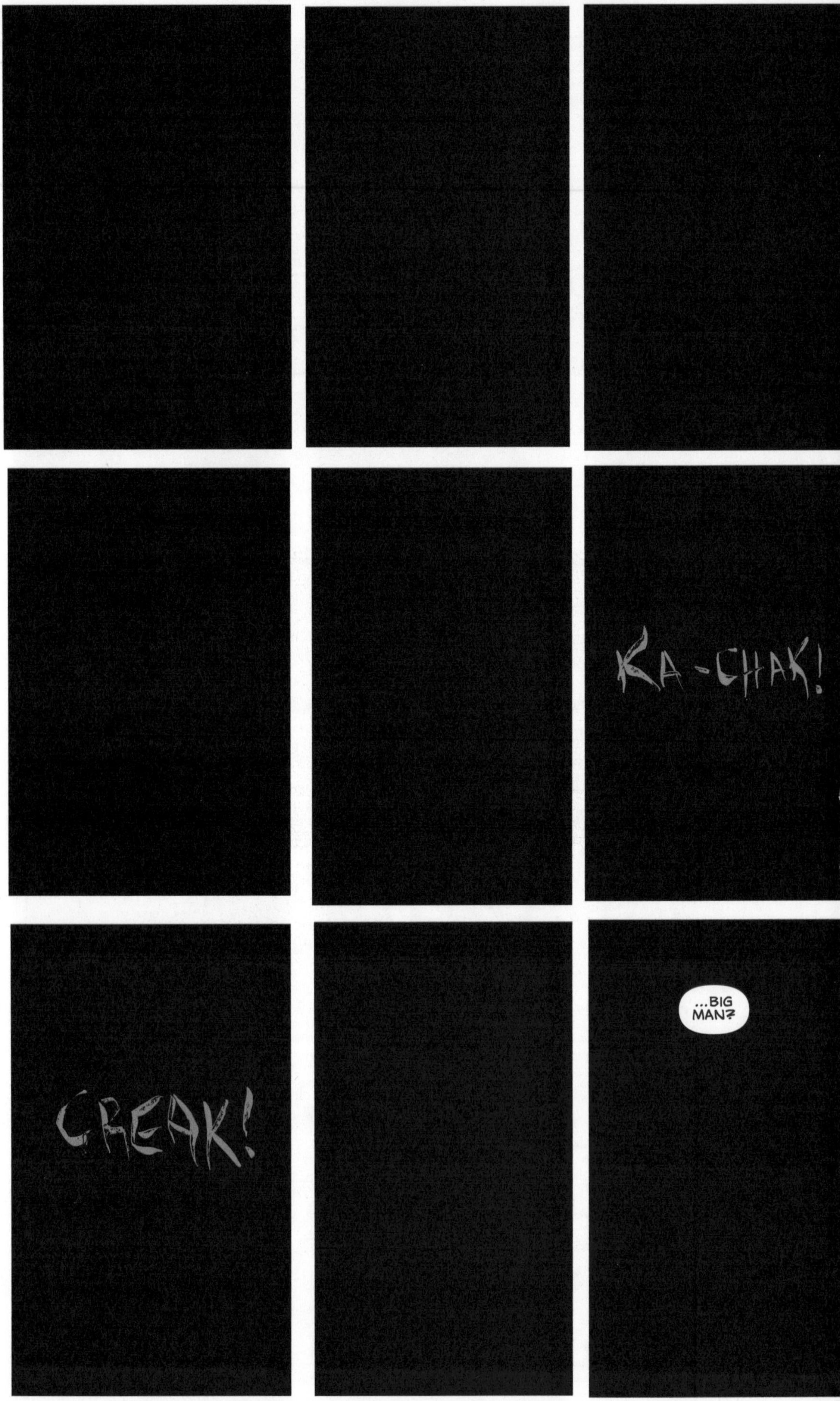
KA-CHAK!
CREAK!
...BIG MAN?

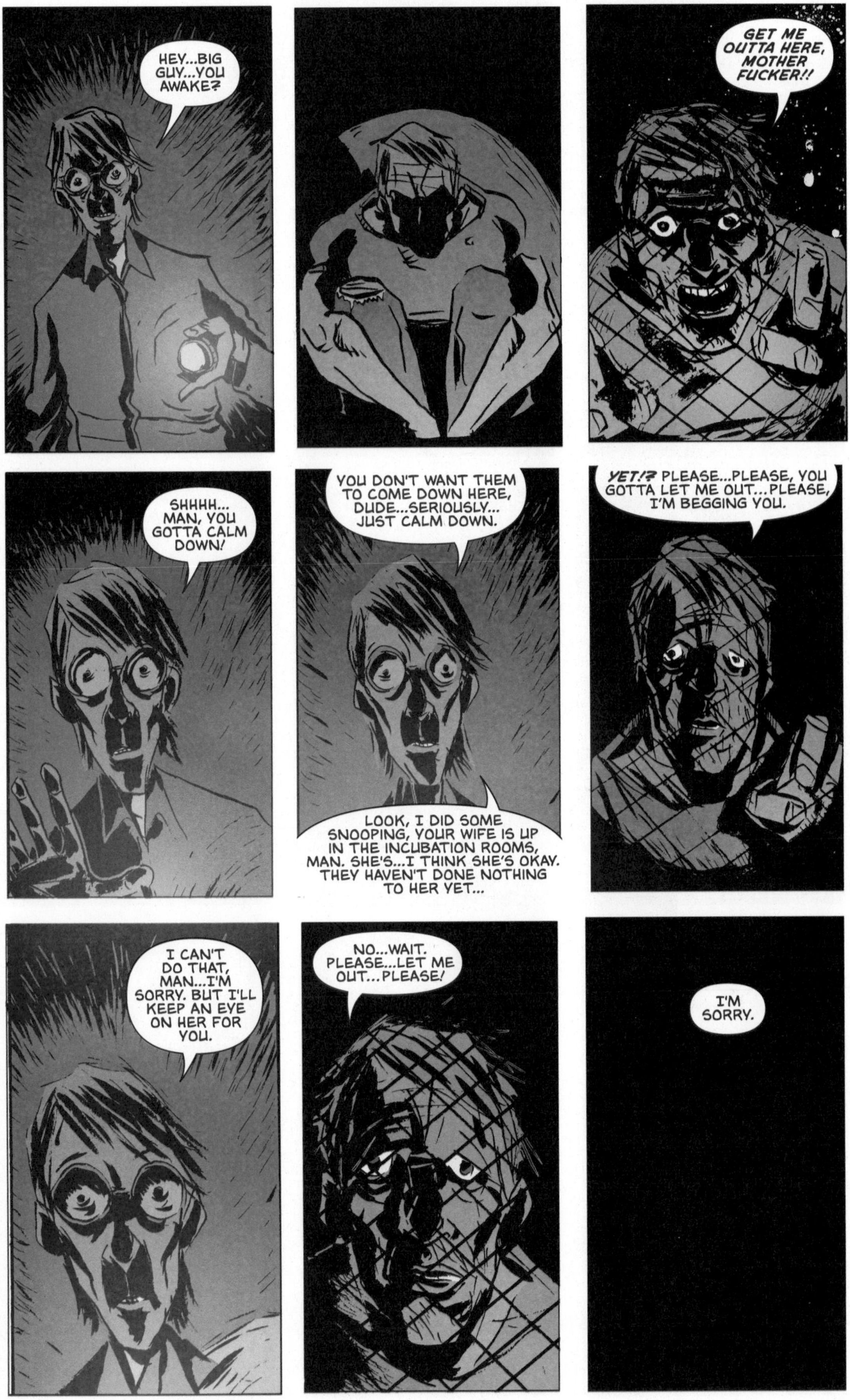
HEY...BIG GUY...YOU AWAKE?
GET ME OUTTA HERE, MOTHER FUCKER!!
SHHHH... MAN, YOU GOTTA CALM DOWN!
YOU DON'T WANT THEM TO COME DOWN HERE, DUDE...SERIOUSLY... JUST CALM DOWN.
LOOK, I DID SOME SNOOPING, YOUR WIFE IS UP IN THE INCUBATION ROOMS, MAN. SHE'S...I THINK SHE'S OKAY. THEY HAVEN'T DONE NOTHING TO HER YET...
YET!? PLEASE...PLEASE, YOU GOTTA LET ME OUT...PLEASE, I'M BEGGING YOU.
I CAN'T DO THAT, MAN...I'M SORRY. BUT I'LL KEEP AN EYE ON HER FOR YOU.
NO...WAIT. PLEASE...LET ME OUT...PLEASE!
I'M SORRY.

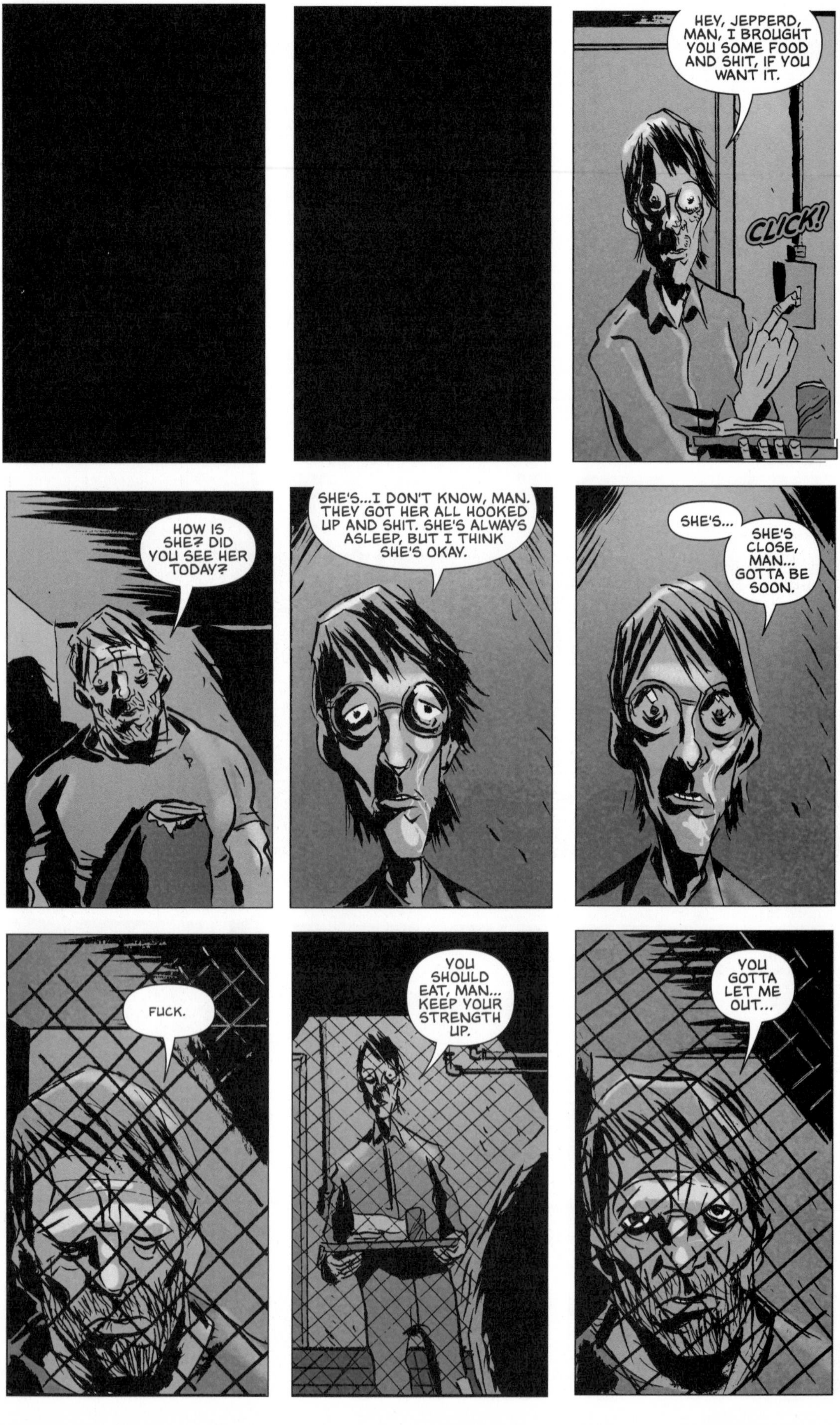
HEY, JEPPERD, MAN, I BROUGHT YOU SOME FOOD AND SHIT, IF YOU WANT IT.
CLICK!
HOW IS SHE? DID YOU SEE HER TODAY?
SHE'S...I DON'T KNOW, MAN. THEY GOT HER ALL HOOKED UP AND SHIT. SHE'S ALWAYS ASLEEP, BUT I THINK SHE'S OKAY.
SHE'S...
SHE'S CLOSE, MAN... GOTTA BE SOON.
FUCK.
YOU SHOULD EAT, MAN... KEEP YOUR STRENGTH UP.
YOU GOTTA LET ME OUT...

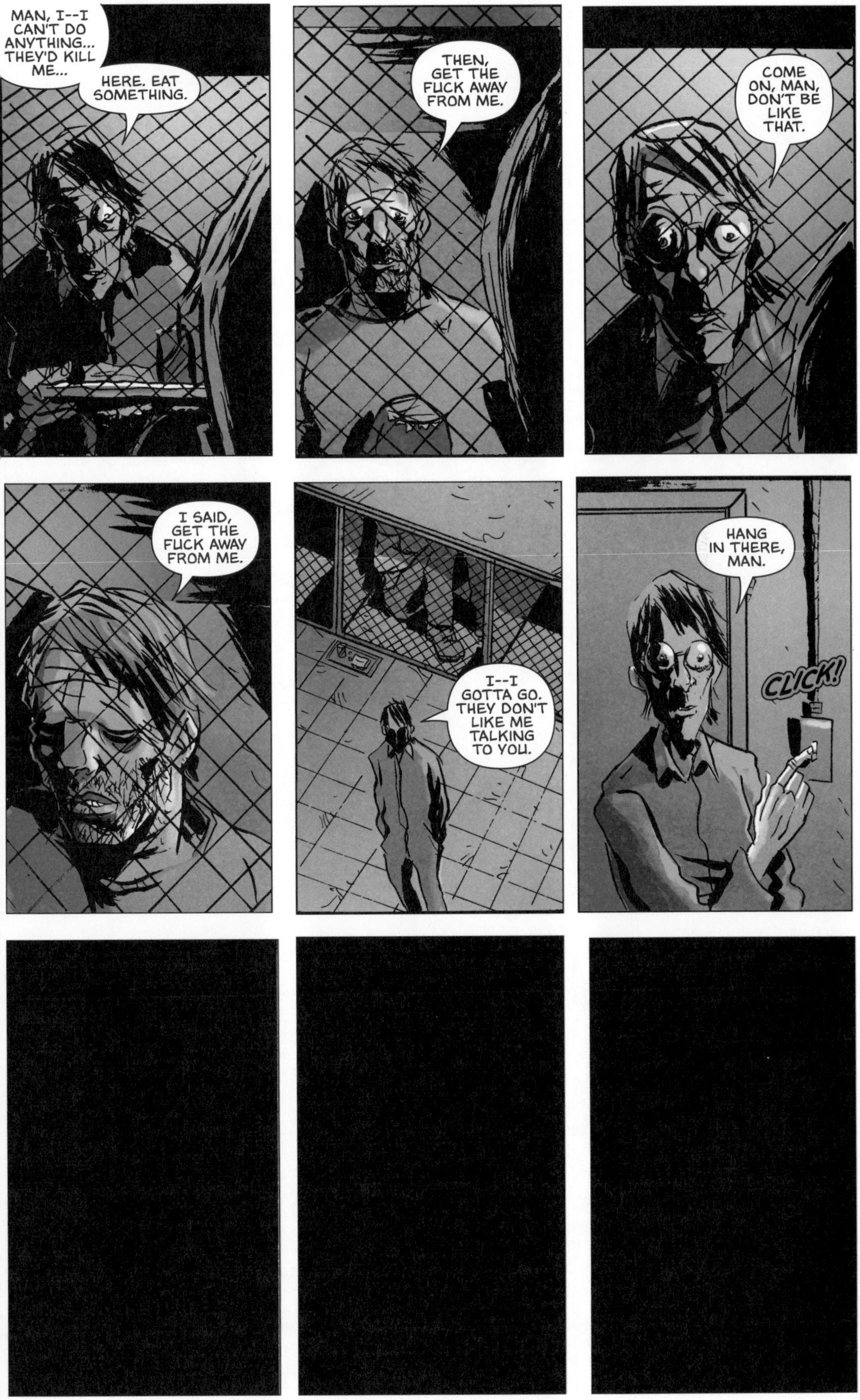
MAN, I--I CAN'T DO ANYTHING... THEY'D KILL ME...
HERE. EAT SOMETHING.
THEN, GET THE FUCK AWAY FROM ME.
COME ON, MAN, DON'T BE LIKE THAT.
I SAID, GET THE FUCK AWAY FROM ME.
I--I GOTTA GO. THEY DON'T LIKE ME TALKING TO YOU.
HANG IN THERE, MAN.
CLICK!

CLICK!

--THE FUCK HAPPENED TO YOU?

JEPPERD...IT'S HAPPENING.

SHE'S IN LABOR.

JOHNNY... YOU GOTTA LET ME OUT.

MAN, NOT THIS AGAIN...YOU KNOW I CAN'T DO THAT.

YES, YOU CAN. YOU WERE FEEDING ME MY DINNER. I ATTACKED YOU, GOT THE KEYS, KNOCKED YOU OUT AND ESCAPED.

NO, DUDE...EVEN IF IT WAS AN ACCIDENT, THEY'D STILL KILL ME. ABBOT AND THOSE GUYS DON'T FUCK AROUND, MAN. LOOK WHAT THEY DID WHEN THEY CAUGHT ME SNOOPING...

MAN, I KNOW IT'S FUCKED-UP HERE, BUT AT LEAST IT'S *SAFE*. IT WASN'T EASY FOR ME TO GET IN. I'M NOT A DOCTOR, NOT A SOLDIER OR NOTHING. COME ON, MAN...

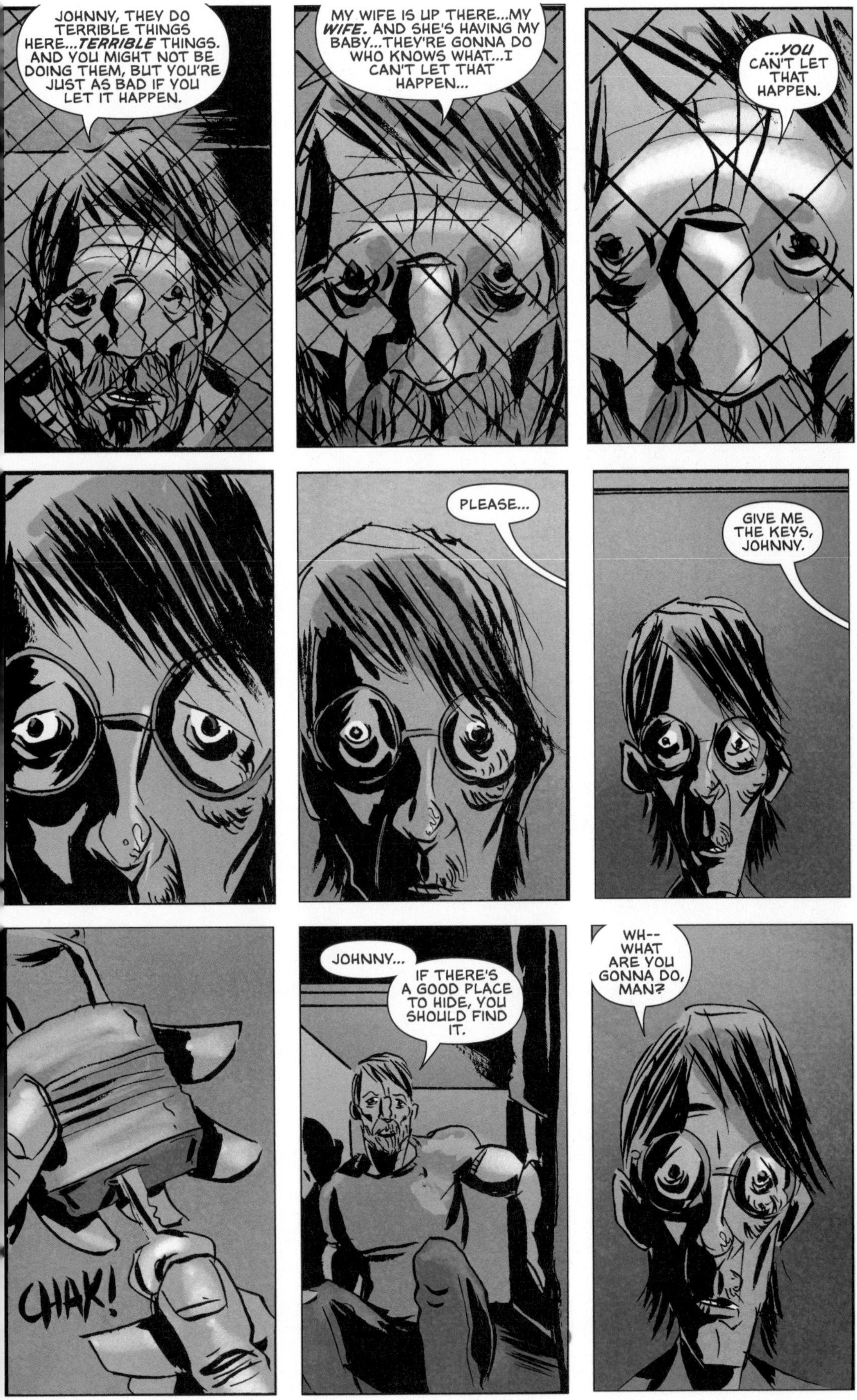
JOHNNY, THEY DO TERRIBLE THINGS HERE...TERRIBLE THINGS. AND YOU MIGHT NOT BE DOING THEM, BUT YOU'RE JUST AS BAD IF YOU LET IT HAPPEN.
MY WIFE IS UP THERE...MY WIFE. AND SHE'S HAVING MY BABY...THEY'RE GONNA DO WHO KNOWS WHAT...I CAN'T LET THAT HAPPEN...
...YOU CAN'T LET THAT HAPPEN.
PLEASE...
GIVE ME THE KEYS, JOHNNY.
CHAK!
JOHNNY...
IF THERE'S A GOOD PLACE TO HIDE, YOU SHOULD FIND IT.
WH-- WHAT ARE YOU GONNA DO, MAN?

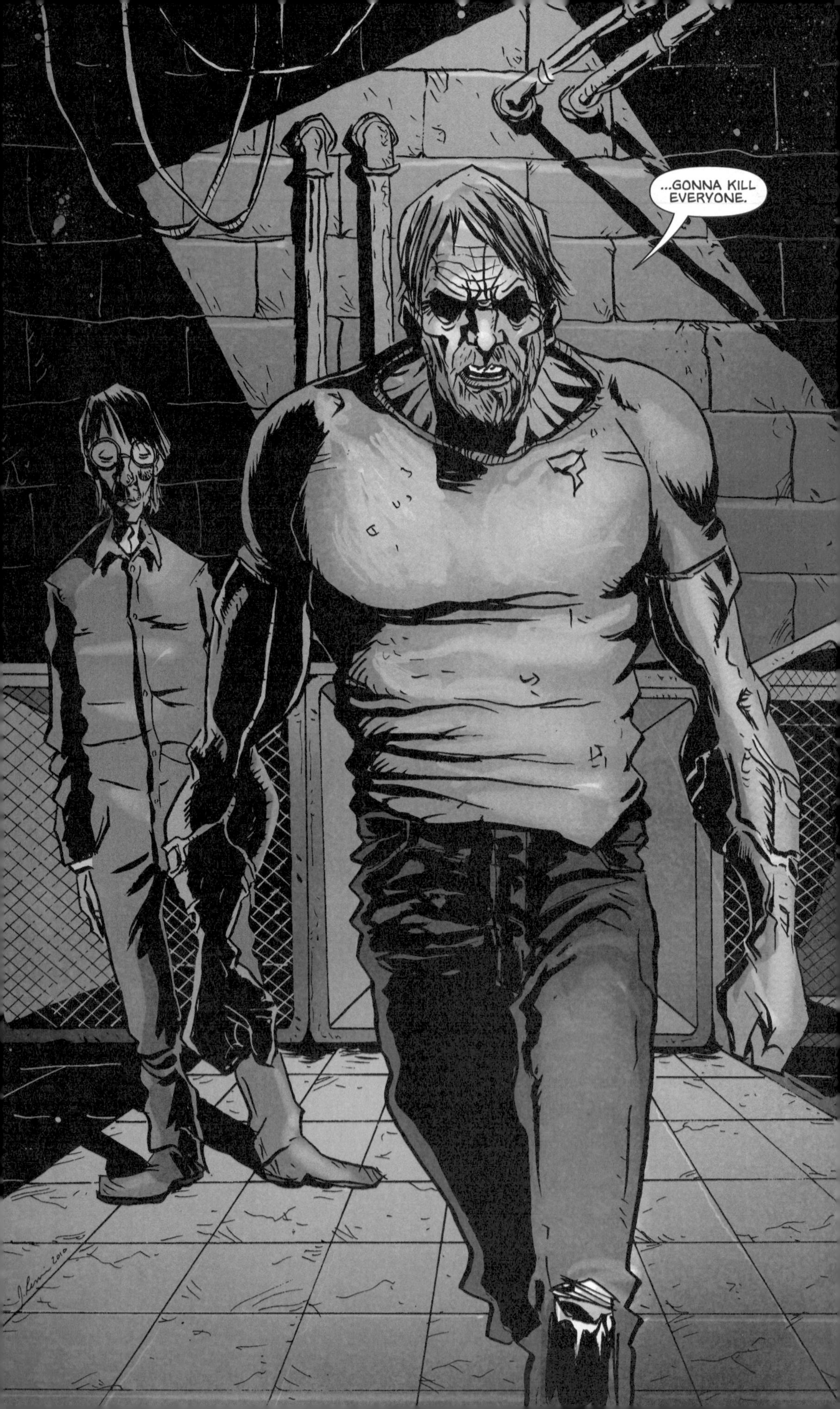
...GONNA KILL EVERYONE.

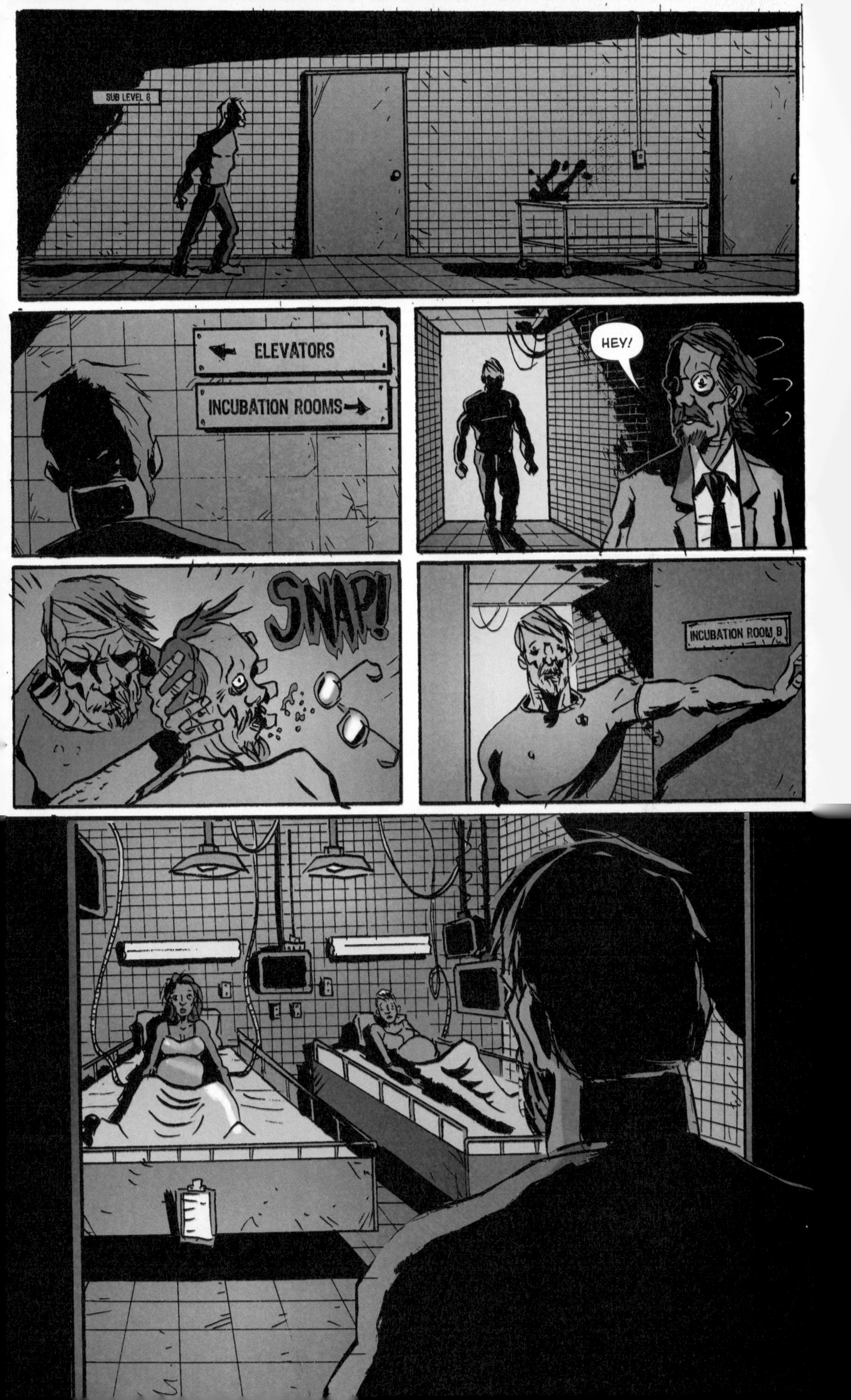

SUB LEVEL 6
ELEVATORS
INCUBATION ROOMS
HEY!
SNAP!
INCUBATION ROOM B

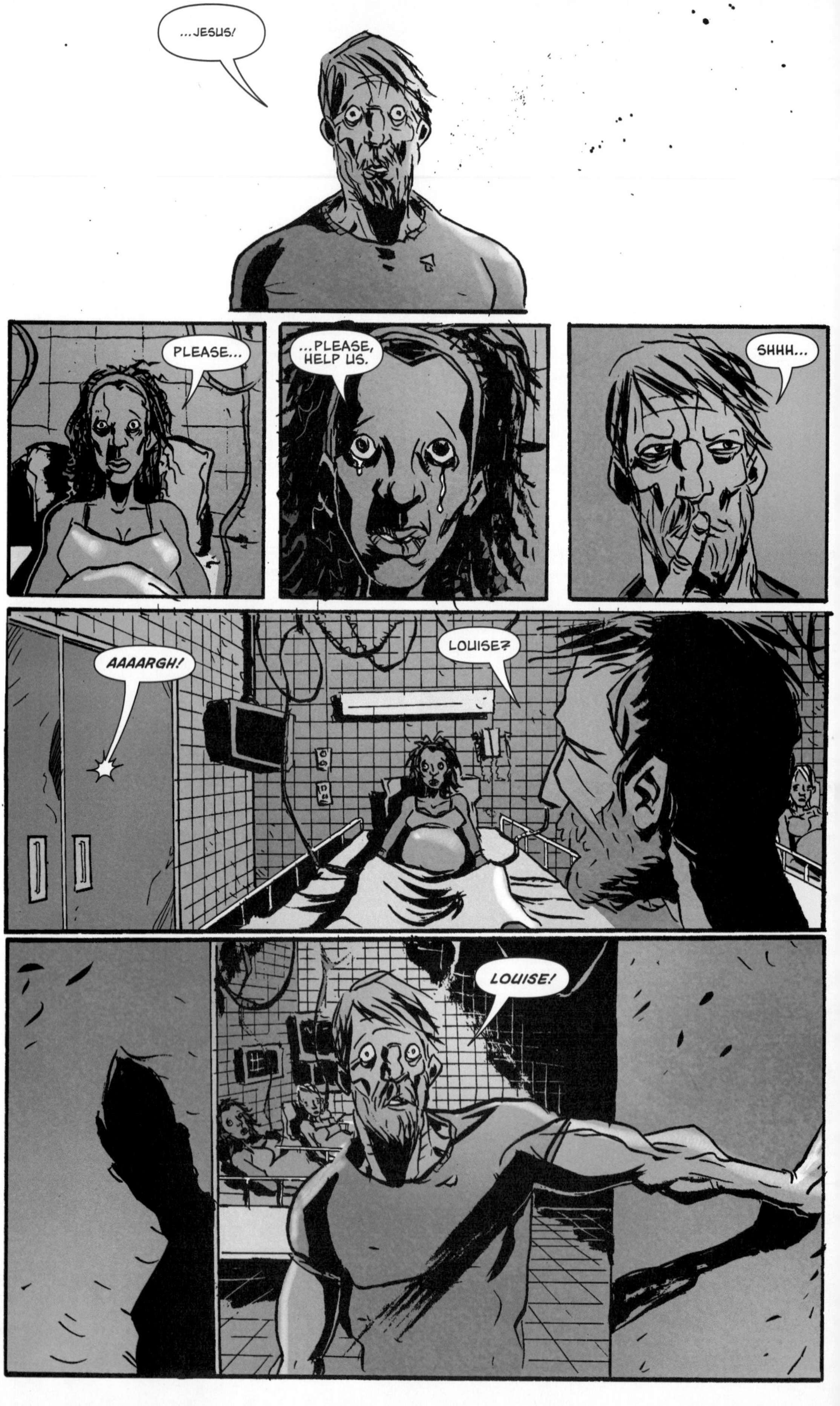
...JESUS!
PLEASE...
...PLEASE, HELP US.
SHHH...
AAAARGH!
LOUISE?
LOUISE!

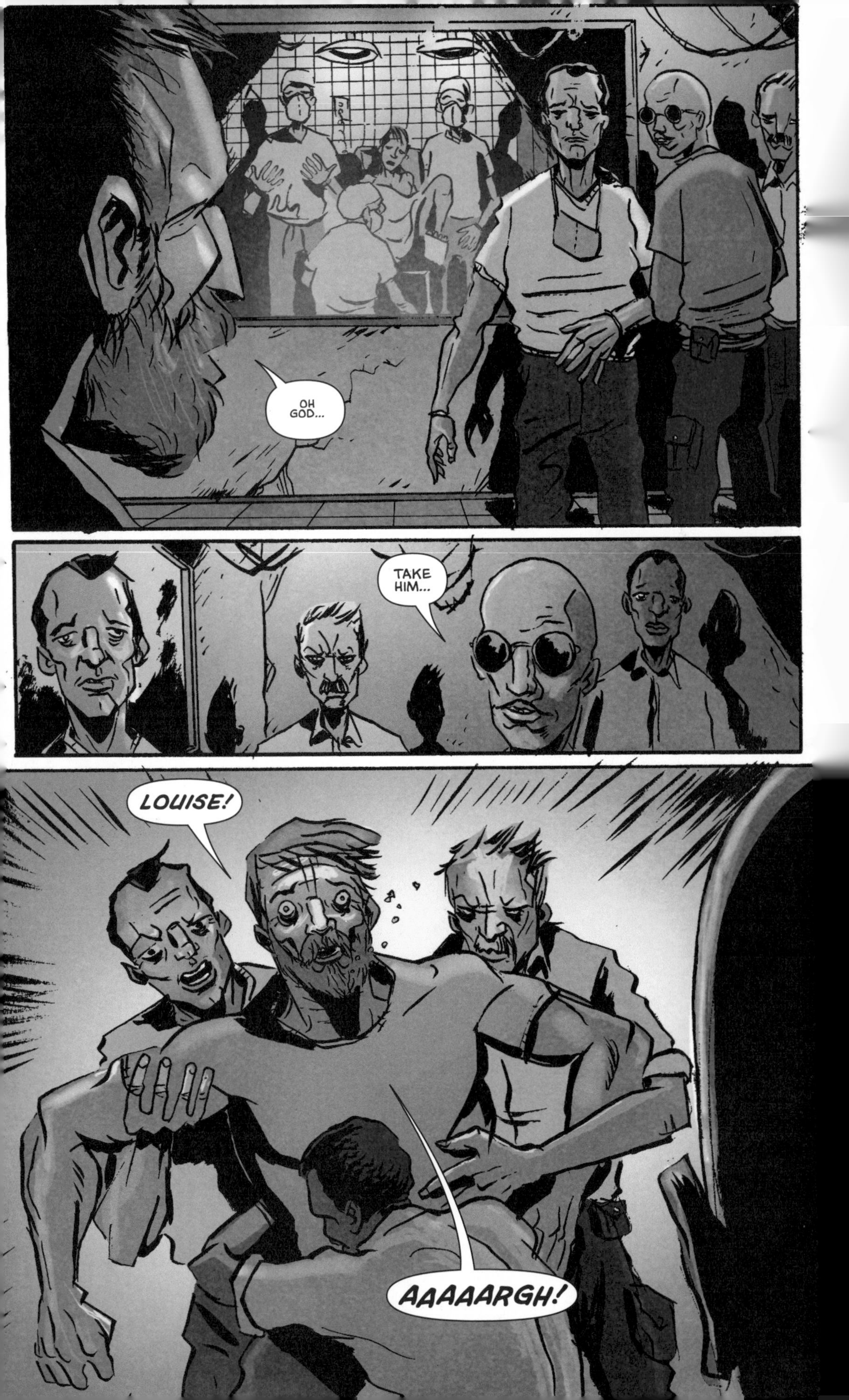
OH GOD...
TAKE HIM...
LOUISE!
AAAAARGH!

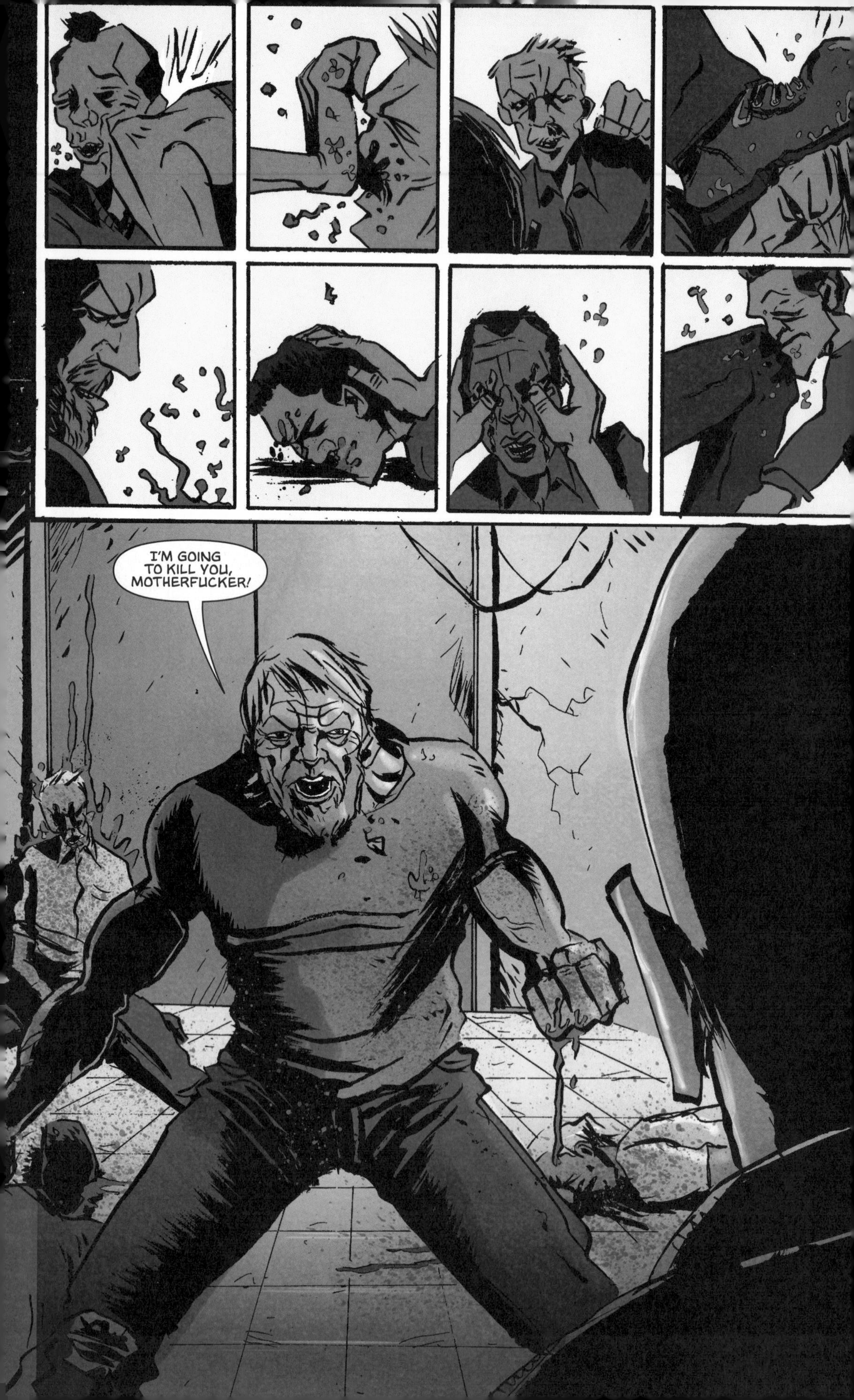
I'M GOING TO KILL YOU, MOTHERFUCKER!

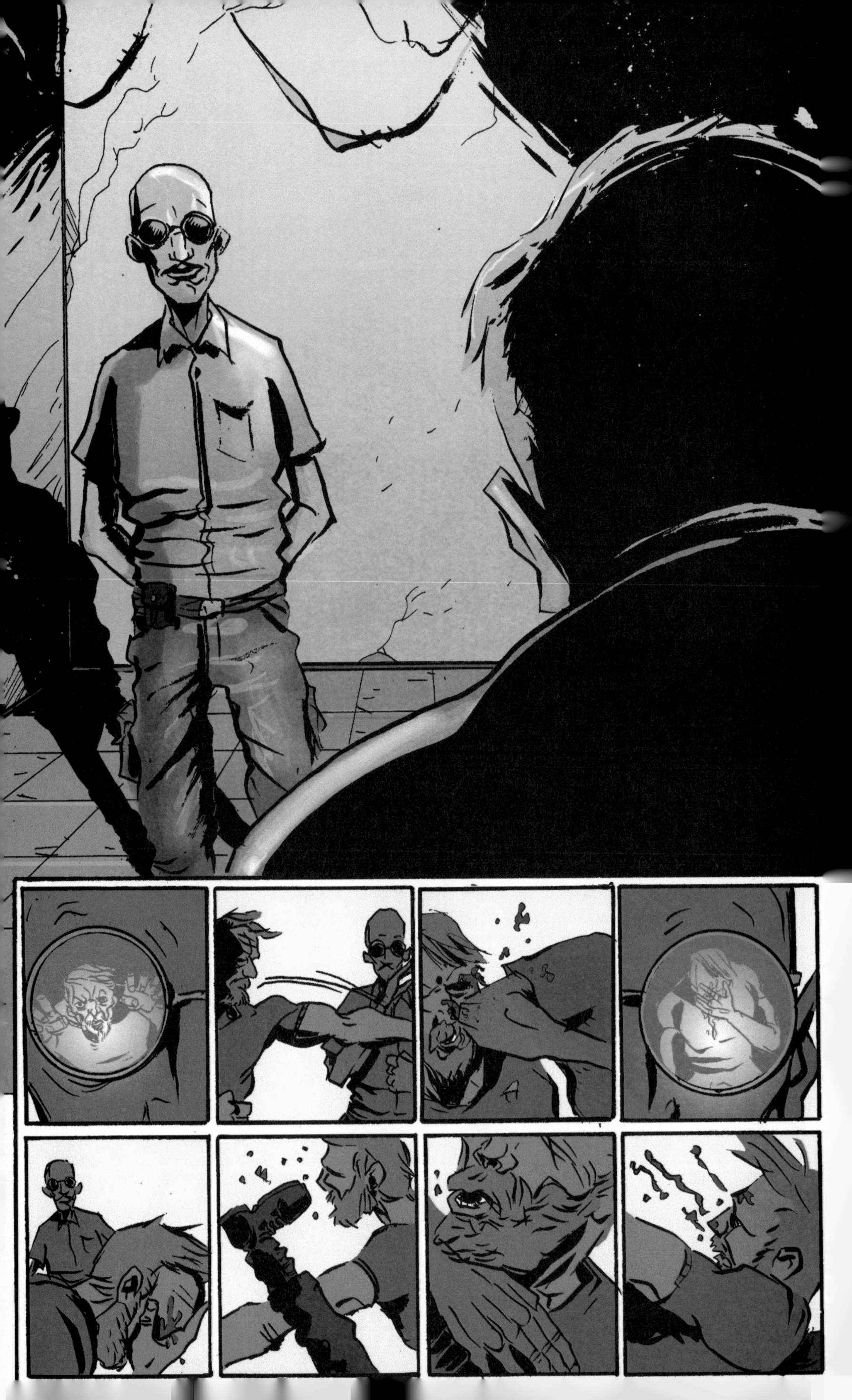

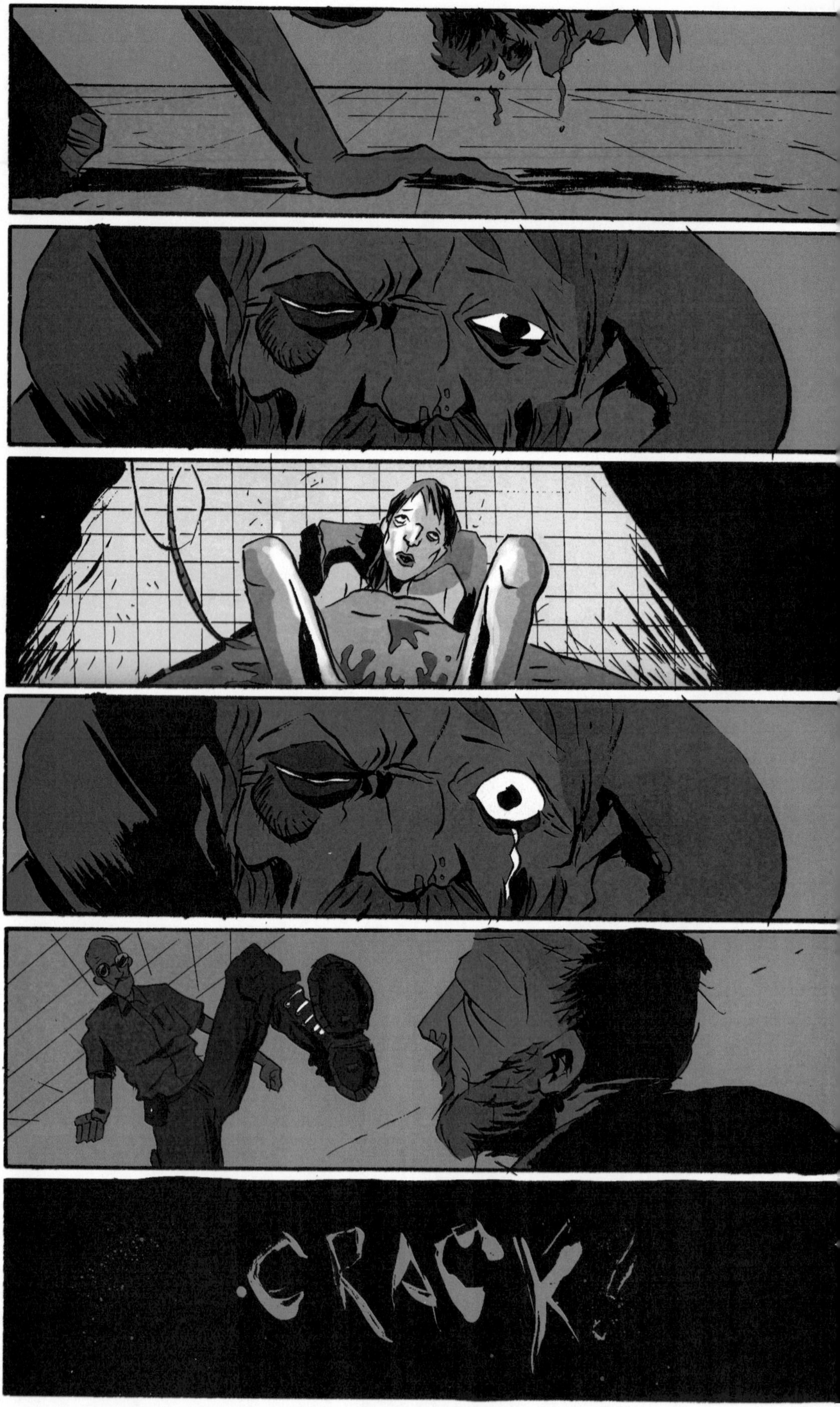
CRACK!

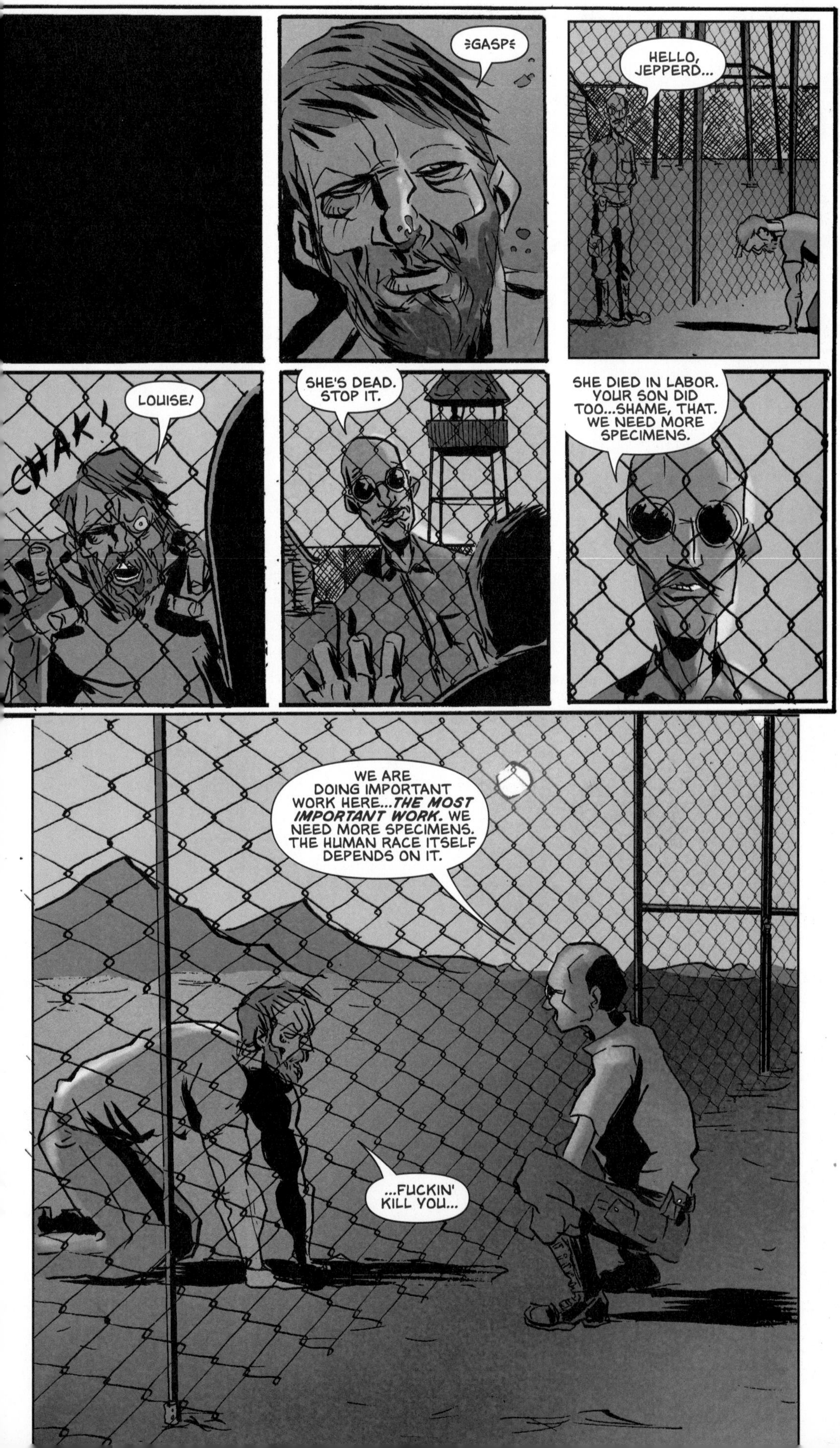

GASP
HELLO, JEPPERD...
CHAK!
LOUISE!
SHE'S DEAD. STOP IT.
SHE DIED IN LABOR. YOUR SON DID TOO...SHAME, THAT. WE NEED MORE SPECIMENS.
WE ARE DOING IMPORTANT WORK HERE...*THE MOST IMPORTANT WORK.* WE NEED MORE SPECIMENS. THE HUMAN RACE ITSELF DEPENDS ON IT.
...FUCKIN' KILL YOU...

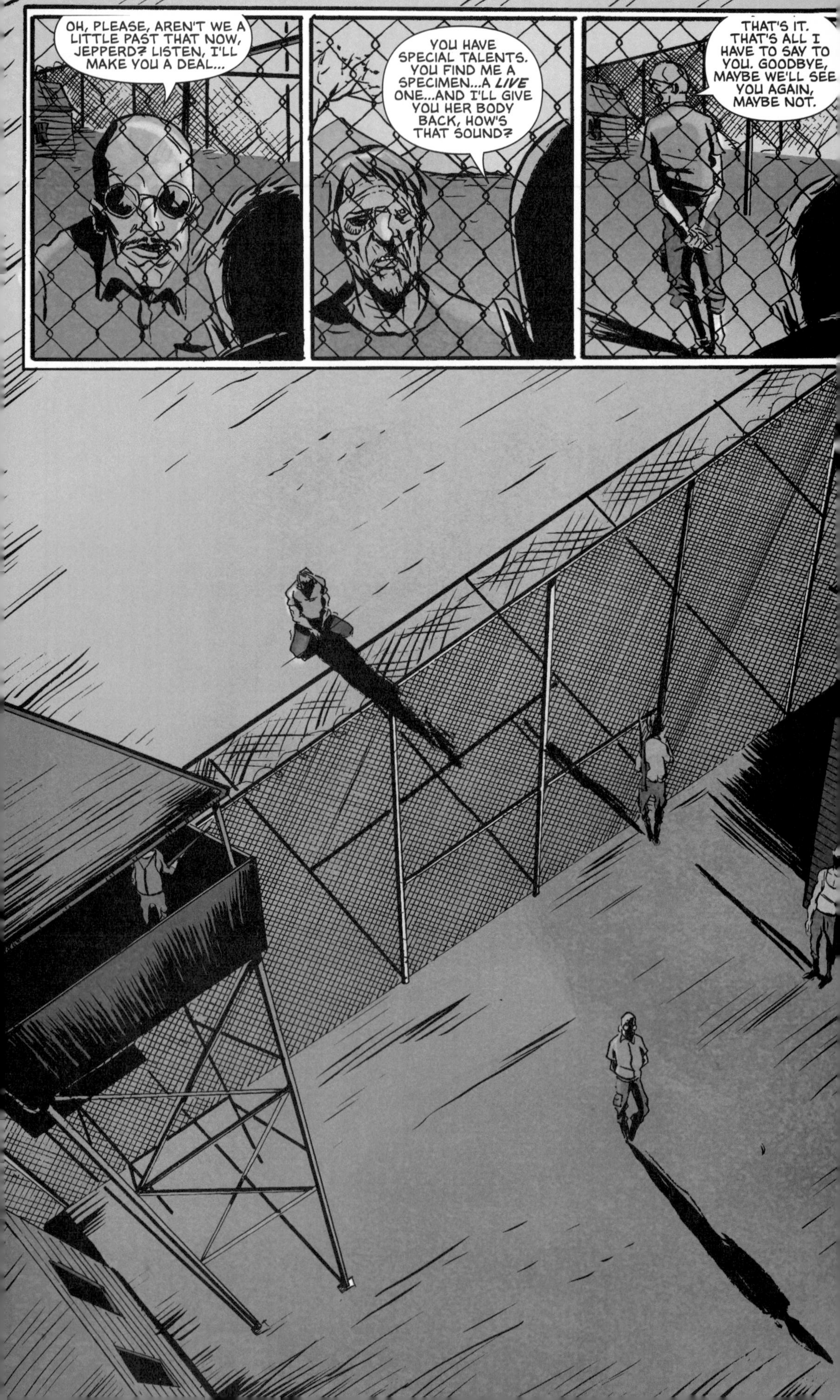
OH, PLEASE, AREN'T WE A LITTLE PAST THAT NOW, JEPPERD? LISTEN, I'LL MAKE YOU A DEAL...
YOU HAVE SPECIAL TALENTS. YOU FIND ME A SPECIMEN...A *LIVE* ONE...AND I'LL GIVE YOU HER BODY BACK, HOW'S THAT SOUND?
THAT'S IT. THAT'S ALL I HAVE TO SAY TO YOU. GOODBYE, MAYBE WE'LL SEE YOU AGAIN, MAYBE NOT.

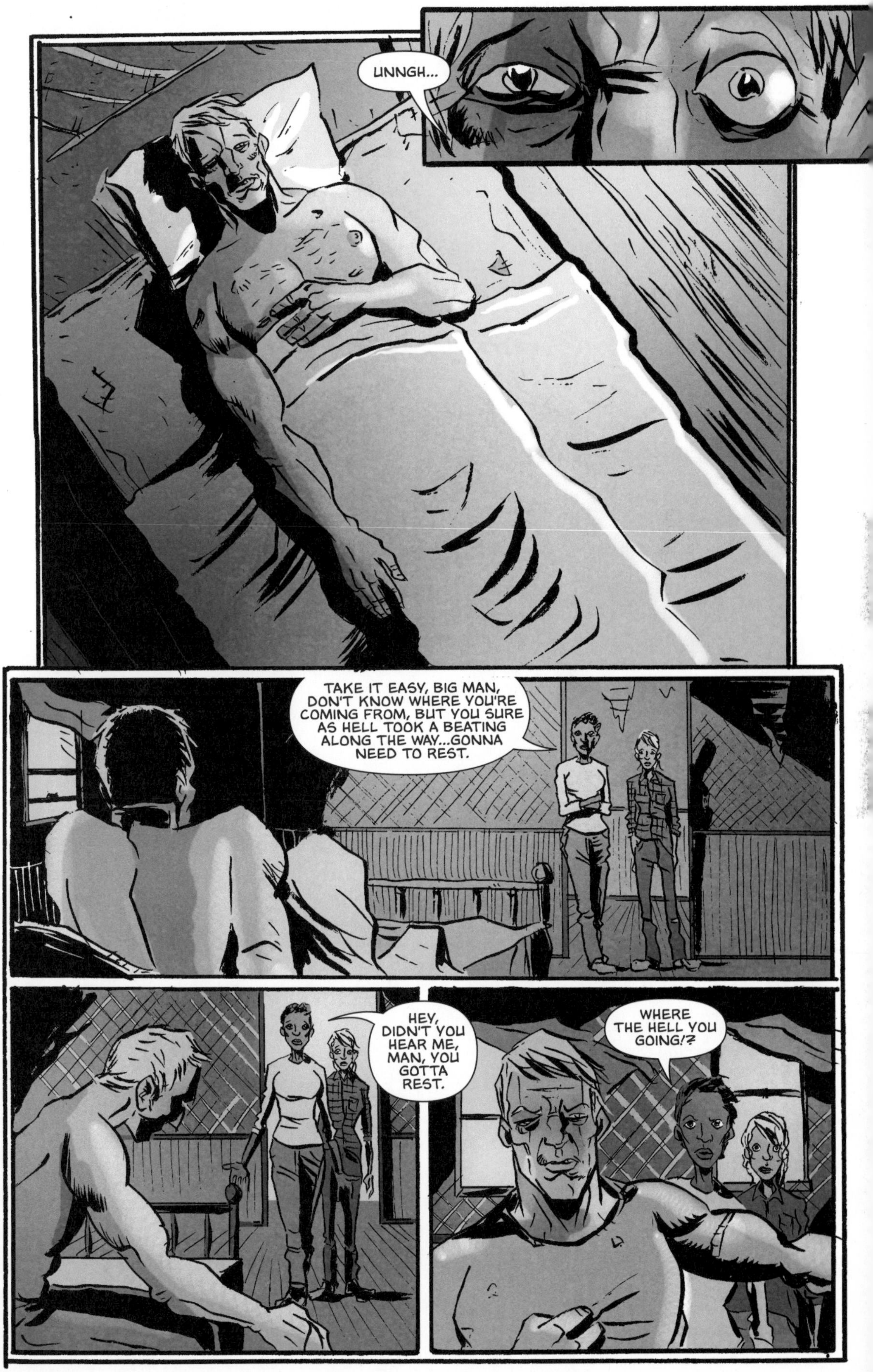
UNNGH...
TAKE IT EASY, BIG MAN, DON'T KNOW WHERE YOU'RE COMING FROM, BUT YOU SURE AS HELL TOOK A BEATING ALONG THE WAY...GONNA NEED TO REST.
HEY, DIDN'T YOU HEAR ME, MAN, YOU GOTTA REST.
WHERE THE HELL YOU GOING!?

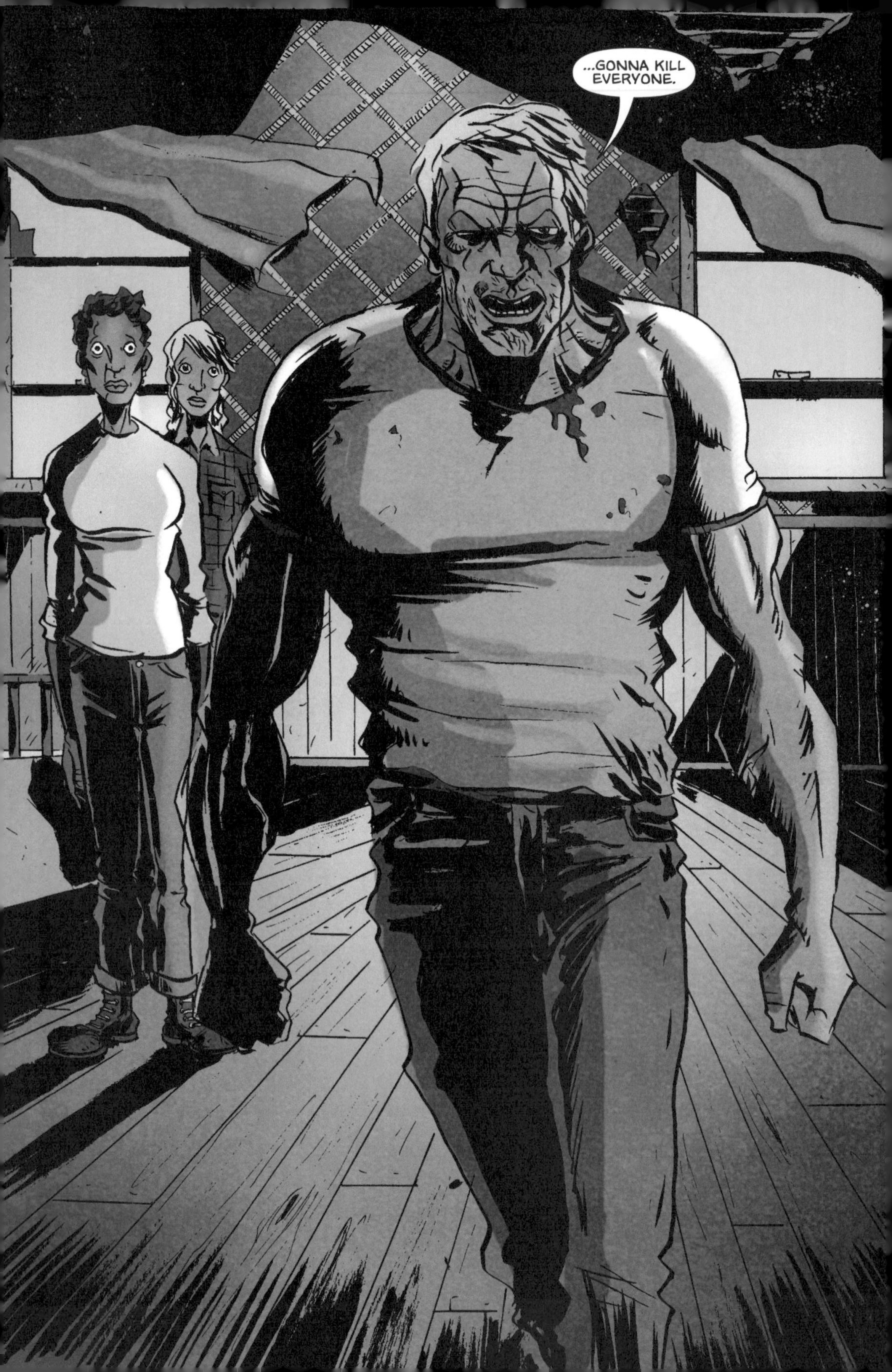
...GONNA KILL EVERYONE.

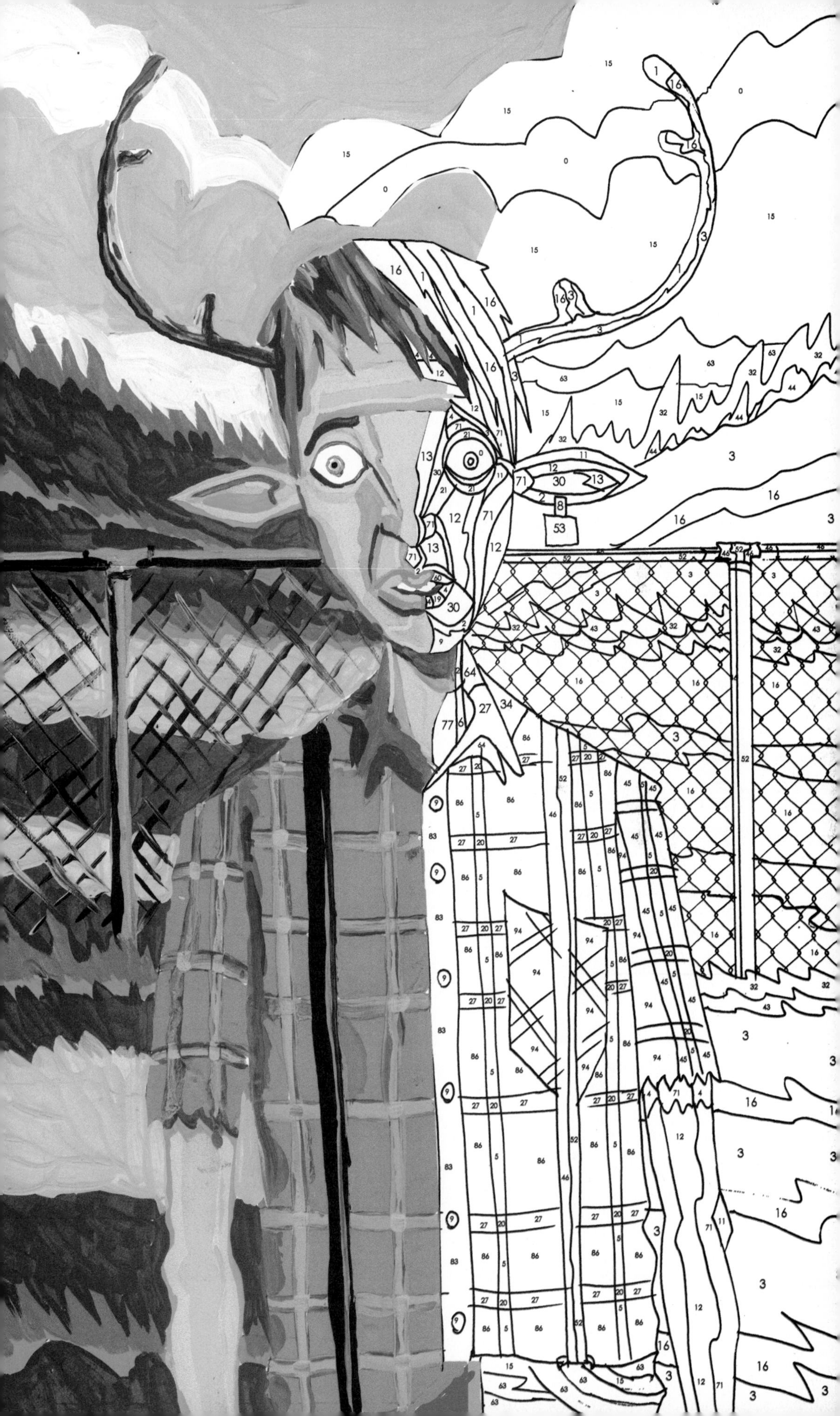

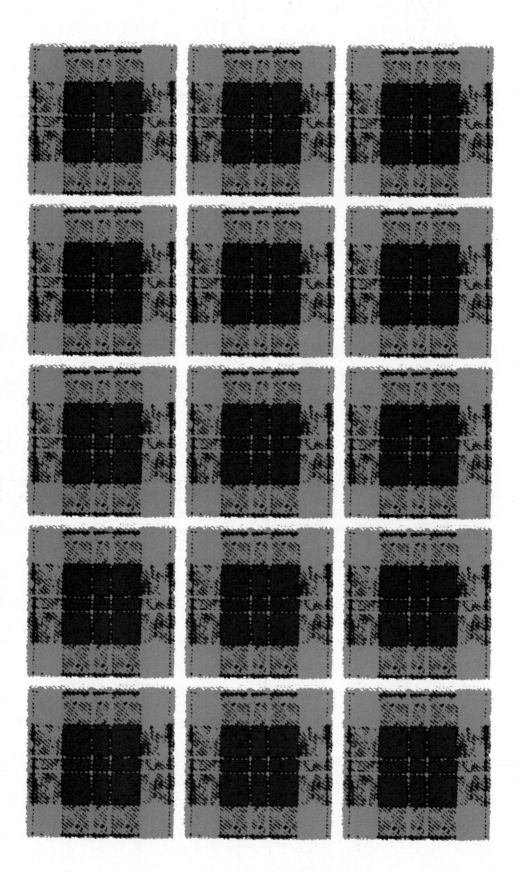

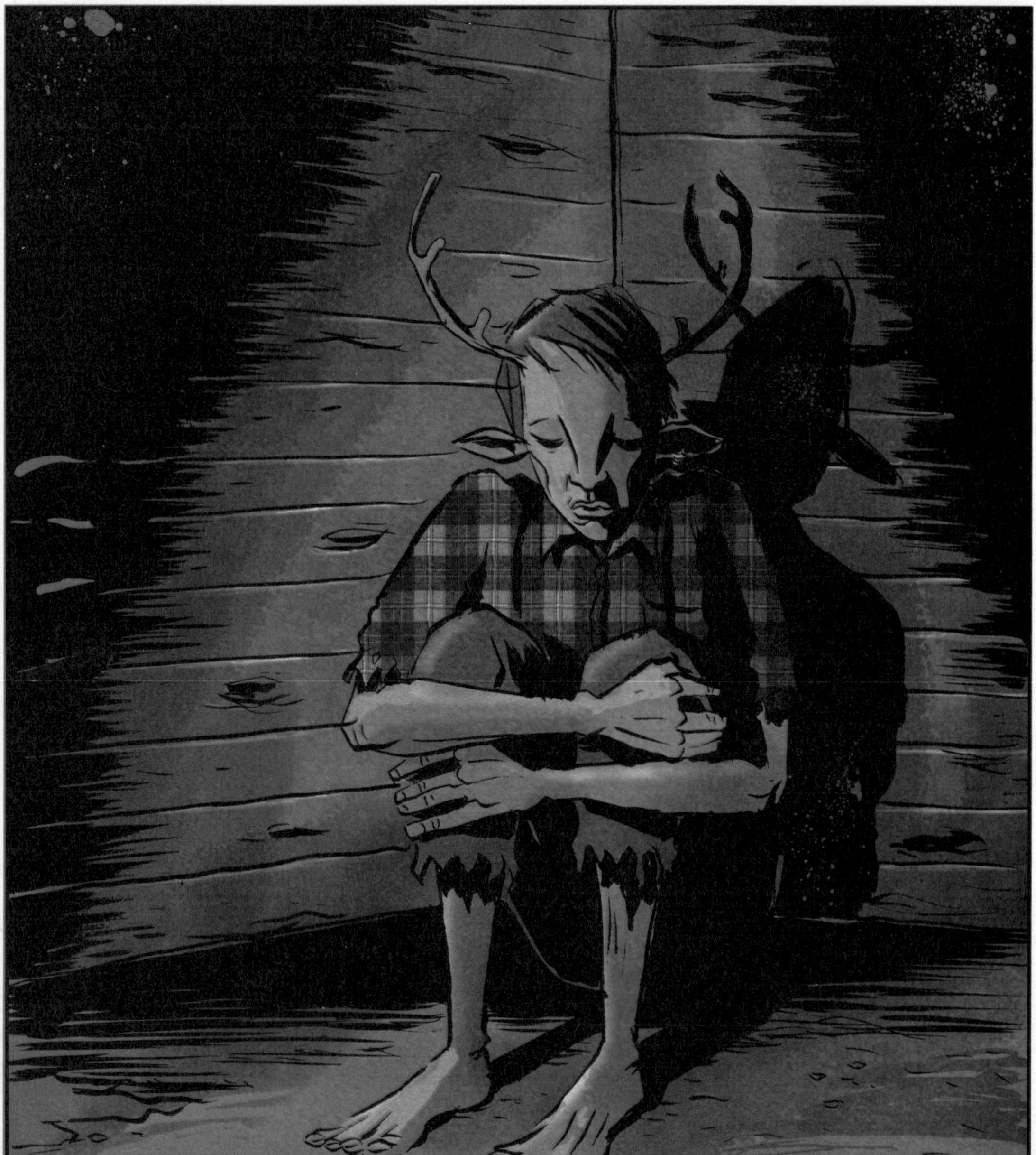

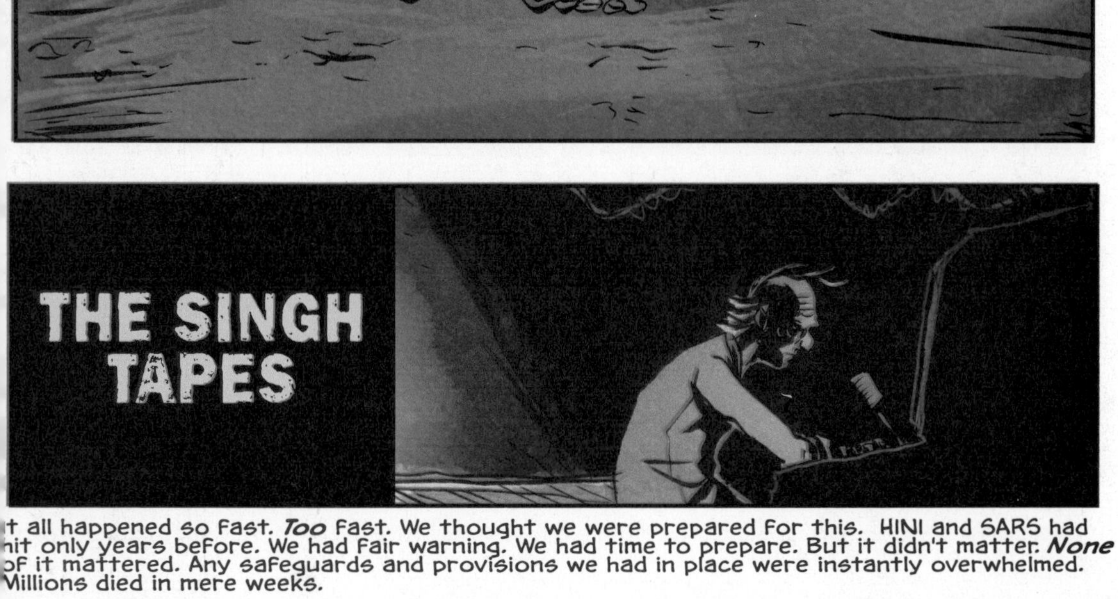
THE SINGH TAPES

t all happened so fast. *Too* fast. We thought we were prepared for this. HINI and SARS had hit only years before. We had fair warning. We had time to prepare. But it didn't matter. ***None*** of it mattered. Any safeguards and provisions we had in place were instantly overwhelmed. Millions died in mere weeks.

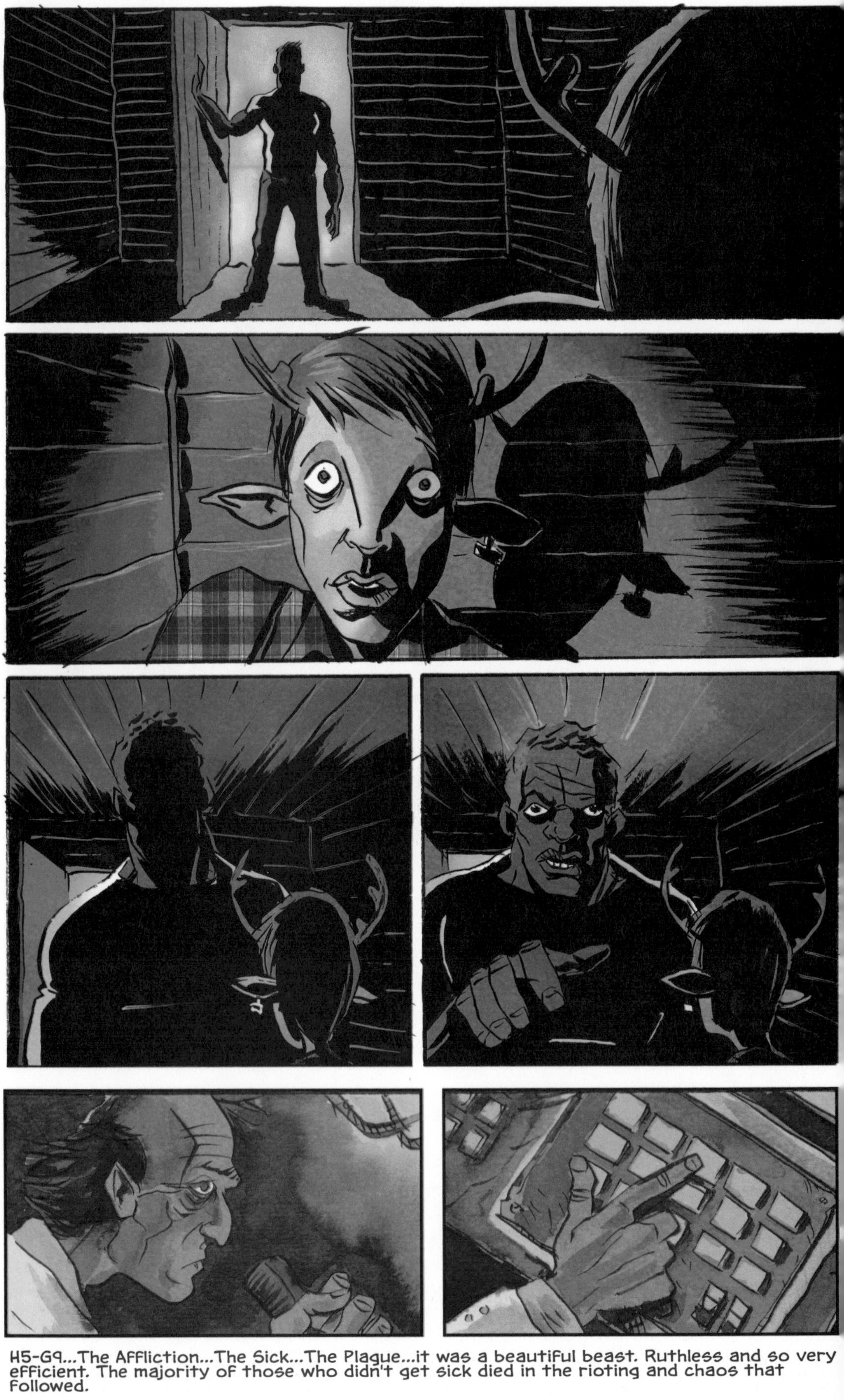

H5-G9...The Affliction...The Sick...The Plague...it was a beautiful beast. Ruthless and so very efficient. The majority of those who didn't get sick died in the rioting and chaos that followed.

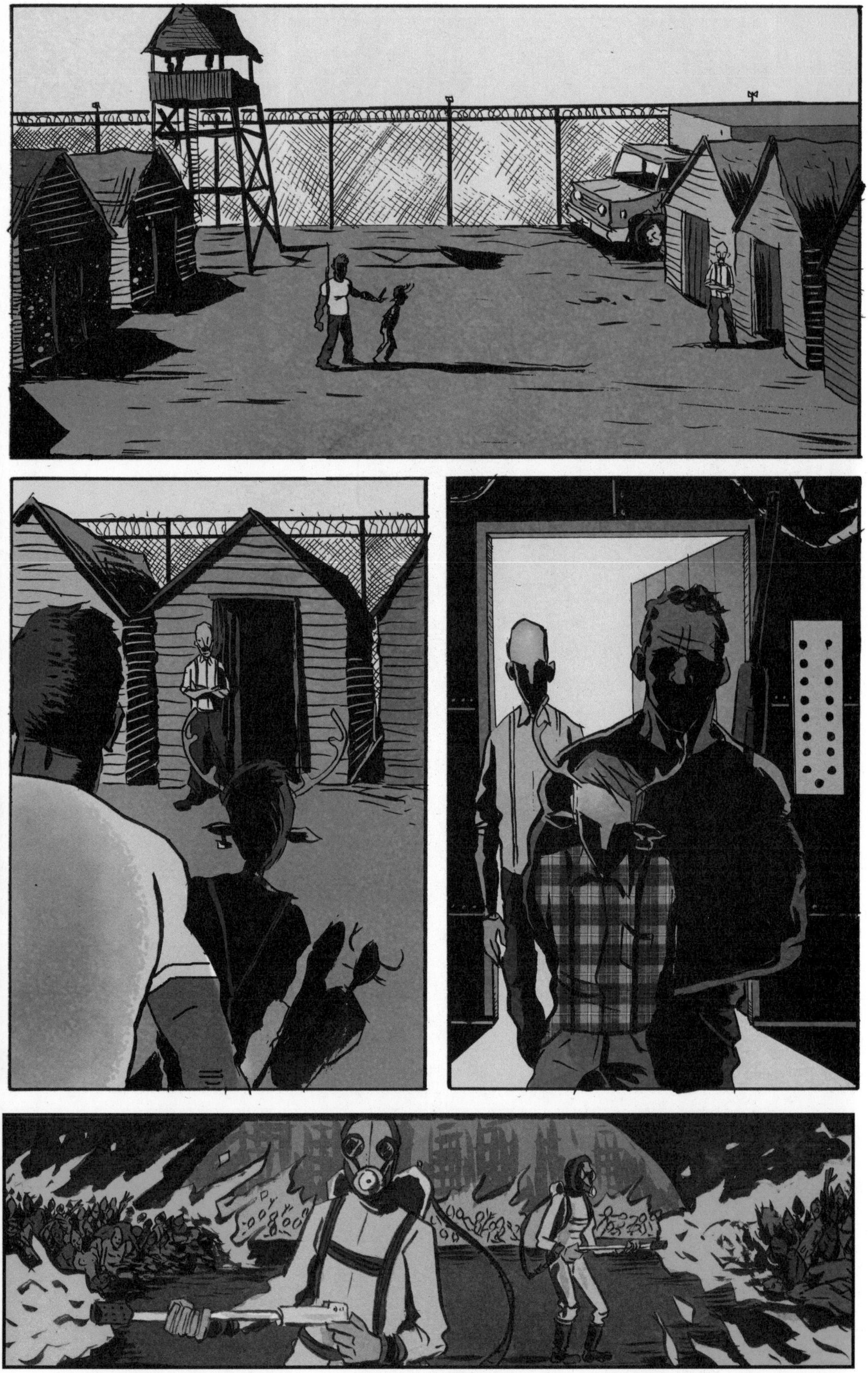

The sheer number of bodies left behind was staggering. Mass graves were--I want to say mass graves were everywhere, but the truth of the matter is that *everywhere* was one big mass grave. Skyscrapers looming behind the bodies...massive, unmarked tombstones.

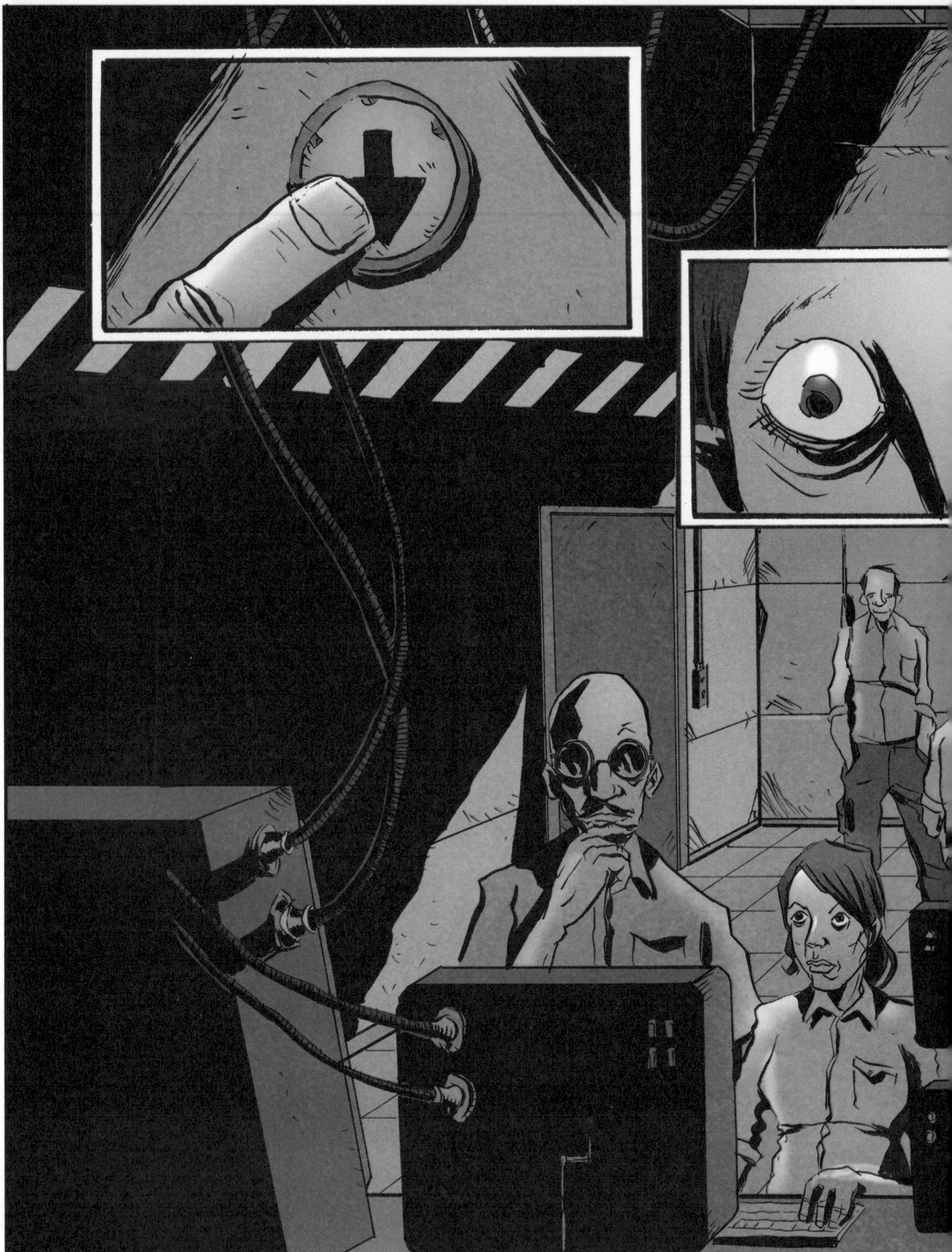

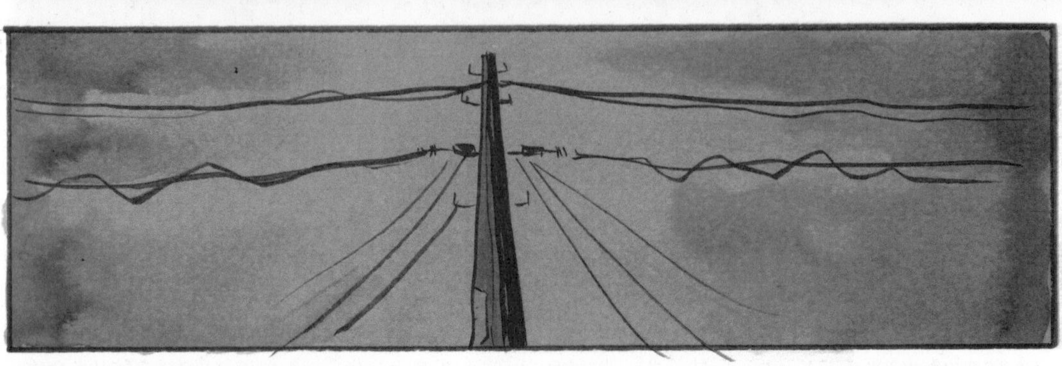

Everything collapsed. Global communication systems...the Internet...all of it obsolete within months. We were cut off from one another...even more alone and terrified.

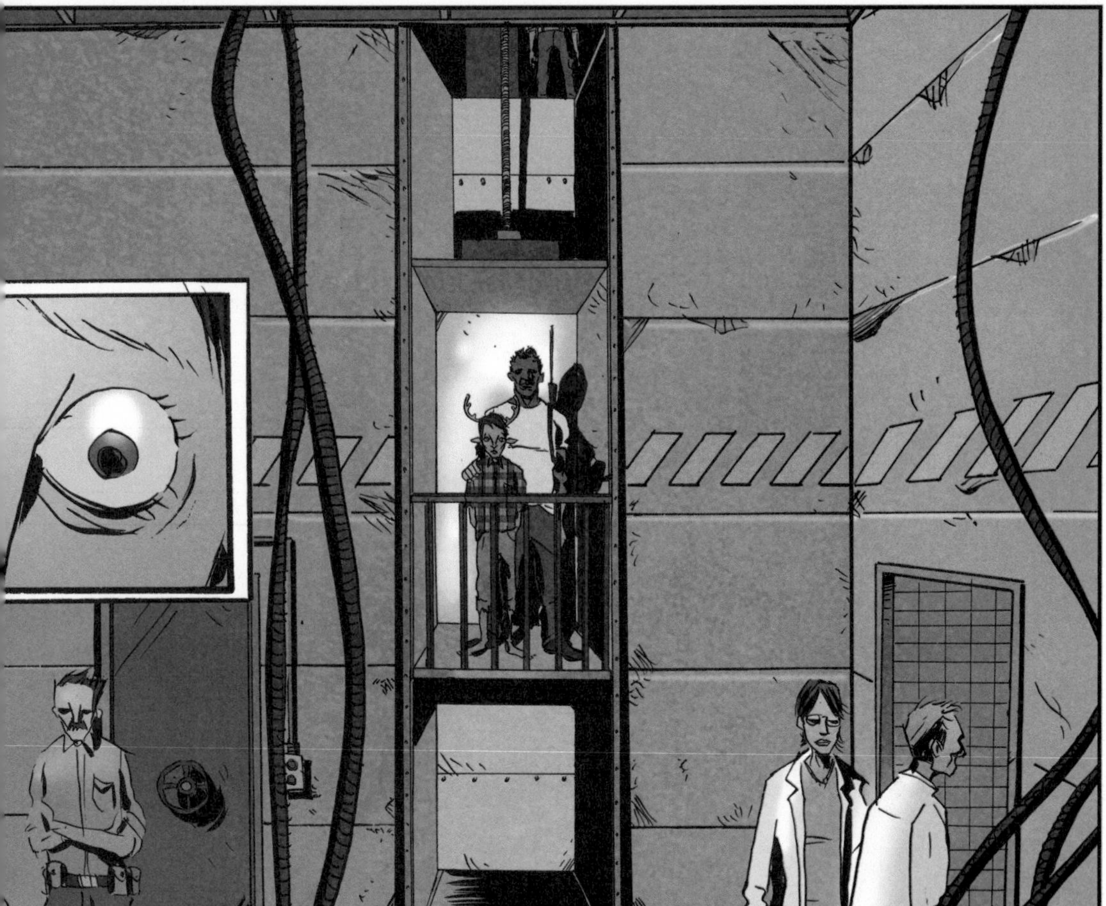

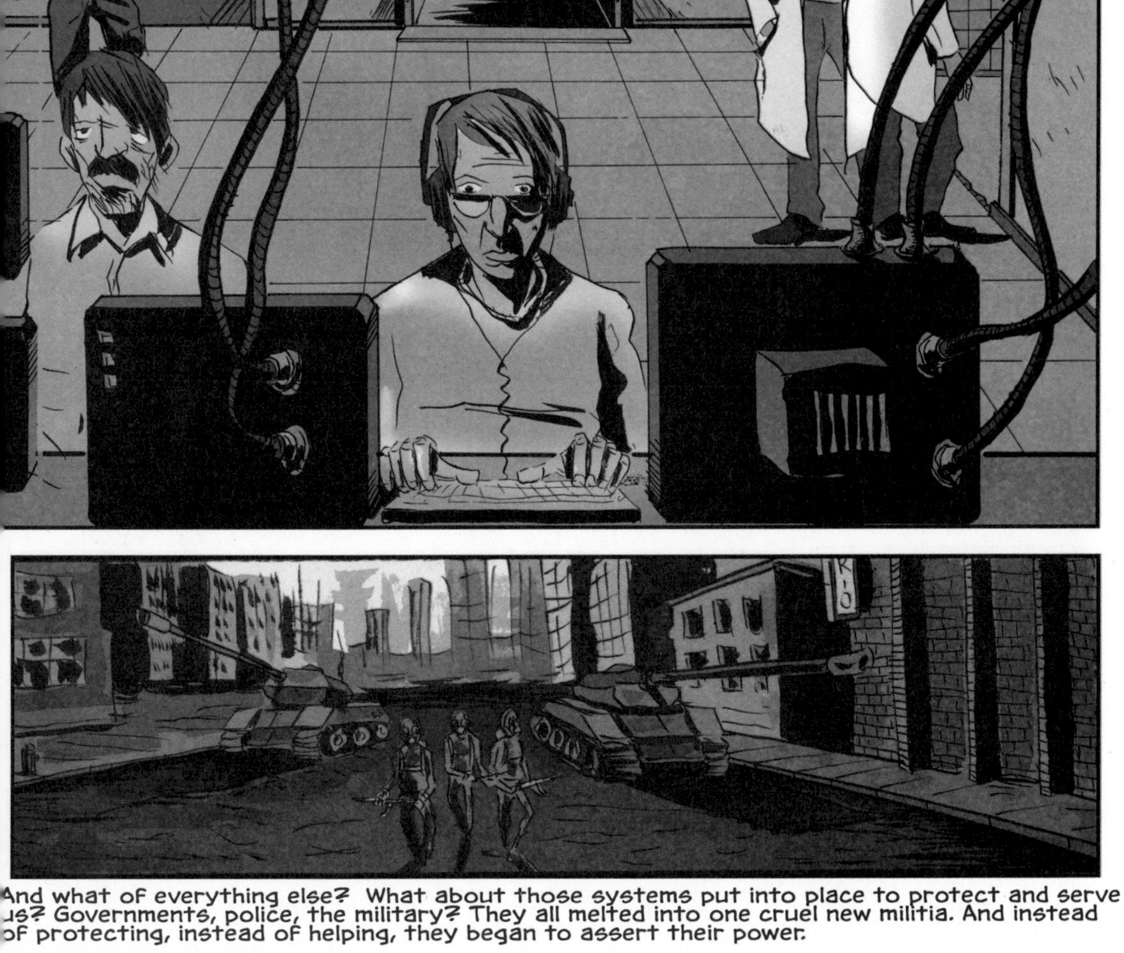

And what of everything else? What about those systems put into place to protect and serve us? Governments, police, the military? They all melted into one cruel new militia. And instead of protecting, instead of helping, they began to assert their power.

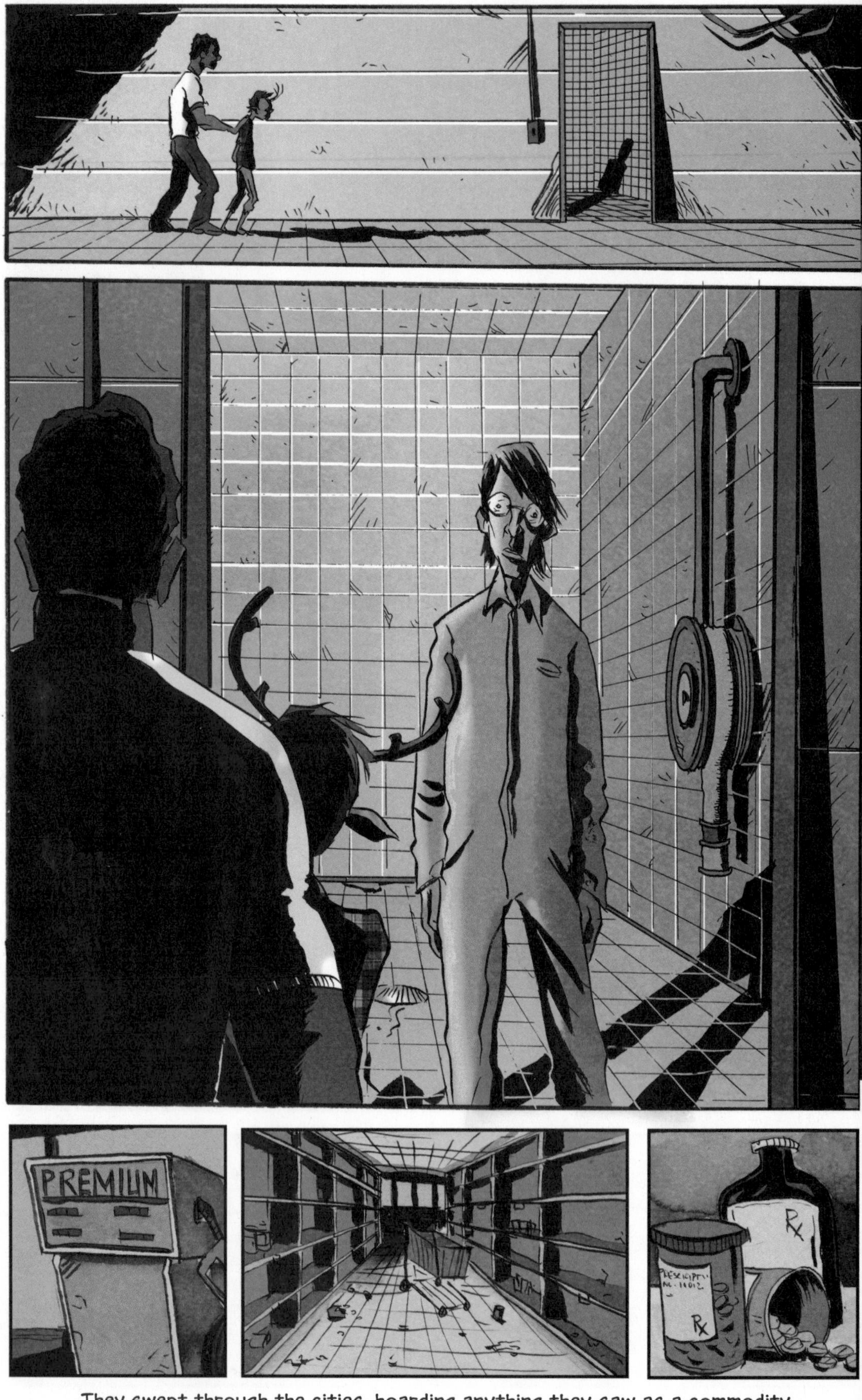
PREMIUM
Rx
Rx

They swept through the cities, hoarding anything they saw as a commodity.
Gasoline, medicine, weapons, food.

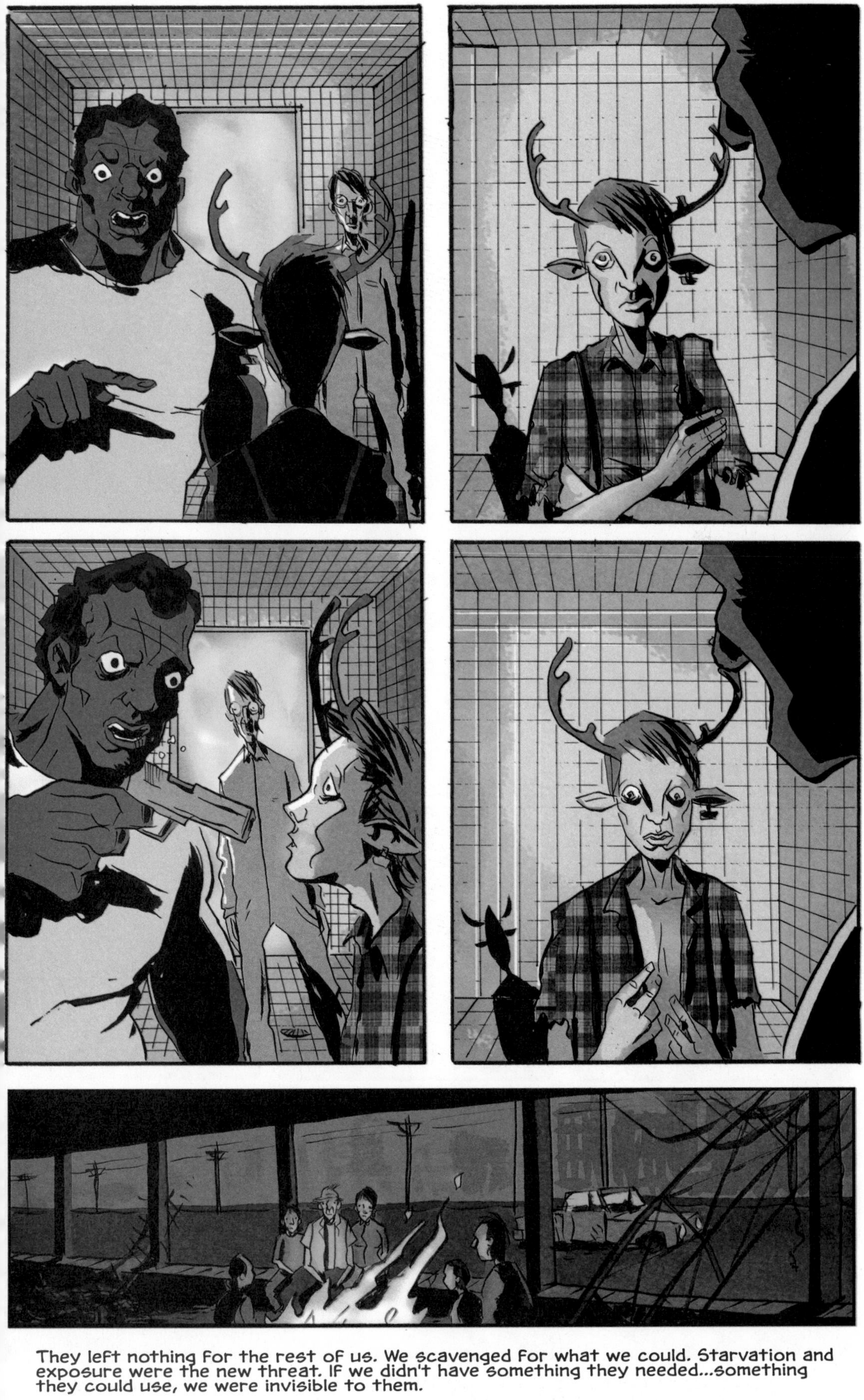

They left nothing for the rest of us. We scavenged for what we could. Starvation and exposure were the new threat. If we didn't have something they needed...something they could use, we were invisible to them.

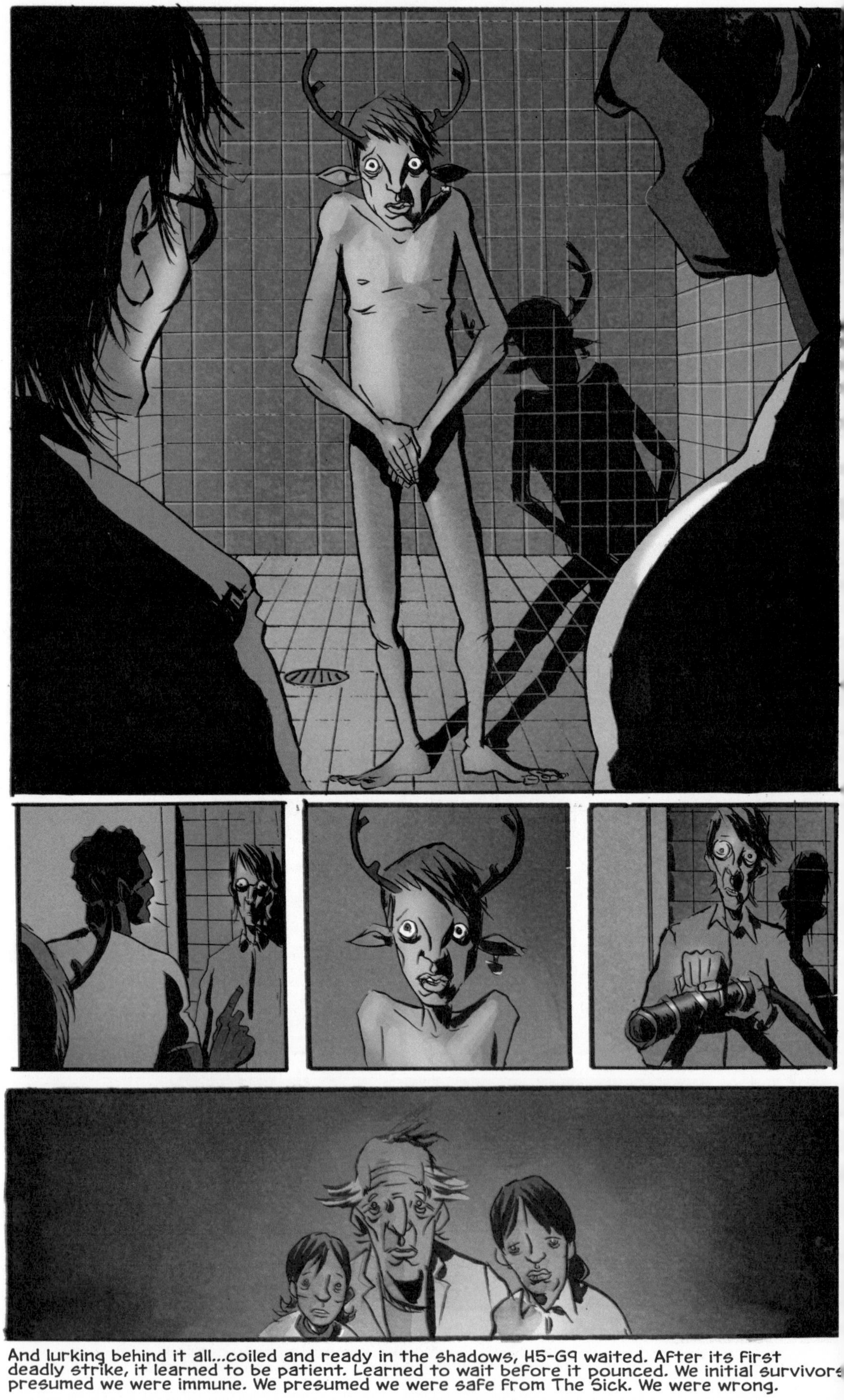

And lurking behind it all...coiled and ready in the shadows, H5-G9 waited. After its first deadly strike, it learned to be patient. Learned to wait before it pounced. We initial survivors presumed we were immune. We presumed we were safe from The Sick. We were wrong.

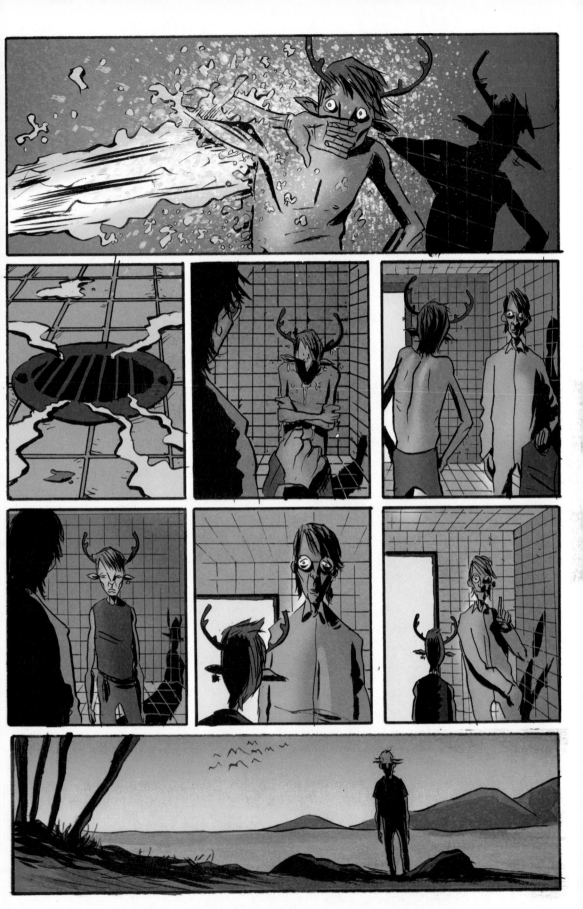

It could take anybody at any time. One day your child looked up at you with her beautiful little eyes...the next she was gone.

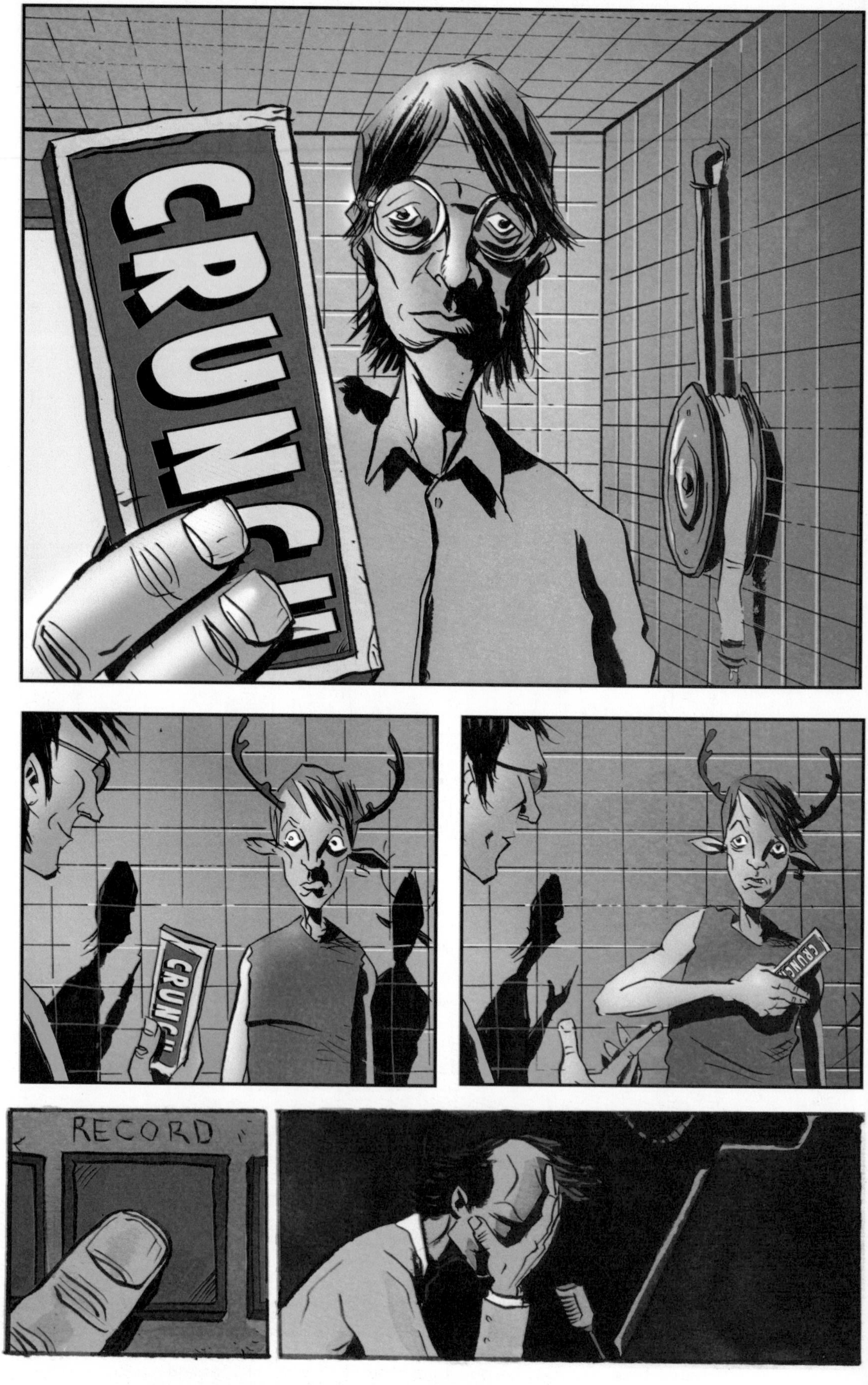
CRUNCH
CRUNCH
CRUNCH
RECORD

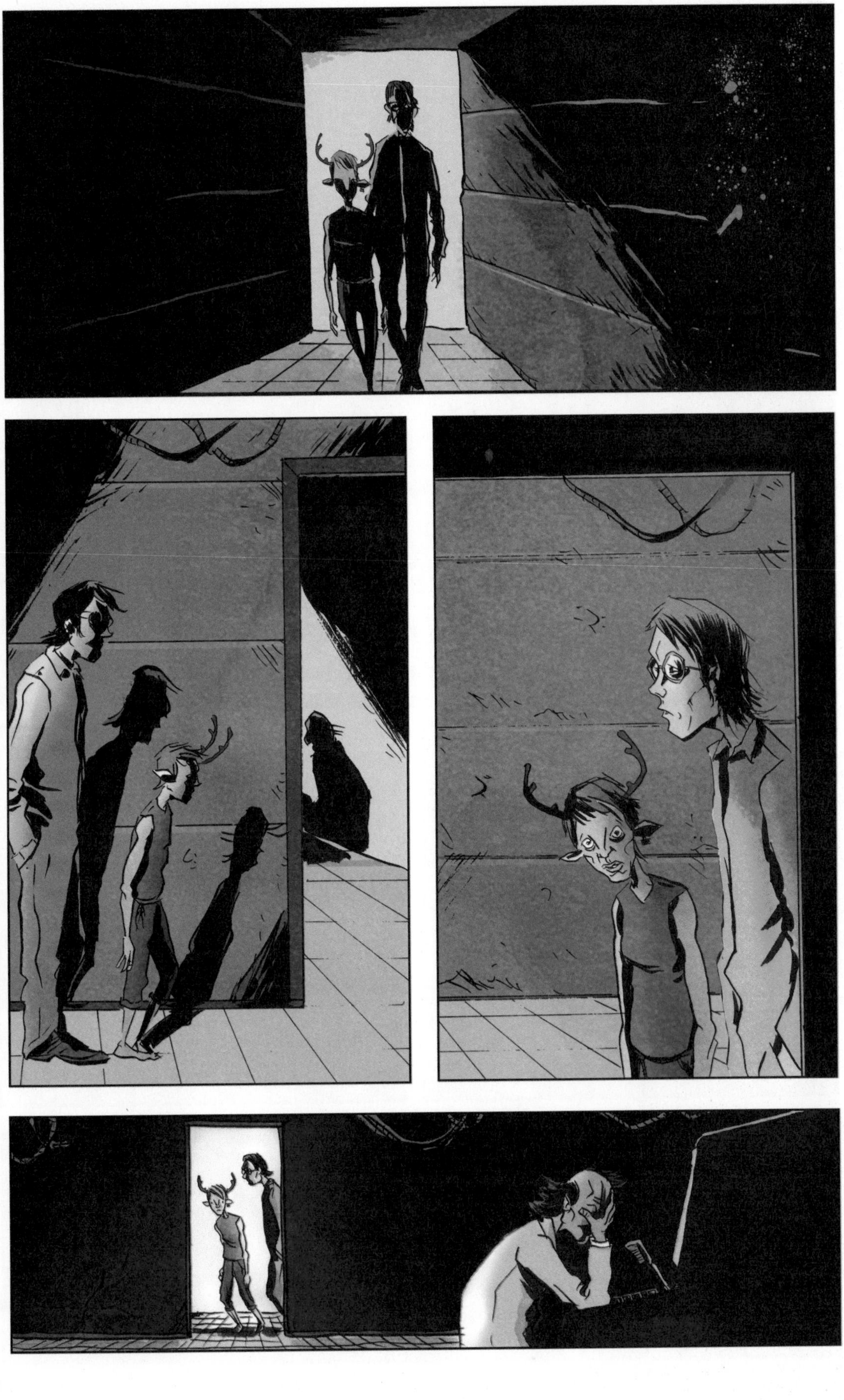

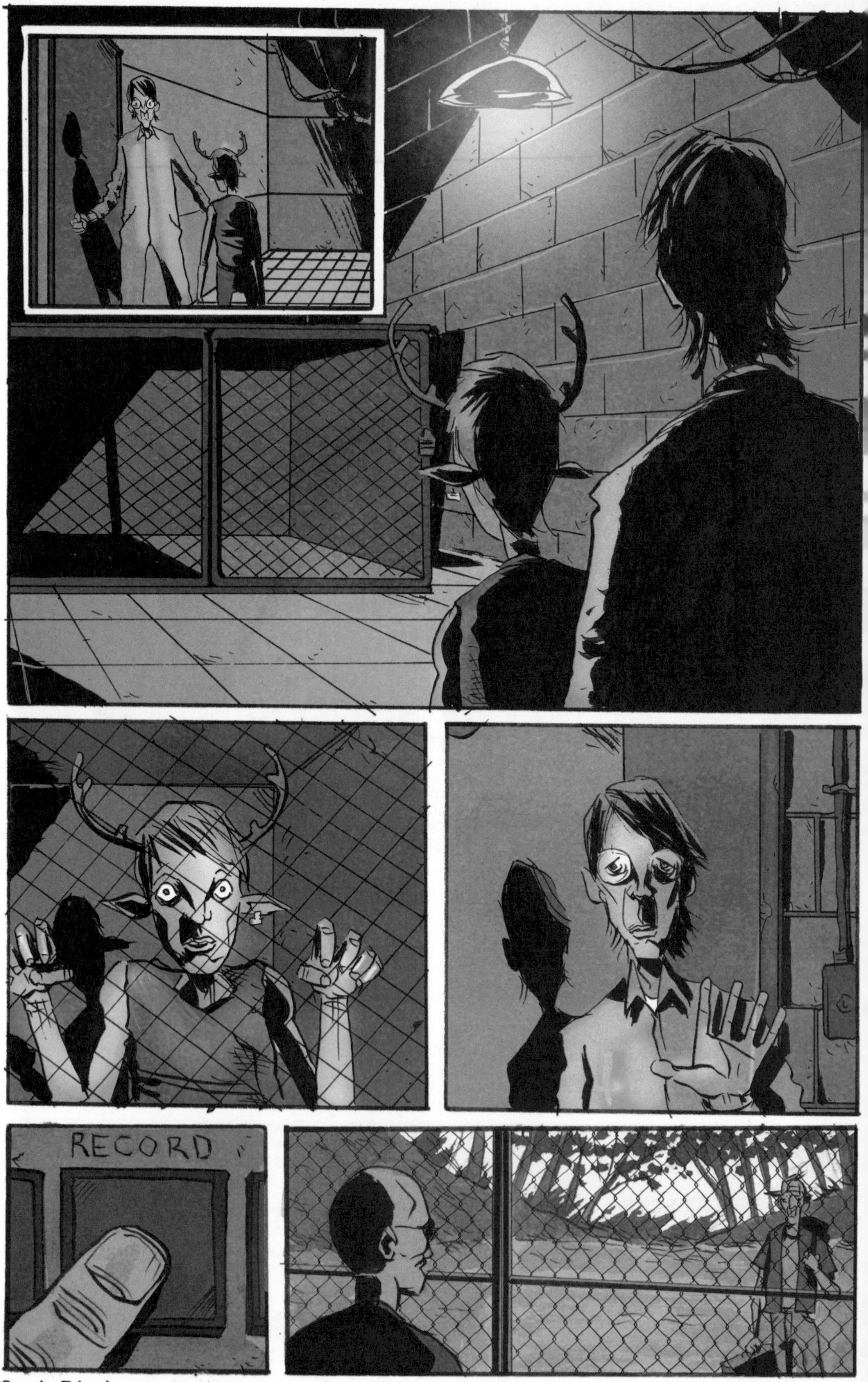
RECORD

If only I had come to them sooner. At least my wife and child would have died in a comfortable bed...in a warm room. Not on the side of the road like filthy vagrants. Would it have made a difference? They would still be dead. But maybe...maybe my work would have been further along by now?

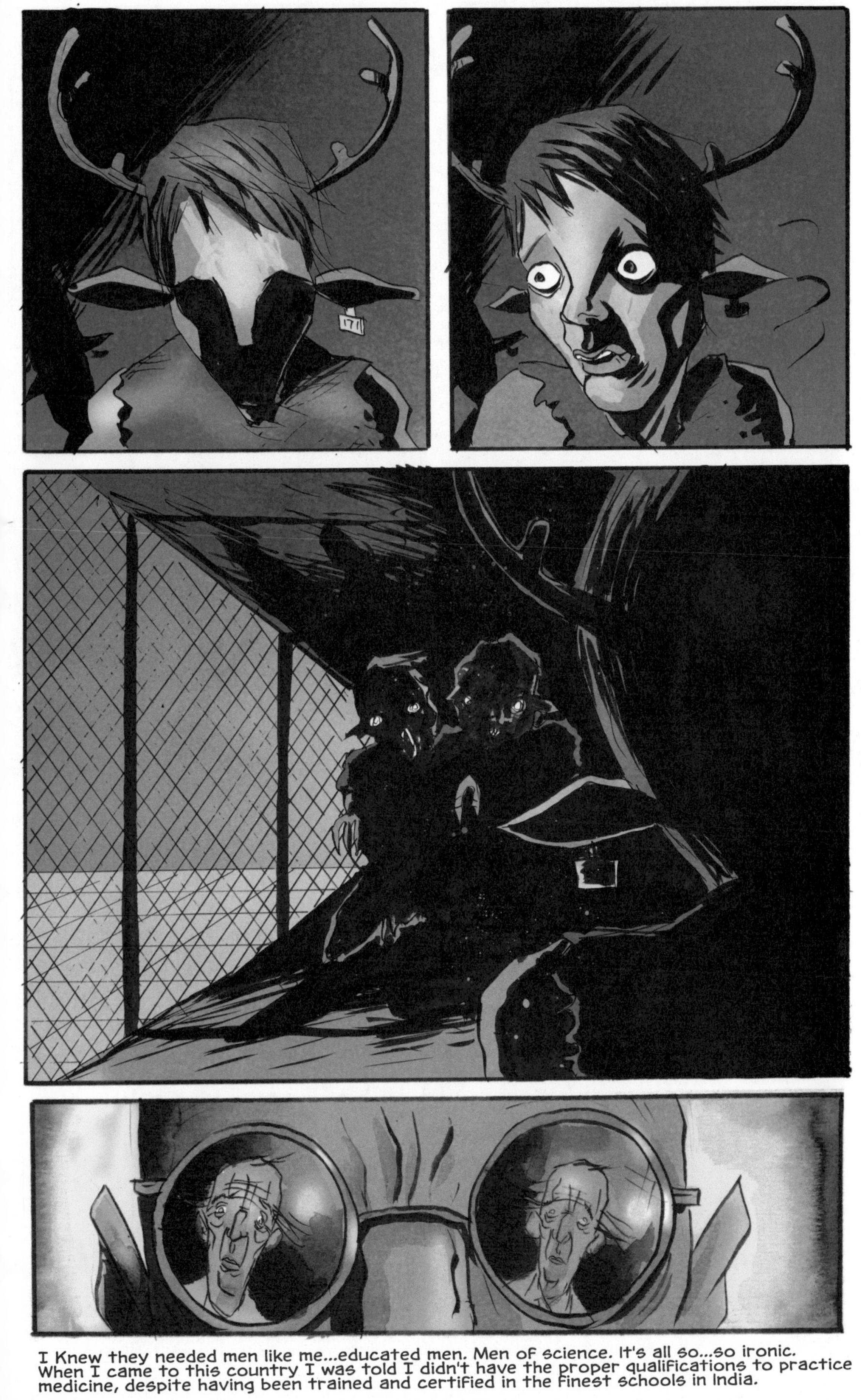

I Knew they needed men like me...educated men. Men of science. It's all so...so ironic. When I came to this country I was told I didn't have the proper qualifications to practice medicine, despite having been trained and certified in the finest schools in India.

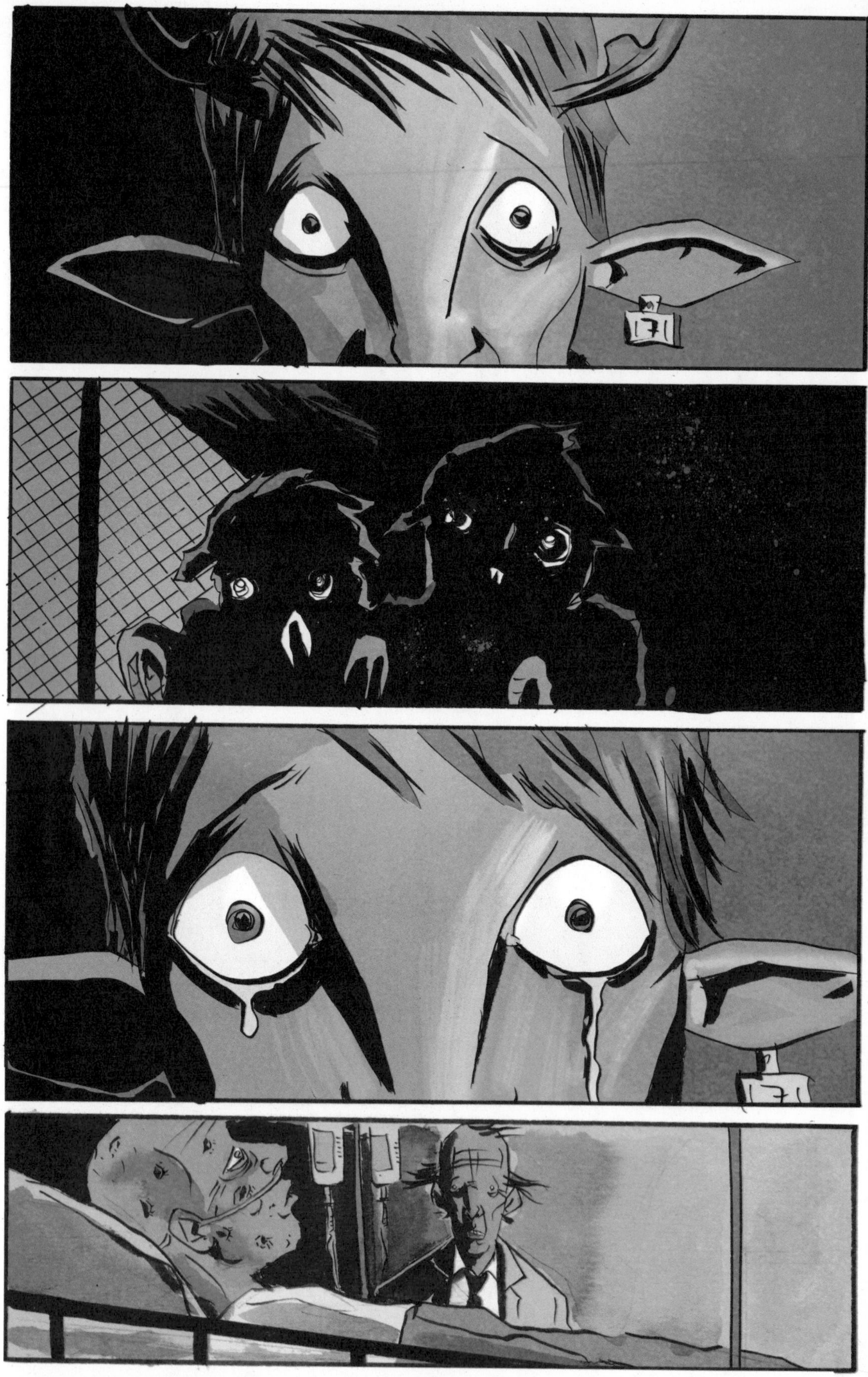

But now...now I was the most desired commodity of all. They needed me. We worked tirelessly...trying to come to some consensus. Trying to make sense of it all. But nothing could make sense of what came next...

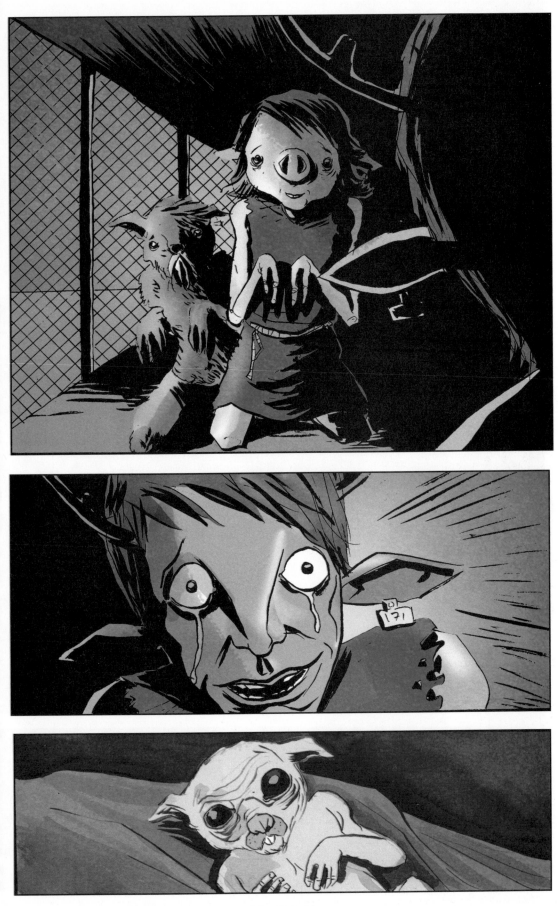

...The Hybrids.

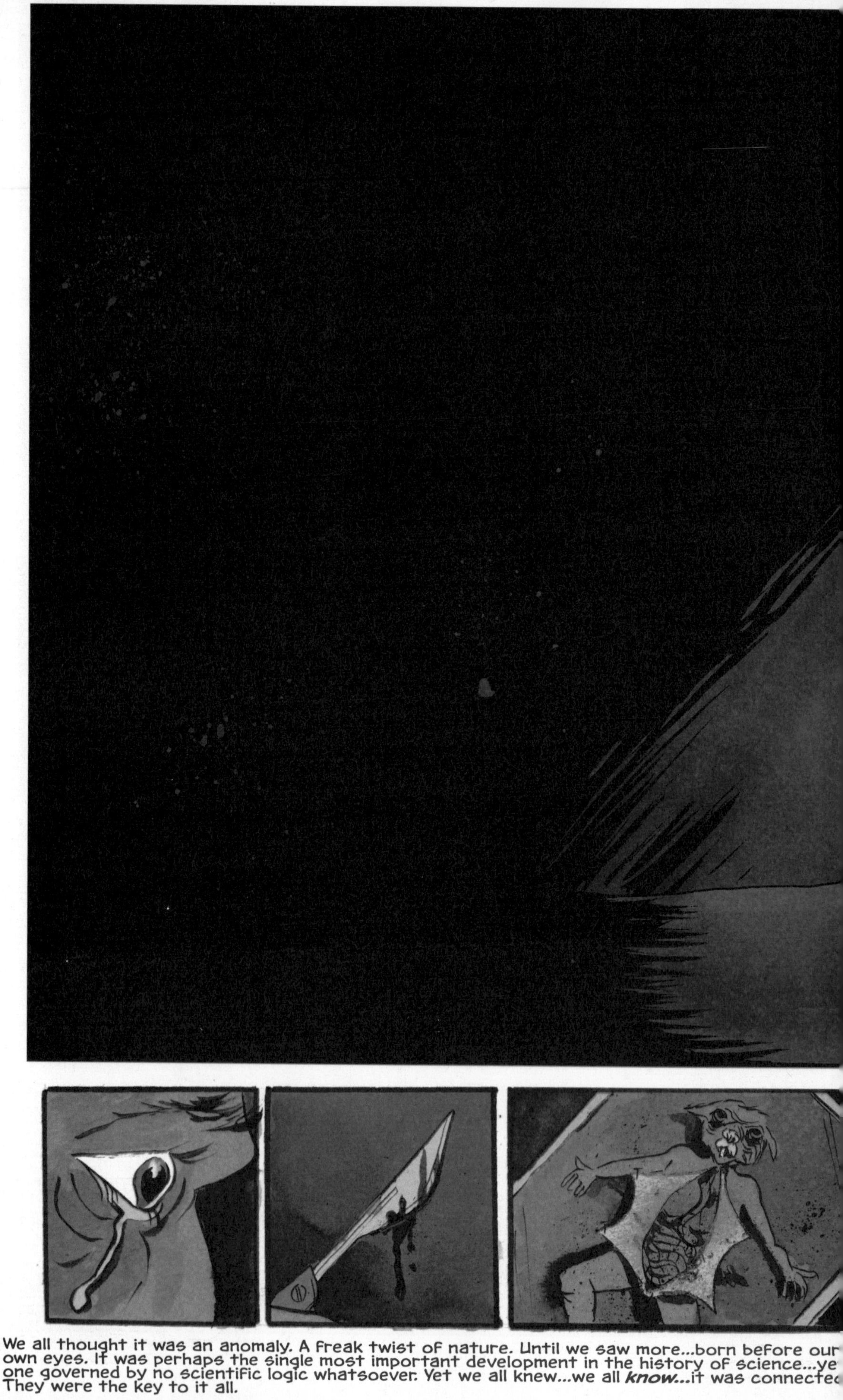

We all thought it was an anomaly. A freak twist of nature. Until we saw more...born before our own eyes. It was perhaps the single most important development in the history of science...ye one governed by no scientific logic whatsoever. Yet we all knew...we all ***know...*** it was connecte They were the key to it all.

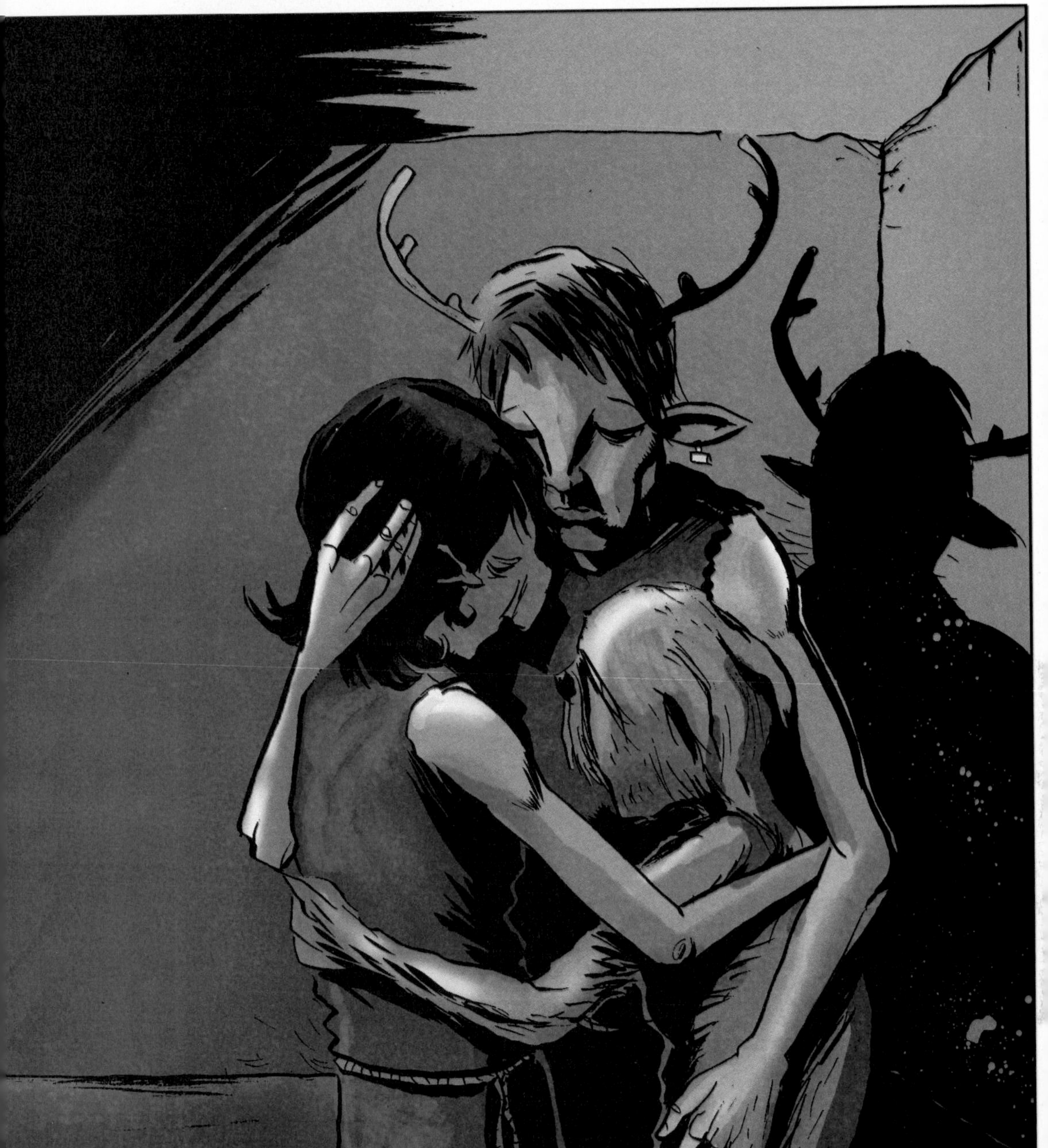

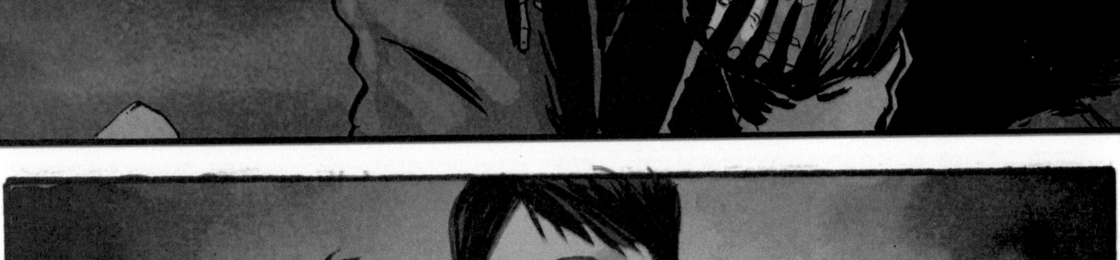

As amazing as they were, once we discovered that they were immune, it became clear we had no choice. H5-G9 did. And still, we can make no sense of it. More and more of my fellow doctors and scientists die, while more and more of them are born. It's a sick race. One I silently fear we cannot win. Is this the end? Is this truly the end?

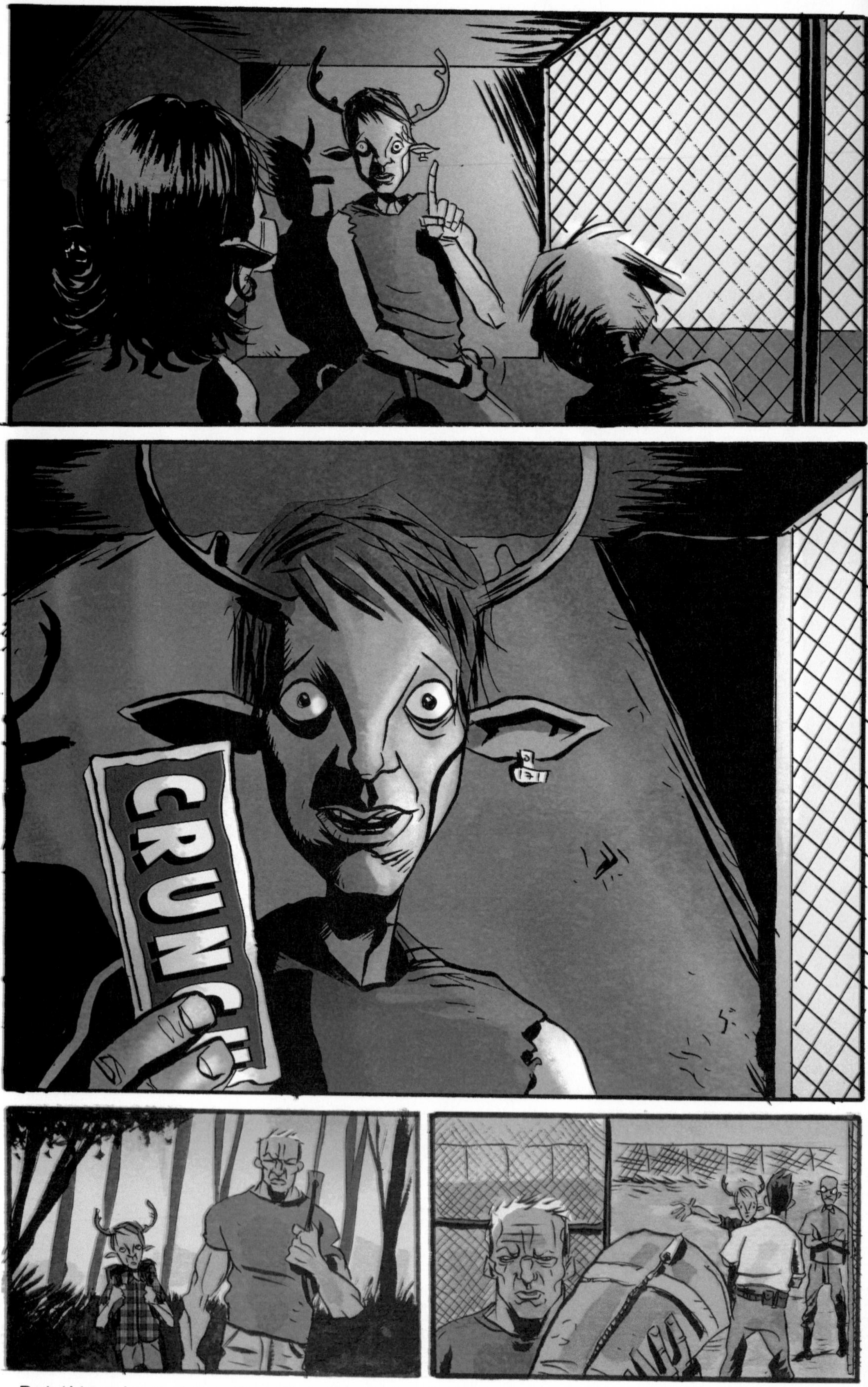
CRUNC

But things have changed again, haven't they? There is hope. *He* is hope. He claims to have been born before the disease hit. I thought he was simply confused until I examined him and saw he wasn't born at all...at least not in any way we know.

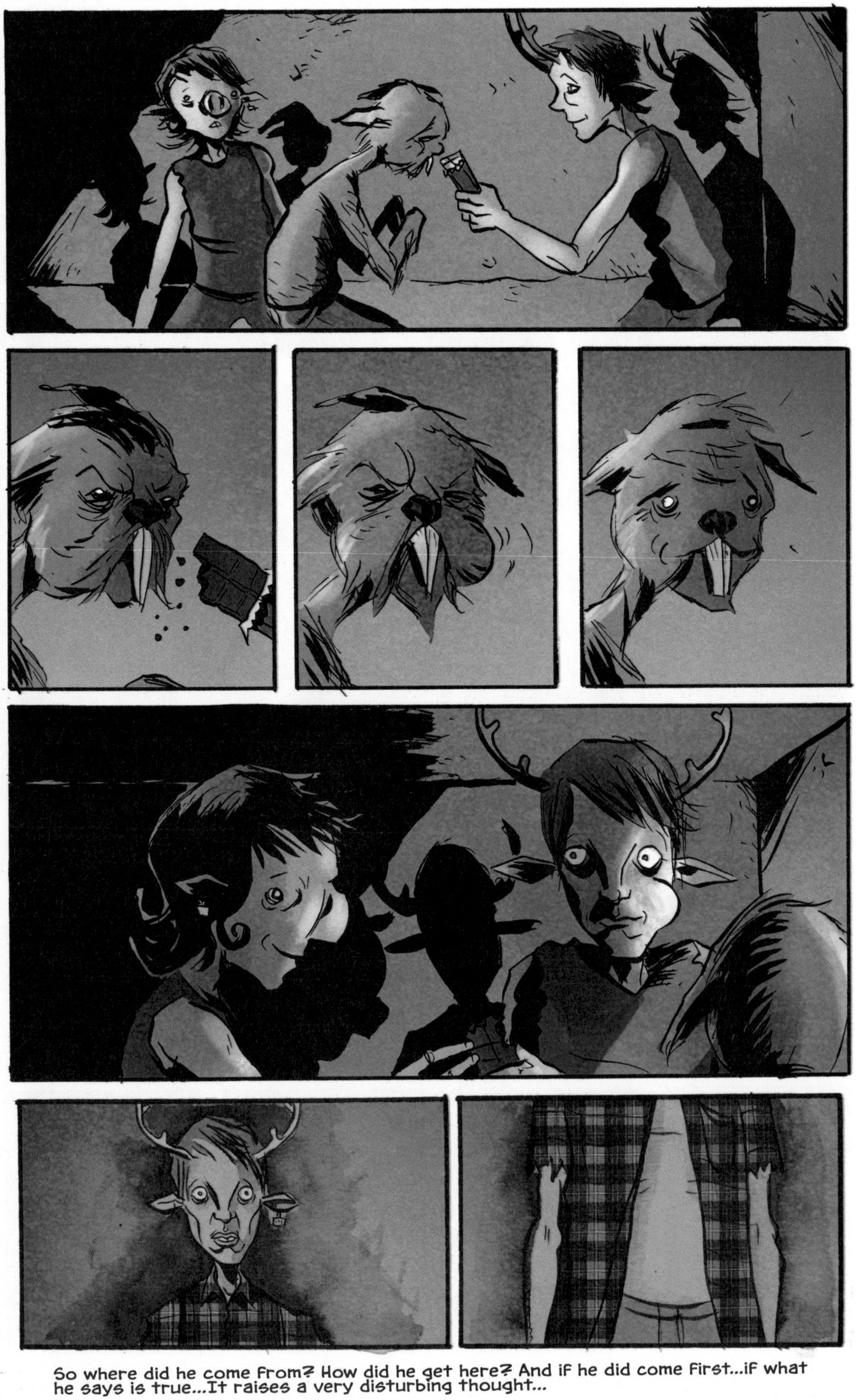

So where did he come from? How did he get here? And if he did come first...if what he says is true...It raises a very disturbing thought...

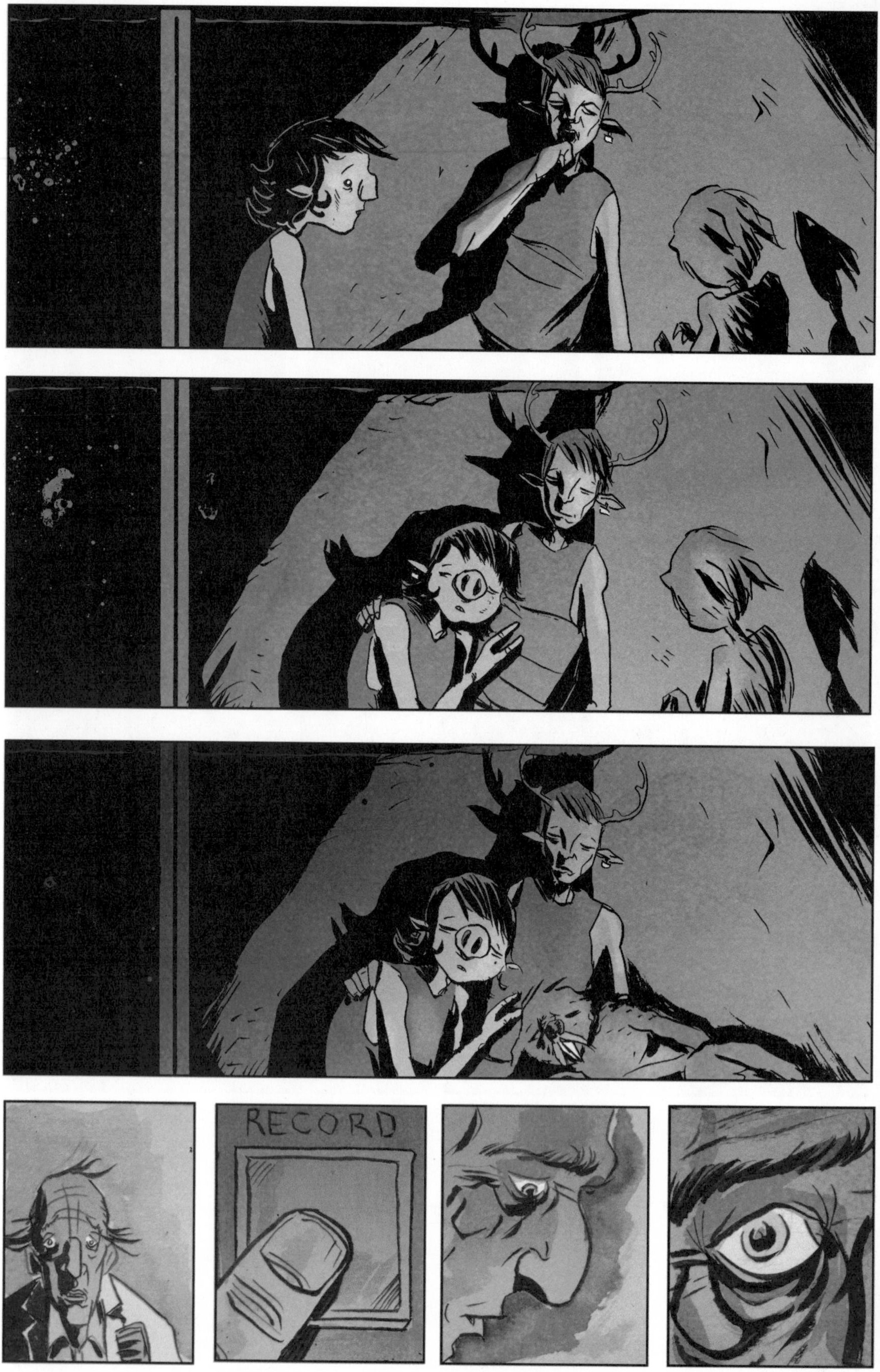
RECORD

What if they aren't the solution at all, but the problem? What if they caused it?

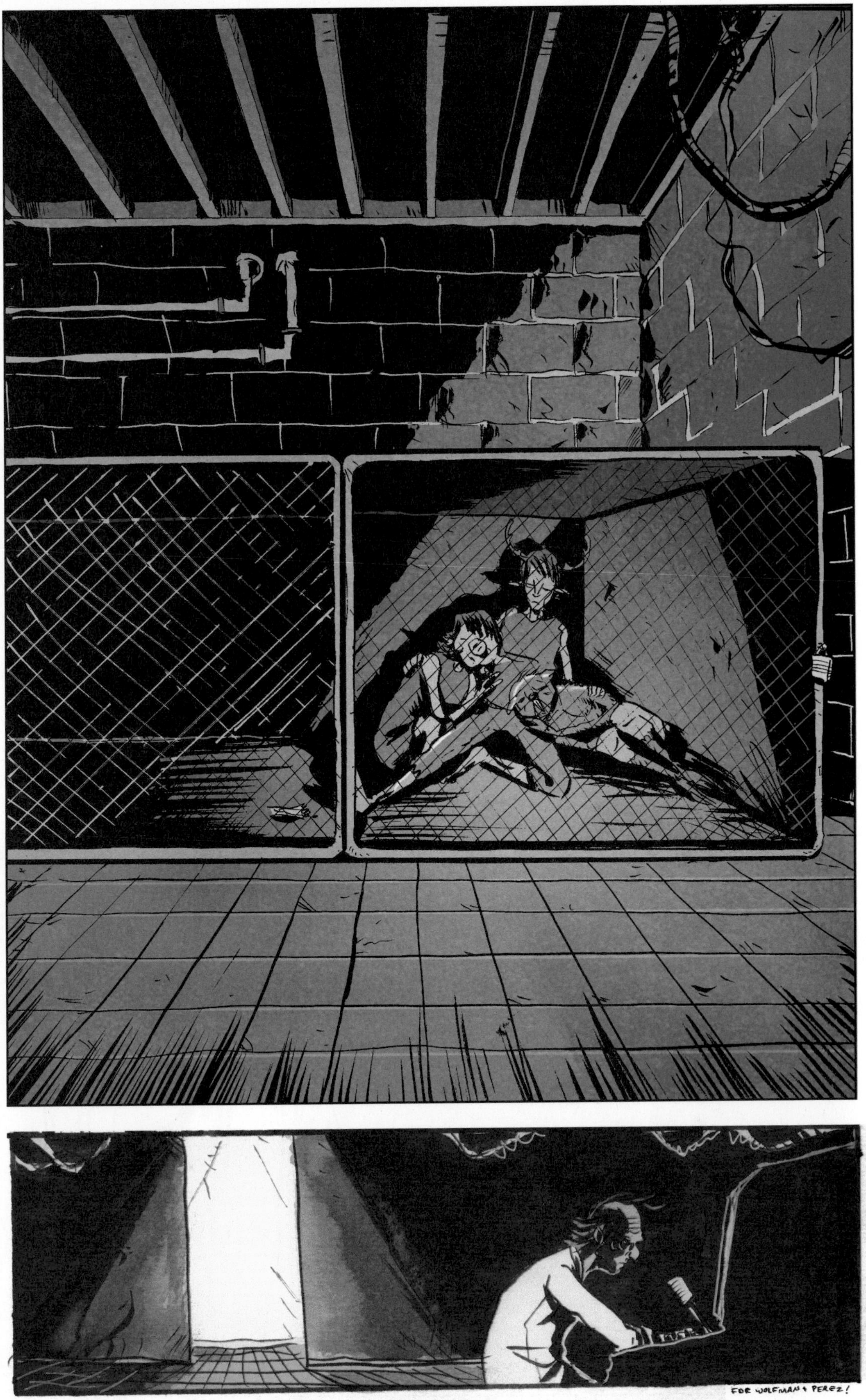
FOR WOLFMAN + PEREZ!

What if ***he*** caused it?

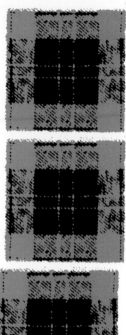

- SWEET TOOTH -
"GUS"

Jeff Lemire 2008

The earliest sketch of Sweet Tooth that I have. As you can see, the final design changed quite a bit. He has deer-like feet here. I'm glad I dropped the cape, it's a bit too Frodo Baggins, I think. I recall I was going to have Jepperd cut Gus's antlers off at one point, thus the toque.

The first sketch of Jepperd. A bit more cartoony than the final version, but looking back I kind of like this look. Jepperd was always going to have the hard, lined face and white hair. I always envisioned him as an older man in his mid-50s. I was really inspired by Garth Ennis and Richard Corben's *Punisher: The End* story about an aging Punisher in a post-apocalyptic world.

SWEET TOOTH SKETCHBOOK
Art and text by
Jeff Lemire

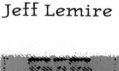

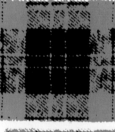

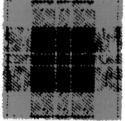

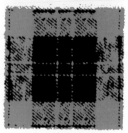

"JEPPERD"

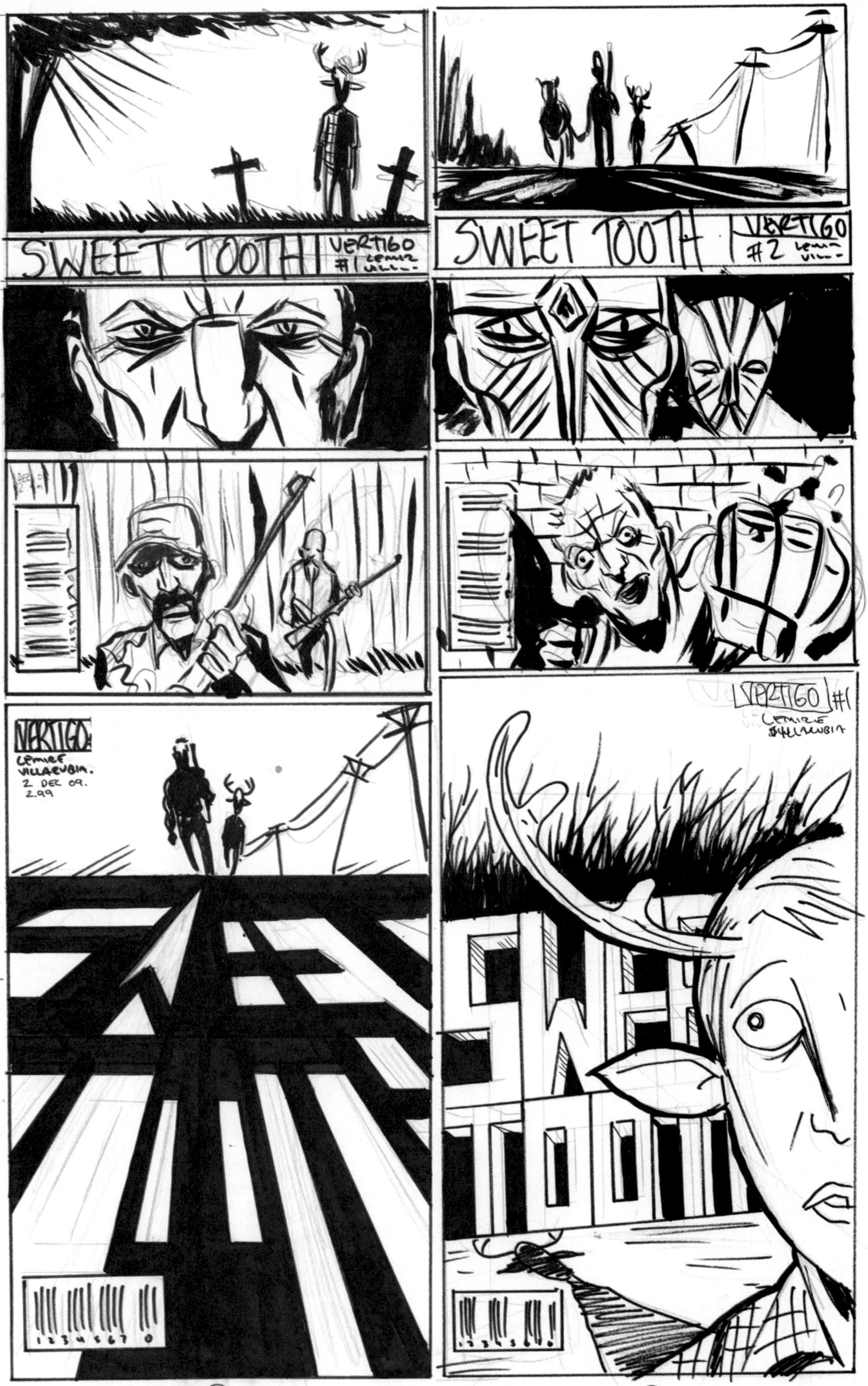
SWEET TOOTH
VERTIGO
#1
SWEET TOOTH
VERTIGO
#2
VERTIGO
LEMIRE
VILLARUBIA.
2 DEC 09.
2.99
VERTIGO #1
2
1

These are four early cover approaches I sketched up for my editor, Bob Schreck. I remember being really into comics legend Carmine Infantino's classic Silver Age cover work, so I was playing around with using the title as part of the artwork like he did so well, so often.

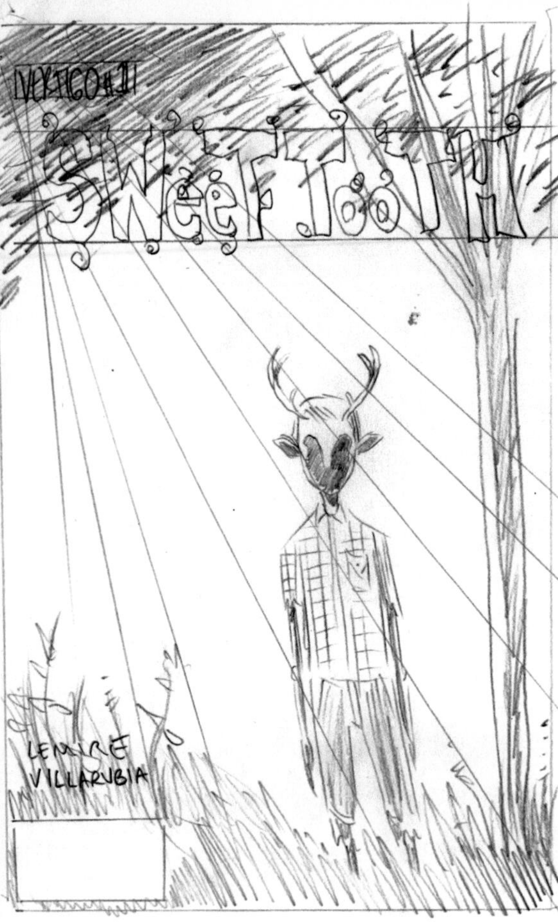
VERTIGO #1
SWEET TOOTH
LEMIRE
VILLARUBIA

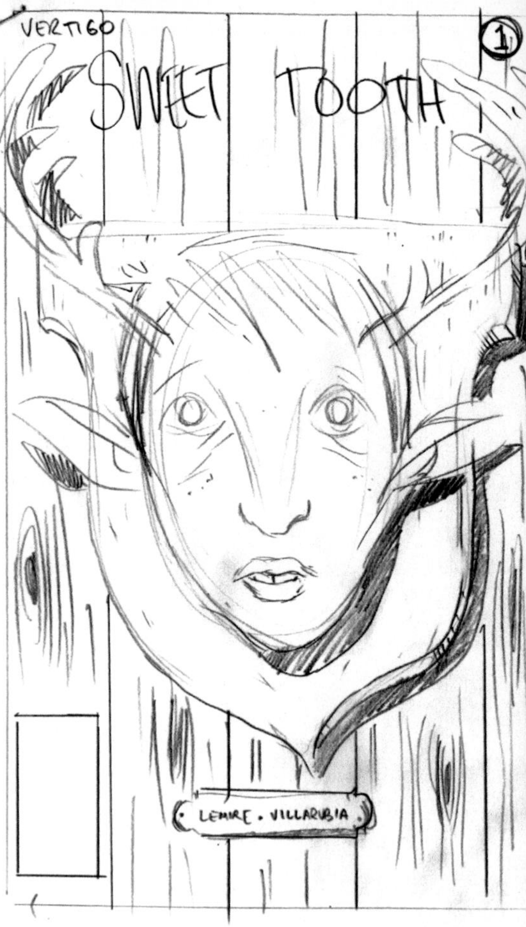
VERTIGO
1
SWEET TOOTH
LEMIRE . VILLARUBIA

Deep In The Woods... From Out of The Deep Woods...

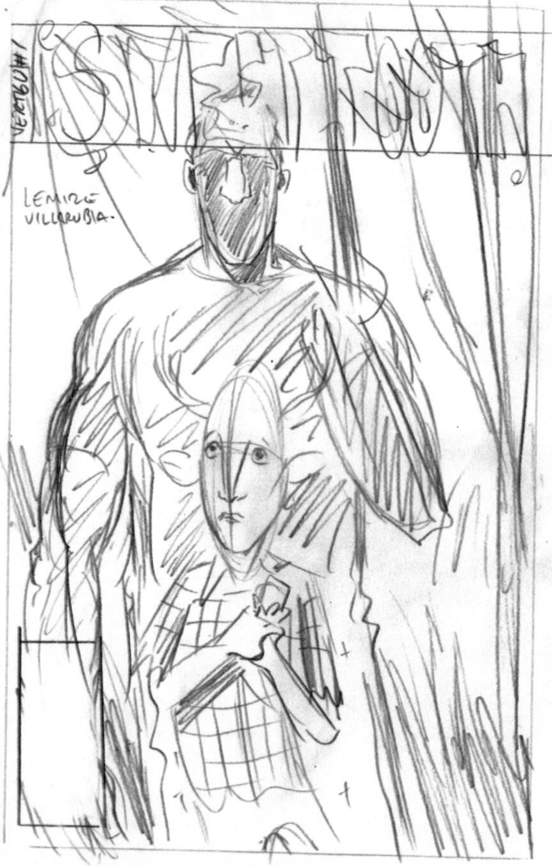
VERTIGO #1
SWEET TOOTH
LEMIRE
VILLARUBIA.

A BOB SCHRECK EXTRAVAGANZA!!!

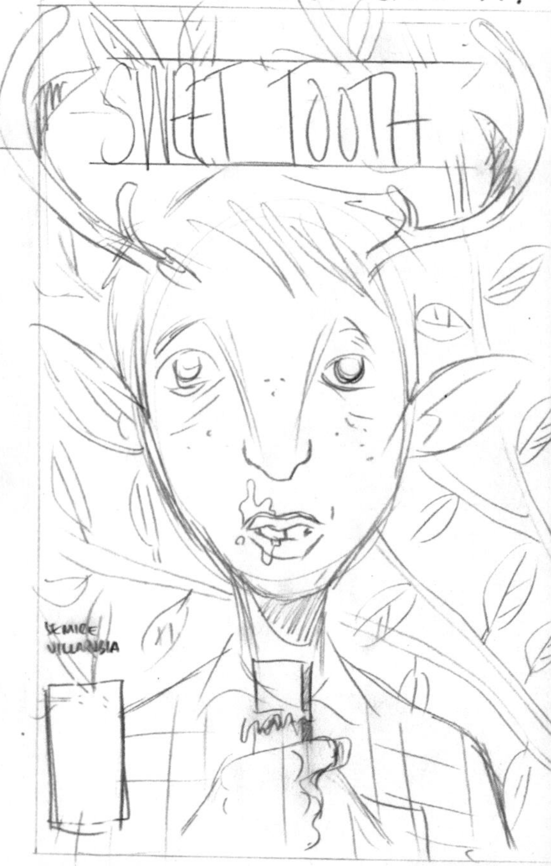
SWEET TOOTH
LEMIRE
VILLARUBIA

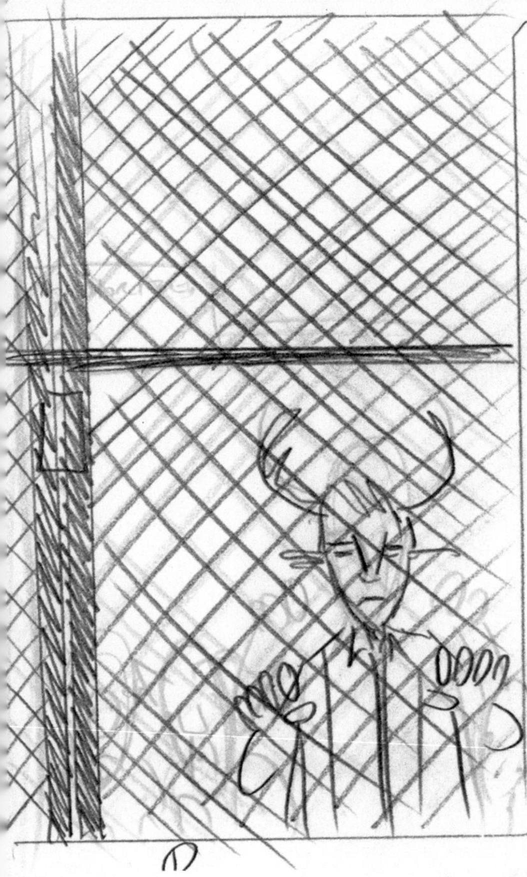

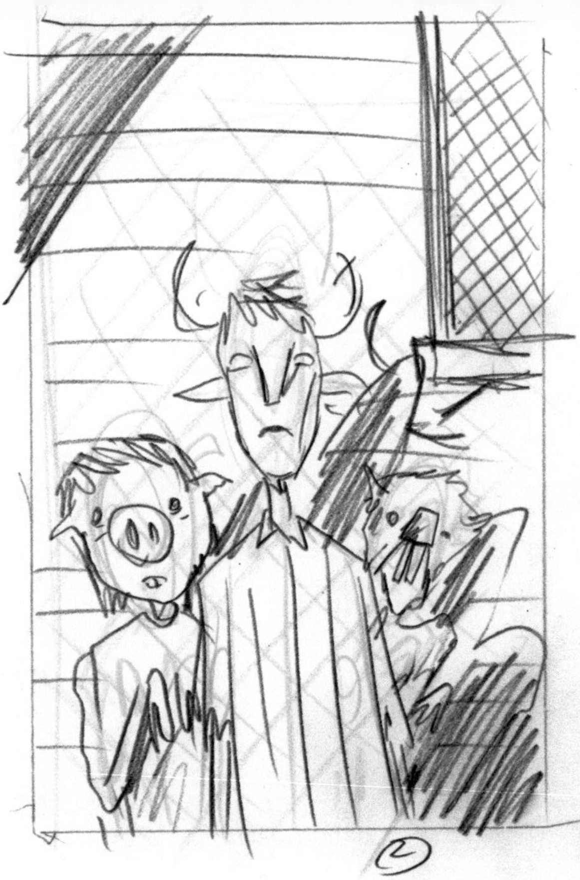

Sweet Tooth Cover Comps. #7

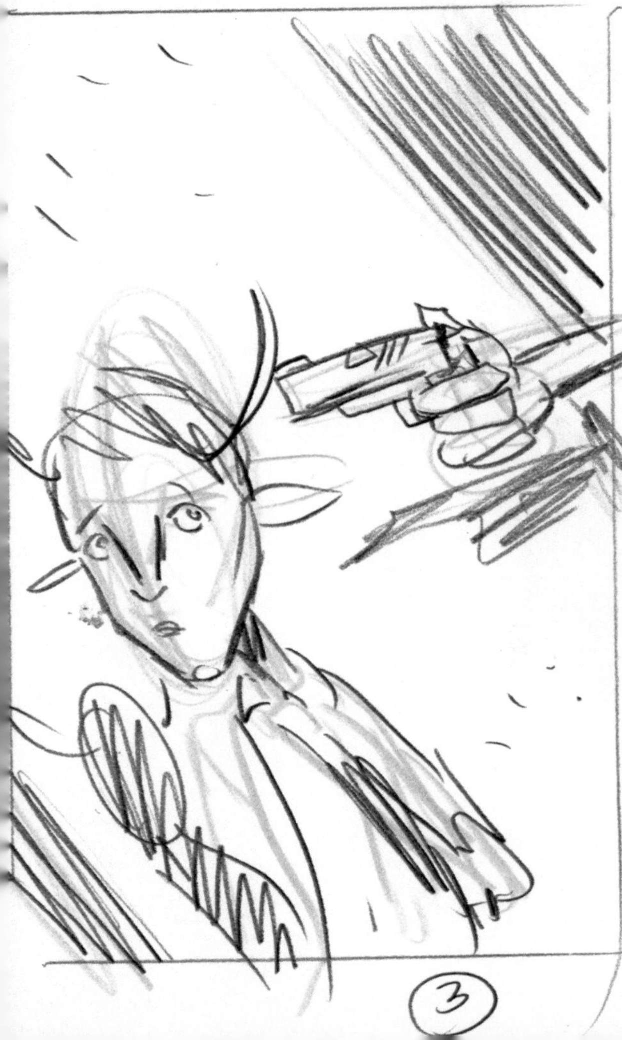

Opposite page: Some more refined cover ideas for Issue 1. Obviously we went with #4 here, and I'd mirror this cover in the final issue as well. One of these first issue ideas, the one with Gus's head mounted on the wall, ended up being the cover for #5.

Cover sketches from Issue 7. The final cover was a combination of ideas #1 and #2. I ended up trading the original art from this cover with my friend artist Rafael Albuquerque for his original art to SUPERBOY #1 that I wrote. Not a bad trade.

1

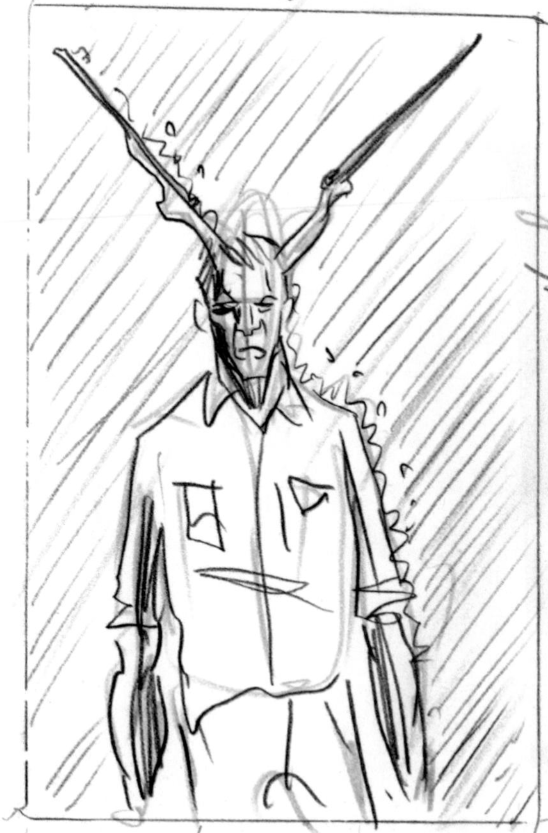

2

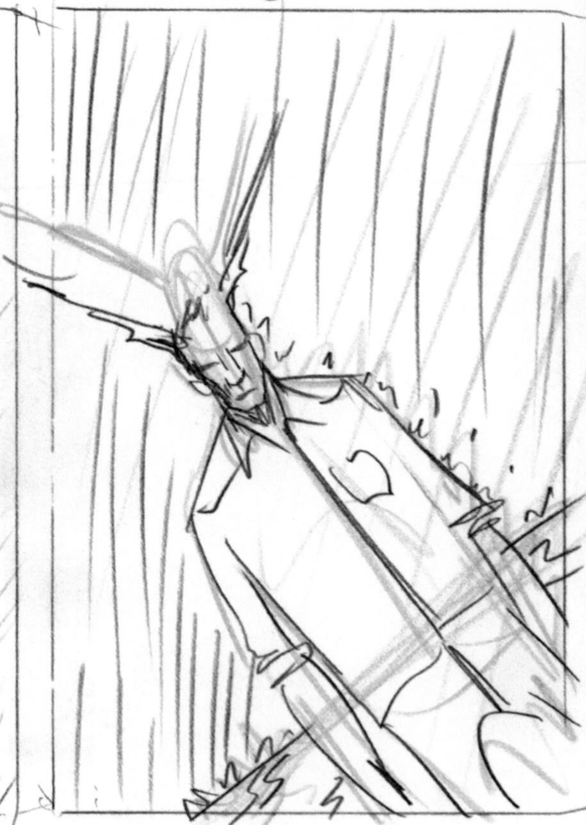

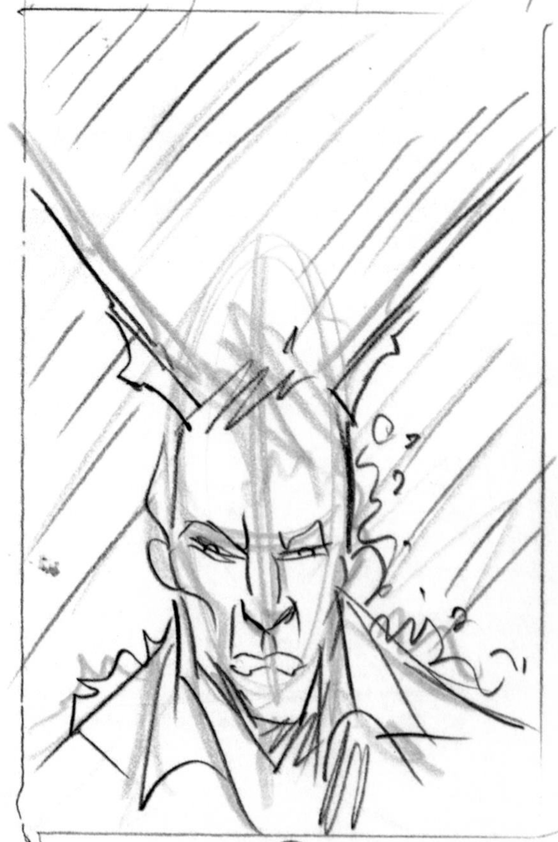

3

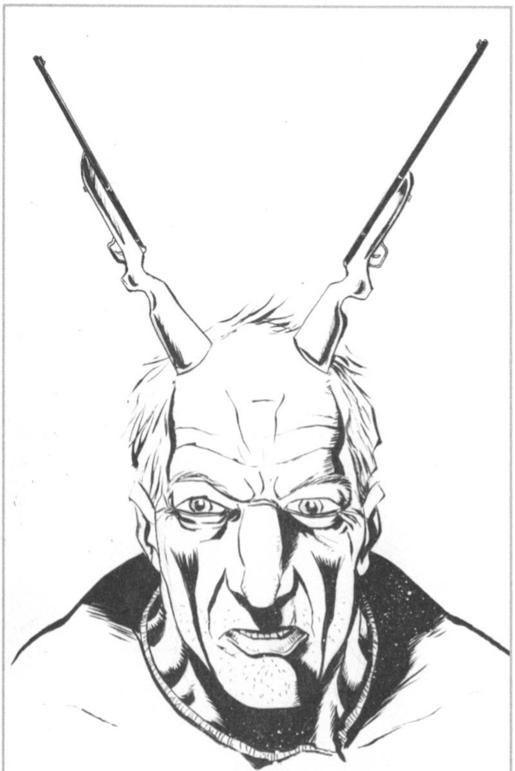

Cover Concepts → Sweet Tooth Issue 6

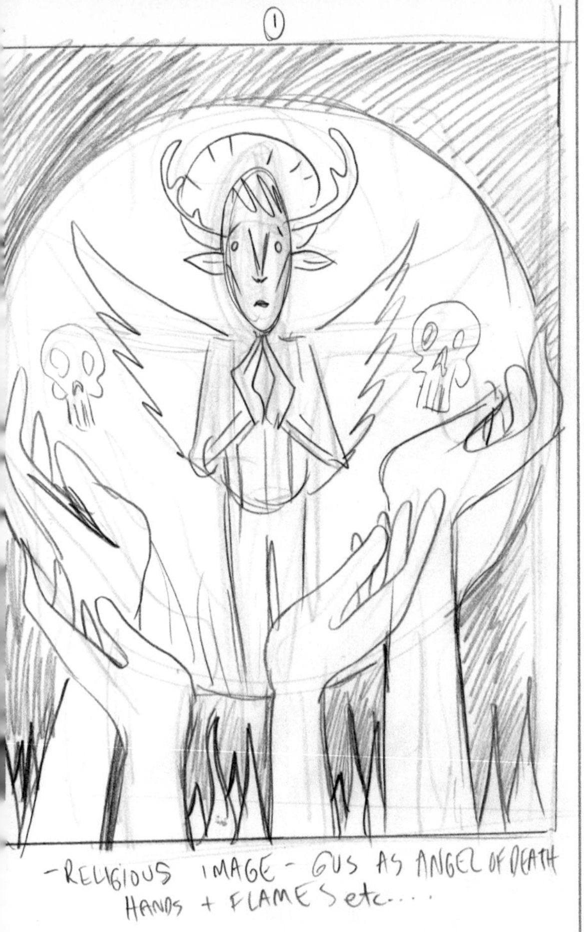
1
-RELIGIOUS IMAGE - GUS AS ANGEL OF DEATH
HANDS + FLAMES etc...

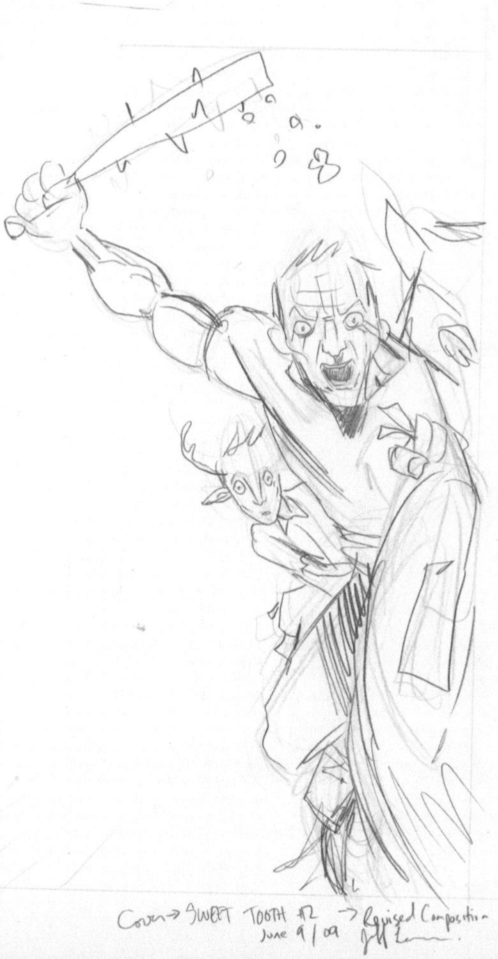
Cover → SWEET TOOTH #2 → Revised Composition
June 9/09

Opposite page: Cover sketches for Issue 6. Shotgun antlers. 'Nuff said.

Opposite page, bottom right: An unused cover. This would have been for Issue 6. We ended up using the concept but going with a full-body shot of Jepperd.

Top: An unused cover sketch I found. I think this was for Issue 10. I like the religious/ stained glass window concept and wish I'd used it at some point.

Bottom: Here are some pencils for a cover for Issue 2 that I never ended up using. I like this better than what we did use for #2 though.

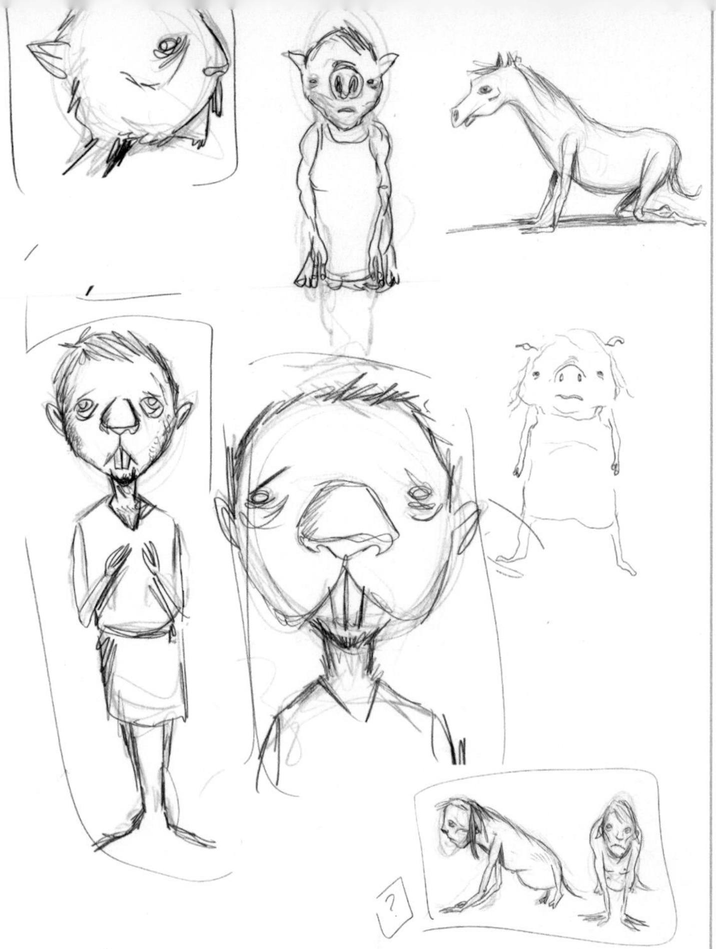

These are the earliest sketches I have fc other Human/Animal Hybrid children. Bobby looked a lot more human here than he ended up being. The sketch of the pig-girl, who would eventually become Wendy, was actually done by my wife, Lesley-Anne. I couldn't get a grip on the pig-girl and this really helped me see where to go with it.

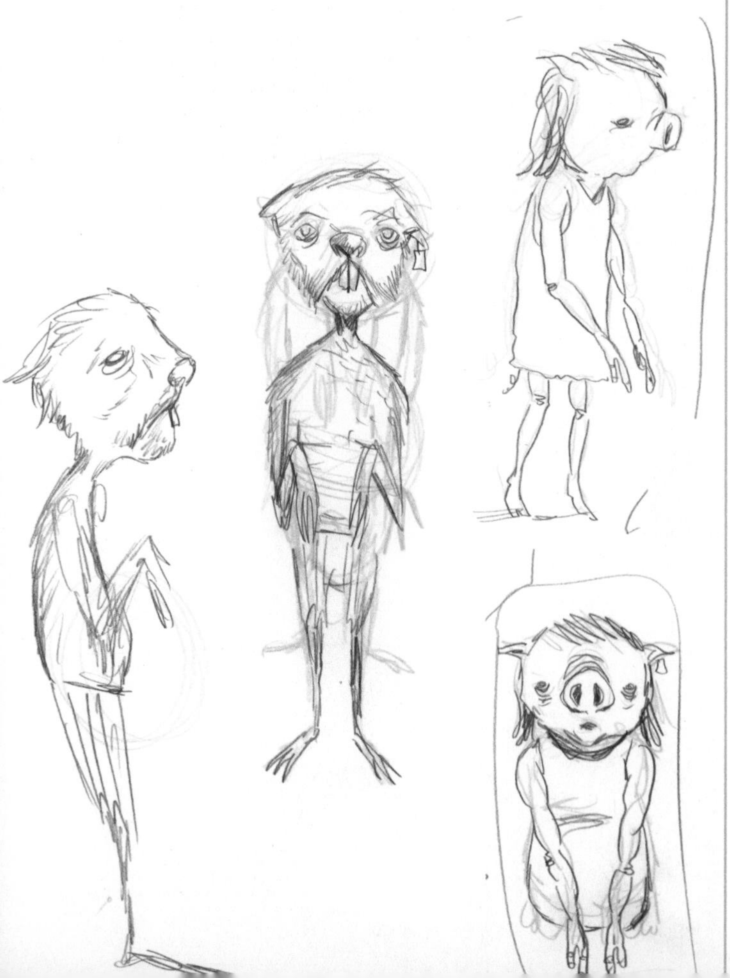

These Bobby and Wendy sketches are much closer to the versions that appear in the book. Bobby was named after my editor, Bob Schreck. Bobby is a groundhog because Bob was born on Groundhog's Day just like my own son, the real Gus. SWEET TOOTH would not exist without Bob. He championed me at Vertigo and got me in the door with THE NOBODY, a graphic novel I did wit him. And he helped get SWEET TOOTH in front of Karen Berger, the book's other guiding light.

"The Sheep Headed Boy"

#93

Buddy. I'm not sure if he ever really looked like a sheep or some mystery animal. Either way, I liked drawing him. The idea was to hint at Jepperd being his Dad by having him be a sheep...Jepperd/Shepherd. Maybe it was a bit too abstract of a connection.

Some early sketches of showing how Gus would age as the series progressed. I never ended up using this. His antlers at the start of the series were much closer to the final version here. In hindsight it would have been good to have them get bigger as the book progressed.

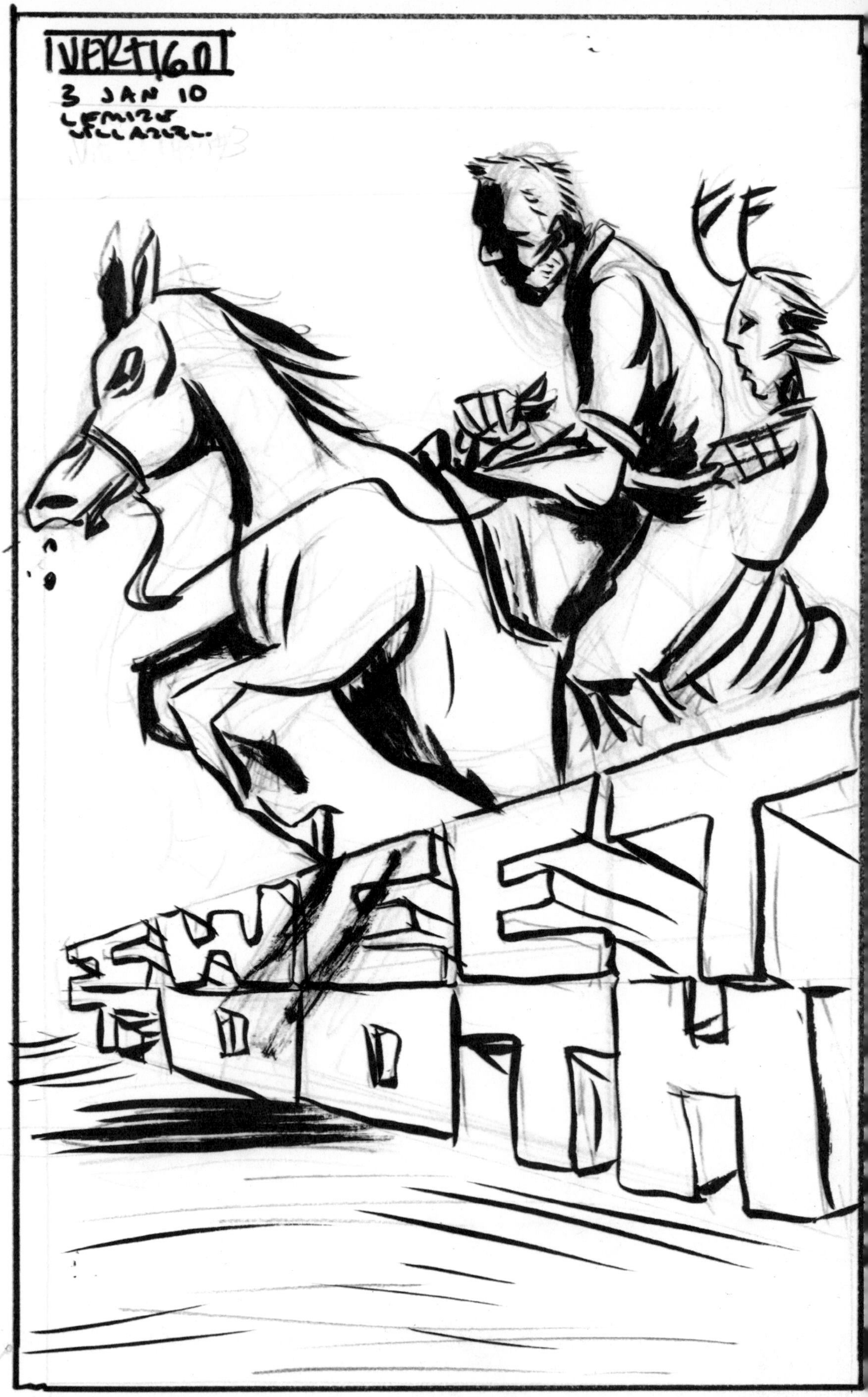
VERTIGO
3 JAN 10

More fun with the title in cover designs.

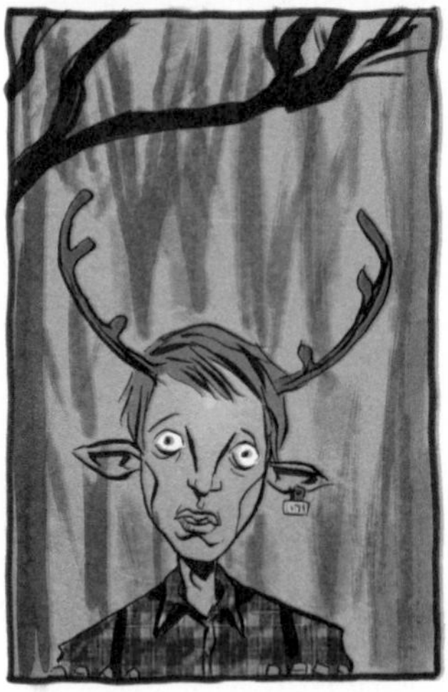

Warning: The following is the original pitch for SWEET TOOTH, which outlines the plan for the entire series run, including big spoilers for the ending. So if you're reading the series for the first time, come back once you've finished Books Two and Three!

"Gus looked just like his Dad, except that Gus had two antlers growing out of his forehead. His Dad told him that so few children had been born after The Accident, that God decided to make them all special. So, they got antlers, or tails, or fur. Gus wouldn't know, he had never seen another child; in fact he had never seen anyone other than his Dad. His Mum had gone to Heaven when Gus was really little, so he didn't really remember her. So now it was just the two of them...alone in the deep woods..."

SWEET TOOTH
Ongoing Series Proposal
Jeff Lemire 2008
For Bob Schreck and Karen Berger

Gus, a young boy born with antlers and deer-like features, has lived his entire life in total isolation with his Father a kind, but zealous man. When Gus's father grows ill and dies, he is finally forced to leave their forest sanctuary.

What he finds outside is beyond his comprehension; an American landscape decimated a decade earlier by a deadly pandemic. Even more remarkable is that Gus is part of a rare new breed of human/animal hybrid children who have emerged in its wake, all apparently immune to the infection.

Jepperd, a hulking drifter, soon takes in Gus and promises to lead him to "The Preserve," a fabled safe-haven for hybrid children. As the two cross this dangerous new American frontier, they begin to develop a deep friendship, one that is torn apart when Jepperd betrays Gus, selling him to a dangerous religious sect who believe hybrids to be the devil incarnate on Earth.

Jepperd is a man who believes in nothing and no one, living only for himself. This mindset has been deeply challenged by his relationship with Gus. And, driven by guilt, he initiates a harrowing rescue. As our first story arc ends, Jepperd and Gus set out across this dangerous and desperate land in search of the real "Preserve," which may or may not even exist at all.

*****

Sweet Tooth is an ongoing series that recasts conventions from both the western and science fiction genres into a startling backdrop for a heartbreaking tale of childhood loss and loneliness, and the unexpected friendships that can emerge in even the darkest of places.

SWEET TOOTH–AN OVERVIEW

From rival bounty hunters to fanatical cults and science militias, the world of Sweet Tooth will be ripe with danger, and will provide plenty of adventure to sustain an ongoing book.

And, while the physical journey of Jepperd and Gus will be satisfying in itself, there is a larger story at work that will carry the book into the future.

It is important to understand that while the search for The Preserve and the mysteries of the hybrids are important, the core of the book is not the promise of some "big reveal", but the evolving relationship between Gus and Jepperd. The search for The Preserve will come to represent everything these two seek. This is the story of a boy's search for a place to call home in a world beyond his understanding, and a man's search to find meaning in a world where nothing lasts, and every morning may be your last.

To use an example, in *The Walking Dead*, finding the source of and cure for the zombie plague is not the focus. It is the relationships, and the lives of the survivors from month to month which propel that book. And, likewise, finding the reasons for the pandemic and the hybrids is not the focus of this book. The real cause of the epidemic, and the hybrids, will never be answered. Whether it was a terrorist attack, or an act of God, it doesn't matter now. These things have happened, this is just the way the world is, and it is beyond their understanding. What is important is staying alive, and keeping some glimmer of hope alive in their hearts, in spite of these insurmountable odds.

Having said that, there is an end point in sight for this story. In the eventual conclusion of the series, Gus and Jepperd will finally find The Preserve, but it will not be at all what they had expected or hoped for. The Preserve will in fact be a vast underground military complex, where the remnants of the military and government lure hybrids and savagely study them in hopes of finding a cure.

In our story's conclusion, Jepperd, who started as an amoral killer, and slowly became a reluctant father figure, will perform the most selfless act possible, sacrificing himself to save Gus.

And Gus, the wide-eyed innocent, hardened by his journey, will in fact become the father figure, leading a group of younger hybrids back to the woods where the story began. There they will form a new community all of their own. And The Preserve they thought a lie will be born after all.